MW01139741

Contents

geometry
problems and solutions
from
Mathematical Olympiads

17th Austrian-Polish Mathematics Competition, 1994

9

On the plane there are given four distinct points A, B, C, D lying (in this order) on a line g, at distances $AB = a$, $BC = b$, $CD = c$.

(a) Construct, whenever possible, a point P, not on g, such that the angles $\angle APB$, $\angle BPC$, $\angle CPD$ are equal.

(b) Prove that a point P with the property as above exists if and only if the following inequality holds: $(a + b)(b + c) < 4ac$.

solution page 85

37th International Mathematical Olympiad, 1996 (Shortlist)

12

Let the sides of two rectangles be $\{a, b\}$ and $\{c, d\}$ respectively, with $a < c \le d < b$ and $ab < cd$. Prove that the first rectangle can be placed within the second one if and only if

$$(b^2 - a^2)^2 \le (bc - ad)^2 + (bd - ac)^2 .$$

solution page 85

37th International Mathematical Olympiad, 1996 (Shortlist)

14

Let $ABCD$ be a convex quadrilateral, and let R_A, R_B, R_C, R_D denote the circumradii of the triangles DAB, ABC, BCD, CDA respectively. Prove that $R_A + R_C > R_B + R_D$ if and only if $\angle A + \angle C > \angle B + \angle D$.

solution page 86

37th International Mathematical Olympiad, 1996 (Shortlist)

15

On the plane are given a point O and a polygon $\mathcal{F}$ (not necessarily convex). Let P denote the perimeter of $\mathcal{F}$, D the sum of the distances from O to the vertices of $\mathcal{F}$, and H the sum of the distances from O to the lines containing the sides of $\mathcal{F}$. Prove that $D^2 - H^2 \ge P^2/4$.

solution page 87

Iranian National Mathematical Olympiad, 1994 (Second Round)

5

Show that if D_1 and D_2 are two skew lines, then there are infinitely many straight lines such that their points have equal distance from D_1 and D_2.

solution page 88

Japan Mathematical Olympiad, 1994 (Final Round)

4

We consider a triangle ABC such that $\angle MAC = 15°$ where M is the midpoint of BC. Determine the possible maximum value of $\angle B$.

solution page 89

30th Spanish Mathematical Olympiad, 1993 (First Round)

4

Let AD be the internal bisector of the triangle ABC ($D \in BC$), E the point symmetric to D with respect to the mid-point of BC, and F the point of BC such that $\angle BAF = \angle EAC$. Show that $\frac{BF}{FC} = \frac{c^3}{b^3}$.

solution page 90

30th Spanish Mathematical Olympiad, 1993 (First Round)

6

An ellipse is drawn taking as major axis the biggest of the sides of a given rectangle, such that the ellipse passes through the intersection point of the diagonals of the rectangle.

Show that, if a point of the ellipse, external to the rectangle, is joined to the extreme points of the opposite side, then three segments in geometric progression are determined on the major axis.

solution page 92

38th Mathematics Competition of the Republic of Slovenia (3rd Grade)

4

Let the point D on the hypotenuse AC of the right triangle ABC be such that $|AB| = |CD|$. Prove that the bisector of the angle $\angle A$, the median through B and the altitude through D of the triangle ABD have a common point.

solution page 93

38th Mathematics Competition of the Republic of Slovenia (4th Grade)

4

Let Q be the mid-point of the side AB of an inscribed quadrilateral $ABCD$ and S the intersection of its diagonals. Denote by P and R the orthogonal projections of S on AD and BC respectively. Prove that $|PQ| = |QR|$.

solution page 94

44th Lithuanian Mathematical Olympiad (Grade XI)

5

In the trapezium $ABCD$, the bases are $AB = a$, $CD = b$, and the diagonals meet at the point O. Find the ratio of the areas of the triangle ABO and trapezium.

solution page 95

44th Lithuanian Mathematical Olympiad (Grade XII)

3

The area of a trapezium equals 2; the sum of its diagonals equals 4. Prove that the diagonals are orthogonal.

solution page 96

Iranian Mathematical Olympiad, 1994

5

Show that if D_1 and D_2 are two skew lines, then there are infinitely many straight lines such that their points have equal distance from D_1 and D_2.

solution page 97

Canadian Mathematical Olympiad, 1999

Let ABC be an equilateral triangle of altitude 1. A circle with radius 1 and centre on the same side of AB as C rolls along the segment AB. Prove that the arc of the circle that is inside the triangle always has the same length.

solution page 98

VIII Nordic Mathematical Contest

A finite set S of points in the plane with integer coordinates is called a *two–neighbour set*, if for each (p, q) in S exactly two of the points $(p + 1, q)$, $(p, q + 1)$, $(p - 1, q)$, $(p, q - 1)$ are in S. For which n does there exist a two-neighbour set which contains exactly n points?

solution page 100

8 th Korean Mathematical Olympiad (First Round)

Consider finitely many points in a plane such that, if we choose any three points A, B, C among them, the area of $\triangle ABC$ is always less than 1. Show that all of these finitely many points lie within the interior or on the boundary of a triangle with area less than 4.

solution page 101

8 th Korean Mathematical Olympiad (First Round)

Let A, B, C be three points lying on a circle, and let P, Q, R be the mid-points of arcs BC, CA, AB, respectively. AP, BQ, CR intersect BC, CA, AB at L, M, N, respectively. Show that

$$\frac{AL}{PL} + \frac{BM}{QM} + \frac{CN}{RN} \geq 9.$$

For which triangle ABC does equality hold?

solution page 102

8 th Korean Mathematical Olympiad (First Round)

Two circles O_1, O_2 of radii r_1, r_2 ($r_1 < r_2$), respectively, intersect at two points A and B. P is any point on circle O_1. Lines PA, PB and circle O_2 intersect at Q and R, respectively.

(i) Express $y = QR$ in terms of r_1, r_2, and $\theta = \angle APB$.

(ii) Show that $y = 2r_2$ is a necessary and sufficient condition that circle O_1 be orthogonal to circle O_2.

solution page 104

8 th Korean Mathematical Olympiad (Final Round)

Let $\triangle ABC$ be an equilateral triangle of side length 1, D a point on BC, and let r_1, r_2 be inradii of triangles ABD, ADC, respectively. Express $r_1 r_2$ in terms of $p = BD$, and find the maximum of $r_1 r_2$.

solution page 106

45th Latvian Mathematical Olympiad, 1994 (11th Grade)

Let $ABCD$ be a convex quadrilateral, $M \in AB$, $N \in BC$, $P \in CD$, $Q \in DA$; $AM = BN = CP = DQ$, and $MNPQ$ is a square. Prove that $ABCD$ is a square, too.

solution page 107

Dutch Mathematical Olympiad, 1994 (Second Round)

A unit square is divided in two rectangles in such a way that the smallest rectangle can be put on the greatest rectangle with every vertex of the smallest on exactly one of the edges of the greatest. Calculate the dimensions of the smallest rectangle.

solution page 109

Dutch Mathematical Olympiad, 1994 (Second Round)

Let P be any point on the diagonal BD of a rectangle $ABCD$. F is the projection of P on BC. H lies on BC such that $BF = FH$. PC intersects AH in Q.

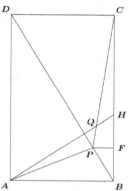

Prove: Area $\triangle APQ =$ Area $\triangle CHQ$.

solution page 111

4th Mathematical Olympiad of the Republic of China (Taiwan), 1995

Let P be a point on the circumscribed circle of $\triangle A_1A_2A_3$. Let H be the orthocentre of $\triangle A_1A_2A_3$. Let B_1 (B_2, B_3 respectively) be the point of intersection of the perpendicular from P to A_2A_3 (A_1A_2, A_2A_3 respectively). It is known that the three points B_1, B_2, B_3 are collinear. Prove that the line $B_1B_2B_3$ passes through the mid-point of the line segment PH.

solution page 112

XI Italian Mathematical Olympiad, 1995

An acute-angled triangle ABC is inscribed in a circle with centre O. Let D be the intersection of the bisector of A with BC and suppose that the perpendicular to AO through D meets the line AC in a point P interior to the segment AC. Show that $AB = AP$.

solution page 114

Bi-National Israel-Hungary Mathematical Competition, 1995

2

Let P, P_1, P_2, P_3, P_4 be five points on a circle. Denote the distance of P from the line P_iP_k by d_{ik}. Prove that $d_{12}d_{34} = d_{13}d_{24}$.

solution page 115

31st Spanish Mathematical Olympiad, 1994 (First Round)

3

The squares of the sides of a triangle ABC are proportional to the numbers 1, 2, 3.

(a) Show that the angles formed by the medians of ABC are equal to the angles of ABC.

(b) Show that the triangle whose sides are the medians of ABC is similar to ABC.

solution page 116

31st Spanish Mathematical Olympiad, 1994 (First Round)

6

Consider the parabolas $y = cx^2 + d$, $x = ay^2 + b$, with $c > 0$, $d < 0$, $a > 0$, $b < 0$. These parabolas have four common points. Show that these four points are concyclic.

solution page 117

31st Spanish Mathematical Olympiad, 1995 (Second Round)

3

A line through the barycentre G of the triangle ABC intersects the side AB at P and the side AC at Q. Show that

$$\frac{PB}{PA} \cdot \frac{QC}{QA} \le \frac{1}{4}.$$

solution page 118

31st Spanish Mathematical Olympiad, 1995 (Second Round)

6

AB is a fixed segment and C a variable point, internal to AB.

Equilateral triangles ACB' and CBA' are constructed, in the same half-plane defined by AB, and another equilateral triangle ABC' is constructed in the opposite half-plane. Show that:

(a) the lines AA', BB' and CC' are concurrent;

(b) if P is the common point of the lines of (a), find the locus of P when C varies on AB;

(c) the centres A'', B'', C'' of the three equilateral triangles also form an equilateral triangle;

(d) the points A'', B'', C'' and P are concyclic.

solution page 119

Bundeswettbewerb Mathematik, 1995 (Second Round)

3

Every diagonal of a given pentagon is parallel to one side of the pentagon. Prove that the ratio of the lengths of a diagonal and its corresponding side is the same for each of the five pairs. Determine the value of this ratio.

solution page 120

Bundeswettbewerb Mathematik, 1996 (First Round)

1

Is it possible to cover a square of length 5 completely with three squares of length 4?

solution page 121

Bundeswettbewerb Mathematik, 1996 (First Round)

3

There are four straight lines in the plane, each three of them determining a triangle. One of these straight lines is parallel to one of the medians of the triangle formed by the other three lines. Prove that each of the other straight lines has the same property.

solution page 123

XLV Lithuanian Mathematical Olympiad, 1996

4

How many sides has the polygon inscribed in a given circle and such that the sum of the squares of its sides is the largest one?

solution page 125

Vietnamese Mathematical Olympiad, 1996 (Category A)

2

Let $Sxyz$ be a trihedron (a figure determined by the intersection of three planes). A plane (P), not passing through S, cuts the rays Sx, Sy, Sz, respectively at A, B, C. In the plane (P), construct three triangles DAB, EBC, FCA such that each has no interior point of triangle ABC and $\triangle DAB = \triangle SAB$, $\triangle EBC = \triangle SBC$, $\triangle FCA = \triangle SCA$. Consider the sphere (T) satisfying simultaneously two conditions:

(i) (T) touches the planes (SAB), (SBC), (SCA), (ABC);

(ii) (T) is inside the trihedron $Sxyz$ and is outside the tetrahedron $SABC$.

Prove that the circumcentre of triangle DEF is the point where (T) touches (P).

solution page 127

Vietnamese Mathematical Olympiad, 1996 (Category B)

2

Let $ABCD$ be a tetrahedron with $AB = AC = AD$, inscribed in a sphere with centre O. Let G be the centre of gravity of triangle ACD, E be the mid-point of BG and F be the mid-point of AE. Prove that OF is perpendicular to BG if and only if OD is perpendicular to AC.

solution page 128

Dutch Mathematical Olympiad, 1993

5

$P_1, P_2, \ldots, P_{11}$ are eleven distinct points on a line, $P_iP_j \leq 1$ for every pair P_i, P_j. Prove that the sum of all (55) distances P_iP_j, $1 \leq i, j \leq 11$ is smaller than 30.

solution page 129

23rd All Russian Olympiad, 1997 (11 Grade, 1st Day)

Two circles intersect at the points A and B. A line is drawn through the point A. This line crosses the first circle again at the point C and it crosses the second circle again at the point D. Let M and N be the mid-points of the arcs BC and BD respectively (these arcs do not contain A). Let K be the mid-point of the segment CD. Prove that the angle MKN is a right angle. (It may be assumed that A lies between C and D).

solution page 130

Fourth National Mathematical Olympiad of Turkey, 1997

Given a square $ABCD$ of side length 2, let M and N be points on the edges $[AB]$ and $[CD]$, respectively. The lines CM and BN meet at P, while the lines AN and MD meet at Q. Show that $|PQ| \geq 1$.

solution page 131

Fourth National Mathematical Olympiad of Turkey, 1997

Given a quadrangle $ABCD$, the circle which is tangential to $[AD]$, $[DC]$ and $[CB]$ touches these edges at K, L and M, respectively. Denote the point at which the line which passes through L and is parallel to AD meets $[KM]$ by N, and the point at which $[LN]$ and $[KC]$ meet by P. Prove that

$$|PL| = |PN|.$$

solution page 132

20th Austrian-Polish Mathematical Competition, 1997

Let P be a parallelepiped, let V be its volume, S its surface area, and L the sum of the lengths of the edges of P. For $t \geq 0$ let P_t be the solid consisting of points having distance from P not greater than t. Prove that the volume of P_t is equal to

$$V + St + \frac{\pi}{4}Lt^2 + \frac{4}{3}\pi t^3.$$

solution page 133

Israel Mathematical Olympiad, 1997

Is there a planar polygon whose vertices have integer coordinates, whose area is $\frac{1}{2}$, such that this polygon is

(a) a triangle with at least two sides longer than 1000?

(b) a triangle whose sides are all longer than 1000?

(c) a quadrangle?

solution page 134

Israel Mathematical Olympiad, 1997

4

Prove that if two altitudes of a tetrahedron intersect, then so do the other two altitudes.

solution page 155

Estonian Mathematical Olympiad, 1997 (Final Round)

4

In a triangle ABC the values of $\tan \angle A$, $\tan \angle B$ and $\tan \angle C$ relate to each other as $1 : 2 : 3$. Find the ratio of the lengths of the sides AC and AB.

solution page 156

Estonian Mathematical Olympiad, 1997 (Final Round)

5

There are n points $(n \geq 3)$ in the plane, no three of which are collinear. Is it always possible to draw a circle through three of these points so that it has no other given points

(a) in its interior? (b) in its interior nor on the circle?

solution page 157

10th Irish Mathematical Olympiad, 1997

2

Let ABC be an equilateral triangle. For a point M inside ABC, let D, E, F be the feet of the perpendiculars from M onto BC, CA, AB, respectively. Find the locus of all such points M for which $\angle FDE$ is a right angle.

solution page 158

10th Irish Mathematical Olympiad, 1997

7

$ABCD$ is a quadrilateral which is circumscribed about a circle Γ (that is, each side of the quadrilateral is tangent to Γ). If $\angle A = \angle B = 120°$, $\angle D = 90°$ and BC has length 1, find, with proof, the length of AD.

solution page 159

Hungary-Israel Bi-National Mathematical Competition, 1997

3

ABC is an acute-angled triangle whose circumcentre is O. The intersection points of the diameters of the circumcircle, passing through A, B, C, with the opposite sides are A_1, B_1, C_1, respectively. The circumradius of the triangle ABC is of length $2p$, where p is a prime. The lengths OA_1, OB_1, OC_1 are integers. What are the lengths of the sides of the triangle?

solution page 140

Hubgary-Israel Bi-National Mathematical Competition, 1997

5

The three squares ACC_1A'', ABB_1A', $BCDE$ are constructed on the sides of a given triangle ABC, outwards. The center of the square $BCDE$ is P. Prove that the three lines $A'C$, $A''B$ and PA pass through one point.

solution page 141

36th Armenian National Mathematical Olympiad, 1997

3

Prove that, for any points A, B, C, D, E, F, the following inequality holds:

$$AD^2 + BE^2 + CF^2 \leq 2(AB^2 + BC^2 + CD^2 + DE^2 + EF^2 + FA^2).$$

solution page 142

Croatian National Mathematical Olympiad, 1997 (IV Class)

2

A circle k and the point K are on the same plane. For every two distinct points P and Q on k, the circle k' contains the points P, Q, and K. Let M be the intersection of the tangent to the circle k' at the point K and the line PQ. Find the locus of the points M when P and Q move over all points on k.

solution page 143

38th IMO Croation Team Selection Test, 1997

1

Three points A, B, C, are given on the same line, such that B is between A and C. Over the segments $\overline{AB}$, $\overline{BC}$, $\overline{AC}$, as diameters, semicircles are constructed on the same side of the line. The perpendicular from B to AC intersects the largest circle at point D. Prove that the common tangent of the two smaller semicircles, different from BD, is parallel to the tangent on the largest semicircle through the point D.

solution page 144

St. Petersburg City Mathematical Olympiad, 1997 (10th Grade)

3

K, L, M, N are the mid-points of sides AB, BC, CD, DA, respectively, of an inscribed quadrangle $ABCD$. Prove that the orthocentres of triangles AKN, BKL, CLM, DMN are vertices of a parallelogram.

solution page 145

St. Petersburg City Mathematical Olympiad, 1997 (11th Grade)

3

Circles S_1 and S_2 intersect at points A and B. A point Q is chosen on S_1. The lines QA and QB meet S_2 at points C and D; the tangents to S_1 at A and B meet at point P. The point Q lies outside S_2, the points C and D lie outside S_1. Prove that the line QP goes through the mid-point of CD.

solution page 146

33rd Spanish Mathematical Olympiad, 1997 (Second Round)

5

Show that for any convex quadrilateral with unit area, the sum of the sides and diagonals is not less than $2(2 + \sqrt{2})$.

solution page 147

7th Japan Mathematical Olympiad, 1997 (Final Round)

1

Prove that, whenever we put ten points in any way on a circle whose diameter is 5, we can find two points whose distance is less than 2.

solution page 148

7th Japan Mathematical Olympiad, 1997 (Final Round)

4

Let A, B, C, D be points in space in a general position. Assume that $AX + BX + CX + DX$ is a minimum at $X = X_0$ ($X_0 \neq A, B, C, D$). Prove that $\angle AX_0B = \angle CX_0D$.

solution page 149

Vietnamese Mathematical Olympiad, 1997

1.

In a plane, let there be given a circle with centre O, with radius R and a point P inside the circle, $OP = d < R$. Among all convex quadrilaterals $ABCD$, inscribed in the circle such that their diagonals AC and BD cut each other orthogonally at P, determine the ones which have the greatest perimeter and the ones which have the smallest perimeter. Calculate these perimeters in terms of R and d.

solution page 150

38 IMO Turkey Team Selection Test, 1997

1

In a triangle ABC which has a right angle at A, let H denote the foot of the altitude belonging to the hypotenuse. Show that the sum of the radii of the incircles of the triangles ABC, ABH, and AHC is equal to $|AH|$.

solution page 151

38 IMO Turkey Team Selection Test, 1997

4

The edge AE of a convex pentagon $ABCDE$ whose vertices lie on the unit circle passes through the centre of this circle. If $|AB| = a$, $|BC| = b$, $|CD| = c$, $|DE| = d$ and $ab = cd = \frac{1}{4}$, compute $|AC| + |CE|$ in terms of a, b, c, d.

solution page 152

Chilean Mathematical Olympiad, 1994

1

Given three straight lines in a plane, that concur at point O, consider the three consecutive angles between them (which, naturally, add up to $180°$). Let P be a point in the plane not on any of these lines, and let A, B, C be the feet of the perpendiculars drawn from P to the three lines. Show that the internal angles of $\triangle ABC$ are equal to those between the given lines.

solution page 153

$ABCDEFGH$ is a cube of edge 2. Let M be the mid-point of $\overline{BC}$ and N the mid-point of $\overline{EF}$. Compute the area of the quadrilateral $AMHN$.

solution page 154

Given a trapezoid $ABCD$, where $\overline{AB}$ and $\overline{DC}$ are parallel, and $\overline{AD} = \overline{DC} = \overline{AB}/2$, determine $\angle ACB$.

solution page 155

In a circle of radius 1 are drawn six equal arcs of circles, radius 1, cutting the original circle as in the figure. Calculate the shaded area.

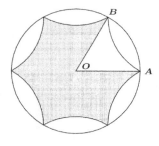

solution page 156

Let $ABCD$ be an $m \times n$ rectangle, with $m, n \in \mathbb{N}$. Consider a ray of light that starts from A, is reflected at an angle of $45°$ on another side of the rectangle, and goes on reflecting in this way.

(a) Show that the ray will finally hit a vertex.

(b) Suppose m and n have no common factor greater than 1. Determine the number of reflections undergone by the ray before it hits a vertex.

solution page 157

Suppose that ten points are given in the plane such that any five of them contains four points which are concyclic. What is the largest number N for which we can correctly say: "At least N of the ten points lie on a circle"? ($4 \le N \le 10$.)

solution page 158

Iranian Mathematical Olympiad, 1997 (Second Round)

3

Suppose that Γ is a semi-circle with centre O and diameter AB. Assume that M is a point on the extension of AB such that $MA > MB$. A line through M intersects Γ at C and D such that $MC > MD$. Circum-circles of the triangles AOC and BOD will intersect at points O and K. Prove that $OK \perp MK$.

solution page 162

Swedish Mathematical Competition, 1997 (Final Round)

1

Let AC be a diameter of a circle. Assume that AB is tangent to the circle at the point A and that the segment BC intersects the circle at D. Show that if $|AC| = 1$, $|AB| = a$, and $|CD| = b$, then

$$\frac{1}{a^2 + \frac{1}{2}} < \frac{b}{a} < \frac{1}{a^2} \, .$$

solution page 163

Swedish Mathematical Competition, 1997 (Final Round)

2

The bisector of the angle B in the triangle ABC intersects the side AC at the point D. Let E be a point on side AB such that $3\angle ACE = 2\angle BCE$. The segments BD and CE intersect at the point P. One knows that $|ED| = |DC| = |CP|$. Find the angles of the triangle.

solution page 164

Ukrainian Mathematical Olympiad, 1998 (9th Grade)

2

A convex polygon with 2000 vertices in a plane is given. Prove that we may mark 1998 points of the plane so that any triangle with vertices which are vertices of the polygon has exactly one marked point as an internal point.

solution page 165

Ukrainian Mathematical Olympiad, 1998 (10th Grade)

3

Let M be an internal point on the side AC of a triangle ABC, and let O be the intersection point of perpendiculars from the mid-points of AM and MC to lines BC and AB, respectively. Find the location of M such that the length of segment OM is minimal.

solution page 166

Ukrainian Mathematical Olympiad, 1998 (11th Grade)

4

A triangle ABC is given. Altitude CD intersects the bisector BK of $\angle ABC$, and the altitude KL of BKC, at the points M and N, respectively. The circumscribed circle of BKN intersects segment AB at the point $P \neq B$. Prove that triangle KPM is isosceles.

solution page 167

Ukrainian Mathematical Olympiad, 1998 (11th Grade)

7

Two spheres with distinct radii are externally tangent at point P. Line segments AB and CD are given such that the first sphere touches them at the points A and C, and the second sphere touches them at the points B and D. Let M and N be the orthogonal projections of the mid-points of segments AC and BD on the line joining the centres of the given spheres. Prove that $PM = PN$.

solution page 168

Vietnamese Mathematical Olympiad, 1998 (Category A, Day 1)

2

Let $ABCD$ be a tetrahedron and AA_1, BB_1, CC_1, DD_1 be diameters of the circumsphere of $ABCD$. Let A_0, B_0, C_0 and D_0 be the centroids of the triangles BCD, CDA, DAB and ABC, respectively. Prove that

(a) the lines A_0A_1, B_0B_1, C_0C_1 and D_0D_1 have a common point, which is denoted by F;

(b) the line passing through F and the mid-point of an edge is perpendicular to its opposite edge.

solution page 169

Vietnamese Mathematical Olympiad, 1998 (Category B, Day 1)

2

Let P be a point lying on a given sphere. Three mutually perpendicular rays from P intersect the sphere at points A, B, and C. Prove that for all such triads of rays from P, the plane of the triangle ABC passes through a fixed point and determine the largest possible value of the area of the triangle ABC.

solution page 170

Vietnamese Mathematical Olympiad, 1998 (Category B, Day 1)

5

Determine the smallest possible value of the following expression

$$\sqrt{x^2 + (y+1)^2} + \sqrt{x^2 + (y-3)^2}$$

where x, y are real numbers such that $2x - y = 2$.

solution page 172

15th Balkan Mathematical Olympiad, 1998

3

Denote by S the set of all points of $\triangle ABC$ except one interior point T. Show that S can be represented as a union of disjoint (line) segments.

solution page 173

1st Mediterranean Mathematical Olympiad, 1998

1

Let $ABCD$ be a square inscribed in a circle. If M is a point on the arc AB show that $MC \cdot MD > 3\sqrt{3} \cdot MA \cdot MB$.

solution page 174

In a triangle ABC, I is the incentre and $D \in (BC)$, $E \in (CA)$, $F \in (AB)$ are the points of tangency of the incircle with the sides of the triangle. Let $M \in (BC)$ be the foot of the interior bisector of $\angle BIC$ and $\{P\} = FE \cap AM$. Prove that DP is the interior bisector of the angle $\angle FDE$.

solution page 175

Let $ABCD$ be a trapezoid ($AB \parallel CD$) and M, N be points on the lines AD and BC, respectively, such that $MN \parallel AB$. Prove that

$$DC \cdot MA + AB \cdot MD = MN \cdot AD.$$

solution page 177

A sphere is inscribed in a given tetrahedron $ABCD$. Its four tangent planes, which are parallel to the faces of the tetrahedron, cut four smaller tetrahedra from the tetrahedron. Prove that the sum of lengths of all their 24 edges is equal to twice the sum of the lengths of the edges of the tetrahedron $ABCD$.

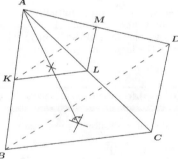

solution page 178

In the exterior of a circle k a point A is given. Show that the diagonals of all trapezoids which are inscribed into the circle k and whose extended arms intersect at the point A intersect at the same point U.

solution page 179

Let O be the centre of the circumcircle of the acute triangle ABC. The lines CO, AO, and BO intersect for the second time the circumcircles of the triangles AOB, BOC, and AOC at C_1, A_1, and B_1, respectively.

Prove that

$$\frac{AA_1}{OA_1} + \frac{BB_1}{OB_1} + \frac{CC_1}{OC_1} \geq 4.5.$$

solution page 180

Let the escribed circle (opposite $\angle A$) of the triangle ABC ($\angle A$, $\angle B$, $\angle C < 120°$) with centre O be tangent to the sides of the triangle AB, BC and CA at points C_1, A_1 and B_1 respectively. Denote the mid-points of the segments AO, BO, and CO by A_2, B_2, and C_2, respectively.

Prove that lines A_1A_2, B_1B_2, and C_1C_2 intersect at the same point. *solution page 182*

Hungary-Israel Mathematical Competition, 1999

$\boxed{2}$

A set of $2n+1$ lines in a plane is drawn. No two of them are parallel, and no three pass through one point. Every three of these lines form a non-right triangle. Determine the maximal number of acute-angled triangles that can be formed. *solution page 184*

12th Korean Mathematical Olympiad, 1999

$\boxed{1}$

Let R, r be the circumradius, and the inradius of $\triangle ABC$, respectively, and let R', r' be the circumradius and inradius of $\triangle A'B'C'$, respectively. Prove that if $\angle C = \angle C'$ and $Rr' = R'r$, then the two triangles are similar. *solution page 186*

Grosman Memorial Mathematical Olympiad, 1999

$\boxed{3}$

For every triangle ABC, denote by $D(ABC)$, the triangle whose vertices are the tangency points of the incircle of ABC (touching the sides of the triangle). The given triangle ABC is not equilateral.

(a) Prove that $D(ABC)$ is also not equilateral.

(b) Find in the sequence of triangles $T_1 = \triangle ABC$, $T_{k+1} = D(T_k)$, $k = 1$, 2, ... a triangle whose largest angle α satisfies the inequality $0 < \alpha - 60° < 0.0001$. *solution page 187*

Grosman Memorial Mathematical Olympiad, 1999

$\boxed{6}$

Six points A, B, C, D, E, F are given in space. The quadrilaterals $ABDE$, $BCEF$, $CDFA$ are parallelograms. Prove that the six mid-points of the sides AB, BC, CD, DE, EF, FA are coplanar. *solution page 189*

Russian Mathematical Olympiad, 1999 (11th Form)

$\boxed{3}$

The incircle of quadrilateral $ABCD$ touches the sides DA, AB, BC, CD in K, L, M, N, respectively. Let S_1, S_2, S_3, S_4 be the incircles of triangles AKL, BLM, CMN, DKN, respectively. Let l_1, l_2, l_3, l_4 be the common external tangents to the pairs S_1 and S_2, S_2 and S_3, S_3 and S_4, S_4 and S_1, different from the sides of quadrilateral $ABCD$. Prove that l_1, l_2, l_3, l_4 intersect in the vertices of a rhombus. *solution page 190*

Russian Mathematical Olympiad, 1999 (11th Form)

7

The plane α passing through the vertex A of tetrahedron $ABCD$ is tangent to the circumsphere of the tetrahedron. Prove that the angles between the lines of intersection of α with the planes ABC, ACD, and ABD are equal if and only if $AB \cdot CD = AC \cdot BD = AD \cdot BC$.

solution page 193

16th Iranian Mathematical Olympiad, 1999 (Second Round)

2

Suppose that $n(r)$ denotes the number of points with integer coordinates on a circle of radius $r > 1$. Prove that,

$$n(r) < 6\sqrt[3]{\pi r^2}\,.$$

solution page 194

16th Iranian Mathematical Olympiad, 1999 (Second Round)

3

Suppose that $ABCDEF$ is a convex hexagon with $AB = BC$, $CD = DE$, and $EF = FA$. Prove that

$$\frac{BC}{BE} + \frac{DE}{DA} + \frac{FA}{FC} \geq \frac{3}{2}\,.$$

solution page 195

16th Iranian Mathematical Olympiad, 1999 (Second Round)

5

In triangle ABC, the angle bisector of $\angle BAC$ meets BC at point D. Suppose that Γ is the circle which is tangent to BC at D and passes through the point A. Let M be the second point of intersection of Γ and AC and BM meets the circle at P. Prove that AP is a median of triangle ABD.

solution page 197

16th Iranian Mathematical Olympiad, 1999 (Second Round)

6

Suppose that ABC is a triangle. If we paint the points of the plane in red and green, prove that either there exist two red points which are one unit apart or three green points forming a triangle equal to ABC.

solution page 198

16th Iranian Mathematical Olympiad, 1999 (Third Round)

3

Suppose that $C_1, \ldots, C_n$ are circles of radius one in the plane such that no two of them are tangent, and the subset of the plane, formed by the union of these circles, is connected. If $S = \{C_i \cap C_j \mid 1 \leq i < j \leq n\}$, prove that $|S| \geq n$.

solution page 199

16th Iranian Mathematical Olympiad, 1999 (Third Round)

5

Suppose that $ABCDEF$ is a convex hexagon with $\angle B + \angle D + \angle F = 360°$ and

$$\frac{AB}{BC} \cdot \frac{CD}{DE} \cdot \frac{EF}{FA} = 1.$$

Prove that

$$\frac{BC}{CA} \cdot \frac{AE}{EF} \cdot \frac{FD}{DB} = 1.$$

solution page 200

Chinese Mathematical Olympiad, 1999

1

In acute triangle $\triangle ABC$, $\angle ACB > \angle ABC$. Point D is on BC such that $\angle ADB$ is obtuse. Let H be the orthocentre of $\triangle ABD$. Suppose point F is inside $\triangle ABC$ and on the circumcircle of $\triangle ABD$. Prove that point F is the orthocentre of $\triangle ABC$ if and only if HD is parallel to CF and H is on the circumcircle of $\triangle ABC$.

solution page 201

Vietnamese Mathematical Olympiad, 1999 (Category A)

2

Let A', B', C' be the respective mid-points of the arcs BC, CA, AB, not containing points A, B, C, respectively, of the circumcircle of the triangle ABC. The sides BC, CA, and AB intersect the pairs of segments $(C'A', A'B')$, $(A'B', B'C')$, and $(B'C', C'A')$ at the pairs of points (M, N), (P, Q), and (R, S), respectively. Prove that $MN = PQ = RS$ if and only if the triangle ABC is equilateral.

solution page 205

Vietnamese Mathematical Olympiad, 1999 (Category A)

5

In three-dimensional space, let Ox, Oy, Oz, Ot be four non-planar distinct rays such that the angles between any two of them have the same measure.

(a) Determine this common measure.

(b) Let Or be another ray different from the above four rays. Let α, β, γ, δ be the angles formed by Or with Ox, Oy, Oz, Ot, respectively. Put

$$p = \cos\alpha + \cos\beta + \cos\gamma + \cos\delta,$$

$$q = \cos^2\alpha + \cos^2\beta + \cos^2\gamma + \cos^2\delta.$$

Prove that p and q are invariant when Or rotates about the point O.

solution page 205

Vietnamese Mathematical Olympiad, 1999 (Category B)

2

Let ABC be a triangle inscribed in the circle $\mathcal{O}$. Locate the position of the points P, not lying in the circle $\mathcal{O}$, of the plane (ABC) with the property that the lines PA, PB, PC intersect the circle $\mathcal{O}$ again at points A', B', C' such that $A'B'C'$ is a right-angled isosceles triangle with $\angle A'B'C' = 90°$.

solution page 207

Vietnamese Mathematical Olympiad, 1999 (Category B)

The base side and the altitude of a regular hexagonal prism $ABCDEF$, $A'B'C'D'E'F'$ are equal to a and h, respectively. Prove that six planes $(AB'F)$, $(CD'B)$, $(EF'D)$, $(D'EC)$, $(F'AE)$ and $(B'CA)$ are tangent to the same sphere. Determine the centre and the radius of this sphere.

solution page 208

16th Balkan Mathematical Olympiad, 1999

Given an acute-angled triangle ABC, let D be the mid-point of the arc BC of the circumcircle of ABC not containing A. The points which are symmetric to D with respect to the line BC and the centre of the circumcircle are denoted by E and F, respectively. Finally, let K stand for the mid-point of $[EA]$. Prove that:

(a) the circle passing through the mid-points of the edges of the triangle ABC, also passes through K;

(b) the line passing through K and the mid-point of $[BC]$ is perpendicular to AF.

solution page 209

16th Balkan Mathematical Olympiad, 1999

Let ABC be an acute-angled triangle; M, N and P are the feet of the perpendiculars from the centroid G of the triangle upon its sides AB, BC and CA respectively. Prove that

$$\frac{4}{27} < \frac{\text{area}(MNP)}{\text{area}(ABC)} \leq \frac{1}{4}.$$

solution page 210

6th Turkish Mathematical Olympiad, 1999 (Second Round)

On the base of the isosceles triangle ABC ($|AB| = |AC|$) we choose a point D such that $|BD| : |DC| = 2 : 1$, and on $[AD]$ we choose a point P such that $m(\widehat{BAC}) = m(\widehat{BPD})$.

Prove that $m(\widehat{DPC}) = m(\widehat{BAC})/2$.

solution page 211

6th Turkish Mathematical Olympiad, 1999 (Second Round)

Given the angle XOY, variable points M and N are considered on the arms $[OX]$ and $[OY]$, respectively, so that $|OM| + |ON|$ is constant. Determine the geometric locus of the mid-point of $[MN]$.

solution page 212

Turkish Team Selection Test for 40th IMO, 1999

Let L and N be the mid-points of the diagonals $[AC]$ and $[BD]$ of the cyclic quadrilateral $ABCD$, respectively. If BD is the bisector of the angle ANC, then prove that AC is the bisector of the angle BLD.

solution page 213

Prove that the plane is not a union of the inner regions of finitely many parabolas. (The outer region of a parabola is the union of the lines not intersecting the parabola. The inner region of a parabola is the set of points of the plane that do not belong to the outer region of the parabola.)

solution page 214

Swiss Mathematical Contest, 1999 (First Day) 1

Two circles intersect each other in points M and N. An arbitrary point A of the first circle, which is not M or N, is connected with M and N, and the straight lines AM and AN intersect the second circle again in the points B and C. Prove that the tangent to the first circle at A is parallel to the straight line BC.

solution page 215

Swiss Mathematical Contest, 1999 (First Day) 5

Let $ABCD$ be a rectangle, P a point on the line CD. Let M and N be the mid-points of AD and BC, respectively. PM intersects AC in Q. Show that MN is the bisector of the angle QNP.

solution page 216

Swiss Mathematical Contest, 1999 (Second Day) 2

A square is partitioned into rectangles whose sides are parallel to the sides of the square. For each rectangle, the ratio of its shorter side to its longer side is determined. Prove that the sum S of these ratios is always at least 1.

solution page 217

50th Polish Mathematical Olympiad, 1999 1

Let D be a point on side BC of triangle ABC such that $AD > BC$. Point E on side AC is defined by the equation $\dfrac{AE}{EC} = \dfrac{BC}{AD - BC}$. Show that $AD > BE$.

solution page 218

Chilean Mathematical Olympiad, 1996 1

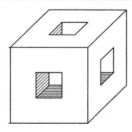

Consider a cube of edge 18 cm. In the centre of three different (and not opposite) faces we bore a square perforation of side 6 cm that goes across the cube as far as the opposite face. We thus obtain the following figure:

Determine the surface area of the resulting solid.

solution page 219

Chilean Mathematical Olympiad, 1996

Two circles intersect at A and B. P is a point on arc $\widehat{AB}$ on one of the circles. PA and PB intersect the other circle at R and S (see figure). If P' is any point on the same arc as P and if R' and S' are the points in which $P'A$ and $P'B$ intersect the second circle, prove that $\widehat{RS} = \widehat{R'S'}$.

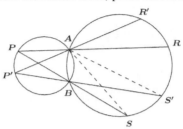

solution page 220

St. Petersburg Mathematical Contest

The point C is on the segment AB. A straight line through C intersects the circle with diameter AB at E and F, the circle with diameter AC again at M, and the circle with diameter BC again at N. Prove that $MF = EN$.

solution page 221

St. Petersburg Mathematical Contest

The sides of a heptagon $A_1A_2A_3A_4A_5A_6A_7$ have equal length. From a point O inside, perpendiculars are dropped to the sides A_1A_2, A_2A_3, ..., A_7A_1, meeting them, and not their extensions, at H_1, H_2, ..., H_7, respectively. Prove that

$$A_1H_1 + A_2H_2 + \cdots + A_7H_7 = H_1A_2 + H_2A_3 + \cdots + H_7A_1.$$

solution page 222

St. Petersburg Mathematical Contest

7

In triangle ABC, the sides satisfy $AB + AC = 2BC$. Prove that the bisector of $\angle A$ is perpendicular to the line segment joining the incentre and circumcentre of ABC.

solution page 223

St. Petersburg Mathematical Contest

Segments AC and BD intersect at point E. Points K and M, on segments AB and CD, respectively, are such that the segment KM passes through E. Prove that $KM \leq \max\{AC, BD\}$.

solution page 224

St. Petersburg Mathematical Contest

The plane is divided into regions by n lines in general positions. Prove that at least $n - 2$ of the regions are triangles.

solution page 226

St. Petersburg Mathematical Contest

29

From each of k points on a plane, a few rays are drawn. No two rays intersect. Prove that one can choose $k-1$ of the segments connecting these points such that they are disjoint from one another and from any of the rays, except possibly at those k points.

solution page 227

St. Petersburg Mathematical Contest

34

A straight line passes through the centre of a regular $2n$–gon. Prove that the sum of distances to this line from the vertices on one side of this line equals the sum of the distances from the remaining vertices.

solution page 250

St. Petersburg Mathematical Contest

39

Each of n lines on a plane is cut by the others into 2 rays and $n-2$ equal segments. Prove that $n = 3$.

solution page 251

St. Petersburg Mathematical Contest

43

H is a given point inside a circle. Prove that a fixed circle passes through the mid-points of the sides of any triangle inscribed in the circle and having H as its orthocentre.

solution page 253

IMO Proposal by the USSR (1985)

25

A triangle T_1 is constructed with the medians of a right triangle T. If R_1 and R are the circumradii of T_1 and T, respectively, prove that $R_1 > 5R/6$.

solution page 254

Leningrad High School Olympiad 1981

4

A plane is partitioned into an infinite set of unit squares by parallel lines. A triangle ABC is constructed with vertices at line intersections. Show that if $|AB| > |AC|$, then $|AB| - |AC| > 1/p$, where p is the perimeter of the triangle. (Grades 8, 9, 10)

solution page 255

Leningrad High School Olympiad 1981

6

In a convex quadrilateral the sum of the distances from any point within the quadrilateral to the four straight lines along which the sides lie is constant. Show that the quadrilateral is a parallelogram. (Grade 9)

solution page 256

Annual Greek High School Competition 1983

2

If **a** and **b** are given nonparallel vectors, solve for x in the equation

$$\frac{a^2 + x\mathbf{a}\cdot\mathbf{b}}{|\mathbf{a}||\mathbf{a} + x\mathbf{b}|} = \frac{b^2 + \mathbf{a}\cdot\mathbf{b}}{|\mathbf{b}||\mathbf{a}+\mathbf{b}|}.$$

solution page 237

Hungarian National Olympiad 1987

2

Cut the regular (equilateral) triangle AXY from rectangle $ABCD$ in such a way that the vertex X is on side BC and the vertex Y is on side CD. Prove that among the three remaining right triangles there are two the sum of whose areas equals the area of the third.

solution page 238

Hungarian National Olympiad 1987

4

Consider points A and B on given rays (semilines) starting from $C\Gamma$ such that the sum $CA + CB$ is a given constant. Show that there is a point $D \neq C$ such that for each position of A and B the circumcircle of triangle ABC passes through D.

solution page 239

British Mathematical Olympiad 1983

1

In the triangle ABC with circumcentre O, $AB = AC$, D is the midpoint of AB, and E is the centroid of triangle ACD. Prove that OE is perpendicular to CD.

solution page 240

West Point Proposals 1984

1

Given six segments $S_1, S_2, \ldots, S_6$ congruent to the edges AB, AC, AD, CD, DB, BC, respectively, of a tetrahedron $ABCD$, show how to construct with straightedge and compass a segment whose length equals that of the *bialtitude* of the tetrahedron relative to opposite edges AB and CD (i.e., the distance between the lines AB and CD).

solution page 241

AustrianPolish Mathematics Competition 1982

2

We are given a unit circle C with center M and a closed convex region R in the interior of C. From every point P of circle C, there are two tangents to the boundary of R that are inclined to each other at $60°$. Prove that R is a closed circular disk with center M and radius $1/2$.

solution page 242

Asian Pacific Mathematical Olympiad 1989

3

Let A_1, A_2, A_3 be three points in the plane, and for convenience, let $A_4 = A_1$, $A_5 = A_2$. For $n = 1, 2$ and 3 suppose that B_n is the midpoint of $A_n A_{n+1}$, and suppose that C_n is the midpoint of $A_n B_n$. Suppose that $A_n C_{n+1}$ and $B_n A_{n+2}$ meet at D_n, and that $A_n B_{n+1}$ and $C_n A_{n+2}$ meet at E_n. Calculate the ratio of the area of triangle $D_1 D_2 D_3$ to the area of triangle $E_1 E_2 E_3$.

solution page 243

Austrian-Polish Mathematics Competition 1985

8

The consecutive vertices of a given convex n-gon are $A_0, A_1, \ldots, A_{n-1}$. The n-gon is partitioned into $n - 2$ triangles by diagonals which are non-intersecting (except possibly at the vertices). Show that there exists an enumeration $\Delta_1, \Delta_2, \ldots, \Delta_{n-2}$ of these triangles such that A_i is a vertex of Δ_i for $1 \leq i \leq n - 2$. How many enumerations of this kind exist?

solution page 244

Leningrad High School Olympiad (Third Round) 1982

2

If in triangle ABC, $C = 2A$ and $AC = 2BC$, show that it is a right triangle. (Grade 8, 9)

solution page 245

Leningrad High School Olympiad (Third Round) 1982

10

In a given tetrahedron $ABCD$, $\angle BAC + \angle BAD = 180°$. If AK is the bisector of $\angle CAD$, determine $\angle BAK$. (Grade 10)

solution page 246

Leningrad High School Olympiad (Third Round) 1982

11

Show that it is possible to place non-zero numbers at the vertices of a given regular n-gon P so that for any set of vertices of P which are vertices of a regular k-gon ($k \leq n$), the sum of the corresponding numbers equals zero. (Grade 10)

solution page 247

3rd Ibero-American Olympiad

1

The angles of a triangle are in arithmetical progression. The altitudes of the triangle are also in arithmetical progression. Show that the triangle is equilateral. *solution page 248*

3rd Ibero-American Olympiad

4

Let ABC be a triangle with sides a, b, c. Each side is divided in n equal parts. Let S be the sum of the squares of distances from each vertex to each one of the points of subdivision of the opposite side (excepting the vertices). Show that

$$\frac{S}{a^2 + b^2 + c^2}$$

is rational.

solution page 249

Spanish Mathematical Olympiad, 1st Round 1985

4

L and M are points on the sides AB and AC, respectively, of triangle ABC such that $\overline{AL} = 2\overline{AB}/5$ and $\overline{AM} = 3\overline{AC}/4$. If BM and CL intersect at P, and AP and BC intersect at N, determine $\overline{BN}/\overline{BC}$.

solution page 250

Second Balkan Mathematical Olympiad

1

Let O be the centre of the circle through the points A, B, C, and let D be the midpoint of AB. Let E be the centroid of the triangle ACD. Prove that the line CD is perpendicular to the line OE if and only if $AB = AC$.

solution page 251

IMO Proposal by Finland (1987)

1

In a Cartesian coordinate system, the circle C_1 has center $O_1 = (-2, 0)$ and radius 3. Denote the point $(1, 0)$ by A and the origin by O. Prove that there is a positive constant c such that for any point X which is exterior to C_1,

$$\overline{OX} - 1 \geq c \, \min\{\overline{AX}, \overline{AX}^2\}.$$

Find the smallest possible c.

solution page 252

IMO Proposal by Poland (1987)

1

Let F be a one-to-one mapping of the plane into itself which maps closed rectangles into closed rectangles. Show that F maps squares into squares. Continuity of F is not assumed.

solution page 253

Singapore MSI Mathematical Competition 1988

2

Suppose $\triangle ABC$ and $\triangle DEF$ in the figure are congruent. Prove that the perpendicular bisectors of AD, BE, and CF intersect at the same point.

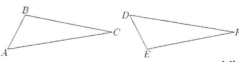

solution page 254

First Selection Test of the Chinese I.M.O. Team 1988

3

In triangle ABC, angle C is $30°$. D is a point on AC and E is a point on BC such that $AD = BE = AB$. Prove that $OI = DE$ and OI is perpendicular to DE, where O and I are respectively the circumcentre and incentre of triangle ABC. *solution page 255*

XIV ALL UNION Mathematical Olympiad U.S.S.R.

2

Side AB of a square $ABCD$ is divided into n segments in such a way that the sum of lengths of the even numbered segments equals the sum of lengths of the odd numbered segments. Lines parallel to AD are drawn through each point of division, and each of the n "strips" thus formed is divided by diagonal BD into a left region and a right region. Show that the sum of the areas of the left regions with odd numbers is equal to the sum of the areas of the right regions with even numbers.

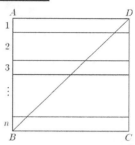

solution page 256

XIV ALL UNION Mathematical Olympiad U.S.S.R.

4

Points M and P are the midpoints of sides BC and CD of convex quadrilateral $ABCD$. If $AM + AP = a$, show that the area of the region $ABCD$ is less than $a^2/2$. *solution page 257*

43rd Mathematical Olympiad (1991-92) in Poland (Final round)

1

Segments AC and BD intersect in point P so that $PA = PD$, $PB = PC$. Let O be the circumcentre of triangle PAB. Prove that lines OP and CD are perpendicular. *solution page 258*

34th IMO Proposal by Canada (1993)

2

Let triangle ABC be such that its circumradius $R = 1$. Let r be the inradius of ABC and let p be the inradius of the orthic triangle $A'B'C'$ of triangle ABC. Prove that $p \leq 1 - 1/3(1 + r)^2$. *solution page 259*

34th IMO Proposal by Spain (1993)

3

Consider the triangle ABC, its circumcircle k of centre O and radius R, and its incircle of centre I and radius r. Another circle K_c is tangent to the sides CA, CB at D, E, respectively, and it is internally tangent to k. Show that I is the midpoint of DE. *solution page 260*

34th IMO Proposal by Spain (1993)

Given the triangle ABC, let D, E be points on the side BC such that $\angle BAD = \angle CAE$. If M and N are respectively, the points of tangency with BC of the incircles of the triangles ABD and ACE, show that

$$\frac{1}{BM} + \frac{1}{MD} = \frac{1}{NC} + \frac{1}{NE}.$$

solution page 261

35th IMO Hong Kong (1994)

ABC is an isosceles triangle with $AB = AC$. Suppose that

(i) M is the midoint of BC and D is the point on the line AM such that OB is perpendicular to AB;

(ii) Q is an arbitrary point on the segment BC different from B and C;

(iii) E lies on the line AB and F on the line AC such that E, Q and F are distinct and collinear.

Prove that OQ is perpendicular to EF if and only if $QE = QF$.

solution page 263

43rd Mathematical Olympiad in Poland

The rectangular $2n$-gon is the base of a regular pyramid with vertex S. A sphere passing through S cuts the lateral edges SA_i in the respective points B_i $(i = 1, 2, \ldots, 2n)$. Show that

$$\sum_{i=1}^{n} SB_{2i-1} = \sum_{i=1}^{n} SB_{2i}.$$

solution page 265

Nordic Mathematical Contest, 1992

Prove that among all triangles with given incircle, the equilateral one has the least perimeter.

solution page 266

10th Iranian Mathematical Olympiad

6

Let O be the intersection of diagonals of the convex quadrilateral $ABCD$. If P and Q are the centres of the circumcircles of AOB and COD show that

$$PQ \geq \frac{AB + CD}{4}.$$

solution page 267

Canadian Mathematical Olympiad 1996

Let $\triangle ABC$ be an isosceles triangle with $AB = AC$. Suppose that the angle bisector of $\angle B$ meets AC at D and that $BC = BD + AD$. Determine $\angle A$.

solution page 268

10th Iranian Mathematical Olympiad (Second Stage Exam)

1

In the right triangle ABC ($A = 90°$), let the internal bisectors of B and C intersect each other at I and the opposite sides D and E respectively. Prove that the area of quadrilateral $BCDE$ is twice the area of the triangle BIC.

solution page 269

10th Iranian Mathematical Olympiad (Second Stage Exam)

5

In the triangle ABC we have $A \leq 90°$ and $B = 2C$. Let the internal bisector of C intersect the median AM (M is the mid-point of BC) at D. Prove that $\angle MDC \leq 45°$. What is the condition for $\angle MDC = 45°$?

solution page 270

6th Korean Mathematical Olympiad (Final Round), 1993

2

Let ABC be a triangle with $\overline{BC} = a$, $\overline{CA} = b$, $\overline{AB} = c$. Find the point P for which

$$a \cdot \overline{AP}^2 + b \cdot \overline{BP}^2 + c \cdot \overline{CP}^2$$

is minimal, and find the minimum.

solution page 272

6th Korean Mathematical Olympiad (Final Round), 1993

6

Let ABC be a triangle with $\overline{BC} = a$, $\overline{CA} = b$ and $\overline{AB} = c$. Let D be the mid-point of the side BC, and let E be the point on BC for which the line segment AE is the bisector of angle A. Let the circle passing through A, D, E intersect with the sides CA, AB at F, G respectively. Finally let H be the point on AB for which $\overline{BG} = \overline{GH}$, i.e. $\overline{BH} = 2\overline{BG}$. Prove that the triangles EBH and ABC are similar and then find the ratio $\frac{\triangle EBH}{\triangle ABC}$ of these areas.

solution page 273

Turkish Mathematical Olympiad, 1993 (Final Selection Test)

2

Let M be the circumcentre of an acute-angled triangle ABC, and assume the circle (BMA) intersects the segment $[BC]$ at P, and the segment $[AC]$ at Q. Show that the line CM is perpendicular to the line PQ.

solution page 274

Turkish Mathematical Olympiad, 1993 (Final Selection Test)

5

On a semicircle with diameter AB and centre O points E and C are marked in such a way that OE is perpendicular to AB, and the chord AC intersects the segment OE at a point D which is interior to the semicircle. Find all values of the angle $\angle CAB$ such that a circle can be inscribed into the quadrilateral $OBCD$.

solution page 275

6th Irish Mathematical Olympiad, 1993

3

The line l is tangent to the circle S at the point A; B and C are points on l on opposite sides of A and the other tangents from B, C to S intersect at a point P. If B, C vary along l in such a way that the product $|AB| \cdot |AC|$ is constant, find the locus of P.

solution page 276

The vertices of six squares coincide in such a way that they enclose triangles; see the picture. Prove that the sum of the areas of the three outer squares (I, II and III) equals three times the sum of the areas of the three inner squares (IV, V and VI).

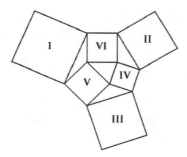

solution page 277

We consider regular n-gons with a fixed circumference 4. We call the distance from the centre of such a n-gon to a vertex r_n and the distance from the centre to an edge a_n.

    a) Determine a_4, r_4, a_8, r_8.

    b) Give an appropriate interpretation for a_2 and r_2.

    c) Prove: $a_{2n} = \frac{1}{2}(a_n + r_n)$ and $r_{2n} = \sqrt{a_{2n} r_n}$.

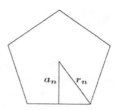

Let $u_0, u_1, u_2, u_3, \ldots$ be defined as follows:

$$u_0 = 0, \quad u_1 = 1; \quad u_n = \frac{1}{2}(u_{n-2} + u_{n-1}) \text{ for } n \text{ even and}$$

$$u_n = \sqrt{u_{n-2} \cdot u_{n-1}} \text{ for } n \text{ odd.}$$

    d) Determine: $\lim_{n \to \infty} u_n$.

solution page 279

Let $\triangle ABC$ be equilateral. On side AB produced, we choose a point P such that A lies between P and B. We now denote a as the length of sides of $\triangle ABC$; r_1 as the radius of incircle of $\triangle PAC$; and r_2 as the exradius of $\triangle PBC$ with respect to side BC. Determine the sum $r_1 + r_2$ as a function of a alone.

solution page 281

A semicircle Γ is drawn on one side of a straight line ℓ. C and D are points on Γ. The tangents to Γ at C and D meet ℓ at B and A respectively, with the center of the semicircle between them. Let E be the point of intersection of AC and BD, and F be the point on ℓ such that EF is perpendicular to ℓ. Prove that EF bisects $\angle CFD$.

solution page 282

A circle ω is tangent to two parallel lines ℓ_1 and ℓ_2. A second circle ω_1 is tangent to ℓ_1 at A and to ω externally at C. A third circle ω_2 is tangent to ℓ_2 at B, to ω externally at D and to ω_1 externally at E. AD intersects BC at Q. Prove that Q is the circumcentre of triangle CDE.

solution page 284

A line ℓ does not meet a circle ω with center O. E is the point on ℓ such that OE is perpendicular to ℓ. M is any point on ℓ other than E. The tangents from M to ω touch it at A and B. C is the point on MA such that EC is perpendicular to MA. D is the point on MB such that ED is perpendicular to MB. The line CD cuts OE at F. Prove that the location of F is independent of that of M.

solution page 286

$ABCD$ is a quadrilateral with BC parallel to AD. M is the midpoint of CD, P that of MA and Q that of MB. The lines DP and CQ meet at N. Prove that N is not outside triangle ABM.

solution page 287

Given five points P_1, P_2, P_3, P_4, P_5 in the plane having integer coordinates, prove that there is at least one pair (P_i, P_j) with $i \neq j$ such that the line P_iP_j contains a point Q having integer coordinates and lying strictly between P_i and P_j.

solution page 288

N is an arbitrary point on the bisector of $\angle BAC$. P and O are points on the lines AB and AN, respectively, such that $\angle ANP = 90° = \angle APO$. Q is an arbitrary point on NP, and an arbitrary line through Q meets the lines AB and AC at E and F respectively. Prove that $\angle OQE = 90°$ if and only if $QE = QF$.

solution page 289

Show that in any triangle, the diameter of the incircle is not bigger than the circumradius.

solution page 290

Canadian Mathematical Olympiad, 1997

4

The point O is situated inside the parallelogram $ABCD$ so that

$$\angle AOB + \angle COD = 180° .$$

Prove that $\angle OBC = \angle ODC$.

solution page 291

Australian Mathematical Olympiad, 1993

6

In the acute-angled triangle ABC, let D, E, F be the feet of altitudes through A, B, C, respectively, and H the orthocentre. Prove that

$$\frac{AH}{AD} + \frac{BH}{BE} + \frac{CH}{CF} = 2.$$

solution page 294

Australian Mathematical Olympiad, 1993

8

The vertices of triangle ABC in the xy–plane have integer coordinates, and its sides do not contain any other points having integer coordinates. The interior of ABC contains only one point, G, that has integer coordinates. Prove that G is the centroid of ABC.

solution page 295

Mathematical Contest Baltic Way, 1992

17

Quadrangle $ABCD$ is inscribed in a circle with radius 1 in such a way that one diagonal, AC, is a diameter of the circle, while the other diagonal, BD, is as long as AB. The diagonals intersect in P. It is known that the length of PC is $\frac{2}{5}$. How long is the side CD?

solution page 296

Mathematical Contest Baltic Way, 1992

18

Show that in a non-obtuse triangle the perimeter of the triangle is always greater than two times the diameter of the circumcircle.

solution page 297

Mathematical Contest Baltic Way, 1992

19

Let C be a circle in the plane. Let C_1 and C_2 be nonintersecting circles touching C internally at points A and B respectively. Let t be a common tangent of C_1 and C_2, touching them at points D and E respectively, such that both C_1 and C_2 are on the same side of t. Let F be the point of intersection of AD and BE. Show that F lies on C.

solution page 298

Mathematical Contest Baltic Way, 1992

20

Let $a \leq b \leq c$ be the sides of a right triangle, and let $2p$ be its perimeter. Show that $p(p-c) = (p-a)(p-b) = S$ (the area of the triangle).

solution page 299

8th Iberoamerican Mathematical Olympiad, 1993 (Mexico)

2

Show that for any convex polygon of unit area, there exists a parallelogram of area 2 which contains the polygon.

solution page 300

8th Iberoamerican Mathematical Olympiad, 1993 (Mexico)

4

Let ABC be an equilateral triangle, and Γ its incircle. If D and E are points of the sides AB and AC, respectively, such that DE is tangent to Γ, show that

$$\frac{AD}{DB} + \frac{AE}{EC} = 1.$$

solution page 301

Italian Mathematical Olympiad, 1994

4

Let r be a line in the plane and let ABC be a triangle contained in one of the half-planes determined by r. Let A', B', C' be the points symmetric to A, B, C with respect to r; draw the line through A' parallel to BC, the line through B' parallel to AC and the line through C' parallel to AB. Show that these three lines have a common point.

solution page 302

10th Iberoamerican Mathematical Olympiad, 1996

5

The inscribed circumference in the triangle ABC is tangent to BC, CA and AB at D, E and F, respectively. Suppose that this circumference meets AD again at its mid-point X; that is, $AX = XD$. The lines XB and XC meet the inscribed circumference again at Y and Z, respectively. Show that $EY = FZ$.

solution page 303

35th International Mathematical Olympiad

4

Let A, B and C be non-collinear points. Prove that there is a unique point X in the plane of ABC such that $XA^2 + XB^2 + AB^2 = XB^2 + XC^2 + BC^2 = XC^2 + XA^2 + CA^2$.

solution page 304

35th International Mathematical Olympiad

5

The incircle of ABC touches BC, CA and AB at D, E and F respectively. X is a point inside ABC such that the incircle of XBC touches BC at D also, and touches CX and XB at Y and Z, respectively. Prove that $EFZY$ is a cyclic quadrilateral.

solution page 305

35th International Mathematical Olympiad

An acute triangle ABC is given. Points A_1 and A_2 are taken on the side BC (with A_2 between A_1 and C), B_1 and B_2 on the side AC (with B_2 between B_1 and A) and C_1 and C_2 on the side AB (with C_2 between C_1 and B) so that

$$\angle AA_1A_2 = \angle AA_2A_1 = \angle BB_1B_2 = \angle BB_2B_1 = \angle CC_1C_2 = \angle CC_2C_1.$$

The lines AA_1, BB_1, and CC_1 bound a triangle, and the lines AA_2, BB_2 and CC_2 bound a second triangle. Prove that all six vertices of these two triangles lie on a single circle.

solution page 506

37th International Mathematical Olympiad

Let P be a point inside triangle ABC such that

$$\angle APB - \angle ACB = \angle APC - \angle ABC.$$

Let D, E be the incentres of triangles APB, APC respectively. Show that AP, BD and CE meet at a point.

solution page 507

36th International Mathematical Olympiad (Shortlist)

Let ABC be a triangle. A circle passing through B and C intersects the sides AB and AC again at C' and B', respectively. Prove that BB', CC' and HH' are concurrent, where H and H' are the orthocentres of triangles ABC and $AB'C'$ respectively.

solution page 509

44th Latvian Mathematical Olympiad, 1994 (2nd Selection Test)

A triangle ABC is given. From the vertex B, n rays are constructed intersecting the side AC. For each of the $n+1$ triangles obtained, an incircle with radius r_i and excircle (which touches the side AC) with radius R_i is constructed. Prove that the expression

$$\frac{r_1 r_2 \ldots r_{n+1}}{R_1 R_2 \ldots R_{n+1}}$$

depends on neither n nor on which rays are constructed.

solution page 510

44th Latvian Mathematical Olympiad, 1994 (3rd Selection Test)

Let $ABCD$ be an inscribed quadrilateral. Its diagonals intersect at O. Let the midpoints of AB and CD be U and V. Prove that the lines through O, U and V, perpendicular to AD, BD and AC respectively, are concurrent.

solution page 511

3rd Mathematical Olympiad of the Republic of China, 1994 (First day)

1

Let $ABCD$ be a quadrilateral with $\overline{AD} = \overline{BC}$ and let $\angle A + \angle B = 120°$. Three equilateral triangles $\triangle ACP$, $\triangle DCQ$ and $\triangle DBR$ are drawn on $\overline{AC}$, $\overline{DC}$ and $\overline{DB}$ away from $\overline{AB}$. Prove that the three new vertices P, Q and R are collinear.

solution page 313

Canadian Mathematical Olympiad, 1998

4

Let ABC be a triangle with $\angle BAC = 40°$ and $\angle ABC = 60°$. Let D and E be the points lying on the sides AC and AB, respectively, such that $\angle CBD = 40°$ and $\angle BCE = 70°$. Let F be the point of intersection of the lines BD and CE. Show that the line AF is perpendicular to the line BC.

solution page 314

Swedish Mathematical Olympiad, 1993

5

A triangle with perimeter $2p$ has sides a, b and c. If possible, a new triangle with the sides $p - a$, $p - b$ and $p - c$ is formed. The process is then repeated with the new triangle. For which original triangles can the process be repeated indefinitely?

solution page 315

Dutch Mathematical Olympiad, 1993 (Second Round)

2

Given is a triangle ABC, $\angle A = 90°$. D is the midpoint of BC, F is the midpoint of AB, E the midpoint of AF and G the midpoint of FB. AD intersects CE, CF and CG respectively in P, Q and R. Determine the ratio $\frac{PQ}{QR}$.

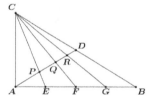

solution page 316

3rd Ukrainian Mathematical Olympiad, 1994

2

A convex polygon and point O inside it are given. Prove that for any $n > 1$ there exist points $A_1, A_2, \ldots, A_n$ on the sides of the polygon such that $\overrightarrow{OA_1} + \overrightarrow{OA_2} + \ldots + \overrightarrow{OA_n} = \overrightarrow{0}$.

solution page 318

Hong Kong Committee - Mock Test, Part I, IMO 1994

1

In a triangle $\triangle ABC$, $\angle C = 2\angle B$. P is a point in the interior of $\triangle ABC$ satisfying that $AP = AC$ and $PB = PC$. Show that AP trisects the angle $\angle A$.

solution page 319

Dutch Mathematical Olympiad, 1993 (Second Round)

In a plane V a circle C is given with centre M. P is a point not on the circle C.

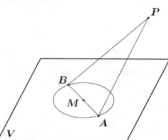

(a) Prove that for a fixed point P, $\overline{AP}^2 + \overline{BP}^2$ is a constant for every diameter AB of the circle C.

(b) Let AB be any diameter of C and P a point on a fixed sphere S not intersecting V. Determine the point(s) P on S such that $\overline{AP}^2 + \overline{BP}^2$ is minimal.

solution page 321

45th Mathematical Olympiad in Poland, 1994 (Final Round)

Let $A_1, A_2, \ldots, A_8$ be the vertices of a parallelepiped and let O be its centre. Show that

$$4(OA_1^2 + OA_2^2 + \cdots + OA_8^2) \leq (OA_1 + OA_2 + \cdots + OA_8)^2.$$

solution page 322

Irish Mathematical Olympiad, 1994

Let A, B, C be three collinear points with B between A and C. Equilateral triangles ABD, BCE, CAF are constructed with D, E on one side of the line AC and F on the opposite side. Prove that the centroids of the triangles are the vertices of an equilateral triangle. Prove that the centroid of this triangle lies on the line AC.

solution page 323

37th International Mathematical Olympiad, 1996 (Shortlist)

9

Let triangle ABC have orthocentre H, and let P be a point on its circumcircle, distinct from A, B, C. Let E be the foot of the altitude BH, let $PAQB$ and $PARC$ be parallelograms, and let AQ meet HR in X. Prove that EX is parallel to AP.

solution page 324

37th International Mathematical Olympiad, 1996 (Shortlist)

Let ABC be an acute-angled triangle with $|BC| > |CA|$, and let O be the circumcentre, H its orthocentre, and F the foot of its altitude CH. Let the perpendicular to OF at F meet the side CA at P. Prove that $\angle FHP = \angle BAC$.

solution page 325

37th International Mathematical Olympiad, 1996 (Shortlist)

Let ABC be equilateral, and let P be a point in its interior. Let
the lines AP, BP, CP meet the sides BC, CA, AB in the points A_1, B_1,
C_1 respectively. Prove that

$$A_1 B_1 \cdot B_1 C_1 \cdot C_1 A_1 \geq A_1 B \cdot B_1 C \cdot C_1 A .$$

solution page 327

37th International Mathematical Olympiad, 1996 (Shortlist)

Let ABC be an acute-angled triangle with circumcentre O and
circumradius R. Let AO meet the circle BOC again in A', let BO meet the
circle COA again in B' and let CO meet the circle AOB again in C'. Prove
that

$$OA' \cdot OB' \cdot OC' \geq 8R^3 .$$

When does equality hold?

solution page 328

Croatian National Mathematics Competition, 1994 (4th Class)

In the plane five points P_1, P_2, P_3, P_4, P_5 are chosen having integer
coordinates. Show that there is at least one pair (P_i, P_j), for $i \neq j$ such that
the line $P_i P_j$ contains a point Q, with integer coordinates, and is strictly
between P_i and P_j.

solution page 330

Croatian National Mathematics Competition, 1994

Construct a triangle ABC if the lengths $|AO|$, $|AU|$ and radius r of
incircle are given, where O is orthocentre and U the centre of the incircle.

solution page 331

Dutch Mathematical Olympiad, 1993 (Second Round)

Given a triangle ABC, $\angle A = 90°$. D is the mid-point of BC, F
is the mid-point of AB, E the midpoint of AF and G the mid-point of FB.
AD intersects CE, CF and CG respectively in P, Q and R. Determine the
ratio $\frac{PQ}{QR}$.

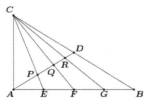

solution page 333

19th Austrian-Polish Mathematics Competition, 1996

2

A convex hexagon $ABCDEF$ satisfies the following conditions:

(a) The opposite sides are parallel (that is, $AB \parallel DE$, $BC \parallel EF$, $CD \parallel FA$).

(b) The distances between the opposite sides are equal (that is, $d(AB, DE) = d(BC, EF) = d(CD, FA)$, where $d(g, h)$ denotes the distance between lines g and h).

(c) $\angle FAB$ and $\angle CDE$ are right angles.

Show that diagonals BE and CF intersect at an angle of $45°$.

solution page 334

3rd Turkish Mathematical Olympiad, 1995

2

For an acute triangle ABC, k_1, k_2, k_3 are the circles with diameters $[BC]$, $[CA]$, $[AB]$, respectively. If K is the radical centre of these circles, $[AK] \cap k_1 = \{D\}$, $[BK] \cap k_2 = \{E\}$, $[CK] \cap k_3 = \{F\}$ and area$(ABC) = u$, area$(DBC) = x$, area$(ECA) = y$, and area$(FAB) = z$, show that $u^2 = x^2 + y^2 + z^2$.

solution page 335

3rd Turkish Mathematical Olympiad, 1995

4

In a triangle ABC with $|AB| \neq |AC|$, the internal and external bisectors of the angle A intersect the line BC at D and E, respectively. If the feet of the perpendiculars from a point F on the circle with diameter $[DE]$ to the lines BC, CA, AB are K, L, M, respectively, show that $|KL| = |KM|$.

solution page 337

37th IMO Turkish Team Selection Test

2

In a parallelogram $ABCD$ with $m(\hat{A}) < 90°$, the circle with diameter $[AC]$ intersects the lines CB and CD at E and F besides C, and the tangent to this circle at A intersects the line BD at P. Show that the points P, F, E are collinear.

solution page 338

37th IMO Turkish Team Selection Test

4

In a convex quadrilateral $ABCD$, Area$(ABC) = $ Area(ADC) and $[AC] \cap [BD] = \{E\}$. The parallels from E to the line segments $[AD]$, $[DC]$, $[CB]$, $[BA]$ intersect $[AB]$, $[BC]$, $[CD]$, $[DA]$ at the points K, L, M, N, respectively. Compute the ratio

$$\frac{\text{Area}(KLMN)}{\text{Area}(ABCD)}.$$

solution page 339

Australian Mathematical Olympiad, 1996

1

Let $ABCDE$ be a convex pentagon such that $BC = CD = DE$ and each diagonal of the pentagon is parallel to one of its sides. Prove that all the angles in the pentagon are equal, and that all sides are equal.

solution page 341

Australian Mathematical Olympiad, 1996

6

Let $ABCD$ be a cyclic quadrilateral and let P and Q be points on the sides AB and AD, respectively, such that $AP = CD$ and $AQ = BC$. Let M be the point of intersection of AC and PQ. Show that M is the mid-point of PQ.

solution page 342

47th Polish Mathematical Olympiad, 1995

2

Given is a triangle ABC and a point P inside it satisfying the conditions: $\angle PBC = \angle PCA < \angle PAB$. Line BP cuts the circumcircle of ABC at B and E. The circumcircle of triangle APE meets line CE at E and F. Show that the points A, P, E, F are consecutive vertices of a quadrilateral. Also show that the ratio of the area of quadrilateral $APEF$ to the area of triangle ABP does not depend on the choice of P.

solution page 343

47th Polish Mathematical Olympiad, 1995

4

Let $ABCD$ be a tetrahedron with

$$\angle BAC = \angle ACD \quad \text{and} \quad \angle ABD = \angle BDC.$$

Show that edges AB and CD have equal lengths.

solution page 344

10th Nordic Mathematical Contest, 1996

3

A circle has the altitude from A in a triangle ABC as a diameter, and intersects AB and AC in the points D and E, respectively, different from A. Prove that the circumcentre of triangle ABC lies on the altitude from A in triangle ADE, or it produced.

solution page 345

Dutch Mathematical Olympiad, 1995

2

On a segment AB a point P is chosen. On AP and PB, isosceles right-angled triangles AQP and PRB are constructed with Q and R on the same side of AB. M is the mid-point of QR. Determine the set of all points M for all points P on the segment AB.

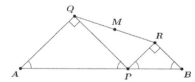

solution page 346

Dutch Mathematical Olympiad, 1995

4

A number of spheres, all with radius 1, are being placed in the form of a square pyramid. First, there is a layer in the form of a square with $n \times n$ spheres. On top of that layer comes the next layer with $(n-1) \times (n-1)$ spheres, and so on. The top layer consists of only one sphere. Determine the height of the pyramid.

solution page 347

XXXIX Republic Competition of Mathematics in Macedonia (Class I)

3

Let h_a, h_b and h_c be the altitudes of the triangle with edges a, b and c, and r be the radius of the inscribed circle in the triangle. Prove that the triangle is equilateral if and only if $h_a + h_b + h_c = 9r$.

solution page 348

XXXIX Republic Competition of Mathematics in Macedonia (Class III)

2

Let AH, BK and CL be the altitudes of arbitrary triangle ABC. Prove that

$$\overline{AK} \cdot \overline{BL} \cdot \overline{CH} = \overline{AL} \cdot \overline{BH} \cdot \overline{CK} = \overline{HK} \cdot \overline{KL} \cdot \overline{LH}.$$

solution page 349

XXXIX Republic Competition of Mathematics in Macedonia (Class III)

4

A finite number of points in the plane are given such that not all of them are collinear. A real number is assigned to each point. The sum of the numbers for each line containing at least two of the given points is zero. Prove that all numbers are zeros.

solution page 350

XXXIX Republic Competition of Mathematics in Macedonia (Class IV)

2

Two circles with radii R and r touch from inside. Find the side of an equilateral triangle having one vertex at the common point of the circles and the other two vertices lying on the two circles.

solution page 351

3rd Macedonian Mathematical Olympiad, 1996

1

Let $ABCD$ be a parallelogram which is not a rectangle and E be a point in its plane, such that $AE \perp AB$ and $BC \perp EC$. Prove that $\angle DAE = \angle CEB$. [Ed. We know this is incorrect — can any reader supply the correct version?]

solution page 352

3rd Macedonian Mathematical Olympiad, 1996

2

Let $\mathcal{P}$ be the set of all polygons in the plane and let $M : \mathcal{P} \to \mathbb{R}$ be a mapping which satisfies:

   (i) $M(P) \geq 0$ for each polygon P;

   (ii) $M(P) = x^2$ if P is an equilateral triangle of side x;

   (iii) If P is a polygon separated into two polygons S and T, then

$$M(P) \ = \ M(S) + M(T); \quad \text{and}$$

   (iv) If P and T are congruent polygons, then $M(P) = M(T)$.

Find $M(P)$ if P is a rectangle with edges x and y.

solution page 555

9th Irish Mathematical Olympiad, 1996

4

Let F be the mid-point of the side BC of the triangle ABC. Isosceles right-angled triangles ABD and ACE are constructed externally on the sides AB and AC with the right angles at D and E, respectively.

   Prove that DEF is a right-angled isosceles triangle.

solution page 556

9th Irish Mathematical Olympiad, 1996

9

Let ABC be an acute-angled triangle and let D, E, F be the feet of the perpendiculars from A, B, C onto the sides BC, CA, AB, respectively. Let P, Q, R be the feet of the perpendiculars from A, B, C onto the lines EF, FD, DE respectively. Prove that the lines AP, BQ, CR (extended) are concurrent.

solution page 557

Georg Mohr Konkurrencen I Matematik, 1996

1

$\angle C$ in $\triangle ABC$ is a right angle and the legs BC and AC are both of length 1. For an arbitrary point P on the leg BC construct points Q, respectively, R, on the hypotenuse, respectively, on the other leg, such that PQ is parallel to AC and QR is parallel to BC. This divides the triangle into three parts.

   Determine positions of the point P on BC such that the rectangular part has greater area than each of the other two parts.

solution page 558

Georg Mohr Konkurrencen I Matematik, 1996

3

This year's idea for a gift is from "BabyMath", namely a series of 9 coloured plastic figures of decreasing sizes, alternating cube, sphere, cube, sphere, etc. Each figure may be opened and the succeeding one may be placed inside, fitting exactly. The largest and the smallest figures are both cubes. Determine the ratio between their side-lengths.

solution page 559

No three diagonals of a convex 1996–gon meet in one point. Prove that the number of the triangles lying in the interior of the 1996–gon and having sides on its diagonals is divisible by 11.

solution page 360

Points A' and C' are taken on the diagonal BD of a parallelogram $ABCD$ so that $AA' \| CC'$. Point K lies on the segment $A'C$, the line AK meets the line $C'C$ at the point L. A line parallel to BC is drawn through K, and a line parallel to BD is drawn through C. These two lines meet at point M. Prove that the points D, M, L are collinear.

solution page 361

In a convex pentagon $ABCDE$, $AB = BC$, $\angle ABE + \angle DBC = \angle EBD$, and $\angle AEB + \angle BDE = 180°$. Prove that the orthocentre of triangle BDE lies on diagonal AC.

solution page 362

Segments AE and CF of equal length are taken on the sides AB and BC of a triangle ABC. The circle going through the points B, C, E and the circle going through the points A, B, F intersect at points B and D. Prove that the line BD is the bisector of angle ABC.

solution page 363

In a triangle ABC the angle A is 60°. A point O is taken inside the triangle such that $\angle AOB = \angle BOC = 120°$. A point D is chosen on the half-line CO such that the triangle AOD is equilateral. The mid-perpendicular to the segment AO meets the line BC at point Q. Prove that the line OQ divides the segment BD into two equal parts.

solution page 364

Through the vertices of a triangle tangents to the circumcircle are constructed. The distances of an arbitrary point of the circle to the straight lines containing the sides of the triangle are equal to a, b and c and to the tangents are equal to x, y and z. Prove that $a^2 + b^2 + c^2 = xy + xz + yz$.

solution page 366

Republic of Moldova XL Mathematical Olympiad, 1996 (11-12)

3

Two disjoint circles C_1 and C_2 with centres O_1 and O_2 are given. A common exterior tangent touches C_1 and C_2 at points A and B, respectively. The segment O_1O_2 cuts C_1 and C_2 at points C and D, respectively. Prove that:

(a) the points A, B, C and D are concyclic;

(b) the straight lines (AC) and (BD) are perpendicular.

solution page 567

Republic of Moldova XL Mathematical Olympiad, 1996 (10)

7

The perpendicular bisector to the side $[BC]$ of a triangle ABC intersects the straight line (AC) at a point M and the perpendicular bisector to the side $[AC]$ intersects the straight line (BC) at a point N. Let O be the centre of the circumcircle to the triangle ABC. Prove that:

(a) points A, B, M, N and O lie on a circle S;

(b) the radius of S equals the radius of the circumcircle of the triangle MNC.

solution page 568

Republic of Moldova XL Mathematical Olympiad, 1996 (11-12)

7

On a sphere distinct points A, B, C and D are chosen so that segments $[AB]$ and $[CD]$ cut each other at point F, and points A, C and F are equidistant to a point E. Prove that the straight lines (BD) and (EF) are perpendicular

solution page 570

31st Canadian Mathematical Olympiad, 1999

Let ABC be an equilateral triangle of altitude 1. A circle with radius 1 and centre on the same side of AB as C rolls along the segment AB. Prove that the arc of the circle that is inside the triangle always has the same length.

solution page 571

Ukrainian Mathematical Olympiad, 1996

A regular polygon with 1996 vertices is given. What minimal number of vertices can we delete so that we do not have four remaining vertices which form: (a) a square? (b) a rectangle?

solution page 572

Ukrainian Mathematical Olympiad, 1996

5

Let O be the centre of the parallelogram $ABCD$, $\angle AOB > \pi/2$. We take the points A_1, B_1 on the half lines OA, OB respectively so that $A_1B_1 \parallel AB$ and $\angle A_1B_1C = \angle ABC/2$.

Prove that $A_1D \perp B_1C$.

solution page 573

XII Italian Mathematical Olympiad, 1996

1

Among the triangles with an assigned side l and with given area S, determine all those for which the product of the three altitudes is maximum.

solution page 374

XII Italian Mathematical Olympiad, 1996

5

Let a circle C and a point A exterior to C be given. For each point P on C construct the square $APQR$, with anticlockwise ordering of the letters A, P, Q, R. Find the locus of the point Q when P runs over C.

solution page 375

South African Mathematical Olympiad, 1995 (Section A)

2

ABC is a triangle with $\angle A > \angle C$, and D is the point on BC such that $\angle BAD = \angle ACB$. The perpendicular bisectors of AD and DC intersect in the point E. Prove that $\angle BAE = 90°$.

solution page 376

South African Mathematical Olympiad, 1995 (Section A)

4

Three circles, with radii p, q, r, and centres A, B, C respectively, touch one another externally at points D, E, F. Prove that the ratio of the areas of $\triangle DEF$ and $\triangle ABC$ equals

$$\frac{2pqr}{(p+q)(q+r)(r+p)} \, .$$

solution page 377

South African Mathematical Olympiad, 1995 (Section B)

1

The convex quadrilateral $ABCD$ has area 1, and AB is produced to E, BC to F, CD to G and DA to H, such that $AB = BE$, $BC = CF$, $CD = DG$ and $DA = AH$. Find the area of the quadrilateral $EFGH$.

solution page 378

South African Mathematical Olympiad, 1995 (Section B)

3

The circumcircle of $\triangle ABC$ has radius 1 and centre O, and P is a point inside the triangle such that $OP = x$. Prove that

$$AP \cdot BP \cdot CP \leq (1+x)^2(1-x) \, ,$$

with equality only if $P = O$.

solution page 379

Taiwan Mathematical Olympiad, 1996

3

Let A and B be two fixed points on a fixed circle. Let a point P move on this circle and let M be a corresponding point such that either M is on the segment PA with $AM = MP + PB$ or M is on the segment PB with $AP + MP = PB$. Determine the locus of such points P.

solution page 381

Croatian Team Selection Test, 1995

1

(a) $n = 2k + 1$ points are given in the plane. Construct an n–gon such that these points are mid-points of its sides.

(b) Arbitrary $n = 2k$, $k > 1$, points are given in the plane. Prove that it is impossible to construct an n–gon, in each case, such that these points are mid-points of its sides.

solution page 382

Croatian Team Selection Test, 1995

2

The side-length of the square $ABCD$ equals a. Two points E and F are given on sides $\overline{BC}$ and $\overline{AB}$ such that the perimeter of the triangle BEF equals $2a$. Determine the angle $\angle EDF$.

solution page 383

Croatian Team Selection Test, 1995

4

Let A_1, A_2, ..., A_n be a regular n–gon inscribed in the circle of radius 1 with the centre at O. A point M is given on the ray OA_1 outside the n–gon. Prove that

$$\sum_{k=1}^{n} \frac{1}{|MA_k|} \geq \frac{n}{|OM|}.$$

solution page 384

13th Iranian Mathematical Olympiad, 1995 (Second Round)

2

Let L be a line in the plane of an acute triangle ABC. Let the lines symmetric to L with respect to the sides of ABC intersect each other in the points A', B' and C'. Prove that the incentre of triangle $A'B'C'$ lies on the circumcircle of triangle ABC.

solution page 385

13th Iranian Mathematical Olympiad, 1995 (Final Round)

3

In triangle ABC we have $\angle A = 60°$. Let O, H, I, and I' be the circumcentre, orthocentre, incentre, and the excentre with respect to A of the triangle ABC. Consider points B' and C' on AC and AB such that $AB = AB'$ and $AC = AC'$. Prove that

(a) Eight points B, C, H, O, I, I', B', and C' are concyclic.

(b) If OH intersects AB and AC in E and F respectively, then triangle AEF has a perimeter equal to $AC + AB$.

(c) $OH = |AB - AC|$.

solution page 386

13th Iranian Mathematical Olympiad, 1995 (Final Round)

5

Let ABC be a non-isosceles triangle. Medians of the triangle ABC intersect the circumcircle in points L, M, N. If L lies on the median of BC and $LM = LN$, prove that $2a^2 = b^2 + c^2$.

solution page 388

13th Iranian Mathematical Olympiad 1995

Points D and E are situated on the sides AB and AC of triangle ABC in such a way that $DE \| BC$. Let P be an arbitrary point inside the triangle ABC. Lines PB and PC intersect DE at F and G, respectively. Let O_1 be the circumcentre of triangle PDG and let O_2 be that of PFE. Show that $AP \perp O_1O_2$.

solution page 589

Estonian Mathematical Contest, 1995 (Final Round)

Let H be the orthocentre of an obtuse triangle ABC and A_1, B_1, C_1 arbitrary points taken on the sides BC, AC, AB, respectively. Prove that the tangents drawn from the point H to the circles with diameters AA_1, BB_1, CC_1 are equal.

solution page 590

10th Mexican Mathematical Olympiad, 1996 (National Contest)

Let $ABCD$ be a quadrilateral and let P and Q be the trisecting points of the diagonal BD (that is, P and Q are the points on the line segment BD for which the lengths BP, PQ and QD are all the same). Let E be the intersection of the straight line through A and P with BC, and let F be the intersection of the straight line through A and Q with DC. Prove the following:

(i) If $ABCD$ is a parallelogram, then E and F are the mid-points of BC and CD, respectively.

(ii) If E and F are the mid-points of BC and CD, respectively, then $ABCD$ is a parallelogram.

solution page 591

10th Mexican Mathematical Olympiad, 1996 (National Contest)

The picture below shows a triangle $\triangle ABC$ in which the length AB is smaller than that of BC, and the length of BC is smaller than that of AC. The points A', B' and C' are such that AA' is perpendicular to BC and the length of AA' equals that of BC; BB' is perpendicular to AC and the length of BB' equals that of AC; CC' is perpendicular to AB and the length of CC' equals that of AB. Moreover $\angle AC'B$ is a 90° angle. Prove that A', B' and C' are collinear.

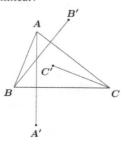

solution page 592

Bi-National Israel-Hungary Competition, 1996

3

A given convex polyhedron has no vertex which is incident with exactly 3 edges. Prove that the number of faces of the polyhedron which are triangles, is at least 8.

solution page 393

Finnish High School Mathematics Contest, 1997 (Final Round)

2

Two circles, of radii R and r, $R > r$, are externally tangent. Consider the common tangent of the circles, not passing through their common point. Determine the maximal radius of a circle drawn in the domain bounded by this tangent line and the circles.

solution page 394

Finnish High School Mathematics Contest, 1997 (Final Round)

5

Let $n \geq 3$. Find a configuration of n points in the plane such that the mutual distance of no pair of points exceeds 1 and exactly n pairs of points have a mutual distance equal to 1.

solution page 396

Georgian Mathematical Olympiad, 1997 (X form)

4

The area of a given trapezoid is 2 cm² and the sum of its diagonals equals 4 cm. Find the altitude of the trapezoid.

solution page 397

Georgian Mathematical Olympiad, 1997 (X form)

5

Prove that in any triangle the following inequality holds: $pR \geq 2S$, where p, R, S are respectively the semiperimeter, the radius of circumcircle and the area of the triangle.

solution page 398

6th ROC Taiwan Mathematical Olympiad, 1997 (Part I)

2

Let AB be a given line segment. Find all possible points C in the plane such that in $\triangle ABC$, the height from the vertex A and the length of the median from the vertex B are equal.

solution page 399

6th ROC Taiwan Mathematical Olympiad, 1997 (Part III)

2

Let $\triangle ABC$ be an acute triangle with circumcentre O and circumradius R. Show that if AO meets the circle OBC again at D, BO meets the circle OCA again at E, and CO meets the circle OAB again at F, then $OD \cdot OE \cdot OF \geq 8R^3$.

solution page 400

Let M be the mid-point of the median AD of the triangle ABC (D belongs to the side BC). The line BM meets the side AC at the point N. Show that AB is tangent to the circumcircle of the triangle NBC if and only if the equality

$$\frac{BM}{MN} = \frac{BC^2}{BN^2}$$

holds.

solution page 401

We have n distinct points $A_1, \dots, A_n$ in the plane. To each point A_i a real number $\lambda_i \neq 0$ is assigned, in such a way that

$$\overline{A_i A_j}^2 = \lambda_i + \lambda_j, \quad \text{for all } i, j \text{ with } i \neq j.$$

Show that

(a) $n \leq 4$.

(b) If $n = 4$, then

$$\frac{1}{\lambda_1} + \frac{1}{\lambda_2} + \frac{1}{\lambda_3} + \frac{1}{\lambda_4} = 0.$$

solution page 405

In tetrahedron $ABCD$ let A', B', C', and D' be the circumcentres of faces BCD, ACD, ABD and ABC. We mean by $S(X, YZ)$, the plane perpendicular from point X to the line YZ. Prove that the planes $S(A, C'D')$, $S(B, D'A')$, $S(C, A'B')$, and $S(D, B'C')$ are concurrent.

solution page 405

Consider a circle of centre O, radius r, and let P be an external point. We draw a chord AB parallel to OP.

(a) Show that $PA^2 + PB^2$ is constant.

(b) Find the length of the chord AB which maximizes the area of the $\triangle ABP$.

solution page 406

The triangle ABC has $\widehat{A} = 90°$, and AD is the altitude from A. The bisectors of the angles $\widehat{ABD}$ and $\widehat{ADB}$ intersect at I_1; the bisectors of the angles $\widehat{ACD}$ and $\widehat{ADC}$ intersect at I_2.

Find the acute angles of $\triangle ABC$, given that the sum of distances from I_1 and I_2 to AD is $BC/4$.

solution page 407

20th Austrian-Polish Mathematical Competition, 1997

1

P is the common point of straight lines l_1 and l_2. Two circles S_1 and S_2 are externally tangent at P and l_1 is their common tangent line. Similarly, two circles T_1 and T_2 are externally tangent at P and l_2 is their common tangent line. The circles S_1 and T_1 have common points P and A, the circles S_1 and T_2 have common points P and B, the circles S_2 and T_2 have common points P and C, and the circles S_2 and T_1 have common points P and D. Prove that the points A, B, C, D lie on a circle if and only if the lines l_1 and l_2 are perpendicular.

solution page 408

20th Austrian-Polish Mathematical Competition, 1997

4

In a convex quadrilateral $ABCD$ the sides AB and CD are parallel, the diagonals AC and BD intersect at point E and points F and G are the orthocentres of the triangles EBC and EAD, respectively. Prove that the midpoint of the segment GF lies on the line k perpendicular to AB such that $E \in k$.

solution page 410

Chinese Mathematical Olympiad, 1997

4

Quadrilateral $ABCD$ is inscribed in a circle. Line AB meets DC at point P. Line AD meets BC at point Q. Tangent lines QE and QF touch the circle at points E and F, respectively. Prove that points P, E and F are collinear.

solution page 411

Swedish Mathematical Competition, 1996 (Final Round)

1

Through an arbitrary interior point of a triangle lines parallel to the sides of the triangle are drawn dividing the triangle into six regions, three of which are triangles. Let the areas of these three triangles be T_1, T_2, and T_3 and let the area of the original triangle be T. Prove that

$$T = (\sqrt{T_1} + \sqrt{T_2} + \sqrt{T_3})^2 .$$

solution page 413

Swedish Mathematical Competition, 1996 (Final Round)

4

A pentagon $ABCDE$ is inscribed in a circle. The angles at A, B, C, D, E form an increasing sequence. Show that the angle at C is $> \pi/2$. Also, prove that this lower bound is best possible.

solution page 414

48th Polish Mathematical Competition, 1997 (Final Round)

3

In a triangular pyramid $ABCD$, the medians of the lateral faces ABD, ACD, BCD drawn from vertex D form equal angles with the corresponding edges AB, AC, BC. Prove that the area of each lateral face is less than the sum of the areas of the two other lateral faces.

solution page 415

Given is a convex pentagon $ABCDE$ with

$$DC = DE \quad \text{and} \quad \angle DCB = \angle DEA = 90°.$$

Let F be the point on AB such that $AF : BF = AE : BC$. Show that

$$\angle FCE = \angle ADE \quad \text{and} \quad \angle FEC = \angle BDC.$$

solution page 416

Consider n points ($n \geq 2$) on the circumference of a circle of radius 1. Let q be the number of segments having those points as endpoints and having length greater than $\sqrt{2}$. Prove that $3q \leq n^2$.

solution page 417

Is there a set A of n points ($n \geq 3$) in the plane such that:

(i) A does not contain three collinear points; and

(ii) given any three points in A, the centre of the circle which contain these points also belongs to A?

solution page 418

Let D be a point of the side $\overline{BC}$ of the acute-angled triangle ABC ($D \neq B$ and $D \neq C$), O_1 be the circumcentre of $\triangle ABD$, O_2 be the circumcentre of $\triangle ACD$ and O be the circumcentre of $\triangle AO_1O_2$. Determine the locus described by the point O when D runs through the side $\overline{BC}$ ($D \neq B$ and $D \neq C$).

solution page 419

Let $ABCD$ be a tetrahedron with $BC = a$, $CA = b$, $AB = c$, $DA = a_1$, $DB = b_1$, $CD = c_1$.

Prove that there exists one and only one point P satisfying the conditions:

$$\begin{aligned}
PA^2 + a_1^2 + b^2 + c^2 &= PB^2 + b_1^2 + c^2 + a^2 \\
&= PC^2 + c_1^2 + a^2 + b^2 = PD^2 + a_1^2 + b_1^2 + c_1^2,
\end{aligned}$$

and that for this point P, we have $PA^2 + PB^2 + PC^2 + PD^2 \geq 4R^2$, where R is the radius of the circumscribed sphere of the tetrahedron $ABCD$. Find a necessary and sufficient condition on the lengths of the edges so that the preceding inequality becomes an equality.

solution page 420

Latvian Mathematical Olympiad, 1997 (1st TST)

The line t has no common points with a circle w centered at O.
Point E lies on t; $OE \perp t$. Point M is another point on t; MA and MB
are tangents to w, A and B being the points of tangency; AB intersects OE
at X.

Prove that X does not depend on M.

solution page 122

Latvian Mathematical Olympiad, 1997 (2nd TST)

An equilateral triangle of side 1 is dissected into n triangles. Prove
that the sum of squares of all sides of all triangles is at least 3.

solution page 123

Latvian Mathematical Olympiad, 1997 (3rd TST)

Let $ABCD$ be a parallelogram. The bisector of A cuts BC at M
and cuts the extension of CD at N. The circumcentre of MCN is O. Prove
that B, O, C, D are concyclic.

solution page 124

Mathematical Olympiad in Bosnia and Herzegovina, 1997 (1st Day)

In an isosceles triangle ABC with the base $\overline{AB}$, point M lies on
the side $\overline{BC}$. Let O be the centre of its circumscribed circle, and S be the
centre of the inscribed circle in the triangle ABC. Prove that:

$$SM \parallel AC \iff OM \perp BS.$$

solution page 125

Mathematical Olympiad in Bosnia and Herzegovina, 1997 (2nd Day)

(a) Let A_1, B_1, C_1 be the points of contact of the circle inscribed
in the triangle ABC and the sides BC, CA, AB, respectively. Let B_1C_1,
A_1C_1, B_1A_1 be the arcs which do not contain points A_1, B_1, C_1 respectively.
Let I_1, I_2, I_3 be their respective arc lengths. Prove the following inequality:

$$\frac{a}{I_1} + \frac{b}{I_2} + \frac{c}{I_3} \geq 9\frac{\sqrt{3}}{\pi}$$

(where a, b, c denote the lengths of sides of the given triangle).

(b) Let $ABCD$ be a tetrahedron with:

$$AB = CD = a,$$
$$BC = AD = b,$$
$$AC = BD = c.$$

Express the height of the tetrahedron in terms of the lengths a, b and c.

solution page 126

Ukranian Mathematical Olympiad, 1999 (11th Grade)

8

Let AA_1, BB_1, CC_1 be the altitudes of acute triangle ABC, let O be an arbitrary point inside the triangle $A_1B_1C_1$. Let us denote by M and N the bases of perpendiculars drawn from O to lines AA_1 and BC, respectively, by P and Q — ones from O to lines BB_1 and CA, respectively, by R and S — ones from O to lines CC_1 and AB, respectively. Prove that the lines MN, PQ, RS are concurrent.

solution page 427

XLIII Mathematical Olympiad of Moldova, 1999 (10th Form)

8

On the sides BC and AB of the equilateral triangle ABC the points D and E, respectively, are taken such that $CD : DB = BE : EA = (\sqrt{5} + 1)/2$. The straight lines AD and CE intersect in the point O. The points M and N are interior points of the segments OD and OC, respectively, such that $MN \parallel BC$ and $AN = 2OM$. The parallel to the straight line AC, drawn through the point O, intersects the segment MC in the point P. Prove that the half-line AP is the bisectrix of the angle MAN.

solution page 428

XLIII Mathematical Olympiad of Moldova, 1999 (11th Form)

8

On the sides BC, AC and AB of the equilateral triangle ABC the points M, N and P, respectively, are considered such that $AP : PB = BM : MC = CN : NA = \lambda$. Find all the values λ for which the circle with the diameter AC covers the triangle bounded by the straight lines AM, BN and CP. (In the case of concurrent straight lines, the mentioned triangle degenerates into a point.)

solution page 429

Italian Team Selection Test, 1999

2

Points D and E are given on the sides AB and AC of $\triangle ABC$ in such a way that DE is parallel to BC and tangent to the incircle of $\triangle ABC$. Prove that

$$DE \leq \tfrac{1}{8}(AB + BC + CA).$$

solution page 431

35th Mongolian Mathematical Olympiad, 1996 (10th Grade)

2

Given an angle $\angle ABC$ and rays ℓ_1, ..., ℓ_{n-1} dividing the angle into n congruent angles, for a line ℓ denote $\ell \cap (AB) = A_1$, $\ell \cap (BC) = A_{n+1}$ and $\ell \cap \ell_i = A_{i+1}$ for $1 \leq i < n$, show that the quotient

$$\frac{\left(\dfrac{1}{|BA_1|} + \dfrac{1}{|BA_{n+1}|}\right)}{\left(\dfrac{1}{|BA_1|} + \dfrac{1}{|BA_2|} + \cdots + \dfrac{1}{|BA_n|} + \dfrac{1}{|BA_{n+1}|}\right)}$$

is a constant which does not depend on ℓ, and find the value of this constant knowing $\angle ABC = \varphi$.

solution page 432

35th Mongolian Mathematical Olympiad, 1996 (10th Grade)

6

A point M lies on the side AC of a triangle ABC. The circle γ with the diameter BM intersects the lines AB, BC, at points P, Q, respectively. Find the locus of intersection points of the tangents of the circle γ at the points P, Q, when the point M varies.

solution page 455

Mongolian Team Selection Test for 40th IMO, 1999

2

Let ABC be a triangle such that $\angle A = 90°$ and $\angle B < \angle C$. The tangent at A to its circumcircle k meets the line BC at D. Let E be the reflection of A across BC, X the foot of the perpendicular from A to BE, and Y the mid-point of AX. Let the line BY meet k again in Z. Prove that the line BD is tangent to the circumcircle of triangle ADZ.

solution page 455

XV Gara Nazionale di Matematica, 1999

1

Given a rectangular sheet with sides a and b, with $a > b$, fold it along a diagonal. Determine the area of the overlapped triangle (the shaded triangle in the picture).

solution page 456

Russian Mathematical Olympiad, 2000

6

The incircle of triangle ABC with centre O touches the side AC at K. Another circle with the same centre intersects each side at two points. The points of intersection on AC are B_1 and B_2, with B_1 closer to A. E is the point of intersection on AB closer to B, and F is the point of intersection on BC closer to B. Let P be the point of intersection of B_2E and B_1F. Prove that B, K, and P are collinear.

solution page 457

Bulgarian Mathematical Olympiad, 2000

2

Let ABC be an acute triangle.

(a) Prove that there exist unique points A', B', and C', on BC, CA, and AB, respectively, such that A' is the mid-point of the orthogonal projection of $B'C'$ onto BC, B' is the mid-point of the orthogonal projection of $C'A'$ onto CA, and C' is the mid-point of the orthogonal projection of $A'B'$ onto AB.

(b) Prove that $A'B'C'$ is similar to the triangle formed by the medians of ABC.

solution page 458

Bulgarian Mathematical Olympiad, 2000

In triangle ABC, we have $CA = CB$. Let D be the mid-point of AB and E an arbitrary point on AB. Let O be the circumcentre of $\triangle ACE$. Prove that the line through D perpendicular to DO, the line through E perpendicular to BC, and the line through B parallel to AC are concurrent.

solution page 440

Belarusian Mathematical Olympiad, 2000

Let $ABCD$ be a quadrilateral with AB parallel to DC. A line ℓ intersects AD, AC, BD, and BC, forming three segments of equal lengths between consecutive points of intersection. Does it follow that ℓ is parallel to AB?

solution page 441

Taiwanese Mathematical Olympiad, 2000

In an acute triangle ABC, $AC > BC$ and M is the mid-point of AB. Let AP be the altitude from A. Let BQ be the altitude from B meeting AP at H. Let the lines AB and PQ meet at R. Prove that the lines RH and CM are perpendicular to each other.

solution page 442

Hungarian Mathematical Olympiad, 2000

Construct the point P inside a given triangle such that the feet of the perpendiculars from P to the sides of the triangle determine a triangle whose centroid is P.

solution page 443

Iranian Mathematical Olympiad, 2000

Triangles $A_3A_1O_2$ and $A_1A_2O_3$ are constructed outside triangle $A_1A_2A_3$, with $O_2A_3 = O_2A_1$ and $O_3A_1 = O_3A_2$. A point O_1 is outside $A_1A_2A_3$ such that $\angle O_1A_3A_2 = \frac{1}{2}\angle A_1O_3A_2$ and $\angle O_1A_2A_3 = \frac{1}{2}\angle A_1O_2A_3$, and T is the foot of the perpendicular from O_1 to A_2A_3. Prove that:

(a) A_1O_1 is perpendicular to O_2O_3;

(b) $\dfrac{A_1O_1}{O_2O_3} = 2\dfrac{O_1T}{A_2A_3}$.

solution page 444

13

Shortlist for IMO, 2000 (India)

Let O be the circumcentre and H the orthocentre of an acute triangle ABC. Prove that there exist points D, E, and F on sides BC, CA, and AB, respectively, such that $OD + DH = OE + EH = OF + FH$ and the lines AD, BE, and CF are concurrent.

solution page 445

Shortlist for IMO, 2000 (Iran)

14

Ten gangsters are standing on a flat surface. The distances between them are all distinct. Simultaneously each of them shoots at the one
among the other nine who is the nearest. At least how many gangsters will
be shot at?

solution page 446

Shortlist for IMO, 2000 (The Netherlands)

16

In the plane we are given two circles intersecting
at X and Y. Prove that there exist four points such that for every circle
touching the two given circles at A and B, and meeting the line XY at C
and D, each of the lines AC, AD, BC, and BD passes through one of those
four points.

solution page 448

Shortlist for IMO, 2000 (United Kingdom)

21

The tangents at B and A to the circumcircle of an
acute triangle ABC meet the tangent at C at T and U, respectively. The
lines AT and BC meet at P, and Q is the mid-point of AP; the lines BU
and CA meet at R, and S is the mid-point of BR.

(a) Prove that $\angle ABQ = \angle BAS$.

(b) Determine, in terms of ratios of side lengths, the triangles for which this
angle is a maximum.

solution page 449

32nd Austrian Mathematical Olympiad

3

We are given a triangle ABC having $k(U, r)$ as its circumcircle. Next
we construct the 'doubled' circle $k(U, 2r)$ and its two tangents parallel to
$c = AB$. Among them we select the one (and designate it c') for which C
lies between c and c'. In a similar way we get the tangents a' and b'.
    Let $A'B'C'$ be the triangle having its sides on a', b', and c', respec-
tively. Prove: The lines joining the mid-points of corresponding sides of the
two triangles intersect in a single point.

solution page 451

32nd Austrian Mathematical Olympiad

6

We are given a semicircle s with diameter AB. On s we choose any two
points C and D such that $AC = CD$. The tangent at C intersects line BD
in a point E. Line AE intersects s at point F.
    Prove that $CD < FD$.

solution page 452

14th Nordic Mathematical Contest

3

In the triangle ABC, the bisector of angle B meets AC at D, and
the bisector of angle C meets AB at E. The bisectors intersect at O, and
$OD = OE$. Prove that either $\triangle ABC$ is isosceles or $\angle BAC = 60°$.

solution page 454

Two circles touch each other externally at A. A common tangent touches one circle at B and the other at C ($B \neq C$). The segments BD and CE are diameters of the circles. Prove that D, A, and C are collinear.

solution page 455

An acute triangle ABC, with $AC \neq BC$, is inscribed in a circle ω. The points A, B, C divide the circle into disjoint arcs $\overset{\frown}{AB}$, $\overset{\frown}{BC}$, and $\overset{\frown}{CA}$. Let M and N be the mid-points of $\overset{\frown}{BC}$ and $\overset{\frown}{AC}$, respectively, and let K be an arbitrary point of $\overset{\frown}{AB}$. Let D be the point of $\overset{\frown}{MN}$ such that $CD \parallel NM$. Let O, O_1, O_2 be the incentres of triangles ABC, CAK, CBK, respectively. Let L be the intersection point of the line DO and the circle ω, where $L \neq D$. Prove that the points K, O_1, O_2, L are concyclic.

solution page 456

The incircle γ of triangle ABC touches the side AB at T. Let D be the point on γ diametrically opposite to T, and let S be the intersection of the line through C and D with the side AB. Show that $AT = SB$.

solution page 458

Let $ABCD$ be a parallelogram, and let K and L be points lying on the sides BC and CD, respectively, such that $BK \cdot AD = DL \cdot AB$. The segments DK and BL intersect at P. Show that $\angle DAP = \angle BAC$.

solution page 459

Points A, B, C, D lie on the line ℓ, in that order. Find the locus of points P in the plane for which $\angle APB = \angle CPD$.

solution page 460

A triangle ABC is given. The mid-points of sides AC and AB are B_1 and C_1, respectively. The centre of the incircle of $\triangle ABC$ is I. The lines $B_1 I$, $C_1 I$ meet the sides AB, AC at C_2, B_2, respectively. Given that the areas of $\triangle ABC$ and $\triangle AB_2C_2$ are equal, what is $\angle BAC$?

solution page 461

Let I and O be the incentre and circumcentre, respectively, of $\triangle ABC$. Assume $\triangle ABC$ is not equilateral (so that $I \neq O$). Prove that $\angle AIO \leq 90°$ if and only if $2BC \leq AB + CA$.

solution page 465

17th Balkan Mathematical Olympiad, 2000

2

Let ABC be a non-isosceles acute triangle, and let E be an interior point of the median AD, with D on BC. Let F be the orthogonal projection of E onto the line BC. Let M be an interior point of the segment EF, and let N and P be the orthogonal projections of M onto the lines AC and AB, respectively. Prove that the bisectors of angles PMN and PEN are parallel.

solution page 464

Israel Mathematical Olympiad, 2001

4

The lengths of the sides of triangle ABC are 4, 5, 6. For any point D on one of the sides, drop the perpendiculars DP, DQ onto the other two sides (P, Q are on the sides). What is the minimal value of PQ?

solution page 466

21st Brazilian Mathematical Olympiad, 2001

1

Let $ABCDE$ be a regular pentagon such that the star $ACEBD$ has area 1. Let P be the point of intersection of AC and BE, and let Q be the point of intersection of BD and CE. Find the area of $APQD$.

solution page 467

49th Mathematical Olympiad of Lithuania, 2000

3

In the triangle ABC, the point D is the mid-point of the side AB. Point E divides BC in the ratio $BE : EC = 2 : 1$. Given that $\angle ADC = \angle BAE$, determine $\angle BAC$.

solution page 468

49th Mathematical Olympiad of Lithuania, 2000

7

A line divides both the area and the perimeter of a triangle into two equal parts. Prove that this line passes through the incentre of the triangle. Does the converse statement always hold?

solution page 469

XXXVI Spanish Mathematical Olympiad, 2000

3

Circles C_1 and C_2 intersect at points A and B. A line r through B intersects C_1 and C_2 again at points P_r and Q_r, respectively. Prove that there is a point M, which depends only on C_1 and C_2, such that the perpendicular bisector of $P_r Q_r$ passes through M.

solution page 471

XXXVI Spanish Mathematical Olympiad, 2000

5

Four points are placed in a square of side 1. Show that the distance between some two of them is less than or equal to 1.

solution page 472

Taiwan Mathematical Olympiad, 2000

In an acute triangle ABC with $|AC| > |BC|$, let M be the mid-point of AB. Let AP be the altitude from A and BQ be the altitude from B. These altitudes meet at H, and the lines AB and PQ meet at R. Prove that the two lines RH and CM are perpendicular.

solution page 473

Kűrschák Mathematical Contest, 2000

Let T be a point in the plane of the non-equilateral triangle ABC which is different from the vertices of the triangle. Let the lines AT, BT, and CT meet the circumcircle of the triangle at A_T, B_T, and C_T, respectively. Prove that there are exactly two points P and Q in the plane for which the triangles $A_P B_P C_P$ and $A_Q B_Q C_Q$ are equilateral. Prove, furthermore, that the line PQ passes through the circumcentre of the triangle ABC.

solution page 474

14th Mexican Mathematical Olympiad

Let A, B, C, and D be circles such that (i) A and B are externally tangent at P, (ii) B and C are externally tangent at Q, (iii) C and D are externally tangent at R, and (iv) D and A are externally tangent at S. Assume that A and C do not intersect and that B and D do not intersect.

(a) Prove that P, Q, R, and S lie on a circle.

(b) Assume further that A and C have radius 2, B and D have radius 3, and the distance between the centres of A and C is 6. Determine the area of $PQRS$.

solution page 475

14th Mexican Mathematical Olympiad

Let ABC be a triangle with $\angle B > 90°$ such that, for some point H on AC, we have $AH = BH$, and BH is perpendicular to BC. Let D and E be the mid-points of AB and BC, respectively. Through H a parallel to AB is drawn, intersecting DE at F. Prove that $\angle BCF = \angle ACD$.

solution page 476

17th Argentinian Mathematical Olympiad

Given a triangle ABC with side AB greater than BC, let M be the mid-point of AC, and let L be the point at which the bisector of $\angle B$ cuts side AC. A straight line is drawn through M parallel to AB, cutting the bisector BL at D, and another straight line is drawn through L parallel to BC, cutting the median BM at E. Show that ED is perpendicular to BL.

solution page 477

XXI Albanian Mathematical Olympiad, 2000 (12th Form)

Let a, b, c be the sides of a triangle, and let α, β, γ be the angles opposite the sides a, b, c, respectively.

(a) Prove that $\gamma = 2\alpha$ if and only if $c^2 = a(a+b)$.

(b) Find all triangles such that a, b, c are natural numbers, b is a prime, and $\gamma = 2\alpha$.

solution page 478

Finland Mathematical Olympiad, 2000 (Final Round)

Let ABC be a right triangle with hypotenuse AB and altitude CF, where F lies on AB. The circle through F centred at B and another circle of the same radius centred at A intersect on the side CB. Determine $FB : BC$.

solution page 479

37th Mongolian Mathematical Olympiad, 2000 (Final Round)

Prove that, if ABC is an acute-angled triangle, then

$$\frac{a^2+b^2}{a+b} \cdot \frac{b^2+c^2}{b+c} \cdot \frac{c^2+a^2}{c+a} \geq 16 \cdot R^2 \cdot r \cdot \frac{m_a}{a} \cdot \frac{m_b}{b} \cdot \frac{m_c}{c}.$$

solution page 480

13th Irish Mathematical Olympiad

Let $ABCDE$ be a regular pentagon with its sides of length one. Let F be the mid-point of AB, and let G and H be points on the sides CD and DE, respectively, such that $\angle GFD = \angle HFD = 30°$. Prove that the triangle GFH is equilateral. A square is inscribed in the triangle GFH with one side of the square along GH. Prove that FG has length

$$t = \frac{2\cos 18°(\cos 36°)^2}{\cos 6°},$$

and that the square has side length $\dfrac{t\sqrt{3}}{2+\sqrt{3}}$.

solution page 481

13th Irish Mathematical Olympiad

Let $ABCD$ be a cyclic quadrilateral and R the radius of the circumcircle. Let a, b, c, d be the lengths of the sides of $ABCD$, and let Q be its area. Prove that

$$R^2 = \frac{(ab+cd)(ac+bd)(ad+bc)}{16Q^2}.$$

Deduce that $R \geq \dfrac{(abcd)^{\frac{3}{4}}}{Q\sqrt{2}}$, with equality if and only if $ABCD$ is a square.

solution page 482

Icelandic Mathematical Contest, 2000

2

Two circles intersect at points P and Q. A line ℓ that intersects the line segment PQ intersects the two circles at the points A, B, C, and D (in that order along the line ℓ). Prove that $\angle APB = \angle CQD$.

solution page 483

Icelandic Mathematical Contest, 2000

5

Triangle ABC is isosceles with a right angle at B and $AB = BC = x$. Point D on the side AB and point E on the side BC are chosen such that $BD = BE = y$. The line segments AE and CD intersect at the point P. What is the area of the triangle APC, expressed in terms of x and y?

solution page 484

XX Colombian Mathematical Olympiad

1

Let ABC be an isosceles triangle with $AB = AC$. Let M be the mid-point of side BC. The circle with diameter AB cuts side AC at point P. The parallelogram $MPDC$ is constructed so that $PD = MC$ and $PD \parallel MC$. Prove that triangles APD and APM are congruent.

solution page 485

53rd Polish Mathematical Olympiad, 2001 (Final Round)

2

On sides AC and BC of an acute-angled triangle ABC, rectangles $ACPQ$ and $BKCL$ are erected outwardly. Assuming that these rectangles have equal areas, show that the vertex C, the circumcentre of triangle ABC, and the mid-point of segment PL are collinear.

solution page 486

2nd Czech-Polish-Slovak Mathematical Olympiad, 2002

5

In an acute-angled triangle ABC with circumcentre O, points P and Q lying respectively on sides AC and BC are such that

$$\frac{AP}{PQ} = \frac{BC}{AB} \quad \text{and} \quad \frac{BQ}{PQ} = \frac{AC}{AB}.$$

Show that the points O, P, Q, and C are concyclic.

solution page 487

Singapore Mathematical Olympiad, 2002 (Open Section, Part A)

7

A circle passes through the vertex C of a rectangle $ABCD$ and touches its sides AB and AD at points M and N, respectively. Suppose the distance from C to MN is 2 cm. Find the area of $ABCD$ in cm^2.

solution page 489

XVIII Italian Mathematical Olympiad, 2002

3

Let A and B be two points of the plane, and let M be the mid-point of AB. Let r be a line, and let R and S be the projections of A and B onto r. Assuming that A, M, and R are not collinear, prove that the circumcircle of triangle AMR has the same radius as the circumcircle of BSM.

solution page 490

British Mathematical Olympiad, 2001 (Round 1)

2

The quadrilateral $ABCD$ is inscribed in a circle. The diagonals AC and BD meet at Q. The sides DA, extended beyond A, and CB, extended beyond B, meet at P.

Given that $CD = CP = DQ$, prove that $\angle CAD = 60°$.

solution page 491

British Mathematical Olympiad, 2001 (Round 2)

1

The altitude from one of the vertices of an acute-angled triangle ABC meets the opposite side at D. From D, perpendiculars DE and DF are drawn to the other two sides. Prove that the length of EF is the same whichever vertex is chosen.

solution page 492

15th Korean Mathematical Olympiad

5

Let ABC be an acute triangle, and let O be its circumcircle. Let the perpendicular line from A to BC meet O at D. Let P be a point on O, and let Q be the foot of the perpendicular line from P to the line AB. Prove that if Q is on the outside of O and $2\angle QPB = \angle PBC$, then D, P, Q are collinear.

solution page 493

Yugoslav Qualification for IMO, 2002 (First Round)

2

Let p be the semiperimeter of the triangle ABC. Let the points E and F lie on the line AB such that $CE = CF = p$. Prove that the circumcircle of the triangle EFC and the circle that touches the side AB and the extension of the sides AC and BC of the triangle ABC meet in one point.

solution page 494

7th Mathematical Olympiad of Bosnia and Herzegovina, 2002

2

Triangle ABC is given in a plane. Draw the bisectors of all three of its angles. Then draw the line that connects the points where the bisectors of angles ABC and ACB meet the sides AC and AB, respectively. Through the point of intersection of the bisector of angle BAC and the previously drawn line, draw another line, parallel to the side BC. Let this line intersect the sides AB and AC in points M and N. Prove that $2MN = BM + CN$.

solution page 495

6

7th Mathematical Olympiad of Bosnia and Herzegovina, 2002

Let the vertices of the convex quadrilateral $ABCD$ and the intersecting point S of its diagonals be integer points in the plane. Let P be the area of the quadrilateral $ABCD$ and P_1 the area of triangle ABS. Prove the following inequality:

$$\sqrt{P} \geq \sqrt{P_1} + \frac{\sqrt{2}}{2}.$$

solution page 496

4th Hong Kong Mathematical Olympiad

There are 212 points inside or on a circle with radius 1. Prove that there are at least 2001 pairs of these points having distances at most 1.

solution page 497

15th Irish Mathematical Olympiad, (First Paper)

In a triangle ABC, $AB = 20$, $AC = 21$, and $BC = 29$. The points D and E lie on the line segment BC, with $BD = 8$ and $EC = 9$. Calculate the angle $\angle DAE$.

solution page 498

15th Irish Mathematical Olympiad, (First Paper)

Let ABC be a triangle whose side lengths are all integers, and let D and E be the points at which the incircle of ABC touches BC and AC, respectively. If $|AD^2 - BE^2| \leq 2$, show that $AC = BC$.

solution page 499

19th Balkan Mathematical Olympiad

Let A_1, A_2, ..., A_n ($n \geq 4$) be points in the plane such that no three of them are collinear. Some pairs of distinct points among A_1, A_2, ..., A_n are connected by line segments in such a way that each point is connected to at least three others. Prove that there exists $k > 1$ and distinct points X_1, X_2, ..., $X_{2k} \in \{A_1, A_2, \ldots, A_n\}$ such that for each $1 \leq i \leq 2k - 1$, X_i is connected to X_{i+1} and X_{2k} is connected to X_1.

solution page 500

Romanian Mathematical Olympiad, 9th Grade

Prove that the mid-points of the altitudes of a triangle are collinear if and only if the triangle is right.

solution page 501

Romanian Mathematical Olympiad, 10th Grade

Let $OABC$ be a tetrahedron such that $OA \perp OB \perp OC \perp OA$, let r be the radius of its inscribed sphere, and let H be the orthocentre of triangle ABC. Prove that $OH \leq r(\sqrt{3} + 1)$.

solution page 502

15th Korean Mathematical Olympiad

2

Let $ABCD$ be a rhombus with $\angle A < 90°$. Let its two diagonals AC and BD meet at a point M. A point O on the line segment MC is selected such that $O \neq M$ and $OB < OC$. The circle centred at O passing through points B and D meets the line AB at point B and a point X (where $X = B$ when the line AB is tangent to the circle) and meets the line BC at point B and a point Y. Let the lines DX and DY meet the line segment AC at P and Q, respectively. Express the value of $\dfrac{OQ}{OP}$ in terms of t when $\dfrac{MA}{MO} = t$.

solution page 503

15th Korean Mathematical Olympiad

4

Suppose that the incircle of $\triangle ABC$ is tangent to the sides AB, BC, CA at points P, Q, R, respectively. Prove the following inequality:

$$\frac{BC}{PQ} + \frac{CA}{QR} + \frac{AB}{RP} \geq 6 \, .$$

solution page 504

X Mathematical Olympiad of Turkey

2

Two circles are externally tangent to each other at a point A and internally tangent to a third circle Γ at points B and C. Let D be the mid-point of the secant of Γ which is tangent to the smaller circles at A. Show that A is the incentre of the triangle BCD if the centres of the circles are not collinear.

solution page 505

X Mathematical Olympiad of Turkey

5

In an acute triangle ABC with $|BC| < |AC| < |AB|$, the points D on side AB and E on side AC satisfy the condition $|BD| = |BC| = |CE|$. Show that the circumradius of the triangle ADE is equal to the distance between the incentre and the circumcentre of the triangle ABC.

solution page 506

Japan Mathematical Olympiad, 2003

A point P lies in a triangle ABC. The edge AC meets the line BP at Q, and AB meets CP at R. Suppose that $AR = RB = CP$ and $CQ = PQ$. Find $\angle BRC$.

solution page 507

Hungarian Mathematical Olympiad, 2003 (First Round)

3

Let ABC be a triangle. We drop a perpendicular from A to the internal bisectors starting from B and C, their feet being A_1 and A_2. In the same way we define B_1, B_2 and C_1, C_2. Prove that

$$2(A_1 A_2 + B_1 B_2 + C_1 C_2) = AB + BC + CA \, .$$

solution page 508

British Mathematical Competition, 2003 (Round I)

2

The triangle ABC, where $AB < AC$, has circumcircle S. The perpendicular from A to BC meets S again at P. The point X lies on the line segment AC, and BX meets S again at Q.

Show that $BX = CX$ if and only if PQ is a diameter of S.

solution page 509

British Mathematical Competition, 2003 (Round II)

2

Let ABC be a triangle, and let D be a point on AB such that $4AD = AB$. The half-line ℓ is drawn on the same side of AB as C, starting from D and making an angle of θ with DA, where $\theta = \angle ACB$. If the circumcircle of ABC meets the half-line ℓ at P, show that $PB = 2PD$.

solution page 510

Kazakh National Mathematical Competition, 2003

2

Angles B and C of triangle ABC are acute. Side KN of rectangle $KLMN$ belongs to segment BC, points L and M belong to segments AB and AC, respectively. Let O be the intersection point of the diagonals of $KLMN$. Let C_1 be the intersection point of lines BO and MN, and let B_1 be the intersection point of lines CO and LK. Prove that lines AO, BB_1, and CC_1 are concurrent.

solution page 511

Ukrainian Mathematical Olympiad, (11 Form)

2

Prove that for any triangle, if S denotes its area and r denotes the radius of its inscribed circle, then
$$\frac{S}{r^2} \geq 3\sqrt{3}.$$

solution page 512

Indian TST for IMO, 2003

1

Let A', B', C' be the mid-points of the sides BC, CA, AB, respectively, of an acute non-isoceles triangle ABC, and let D, E, F be the feet of the altitudes through the vertices A, B, C on these sides, respectively. Consider the arc DA' of the nine-point circle of triangle ABC lying outside the triangle. Let the point of trisection of this arc closer to A' be A''. Define analogously the points B'' (on arc EB') and C'' (on arc FC'). Show that triangle $A''B''C''$ is equilateral.

solution page 513

Indian TST for IMO, 2003

8

Let ABC be a triangle, and let r, r_1, r_2, r_3 denote its inradius and the exradii opposite the vertices A, B, C, respectively. Suppose $a > r_1$, $b > r_2$, $c > r_3$. Prove that

(a) triangle ABC is acute, (b) $a + b + c > r + r_1 + r_2 + r_3$.

solution page 514

German Mathematical Olympiad, 2003

2

In the interior of a triangle ABC, circles K_1, K_2, K_3, and K_4 of the same radii are defined such that K_1, K_2, and K_3 touch two sides of the triangle and K_4 touches K_1, K_2, and K_3, as shown in the figure.

Prove that the centre of K_4 is located on the line through the incentre and the circumcentre.

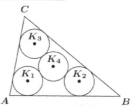

solution page 515

German Mathematical Olympiad, 2003

4

Let A_1, B_1, and C_1 be the midpoints of the sides of the acute-angled triangle ABC. The 6 lines through these points perpendicular to the other sides meet in the points A_2, B_2, and C_2, as shown in the figure. Prove that the area of the hexagon $A_1C_2B_1A_2C_1B_2$ equals half of the area of $\triangle ABC$.

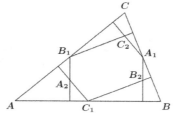

solution page 516

38th Mongolian Mathematical Olympiad

3

The incircle of triangle ABC with $AB \neq BC$ touches sides BC and AC at points A_1 and B_1, respectively. The segments AA_1 and BB_1 meet the incircle at A_2 and B_2, respectively. Prove that the lines AB, A_1B_1, and A_2B_2 are concurrent.

solution page 517

38th Mongolian Mathematical Olympiad

6

Let A_1, B_1, and C_1 be the respective mid-points of the sides BC, AC, and AB of triangle ABC. Take a point K on the segment C_1A_1 and a point L on the segment A_1B_1 such that

$$\frac{C_1K}{KA_1} = \frac{BC + AC}{AC + AB} \quad \text{and} \quad \frac{A_1L}{LB_1} = \frac{AC + AB}{AB + BC}.$$

Let $S = BK \cap CL$. Show that $\angle C_1A_1S = \angle B_1A_1S$.

solution page 518

Iranian Mathematical Olympiad, 2002 (First Round)

4

Let A and B be two fixed points in the plane. Let $ABCD$ be a convex quadrilateral such that $AB = BC$, $AD = DC$, and $\angle ADC = 90°$. Prove that there is a fixed point P such that, for every such quadrilateral $ABCD$ on the same side of the line AB, the line DC passes through P.

solution page 519

In a triangle ABC, define C_a to be the circle tangent to AB, to AC, and to the incircle of the triangle ABC, and let r_a be the radius of C_a. Define r_b and r_c in the same way. Prove that $r_a + r_b + r_c \geq 4r$, where r is the inradius of the triangle ABC.

solution page 520

Let ABC be a triangle. We drop a perpendicular from A to the internal bisectors starting from B and C, their feet being A_1 and A_2. In the same way we define B_1, B_2 and C_1, C_2. Prove that

$$2(A_1A_2 + B_1B_2 + C_1C_2) = AB + BC + CA.$$

solution page 521

Find the area of the convex pentagon $ABCDE$, given that $AB = BC$, $CD = DE$, $\angle ABC = 150°$, $\angle CDE = 30°$, and $BD = 2$.

solution page 523

The quadrilateral $ABCD$ is cyclic and has the property that $AB = BC = AD + CD$. Given that $\angle BAD = \alpha$ and that the diagonal $AC = d$, find the area of the triangle ABC.

solution page 524

Prove that a right-angled triangle can be inscribed in the parabola $y = x^2$ so that its hypotenuse is parallel to the x–axis if and only if the altitude from the right angle is equal to 1. (A triangle is inscribed in a parabola if all three vertices of the triangle are on the parabola.)

solution page 525

The diagonals A_1A_4, A_2A_5, and A_3A_6 of the convex hexagon $A_1A_2A_3A_4A_5A_6$ meet at a point K. Given that $A_2A_1 = A_2A_3 = A_2K$, $A_4A_3 = A_4A_5 = A_4K$, and $A_6A_5 = A_6A_1 = A_6K$, prove that the hexagon is cyclic.

solution page 526

Distinct points $A_0, A_1, \ldots, A_{1000}$ on one side of an angle
and distinct points $B_0, B_1, \ldots, B_{1000}$ on the other side are spaced so that
$A_0A_1 = A_1A_2 = \cdots = A_{999}A_{1000}$ and $B_0B_1 = B_1B_2 = \cdots = B_{999}B_{1000}$.
Find the area of the quadrilateral $A_{999}A_{1000}B_{1000}B_{999}$ if the areas of the
quadrilaterals $A_0A_1B_1B_0$ and $A_1A_2B_2B_1$ are equal to 5 and 7, respectively.

solution page 527

A quadrilateral $ABCD$ is cyclic with $AB = 2AD$ and
$BC = 2CD$. Given that $\angle BAD = \alpha$, and diagonal $AC = d$, find the area
of the triangle ABC.

solution page 528

Let $ABCD$ be a cyclic quadrilateral. Let P, Q, R be the feet of the
perpendiculars from D to the lines BC, CA, AB, respectively. Show that
$PQ = QR$ if and only if the bisectors of $\angle ABC$ and $\angle ADC$ are concurrent
with AC.

solution page 529

Let ABC be a triangle, and let P be a point in its interior. Denote by
D, E, F the feet of the perpendiculars from P to the lines BC, CA, AB,
respectively. Suppose that $AP^2 + PD^2 = BP^2 + PE^2 = CP^2 + PF^2$.
Denote by I_A, I_B, I_C the excentres of the triangle ABC. Prove that P is
the circumcentre of the triangle $I_AI_BI_C$.

solution page 530

Let ABC be an isosceles triangle with $AC = BC$, whose incentre is I.
Let P be a point on the circumcircle of the triangle AIB lying inside the
triangle ABC. The lines through P parallel to CA and CB meet AB at D
and E, respectively. The line through P parallel to AB meets CA and CB
at F and G, respectively. Prove that the lines DF and EG intersect on the
circumcircle of the triangle ABC.

solution page 531

Let a, b, and c denote the sides of a triangle opposite the angles A, B,
and C, respectively. Let r be the inradius and R the circumradius of the
triangle. If $\angle A \geq 90°$, prove that

$$\frac{r}{R} \leq \frac{a \sin A}{a + b + c}.$$

solution page 533

Hungarian National Olympiad, 2003, Grade11, Final Round

Let ABC be an acute triangle, and let P be a point on side AB. Draw lines through P parallel to AC and BC, and let them cut BC and AC at X and Y, respectively. Construct (with straightedge and compass) the point P which gives the shortest length XY. Prove that the shortest XY is perpendicular to the median of ABC through C.

solution page 534

Hungarian National Olympiad, 2003, Grade11, First Round

Consider the three disjoint arcs of a circle determined by three points on the circle. For each of these arcs, draw a circle centred at the mid-point of the arc and passing through the end-points of the arc. Prove that the three circles have a common point.

solution page 536

Finnish High School Math Contest, 2004, Final Round

Two circles with radii r and R are externally tangent at a point P. Determine the length of the segment cut from the common tangent through P by the other common tangents.

solution page 537

XX Olimpiadi Italiane Della Matematika, Cesenatico, 2004

2

Let r and s be two parallel lines in the plane, and P and Q two points such that $P \in r$ and $Q \in s$. Consider circles C_P and C_Q such that C_P is tangent to r at P, C_Q is tangent to s at Q, and C_P and C_Q are tangent externally to each other at some point, say T. Find the locus of T when (C_P, C_Q) varies over all pairs of circles with the given properties.

solution page 538

XX Olimpiadi Italiane Della Matematika, Cesenatico, 2004

Let P be a point inside the triangle ABC. Say that the lines AP, BP, and CP meet the sides of ABC at A', B', and C', respectively. Let

$$x = \frac{AP}{PA'}, \quad y = \frac{BP}{PB'}, \quad z = \frac{CP}{PC'}.$$

Prove that $xyz = x + y + z + 2$.

solution page 539

17th Irish Mathematical Olympiad, 2004, First Paper

Let AB be a chord of length 6 of a circle of radius 5 centred at O. Let $PQRS$ denote the square inscribed in the sector OAB such that P is on the radius OA, S is on the radius OB, and Q and R are points on the arc of the circle between A and B. Find the area of $PQRS$.

solution page 540

17th Irish Mathematical Olympiad, 2004, Second Paper

2

Let A and B be distinct points on a circle T. Let C be a point distinct from B such that $|AB| = |AC|$ and such that BC is tangent to T at B. Suppose that the bisector of $\angle ABC$ meets AC at a point D inside T. Show that $\angle ABC > 72°$.

solution page 541

New Zealand IMO Squad Selection Problems, 2004

1

Let I be the incentre of triangle ABC, and let A', B', and C' be the reflections of I in BC, CA, and AB, respectively. The circle through A', B', and C' passes also through B. Find the angle $\angle ABC$.

solution page 542

New Zealand IMO Squad Selection Problems, 2004

5

Let I be the incentre of triangle ABC. Let points $A_1 \neq A_2$ lie on the line BC, points $B_1 \neq B_2$ lie on the line AC, and points $C_1 \neq C_2$ lie on the line AB so that $AI = A_1I = A_2I$, $BI = B_1I = B_2I$, $CI = C_1I = C_2I$. Prove that $A_1A_2 + B_1B_2 + C_1C_2 = P$, where P is the perimeter of $\triangle ABC$.

solution page 543

21st Balkan Mathematical Olympiad, 2004

3

Let O be the circumcentre of the acute triangle ABC. The circles centred at the mid-points of the triangle's sides and passing through O intersect one another at the points K, L, and M. Prove that O is the incentre of triangle KLM.

solution page 544

Thai Mathematical Olympiad, 2003

1

Triangle ABC has $\angle A = 70°$ and $CA + AI = BC$, where I is the incentre of triangle ABC. Find $\angle B$.

solution page 545

Thai Mathematical Olympiad, 2003

6

Let $ABCD$ be a convex quadrilateral. Prove that

$$[ABCD] \leq \tfrac{1}{4}\left(AB^2 + BC^2 + CD^2 + DA^2\right).$$

solution page 546

Thai Mathematical Olympiad, 2003

9

Given a right triangle ABC with $\angle B = 90°$, let P be a point on the angle bisector of $\angle A$ inside ABC and let M be a point on the side AB (with $A \neq M \neq B$). Lines AP, CP, and MP intersect BC, AB, and AC at D, E, and N, respectively. Suppose that $\angle MPB = \angle PCN$ and $\angle NPC = \angle MBP$. Find $[APC]/[ACDE]$.

solution page 547

25th Albanian Mathematical Olympiad, Test 1

2

Let M, N, and P be the respective mid-points of sides BC, CA, and AB of triangle ABC, and let G be the intersection point of its medians. Prove that if $BN = \frac{\sqrt{3}}{2} AB$ and $BMGP$ is a cyclic polygon, then triangle ABC is equilateral.

solution page 549

25th Albanian Mathematical Olympiad, Test 2

5

In an acute-angled triangle ABC, Let H be the orthocenter, and let d_a, d_b, and d_c be the distances from H to the sides BC, CA, and AB, respectively. Prove that $d_a + d_b + d_c \leq 3r$, where r is the radius of the incircle of triangle ABC.

solution page 550

44th Ukrainian Mathematical Olympiad, 11th Form, Final Round

2

The acute-angled triangle ABC is given. Let O be the centre of its circumcircle. The perpendicular bisector of the side AC intersects the side AB and the line BC at the points P and Q, respectively. Prove that $\angle PQB = \angle PBO$.

solution page 552

44th Ukrainian Mathematical Olympiad, 11th Form, Final Round

10

Let ω be the inscribed circle of the triangle ABC. Let L, N, and E be the points of tangency of ω with the sides AB, BC, and CA, respectively. Lines LE and BC intersect at the point H, and lines LN and AC intersect at the point J (all the points H, J, N, E lie on the same side of the line AB). Let O and P be the mid-points of the segments EJ and NH, respectively. Find $S(HJNE)$ if $S(ABOP) = u^2$ and $S(COP) = v^2$. (Here $S(\mathcal{F})$ is the area of figure $\mathcal{F}$).

solution page 553

Kurshak Mathematics Competition, 2003

1

Let EF be a diameter of the circle Γ, and let e be the tangent line to Γ at E. Let A and B be any two points of e such that E is an interior point of the segment AB, and $AE \cdot EB$ is a fixed constant. Let AF and BF meet Γ at A' and B', respectively. Prove that all such segments $A'B'$ pass through a common point.

solution page 555

Hellenic Mathematics Competition, 2004

3

A circle (O, r) and a point A outside the circle are given. From A we draw a straight line ε, different from the line AO, which intersects the circle at B and Γ, with B between A and Γ. Next we draw the symmetric line of ε with respect to the axis AO, which intersects the circle at E and Δ, with E between A and Δ.

Prove that the diagonals of the quadrilateral $B\Gamma\Delta E$ pass through a fixed point; that is, they always intersect at the same point, independent of the position of the line ε.

solution page 556

Vietnamese Mathematical Olympiad, 2004

Let ABC be a triangle in a plane. The internal angle bisector of $\angle ACB$ cuts the side AB at D.

Consider an arbitrary circle Γ_1 passing through C and D so that the lines BC and CA are not its tangents. This circle cuts the lines BC and CA again at M and N, respectively.

(a) Prove that there exists a circle Γ_2 touching the line DM at M and touching the line DN at N.

(b) The circle Γ_2 from part (a) cuts the lines BC and CA again at P and Q, respectively. Prove that the measures of the segments MP and NQ are constant as Γ_1 varies.

solution page 557

Vietnamese Mathematical Olympiad, 2004

Given an acute triangle ABC inscribed in a circle Γ in a plane, let H be its orthocentre. On the arc BC of Γ not containing A, take a point P distinct from B and C. Let D be the point such that $\overrightarrow{AD} = \overrightarrow{PC}$. Let K be the orthocentre of triangle ACD, and let E and F be the orthogonal projections of K onto the lines BC and AB, respectively. Prove that the line EF passes through the mid-point of HK.

solution page 559

Taiwanese Mathematical Olympiad, 2004

Suppose that the points D and E lie on the circumcircle of $\triangle ABC$, ray $\overrightarrow{AD}$ is the interior angle bisector of $\angle BAC$, and ray $\overrightarrow{AE}$ is the exterior angle bisector of $\angle BAC$. Let F be the symmetrical point of A with respect to D, and let G be the symmetrical point of A with respect to E. Prove that, if the circumcircle of $\triangle ADG$ and the circumcircle of $\triangle AEF$ intersect at P, then AP is parallel to BC.

solution page 560

Taiwanese Mathematical Olympiad, 2004

Let O and H be the circumcentre and orthocentre of an acute triangle ABC. Suppose that the bisectrix of $\angle BAC$ intersects the circumcircle of $\triangle ABC$ at D, and that the points E and F are symmetrical points of D with respect to BC and O, respectively. If AE and FH intersect at G and if M is the mid-point of BC, prove that GM is perpendicular to AF.

solution page 561

Albanian Mathematical Olympiad, 2004 (Test 2)

In an acute-angled triangle ABC, let H be the orthocentre, and let d_a, d_b, and d_c be the distances from H to the sides BC, CA, and AB, respectively. Prove that $d_a + d_b + d_c \leq 3r$, where r is the radius of the incircle of triangle ABC.

solution page 562

25th Brazilian Mathematical Olympiad, 2003

3

Let $ABCD$ be a rhombus. Let E, F, G, and H be points on the sides AB, BC, CD, and DA, respectively, so that EF and GH are tangent to the incircle of $ABCD$. Show that EH and FG are parallel.

solution page 563

Republic of Moldova Team Selection Test, 2004

7

Let ABC be an acute-angled triangle with orthocentre H and circumcentre O. The inscribed and circumscribed circles have radii r and R, respectively. If P is an arbitrary point of the segment $[OH]$, prove that $6r \leq PA + PB + PC \leq 3R$.

solution page 564

Republic of Moldova Team Selection Test, 2004

11

Let ABC be an isosceles triangle with $AC = BC$, and let I be its incentre. Let P be a point on the circumcircle of the triangle AIB lying inside the triangle ABC. The straight lines through P parallel to CA and CB meet AB at D and E, respectively. The line through P parallel to AB meets CA and CB at F and G, respectively. Prove that the straight lines DF and GE intersect on the circumcircle of the triangle ABC.

solution page 565

Singapore Mathematical Olympiad, 2004

3

Let AD be the common chord of two circles Γ_1 and Γ_2. A line through D intersects Γ_1 at B and Γ_2 at C. Let E be a point on the segment AD different from A and D. The line CE intersects Γ_1 at P and Q. The line BE intersects Γ_2 at M and N.

(i) Prove that P, Q, M, and N lie on the circumference of a circle Γ_3.

(ii) If the centre of Γ_3 is O, prove that OD is perpendicular to BC.

solution page 566

18th Nordic Mathematical Contest, 2004

4

Let a, b, c, and R be the side lengths and the circumradius of a triangle. Show that

$$\frac{1}{ab} + \frac{1}{bc} + \frac{1}{ca} \geq \frac{1}{R^2}.$$

solution page 567

17th Irish Mathematical Olympiad, 2004

2

Let A and B be distinct points on a circle T. Let C be a point distinct from B such that $|AB| = |AC|$ and such that BC is tangent to T at B. Suppose that the bisector of $\angle ABC$ meets AC at a point D inside T. Show that $\angle ABC > 72°$.

solution page 568

Taiwan Mathematical Olympiad, 2005

1

A $\triangle ABC$ is given with side lengths a, b, and c. A point P lies inside $\triangle ABC$, and the distances from P to the three sides are p, q, and r, respectively. Prove that

$$R \leq \frac{a^2 + b^2 + c^2}{18\sqrt[3]{pqr}},$$

where R is the circumradius of $\triangle ABC$. When does equality hold?

solution page 569

German Mathematical Olympiad, 2005

2

Let A, B, and C be three distinct points on the circle k. Let the lines h and g each be perpendicular to BC with h passing through B and g passing through C. The perpendicular bisector of AB meets h in F and the perpendicular bisector of AC meets g in G. Prove that the product $|BF| \cdot |CG|$ is independent of the choice of A, whenever B and C are fixed.

solution page 570

German Mathematical Olympiad, 2005

3

A lamp is placed at each lattice point (x, y) in the plane (that is, x and y are both integers). At time $t = 0$ exactly one lamp is switched on. At any integer time $t \geq 1$, exactly those lamps are switched on which are at a distance of 2005 from some lamp which is already switched on. Prove that every lamp will be switched on at some time.

solution page 571

Hungarian Mathematical Olympiad, 2005 (First Round)

1

The quadrilateral $ABCD$ is cyclic. Prove that

$$\frac{AC}{BD} = \frac{DA \cdot AB + BC \cdot CD}{AB \cdot BC + CD \cdot DA}.$$

solution page 572

Hungarian Mathematical Olympiad, 2005 (Final Round)

1

Let $ABCD$ be a trapezoid with parallel sides AB and CD. Let E be a point on the side AB such that EC and AD are parallel. Further, let the area of the triangle determined by the lines AC, BD, and DE be t, and the area of ABC be T. Determine the ratio $AB : CD$, if $t : T$ is maximal.

solution page 573

Hungarian Mathematical Olympiad, 2005 (Second Round, 11 Grade)

2

In triangle ABC, the points B_1 and C_1 are on BC, point B_2 is on AB, and point C_2 is on AC such that the segment B_1B_2 is parallel to AC and the segment C_1C_2 is parallel to AB. Let the lines B_1B_2 and C_1C_2 meet at D. Denote the areas of triangles BB_1B_2 and CC_1C_2 by b and c, respectively.

(a) Prove that if $b = c$, then the centroid of ABC is on the line AD.

(b) Find the ratio $b : c$ if D is the incentre of ABC and $AB = 4$, $BC = 5$, and $CA = 6$.

solution page 574

Triangle ABC is acute angled, $\angle BAC = 60°$, $AB = c$, and $AC = b$ with $b > c$. The orthocentre and the circumcentre of ABC are M and O, respectively. The line OM intersects AB and CA at X and Y, respectively.

(a) Prove that the perimeter of triangle AXY is $b + c$.

(b) Prove that $OM = b - c$.

solution page 576

Let A, B, and C be three points on a line with B between A and C. Let Γ_1, Γ_2, and Γ_3 be semicircles, all on the same side of AC, and with AC, AB, and BC as diameters, respectively. Let l be the line perpendicular to AC through B. Let Γ be the circle which is tangent to the line l, tangent to Γ_1 internally, and tangent to Γ_3 externally. Let D be the point of contact of Γ and Γ_3. The diameter of Γ through D meets l in E. Show that $AB = DE$.

solution page 577

Let ABC be a triangle and let P be an exterior point in the plane of the triangle. Let AP, BP, and CP meet the (possibly extended) sides BC, CA, and AB in D, E, and F, respectively. If the areas of the triangles PBD, PCE, and PAF are all equal, prove that their common area is equal to the area of the triangle ABC.

solution page 579

Let PQR be an acute triangle. Let SRP, TPQ, and UQR be isosceles triangles exterior to PQR, with $SP = SR$, $TP = TQ$, and $UQ = UR$, such that $\angle PSR = 2\angle QPR$, $\angle QTP = 2\angle RQP$, and $\angle RUQ = 2\angle PRQ$. Let S', T', and U' be the points of intersection of SQ and TU, TR and US, and UP and ST, respectively. Determine the value of

$$\frac{SQ}{SS'} + \frac{TR}{TT'} + \frac{UP}{UU'}.$$

solution page 581

Through a point P exterior to a given circle pass a secant and a tangent to the circle. The secant intersects the circle at A and B, and the tangent touches the circle at C on the same side of the diameter through P as A and B. The projection of C onto the diameter is Q. Prove that QC bisects $\angle AQB$.

solution page 582

17

Mathematical Competition Baltic Way, 2004

Consider a rectangle with sides of lengths 3 and 4, and on each side pick an arbitrary point that is not a corner. Let x, y, z, and u be the lengths of the sides of the quadrilateral spanned by these points. Prove that

$$25 \leq x^2 + y^2 + z^2 + u^2 \leq 50.$$

solution page 583

Mathematical Competition Baltic Way, 2004

A ray emanating from the vertex A of the triangle ABC intersects the side BC at X and the circumcircle of ABC at Y. Prove that

$$\frac{1}{AX} + \frac{1}{XY} \geq \frac{4}{BC}.$$

solution page 584

Mathematical Competition Baltic Way, 2004

In triangle ABC let D be the midpoint of BC and let M be a point on the side BC such that $\angle BAM = \angle DAC$. Let L be the second intersection point of the circumcircle of triangle CAM with AB, and let K be the second intersection point of the circumcircle of triangle BAM with the side AC. Prove that $KL \parallel BC$.

solution page 585

20

Mathematical Competition Baltic Way, 2004

Three circular arcs w_1, w_2, and w_3 with common end-points A and B are on the same side of the line AB, and w_2 lies between w_1 and w_3. Two rays emanating from B intersect these arcs at M_1, M_2, M_3 and K_1, K_2, K_3, respectively. Prove that

$$\frac{M_1 M_2}{M_2 M_3} = \frac{K_1 K_2}{K_2 K_3}.$$

solution page 586

XIX Olimpíada Iberoamericana de Matemática, 2004

Let A be a fixed exterior point with respect to a given circle with centre O and radius r. Let M be a point on the circle and let N be diametrically opposite to M with respect to O. Find the locus of the centres of the circles passing through A, M, and N, as the point M is varied on the circle.

solution page 587

5

XIX Olimpíada Iberoamericana de Matemática, 2004

In a scalene triangle ABC, the interior bisectors of the angles A, B, and C meet the opposite sides at points A', B', and C' respectively. Let A'' be the intersection of BC with the perpendicular bisector of AA', let B'' be the intersection of AC with the perpendicular bisector of BB', and let C'' be the intersection of AB with the perpendicular bisector of CC'. Prove that A'', B'', and C'' are collinear.

solution page 588

Swedish Mathematical Contest, 2005

1

The cities A, B, C, D, and E are connected by straight roads (more than two cities may lie on the same road). The distance from A to B, and from C to D, is 3 km. The distance from B to D is 1 km, from A to C it is 5 km, from D to E it is 4 km, and finally, from A to E it is 8 km. Determine the distance from C to E.

solution page 589

Swedish Mathematical Contest, 2005

6

Let $2n$ (where $n \geq 1$) points lie in the plane so that no straight line contains more than two of them. Paint n of the points blue and paint the other n points yellow. Show that there are n segments, each with one blue endpoint and one yellow endpoint, such that each of the $2n$ points is an endpoint of one of the n segments and none of the segments have a point in common.

solution page 590

Swedish Mathematical Contest, 2005 (Final Round)

1

Two circles in the plane of the same radius R intersect at a right angle. How large is the area of the region which lies inside both circles?

solution page 591

Abel Mathematical Competition, 2005

3

(a) Let $\triangle ABC$ be isosceles with $AB = AC$, and let D be the midpoint of BC. The points P and Q lie respectively on the segments AD and AB such that $PQ = PC$ and $Q \neq B$. Show that $\angle PQC = \frac{1}{2}\angle BAC$.

(b) Let $ABCD$ be a rhombus with $\angle BAD = 60°$. Let F, G, and H be points on the segments AD, CA, and DC respectively such that $DFGH$ is a parallelogram. Show that $\triangle BHF$ is equilateral.

solution page 592

19th Lithuanian Mathematical Team Contest, 2004

17

Let a, b, and c be the sides of a triangle and let x, y, and z be real numbers such that $x + y + z = 0$. Prove that

$$a^2 yz + b^2 zx + c^2 xy \leq 0.$$

solution page 593

19th Lithuanian Mathematical Team Contest, 2004

18

Points M and N are on the sides AB and BC of the triangle ABC, respectively. It is given that $\frac{AM}{MB} = \frac{BN}{NC} = 2$ and $\angle ACB = 2\angle MNB$. Prove that ABC is an isosceles triangle.

solution page 594

The two diagonals of a trapezoid divide it into four triangles. The areas of three of them are 1, 2, and 4 square units. What values can the area of the fourth triangle have?

solution page 595

The ratio of the lengths of the diagonals of a rhombus is $a : b$. Find the ratio of the area of the rhombus to the area of an inscribed circle.

solution page 596

Let H be the orthocentre of an acute-angled triangle ABC. Prove that the midpoints of AB and CH and the intersection point of the interior bisectors of $\angle CAH$ and $\angle CBH$ are collinear.

solution page 597

Given are a circle and its diameter PQ. Let t be a tangent to the circle, touching it at T, and let A be the intersection of the lines t and PQ. Let p and q be the tangents to the circle at P and Q respectively, and let

$$PT \cap q = \{N\} \quad \text{and} \quad QT \cap p = \{M\}.$$

Prove that the points A, M, and N are collinear.

solution page 599

Triangle ABC is equilateral, D is a point inside the triangle such that $DA = DB$, and E is a point that satisfies the conditions $\angle DBE = \angle DBC$ and $BE = AB$. How large is the angle $\angle DEB$?

solution page 601

Let h be the altitude from A in an acute triangle ABC. Prove that

$$(b + c)^2 \geq a^2 + 4h^2,$$

where a, b, and c are the lengths of the sides opposite A, B, and C respectively.

solution page 602

geometry
problems and solutions from Mathematical Olympiads

On the plane there are given four distinct points A, B, C, D lying (in this order) on a line g, at distances $AB = a$, $BC = b$, $CD = c$.

(a) Construct, whenever possible, a point P, not on g, such that the angles $\angle APB$, $\angle BPC$, $\angle CPD$ are equal.

(b) Prove that a point P with the property as above exists if and only if the following inequality holds: $(a + b)(b + c) < 4ac$.

Solution

(a) If P is a solution, then the lines PB and PC are interior bisectors in $\triangle APC$ and $\triangle BPD$ respectively. Hence we have: $\dfrac{PA}{PC} = \dfrac{BA}{BC}$ and $\dfrac{PB}{PD} = \dfrac{CB}{CD}$ and P is simultaneously on $E_1 = \left\{ M : \dfrac{MA}{MC} = \dfrac{a}{b} \right\}$ and $E_2 = \left\{ M : \dfrac{MB}{MD} = \dfrac{b}{c} \right\}$.

In the general case where $a \neq b$, denoting by B' the harmonic conjugate of B with respect to A and C, E_1 is the circle with diameter BB' and, when $a = b$, E_1 is the perpendicular bisector of the segment AC. Similar results hold for E_2.

Conversely, we may construct E_1 and E_2 and, assuming that they are secant, choose for P one of their two distinct points of intersection symmetrical about g. From $\dfrac{PA}{PC} = \dfrac{BA}{BC}$, we deduce that PB is one of the bisectors of $\angle APC$, more precisely the interior bisector in $\triangle APC$ since B is between A and C. Hence $\angle APB = \angle BPC$. Similarly $\angle BPC = \angle CPD$ and finally: $\angle APB = \angle BPC = \angle CPD$.

(b) The above construction provides a point P solution whenever E_1 and E_2 are secant. We first examine the general case where $a \neq b$ and $b \neq c$: E_1 and E_2 are circles with centres I_1, I_2 and radii r_1, r_2 respectively. These circles are secant if and only if:

$$|r_1 - r_2| < I_1 I_2 < r_1 + r_2 \qquad (1)$$

Let us denote by k the real number such that $\overline{BI_1} = \dfrac{k}{b} \overline{BC}$ (so that $|k| = r_1$).

We may compute: $\overline{I_1 A} = -\dfrac{k + a}{b} \overline{BC}$ and $\overline{I_1 C} = \dfrac{b - k}{b} \overline{BC}$, and from the Newton's relation, $\overline{I_1 B}^2 = \overline{I_1 A} \cdot \overline{I_1 C}$, we obtain easily $k = \dfrac{ab}{a - b}$, so that $r_1 = \dfrac{ab}{|a - b|}$. Similarly: $r_2 = \dfrac{cb}{|c - b|}$.

We also compute: $\overline{I_1 I_2} = \dfrac{b^2 - ac}{(b - a)(b - c)} \overline{BC}$ so that $I_1 I_2 = \dfrac{b|b^2 - ac|}{|b - a|\,|b - c|}$.

The condition (1) may now be successively written:

$$\big| c|a - b| - a|c - b| \big| \; < \; |b^2 - ac| \; < \; a|c - b| + c|a - b|$$

$$a^2(c - b)^2 + c^2(a - b)^2 - 2ac|a - b|\,|c - b| \; < \; (b^2 - ac)^2$$
$$< \; a^2(c - b)^2 + c^2(a - b)^2 + 2ac|a - b|\,|c - b|$$

$$\big| (b^2 - ac)^2 - a^2(c - b)^2 + c^2(a - b)^2 \big| \; < \; 2ac|a - b|\,|c - b|$$

$$|a - b|\,|c - b|\,|b^2 + b(a + c) - ac| \; < \; 2ac|a - b|\,|c - b|$$

$$-2ac \; < \; b^2 + b(a + c) - ac \; < \; 2ac$$

$$-ac \; < \; b^2 + b(a + c) \; < \; 3ac .$$

Since $b^2 + b(a + c)$ is positive, the latter condition is equivalent to $b^2 + b(a + c) < 3ac$ or $(a + b)(b + c) < 4ac$.

E_1 and E_2 are both lines when $a = b = c$, but in this case they are strictly parallel so that no point P exists (and the condition $(a + b)(b + c) < 4ac$ is not true either).

Lastly, suppose for instance that E_1 is a line and E_2 is a circle (that is, $a = b$ and $b \neq c$). Since E_1 is perpendicular to g at B, E_1 and E_2 are secant if and only if $I_2 B < r_2$. We obtain easily: $I_2 B = \dfrac{b^2}{|c - b|}$ and the condition becomes: $b < c$ (and the inequality $(a + b)(b + c) < 4ac$ reduces to $b < c$ as well). The proof of (b) is now complete.

Let the sides of two rectangles be $\{a, b\}$ and $\{c, d\}$ respectively, with $a < c \leq d < b$ and $ab < cd$. Prove that the first rectangle can be placed within the second one if and only if

$$(b^2 - a^2)^2 \leq (bc - ad)^2 + (bd - ac)^2 .$$

Solution

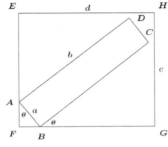

Let $ABCD$ and $EFGH$ denote respectively the first and second rectangle.

$ABCD$ can be placed within $EFGH$ if and only if

$$\begin{cases} a\cos\theta + b\sin\theta \leq c, \\ b\cos\theta + a\sin\theta \leq d. \end{cases}$$

This means that the point of intersection of $a\cos\theta + b\sin\theta = c$ and $b\cos\theta + a\sin\theta = d$, which is $\left(\frac{bd-ac}{b^2-a^2}, \frac{bc-ad}{b^2-a^2}\right)$, lies outside or on the unit circle, or equivalently

$$(b^2 - a^2)^2 \leq (bd - ac)^2 + (bc - ad)^2 .$$

Let $ABCD$ be a convex quadrilateral, and let R_A, R_B, R_C, R_D denote the circumradii of the triangles DAB, ABC, BCD, CDA respectively. Prove that $R_A + R_C > R_B + R_D$ if and only if $\angle A + \angle C > \angle B + \angle D$.

Solution

Let the diagonals meet in E. We may suppose that $\angle AED > 90°$. Then all of $\angle EDA$, $\angle DAE$, $\angle EBC$, $\angle BCE$ are acute. Label them as θ, ϕ, ϕ', θ', respectively. Then $\theta + \phi = \theta' + \phi'$.

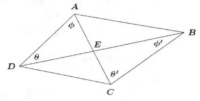

Now, if A, B, C and D were concyclic we would have $\phi = \phi'$ and $\theta = \theta'$.

On the other hand, if $\angle A + \angle C > 180°$, then $\theta < \theta'$ and $\phi > \phi'$. This is easily seen by drawing a circumcircle of $\triangle ABC$ and examining the possible locations of B on the extension of DE.

The purpose of isolating acute angles was for a convenient application of the Sine Law. We have

$$R_A = \frac{AB}{2\sin\theta}, \quad R_B = \frac{AB}{2\sin\theta'}, \quad R_C = \frac{DC}{2\sin\phi'}, \quad R_D = \frac{DC}{2\sin\phi}.$$

Thus if $\angle A + \angle C = 180°$ then $\phi' = \phi$ and $\theta = \theta'$ and therefore $R_A + R_C = R_B + R_D$.

More generally,

$$\angle A + \angle C > \angle B + \angle D \iff \angle A + \angle C > 180°$$
$$\implies \phi' < \phi, \quad \theta < \theta'$$
$$\impliedby R_C > R_D, \quad R_A > R_B$$
$$\implies R_A + R_C > R_B + R_D.$$

The fact that we have equivalence follows by symmetry.

On the plane are given a point O and a polygon $\mathcal{F}$ (not necessarily convex). Let P denote the perimeter of $\mathcal{F}$, D the sum of the distances from O to the vertices of $\mathcal{F}$, and H the sum of the distances from O to the lines containing the sides of $\mathcal{F}$. Prove that $D^2 - H^2 \geq P^2/4$.

Solution

We shall prove that $D^2 - H^2 \geq P^2/4$ for any n–gon. We use "induction" on n.

If $n = 2$, the inequality $D^2 - H^2 \geq P^2/4$ is equivalent to $(a+b)^2 - 4h^2 \geq c^2$.

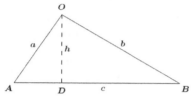

To prove this, consider a line (L) passing through O and parallel to AB, and let B_1 be the image of B under reflection in (L). Then $OA + OB = OA + OB_1 \geq AB_1$; that is $a + b \geq \sqrt{4h^2 + c^2}$, as required.

Now, let the n–gon $\mathcal{F}$ be $P_1 P_2 \ldots P_n$ and let $d_i = OP_i$, $p_i = P_i P_{i+1}$, $h_i = $ distance from O to $P_i P_{i+1}$. Then by the "induction hypothesis" we have for each i

$$d_i + d_{i+1} \geq \sqrt{4h_i^2 + p_i^2}\,.$$

Summing these inequalities over $i = 1, 2, \ldots, n$ we obtain

$$2D \geq \sum_i \sqrt{4h_i^2 + p_i^2}\,,$$

or equivalently
$$4D^2 \geq \left(\sum_i \sqrt{4h_i^2 + p_i^2}\right)^2.$$

Now, $4H^2 + P^2 = 4(\sum_i h_i)^2 + (\sum_i p_i)^2$, so if we prove that

$$\sum_i \sqrt{4h_i^2 + p_i^2} \geq \sqrt{4\left(\sum_i h_i\right)^2 + \left(\sum_i p_i\right)^2}\,,$$

then we are done. But the above inequality follows from the triangle inequality applied to the sum of the vectors $(2h_i, p_i)$.

Show that if D_1 and D_2 are two skew lines, then there are infinitely many straight lines such that their points have equal distance from D_1 and D_2.

Solution

Let H_1 on D_1, H_2 on D_2 be such that: $H_1H_2 \perp D_1$ and $H_1H_2 \perp D_2$ and let O be the midpoint of H_1H_2. We will work in the following system of rectangular axes: we take O as origin, the z-axis along H_1H_2 and, as x-axis and y-axis, we take the bisectors of the angle formed at O by the parallels to D_1 and D_2. Then there exist non-zero real numbers a and m such that:

D_1 is the intersection of the planes $(P_1) : z = a$ and $(Q_1) : y = mx$;

D_2 is the intersection of the planes $(P_2) : z = -a$ and $(Q_2) : y = -mx$.

Now, let $A(\alpha, 0, 0)$ be a point lying on the x-axis and Δ_A be the line through A directed by $\vec{u}(0, 1, t)$. We show that it is possible to choose t (depending on α) such that each point $M(\alpha, k, kt)$, $(k \in \mathbb{R})$ of Δ_A has equal distance from D_1 and D_2.

As the planes (P_1) and (Q_1) are perpendicular, we have:

$$[d(M, D_1)]^2 = [d(M, P_1)]^2 + [d(M, Q_1)]^2 = (kt - a)^2 + \frac{(k - m\alpha)^2}{1 + m^2}.$$

Similarly: $[d(M, D_2)]^2 = (kt + a)^2 + \dfrac{(k + m\alpha)^2}{1 + m^2}$.

Hence, $d(M, D_1) = d(M, D_2)$ is equivalent to $4k \left(at + \dfrac{m\alpha}{1 + m^2} \right) = 0$

so that, by choosing $t = -\dfrac{m\alpha}{a(1 + m^2)}$, we have $d(M, D_1) = d(M, D_2)$ for all M on Δ_A.

Since $\Delta_A \neq \Delta_B$ whenever $A \neq B$ on the x-axis (Δ_A and Δ_B are in strictly parallel planes), the family of lines Δ_A, when α takes all real values, answers the question.

We consider a triangle ABC such that $\angle MAC = 15°$ where M is the midpoint of BC. Determine the possible maximum value of $\angle B$.

Solution

Let $\Gamma(O, R)$ be the circumcircle of $\triangle AMC$, with centre O and radius R. Denote $\angle B = \beta$. Now β has its maximum when AB touches Γ at A. We denote $\angle BAM = \angle ACM = x$.

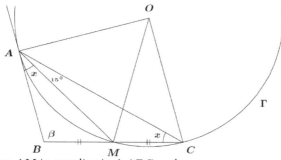

Since AM is a median in $\triangle ABC$ we have:

$$\sin x : \sin 15° = \sin \beta : \sin x,$$
$$2 \sin^2 x = 2 \sin \beta \sin 15°,$$
$$1 - \cos 2x = \cos(\beta - 15°) - \cos(\beta + 15°).$$

Since $\beta + 15° + 2x = 180°$, we have $2x = 165° - \beta$. Thus $1 + \cos(\beta + 15°) = \cos(\beta - 15°) - \cos(\beta + 15°)$, or

$$2\cos(\beta + 15°) - \cos(\beta - 15°) + 1 = 0. \qquad (1)$$

It is easy to verify that this is satisfied by $\beta = 105°$.

Write $\beta = 105° + y$. From (1) we obtain

$$2\cos(120° + y) - \cos(90° + y) + 1 = 0,$$
$$2\cos 120° \cos y - 2\sin 120° \sin y + \sin y + 1 = 0,$$
$$1 - \cos y = \sin y \left(\sqrt{3} - 1\right),$$
$$2\sin^2 \left(\frac{1}{2}\right) y = 2\sin \left(\frac{1}{2}y\right) \cos \left(\frac{1}{2}y\right) \left(\sqrt{3} - 1\right).$$

Therefore, $\sin \left(\frac{1}{2}y\right) = 0 \implies y = 0$ or

$$\tan \left(\frac{1}{2}y\right) = \sqrt{3} - 1$$
$$\implies y = 72.4\ldots°$$
$$\implies \beta = 177.4\ldots°.$$

Since $x > 15°$, this does not hold. So β has a maximum of $105°$.

Let AD be the internal bisector of the triangle ABC ($D \in BC$), E the point symmetric to D with respect to the mid-point of BC, and F the point of BC such that $\angle BAF = \angle EAC$. Show that $\frac{BF}{FC} = \frac{c^3}{b^3}$.

Solution

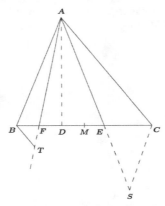

Let T be the point on AF such that $BT \parallel AC$ and let S be the point on AE such that $CS \parallel AB$. Then $\angle ABT + \angle BAC = 180°$ and $\angle ACS + \angle BAC = 180°$.

Thus we have $\angle ABT = \angle ACS$. Since $\angle BAT = \angle BAF = \angle CAE = \angle CAS$ we have $\triangle ABT \sim \triangle ACS$ so that

$$\frac{BT}{CS} = \frac{AB}{AC} = \frac{c}{b}. \tag{1}$$

As $BT \parallel AC$ we get

$$\frac{BF}{FC} = \frac{BT}{AC} = \frac{BT}{b}. \tag{2}$$

As $AB \parallel CS$ we have

$$\frac{BE}{EC} = \frac{AB}{CS} = \frac{c}{CS}. \tag{3}$$

Let M be the mid-point of BC.

Since E is the point symmetric to D with respect to M we have

$$EC = BD \quad \text{and} \quad BE = DC,$$

so that $\dfrac{BE}{EC} = \dfrac{DC}{BD}$.

Since AD is the bisector of $\angle BAC$, we get $\dfrac{DC}{BD} = \dfrac{AC}{AB} = \dfrac{b}{c}$. Thus we have

$$\frac{BE}{EC} = \frac{b}{c}. \tag{4}$$

From (3) and (4) we have

$$\frac{c}{CS} = \frac{b}{c}, \quad \text{so that} \quad CS = \frac{c^2}{b}.$$

Hence, from (1), we get $BT = \dfrac{c^3}{b^2}$; whence from (2), $\dfrac{BF}{FC} = \dfrac{c^3}{b^3}$.

An ellipse is drawn taking as major axis the biggest of the sides of
a given rectangle, such that the ellipse passes through the intersection point
of the diagonals of the rectangle.

Show that, if a point of the ellipse, external to the rectangle, is joined
to the extreme points of the opposite side, then three segments in geometric
progression are determined on the major axis.

Solution

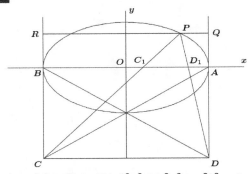

An equation of the ellipse E is $b^2x^2 + a^2y^2 - a^2b^2 = 0$. The rectangle
$ABCD$ has sides $AB = CD = 2a$, $AD = BC = 2b$. A point P of E is
$P(a\cos\varphi, b\sin\varphi)$, with $\sin\varphi > 0$. Let the line through P parallel to AB
meet BC and AD in R and Q, respectively. Let PD and PC meet the major
axis at D_1, C_1 respectively.

From $\triangle DPQ$ and $\triangle DD_1A$, we have

$$D_1A : PQ = 2b : (2b + b\sin\varphi), \qquad D_1A : a(1 - \cos\varphi) = 2 : (2 + \sin\varphi);$$

$$\implies \quad D_1A = \frac{2a(1 - \cos\varphi)}{2 + \sin\varphi}. \tag{1}$$

In the same way, from $\triangle PCD$ and $\triangle PC_1D_1$, we have

$$C_1D_1 = \frac{2a\sin\varphi}{2 + \sin\varphi}, \tag{2}$$

and from $\triangle CPR$ and $\triangle CC_1B$, we have

$$BC_1 = \frac{2a(1 + \cos\varphi)}{2 + \sin\varphi}. \tag{3}$$

From (1), (2) and (3) $D_1A : C_1D_1 : BC_1 = (1 - \cos\varphi) : \sin\varphi : (1 + \cos\varphi)$.
And as $\sin^2\varphi = 1 - \cos^2\varphi$ the three segments are in geometric progression
indeed.

Let the point D on the hypotenuse AC of the right triangle ABC be such that $|AB| = |CD|$. Prove that the bisector of the angle $\angle A$, the median through B and the altitude through D of the triangle ABD have a common point.

Solution

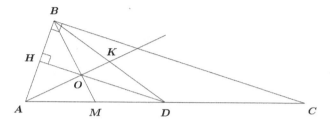

Let M be the foot of the median from B, K the point of intersection of the angle bisector with BD and H the foot of the altitude from D in $\triangle ABD$.

We use Ceva's Theorem to prove that AM, DH and AK have a common point.

$$\frac{MA}{MD} = 1 \qquad \text{(because } BM \text{ is a median)}$$

$$\frac{KD}{KB} = \frac{AD}{AB} \qquad \text{(Bisector Property)}$$

$$\triangle AHD \sim \triangle ABC \implies \frac{HB}{HA} = \frac{DC}{DA} = \frac{AB}{AD}.$$

Thus

$$\frac{MA}{MD} \cdot \frac{KD}{KB} \cdot \frac{HB}{HA} = \frac{AD}{AB} \cdot \frac{AB}{AD} = 1.$$

Let Q be the mid-point of the side AB of an inscribed quadrilateral $ABCD$ and S the intersection of its diagonals. Denote by P and R the orthogonal projections of S on AD and BC respectively. Prove that $|PQ| = |QR|$.

Solution

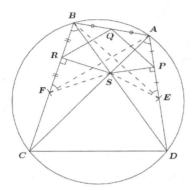

Let E be the point symmetric to A with respect to P, and let F be the point symmetric to B with respect to R. Then we have

$$SE = SA, \quad \angle SEA = \angle SAE,$$

and $$SF = SB, \quad \angle SFB = \angle SBF.$$

As A, B, C, D are concyclic we get $\angle CAD = \angle CBD$. Thus,

$$\angle SEA = \angle SAE = \angle SBF = \angle SFB.$$

Consequently we have $\angle ASE = \angle BSF$. Thus we get

$$\angle BSE = \angle BSA + \angle ASE = \angle BSA + \angle BSF = \angle FSA.$$

Since $SB = SF$ and $SE = SA$, we have

$$\triangle SEB \equiv \triangle SAF. \qquad (SAS)$$

Thus we get $EB = AF$. Since P, Q, R are mid-points of AE, AB, BF respectively, we have

$$PQ = \frac{1}{2}EB \quad \text{and} \quad QR = \frac{1}{2}AF.$$

Therefore we have $PQ = QR$.

In the trapezium $ABCD$, the bases are $AB = a$, $CD = b$, and the diagonals meet at the point O. Find the ratio of the areas of the triangle ABO and trapezium.

Solution

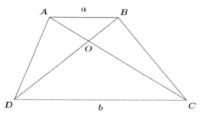

Since triangles with the same height have areas in proportion to their bases and since $\triangle AOB \sim \triangle COD$, we have

$$\frac{[DOA]}{[AOB]} = \frac{OD}{OB} = \frac{b}{a} \quad \text{or} \quad [DOA] = \frac{b}{a}[AOB],$$

where $[\mathcal{P}]$ denotes the area of polygon $[\mathcal{P}]$.

Also, since the areas of similar triangles are proportional to the squares on corresponding sides,

$$\frac{[COD]}{[AOB]} = \frac{b^2}{a^2} \quad \text{or} \quad [COD] = \frac{b^2}{a^2}[AOB].$$

Finally, since $\triangle ABD$ and $\triangle ABC$ have the same base and equal altitude $[ABD] = [ABC]$, and since

$$[ABD] = [AOB] + [DOA], \quad [ABC] = [AOB] + [BOC],$$

it follows that $[DOA] = [BOC]$.

Consequently,

$$\begin{aligned}
[ABCD] &= [AOB] + [BOC] + [COD] + [DOA] \\
&= [AOB] + 2[DOA] + [COD];
\end{aligned}$$

that is,

$$[ABCD] = \left(1 + 2 \cdot \frac{b}{a} + \frac{b^2}{a^2}\right)[AOB],$$

giving

$$[ABCD] = \left(\frac{a+b}{a}\right)^2 [AOB],$$

and

$$\frac{[AOB]}{[ABCD]} = \left(\frac{a}{a+b}\right)^2.$$

The area of a trapezium equals 2; the sum of its diagonals equals 4. Prove that the diagonals are orthogonal.

Solution

If a and b are the diagonal lengths and θ the angle between them, then the area $2 = \frac{1}{2}ab\sin\theta$. Since $4 = a + b \geq 2\sqrt{ab}$, the maximum value of ab is 4. Hence $\sin\theta = 1$, so that $\theta = \pi/2$.

Show that if D_1 and D_2 are two skew lines, then there are infinitely many straight lines such that their points have equal distance from D_1 and D_2.

Solution

Rename the lines l and m. Fix points A and B on l a unit distance apart. For each A' on m there are two points B' and B'' on m that are a unit distance from A'. There is a unique rotation that takes A and B to A' and B', and another taking them to A' and B''; the points of the axes of these two rotations are equidistant from l and m since the perpendicular from an axis point to l is taken by the rotation to the perpendicular from that point to m. Each A' leads to a different pair of lines. (To see that the rotation exists as claimed, take as mirror 1 the plane of points equidistant from A and A'; if B^* is the image of B under reflection in mirror 1 then take mirror 2 to be the perpendicular bisector (necessarily through A') of B^* and either B' or B''. The product of reflections in these two mirrors is a rotation about their line of intersection.)

Let ABC be an equilateral triangle of altitude 1. A circle with radius 1 and centre on the same side of AB as C rolls along the segment AB. Prove that the arc of the circle that is inside the triangle always has the same length.

Solution

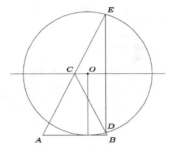

Let D and E be the intersections of BC and extended AC, respectively, with the circle.

Since $CO \parallel AB$ (because both the altitude and the radius are 1) $\angle BCO = 60°$ and therefore $\angle ECO = 180° - \angle ACB - \angle BCO = 60°$.

Since a circle is always symmetric about its diameter and line CE is a reflection of line CB in CO, line segment CE is a reflection of line segment CD.

Therefore $CE = CD$.

Therefore $\triangle CED$ is an isosceles triangle.

Therefore $\angle CED = \angle CDE$ and $\angle CED + \angle CDE = \angle ACB = 60°$.

$\angle CED = 30°$ regardless of the position of centre O. Since $\angle CED$ is also the angle subtended from the arc inside the triangle, if CED is constant, the arc length is also constant.

Solution 2

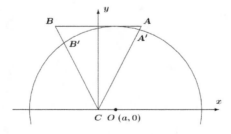

Place C at the origin, point A at $\left(\frac{1}{\sqrt{3}}, 1\right)$ and point B at $\left(-\frac{1}{\sqrt{3}}, 1\right)$. Then $\triangle ABC$ is equilateral with altitude of length 1.

Let O be the centre of the circle. Because the circle has radius 1, and since it touches line AB, the locus of O is on the line through C parallel to AB (since C is length 1 away from AB); that is, the locus of O is on the x–axis.

Let point O be at $(a, 0)$. Then $-\frac{1}{\sqrt{3}} \leq a \leq \frac{1}{\sqrt{3}}$ since we have the restriction that the circle rolls along AB.

Now, let A' and B' be the intersection of the circle with CA and CB, respectively. The equation of CA is $y = \sqrt{3}\, x$, $0 \leq x \leq \frac{1}{\sqrt{3}}$, of CB is $y = -\sqrt{3}\, x$, $-\frac{1}{\sqrt{3}} \leq x \leq 0$, and of the circle is $(x - a)^2 + y^2 = 1$.

We solve for A' by substituting $y = \sqrt{3}\, x$ into $(x - a)^2 + y^2 = 1$ to get $x = \dfrac{a \pm \sqrt{4 - 3a^2}}{4}$.

Visually, we can see that solutions represent the intersection of AC extended and the circle, but we are only concerned with the greater x–value — this is the solution that is on AC, not on AC extended. Therefore

$$x = \frac{a + \sqrt{4 - 3a^2}}{4}, \qquad y = \sqrt{3}\left(\frac{a + \sqrt{4 - 3a^2}}{4}\right).$$

Likewise we solve for B', but we take the lesser x–value to get

$$x = \frac{a - \sqrt{4 - 3a^2}}{4}, \qquad y = -\sqrt{3}\left(\frac{a - \sqrt{4 - 3a^2}}{4}\right).$$

Let us find the length of $A'B'$:

$$
\begin{aligned}
|A'B'|^2 &= \left(\frac{a + \sqrt{4 - 3a^2}}{4} - \frac{a - \sqrt{4 - 3a^2}}{4}\right)^2 + \\
&\qquad \left(\left(\sqrt{3}\,\frac{a + \sqrt{4 - 3a^2}}{4}\right) - \left(-\sqrt{3}\,\frac{a - \sqrt{4 - 3a^2}}{4}\right)\right)^2 \\
&= \frac{4 - 3a^2}{4} + 3\,\frac{a^2}{4} = 1,
\end{aligned}
$$

which is independent of a.

Consider the points O, A' and B'. $\triangle OA'B'$ is an equilateral triangle (because $A'B' = OA' = OB' = 1$).

Therefore $\angle A'OB' = \frac{\pi}{3}$ and arc $A'B' = \frac{\pi}{3}$, a constant.

A finite set S of points in the plane with integer coordinates is called a *two-neighbour set*, if for each (p, q) in S exactly two of the points $(p + 1, q)$, $(p, q + 1)$, $(p - 1, q)$, $(p, q - 1)$ are in S. For which n does there exist a two-neighbour set which contains exactly n points?

Solution

Put the points in the coordinate plane. Let (x, y) be even if $x + y = 0 \pmod 2$ and odd otherwise. Note that the even (odd) points have only odd (even) neighbours. So, if we have k even points, we will count $2k$ odd neighbours. But each odd point has two even neighbours, so each point was counted twice and there are k odd points as well. This means the number of points is even (it is equal to $2k$). 4 works by taking a 2 by 2 square $2k$, $k > 3$ works by starting with a 3 by 3 square with centre removed and then stretching it appropriately. Finally, it is evident that a set of six points does not work.

Consider finitely many points in a plane such that, if we choose any three points A, B, C among them, the area of $\triangle ABC$ is always less than 1. Show that all of these finitely many points lie within the interior or on the boundary of a triangle with area less than 4.

Solution

Let ABC be the triangle having the maximal area $[ABC]$. Then $[ABC] \leq 1$. Let $A'B'C'$ be the triangle whose medial triangle is ABC. Then $[A'B'C'] \leq 4[ABC] \leq 4$. We will show that $A'B'C'$ contains all n of the points.

Assume, for a contradiction, that there is a point, D, outside $A'B'C'$. Then ABC and D lie on different sides of at least one of the lines $A'B'$, $B'C'$, $C'A'$.

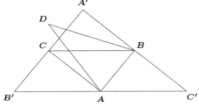

Then $[ABD] \geq [ABC]$, contradicting the maximality of $[ABC]$.

Let A, B, C be three points lying on a circle, and let P, Q, R be the mid-points of arcs BC, CA, AB, respectively. AP, BQ, CR intersect BC, CA, AB at L, M, N, respectively. Show that

$$\frac{AL}{PL} + \frac{BM}{QM} + \frac{CN}{RN} \geq 9.$$

For which triangle ABC does equality hold?

Solution

To be definite, we have taken P to lie on the arc BC that does not contain A.

Since P is the mid-point of BC, $\angle BAP = \angle PAC$ and AL is the internal bisector of the angle A of triangle ABC formed by joining the points A, B, C.

Let $AA_0 = h_a$ be the altitude from A and let P_0 be the foot of the perpendicular from P to the side BC.

The right triangles AA_0L and PP_0L are similar, so

$$\frac{AL}{PL} = \frac{AA_0}{PP_0} \qquad \text{or} \qquad \frac{AL}{PL} = \frac{h_a}{PP_0}. \tag{1}$$

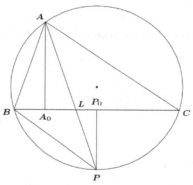

If the lengths of the sides of $\triangle ABC$ are $BC = a$, $CA = b$ and $AB = c$, then the area of $\triangle ABC$ is $\frac{1}{2}a \cdot h_a$ and also $\frac{1}{2}bc \cdot \sin A$; hence

$$h_a = \frac{bc \sin A}{a}.$$

In $\triangle BP_0P$, we have $\angle P_0BP = \angle CBP = \frac{1}{2}\angle A$ (since both $\angle CBP$ and $\angle A/2$ are inscribed in the circular arc PC). Hence

$$PP_0 \;=\; BP_0 \cdot \tan \frac{A}{2} \;=\; \frac{a}{2} \cdot \tan \frac{A}{2}.$$

Substituting these expressions for h_a and PP_0 in (1) gives

$$\frac{AL}{PL} \;=\; \frac{4bc\cos^2 \frac{A}{2}}{a^2}.$$

Since $\cos^2 \dfrac{A}{2} \;=\; \dfrac{s(s-a)}{bc}$ where $s \;=\; \dfrac{a+b+c}{2}$, this is equivalent to

$$
\begin{aligned}
\frac{AL}{PL} \;&=\; \frac{2s}{a} \cdot \frac{2(s-a)}{a} \\
&=\; \left(1 + \frac{b}{a} + \frac{c}{a}\right)\left(-1 + \frac{b}{a} + \frac{c}{a}\right) \\
&=\; \left(\frac{b}{a} + \frac{c}{a}\right)^2 - 1.
\end{aligned}
$$

We have conducted our discussions with respect to the side BC of $\triangle ABC$. Applying the same reasoning to either of the other sides instead, we obtain

$$
\begin{aligned}
\frac{AL}{PL} \;&+\; \frac{BM}{QM} \;+\; \frac{CN}{RN} \\
&=\; \left[\left(\frac{b}{a} + \frac{c}{a}\right)^2 - 1\right] + \left[\left(\frac{c}{b} + \frac{a}{b}\right)^2 - 1\right] + \left[\left(\frac{a}{c} + \frac{b}{c}\right)^2 - 1\right] \\
&=\; \left(\frac{a^2}{b^2} + \frac{b^2}{a^2}\right) + \left(\frac{b^2}{c^2} + \frac{c^2}{b^2}\right) + \left(\frac{c^2}{a^2} + \frac{a^2}{c^2}\right) \\
&\quad +2\left(\frac{ab}{c^2} + \frac{bc}{a^2} + \frac{ca}{b^2}\right) - 3.
\end{aligned}
$$

According to the arithmetic mean–geometric mean inequality,

$$\frac{a^2}{b^2} + \frac{b^2}{a^2} \geq 2, \qquad \frac{b^2}{c^2} + \frac{c^2}{b^2} \geq 2,$$

$$\frac{c^2}{a^2} + \frac{a^2}{c^2} \geq 2, \qquad \frac{ab}{c^2} + \frac{bc}{a^2} + \frac{ca}{b^2} \geq 3.$$

Therefore,

$$\frac{AL}{PL} + \frac{BM}{QM} + \frac{CN}{RN} \;\geq\; 2 + 2 + 2 + 2\cdot 3 - 3 \;=\; 9.$$

Equality occurs when $a = b = c$; that is, when $\triangle ABC$ is equilateral.

Two circles O_1, O_2 of radii r_1, r_2 $(r_1 < r_2)$, respectively, intersect at two points A and B. P is any point on circle O_1. Lines PA, PB and circle O_2 intersect at Q and R, respectively.

(i) Express $y = QR$ in terms of r_1, r_2, and $\theta = \angle APB$.

(ii) Show that $y = 2r_2$ is a necessary and sufficient condition that circle O_1 be orthogonal to circle O_2.

Solution

(i) In figure 1, $\angle PBA = \angle PQR$, both being supplements of $\angle ABR$.

Let W_1 and W_2 be the centres of O_1 and O_2. In Figure 2, the line W_1W_2, joining the centres of the intersecting circles, is perpendicular to their common chord AB which subtends at the centre W_1 (respectively W_2) twice the angle it subtends at P (respectively Q) on the circumference O_1 (respectively O_2), implying

$$\angle QPB = \angle W_2W_1B \quad \text{and} \quad \angle BQP = \angle BW_2W_1.$$

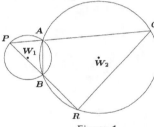 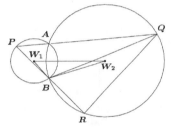

Figure 1.   Figure 2.

The similar triangles $\triangle PAB \sim \triangle PRQ$ and $\triangle PBQ \sim \triangle W_1BW_2$ yield

$$\frac{QR}{AB} = \frac{PQ}{PB}, \qquad \frac{PQ}{PB} = \frac{W_1W_2}{W_1B},$$

whence

$$y = QR = \frac{AB}{W_1B} \cdot W_1W_2 \qquad (\overline{QR} \text{ is constant}).$$

Since $\sin\theta = \dfrac{AB/2}{W_1B}$, we have $\dfrac{AB}{W_1B} = 2\sin\theta$, and hence

$$y = 2 \cdot W_1W_2 \cdot \sin\theta.$$

By the Law of Sines, applied to $\triangle W_1W_2B$ with $\angle BW_2W_1 = \alpha$,

$$\frac{W_2B}{\sin\theta} = \frac{W_1B}{\sin\alpha}; \quad \text{that is,} \quad \sin\alpha = \frac{r_1}{r_2}\sin\theta.$$

Hence

$$W_1 W_2 = r_1 \cos\theta + r_2 \cos\alpha$$

$$= r_1 \cos\theta + r_2 \sqrt{1 - \left(\frac{r_1}{r_2}\sin\theta\right)^2}$$

$$= r_1 \cos\theta + \sqrt{r_2^2 - r_1^2 \sin^2\theta}\,.$$

We conclude that

$$y = 2\left(r_1 \cos\theta + \sqrt{r_2^2 - r_1^2 \sin^2\theta}\right)\sin\theta\,.$$

(ii) In the equation $y = 2r_2$, we replace y by

$$2 \cdot \left(r_1 \cos\theta + \sqrt{r_2^2 - r_1^2 \sin^2\theta}\right)\sin\theta$$

and write it in the form

$$\left(\sqrt{r_2^2 - r_1^2 \sin^2\theta}\right)\sin\theta = r_2 - r_1 \sin\theta\cos\theta\,,$$

which is equivalent to the one obtained by squaring both sides; that is,

$$(r_2^2 - r_1^2 \sin^2\theta)\sin^2\theta = r_2^2 - 2r_1 r_2 \sin\theta\cos\theta + r_1^2 \sin^2\theta\cos^2\theta\,,$$

which is equivalent to

$$(r_2 \cos\theta - r_1 \sin\theta)^2 = 0\,.$$

This, in turn, is equivalent to

$$\tan\theta = \frac{r_2}{r_1}\,,$$

or finally

$$\angle W_1 B W_2 = 90°\,.$$

(Of course, this angle is the same at both intersections A and B).

Since the tangent line to a circle is perpendicular to the radius at the point of contact, the angle between the tangents at both intersections A and B is 90° and O_1, O_2 cut orthogonally.

Let $\triangle ABC$ be an equilateral triangle of side length 1, D a point on BC, and let r_1, r_2 be inradii of triangles ABD, ADC, respectively. Express $r_1 r_2$ in terms of $p = BD$, and find the maximum of $r_1 r_2$.

Solution

By the Law of Cosines, applied to $\triangle ABD$,

$$\overline{AD}^2 = 1^2 + p^2 - 2 \cdot 1 \cdot p \cdot \cos 60°,$$

so that

$$\overline{AD} = \sqrt{p^2 - p + 1}.$$

The area of $\triangle ABD$ may be expressed as $\frac{1}{2} \cdot 1 \cdot p \cdot \sin 60° = \frac{p\sqrt{3}}{4}$ and also as $\frac{1 + p + \sqrt{p^2 - p + 1}}{2} \cdot r_1$. Equating these and solving for r_1, we get

$$r_1 = \frac{\sqrt{3}\left(1 + p - \sqrt{p^2 - p + 1}\right)}{6}.$$

In the same way, (or substituting $1 - p$ for p into the above result) we find that the inradius r_2 of triangle ADC satisfies

$$r_2 = \frac{\sqrt{3}\left(2 - p - \sqrt{p^2 - p + 1}\right)}{6}.$$

Therefore,

$$r_1 r_2 = \frac{1 - \sqrt{p^2 - p + 1}}{4} = \frac{1 - \sqrt{(p - \frac{1}{2})^2 + \frac{3}{4}}}{4}.$$

Maximizing $\frac{1 - \sqrt{(p - \frac{1}{2})^2 + \frac{3}{4}}}{4}$ is equivalent to minimizing $(p - \frac{1}{2})^2 + \frac{3}{4}$. Since $(p - \frac{1}{2})^2 + \frac{3}{4}$ is a minimum when the square is zero, the product $r_1 r_2$ takes on its maximum value

$$\frac{2 - \sqrt{3}}{8} \quad \text{for} \quad p = \frac{1}{2}.$$

Let $ABCD$ be a convex quadrilateral, $M \in AB$, $N \in BC$, $P \in CD$, $Q \in DA$; $AM = BN = CP = DQ$, and $MNPQ$ is a square. Prove that $ABCD$ is a square, too.

Solution

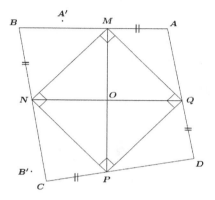

Let O be the centre of $MNPQ$, and r the rotation with centre O and angle $\pm\frac{\pi}{2}$ such that $r(M) = N$. We have

$$
\begin{aligned}
M &\to N \\
N &\to P \qquad A \to A' \\
P &\to Q \qquad B \to B' \\
Q &\to M\,.
\end{aligned}
$$

Then $(NB) \to (PB')$ so $(NB) \perp (PB')$. Thus

$$(NC) \perp (PB')\,. \tag{1}$$

Moreover

$$
\begin{aligned}
PB' &= NB \\
&= PC\,. \tag{2}
\end{aligned}
$$

From (1) and (2), we deduce that $B' \in (BC)$ or B' is on the other side of (BC) than P.

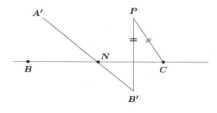

But $A' \in (B'N)$ and $A' \notin (BN)$ so that A' is on the same side of (BC) as M.

$$\text{So} \quad \angle MNA' \leq \angle MNB.$$

But rotations preserve angles, so that $\angle QMA = \angle MNA'$.

$$\text{Thus} \quad \angle QMA \leq \angle MNB,$$

and by symmetry

$$\angle QMA \leq \angle MNB \leq \angle NPC \leq \angle PQD \leq \angle QMA.$$

Thus, they are all equal to a common value, θ, say. From this

$$\angle BMN = \frac{\pi}{2} - \angle QMA = \frac{\pi}{2} - \angle MNB = \angle CNP.$$

Similarly,

$$\angle BMN = \angle CNP = \angle DPQ = \angle AQM = \frac{\pi}{2} - \angle QMA.$$

Then $\angle A = \angle B = \angle C = \angle D = \frac{\pi}{2}$, and $ABCD$ is a rectangle. Further, by Pythagoras' Theorem,

$$BM^2 = MN^2 - BN^2 = MQ^2 - AM^2 = AQ^2.$$

Thus $BM = AQ$ and $BA = MB + MA = AQ + QD = AD$. Then the rectangle is a square.

Dutch Mathematical Olympiad, 1994 (Second Round)

A unit square is divided in two rectangles in such a way that the smallest rectangle can be put on the greatest rectangle with every vertex of the smallest on exactly one of the edges of the greatest. Calculate the dimensions of the smallest rectangle.

Solution

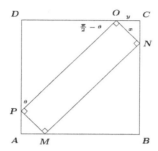

The problem is to calculate $x = ON = PM$ (we have $OP = MN = 1$). Let $\theta = \angle NOC$, $y = OC$. Then $\angle DOP = \frac{\pi}{2} - \theta$, etc.

We deduce that

$$NOC \text{ and } PMA \text{ are isometric (congurent)} \qquad (1)$$
$$NOC, \ OPD \text{ are similar.} \qquad (2)$$

We have $NC^2 = ON^2 - OC^2$. Then $NC = PA = \sqrt{x^2 - y^2}$ (and $y < x$). So we get

$$OD = 1 - x - y$$
$$DP = 1 - PA = 1 - \sqrt{x^2 - y^2}, \qquad (3)$$

and

$$DP^2 = OP^2 - OD^2 = 1 - (1 - x - y)^2. \qquad (4)$$

From (3) and (4) we get

$$2\sqrt{x^2 - y^2} = 2x^2 - 2x + 1 - 2y + 2xy. \qquad (5)$$

But from (2), $\frac{CN}{ON} = \frac{OD}{OP}$, which gives

$$\sqrt{x^2 - y^2} = x(1 - x - y). \qquad (6)$$

By (5) and (6)

$$2y(1 - 2x) = (1 - 2x)^2.$$

Then $x = \frac{1}{2}$ or $y = \frac{1}{2} - x$.

If $x = \frac{1}{2}$ then $y < \frac{1}{2}$ and from (6)

$$\sqrt{\left(\frac{1}{2} - y\right)\left(\frac{1}{2} + y\right)} = \frac{1}{2}\left(\frac{1}{2} - y\right),$$

and then

$$\frac{1}{2} + y = \frac{1}{4}\left(\frac{1}{2} - y\right),$$

so $y < 0$, a contradiction, so $x \neq \frac{1}{2}$.

Thus $y = \frac{1}{2} - x$, or $x + y = \frac{1}{2}$.

Using (6) again, we obtain

$$\left(2x - \frac{1}{2}\right)\frac{1}{2} = \frac{1}{4}x^2;$$

that is, $x^2 - 4x + 1 = 0$ with $x < 1$.

Thus $x = 2 - \sqrt{3}$.

Let P be any point on the diagonal BD of a rectangle $ABCD$. F is the projection of P on BC. H lies on BC such that $BF = FH$. PC intersects AH in Q.

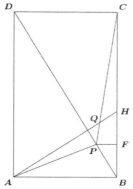

Prove: Area $\triangle APQ =$ Area $\triangle CHQ$.

Solution

Join AC and PH.

Since F is the midpoint of BH, $\triangle PBH$ is an isosceles triangle, and

$$\angle PBH = \angle DBC = \angle PHB. \qquad (1)$$

Triangles $\triangle ACB$ and $\triangle DCB$ are congruent. So

$$\angle DBC = \angle ACB. \qquad (2)$$

From (1) and (2)

$$\angle PHB = \angle ACB. \qquad (3)$$

Thus PH is parallel to AC, and the area of $\triangle APC =$ area of $\triangle ACH$. $[APC] - [AQC] = [ACH] - [AQC]$. Thus $[APQ] = [CHQ]$, as required. ($[XYZ]$ means, as usual, the area of $\triangle XYZ$.)

Let P be a point on the circumscribed circle of $\triangle A_1 A_2 A_3$. Let H be the orthocentre of $\triangle A_1 A_2 A_3$. Let B_1 (B_2, B_3 respectively) be the point of intersection of the perpendicular from P to $A_2 A_3$ ($A_1 A_2$, $A_2 A_3$ respectively). It is known that the three points B_1, B_2, B_3 are collinear. Prove that the line $B_1 B_2 B_3$ passes through the mid-point of the line segment PH.

Solution

The line $B_1 B_2 B_3$ is known as the Simson line.

Let C_1, C_2, C_3 be such that B_1, B_2, B_3 are the mid-points of PC_1, PC_2, PC_3, respectively.

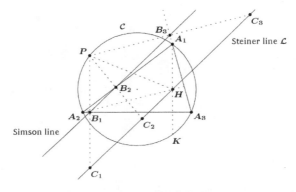

It is known that C_1, C_2, C_3 are collinear. The line $C_1 C_2 C_3$ is the Steiner line, $\mathcal{L}$. (The Steiner line is the image of the Simson line by the homothetic transformation with centre P and ratio 2.)

It suffices to show that H is on the Steiner line.

If P is one of A_1, A_2, A_3, then $\mathcal{L}$ is an altitude in $\triangle A_1 A_2 A_3$ and $H \in \mathcal{L}$.

If $P \notin \{A_1, A_2, A_3\}$, let K be symmetric with H with respect to $A_2 A_3$. It is known that K is on the circle $\mathcal{C}$.

If H is among C_1, C_2, C_3, clearly $H \in \mathcal{L}$. Otherwise, with angles evaluated modulo π: [Ed. $(AB; CD)$, means the angle from the line segment AB to the line segment CD.]

$$
\begin{aligned}
(C_1 H; C_2 H) &= (C_1 H; C_1 P) + (C_1 P; C_2 P) + (C_2 P; C_2 H) \\
(C_1 H; C_1 P) &= (KH; KP) \quad \text{symmetry in } A_2 A_3 \\
&= (K A_1; KP) \\
&= (A_2 A_1; A_2 P) \quad \text{concyclic.}
\end{aligned}
$$

Similarly

$$
(C_2 P; C_2 H) = (A_1 P; A_1 A_2).
$$

Thus

$$\begin{aligned}
(C_1H; C_2H) &= (A_2A_1; A_2P) + (C_1P; C_2P) + (A_1P; A_1A_2) \\
&= (A_1P; A_2A_1) + (A_2A_1; A_2P) + (C_1P; C_2P) \\
&= (PA_1; PA_2) + (C_1P; C_2P) \,.
\end{aligned}$$

Moreover

$$\begin{aligned}
(C_1P; C_2P) &= (B_1P; B_2P) \\
&= (B_1P; PA_2) + (PA_2; PA_1) + (PA_1; B_2P) \,.
\end{aligned}$$

Then

$$\begin{aligned}
(C_1H; C_2H) &= (B_1P; PA_2) + (PA_1; B_2P) \\
&= \underbrace{(B_1P; B_1A_2)}_{(\pi/2)} + (B_1A_2; PA_2) \\
&\qquad + (PA_1; A_1B_2) + \underbrace{(A_1B_2; B_2P)}_{(\pi/2)} \\
&= (A_3P; PA_2) + (PA_1; A_1A_3) \\
&= (A_2A_3; A_2P) + (A_2P; A_2A_1) \quad \text{(concyclic)} \\
&= 0 \,(\mathrm{mod}\ \pi)\,.
\end{aligned}$$

Then C_1, C_2, H are collinear and in all cases $H \in \mathcal{L}$.

An acute-angled triangle ABC is inscribed in a circle with centre O.
Let D be the intersection of the bisector of A with BC and suppose that the perpendicular to AO through D meets the line AC in a point P interior to the segment AC. Show that $AB = AP$.

Solution

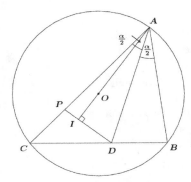

Since ABC is acute, O is interior to ABC, $P \in AC$, so O is interior to ADC. We have $\angle AOC = 2\beta$ and $OA = OC$, therefore $\angle CAO = \frac{1}{2}(\pi - 2\beta) = \frac{\pi}{2} - \beta$. Thus

$$\angle OAD = \frac{\alpha}{2} - \angle CAO = \frac{\alpha}{2} + \beta - \frac{\pi}{2}.$$

Let $I = PD \cap AO$. We have that $\triangle AID$ is right-angled at I.

Then

$$\angle PDA = \angle IDA = \frac{\pi}{2} - \angle OAD$$
$$= \pi - \frac{\alpha}{2} - \beta = \angle BDA.$$

We deduce that triangles ABD and APD are similar with AD in common. Therefore triangles ABD and APD are isometric, so that $AP = AB$.

Let P, P_1, P_2, P_3, P_4 be five points on a circle. Denote the distance of P from the line P_iP_k by d_{ik}. Prove that $d_{12}d_{34} = d_{13}d_{24}$.

Solution

Let D denote the diameter of the circle.

We have $d_{ik} \cdot P_iP_k = 2[PP_iP_k] = PP_i \cdot PP_k \cdot \sin \angle P_iPP_k$. Hence

$$d_{ik} = \frac{PP_i \cdot PP_k \cdot \sin \angle P_iPP_k}{P_iP_k} = \frac{PP_i \cdot PP_k}{D}.$$

It is now obvious that

$$d_{12}d_{34} = d_{13}d_{24} = (d_{14}d_{23}) = \frac{1}{D^2} \prod_{i=1}^{4} PP_i.$$

The squares of the sides of a triangle ABC are proportional to the numbers 1, 2, 3.

(a) Show that the angles formed by the medians of ABC are equal to the angles of ABC.

(b) Show that the triangle whose sides are the medians of ABC is similar to ABC.

Solution

(b) Let us say that $a^2 : b^2 : c^2 = 1 : 2 : 3$; that is, $a^2 = t$, $b^2 = 2t$, $c^2 = 3t$. Let m_a, m_b, m_c denote the medians passing through A, B, C respectively.

Then $4m_a^2 = 2b^2 + 2c^2 - a^2 = 9t$, $4m_b^2 = 2a^2 + 2c^2 - b^2 = 6t$, $4m_c^2 = 2a^2 + 2b^2 - c^2 = 3t$. Thus, $m_c^2 : m_b^2 : m_a^2 = 1 : 2 : 3 = a^2 : b^2 : c^2$. Hence $m_c : m_b : m_a = a : b : c$. This proves (b).

(a) Let A', B', C' be the mid-points of BC, AC, AB, and let G be the centroid of ABC. Extend GC' to H so that $GC' = C'H$.

Then $AG = \frac{2}{3}m_a$, $AH = BG = \frac{2}{3}m_b$, $GH = \frac{2}{3}m_c$. Hence, by what was proved in (b), $ABC \sim AGH$. Consequently, $\angle GAH = \angle BAC \equiv \alpha$, $\angle HGA = \angle CBA \equiv \beta$, $\angle AHG = \angle ACB \equiv \gamma$. We can now fill in our diagram as follows:

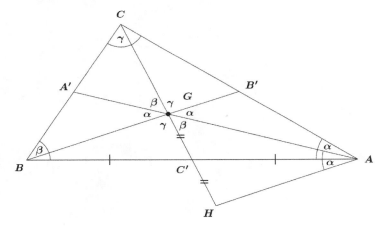

This proves (a).

Consider the parabolas $y = cx^2 + d$, $x = ay^2 + b$, with $c > 0$, $d < 0$, $a > 0$, $b < 0$. These parabolas have four common points. Show that these four points are concyclic.

Solution

Solution I. Let $M_k(x_k, y_k)$ ($k = 1, 2, 3, 4$) be the four common points. We suppose that they are distinct (otherwise there is nothing to prove). We have: $y_k = cx_k^2 + d$ and $x_k = ay_k^2 + b$. Multiplying the first equality by a and the second one by c, adding and rearranging, we obtain:

$$x_k^2 + y_k^2 - \frac{1}{a}x_k - \frac{1}{c}x_k + \frac{ad + bc}{ac} = 0 \qquad (k = 1, 2, 3, 4).$$

Now, the equation $x^2 + y^2 - \frac{1}{a}x - \frac{1}{c}y + \frac{ad+bc}{ac} = 0$ defines either $\emptyset$, or a singleton, or a circle. Since it is satisfied by (x_k, y_k) ($k = 1, 2, 3, 4$), it does define a circle and the points M_k are concyclic.

Solution II. We introduce the complex representation of the points $M_k : z_k = x_k + iy_k$. We have to show that the cross-ratio

$$\frac{z_4 - z_1}{z_3 - z_1} \bigg/ \frac{z_4 - z_2}{z_3 - z_2}$$

is a real number.

Since $y_1 = cx_1^2 + d$, $y_3 = cx_3^2 + d$, we obtain $z_3 - z_1 = (x_3 - x_1)(1 + ic(x_3 + x_1))$ and analogous results for $z_4 - z_1$, $z_4 - z_2$, $z_3 - z_2$.

It is easy to see that we actually have to show that the product

$$P = (1 + ic(x_1 + x_4))(1 + ic(x_2 + x_3))(1 - ic(x_1 + x_3))(1 - ic(x_2 + x_4))$$

is a real number.

But, by eliminating y between $y = cx^2 + d$ and $x = ay^2 + b$, we see that x_1, x_2, x_3, x_4 are the roots of $ac^2x^4 + 2acdx^2 - x + ad^2 + b$, so that $x_1 + x_2 + x_3 + x_4 = 0$. By multiplying out the first two factors and the last two factors of P, it follows that P is a real number, as required.

A line through the barycentre G of the triangle ABC intersects the side AB at P and the side AC at Q. Show that

$$\frac{PB}{PA} \cdot \frac{QC}{QA} \leq \frac{1}{4}.$$

Solution

Let $u = \frac{PB}{PA}$, $v = \frac{QC}{QA}$. We will show that $u + v = 1$. It will then follow that $uv = u(1 - u) = \frac{1}{4} - \left(\frac{1}{2} - u\right)^2 \leq \frac{1}{4}$.

That $u + v = 1$ is a special case of the theorem below.

Theorem. Suppose ABC is any triangle and P, Q, R are arbitrary points on the sides AB, AC, BC. Let G be the intersection of PQ and AR. Let $BR : RC = \lambda_1 : \lambda_2$, where $\lambda_1 + \lambda_2 = 1$. Then

$$\frac{GR}{GA} = \lambda_2 \frac{PB}{PA} + \lambda_1 \frac{QC}{QA}.$$

Proof. Draw lines through B and C that are parallel to AR, and extend PQ to meet these lines at M and N, as in the diagram.

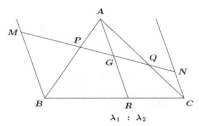

$$\lambda_1 : \lambda_2$$

Then $GR = \lambda_2 MB + \lambda_1 NC$, so that $\frac{GR}{GA} = \lambda_2 \frac{MB}{GA} + \lambda_1 \frac{NC}{GA}$. Therefore, $\frac{GR}{GA} = \lambda_2 \frac{PB}{PA} + \lambda_1 \frac{QC}{QA}$.   Q.E.D.

When G is the barycentre (centroid), we have $\frac{GR}{GA} = \frac{1}{2}$ and $\lambda_1 = \lambda_2 = \frac{1}{2}$. Consequently, $1 = \frac{PB}{PA} + \frac{QC}{QA}$, as asserted at the outset.

AB is a fixed segment and C a variable point, internal to AB. Equilateral triangles ACB' and CBA' are constructed, in the same half-plane defined by AB, and another equilateral triangle ABC' is constructed in the opposite half-plane. Show that:

(a) the lines AA', BB' and CC' are concurrent;

(b) if P is the common point of the lines of (a), find the locus of P when C varies on AB;

(c) the centres A'', B'', C'' of the three equilateral triangles also form an equilateral triangle;

(d) the points A'', B'', C'' and P are concyclic.

Solution

(a) The rotation with centre C and angle $60°$ transforms B' into A and B into A'. Hence the lines AA' and BB' make an angle of $60°$ and, if we denote by P their point of intersection, we have: $\angle APB = 120°$, from which we deduce that the points A, P, B, C' are concyclic (with P and C' in different half-planes defined by AB). Therefore, $\angle C'PB = \angle C'AB = 60°$ and the line $C'P$ makes an angle of $60°$ with the line BB'.

Now, by the same reasoning as at the beginning, the line CC' also makes an angle of $60°$ with the line BB'. Thus, the lines CC' and $C'P$ coincide and AA', BB' and CC' are concurrent at P.

(b) From (a) P belongs to the arc AB subtending $120°$ on the segment AB. Conversely, if M is any point of this arc, let us first construct C' such that $\triangle ABC'$ is equilateral, and M and C' are not in the same half-plane defined by AB, and then C is the point of intersection of MC' and AB. The points A' and B' being obtained, the lines AA' and BB' intersect at the point P of CC' such that $\angle APB = 120°$; that is at M. Thus, $M = P$ and M is a point of the locus.

In conclusion, we find that the locus is the arc AB subtending $120°$ on the segment AB.

(c) The circles $(AB'C)$ and $(A'BC)$ intersect at P and C and have respective centres B'' and A''. Thus, $A''B'' \perp PC$. Similarly, $A''C'' \perp PB$. The lines $A''B''$ and $A''C''$ make the same angle as PC and PB; that is $60°$. We have the same result for lines $A''B''$ and $B''C''$ and for lines $B''C''$ and $A''C''$ so that $\triangle A''B''C''$ is equilateral.

(d) $\triangle A''PC$ is isosceles at A'', so that

$$\angle A''PC = \angle PCA'' = \left(\frac{1}{2}\right)(180° - \angle PA''C) = 90° - \angle CBP$$
$$= 90° - (120° - \angle BCP) = \angle BCP - 30°.$$

Similarly, $\angle B''PC = \angle ACP - 30°$. Hence

$$\angle B''PA'' = \angle B''PC + \angle A''PC = \angle BCP + \angle ACP - 60°$$
$$= 180° - 60° = 120°$$

and P is on the circle $(A''B''C'')$.

Every diagonal of a given pentagon is parallel to one side of the pentagon. Prove that the ratio of the lengths of a diagonal and its corresponding side is the same for each of the five pairs. Determine the value of this ratio.

Solution

In the pentagon $ABCDE$, we assume that $AB\|CE$, $BC\|AD$, $CD\|BE$, $DE\|CA$, and $EA\|DB$. As shown in figure 1 on the next page, we label the intersections of diagonals.

Since $ATDE$ and $SCDE$ are both parallelograms we get:

$AT = ED = SC$, so that $AS + ST = ST + TC$. Thus we have $AS = TC$. Hence $CE : AB = CS : SA = AT : TC = AD : BC$.

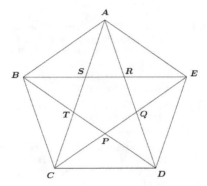

Figure 1.

Similarly we have

$$AD : BC = BE : CD = CA : DE = DB : EA .$$

We put

$$\frac{CE}{AB} = \frac{AD}{BC} = \frac{BE}{CD} = \frac{CA}{DE} = \frac{DB}{EA} = k .$$

Thus we have

$$\frac{CS}{SA} = \frac{CE}{AB} = k , \qquad \frac{DT}{BT} = \frac{AD}{BC} = k ,$$

and $\dfrac{DR}{RA} = \dfrac{BD}{AE} = k$, so that $\dfrac{DB}{BT} = \dfrac{k+1}{1}$ and $\dfrac{TS}{SA} = \dfrac{k-1}{1}$.

By Menelaus' Theorem for $\triangle ATD$ we get

$$\frac{DB}{BT} \cdot \frac{TS}{SA} \cdot \frac{AR}{RD} = 1 .$$

Therefore we have $\frac{k+1}{1} \cdot \frac{k-1}{1} \cdot \frac{1}{k} = 1$. Thus $k^2 - k - 1 = 0$, from which we obtain $k = \frac{1+\sqrt{5}}{2}$.

Is it possible to cover a square of length 5 completely with three squares of length 4?

Solution

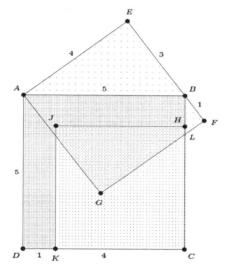

This is a diagram showing the 5×5 square, $ABCD$, covered by two of the three available 4×4 squares. One 4×4 square shown is $JHCK$, and the other one is $AEFG$. The third 4×4 square is not shown, but occupies a similar position to square $AEFG$, except that it is reflected over a line joining AC. The reason that this square is not shown will be explained shortly.

The square $JHCK$ covers a 4×4 area of the square $ABCD$, and so leaves an L-shaped area (the polygon $ABHJKD$) left to be covered by the other two squares. To cover this L-shaped area with two squares, each square must cover, at the very least, half of this L-shaped area.

The square $AEFG$ does cover over half of the area. This can be proven as follows: Using Pythagoras' Theorem, the line EB can be calculated because it forms the triangle AEB and $AB = 5$, and $AE = 4$. Therefore, since $AB^2 = EB^2 + AE^2$, $EB^2 = 5^2 - 4^2$, or 9, so $EB = 3$.

On the left side of the diagram, $\angle BAG$ must be greater than $\angle BAC$. Since BAC is the diagonal of a square, $\angle BAC = 45°$. To find $\angle BAG$, we must first find $\angle EAB$ (since $\angle EAB$ and $\angle BAG$ are complementary). The sine of $\angle EAB$ is $\frac{3}{5}$, so when the inverse sine is taken for $\angle EAB$, the angle is $36.870°$. Subtract this angle from $90°$, and we get $(90° - 36.870°)$ or $53.130°$. Thus, $\angle BAG$ is approximately $53°$, and $53° > 45°$. Thus $\angle BAG$ is greater than $\angle BAC$.

On the right side of the diagram, point L must extend past point H on the line BC, or BL must be greater than BH (and BH is 1 unit long). Since BL is the hypotenuse of $\triangle BFL$, and BF is 1, then BL must be greater than 1. Thus BL is greater than BH.

When the third unit four square is placed as the reflection of $AEFG$ over the line AC, then this square will cover a similar area to $AEFG$. Both squares together will completely cover the aforementioned L-shaped area, and together with square $JHCK$, the unit five square is completely covered with three unit four squares.

There are four straight lines in the plane, each three of them determining a triangle. One of these straight lines is parallel to one of the medians of the triangle formed by the other three lines. Prove that each of the other straight lines has the same property.

Solution 1

Let the four lines be a, b, c, d, and let $\triangle ABC$ be determined by a, b, and c as shown in the figure. The line d intersects BC, CA, AB at P, Q, R respectively.

We assume that the median AM of $\triangle ABC$ is parallel to d. Let X be a point on AC such that $PX \parallel AB$. Since $PX \parallel AB$ and $AM \parallel PQ$, we have

$$\frac{AC}{CX} = \frac{BC}{CP} = \frac{2MC}{CP} = 2 \cdot \frac{AC}{CQ}.$$

Thus $CQ = 2CX$; that is, $CX = XQ$.

Hence median PX of $\triangle PCQ$ is parallel to c. Let Y be a point on AB

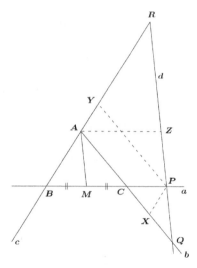

Thus $BR = 2BY$; that is, $BY = YR$.

Hence median PY of $\triangle PBR$ is parallel to b. Let Z be a point on QR such that $AZ \parallel BP$. Since $AZ \parallel BP$ and $AM \parallel PQ$ we have

$$\frac{ZP}{ZQ} = \frac{AC}{AQ} = \frac{MC}{MP} = \frac{BM}{MP} = \frac{BA}{AR} = \frac{ZP}{ZR}.$$

Thus $ZQ = ZR$.

Hence median AZ of $\triangle AQR$ is parallel to a.

We denote the four straight lines by L_1, L_2, L_3, L_4, and we suppose that the names are chosen so that L_4 is parallel to one of the medians of the triangle formed by L_1, L_2, L_3. More precisely, let L_2, L_3 intersect at A, L_3, L_1 intersect at B, L_1, L_2 intersect at C and let us suppose $L_4 \| AM$ where M is the mid-point of BC. We shall work in the system of axes with origin A, and AB, AC as x–axis and y–axis respectively. Thus we have

$$A(0,0); \quad B(1,0); \quad C(0,1); \quad M\left(\frac{1}{2}, \frac{1}{2}\right)$$

and AM has equation $y = x$.

We readily find:

$$L_1 : x + y = 1; \quad L_2 : x = 0; \quad L_3 : y = 0, \quad \text{and } L_4 : x - y = k,$$

where $k \neq 0$, 1, -1 [this condition on k ensures that L_4 determines a real triangle with any two of the three lines L_1, L_2, L_3].

It is now easy to compute the coordinates of the points A', B', C' where L_4 intersects L_1, L_2, L_3 respectively:

$$A'\left(\frac{1+k}{2}, \frac{1-k}{2}\right); \quad B'(0, -k); \quad C'(k, 0).$$

The mid-point I of BC' has coordinates $(\frac{1+k}{2}, 0)$ so that $\overrightarrow{A'I} = (0, \frac{k-1}{2})$. Hence the median $A'I$ (of the triangle formed by L_1, L_3, L_4) is parallel to L_2.

Similarly, the mid-point J of CB' has coordinates $(0, \frac{1-k}{2})$ and $\overrightarrow{A'J} = (-\frac{1+k}{2}, 0)$ is parallel to L_3.

Lastly, the mid-point K of $B'C'$ has coordinates $(\frac{k}{2}, -\frac{k}{2})$ and $\overrightarrow{AK} = (\frac{k}{2}, -\frac{k}{2})$ is parallel to L_1.

How many sides has the polygon inscribed in a given circle and such that the sum of the squares of its sides is the largest one?

We will prove that the "maximal" polygon is the equilateral triangle.

Lemma. Let $\mathcal{P} = A_1 A_2 \ldots A_n$ be a convex polygon with $n \geq 5$ sides. Then $\mathcal{P}$ has an obtuse angle.

Proof of the lemma. We have $\sum_{i=1}^{n} \widehat{A_i} = (n-2)\pi$. Suppose, on the contrary, that each $\widehat{A_i} \leq \frac{\pi}{2}$. Then, $\sum_{i}^{n} A_i \leq \frac{n\pi}{2}$. Thus $(n-2)\pi \leq \frac{n\pi}{2}$. Then $n \leq 4$, which is a contradiction.

Let $\mathcal{P}$ be a convex polygon with $n \geq 4$ sides and with an obtuse angle. Let $\widehat{B} > \frac{\pi}{2}$ and A, C be the neighbouring vertices of B. Then, from the Law of Cosines:

$$AC^2 = AB^2 + BC^2 - 2AB \cdot BC \cos \widehat{B} > AB^2 + BC^2 .$$

Thus, $\mathcal{P}$ is not maximal, because we have a larger sum by deleting B. Then, using the above lemma: if a "maximal" polygon exists, it has $n \leq 4$ sides, and no obtuse angle.

Let $\mathcal{P}_n$ be a convex polygon with $n \leq 4$ sides, no obtuse angle, inscribed in the circle $\mathcal{C}$ with centre O and radius R.

Let $n = 4$. The proof of the lemma may be used to prove that all angles of $\mathcal{P}_n$ are $\frac{\pi}{2}$ (because they are $\leq \frac{\pi}{2}$). Then $\mathcal{P}_4$ is a rectangle.

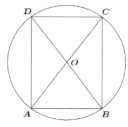

Pythagoras' Theorem leads to:

$$AB^2 + BC^2 = 4R^2 = CD^2 + DA^2 .$$

Thus the sum of the squares of the sides is $S_4 = 8R^2$. Note that S_4 is independent of the rectangle.

Let $n = 3$. Suppose that $\triangle ABC$ is a non-obtuse triangle inscribed in $\mathcal{C}$. Let G be the centre of gravity of $\triangle ABC$. For any point M, we have

$$AM^2 + BM^2 + CM^2 = AG^2 + BG^2 + CG^2 + 3GM^2 . \tag{1}$$

Then

$$AG^2 + BG^2 + CG^2 + 3GO^2 = 3R^2. \qquad (2)$$

Moreover, for $M = A$, we have $AB^2 + AC^2 = 4AG^2 + BG^2 + CG^2$. We also have the same relation for $M = B$, $M = C$.

Then, summing these three relations, we obtain

$$2(AB^2 + BC^2 + CA^2) = 6(AG^2 + BG^2 + CG^2)$$

and, using (2) we get

$$AB^2 + BC^2 + CA^2 = 9(R^2 - OG^2).$$

We deduce that the sum of the squares is $S_2 \leq 9R^2$ with equality if and only if $O = G$; that is, $\triangle ABC$ is equilateral.

Then, the "maximal" polygon exists; it is the equilateral triangle and the sum is $S = 9R^2$.

Vietnamese Mathematical Olympiad, 1996 (Category A)

Let $Sxyz$ be a trihedron (a figure determined by the intersection of three planes). A plane (P), not passing through S, cuts the rays Sx, Sy, Sz, respectively at A, B, C. In the plane (P), construct three triangles DAB, EBC, FCA such that each has no interior point of triangle ABC and $\triangle DAB = \triangle SAB$, $\triangle EBC = \triangle SBC$, $\triangle FCA = \triangle SCA$. Consider the sphere (T) satisfying simultaneously two conditions:

(i) (T) touches the planes (SAB), (SBC), (SCA), (ABC);

(ii) (T) is inside the trihedron $Sxyz$ and is outside the tetrahedron $SABC$.

Prove that the circumcentre of triangle DEF is the point where (T) touches (P).

Solution

Let Ω be the centre of (T) and O, O' be the points where (T) touches the planes (ABC) and (SBC), respectively. Since $\Omega O \perp (ABC)$ and $\Omega O' \perp (SBC)$, BC is orthogonal to ΩO and $\Omega O'$ so that BC is orthogonal to the plane $(\Omega O O')$. Hence, the (orthogonal) projection ω of Ω onto BC is the projection of O and of O' onto BC as well. Therefore,

$$O\omega \perp BC, \qquad O'\omega \perp BC. \tag{1}$$

Moreover, since $\Omega O = \Omega O'$ (equal to the radius R of (T)), we also have

$$O\omega = O'\omega, \tag{2}$$

by Pythagoras' Theorem. From (1) and (2), we easily deduce that the rotation with axis BC which transforms S into E, also transforms O' into O. Thus, $SO' = OE$.

Similarly, if (T) touches (SAB) at O'' and (SCA) at O''', we have $SO'' = OD$ and $SO''' = OF$. Since $SO' = SO'' = SO''' (= \sqrt{S\Omega^2 - R^2})$, we obtain $OE = OD = OF$, so that O is actually the circumcentre of $\triangle DEF$.

Let $ABCD$ be a tetrahedron with $AB = AC = AD$, inscribed in a sphere with centre O. Let G be the centre of gravity of triangle ACD, E be the mid-point of BG and F be the mid-point of AE. Prove that OF is perpendicular to BG if and only if OD is perpendicular to AC.

Solution

[The vector from the origin to the point X is denoted by X.] We have

$$(\mathbf{O} - \mathbf{F}) \cdot (\mathbf{B} - \mathbf{G})$$
$$= \frac{1}{2}(\mathbf{A} + \mathbf{E}) \cdot (\mathbf{B} - \mathbf{G}) = \frac{1}{4}((2\mathbf{A} + \mathbf{B} + \mathbf{G}) \cdot (\mathbf{B} - \mathbf{G}))$$
$$= \frac{1}{36}\left(18\mathbf{A} \cdot \mathbf{B} - 6\mathbf{A} \cdot (\mathbf{A} + \mathbf{C} + \mathbf{D}) + 9\mathbf{B}^2 - (\mathbf{A} + \mathbf{C} + \mathbf{D})^2\right)$$
$$= \frac{1}{36}\left(2\mathbf{A} \cdot \mathbf{D} - 2\mathbf{C} \cdot \mathbf{D}\right) .$$

Hence, $OF \perp BG$ if and only if $OD \perp AC$.

$P_1, P_2, \ldots, P_{11}$ are eleven distinct points on a line, $P_iP_j \leq 1$ for every pair P_i, P_j. Prove that the sum of all (55) distances P_iP_j, $1 \leq i, j \leq 11$ is smaller than 30.

Solution

More generally, consider n distinct adjacent points $P_1, P_2, \ldots, P_n$ on a line ($n \geq 2$) such that $P_iP_j \leq 1$ for every pair P_i, P_j. We shall prove by induction on m that if $n = 2m + 1 > 3$, then $\sum_{1 \leq i < j \leq n} P_iP_j < m(m+1)$.

First, note that, if $n = 3$, then $P_1P_2 + P_2P_3 + P_1P_3 = 2P_1P_3 \leq 2$, with equality if and only if $P_1P_3 = 1$. Now, if $n = 5$, then $\sum_{1 < i < j < 5} P_iP_j < 2$ (since $P_2P_43 < P_1P_5 \leq 1$). Therefore,

$$\sum_{1 \leq i < j \leq 5} P_iP_j = \sum_{1 < i < j < 5} P_iP_j + P_1P_5 + \sum_{1 < k < 5} (P_1P_k + P_kP_5)$$

$$= \sum_{1 < i < j < 5} P_iP_j + P_1P_5 + \sum_{1 < k < 5} P_1P_5$$

$$= \sum_{1 < i < j < 5} P_iP_j + 4P_1P_5 < 2 + 4 = 6.$$

Suppose that the result is true for some $n = 2m + 1 > 3$. We show that it is also true for $n + 2$. Indeed, by the inductive hypothesis, we have $\sum_{1 < i < j < n+1} P_iP_j < m(m+1)$. Hence,

$$\sum_{1 \leq i < j \leq n+2} P_iP_j = \sum_{1 < i < j < n+2} P_iP_j + P_1P_{n+2} + \sum_{1 < k < n+2} (P_1P_k + P_kP_{n+2})$$

$$= \sum_{1 < i < j < n+2} P_iP_j + P_1P_{n+2} + \sum_{1 < k < n+2} P_1P_{n+2}$$

$$= \sum_{1 < i < j < n+2} P_iP_j + (n+1)P_1P_{n+2}$$

$$< m(m+1) + (n+1) = (m+2)(m+1).$$

The proof is complete.

Two circles intersect at the points A and B. A line is drawn through the point A. This line crosses the first circle again at the point C and it crosses the second circle again at the point D. Let M and N be the mid-points of the arcs BC and BD respectively (these arcs do not contain A). Let K be the mid-point of the segment CD. Prove that the angle MKN is a right angle. (It may be assumed that A lies between C and D).

Solution

From $\angle CMB = 180° - \angle CAB = \angle BAD = 180° - \angle BND$, we get $\angle CMB + \angle BND = 180°$. Thus, the composition $R_N \circ R_M$ of the rotations R_M (centre M, transforming C into B) and R_N (centre N, transforming B into D) is a symmetry about a point. But, since $MC = MB$ and $NB = ND$, we have $R_N \circ R_M(C) = D$ so that $R_N \circ R_M$ is the symmetry about K.

Now, let $M' = R_N \circ R_M(M) = R_N(M)$. The triangle MNM' is isosceles ($NM = NM'$) and K is the mid-point of MM'. It follows that $NK \perp MM'$ and $\angle MKN = 90°$.

Next we give Seimiya's solution.

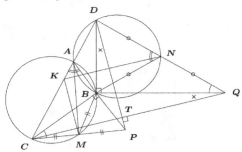

Let P be a point on CM produced beyond M such that $CM = MP$, and let Q be a point on DN produced beyond N such that $DN = NQ$.

Since M is the mid-point of arc BC, we get $BM = CM$, so that $BM = CM = MP$. Hence, $\angle CBP = 90°$.

Similarly, we get $BN = DN = NQ$ and $\angle DBQ = 90°$. Thus, we have

$$\angle BQD = \tfrac{1}{2}\angle BND = \tfrac{1}{2}\angle BAC = \angle BAM = \angle BCM = \angle BCP.$$

Since $\angle CBP = 90° = \angle DBQ$, we have $\triangle BCP \sim \triangle BQD$.

Since $\triangle BCP$ and $\triangle BQD$ are directly similar, we get $\triangle BCQ \sim \triangle BPD$, so that $\angle BQC = \angle BDP$. Let T be the intersection of CQ and DP. Since $\angle BQC = \angle BDP$, we get $\angle BQT = \angle BDT$, so that $\angle DTQ = \angle DBQ = 90°$; that is, $DP \perp CQ$. Since K, M and N are mid-points of CD, CP and DQ, respectively, we have

$$KM \parallel DP \quad \text{and} \quad KN \parallel CQ.$$

Because $DP \perp CQ$, we get $KM \perp KN$. Therefore, $\angle MKN = 90°$.

Given a square $ABCD$ of side length 2, let M and N be points on the edges $[AB]$ and $[CD]$, respectively. The lines CM and BN meet at P, while the lines AN and MD meet at Q. Show that $|PQ| \geq 1$.

Solution

More generally we replace the square by a rectangle with $AB = 2\ell$ and $CB = 2w$, and show that $|PQ| \geq \ell$.

Let the rectangular coordinates be $A(-\ell, w)$, $M(a, w)$, $B(\ell, w)$, $C(\ell, -w)$, $N(b, -w)$, and $D(-\ell, -w)$. The equations of lines AN and MD are

$$\frac{y - w}{2w} = -\frac{-(x + \ell)}{\ell + b} \quad \text{and} \quad \frac{y - w}{2w} = \frac{x - a}{a + \ell}.$$

Solving them gives point Q:

$$x_Q = \frac{ab - \ell^2}{a + b + 2\ell}, \quad y_Q = \frac{w(b - a)}{a + b + 2\ell}.$$

The equations of lines BN and MC are

$$\frac{y - w}{2w} = \frac{x - \ell}{\ell - b} \quad \text{and} \quad \frac{y - w}{2w} = \frac{x - a}{a - \ell},$$

and their point of intersection P is given by

$$x_P = \frac{ab - \ell^2}{a + b - 2\ell}, \quad y_P = \frac{w(b - a)}{a + b - 2\ell}.$$

We now need to show that $|PQ|^2 \geq \ell^2$ or

$$16[(ab - \ell^2)^2 + w^2(b - a)^2] \geq [4\ell^2 - (a + b)^2]^2.$$

Since $-\ell \leq a, b \leq \ell$, it suffices to have

$$4(\ell^2 - ab) \geq 4\ell^2 - (a + b)^2$$

or $(a - b)^2 \geq 0$. There is equality if and only if $a = b$.

Given a quadrangle $ABCD$, the circle which is tangential to $[AD]$, $[DC]$ and $[CB]$ touches these edges at K, L and M, respectively. Denote the point at which the line which passes through L and is parallel to AD meets $[KM]$ by N, and the point at which $[LN]$ and $[KC]$ meet by P. Prove that

$$|PL| = |PN|.$$

Solution

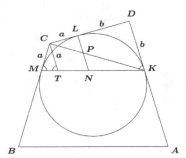

Since CM, CL, DL and DK are tangent to the circle, we have $CM = CL$ and $DL = DK$. We put $CM = CL = a$ and $DL = D = b$.

Let T be the point on MK such that $CT \parallel DK$. Then $\angle CTM = \angle DKM = \angle CMK = \angle CMT$. Thus, $CT = CM = a$. Since $LP \parallel DK$, we get $\dfrac{LP}{DK} = \dfrac{CL}{CD}$; that is, $\dfrac{LP}{b} = \dfrac{a}{a+b}$. Thus,

$$LP = \frac{ab}{a+b}. \tag{1}$$

Since $CT \parallel LN \parallel DK$, it follows that

$$\frac{PN}{CT} = \frac{KP}{KC} = \frac{DL}{DC} = \frac{b}{a+b}.$$

Since $CT = a$, we obtain

$$PN = \frac{ab}{a+b}. \tag{2}$$

From (1) and (2), we obtain $LP = PN$.

Let P be a parallelepiped, let V be its volume, S its surface area, and L the sum of the lengths of the edges of P. For $t \geq 0$ let P_t be the solid consisting of points having distance from P not greater than t. Prove that the volume of P_t is equal to

$$V + St + \frac{\pi}{4}Lt^2 + \frac{4}{3}\pi t^3 .$$

Solution

It is a known result [1] that the volume $V(P_t)$ of a parallel body of a convex polyhedron P at a distance t from P is the sum of

(a) $V(P)$,

(b) the volumes of right prisms of height t whose bases are the faces of P, altogether a volume St, where S is the total surface area of P,

(c) the volumes of the cylindrical segments whose heights are the lengths e_i of the edges and whose bases are circular sectors of radius t and centre angles α_i equal to the angles between the normals to the faces intersecting in e_i, and

(d) the volumes of the spherical sectors at the vertices of P, which altogether equal the volume of one spherical ball of radius t.

Thus,

$$V(P_t) = V(P) + St + \left(\sum \frac{e_i \alpha_i}{2}\right) t^2 + \frac{4\pi t^3}{3} .$$

For the special case where P is a rectangular parallelepiped, $\alpha_i = \frac{\pi}{2}$, and the given result follows. The result for general parallelepipeds is not valid.

Is there a planar polygon whose vertices have integer coordinates, whose area is $\frac{1}{2}$, such that this polygon is

(a) a triangle with at least two sides longer than 1000?

(b) a triangle whose sides are all longer than 1000?

(c) a quadrangle?

Solution

(a) Yes. Just consider the one with vertices $(0, 0)$, $(1, 0)$, and $(1001, 1)$.

(b) Yes. Consider a triangle with integer coordinates $(0, 0)$, (a, b), and (c, d) where the three sides are > 1000. The area is given by $|ad - bc|/2$. Thus, we need $ad - bc = \pm 1$. For instance, let $(a, b) = (1000, 999)$ and $(c, d) = (10001, 9991)$. We can even make all the sides arbitrarily large. We first would choose a and b to be arbitrarily large and relatively prime. Then we can find arbitrarily large c and d satisfying $|ad - bc| = 1$. For example, for the choice of (a, b) above, $(c, d) = (1000m + 1, 999m + 1)$ for large m.

(c) No. By Pick's Theorem, the area of such a quadrangle is $I + \frac{B}{2} - 1$ where I is the number of interior lattice points and B is the number of boundary lattice points. Since B is at least 4, the area of any quadrangle is at least 1

Prove that if two altitudes of a tetrahedron intersect, then so do the other two altitudes.

Solution

Suppose that the altitudes AH and BK of tetrahedron $ABCD$ concur, say at U (with H and K in the planes (BCD) and (ACD), respectively). Since CD is orthogonal to AH and BK, CD is orthogonal to the plane (ABU), and hence to AB.

Conversely, suppose $AB \perp CD$ and let B' be the foot of the altitude from B in $\triangle BCD$. Then CD is orthogonal to the plane (ABB'), hence to AB', so that B' is also the foot of the altitude from A in $\triangle ACD$. Thus, AH and BK are both contained in the plane (ABB') and, as such, are concurrent (obviously they cannot be parallel).

It follows that the concurrency of AH and BK is *equivalent* to the condition $AB \perp CD$, and therefore also to the concurrency of the altitudes issued from C and D. This completes the proof.

Comment. With the hypotheses above, UB' is the third altitude in $\triangle ABB'$ (the first two being AH and BK) so that $UB' \perp AB$ and $UB' \perp CD$. Reasoning similarly with the intersection V of the altitudes from C and D, we may conclude that, when $V \neq U$, the line UV is the common perpendicular to the orthogonal lines AB and CD.

In a triangle ABC the values of $\tan \angle A$, $\tan \angle B$ and $\tan \angle C$ relate to each other as $1 : 2 : 3$. Find the ratio of the lengths of the sides AC and AB.

Solution

From $\tan B = 2 \tan A$, $\tan C = 3 \tan A$ and the well-known relation $\tan A + \tan B + \tan C = \tan A \tan B \tan C$, we obtain $6 \tan A = 6(\tan A)^3$.

Certainly $\tan A \neq 0$; hence, $\tan A = 1$ or $\tan A = -1$. But the latter cannot hold since otherwise all the angles of $\triangle ABC$ would be obtuse. Thus, $\tan A = 1$ and $A = 45°$.

Now, let H be the foot of the altitude from C. We have

$$\frac{CH}{AH} = \tan A = 1, \quad \frac{CH}{BH} = \tan B = 2,$$

and $H \in [AB]$ (since A, B are acute). It follows that

$$AB = AH + HB = \frac{3}{2}CH.$$

Since we clearly have $AC = CH\sqrt{2}$, we finally get $\dfrac{AC}{AB} = \dfrac{2\sqrt{2}}{3}$.

There are n points ($n \geq 3$) in the plane, no three of which are collinear. Is it always possible to draw a circle through three of these points so that it has no other given points

(a) in its interior?   (b) in its interior nor on the circle?

Solution

(a) Yes. Let E be a set of $n \geq 3$ points in the plane, no three of which are collinear. Let P, Q be two adjacent vertices of the convex hull of E. We then have P, Q in E. For each point $M \in E - \{P, Q\}$, let Γ_M denote the circle through M, P, Q; and let M' denote the intersection of Γ_M and the perpendicular bisector of $[PQ]$ which is on the same side of (PQ) as M.

Since three points in E are never collinear, and from the choice of P and Q, all the points in $E - \{P, Q\}$ are on the same side of (PQ). Since E is finite, we may consider a point $A \in E$ such that the distance from A' to (PQ) is minimal.

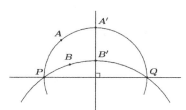

Suppose that $B \in E$ is interior to Γ_A. Then the arc of Γ_B whose endpoints are P and Q, and which contains B (and B'), is in the interior of Γ_A (P and Q excepted). Thus,

$$ 0 < d(B', (PQ)) < d(A', (PQ)), $$

which contradicts the minimality of A'. Then Γ_A has no other point of E in its interior, and we are done.

(b) For $n = 3$, the answer is obviously yes. For $n \geq 4$, the answer is no. It suffices to choose the n points on a given circle.

Let ABC be an equilateral triangle. For a point M inside ABC, let D, E, F be the feet of the perpendiculars from M onto BC, CA, AB, respectively. Find the locus of all such points M for which $\angle FDE$ is a right angle.

Solution

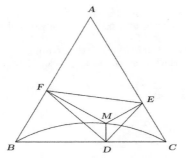

For all interior points M whose projections onto BC, CA, AB are D, E, F, respectively, points B, D, M, F are concyclic (they lie on the circle with diameter BM). Similarly, M, D, C, E are concyclic. It follows that $\angle FBM = \angle FDM$ and $\angle ECM = \angle EDM$. Therefore,

$$\angle FDE = \angle FBM + \angle ECM.$$

Thus,

$$\angle FDE = 90° \iff \angle FBM + \angle ECM = 90°$$
$$\iff \angle MBD + \angle MCD = 30°$$
$$\text{(since } \angle B = \angle C = 60°)$$
$$\iff \angle BMC = 150°.$$

We may now conclude that the locus of M is the arc of the circle interior to $\triangle ABC$ subtending $150°$ on the line segment BC (as shown in the figure).

$ABCD$ is a quadrilateral which is circumscribed about a circle Γ (that is, each side of the quadrilateral is tangent to Γ). If $\angle A = \angle B = 120°$, $\angle D = 90°$ and BC has length 1, find, with proof, the length of AD.

Solution

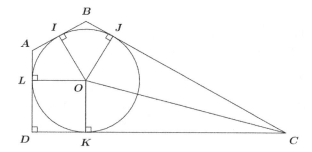

Let O be the centre of Γ, and let I, J, K, and L be the points at which AB, BC, CD, and DA touch Γ, respectively. Triangle IBJ is isosceles with $\angle B = 120°$. Therefore, $\angle BIJ = \angle BJI = 30°$; whence, $\angle OIJ = 60°$. It follows that $\triangle IOJ$ is equilateral and, consequently, $IJ = OI = OJ = R$, the radius of Γ. Since $\frac{\sqrt{3}}{2} = \cos 30° = \frac{IJ/2}{BJ}$, we get $BJ = \frac{R}{\sqrt{3}}$.

Now, observing that $OKDL$ is a square and that $\triangle IOJ$ and $\triangle IOL$ are equilateral triangles, we obtain $\angle KOJ = 150°$. Then $\angle OCJ = 15°$; whence, $2 - \sqrt{3} = \tan 15° = \frac{OJ}{CJ}$. This implies that $CJ = R(2 + \sqrt{3})$. The relation $1 = BC = BJ + CJ$ now yields $R = \frac{\sqrt{3}}{4 + 2\sqrt{3}}$. Using $DL = R$ and $AL = BJ = \frac{R}{\sqrt{3}}$, we can compute $AD = AL + DL = \frac{R}{\sqrt{3}} + R$, which readily gives $AD = \frac{\sqrt{3} - 1}{2}$.

ABC is an acute-angled triangle whose circumcentre is O. The intersection points of the diameters of the circumcircle, passing through A, B, C, with the opposite sides are A_1, B_1, C_1, respectively. The circumradius of the triangle ABC is of length $2p$, where p is a prime. The lengths OA_1, OB_1, OC_1 are integers. What are the lengths of the sides of the triangle?

Solution

The circumcentre O lies in the interior of ABC, and $OA = OB = OC = 2p$. Let $OA_1 = r$, $OB_1 = s$, $OC_1 = t$. Thus, r, s, t are positive integers.

Assertion I. $r = s = t = p$.

Proof. We have
$$\frac{OA_1}{AA_1} + \frac{OB_1}{BB_1} + \frac{OC_1}{CC_1} = \frac{[OBC]}{[ABC]} + \frac{[OAC]}{[ABC]} + \frac{[OAB]}{[ABC]} = \frac{[ABC]}{[ABC]};$$
that is,
$$\frac{r}{r+2p} + \frac{s}{s+2p} + \frac{t}{t+2p} = 1.$$
This is equivalent to
$$r(s+2p)(t+2p) + s(r+2p)(t+2p) + t(r+2p)(s+2p)$$
$$= (r+2p)(s+2p)(t+2p). \quad (1)$$

It follows that $2rst \equiv 0 \pmod{2p}$; hence, $p \mid rst$. Witout loss of generality, suppose $p \mid r$. Since $0 < r < 2p$, we have $r = p$. Replacing r by p in (1), we obtain
$$3s(t+2p) + 3t(s+2p) = 2(s+2p)(t+2p), \quad (2)$$

which implies $4st \equiv 0 \pmod{2p}$; that is, $p \mid 2st$. Thus, either $p = 2$ or $p \mid st$.

(i) Suppose $p = 2$. Equation (2) reduces to $st + s + t = 8$; that is, $(s+1)(t+1) = 9$. Therefore, $s = t = 2$. Also $r = p = 2$.

(ii) Suppose $p \mid st$. Without loss of generality, $p \mid s$. Since $0 < s < 2p$, we have $s = p$. It then follows easily from equation (2) that $t = p$.

Assertion I has now been proved.

Assertion II. $AB = AC = BC = 2p\sqrt{3}$.

Proof. We have three pairs of congruent triangles: $\triangle OAB_1 \cong \triangle OBA_1$, $\triangle OBC_1 \cong \triangle OCB_1$, $\triangle OCA_1 \cong \triangle OAC_1$. Let
$$X = [OAB_1] = [OBA_1],$$
$$Y = [OBC_1] = [OCB_1],$$
$$Z = [OAC_1] = [OCA_1].$$

Since $AO : OA_1 = 2 : 1$, we have $Y + Z = 2X$ and $X + Y = 2Z$, from which it follows easily that $X = Z$. Consequently, $BA_1 = CA_1$; hence, $OA_1 \perp BC$ and $BA_1 = CA_1 = p\sqrt{3}$. Therefore, $BC = 2p\sqrt{3}$. Similarly, $AB = AC = 2p\sqrt{3}$.

The three squares ACC_1A'', ABB_1A', $BCDE$ are constructed on the sides of a given triangle ABC, outwards. The center of the square $BCDE$ is P. Prove that the three lines $A'C$, $A''B$ and PA pass through one point.

Solution

We may assume $\angle A(= \angle BAC) < 90°$. Say $A'C$ meets AB at R, AP meets BC at S, and $A''B$ meets AC at T. Draw $A'B$, $A''C$, BP, and CP.

$$\frac{AR}{RB} = \frac{[A'AC]}{[A'BC]} = \frac{A'A \cdot AC \cdot \sin(A + 90°)}{A'B \cdot BC \cdot \sin(B + 45°)}$$

$$= \frac{1}{\sqrt{2}} \cdot \frac{AC}{BC} \cdot \frac{\sin(A + 90°)}{\sin(B + 45°)},$$

$$\frac{BS}{SC} = \frac{[ABP]}{[ACP]} = \frac{AB \cdot BP \cdot \sin(B + 45°)}{AC \cdot CP \cdot \sin(C + 45°)} = \frac{AB}{AC} \cdot \frac{\sin(B + 45°)}{\sin(C + 45°)},$$

$$\frac{CT}{TA} = \frac{[A''CB]}{[A''AB]} = \frac{A''C \cdot BC \cdot \sin(C + 45°)}{A''A \cdot AB \cdot \sin(A + 90°)}$$

$$= \frac{\sqrt{2}}{1} \cdot \frac{BC}{AB} \cdot \frac{\sin(C + 45°)}{\sin(A + 90°)}.$$

It follows easily that $\frac{AR}{RB} \cdot \frac{BS}{SC} \cdot \frac{CT}{TA} = 1$. Hence, $A'C$, $A''B$, and PA are concurrent.

Prove that, for any points A, B, C, D, E, F, the following inequality holds:

$$AD^2 + BE^2 + CF^2 \leq 2(AB^2 + BC^2 + CD^2 + DE^2 + EF^2 + FA^2).$$

Solution

Let $\vec{A}$, $\vec{B}$, $\vec{C}$, $\vec{D}$, $\vec{E}$, $\vec{F}$ denote the respective vectors AB, BC, CD, DE, EF, FA. Then the inequality can be rewritten as

$$\left(\vec{A} + \vec{B} + \vec{C}\right)^2 + \left(\vec{B} + \vec{C} + \vec{D}\right)^2 + \left(\vec{C} + \vec{D} + \vec{E}\right)^2$$
$$\leq 2\left(\vec{A}^2 + \vec{B}^2 + \vec{C}^2 + \vec{D}^2 + \vec{E}^2 + \vec{F}^2\right).$$

Replacing $\vec{F}$ by $-\left(\vec{A} + \vec{B} + \vec{C} + \vec{D} + \vec{E}\right)$, the inequality can be rewritten in terms of a sum of squares:

$$\left(\vec{A} + \vec{B} + \vec{D} + \vec{E}\right)^2 + \left(\vec{A} + \vec{C} + \vec{E}\right)^2 + \left(\vec{A} + \vec{D}\right)^2 + \left(\vec{B} + \vec{E}\right)^2 \geq 0.$$

Thus, the inequality holds.

There is equality if and only if $\vec{A} + \vec{C} + \vec{E} = \vec{A} + \vec{D} = \vec{B} + \vec{E} = \vec{0}$. This requires that $ABCDEF$ be a planar centro-symmetric hexagon whose sides are parallel to the three main diagonals. Here, any side length is half the length of its parallel main diagonal.

A circle k and the point K are on the same plane. For every two distinct points P and Q on k, the circle k' contains the points P, Q, and K. Let M be the intersection of the tangent to the circle k' at the point K and the line PQ. Find the locus of the points M when P and Q move over all points on k.

Solution

First two easy particular cases:

If K lies on k, the locus of M is clearly the tangent to k at K.

If K is the centre O of k, the tangent to k' at K is always parallel to PQ. Thus, the locus of M is empty.

Now to the general case where $K \notin k$ and $K \neq 0$ (Figure 1). Since the line PQ is the radical axis of k and k', the point M has the same power with respect to k and k'. The relation $MO^2 - R^2 = MK^2$ (in which R denotes the radius of k) follows immediately and shows that M belongs to the line L whose points N are characterized by $NO^2 - NK^2 = R^2$.

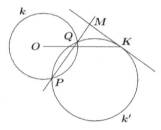

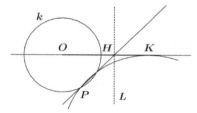

Figure 1   Figure 2

Conversely, let N be any point on L. Then

$$NO^2 - R^2 = NK^2. \qquad (1)$$

Choose any point P on k, not on NK and not a point of tangency of k with a circle tangent to NK at K [this leaves infinitely many choices!]. Then there exists a unique circle Γ through P and tangent to NK at K: its centre is the point of intersection of the perpendicular bisector of KP and the perpendicular to NK at K. The circle Γ cuts k again at Q distinct from P (by the choice of P), and the line PQ is the radical axis of Γ ($= k'$) and k. Thus, PQ passes through any point that has the same power with respect to the two circles. In particular, PQ passes through N, in view of (1). Thus, $N = M$ is a point of the locus. In conclusion, the locus we seek is the line L.

Note. This line L is the perpendicular to OK at the point H defined by $IH = \frac{1}{2}R^2/OK$, where I is the mid-point of OK. Observe that K is not on L (since $K \notin k$) and that L is exterior to k (since $NO^2 > R^2$ for all N on L). The line L can easily be constructed by remarking that H is also the intersection of OK with the line through the common points of k and a circle tangent to OK at K (see Figure 2).

Three points A, B, C, are given on the same line, such that B is be-tween A and C. Over the segments $\overline{AB}$, $\overline{BC}$, $\overline{AC}$, as diameters, semicircles are constructed on the same side of the line. The perpendicular from B to AC intersects the largest circle at point D. Prove that the common tangent of the two smaller semicircles, different from BD, is parallel to the tangent on the largest semicircle through the point D.

Solution

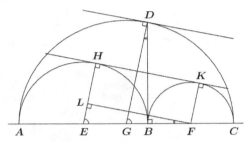

Let the semicircles with diameters AB, BC, and AC be $\Gamma_1(E, R_1)$, $\Gamma_2(F, R_2)$, and $\Gamma_3(G, R_1 + R_2)$, respectively. Assume $R_1 > R_2$. The common tangent to Γ_1 and Γ_2 touches Γ_1 at H and Γ_2 at K. Let $L \in EH$ such that $FL \| KH$. Thus, $GD = EF = R_1 + R_2$, $GB = EL = R_1 - R_2$, and $\angle ELF = \angle GBD = 90°$. We see that $\triangle ELF \cong \triangle GBD$, and therefore, $\angle FEL = \angle BGD$. This implies that EH is parallel to GD. We conclude that the tangent to Γ_3 at D is parallel to KH.

K, L, M, N are the mid-points of sides AB, BC, CD, DA, respectively, of an inscribed quadrangle $ABCD$. Prove that the orthocentres of triangles AKN, BKL, CLM, DMN are vertices of a parallelogram.

Solution

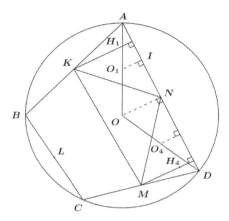

Let O be the centre of the circle $(ABCD)$, and let H_1, H_2, H_3, H_4 be the orthocentres of triangles AKN, BKL, CLM, DMN, respectively. Note that $\triangle AKN$ is the homothetic image of $\triangle ABD$ under the homothety with centre A and factor $\frac{1}{2}$. It follows that the circumcentre O_1 of $\triangle AKN$ is the mid-point of AO. Denoting by I the mid-point of AN, we thus have $\overrightarrow{O_1 I} = \frac{1}{2}\overrightarrow{ON}$. Using the well-known relation $\overrightarrow{KH_1} = 2\overrightarrow{O_1 I}$, we deduce that $\overrightarrow{KH_1} = \overrightarrow{ON}$.

Similarly, $\overrightarrow{MH_4} = \overrightarrow{ON}$. It then follows that $\overrightarrow{KH_1} = \overrightarrow{MH_4}$. Hence, $\overrightarrow{H_1 H_4} = \overrightarrow{KM}$. In the same way, $\overrightarrow{H_2 H_3} = \overrightarrow{KM}$. Thus, $\overrightarrow{H_1 H_4} = \overrightarrow{H_2 H_3}$, which means that $H_1 H_2 H_3 H_4$ is a parallelogram.

Circles S_1 and S_2 intersect at points A and B. A point Q is chosen on S_1. The lines QA and QB meet S_2 at points C and D; the tangents to S_1 at A and B meet at point P. The point Q lies outside S_2, the points C and D lie outside S_1. Prove that the line QP goes through the mid-point of CD.

Solution

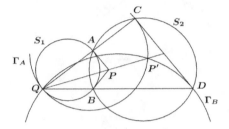

Since $QA \cdot QC = QB \cdot QD$, points A, C as well as B, D are inverse points through an inversion with centre Q. This inversion transforms the line CD into S_1 and the lines AP, BP into circles Γ_A, Γ_B passing through Q and tangent to CD at C, D, respectively. Let P' be the inverse of P. We see that Γ_A, Γ_B intersect at Q and P' and that CD is a common exterior tangent (at C, D) to Γ_A, Γ_B. As is well-known, QP' meets CD at its mid-point. Since Q, P, P' are collinear, the desired result is obtained.

Show that for any convex quadrilateral with unit area, the sum of the sides and diagonals is not less than $2(2 + \sqrt{2})$.

Solution

Let θ be the angle between the diagonals. Then the area is equal to $\frac{1}{2}d_1 d_2 \sin\theta$. Then $d_1 d_2 \geq 2$, with equality when the diagonals are perpendicular. By the AM–GM Inequality, $d_1 + d_2 \geq 2\sqrt{2}$, with equality when the diagonals are equal and perpendicular.

If $s = \dfrac{a + b + c + d}{2}$, and B, D are opposite angles, then we have

$$(\text{area})^2 = (s-a)(s-b)(s-c)(s-d) - (abcd)\cos^2\left(\frac{B+D}{2}\right).$$

Hence, $(s-a)(s-b)(s-c)(s-d) \geq 1$. By the AM–GM Inequality,

$$4 \leq (s-a) + (s-b) + (s-c) + (s-d) = a+b+c+d,$$

with equality when $a = b = c = d$.

We conclude that the sum of the sides and diagonals is at least $2(2 + \sqrt{2})$, with equality for a square.

Prove that, whenever we put ten points in any way on a circle whose diameter is 5, we can find two points whose distance is less than 2.

Solution

A circle whose diameter is 5 has a circumference slightly less than 16 units. Divide the circumference into 8 arcs of equal length. Then the 8 arcs are of length slightly less than 2. Since there are 8 arcs, by the Pigeonhole Principle at least one of these arcs has 2 points on it. Since the arcs are less than 2 units, the distance between these two points is less than 2.

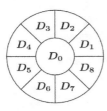

Figure 1

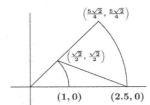

Figure 2

A disc whose diameter is 5 can be divided up as shown in Figure 1. Here the boundary of D_0 is a circle of radius 2 and is not included in D_0. It is easy to see that the distance between any two points in D_i is less than 2 (see Figure 2).

Let A, B, C, D be points in space in a general position. Assume that $AX + BX + CX + DX$ is a minimum at $X = X_0$ ($X_0 \neq A, B, C, D$). Prove that $\angle AX_0 B = \angle CX_0 D$.

Solution

Let (x_1, y_1, z_1), ..., (x_4, y_4, z_4) be the coordinates of A, B, C, D, respectively, and let (x, y, z) be the coordinates of X. We set

$$f(X) = AX + BX + CX + DX$$
$$= \sum_{i=1}^{4} \sqrt{(x - x_i)^2 + (y - y_i)^2 + (z - z_i)^2}\,.$$

Then

$$\frac{\partial f}{\partial x} = \sum_{i=1}^{4} \frac{(x - x_i)}{\sqrt{(x - x_i)^2 + (y - y_i)^2 + (z - z_i)^2}}\,,$$

and similarly for $\dfrac{\partial f}{\partial y}$ and $\dfrac{\partial f}{\partial z}$. Since f has a minimum at $X = X_0$, we have $\left.\dfrac{\partial f}{\partial x}\right|_{X_0} = \left.\dfrac{\partial f}{\partial y}\right|_{X_0} = \left.\dfrac{\partial f}{\partial z}\right|_{X_0} = 0$. Thus, we obtain

$$\frac{\overrightarrow{AX_0}}{AX_0} + \frac{\overrightarrow{BX_0}}{BX_0} + \frac{\overrightarrow{CX_0}}{CX_0} + \frac{\overrightarrow{DX_0}}{DX_0} = 0\,,$$

which implies

$$\frac{\overrightarrow{AX_0}}{AX_0} \cdot \frac{\overrightarrow{BX_0}}{BX_0} = \frac{\overrightarrow{CX_0}}{CX_0} \cdot \frac{\overrightarrow{DX_0}}{DX_0}\,.$$

Hence, $\angle AX_0 D = \angle CX_0 D$.

In a plane, let there be given a circle with centre O, with radius R and a point P inside the circle, $OP = d < R$. Among all convex quadrilaterals $ABCD$, inscribed in the circle such that their diagonals AC and BD cut each other orthogonally at P, determine the ones which have the greatest perimeter and the ones which have the smallest perimeter. Calculate these perimeters in terms of R and d.

Solution

Let $ABCD$ be a quadrilateral satisfying the given conditions, and let p denote its perimeter. Then

$$\begin{aligned} p^2 &= (AB + BC + CD + DA)^2 \\ &= AB^2 + CD^2 + BC^2 + DA^2 + 2(AB \cdot CD + AD \cdot BC) \\ &\quad + 2(AB \cdot AD + CB \cdot CD) + 2(BA \cdot BC + DA \cdot DC). \end{aligned}$$

Now

$$AB^2 + CD^2 = BC^2 + DA^2 = 4R^2. \tag{1}$$

Ptolemy's Theorem gives us

$$AB \cdot CD + AD \cdot BC = AC \cdot BD.$$

Also, with some work one obtains $AC^2 + BD^2 = 8R^2 - 4d^2$. Hence,

$$2AC \cdot BD = (AC + BD)^2 - 8R^2 + 4d^2. \tag{2}$$

Thus,

$$2(AB \cdot CD + AD \cdot BC) = (AC + BD)^2 - 8R^2 + 4d^2. \tag{3}$$

Furthermore,

$$2(AB \cdot AD + CB \cdot CD) = 4R \cdot AC, \tag{4}$$

and

$$2(BA \cdot BC + DA \cdot DC) = 4R \cdot BD. \tag{5}$$

Using (1), (3), (4), and (5) in our expression for p^2, we get

$$p^2 = (AC + BD)^2 + 4R(AC + BD) + 4d^2.$$

Consequently, the maximum (respectively, minimum) of p corresponds to the maximum (respectively, minimum) of $AC + BD$, which, in view of (2), corresponds to the maximum (respectively, minimum) of $AC \cdot BD$. Noting that

$$2AC \cdot BD = 8R^2 - 4d^2 - (AC - BD)^2,$$

we conclude that the maximum (respectively, minimum) of p corresponds to the minimum (respectively, maximum) of $|AC - BD|$. It follows that p is maximized when $AC = BD$, and p is minimized when $AC = 2R$ and $BD = 2\sqrt{R^2 - d^2}$ (the maximum and minimum possible lengths for a chord through P). Hence,

$$p_{\max}^2 = 16R^2 - 4d^2 + 8R\sqrt{4R^2 - 2d^2},$$

and

$$p_{\min}^2 = 16R^2 + 16R\sqrt{R^2 - d^2}.$$

In a triangle ABC which has a right angle at A, let H denote the foot of the altitude belonging to the hypotenuse. Show that the sum of the radii of the incircles of the triangles ABC, ABH, and AHC is equal to $|AH|$.

Solution

Triangles HBA, HAC, ABC are similar. Let r_1, r_2, r be the radii of the incircles of these triangles, respectively. Then

$$\frac{r_1}{AB} = \frac{r_2}{AC} = \frac{r}{BC} = \frac{r_1 + r_2 + r}{AB + AC + BC}.$$

Thus,

$$r_1 + r_2 + r = \frac{r(AB + AC + BC)}{BC} = \frac{2[ABC]}{BC} = \frac{BC \cdot AH}{BC} = AH$$

The edge AE of a convex pentagon $ABCDE$ whose vertices lie on the unit circle passes through the centre of this circle. If $|AB| = a$, $|BC| = b$, $|CD| = c$, $|DE| = d$ and $ab = cd = \frac{1}{4}$, compute $|AC| + |CE|$ in terms of a, b, c, d.

Solution

Let $|AC| = x$, $|CE| = y$, $|AD| = p$, $|BE| = q$. The angles ABE, ACE, ADE are each $90°$, so that $a^2 + q^2 = x^2 + y^2 = p^2 + d^2 = 4$. By Ptolemy's Theorem, $dx + 2c = py$; whence, $d^2x^2 + x + 4c^2 = p^2y^2$. Therefore,

$$
\begin{aligned}
x &= (4 - d^2)y^2 - 4c^2 - d^2x^2 = 4y^2 - 4c^2 - d^2(x^2 + y^2) \\
&= 4y^2 - 4c^2 - 4d^2 .
\end{aligned}
$$

Analogously, the relation $ay + 2b = qx$ leads to $y = 4x^2 - 4a^2 - 4b^2$.

Consequently, $x + y = 16 - 4(a^2 + b^2 + c^2 + d^2)$.

Given three straight lines in a plane, that concur at point O, consider the three consecutive angles between them (which, naturally, add up to $180°$). Let P be a point in the plane not on any of these lines, and let A, B, C be the feet of the perpendiculars drawn from P to the three lines. Show that the internal angles of $\triangle ABC$ are equal to those between the given lines.

Solution

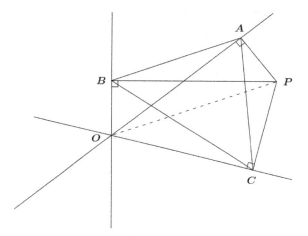

The points O, C, P, A, B lie on the circle having $\overline{OP}$ as diameter. Therefore, $\angle ABC = \angle AOC$ and $\angle ACB = \angle AOB$. As a consequence, $\angle BAC$ is equal to the third consecutive angle at O.

$ABCDEFGH$ is a cube of edge 2. Let M be the mid-point of $\overline{BC}$ and N the mid-point of $\overline{EF}$. Compute the area of the quadrilateral $AMHN$.

Solution

Since clearly $\overrightarrow{NH} = \overrightarrow{AM}$, the four points A, M, H, and N are co-planar. Since $\triangle ENH$, $\triangle FNA$, $\triangle BMA$, and $\triangle CMH$ are right triangles whose sides have lengths 1 and 2, we see that these triangles are congruent and $AM = MH = HN = NA$. Quadrilateral $NHMA$ is thus a rhombus.

Let us find the length of its diagonals AH and NM.

By applying the Pythagorean Theorem in right triangle $\triangle EHC$, we have $EC = \sqrt{EH^2 + HC^2} = 2\sqrt{2}$. Noticing that $NM = EC$, we get $NM = 2\sqrt{2}$. By the same reasoning, we see that $AC = 2\sqrt{2}$. Applying the Pythagorean Theorem in $\triangle ACH$, we get $AH = \sqrt{AC^2 + HC^2} = 2\sqrt{3}$.

Now, the area of a rhombus is half the product of the lengths of its diagonals. Hence, we obtain $2\sqrt{6}$ as the area.

Given a trapezoid $ABCD$, where $\overline{AB}$ and $\overline{DC}$ are parallel, and $\overline{AD} = \overline{DC} = \overline{AB}/2$, determine $\angle ACB$.

Solution

Let M be the mid-point of AB, and let E be the point of intersection of AD and BC. Since $DC = AB/2$ and $DC \| AB$, we see by Thales that D is the mid-point of AE and C is the mid-point of BE. Thus, M, D, and C are the mid-points of the sides of $\triangle ABE$. By the Mid-point Theorem, $AMCD$ is a parallelogram and $MC = AD = AB/2$.

In $\triangle ABC$, MC is a median which is half the length of the side AB. Hence, $\triangle ABC$ has a right angle at C. That is, $\angle ACB = 90°$.

In a circle of radius 1 are drawn six equal arcs of circles, radius 1, cutting the original circle as in the figure. Calculate the shaded area.

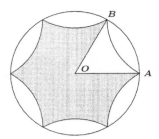

Solution

Since both arcs passing through A and B are of radius 1, they are symmetric about the line AB. Hence, the area enclosed by these two arcs is cut in half by the line segment AB. If line segments are drawn through all vertices of the hexagonal star, we get a regular hexagon inscribed in the circle. From this we can easily calculate the area of the total white border, for it will be twice the area between the circle and the hexagon.

The hexagon's area is six times the area of an equilateral triangle of side 1, namely $6 \cdot \frac{\sqrt{3}}{4} = \frac{3\sqrt{3}}{2}$. The circle has area $\pi r^2 = \pi$. Hence, the hexagonal star has area $\pi - 2\left(\pi - \frac{3\sqrt{3}}{2}\right) = 3\sqrt{3} - \pi$.

Thus, since the shaded area has only $5/6$ the area of the hexagonal star, its area is $\frac{5}{6}(3\sqrt{3} - \pi)$.

Let $ABCD$ be an $m \times n$ rectangle, with $m, n \in \mathbb{N}$. Consider a ray of light that starts from A, is reflected at an angle of $45°$ on another side of the rectangle, and goes on reflecting in this way.

(a) Show that the ray will finally hit a vertex.

(b) Suppose m and n have no common factor greater than 1. Determine the number of reflections undergone by the ray before it hits a vertex.

Solution

(a) Extend the rectangle in all directions to form a Cartesian grid. (The example in the figure below has $m = 3$ and $n = 2$.)

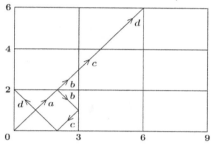

The actual path is mirrored by a straight line with equation $y = x$. The ray of light will eventually hit the vertex corresponding to the vertex (mn, mn) in the extension.

(b) The ray crosses $m - 1$ lines in one direction and $n - 1$ in the other (in the extension). Thus, the number of reflections is $m + n - 2$.

Suppose that ten points are given in the plane such that any five of them contains four points which are concyclic. What is the largest number N for which we can correctly say: "At least N of the ten points lie on a circle"? ($4 \leq N \leq 10$.)

Solution

The answer is 9.

More generally, let $n \geq 5$ be an integer. Let S be a set of n points in the plane such that among any five of them, four are concyclic. Denote by $f(n)$ the largest integer k for which we can correctly say: "At least k of the n points lie on a circle".

We will prove the following claim.

Claim. $f(6) = 4$, and $f(n) = n - 1$ if $n \geq 5$ and $n \neq 6$.

Lemma. There do not exist seven distinct points M_1, M_2, ..., M_7 in the plane such that each of the following seven sets is concyclic and the seven circles thus defined are distinct.

(1)　　M_1, M_2, M_3, M_4　　　　(2)　　M_1, M_2, M_5, M_6

(3)　　M_3, M_4, M_5, M_6　　　　(4)　　M_2, M_3, M_5, M_7

(5)　　M_1, M_4, M_5, M_7　　　　(6)　　M_1, M_3, M_6, M_7

(7)　　M_2, M_4, M_6, M_7

Proof of the Lemma. Suppose, for the purpose of contradiction, that there exist 7 such points. Let f be an inversion with pole M_1. Let $P_i = f(M_i)$ for $i = 2, \ldots, 7$. Then we have

(1') P_2, P_3, P_4 are collinear.

(2') P_2, P_5, P_6 are collinear.

(3') P_3, P_4, P_5, P_6 lie on a circle, say Γ.

(4') P_2, P_3, P_5, P_7 are concyclic.

(5') P_4, P_5, P_7 are collinear.

(6') P_3, P_6, P_7 are collinear.

(7') P_2, P_4, P_6, P_7 are concyclic.

Case 1. $P_3P_4P_5P_6$ is convex. Then P_2 and P_7 are exterior to Γ.

Subcase (a). P_3 lies between P_2 and P_4. Then P_6 lies between P_2 and P_5.

If P_6 lies between P_7 and P_3, then P_5 lies between P_7 and P_4 (as in the diagram on the right). It follows that P_6 is interior to triangle $P_2P_4P_7$. Thus, (7') cannot be satisfied.

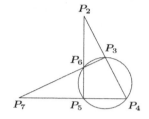

If P_3 lies between P_7 and P_6, then P_4 lies between P_7 and P_5. It then follows that P_3 is interior to triangle $P_2P_5P_7$. Thus, (4') cannot be satisfied.

Subcase (b). P_4 lies between P_2 and P_3. Then P_5 lies between P_2 and P_6. As above, we prove that either (4') or (7') is not satisfied.

Case 2. $P_3P_4P_6P_5$ is convex. Then P_2 is exterior to Γ, and P_7 is interior to the quadrilateral $P_3P_4P_6P_5$.

Subcase (a). P_3 lies between P_2 and P_4. Then P_5 lies between P_2 and P_6 (as in the diagram on the right). It follows that P_7 is interior to triangle $P_2P_4P_6$. Thus, (7') cannot be satisfied.

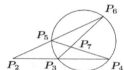

Subcase (b). P_4 lies between P_2 and P_3. Then P_6 lies between P_2 and P_5. It follows that P_7 is interior to triangle $P_2P_3P_5$. Thus, (4') cannot be satisfied.

Case 3. $P_3P_5P_4P_6$ is convex. We proceed as in the second case, just interchanging P_2 and P_7.

In each case, we obtain a contradiction. Thus, the lemma is proved.

Proof of the Claim. First we note that if we choose $n-1$ points on a circle Γ and another point not on Γ, the set S of these n points satisfies the requirement that among any five points of S, four are concyclic. Thus, $f(n) \leq n-1$. Moreover, it is clear that $f(n) \geq 4$. Then $f(5) = 4$. The following configuration shows that $f(6) = 4$.

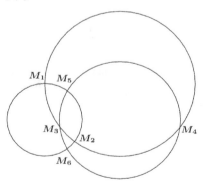

From now on, we suppose that S is a set of $n \geq 7$ points satisfying the requirement in the problem. Suppose (for the purpose of contradiction) that not more than $n - 2$ of the points of S are concyclic.

Let Γ_1 be a circle containing at least four of the n points. With no loss of generality, we may suppose that each of the points M_1, M_2, M_3, M_4 belongs to Γ_1, and that $M_5 \notin \Gamma_1$, and $M_6 \notin \Gamma_1$.

Given the set $\{M_1, M_2, M_3, M_5, M_6\}$, since $M_5, M_6 \notin \Gamma_1$, then among the four concyclic points in this set, we must have M_5, M_6, and exactly two of the three other points. With no loss of generality, we may suppose that M_1, M_2, M_5, M_6 lie on a circle, say Γ_2, where $\Gamma_1 \neq \Gamma_2$.

Given the set $\{M_1, M_3, M_4, M_5, M_6\}$, if M_1 is among the four concyclic points in this set, then without loss of generality M_1, M_i, M_5, M_6 are concyclic for some $i \in \{3, 4\}$. But M_1, M_2, M_5, M_6 are concyclic too, and hence M_1, M_2, M_i, M_5, M_6 are concyclic. Thus, $M_5 \in \Gamma_1$, a contradiction. It follows that M_3, M_4, M_5, M_6 lie on a circle, say Γ_3, and $\Gamma_3 \neq \Gamma_i$ for $i \in \{1, 2\}$.

Let us suppose (for the purpose of contradiction) that Γ_1 contains at least 5 of the points of S. Then $M_7 \in \Gamma_1$ for some point $M_7 \in S$. Given the set $\{M_1, M_3, M_5, M_6, M_7\}$, we know that four of these points have to be concyclic.

- If M_1, M_3, M_5, M_6 are concyclic, then $M_3 \in \Gamma_2$, and hence $\Gamma_1 = \Gamma_2$, a contradiction.

- If M_1, M_3, M_5, M_7 are concyclic, then $M_5 \in \Gamma_1$, a contradiction.

- If M_1, M_3, M_6, M_7 are concyclic, then $M_6 \in \Gamma_1$, a contradiction.

- If M_1, M_5, M_6, M_7 are concyclic, then $M_7 \in \Gamma_2$ and hence $\Gamma_1 = \Gamma_2$, a contradiction.

- If M_3, M_5, M_6, M_7 are concyclic, then $M_7 \in \Gamma_3$ and hence $\Gamma_1 = \Gamma_3$, a contradiction.

In each case, we obtain a contradiction. It follows that Γ_1 contains exactly 4 points of S.

From the choice of Γ_1, we deduce that every circle which contains at least 4 points of S, contains exactly 4 points of S. Thus, $M_i \notin \Gamma_1 \cup \Gamma_2 \cup \Gamma_3$ for $i = 7, \ldots, n$.

Let P be any one of the points M_i of S where $i \geq 7$. Given the set $\{M_1, M_2, M_3, M_5, P\}$, since $M_5 \notin \Gamma_1$ and $P \notin \Gamma_1$, the four concyclic points from this set must include both M_5 and P. Similarly, since $P \notin \Gamma_2$, the four concyclic points must also include M_3.

Case 1. M_2, M_3, M_5, P lie on a circle Γ_4.

Given the set $\{M_1, M_2, M_4, M_5, P\}$, arguing as above, we see that the points M_4, M_5, and P must all be included among the four concyclic points. If M_2, M_4, M_5, P are concyclic, then M_2, M_3, M_4, M_5, P are concyclic, which implies that $M_5 \in \Gamma_1$, a contradiction. Therefore, M_1, M_4, M_5, P lie on a circle Γ_5.

Given the set $\{M_1, M_2, M_3, M_6, P\}$, a similar argument shows that M_1, M_3, M_6, P lie on a circle Γ_6.

Given the set $\{M_2, M_4, M_5, M_6, P\}$, a similar argument shows that M_2, M_4, M_6, P lie on a circle Γ_7.

It follows that the seven points M_1, M_2, M_3, M_4, M_5, M_6, P violate the lemma (the seven circles are Γ_1, Γ_2, $\ldots$, Γ_7).

Case 2. M_1, M_3, M_5, P are concyclic.

In the same manner as in case 1 above, by interchanging the roles of M_1 and M_2, we prove that the seven points M_2, M_1, M_3, M_4, M_5, M_6, P violate the lemma.

It follows that, if $n \geq 7$, then at least $n - 1$ of the points of S are concyclic. That is, if $n \geq 7$, then $f(n) \geq n - 1$. The claim is now proved.

Suppose that Γ is a semi-circle with centre O and diameter AB.
Assume that M is a point on the extension of AB such that $MA > MB$.
A line through M intersects Γ at C and D such that $MC > MD$. Circum-
circles of the triangles AOC and BOD will intersect at points O and K.
Prove that $OK \perp MK$.

Solution

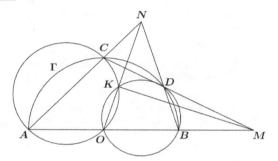

Let N be the point of intersection of AC and BD. The points M and
N are conjugate with respect to the circle containing Γ. (We will call this
circle Γ as well.) Denote by p, p', p'' the powers of N with respect to the
circles Γ, (AOC), (BOD), respectively. Then $p = NA \cdot NC = NB \cdot ND$,
$p' = NA \cdot NC$, and $p'' = NB \cdot ND$. Thus, $p' = p''$; whence, N lies on the
radical axis OK of the circles (AOC) and (BOD).

Let R be the radius of Γ. From $p = NO^2 - R^2 = NK \cdot NO$, we deduce
that $OK \cdot ON = R^2$, which implies that N and K are conjugate with respect
to Γ. Since K and M are both conjugates of N, we see that MK is the polar
of N with respect to Γ and, as such, is perpendicular to the line $ON (= OK)$
joining N to the centre O of Γ.

Let AC be a diameter of a circle. Assume that AB is tangent to the circle at the point A and that the segment BC intersects the circle at D. Show that if $|AC| = 1$, $|AB| = a$, and $|CD| = b$, then

$$\frac{1}{a^2 + \frac{1}{2}} < \frac{b}{a} < \frac{1}{a^2}\,.$$

Solution

Let $\theta = \angle ACD$. Note that $0 < \theta < 90°$. We have $\tan\theta = \dfrac{|AB|}{|AC|} = a$ and $\cos\theta = \dfrac{|CD|}{|AC|} = b$, since $\angle CAB = \angle CDA = 90°$.

Now, $\dfrac{b}{a} < \dfrac{1}{a^2}$ holds, since this is equivalent to $ab < 1$, or $\sin\theta < 1$, which is true. Also, $\dfrac{1}{a^2 + 1/2} < \dfrac{b}{a}$ holds, being successively equivalent to

$$2a^2 - 2\frac{a}{b} + 1 \;>\; 0\,,$$

$$2(\tan\theta)^2 - 2\left(\frac{\tan\theta}{\cos\theta}\right) + 1 \;>\; 0\,,$$

$$2(\sin\theta)^2 - 2\sin\theta + (\cos\theta)^2 \;>\; 0\,,$$

$$(\sin\theta - 1)^2 \;>\; 0\,,$$

which is true as well.

The bisector of the angle B in the triangle ABC intersects the side AC at the point D. Let E be a point on side AB such that $3\angle ACE = 2\angle BCE$. The segments BD and CE intersect at the point P. One knows that $|ED| = |DC| = |CP|$. Find the angles of the triangle.

Solution

We set $\angle ABD = \angle DBC = \beta$ and $3\angle ACE = 2\angle BCE = 6\alpha$. Then $\angle ACE = 2\alpha$ and $\angle BCE = 3\alpha$. Since $CP = CD$, we see that $\angle CPD = \angle CDP$. Since

$$\angle CPD = \angle PBC + \angle PCB = \beta + 3\alpha,$$

and since

$$\angle CDP = \angle CDB = \angle A + \angle ABD = \angle A + \beta,$$

we must have $\beta + 3\alpha = \angle A + \beta$, which implies that $\angle A = 3\alpha$. Therefore,

$$\angle BEC = \angle A + \angle ACE = 3\alpha + 2\alpha = 5\alpha.$$

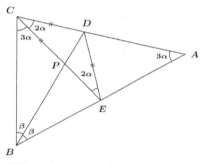

Since $DE = DC$, we have $\angle DEC = \angle DCE = 2\alpha$. Therefore,

$$\angle BED = \angle BEC + \angle DEC = 5\alpha + 2\alpha = 7\alpha.$$

By the Law of Sines for $\triangle BDE$ and $\triangle BDC$, we have

$$\frac{\sin BED}{BD} = \frac{\sin EBD}{DE} = \frac{\sin CBD}{DC} = \frac{\sin BCD}{BD}.$$

Thus, $\sin BED = \sin BCD$. Hence, either $\angle BED = \angle BCD$ or $\angle BED + \angle BCD = 180°$. Since $\angle BED = 7\alpha$ and $\angle BCD = 5\alpha$, we see that $\angle BED \neq \angle BCD$. Thus, $\angle BED + \angle BCD = 180°$. This further implies that B, C, D, and E are concyclic. Therefore, $\angle EBD = \angle ECD$; that is, $\beta = 2\alpha$. By examining the interior angles of $\triangle ABC$, we have $3\alpha + 2\beta + 5\alpha = 180°$. Consequently, we have

$$3\alpha + 4\alpha + 5\alpha = 180°,$$

from which we get $\alpha = 15°$.

Hence, $\angle A = 3\alpha = 45°$, $\angle B = 2\beta = 4\alpha = 60°$, and $\angle C = 5\alpha = 75°$. (It is easy to verify that this triangle satisfies the required conditions.)

A convex polygon with 2000 vertices in a plane is given.
Prove that we may mark 1998 points of the plane so that any triangle with vertices which are vertices of the polygon has exactly one marked point as an internal point.

Solution

More generally, for any integer $n \geq 3$, we prove the result with the numbers n and $n - 2$ instead of 2000 and 1998, respectively.

Let $\mathcal{K}$ be a convex n–gon in the plane. Since $\mathcal{K}$ has a finite number of vertices, the number of lines that pass through at least two of these vertices is finite. Thus, we may consider an orthonormal coordinate system $\mathcal{R}$ such that, in $\mathcal{R}$, the x–coordinates of the vertices of $\mathcal{K}$ are pairwise distinct. Let $P_i(x_i, y_i)$, for $i = 1, 2, \ldots, n$, be the vertices of $\mathcal{K}$, ordered so that $x_1 < x_2 < \cdots < x_n$.

For $i \neq j$, let Δ_{ij} be the line $(P_i P_j)$. Denote by $d(P_k, \Delta_{ij})$ the distance from P_k to Δ_{ij}. Since there is a finite number of lines Δ_{ij}, we may consider the minimum of the set of distances $d(P_k, \Delta_{ij})$, for i, j, k pairwise distinct. Let d denote this minimum. Since the vertices P_i are in convex position, we have $d > 0$.

For $i = 2, \ldots, n - 1$, exactly one of the two points with coordinates $\left(x_i, y_i \pm \frac{d}{2}\right)$ is an interior point of $\mathcal{K}$. Denote this point by M_i. The construction of the points M_i ensures that M_i is an exterior point of any of the triangles $P_a P_b P_c$ where $i \notin \{a, b, c\}$. Moreover, M_i is an interior point of $P_i P_j P_k$ if and only if $j < i < k$ or $k < i < j$. Thus, each one of the triangles $P_a P_b P_c$ contains exactly one point M_i. We mark these points, and the conclusion follows.

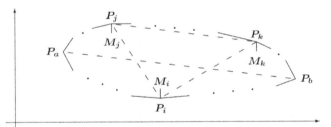

Let M be an internal point on the side AC of a triangle ABC, and let O be the intersection point of perpendiculars from the mid-points of AM and MC to lines BC and AB, respectively. Find the location of M such that the length of segment OM is minimal.

Solution

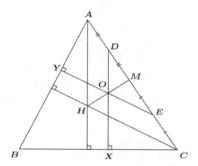

Let D and E be the mid-points of AM and CM, respectively. Let X and Y be the feet of the perpendiculars from D to BC and from E to AB, respectively. Let H be the orthocentre of $\triangle ABC$.

Since $AH \perp BC$ and $DX \perp BC$, we have $AH \parallel DX$. Because D is the mid-point of AM, we see that DX passes through the mid-point of HM. Similarly, EY passes through the mid-point of HM. Therefore, the intersection of DX and EY is the mid-point of HM. Thus, O is the mid-point of HM. Hence, $OM = \frac{1}{2}HM$. We conclude that OM is minimal when HM is minimal.

Let P be the foot of the altitude from B to AC. Then P is also the foot of the perpendicular from H to AC. If $\angle BAC$ and $\angle BCA$ are acute, then P is an internal point of the side AC, and the length of HM may be minimized by taking $M = P$. If $\angle BAC \geq 90°$ or $\angle BCA \geq 90°$, then P is not an internal point of AC, and there is no choice for M that minimizes the length of HM.

Thus, the length of OM is minimal when M is the foot of the altitude from B to AC, provided that $\angle BAC$ and $\angle BCA$ are acute. Otherwise, there is no minimal length.

A triangle ABC is given. Altitude CD intersects the bisector BK of $\angle ABC$, and the altitude KL of BKC, at the points M and N, respectively. The circumscribed circle of BKN intersects segment AB at the point $P \neq B$. Prove that triangle KPM is isosceles.

Solution

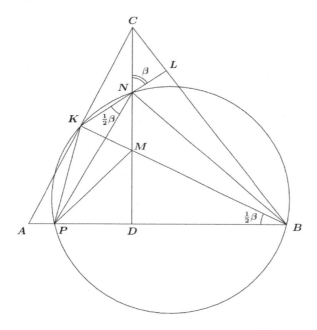

Quadrilateral $PBNK$ can be inscribed in a circle. Therefore,

$$\angle KNP \; = \; \angle KBP = \tfrac{1}{2}\beta , \tag{1}$$

where $\beta \; = \; \angle ABC$. We also observe that $\angle NCL \; = \; 90° - \beta$, since $CD \perp AB$. This implies that $\angle CNL = \beta$, since $KL \perp BC$. Then

$$\angle KNM \; = \; \angle CNL \; = \; \beta . \tag{2}$$

From (1) and (2), we conclude that $\angle KNP = \angle MNP = \tfrac{1}{2}\beta$. Thus, NP is the bisector of $\angle KNM$. Furthermore, since $\angle KMN$ is an exterior angle of $\triangle MBC$, we have

$$\angle KMN \; = \; \angle MBC + \angle MCB \; = \; \tfrac{1}{2}\beta + (90° - \beta) \; = \; 90° - \tfrac{1}{2}\beta .$$

It follows that $NP \perp KM$. This can happen only when $PK = PM$.

Two spheres with distinct radii are externally tangent at point P. Line segments AB and CD are given such that the first sphere touches them at the points A and C, and the second sphere touches them at the points B and D. Let M and N be the orthogonal projections of the mid-points of segments AC and BD on the line joining the centres of the given spheres. Prove that $PM = PN$.

Solution

Let S (centre O, radius R) and S' (centre O', radius R') be the given spheres. Denote by I, J, K, L the respective mid-points of segments AB, BD, DC, AC, so that M and N are the respective orthogonal projections of L and J onto OO'. Let $\vec{U} = \overrightarrow{OO'}/\|\overrightarrow{OO'}\|$, a unit vector in the direction of $\overrightarrow{OO'}$. For any point Z, we denote by $\vec{Z}$ the vector $\overrightarrow{PZ}$.

Now, $\vec{N}$ points in the same direction as $\vec{U}$ and $\vec{M}$ points in the opposite direction. Therefore, $PN = \vec{N} \cdot \vec{U}$ and $PM = -\vec{M} \cdot \vec{U}$. Note also that $\vec{N} \cdot \vec{U} = \vec{J} \cdot \vec{U}$ and $\vec{M} \cdot \vec{U} = \vec{L} \cdot \vec{U}$, since M and N are the orthogonal projections of L and J onto OO'. Thus,

$$PN - PM = \vec{J} \cdot \vec{U} + \vec{L} \cdot \vec{U} = (\vec{J} + \vec{L}) \cdot \vec{U}.$$

We have

$$\vec{J} + \vec{L} = (\vec{B} + \vec{D}) + (\vec{A} + \vec{C}) = (\vec{A} + \vec{B}) + (\vec{C} + \vec{D}) = \vec{I} + \vec{K}.$$

Hence, $PN - PM = (\vec{I} + \vec{K}) \cdot \vec{U}$.

But

$$IO^2 - IO'^2 = (IO^2 - R^2) - (IO'^2 - R'^2) + R^2 - R'^2$$
$$= IA^2 - IB^2 + R^2 - R'^2 = R^2 - R'^2 = PO^2 - PO'^2.$$

Thus, I belongs to the plane orthogonal to OO' through P (which is the radical plane of S, S'). It follows that $\vec{U} \cdot \vec{I} = 0$. Similarly, $\vec{U} \cdot \vec{K} = 0$, and we get $PN - PM = 0$, as required.

Let $ABCD$ be a tetrahedron and AA_1, BB_1, CC_1, DD_1 be diameters of the circumsphere of $ABCD$. Let A_0, B_0, C_0 and D_0 be the centroids of the triangles BCD, CDA, DAB and ABC, respectively. Prove that

(a) the lines A_0A_1, B_0B_1, C_0C_1 and D_0D_1 have a common point, which is denoted by F;

(b) the line passing through F and the mid-point of an edge is perpendicular to its opposite edge.

Solution

Take the origin at the circumcentre O of $ABCD$ and set $\overrightarrow{a} = \overrightarrow{OA}$. Then $\overrightarrow{OA_1} = -\overrightarrow{a}$, since AA_1 is a diameter. Define $\overrightarrow{b}$, $\overrightarrow{c}$, and $\overrightarrow{d}$ similarly. If A_0 is the centroid of $\triangle BCD$, then $\overrightarrow{OA_0} = \frac{1}{3}(\overrightarrow{b} + \overrightarrow{c} + \overrightarrow{d})$.

The line A_0A_1 has vector equation

$$\overrightarrow{r} = \tfrac{1}{3}(\overrightarrow{b} + \overrightarrow{c} + \overrightarrow{d}) + t(-\overrightarrow{a} - \tfrac{1}{3}\overrightarrow{b} - \tfrac{1}{3}\overrightarrow{c} - \tfrac{1}{3}\overrightarrow{d}).$$

For $t = -\frac{1}{2}$, we have $\overrightarrow{r} = \frac{1}{2}(\overrightarrow{a} + \overrightarrow{b} + \overrightarrow{c} + \overrightarrow{d})$. By symmetry, this point lies on B_0B_1, C_0C_1, and D_0D_1 also. Thus, we may use this point as the point F to establish part (a).

Let L be the mid-point of AB. Then, we have $\overrightarrow{OL} = \frac{1}{2}(\overrightarrow{a} + \overrightarrow{b})$ and $\overrightarrow{LF} = \frac{1}{2}(\overrightarrow{c} + \overrightarrow{d})$. Now

$$\overrightarrow{LF} \cdot \overrightarrow{CD} = \frac{1}{2}(\overrightarrow{c} + \overrightarrow{d}) \cdot (\overrightarrow{d} - \overrightarrow{c}) = \frac{1}{2}\|\overrightarrow{d}\|^2 - \frac{1}{2}\|\overrightarrow{c}\|^2 = 0,$$

because $\|\overrightarrow{a}\| = \|\overrightarrow{b}\| = \|\overrightarrow{c}\| = \|\overrightarrow{d}\| = R$, the radius of the circumcircle.

Let P be a point lying on a given sphere. Three mutually perpendicular rays from P intersect the sphere at points A, B, and C. Prove that for all such triads of rays from P, the plane of the triangle ABC passes through a fixed point and determine the largest possible value of the area of the triangle ABC.

Solution

Let O be the centre of the sphere, and let I, J, K, L, M, N be the respective mid-points of BC, CA, AB, PA, PB, PC. As the centre of the circumcircle of $\triangle BPC$, the point I is the orthogonal projection of O onto the plane (BPC). Thus, OI is parallel to PA. Similarly, $OJ \parallel PB$ and $OK \parallel PC$. It follows that the points O, I, N, J, L, P, M, K are the vertices of a right-angled parallelepiped.

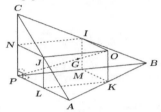

Let G be the centroid of $\triangle ABC$. We have

$$\overrightarrow{PO} = \overrightarrow{PL} + \overrightarrow{LK} + \overrightarrow{KO} = \frac{1}{2}\overrightarrow{PA} + \frac{1}{2}\overrightarrow{PB} + \frac{1}{2}\overrightarrow{PC} = \frac{1}{2}(3\overrightarrow{PG}),$$

and hence, $\overrightarrow{PG} = \frac{2}{3}\overrightarrow{PO}$. Then G is fixed, since P and O are fixed.

Since $PABC$ is a right-angled tetrahedron, the area $[ABC]$ of the triangle ABC satisfies the well-known Pythagoras-like relation

$$[ABC]^2 = [APC]^2 + [BPC]^2 + [BPA]^2 .$$

Thus, $[ABC]^2 = \frac{1}{4}(PA^2 PC^2 + PC^2 PB^2 + PB^2 PA^2)$. Then

$$[ABC]^2 \leq \frac{1}{4}(PA^4 + PB^4 + PC^4)$$

(since $xy + yz + zx \leq x^2 + y^2 + z^2$ for positive numbers x, y, z).

On the other hand,

$$
\begin{aligned}
PA^4 + PB^4 + PC^4 &= (PA^2 + PB^2 + PC^2)^2 \\
&\quad -2(PA^2 PC^2 + PC^2 PB^2 + PB^2 PA^2),
\end{aligned}
$$

and

$$
\begin{aligned}
PA^2 + PB^2 + PC^2 &= (2PL)^2 + (2PM)^2 + (2PN)^2 \\
&= 4(PL^2 + LK^2 + KO^2) = 4PO^2 = 4r^2 ,
\end{aligned}
$$

where r denotes the radius of the given sphere.

Thus, $[ABC]^2 \leq \frac{1}{4}((4r^2)^2 - 2(4[ABC]^2))$; whence, $[ABC] \leq \frac{2r^2}{\sqrt{3}}$.

Furthermore, the value $\frac{2r^2}{\sqrt{3}}$ is attained when $PA = PB = PC = \frac{2r}{\sqrt{3}}$; that is, when P, A, B, C are four vertices of a cube inscribed in the sphere.

In conclusion, the maximal value of $[ABC]$ is $\frac{2r^2}{\sqrt{3}}$.

Determine the smallest possible value of the following expression

$$\sqrt{x^2 + (y+1)^2} + \sqrt{x^2 + (y-3)^2}$$

where x, y are real numbers such that $2x - y = 2$.

Solution

Let ℓ be the line with equation $2x - y = 2$. Let $A = (0, -1)$ and $B = (0, 3)$. Let A' be the reflection of A across the line ℓ; then $A' = \left(\frac{4}{5}, -\frac{7}{5}\right)$. Let N be the point of intersection of $A'B$ and ℓ; then $N = \left(\frac{2}{3}, -\frac{2}{3}\right)$.

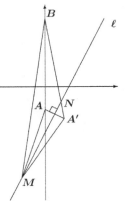

Let $M = (x, y)$ be an arbitrary point on the line ℓ. By symmetry, $MA = MA'$. Thus,

$$\sqrt{x^2 + (y+1)^2} + \sqrt{x^2 + (y-3)^2}$$
$$= MA + MB = MA' + MB.$$

By the Triangle Inequality, we have

$$MA' + MB \geq A'B = 2\sqrt{5},$$

with equality if and only if $M = N$.

Finally,

$$\sqrt{x^2 + (y+1)^2} + \sqrt{x^2 + (y-3)^2} \geq 2\sqrt{5}.$$

Equality holds only if $(x, y) = \left(\frac{2}{3}, -\frac{2}{3}\right)$.

Denote by S the set of all points of $\triangle ABC$ except one interior point T. Show that S can be represented as a union of disjoint (line) segments.

Solution

Lemma. If $MNPQ$ is a trapezoid, with MN parallel to PQ, then the set S of all the points interior to, or on the boundary of, $MNPQ$ except the line segment $[MN]$, can be represented as a union of disjoint line segments.

Proof. For any point X on the half-open segment $[QM[$, let Y_X be the point on the half-open segment $[PN[$ such that XY_X is parallel to MN. Then we have

$$S = \bigcup_{X \in [QM[} [XY_X],$$

which proves the lemma.

Let T be an interior point of the triangle ABC. Let ℓ_1, ℓ_2, ℓ_3 be the lines through T parallel to AB, BC, CA, respectively. Let D, E, F be the respective intersections of ℓ_1 with BC, of ℓ_2 with AC, and of ℓ_3 with AB.

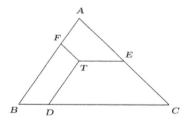

To get the conclusion, it suffices to see that S is the disjoint union of the three trapezoids $TFBD - [TD]$, $TDCE - [TE]$, $TEAF - [TF]$, and to use the lemma in these three cases.

Let $ABCD$ be a square inscribed in a circle. If M is a point on the arc $\overline{AB}$ show that $MC \cdot MD > 3\sqrt{3} \cdot MA \cdot MB$.

Solution

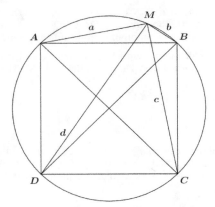

Without loss of generality, let the side of the square be equal to 1. Write $MA = a$, $MB = b$, $MC = c$, $MD = d$.

By Ptolemy's Theorem for $DAMB$ we have

$$b + a\sqrt{2} = d,$$

and for $AMBC$ we have

$$a + b\sqrt{2} = c.$$

Hence,

$$cd = \sqrt{2}a^2 + \sqrt{2}b^2 + 3ab,$$

which, by the AM-GM Inequality, yields

$$cd \geq (3 + 2\sqrt{2})ab > 3\sqrt{3}ab.$$

The last inequality is justified by observing that

$$3 + 2\sqrt{2} > 3\sqrt{3} \iff 17 + 12\sqrt{2} > 27 \iff 12\sqrt{2} > 10,$$

which is clearly true.

In a triangle ABC, I is the incentre and $D \in (BC)$, $E \in (CA)$, $F \in (AB)$ are the points of tangency of the incircle with the sides of the triangle. Let $M \in (BC)$ be the foot of the interior bisector of $\angle BIC$ and $\{P\} = FE \cap AM$. Prove that DP is the interior bisector of the angle $\angle FDE$.

Solution

Let X, Y be points on AM such that $BX \parallel CY \parallel FE$. Since $\triangle BMX$ and $\triangle CMY$ are similar, and $\angle BIM = \angle CIM$, we have

$$\frac{CY}{BX} = \frac{CM}{BM} = \frac{CI}{BI}.$$

Since $EP \parallel CY$, $FP \parallel BX$ and $AE = AF$, we have

$$\frac{EP}{FP} = \frac{EP}{CY} \cdot \frac{BX}{FP} \cdot \frac{CY}{BX} = \frac{AE}{AC} \cdot \frac{AB}{AF} \cdot \frac{CY}{BX} = \frac{AB}{AC} \cdot \frac{CI}{BI}. \qquad (1)$$

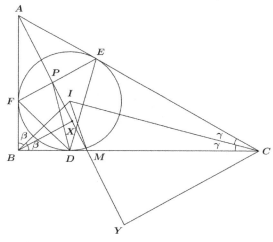

Let $\angle ABC = 2\beta$ and $\angle ACB = 2\gamma$. Then

$$\angle ABI = \angle IBC = \beta \quad \text{and} \quad \angle ACI = \angle ICB = \gamma.$$

By the Law of Sines for $\triangle ABC$ and $\triangle IBC$, we get

$$\frac{AB}{AC} = \frac{\sin 2\gamma}{\sin 2\beta} = \frac{2 \sin \gamma \cos \gamma}{2 \sin \beta \cos \beta} = \frac{\sin \gamma \cos \gamma}{\sin \beta \cos \beta},$$

and

$$\frac{CI}{BI} = \frac{\sin \beta}{\sin \gamma}.$$

Thus, from (1),

$$\frac{EP}{FP} = \frac{\sin \gamma \cos \gamma}{\sin \beta \cos \beta} \cdot \frac{\sin \beta}{\sin \gamma} = \frac{\cos \gamma}{\cos \beta}. \qquad (2)$$

Let r be the radius of the incircle. Then

$$DE = 2r \sin \angle DFE = 2r \sin \angle EDC = 2r \sin(90° - \gamma) = 2r \cos \gamma.$$

Similarly, we have $DF = 2r \cos \beta$. Hence,

$$\frac{DE}{DF} = \frac{2r \cos \gamma}{2r \cos \beta} = \frac{\cos \gamma}{\cos \beta}. \qquad (3)$$

From (2) and (3) we obtain $\frac{EP}{FP} = \frac{DE}{DF}$.

Therefore, DP is the interior bisector of $\angle FDE$.

Let $ABCD$ be a trapezoid ($AB \parallel CD$) and M, N be points on the lines AD and BC, respectively, such that $MN \parallel AB$. Prove that

$$DC \cdot MA + AB \cdot MD = MN \cdot AD.$$

Solution

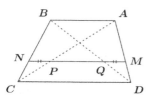

Let MN meet AC and BD at the points P and Q, respectively. Since $PM \parallel AB \parallel CD$, we have $PM \parallel CD$. Thus, $\dfrac{MA}{AD} = \dfrac{MP}{DC}$; that is,

$$DC \cdot MA = MP \cdot AD. \quad (1)$$

Since $MN \parallel AB$ and $MN \parallel DC$, we have

$$\frac{NP}{BA} = \frac{CP}{CA} = \frac{DM}{DA} = \frac{QM}{BA}.$$

Therefore,

$$NP = QM. \quad (2)$$

Since $\dfrac{QM}{BA} = \dfrac{DM}{DA}$, then

$$AB \cdot MD = QM \cdot AD.$$

Hence, using (2),

$$AB \cdot MD = NP \cdot AD. \quad (3)$$

From (1) and (3) it follows that

$$\begin{aligned}
DC \cdot MA + AB \cdot MD &= MP \cdot AD + NP \cdot AD \\
&= (MP + NP) \cdot AD = MN \cdot AD.
\end{aligned}$$

A sphere is inscribed in a given tetrahedron $ABCD$. Its four tangent planes, which are parallel to the faces of the tetrahedron, cut four smaller tetrahedra from the tetrahedron. Prove that the sum of lengths of all their 24 edges is equal to twice the sum of the lengths of the edges of the tetrahedron $ABCD$.

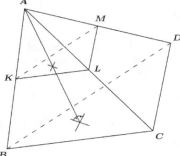

Solution

Denote by r the radius of the inscribed sphere and by U_A, U_B, U_C, U_D the four heights of the given tetrahedron, labelled according to the vertices from which they emanate. The smaller tetrahedron $AKLM$ (see figure) is homothetic (with centre A) to the whole tetrahedron $ABCD$. Thus, the ratio of the sum of the edge lengths of $AKLM$ to the sum of the edge lengths of $ABCD$ is the same as the ratio of their heights from the common vertex A. This ratio is $(U_A - 2r) : U_A$ (since $2r$ is the distance between the parallel planes KLM and BCD, both of which are tangent to the inscribed sphere). A similar argument applies to the other three small tetrahedra.

Our task is then to show that

$$\frac{U_A - 2r}{U_A} + \frac{U_B - 2r}{U_B} + \frac{U_C - 2r}{U_C} + \frac{U_D - 2r}{U_D} = 2 ,$$

or equivalently,

$$r \left(\frac{1}{U_A} + \frac{1}{U_B} + \frac{1}{U_C} + \frac{1}{U_D} \right) = 1 .$$

We prove this by an argument involving the volume V and surface area S of the tetrahedron $ABCD$. Let S_X denote the area of the face not containing the vertex X. Then $S = S_A + S_B + S_C + S_D$. Furthermore,

$$V = \tfrac{1}{3}S_A U_A = \tfrac{1}{3}S_B U_B = \tfrac{1}{3}S_C U_C = \tfrac{1}{3}S_D U_D ,$$

and $V = \tfrac{1}{3}rS$. Combining these formulas, we obtain

$$r \left(\frac{1}{U_A} + \frac{1}{U_B} + \frac{1}{U_C} + \frac{1}{U_D} \right) = \frac{3V}{S} \left(\frac{S_A}{3V} + \frac{S_B}{3V} + \frac{S_C}{3V} + \frac{S_D}{3V} \right) = 1 ,$$

which completes the proof.

In the exterior of a circle k a point A is given. Show that the diagonals of all trapezoids which are inscribed into the circle k and whose extended arms intersect at the point A intersect at the same point U.

Solution

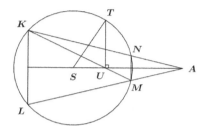

Let S be the centre of the circle k, and let $KLMN$ be an inscribed trapezoid whose extended arms KN and LM intersect at A (see figure). We use the axial symmetry of the trapezoid $KLMN$ with respect to the line AS to conclude that the intersection U of its diagonals must also lie on this line. Let T be one of the endpoints of the chord of the circle k which is perpendicular to SA and passes through U. The power of the point U with respect to the circle k is $|KU| \cdot |MU| = |TU|^2$. Considering the triangle KAM, in which AU bisects $\angle KAM$, we see that

$$|AU|^2 = |AK| \cdot |AM| - |KU| \cdot |MU| = |AK| \cdot |AN| - |TU|^2.$$

Hence,

$$|AK| \cdot |AN| = |AU|^2 + |TU|^2 = |AT|^2.$$

Since $|AK| \cdot |AN| = |AT|^2$, the point T is the point of tangency of one of the two tangents to k passing through the point A. These two tangents are independent of the choice of the trapezoid $KLMN$. Hence, the same is true for the point U.

Let us also remark that, by the Theorem of Euclid, the leg ST of the right triangle ATS satisfies $|ST|^2 = |SU| \cdot |SA|$, showing that U and A are images of each other in the inversion with respect to the circle k.

Let O be the centre of the circumcircle of the acute triangle ABC. The lines CO, AO, and BO intersect for the second time the circumcircles of the triangles AOB, BOC, and AOC at C_1, A_1, and B_1, respectively.

Prove that

$$\frac{AA_1}{OA_1} + \frac{BB_1}{OB_1} + \frac{CC_1}{OC_1} \geq 4.5 .$$

Solution

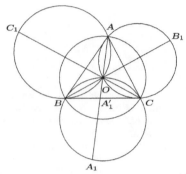

Let Γ be the circumcircle of $\triangle ABC$, and let R be its radius. Let f be the inversion in Γ. For any point P distinct from O, let $P' = f(P)$. Then $A' = A$, $B' = B$, and $C' = C$. The image of the circumcircle of $\triangle OBC$ is a line containing B' and C' and is therefore the line BC. Since the line through A, O, and A_1 is mapped onto itself by f, we deduce that A_1' is the intersection of this line with BC, and we have

$$OA_1 \cdot OA_1' = R^2 . \qquad (1)$$

For any points M and N distinct from O, it is well known that

$$M'N' = \frac{R^2 \cdot MN}{OM \cdot ON} .$$

Thus,

$$AA_1 = \frac{R^2 \cdot AA_1'}{OA \cdot OA_1'} ,$$

and hence, using (1),

$$\frac{AA_1}{OA_1} = \frac{R^2 \cdot AA_1'}{OA \cdot OA_1'} \cdot \frac{OA_1'}{R^2} = \frac{AA_1'}{OA} . \qquad (2)$$

Let I and J be the respective orthogonal projections of A and O onto the line BC. Let $x = [OBC]$ and $S = [ABC]$. From Thales' Theorem, we have

$$\frac{OA_1'}{AA_1'} = \frac{OJ}{AI} = \frac{x}{S} .$$

Since O is interior to $\triangle ABC$ (because $\triangle ABC$ is acute), it follows that $OA = AA'_1 - OA'_1$, and therefore

$$\frac{OA}{AA'_1} = 1 - \frac{OA'_1}{AA'_1} = \frac{S-x}{S}.$$

Then, using (2),

$$\frac{AA_1}{OA_1} = \frac{S}{S-x}.$$

Similarly,

$$\frac{BB_1}{OB_1} = \frac{S}{S-y} \quad \text{and} \quad \frac{CC_1}{OC_1} = \frac{S}{S-z},$$

where $y = [OAC]$ and $z = [OAB]$. Then

$$\frac{AA_1}{OA_1} + \frac{BB_1}{OB_1} + \frac{CC_1}{OC_1} = \frac{S}{S-x} + \frac{S}{S-y} + \frac{S}{S-z}. \tag{3}$$

We have x, y, $z > 0$ and $S = x + y + z$. From the Cauchy-Schwarz Inequality, we have

$$\left(\frac{S}{S-x} + \frac{S}{S-y} + \frac{S}{S-z} \right) \left((S-x) + (S-y) + (S-z) \right)$$

$$\geq \left(\sqrt{S} + \sqrt{S} + \sqrt{S} \right)^2 ;$$

that is, $2S \left(\dfrac{S}{S-x} + \dfrac{S}{S-y} + \dfrac{S}{S-z} \right) \geq 9S$. Thus,

$$\frac{S}{S-x} + \frac{S}{S-y} + \frac{S}{S-z} \geq \frac{9}{2}. \tag{4}$$

The result follows directly from (3) and (4). Note that equality occurs if and only if $\triangle ABC$ is equilateral.

Let the escribed circle (opposite $\angle A$) of the triangle ABC ($\angle A$, $\angle B$, $\angle C < 120°$) with centre O be tangent to the sides of the triangle AB, BC and CA at points C_1, A_1 and B_1 respectively. Denote the mid-points of the segments AO, BO, and CO by A_2, B_2, and C_2, respectively.

Prove that lines $A_1 A_2$, $B_1 B_2$, and $C_1 C_2$ intersect at the same point.

Solution

We will use areal coordinates. The following coordinates are known:

$$A: (1,0,0); \quad B: (0,1,0); \quad C: (0,0,1);$$

$$A_1: \frac{1}{2a}(0, a-b+c, a+b-c);$$

$$B_1: \frac{1}{2b}(b-c-a, 0, a+b+c);$$

$$C_1: \frac{1}{2c}(c-a-b, a+b+c, 0);$$

$$O: \frac{1}{b+c-a}(-a, b, c).$$

The coordinates of the mid-point of a line segment are the averages of the coordinates of the endpoints. Thus, the coordinates of A_2, B_2, and C_2 are:

$$A_2: \frac{1}{2(b+c-a)}(b+c-2a, b, c);$$

$$B_2: \frac{1}{2(b+c-a)}(-a, 2b+c-a, c);$$

$$C_2: \frac{1}{2(b+c-a)}(-a, b, 2c+b-a).$$

The equation of $A_1 A_2$ is

$$\det \begin{pmatrix} x & y & z \\ b+c-2a & b & c \\ 0 & a-b+c & a+b-c \end{pmatrix} = 0,$$

which, on expansion, becomes

$$x(b-c)(a+b+c) - y(b+c-2a)(a+b-c)$$
$$+ z(b+c-2a)(a-b+c) = 0.$$

Similarly, $B_1 B_2$ has the equation

$$x(a+b+c)(2b+c-a) + y(a+c)(a+b-c)$$
$$+ z(a-b+c)(2b+c-a) = 0,$$

and $C_1 C_2$ has the equation

$$x(a+b+c)(2c+b-a) + y(a+b-c)(2c+b-a)$$
$$+ z(a+b)(a-b+c) = 0.$$

The three lines meet at the point with unnormalized areal coordinates

$$x = \frac{(b+c)(2a-b-c)}{a+b+c},$$

$$y = \frac{(2b+c-a)(c-a)}{a+b-c},$$

$$z = \frac{(2c+b-a)(b-a)}{a-b+c}.$$

A set of $2n+1$ lines in a plane is drawn. No two of them are parallel, and no three pass through one point. Every three of these lines form a non-right triangle. Determine the maximal number of acute-angled triangles that can be formed.

Solution

Let $\ell_1, \ell_2, \ldots, \ell_{2n+1}$ be the lines, and let M_{ij} be the common point of ℓ_i and ℓ_j (for $i \neq j$). Consider that we are in the complex plane $(O, \overrightarrow{u}, \overrightarrow{v})$.

Let L be an arbitrary line, distinct from and not parallel to any of the ℓ_i's, and such that none of the M_{ij}'s belongs to L. Let α_i be the angle between the lines L and ℓ_i (mod π).

Then, the triangle formed by the lines ℓ_i, ℓ_j, ℓ_k is $M_{ij}M_{jk}M_{ki}$, and

$$2(\overrightarrow{M_{ij}M_{ik}}, \overrightarrow{M_{ij}M_{kj}}) \;=\; 2(L, \ell_i) + 2(\ell_j, L) \;=\; 2(\alpha_i - \alpha_j) \pmod{2\pi} \,.$$

Let P_i be the point on the unit circle Γ with center O such that

$$(\overrightarrow{u}, \overrightarrow{OP_i}) \;=\; 2\alpha_i \pmod{2\pi} \,.$$

Then, for i, j, k pairwise distinct, we have

$$\begin{aligned}
2(\overrightarrow{P_kP_j}, \overrightarrow{P_kP_i}) &= (\overrightarrow{OP_j}, \overrightarrow{OP_i}) = 2(\alpha_i - \alpha_j) \\
&= 2(\overrightarrow{M_{ij}M_{ik}}, \overrightarrow{M_{ij}M_{kj}}) \pmod{2\pi} \,.
\end{aligned}$$

Thus, $\angle P_iP_kP_j = \angle M_{ik}M_{ij}M_{kj}$. It follows that $\angle M_{ik}M_{ij}M_{kj}$ is acute if and only if $\angle P_iP_kP_j$ is acute, and $\angle M_{ik}M_{ij}M_{kj}$ is obtuse if and only if $\angle P_iP_kP_j$ is obtuse (since there is no right triangle).

Moreover, we note that if points P_1, P_2, $\ldots$, P_{2n+1} are given on Γ, then we may find some lines ℓ_1, ℓ_2, $\ldots$, ℓ_{2n+1} such that the construction above leads to the given P_i's.

Therefore, the problem is equivalent to finding the maximum number of acute triangles formed by the P_i's. That is, it is equivalent to finding the minimum number of obtuse triangles formed by these points. But the triangle $P_iP_kP_j$ is obtuse if and only if P_i, P_j, and P_k belong to one semicircle defined on Γ.

Let $i \in \{1, 2, \ldots, 2n+1\}$ be fixed. Suppose that there are d_i points on one side of the diameter with endpoint P_i. Then there are $2n - d_i$ points on the other side of it (since there is no right triangle). The number of obtuse triangles with vertex P_i and an acute angle at P_i is

$$\begin{aligned}
N_i &= \binom{d_i}{2} + \binom{2n - d_i}{2} = d_i^2 + 2n^2 - 2nd_i - n \\
&= (d_i - n)^2 + n^2 - n \geq n^2 - n \,,
\end{aligned}$$

with equality if and only if $d_i = n$.

Summing over i, we count each obtuse triangle exactly twice. Thus, the number of obtuse triangles is

Since there are exactly $\binom{2n+1}{3} = \dfrac{(2n+1)n(2n-1)}{3}$ triangles formed by the P_i's, it follows that the number of acute triangles is at most

$$\frac{(2n+1)n(2n-1)}{3} - \frac{(2n+1)n(n-1)}{2} = \frac{n(n+1)(2n+1)}{6}.$$

This value is achieved if, for example, we choose the P_i's as the vertices of a regular $(2n+1)$-gon inscribed in Γ.

Thus, the maximal number of acute triangles is $\dfrac{n(n+1)(2n+1)}{6}$.

12th Korean Mathematical Olympiad, 1999

Let R, r be the circumradius, and the inradius of $\triangle ABC$, respectively, and let R', r' be the circumradius and inradius of $\triangle A'B'C'$, respectively. Prove that if $\angle C = \angle C'$ and $Rr' = R'r$, then the two triangles are similar.

Solution

It is well known

$$\cos A + \cos B + \cos C \;=\; 1 + \frac{R}{r}\,.$$

Since $\dfrac{R}{r} = \dfrac{R'}{r'}$, we have

$$\cos A + \cos B + \cos C \;=\; \cos A' + \cos B' + \cos C'\,.$$

Since $C = C'$, we deduce that $\cos A + \cos B = \cos A' + \cos B'$; that is,

$$2\cos\left(\frac{A+B}{2}\right)\cos\left(\frac{A-B}{2}\right) \;=\; 2\cos\left(\frac{A'+B'}{2}\right)\cos\left(\frac{A'-B'}{2}\right)\,.$$

Now, note that $A + B = \pi - C = \pi - C' = A' + B'$. Thus,

$$\cos\left(\frac{A-B}{2}\right) \;=\; \cos\left(\frac{A'-B'}{2}\right)\,.$$

With no loss of generality, we may suppose that $A \geq B$ and $A' \geq B'$. Then $A - B = A' - B'$. Since we also have $A + B = A' + B'$, we deduce that $A = A'$ and $B = B'$. Then $\triangle ABC$ is similar to $\triangle A'B'C'$.

For every triangle ABC, denote by $D(ABC)$, the triangle whose vertices are the tangency points of the incircle of ABC (touching the sides of the triangle). The given triangle ABC is not equilateral.

(a) Prove that $D(ABC)$ is also not equilateral.

(b) Find in the sequence of triangles $T_1 = \triangle ABC$, $T_{k+1} = D(T_k)$, $k = 1, 2, \ldots$ a triangle whose largest angle α satisfies the inequality $0 < \alpha - 60° < 0.0001$.

Solution

(a) Let I be the incentre of $\triangle ABC$, and let D, E, F be the points of tangency of the incircle opposite A, B, C, respectively, as in the diagram below. Thus, $D(ABC) = \triangle DEF$.

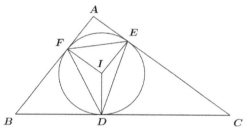

Since $\angle IFA = \angle IEA = 90°$, we have $\angle FIE = 180° - A = B + C$ and $\angle FDE = \frac{1}{2}\angle FIE = \frac{1}{2}(B + C)$. Similarly, $\angle DEF = \frac{1}{2}(A + C)$ and $\angle EFD = \frac{1}{2}(A + B)$.

If $\triangle DEF$ is equilateral, then $A + B = A + C = B + C = 120°$, from which it follows that $A = B = C = 60°$, and $\triangle ABC$ is equilateral. Hence, since $\triangle ABC$ is not equilateral, neither is $\triangle DEF$.

(b) For each $k = 1, 2, \ldots$, let the vertices of T_k be A_k, B_k, C_k, and let $\alpha_k = \angle A_k$, $\beta_k = \angle B_k$, and $\gamma_k = \angle C_k$. We may suppose, without loss of generality, that the vertices are labelled so that $\alpha_k \geq \beta_k \geq \gamma_k$. Then, from the proof of part (a), we see that

$$\alpha_{k+1} = \tfrac{1}{2}(\alpha_k + \beta_k), \qquad \beta_{k+1} = \tfrac{1}{2}(\alpha_k + \gamma_k), \qquad \gamma_{k+1} = \tfrac{1}{2}(\beta_k + \gamma_k),$$

for $k = 1, 2, \ldots$. By solving this system of difference equations, we obtain for $n = 0, 1, 2, \ldots,$

$$\alpha_{2n+1} = \frac{1}{3}\left(1 + \frac{1}{2^{2n-1}}\right)\alpha_1 + \frac{1}{3}\left(1 - \frac{1}{2^{2n}}\right)(\beta_1 + \gamma_1),$$

$$\beta_{2n+1} = \frac{1}{3}\left(1 + \frac{1}{2^{2n-1}}\right)\beta_1 + \frac{1}{3}\left(1 - \frac{1}{2^{2n}}\right)(\alpha_1 + \gamma_1),$$

$$\gamma_{2n+1} = \frac{1}{3}\left(1 + \frac{1}{2^{2n-1}}\right)\gamma_1 + \frac{1}{3}\left(1 - \frac{1}{2^{2n}}\right)(\alpha_1 + \beta_1).$$

We can then simplify the largest angle:

$$\begin{aligned}
\alpha_{2n+1} &= \frac{1}{3}\left(1+\frac{1}{2^{2n-1}}\right)\alpha_1 + \frac{1}{3}\left(1-\frac{1}{2^{2n}}\right)(180° - \alpha_1) \\
&= \left(1-\frac{1}{2^{2n}}\right)60° + \left(\frac{1}{2^{2n}}\right)\alpha_1 \\
&= 60° + \frac{1}{2^{2n}}(\alpha_1 - 60°).
\end{aligned}$$

Since $60° < \alpha_1 < 180°$, we have $60° < \alpha_{2n+1} < 60° + \frac{1}{2^{2n}}120°$. To obtain $0 < \alpha_{2n+1} - 60° < 0.0001$, it is sufficient to choose n so that $120/2^{2n} < 0.0001$; that is, $2^{2n} > 1200000$. The smallest such n is 11, since $2^{20} \approx 1024^2 \approx 1000000$. Hence, the largest angle of triangle T_{23} satisfies the given inequality.

Six points A, B, C, D, E, F are given in space. The quadrilaterals $ABDE$, $BCEF$, $CDFA$ are parallelograms. Prove that the six mid-points of the sides AB, BC, CD, DE, EF, FA are coplanar.

Solution

Let I, J, K, L, M, N be the mid-points of AB, BC, CD, DE, EF, FA, respectively, and let $\mathcal{P}$ and $\mathcal{Q}$ be the planes determined by M, N, I and J, K, L, respectively. We are required to prove that $\mathcal{P} = \mathcal{Q}$. It suffices to show that the lines IL and JM are both contained in $\mathcal{P}$ and $\mathcal{Q}$ and are concurrent.

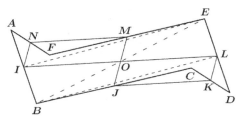

Let O be the mid-point of BE. Then, $IOMN$ is the Varignon Parallelogram of $ABEF$; hence, $O \in \mathcal{P}$. Similarly, $O \in \mathcal{Q}$ [using $JKLO$]. Since $\overrightarrow{IB} = \frac{1}{2}\overrightarrow{AB} = \frac{1}{2}\overrightarrow{ED} = \overrightarrow{EL}$, we see that $IBLE$ is a parallelogram, and therefore O is the mid-point of IL. Thus, the line IL is contained in $\mathcal{P}$ (since O and I are in $\mathcal{P}$) and in $\mathcal{Q}$ (since O and L are in $\mathcal{Q}$). In a similar way, we see that O is the mid-point of JM. It follows that JM is contained in both $\mathcal{P}$ and $\mathcal{Q}$. To complete the proof, we observe that IL and JM clearly concur at O.

The incircle of quadrilateral $ABCD$ touches the sides DA, AB, BC, CD in K, L, M, N, respectively. Let S_1, S_2, S_3, S_4 be the incircles of triangles AKL, BLM, CMN, DKN, respectively. Let l_1, l_2, l_3, l_4 be the common external tangents to the pairs S_1 and S_2, S_2 and S_3, S_3 and S_4, S_4 and S_1, different from the sides of quadrilateral $ABCD$. Prove that l_1, l_2, l_3, l_4 intersect in the vertices of a rhombus.

Solution

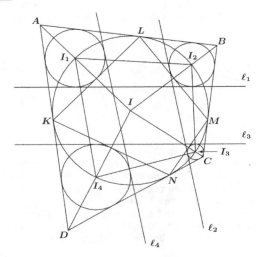

Let r be the radius of the incircle of quadrilateral $ABCD$. Let

$$\alpha = \tfrac{1}{2}\angle A, \quad \beta = \tfrac{1}{2}\angle B, \quad \gamma = \tfrac{1}{2}\angle C, \quad \delta = \tfrac{1}{2}\angle D.$$

Note that $\alpha + \beta + \gamma + \delta = 180°$.

Triangles AKI and ALI are congruent, since they are right-angled, with a common hypotenuse and $KI = LI = r$. Therefore, $AK = AL$ and $\angle IAK = \angle IAL = \alpha$. Since AI is the bisector of $\angle A$ in the isosceles triangle KAL, we have $AI \perp KL$. Then, since $\angle ALI = 90°$, we see that $\angle KLI = \angle IAL = \alpha$ (and also $\angle LKI = \alpha$). Hence, $KL = 2r\cos\alpha$.

Let I_1 be the point at which the incircle of $ABCD$ intersects the line segment AI, and let r_1 be the distance from I_1 to AL (which equals the distance from I_1 to AK). We claim that I_1 and r_1 are the centre and radius of S_1. To prove this, first note that $AI = AI_1 + r$, with $AI = r\csc\alpha$ and $AI_1 = r_1\csc\alpha$. Thus, we have $r\csc\alpha = r_1\csc\alpha + r$; that is,

$$r_1 = r(1 - \sin\alpha). \tag{1}$$

Since the distance from I to KL is $r \sin \angle KLI = r \sin \alpha$, the distance from I_1 to KL is $r - r \sin \alpha = r_1$. We conclude that the point I_1 is the same distance r_1 from each side of $\triangle AKL$, which proves the claim.

Similar considerations apply to the incircles S_2, S_3, and S_4. We denote their centres by I_2, I_3, and I_4, and their radii by r_2, r_3, and r_4, respectively.

Now consider $\triangle II_1I_2$. It is isosceles, with $II_1 = II_2 = r$. Since $\angle I_1II_2 = \angle AIB = 180° - \alpha - \beta$, we have

$$\angle II_1I_2 = \angle II_2I_1 = \tfrac{1}{2}(\alpha + \beta)\,, \tag{2}$$

and hence,

$$I_1I_2 = 2r \cos\left[\tfrac{1}{2}(\alpha + \beta)\right]\,. \tag{3}$$

Let θ be the angle between the lines I_1I_2 and ℓ_2 that contains the point I in its interior. We will prove that $\theta = \gamma + \tfrac{1}{2}(\alpha + \beta)$.

Case 1. $\beta < \gamma$ (or, equivalently, $r_2 > r_3$, as in the figure).

Then the lines BC and ℓ_2 meet on the extension of BC beyond C. Let the point where they meet be denoted by S, and let T be the point where ℓ_2 intersects I_1I_2. Thus, $\angle I_1TS = \theta$.

From (2), by symmetry, we have $\angle II_2I_3 = \tfrac{1}{2}(\beta + \gamma)$. This angle is exterior to $\triangle I_2BS$ opposite the interior angles $\angle I_2BS = \beta$ and $\angle I_2SB$. Therefore, $\angle I_2SB = \tfrac{1}{2}(\beta + \gamma) - \beta = \tfrac{1}{2}(\gamma - \beta)$. Since SI_2 bisects $\angle TSB$, we also have $\angle I_2ST = \tfrac{1}{2}(\gamma - \beta)$.

Now θ is an exterior angle of $\triangle TI_2S$ opposite the interior angles $\angle I_2ST = \tfrac{1}{2}(\gamma - \beta)$ and $\angle TI_2S = \tfrac{1}{2}(\alpha + \beta) + \tfrac{1}{2}(\beta + \gamma) = \beta + \tfrac{1}{2}(\alpha + \gamma)$. Therefore,

$$\theta = \beta + \tfrac{1}{2}(\alpha + \gamma) + \tfrac{1}{2}(\gamma - \beta) = \gamma + \tfrac{1}{2}(\alpha + \beta)\,.$$

Case 2. $\beta = \gamma$ (or, equivalently, $r_2 = r_3$).

Then the three lines BC, I_2I_3, and ℓ_2 are parallel. Hence,

$$\theta = \angle I_1I_2I_3 = \tfrac{1}{2}(\alpha+\beta)+\tfrac{1}{2}(\beta+\gamma) = \beta+\tfrac{1}{2}(\alpha+\gamma) = \gamma+\tfrac{1}{2}(\alpha+\beta)\,.$$

Case 3. $\beta > \gamma$ (or, equivalently, $r_2 < r_3$).

Then the lines BC and ℓ_2 meet on the extension of BC beyond B. The angle at which they meet is $\beta - \gamma$ (from Case 1, with β and γ interchanged). An argument similar to that of Case 1, leads to $\theta = \gamma + \tfrac{1}{2}(\alpha + \beta)$.

In all three cases,

$$\theta = \gamma + \tfrac{1}{2}(\alpha + \beta) = \gamma + \tfrac{1}{2}(180° - \gamma - \delta) = 90° + \tfrac{1}{2}(\gamma - \delta)\,.$$

By symmetry, the angle between I_1I_2 and ℓ_4 which contains I in its interior is $90° + \tfrac{1}{2}(\delta - \gamma)$. Since the sum of this angle and θ is $180°$, the lines ℓ_2 and ℓ_4 are parallel. Similarly, ℓ_1 and ℓ_3 are parallel. Thus, ℓ_1, ℓ_2, ℓ_3, ℓ_4 intersect in the vertices of a parallelogram.

Since θ is one of the two angles between $I_1 I_2$ and ℓ_2 (the other being $180° - \theta$), the perpendicular distance between the lines parallel to ℓ_2 that pass through I_1 and I_2 is $I_1 I_2 \sin \theta = I_1 I_2 \cos[\frac{1}{2}(\gamma - \delta)]$, where $I_1 I_2$ is given by (3). Therefore, the perpendicular distance between ℓ_2 and ℓ_4 is

$$
\begin{aligned}
2r \cos\left[\tfrac{1}{2}(\alpha + \beta)\right] &\cos\left[\tfrac{1}{2}(\gamma - \delta)\right] - r_1 - r_2 \\
&= r \cos\left[\tfrac{1}{2}(\alpha + \beta + \gamma - \delta)\right] + r \cos\left[\tfrac{1}{2}(\alpha + \beta - \gamma + \delta)\right] - r_1 - r_2 \\
&= r \cos\left[\tfrac{1}{2}(180° - 2\delta)\right] + r \cos\left[\tfrac{1}{2}(180° - 2\gamma)\right] - r_1 - r_2 \\
&= r \sin \delta + r \sin \gamma - r_1 - r_2 \\
&= (r - r_4) + (r - r_3) - r_1 - r_2 \;=\; 2r - (r_1 + r_2 + r_3 + r_4).
\end{aligned}
$$

This, by symmetry, is equal to the perpendicular distance between ℓ_1 and ℓ_3. Hence, ℓ_1, ℓ_2, ℓ_3, ℓ_4 intersect in the vertices of a rhombus.

The plane α passing through the vertex A of tetrahedron $ABCD$ is tangent to the circumsphere of the tetrahedron. Prove that the angles between the lines of intersection of α with the planes ABC, ACD, and ABD are equal if and only if $AB \cdot CD = AC \cdot BD = AD \cdot BC$.

Solution

Let K be the centre of the circumsphere of $ABCD$. Without loss of generality, assume that the radius of the sphere is 1. Take A to be the origin of vectors, and denote $\overrightarrow{AB}$, $\overrightarrow{AC}$, $\overrightarrow{AD}$, and $\overrightarrow{AK}$ by b, c, d, and k, respectively. Since $KB = 1$ and $|\mathbf{k}| = 1$, we have

$$1 \; = \; KB^2 \; = \; |\mathbf{k} - \mathbf{b}|^2 \; = \; 1 + |\mathbf{b}|^2 - 2(\mathbf{k} \cdot \mathbf{b}) \,.$$

Therefore, $|\mathbf{b}|^2 = 2(\mathbf{k} \cdot \mathbf{b})$. Similarly, $|\mathbf{c}|^2 = 2(\mathbf{k} \cdot \mathbf{c})$ and $|\mathbf{d}|^2 = 2(\mathbf{k} \cdot \mathbf{d})$.

A vector normal to the plane α at A is k, and a vector normal to the plane ABC is b $\times$ c. Hence, a vector along the line of intersection of α with the plane ABC is

$$\mathbf{k} \times (\mathbf{c} \times \mathbf{b}) \; = \; (\mathbf{k} \cdot \mathbf{b})\mathbf{c} - (\mathbf{k} \cdot \mathbf{c})\mathbf{b} \; = \; \tfrac{1}{2} \left(|\mathbf{b}|^2 \mathbf{c} - |\mathbf{c}|^2 \mathbf{b} \right) \,.$$

Similarly, a vector along the line of intersection of α with the plane ACD is $\tfrac{1}{2} \left(|\mathbf{c}|^2 \mathbf{d} - |\mathbf{d}|^2 \mathbf{c} \right)$, and a vector along the line of intersection of α with the plane ADB is $\tfrac{1}{2} \left(|\mathbf{d}|^2 \mathbf{b} - |\mathbf{b}|^2 \mathbf{d} \right)$.

Let h, i, j be scaled versions of these vectors as follows:

$$\begin{aligned}
\mathbf{h} &= |\mathbf{d}|^2 \left(|\mathbf{b}|^2 \mathbf{c} - |\mathbf{c}|^2 \mathbf{b} \right) \,, \\
\mathbf{i} &= |\mathbf{b}|^2 \left(|\mathbf{c}|^2 \mathbf{d} - |\mathbf{d}|^2 \mathbf{c} \right) \,, \\
\mathbf{j} &= |\mathbf{c}|^2 \left(|\mathbf{d}|^2 \mathbf{b} - |\mathbf{b}|^2 \mathbf{d} \right) \,.
\end{aligned}$$

Then h, i, j are coplanar, since they all lie in α. Also, we have $\mathbf{h} + \mathbf{i} + \mathbf{j} = 0$. We calculate

$$\begin{aligned}
|\mathbf{h}|^2 &= |\mathbf{d}|^4 \Big| |\mathbf{b}|^2 \mathbf{c} - |\mathbf{c}|^2 \mathbf{b} \Big|^2 \\
&= |\mathbf{d}|^4 \left(|\mathbf{b}|^4 |\mathbf{c}|^2 + |\mathbf{c}|^4 |\mathbf{b}|^2 - 2|\mathbf{b}|^2 |\mathbf{c}|^2 \mathbf{b} \cdot \mathbf{c} \right) \\
&= |\mathbf{d}|^4 |\mathbf{b}|^2 |\mathbf{c}|^2 \left(|\mathbf{b}|^2 + |\mathbf{c}|^2 - 2\mathbf{b} \cdot \mathbf{c} \right) \\
&= |\mathbf{d}|^4 |\mathbf{b}|^2 |\mathbf{c}|^2 |\mathbf{b} - \mathbf{c}|^2 \; = \; |\mathbf{b}|^2 |\mathbf{c}|^2 |\mathbf{d}|^2 (AD^2 BC^2) \,;
\end{aligned}$$

that is, $|\mathbf{h}| = |\mathbf{b}||\mathbf{c}||\mathbf{d}|(AD \cdot BC)$. Similarly, $|\mathbf{i}| = |\mathbf{b}||\mathbf{c}||\mathbf{d}|(AB \cdot CD)$ and $|\mathbf{j}| = |\mathbf{b}||\mathbf{c}||\mathbf{d}|(AC \cdot BD)$.

Now we apply the known result that three coplanar vectors h, i, j such that $\mathbf{h} + \mathbf{i} + \mathbf{j} = 0$ make angles of $120°$ with one another if and only if $|\mathbf{h}| = |\mathbf{i}| = |\mathbf{j}|$. (One interpretation of this is that three coplanar forces with resultant zero are equally inclined to each other if and only if they are of equal magnitude.) We conclude that our particular vectors h, i, j make angles of $120°$ with one another if and only if $AD \cdot BC = AB \cdot CD = AC \cdot BD$, which is the required condition.

Suppose that $n(r)$ denotes the number of points with integer coordinates on a circle of radius $r > 1$. Prove that,

$$n(r) < 6\sqrt[3]{\pi r^2} \, .$$

Solution

If $n \leq 8$, then, since $r > 1$ and $6\sqrt[3]{\pi} > 8$, we have $n < 6\sqrt[3]{\pi r^2}$, as required. Now suppose that for some $r > 1$ we have $n > 8$. Let the points with integer coordinates that lie on the circle be $P_1, P_2, \ldots, P_n$, in counterclockwise order. Since $\overparen{P_1 P_3} + \overparen{P_2 P_4} + \cdots + \overparen{P_n P_2} = 4\pi$, one of the arcs $\overparen{P_i P_{i+2}}$ is at most $4\pi/n$. The triangle $P_i P_{i+1} P_{i+2}$ is inscribed in an arc of angle at most $4\pi/n$.

To simplify the notation, write A, B, C in place of P_i, P_{i+1}, P_{i+2}, respectively. Let $\theta = \overparen{AC}$ and $t = \overparen{AB}$. Then $0 < t < \theta \leq 4\pi/n$, and

$$
\begin{aligned}
[ABC] = \frac{abc}{4r} &= \frac{\left(2r \sin \frac{t}{2}\right)\left(2r \sin \frac{\theta}{2}\right)\left(2r \sin \frac{\theta-t}{2}\right)}{4r} \\
&\leq 2r^2 \left(\frac{t}{2}\right)\left(\frac{\theta}{2}\right)\left(\frac{\theta-t}{2}\right) = \frac{r^2 \theta t (\theta - t)}{4} \\
&\leq \frac{r^2 \theta \left(\frac{\theta}{2}\right)^2}{4} = \frac{r^2 \theta^3}{16} \leq \frac{r^2 \left(\frac{4\pi}{n}\right)^3}{16} = \frac{4r^2 \pi^3}{n^3} \, .
\end{aligned}
$$

Thanks to Pick's Theorem, we know that $[ABC] \geq \frac{1}{2}$. Therefore,

$$\frac{1}{2} \leq \frac{4r^2 \pi^3}{n^3} \, ,$$

$$n \leq \sqrt[3]{8r^2 \pi^3} = 2\pi \sqrt[3]{r^2} < 6\sqrt[3]{\pi r^2} \, .$$

Suppose that $ABCDEF$ is a convex hexagon with $AB = BC$, $CD = DE$, and $EF = FA$. Prove that

$$\frac{BC}{BE} + \frac{DE}{DA} + \frac{FA}{FC} \geq \frac{3}{2}.$$

Solution

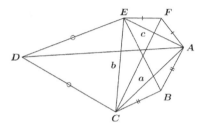

We put $AC = a$, $CE = b$, and $AE = c$. By the well-known generalization of Ptolemy's Theorem for quadrilateral $ABCE$, we have

$$AC \cdot BE \leq AB \cdot CE + BC \cdot AE = BC(CE + AE);$$

that is, $a \cdot BE \leq BC(b + c)$. Hence,

$$\frac{BC}{BE} \geq \frac{a}{b + c}.$$

Similarly,

$$\frac{DE}{DA} \geq \frac{b}{c + a} \quad \text{and} \quad \frac{FA}{FC} \geq \frac{c}{a + b}.$$

Thus,

$$\frac{BC}{BE} + \frac{DE}{DA} + \frac{FA}{FC} \geq \frac{a}{b + c} + \frac{b}{c + a} + \frac{c}{a + b}. \tag{1}$$

By the AM–GM Inequality, we have

$$\left(\frac{1}{b + c} + \frac{1}{c + a} + \frac{1}{a + b}\right) \geq 3\sqrt[3]{\frac{1}{b + c} \cdot \frac{1}{c + a} \cdot \frac{1}{a + b}} \tag{2}$$

and

$$(b + c) + (c + a) + (a + b) \geq 3\sqrt[3]{(b + c)(c + a)(a + b)};$$

that is,

$$a + b + c \geq \frac{3}{2}\sqrt[3]{(b + c)(c + a)(a + b)}; \tag{3}$$

Multiplying (2) by (3), we get

$$\frac{a+b+c}{b+c} + \frac{a+b+c}{c+a} + \frac{a+b+c}{a+b} \geq \frac{9}{2},$$

which simplifies to

$$\frac{a}{b+c} + \frac{b}{c+a} + \frac{c}{a+b} \geq \frac{3}{2}. \tag{4}$$

Finally, from (1) and (4),

$$\frac{BC}{BE} + \frac{DE}{DA} + \frac{FA}{FC} \geq \frac{3}{2}.$$

In triangle ABC, the angle bisector of $\angle BAC$ meets BC at point D. Suppose that Γ is the circle which is tangent to BC at D and passes through the point A. Let M be the second point of intersection of Γ and AC and BM meets the circle at P. Prove that AP is a median of triangle ABD.

Solution

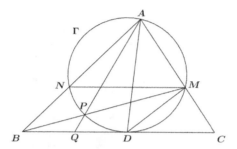

Let N be the second point of intersection of Γ and AB, and let AP meet BC at Q. Recalling that the angle between a tangent and a chord is equal to the angle subtended by the chord at a point on the circumference on the opposite side of the chord, we get $\angle MDC = \angle CAD = \frac{1}{2}\angle A$. Then

$$\begin{aligned}
\angle ADM &= \angle ADC - \angle MDC \\
&= (180° - \angle CAD - \angle DCA) - \angle MDC \\
&= (180° - \tfrac{1}{2}\angle A - \angle C) - \tfrac{1}{2}\angle A \\
&= 180° - \angle A - \angle C = \angle B .
\end{aligned}$$

Also, $\angle ADM = \angle ANM$, since these angles are subtended by the same arc of Γ. Thus, $\angle ANM = \angle B$ (which shows that NM is parallel to BC). Hence, $\angle QPB = \angle APM = \angle ANM = \angle B$. Since we also have $\angle BQP = \angle BQA$, the triangles BPQ and ABQ are similar. Then, from the proportional sides, we get

$$\frac{BQ}{QA} = \frac{QP}{BQ},$$

giving $BQ^2 = QP \cdot QA$. We also have $QP \cdot QA = QD^2$ (the power of the point Q with respect to Γ). Hence $BQ = QD$, establishing AP as a median of $\triangle ABD$.

Suppose that ABC is a triangle. If we paint the points of the plane in red and green, prove that either there exist two red points which are one unit apart or three green points forming a triangle equal to ABC.

Solution

With no loss of generality, we may suppose that there exists at least one red point (if not, the conclusion holds trivially) and that the sides of ABC have lengths a, b, c with $a \leq b$ and $a \leq c$.

Assume, for the purpose of contradiction, that there exist neither two red points which are one unit apart nor three green points forming a triangle equal to ABC.

Suppose that there are two red points M and N such that $MN = a$. Let P be such that triangle PMN is equal to triangle ABC. Let Γ_P, Γ_M, and Γ_N be the circles of radius 1 centred at P, M, and N, respectively. Then Γ_M and Γ_N are entirely green. If Γ_P is entirely red, then, since Γ_P has radius 1, there are two red points on Γ_P which are one unit apart—a contradiction. Therefore, there must be a green point on Γ_P, say X. From M and N, using the translation with vector $\overrightarrow{PX}$, we construct green points Y on Γ_M and Z on Γ_N such that XYZ is a green triangle equal to ABC, giving a contradiction.

Thus, there do not exist red points M and N such that $MN = a$.

Now, let Ω be a red point, and let C_Ω be the circle with radius a and centre Ω. From above, C_Ω is entirely green. Let $U \in C_\Omega$. Let $V \in C_\Omega$ be a point such that $UV = a$. (Thus, $\angle U\Omega V = \frac{\pi}{3}$ (mod 2π).) Since U and V both lie on C_Ω, they are both green. Since $a = \min\{a, b, c\}$, there exists a point T outside C_Ω such that the triangle TUV is equal to ABC. Clearly, T must be red (if not, we would have a green triangle equal to ABC).

When we rotate U on C_Ω the set of corresponding points T is a circle Γ with centre Ω and radius $r > a$. Since Γ is entirely red, we may find two red points on it, say M and N, such that $MN = a$, a final contradiction.

Suppose that $C_1, \ldots, C_n$ are circles of radius one in the plane such that no two of them are tangent, and the subset of the plane, formed by the union of these circles, is connected. If $S = \{C_i \cap C_j \mid 1 \le i < j \le n\}$, prove that $|S| \ge n$.

Solution

For each i, denote by $n(C_i)$ the number of elements of S which belong to C_i. Since the union of the circles is connected, we have $n(C_i) > 0$. For each $M \in S$, denote by $n(M)$ the number of circles C_i which contain M. Thus, $n(M) \ge 2$.

Let $M \in S$, and let C_i be any of the given unit circles such that $M \in C_i$. Since there is no tangency, each of the $n(M) - 1$ other circles which contain M must intersect C_i in another point. These points are pairwise distinct, because, for any two given points of the plane, there are at most two unit circles which contain the two of them. Thus, in addition to M, the circle C_i contains at least $n(M) - 1$ other elements of S. It follows that, for each $M \in S$ and each circle C_i such that $M \in C_i$, we have $n(M) \le n(C_i)$.

Let $N = \sum\limits_{(M, C_i)} \dfrac{1}{n(C_i)}$, where the sum is for the pairs (M, C_i) such that C_i is one of the given unit circles and $M \in S \cap C_i$. We have

$$N = \sum_{C_i} \left(\sum_{M \in C_i \cap S} \frac{1}{n(C_i)} \right) = \sum_{C_i} n(C_i) \frac{1}{n(C_i)} = n.$$

On the other hand, since $n(M) \le n(C_i)$, we have

$$N \le \sum_{(M, C_i)} \frac{1}{n(M)} = \sum_{M \in S} \left(\sum_{C_i : M \in C_i} \frac{1}{n(M)} \right)$$

$$= \sum_{M \in S} n(M) \frac{1}{n(M)} = \sum_{M \in S} 1 = |S|.$$

Thus, $|S| \ge n$.

Suppose that $ABCDEF$ is a convex hexagon with $\angle B + \angle D + \angle F = 360°$ and

$$\frac{AB}{BC} \cdot \frac{CD}{DE} \cdot \frac{EF}{FA} = 1.$$

Prove that

$$\frac{BC}{CA} \cdot \frac{AE}{EF} \cdot \frac{FD}{DB} = 1.$$

Solution

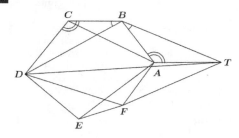

Since $\angle B + \angle D + \angle F = 360°$, we get

$$\angle A + \angle C + \angle E = 360°. \tag{1}$$

We construct $\triangle BAT$ directly similar to $\triangle BCD$, as shown in the figure. Then $\angle CBA = \angle DBT$ and $BC/AB = DB/BT$. Therefore, $\triangle BCA \sim \triangle BDT$. Hence,

$$\frac{BC}{CA} = \frac{BD}{DT}. \tag{2}$$

Since $\triangle BCD \sim \triangle BAT$, we have

$$\frac{AB}{BC} = \frac{AT}{CD}. \tag{3}$$

Since $\frac{AB}{BC} \cdot \frac{CD}{DE} \cdot \frac{EF}{FA} = 1$, from (3) we see that $\frac{AT}{CD} \cdot \frac{CD}{DE} \cdot \frac{EF}{FA} = 1$; that is,

$$\frac{FA}{AT} = \frac{EF}{DE}. \tag{4}$$

From (1), we have $\angle BCD + \angle BAF + \angle FED = 360°$. Since $\angle BAT + \angle BAF + \angle FAT = 360°$, we find that $\angle FAT = \angle FED$. This together with (4) implies that $\triangle FAT \sim \triangle FED$. Then $\triangle FAE \sim \triangle FTD$, which implies that

$$\frac{AE}{EF} = \frac{TD}{DF}. \tag{5}$$

From (2) and (5) we obtain

$$\frac{BC}{CA} \cdot \frac{AE}{EF} = \frac{BD}{DT} \cdot \frac{TD}{DF} = \frac{BD}{DF},$$

and hence,

$$\frac{BC}{CA} \cdot \frac{AE}{EF} \cdot \frac{FD}{DB} = 1.$$

In acute triangle $\triangle ABC$, $\angle ACB > \angle ABC$. Point D is on BC such that $\angle ADB$ is obtuse. Let H be the orthocentre of $\triangle ABD$. Suppose point F is inside $\triangle ABC$ and on the circumcircle of $\triangle ABD$. Prove that point F is the orthocentre of $\triangle ABC$ if and only if HD is parallel to CF and H is on the circumcircle of $\triangle ABC$.

Solution

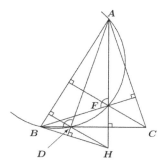

Figure 1

First let us suppose that F is the orthocentre of $\triangle ABC$ (see Figure 1). Then $CF \perp AB$. As H is the orthocentre of $\triangle ABD$, we have $HD \perp AB$. Thus, $HD \parallel CF$.

Since A, B, D, and F are concyclic,

$$\angle AFB = \angle ADB. \tag{1}$$

As F and H are orthocentres of $\triangle ABC$ and $\triangle ABD$, respectively, we have $AF \perp BC$, $BF \perp AC$, $AD \perp BH$, and $BD \perp AH$. It follows that $\angle AFB + \angle ACB = 180°$ and $\angle ADB + \angle AHB = 180°$. Then, using (1), $\angle ACB = \angle AHB$. Therefore A, B, C, and H are concyclic.

Now we consider the converse (see Figure 2). Assume that $HD \parallel CF$ and that A, B, C, and H are concyclic. Since A, B, D, and F are concyclic, $\angle AFB = \angle ADB$. Since A, B, C, and H are concyclic, $\angle ACB = \angle AHB$. As H is the orthocentre of $\triangle ABD$, we have $\angle ADB + \angle AHB = 180°$. Thus, $\angle AFB + \angle ACB = 180°$.

Let G be the reflection of F through AB. Then $\angle AGB = \angle AFB$ and $\angle ABG = \angle ABF$. Thus,

$$\angle AGB + \angle ACB = \angle AFB + \angle ACB = 180°.$$

Hence, A, G, B, and C are concyclic.

Since $CF \parallel HD$ and $HD \perp AB$, we have $CF \perp AB$. Then, since $FG \perp AB$, the points C, F, and G must be collinear. Hence,

$$\angle ACF = \angle ACG = \angle ABG = \angle ABF.$$

Since $CF \perp AB$, we have $\angle ACF + \angle BAC = 90°$, which gives us $\angle ABF + \angle BAC = 90°$. Then $BF \perp AC$. Thus, F is the orthocentre of $\triangle ABC$.

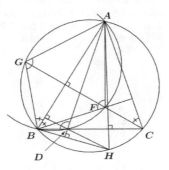

Figure 2

Let A', B', C' be the respective mid-points of the arcs BC, CA, AB, not containing points A, B, C, respectively, of the circumcircle of the triangle ABC. The sides BC, CA, and AB intersect the pairs of segments $(C'A', A'B')$, $(A'B', B'C')$, and $(B'C', C'A')$ at the pairs of points (M, N), (P, Q), and (R, S), respectively. Prove that $MN = PQ = RS$ if and only if the triangle ABC is equilateral.

Solution

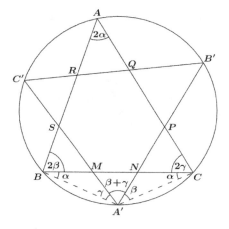

We put $\angle BAC = 2\alpha$, $\angle ABC = 2\beta$, and $\angle ACB = 2\gamma$. Then $\alpha + \beta + \gamma = \frac{\pi}{2}$. Since A' is the mid-point of the arc BC, we have

$$\angle A'AB = \angle A'CB = \angle A'BC = \angle A'AC = \alpha.$$

Also, $\angle B'A'C = \angle B'BC = \beta$ and $\angle BA'C' = \angle BCC' = \gamma$. Hence,

$$\angle A'NM = \angle A'CB + \angle B'A'C = \alpha + \beta,$$

and

$$\angle A'MN = \angle A'BC + \angle BA'C' = \alpha + \gamma.$$

Then

$$\begin{aligned}
\angle MA'N &= 180° - \angle A'NM - \angle A'MN \\
&= 180° - (2\alpha + \beta + \gamma) = \beta + \gamma.
\end{aligned}$$

Let R be the circumradius of $\triangle ABC$. Then

$$BA' = 2R\sin \angle A'CB = 2R\sin\alpha. \tag{1}$$

Applying the Law of Sines to $\triangle A'BM$ and $\triangle A'MN$, we get

$$\frac{MA'}{BA'} = \frac{\sin \angle A'BM}{\sin \angle A'MB} = \frac{\sin \alpha}{\sin(\pi - \alpha - \gamma)} = \frac{\sin \alpha}{\sin(\alpha + \gamma)} = \frac{\sin \alpha}{\cos \beta},$$

and

$$\frac{MN}{MA'} = \frac{\sin \angle MA'N}{\sin \angle A'NM} = \frac{\sin(\beta + \gamma)}{\sin(\alpha + \beta)} = \frac{\cos \alpha}{\cos \gamma}.$$

Hence,

$$\frac{MN}{BA'} = \frac{MN}{MA'} \cdot \frac{MA'}{BA'} = \frac{\cos \alpha}{\cos \gamma} \cdot \frac{\sin \alpha}{\cos \beta}. \qquad (2)$$

It follows from (1) and (2) that

$$MN = \frac{\sin \alpha \cos \alpha}{\cos \beta \cos \gamma} \cdot BA' = 2R\frac{\sin^2 \alpha \cos \alpha}{\cos \beta \cos \gamma} = \frac{R(\sin 2\alpha)^2}{2\cos \alpha \cos \beta \cos \gamma}.$$

Similarly, we have

$$PQ = \frac{R(\sin 2\beta)^2}{2\cos \alpha \cos \beta \cos \gamma} \quad \text{and} \quad RS = \frac{R(\sin 2\gamma)^2}{2\cos \alpha \cos \beta \cos \gamma}.$$

Thus, $MN = PQ = RS$ if and only if $(\sin 2\alpha)^2 = (\sin 2\beta)^2 = (\sin 2\gamma)^2$, which is true if and only if $\sin 2\alpha = \sin 2\beta = \sin 2\gamma$. This is equivalent to $\alpha = \beta = \gamma$, which means that $\triangle ABC$ is equilateral.

In three-dimensional space, let Ox, Oy, Oz, Ot be four non-planar distinct rays such that the angles between any two of them have the same measure.

(a) Determine this common measure.

(b) Let Or be another ray different from the above four rays. Let α, β, γ, δ be the angles formed by Or with Ox, Oy, Oz, Ot, respectively. Put

$$p = \cos\alpha + \cos\beta + \cos\gamma + \cos\delta,$$

$$q = \cos^2\alpha + \cos^2\beta + \cos^2\gamma + \cos^2\delta.$$

Prove that p and q are invariant when Or rotates about the point O.

Solution

Let $XYZT$ be a regular tetrahedron with centre O and circumradius 1. Let the four unit vectors from O to X, Y, Z, and T be denoted by x, y, z, and t, respectively. These four vectors make equal angles with each other. Also, $x + y + z + t = 0$, since O is the centroid. Expanding $|x + y + z + t|^2 = 0$, we get $4 + 12\cos\theta = 0$, or $\theta = \cos^{-1}(-1/3)$, where θ is the angle between any two of the vectors.

(b) Let v be the vector of the form $c_0 x + c_1 y + c_2 z + c_3 t$ such that v is parallel to the ray Or and $\sum_{k=0}^{3} c_k = 1$. It will suffice to show that p and q are independent of c_0, c_1, c_2, and c_3. We have

$$\cos\alpha = x \cdot \frac{v}{|v|} = \frac{c_0 - \frac{1}{3}(c_1 + c_2 + c_3)}{|v|} = \frac{4c_0 - 1}{3|v|},$$

with similar expressions for $\cos\beta$, $\cos\gamma$, and $\cos\delta$. Also,

$$|v|^2 = \sum_{k=0}^{3} c_k^2 - \frac{2}{3} \sum_{i<j} c_i c_j$$

$$= \sum_{k=0}^{3} c_k^2 - \frac{1}{3}\left(1 - \sum_{k=0}^{3} c_k^2\right) = \frac{1}{3}\left(4\sum_{k=0}^{3} c_k^2 - 1\right).$$

Hence, $p = \dfrac{1}{3|v|} \sum_{k=0}^{3}(4c_k - 1) = 0$, and

$$q = \frac{1}{9|v|^2} \sum_{k=0}^{3}(4c_k - 1)^2 = \frac{1}{9|v|^2}\left(16\sum_{k=0}^{3} c_k^2 - 8\sum_{k=0}^{3} c_k + 4\right)$$

$$= \frac{4}{9|v|^2}\left(4\sum_{k=0}^{3} c_k^2 - 1\right) = \frac{4}{3}.$$

These results generalize to E^n, where we have $n+1$ concurrent rays such that the angle between any two of them has the same measure. We start with $n+1$ unit vectors, $x_0, x_1, \ldots, x_n$, from the centroid to the vertices of a regular simplex $X_0 X_1 \cdots X_n$. Expanding $|x_0 + x_1 + \cdots + x_n|^2 = 0$ gives

$$n + 1 + 2 \binom{n+1}{2} \cos\theta = 0,$$

which yields $\cos\theta = -1/n$, or $\theta = \cos^{-1}(-1/n)$.

Next, let $v = c_0 x_0 + c_1 x_1 + \cdots + c_n x_n$ such that the angle between v and x_k is α_k and $\sum_{k=0}^{n} c_k = 1$. Then

$$\cos\alpha_k = x_k \cdot \frac{v}{|v|} = \frac{(n+1)c_k - 1}{n|v|} \quad \text{and} \quad n|v|^2 = (n+1) \sum_{k=0}^{n} c_k^2 - 1.$$

Hence, $\sum_{k=0}^{n} \cos\alpha_k = 0$ and

$$\sum_{k=0}^{n} \cos^2 \alpha_k = \frac{(n+1)\left((n+1)\sum_{k=0}^{n} c_k^2 - 1\right)}{n^2 |v|^2} = \frac{n+1}{n}.$$

Let ABC be a triangle inscribed in the circle $\mathcal{O}$. Locate the position of the points P, not lying in the circle $\mathcal{O}$, of the plane (ABC) with the property that the lines PA, PB, PC intersect the circle $\mathcal{O}$ again at points A', B', C' such that $A'B'C'$ is a right-angled isosceles triangle with $\angle A'B'C' = 90°$.

Solution

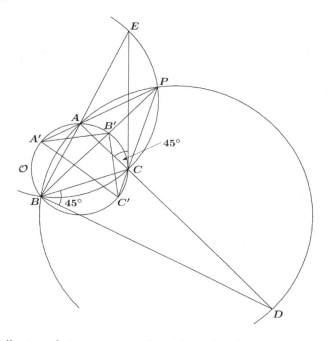

In the following solution we assume that $\angle A > 45°$ and $\angle C > 45°$. But the following construction and proof work in other cases with minor changes.

Let D be the point on AC produced beyond C such that $\angle CBD = 45°$, and let E be the point on AB produced beyond A such that $\angle ACE = 45°$. Let P be the intersection of the circumcircles of $\triangle ABD$ and $\triangle BCE$ other than B.

Claim. Then P is the point we are looking for.

Proof. Let A', B', and C' be the points of intersection of PA, PB, and PC with circle O other than A, B, and C. Then

$$\angle B'A'C' = \angle B'CP = \angle BB'C - \angle BPC$$
$$= \angle BAC - \angle BEC = \angle ACE = 45°,$$

and $\quad \angle B'C'A' = \angle B'AP = \angle AB'B - \angle APB$
$$= \angle ACB - \angle ADB = \angle CBD = 45°.$$

Hence, $\triangle A'B'C'$ is a right-angled isosceles triangle with $\angle A'B'C' = 90°$.

The base side and the altitude of a regular hexagonal prism $ABCDEF$, $A'B'C'D'E'F'$ are equal to a and h, respectively. Prove that six planes $(AB'F)$, $(CD'B)$, $(EF'D)$, $(D'EC)$, $(F'AE)$ and $(B'CA)$ are tangent to the same sphere. Determine the centre and the radius of this sphere.

Solution

First, note the misprint in the question: the second of the six planes should be $(CD'B)$, not $(CD'B')$. [*Ed.* This has been corrected already in the problem statement above.]

We introduce rectangular coordinates (x, y, z) such that the hexagons $ABCDEF$ and $A'B'C'D'E'F'$ lie in the planes $z = 0$ and $z = h$, respectively, and the coordinates of A, B, C, D, E, F are as follows:

$$A = a\left(-\frac{1}{2}, \frac{\sqrt{3}}{2}, 0\right), \quad B = a\left(\frac{1}{2}, \frac{\sqrt{3}}{2}, 0\right), \quad C = a(1, 0, 0),$$

$$D = a\left(\frac{1}{2}, -\frac{\sqrt{3}}{2}, 0\right), \quad E = a\left(-\frac{1}{2}, -\frac{\sqrt{3}}{2}, 0\right), \quad F = a(-1, 0, 0).$$

(The coordinates of A', B', C', D', E', F' are the same except that their z-coordinates have the value h instead of 0.)

Note that the three planes $(AB'F)$, $(CD'B)$, and $(EF'D)$ are placed symmetrically around the prism under a rotation of $120°$, as are the three planes $(D'EC)$, $(F'AE)$, and $(B'CA)$. Therefore, if there is a sphere with centre on the z-axis which is tangent to the planes $(AB'F)$ and $(D'EC)$, then this sphere will be tangent to all six planes.

The planes $(AB'F)$ and $(D'EC)$ have the respective equations

$$\frac{x}{a} - \frac{1}{\sqrt{3}}\frac{y}{a} - \frac{z}{h} + 1 = 0 \quad \text{and} \quad \frac{x}{a} - \sqrt{3}\frac{y}{a} - \frac{z}{h} - 1 = 0.$$

We now look for a point $(0, 0, k)$ which is the same distance r from these two planes. This condition gives us

$$r = \frac{a}{\mu}\left|1 - \frac{k}{h}\right| = \frac{a}{\nu}\left|1 + \frac{k}{h}\right|,$$

where

$$\mu = \sqrt{\frac{4}{3} + \left(\frac{a}{h}\right)^2} \quad \text{and} \quad \nu = \sqrt{4 + \left(\frac{a}{h}\right)^2}.$$

Solving for k, we obtain two solutions, with corresponding values for r:

$$k = \left(\frac{\nu - \mu}{\nu + \mu}\right)h = \frac{3}{8}(\nu - \mu)^2 h, \qquad r = \frac{3}{4}a(\nu - \mu);$$

$$k = \left(\frac{\nu + \mu}{\nu - \mu}\right)h = \frac{3}{8}(\nu + \mu)^2 h, \qquad r = \frac{3}{4}a(\nu + \mu).$$

We have found *two* spheres that meet the requirements in the problem. Their centres are on the axis of symmetry of the prism at $(0, 0, k)$, where the two values of k and the corresponding values of the radius r are given by the equations above.

Given an acute-angled triangle ABC, let D be the mid-point of the arc BC of the circumcircle of ABC not containing A. The points which are symmetric to D with respect to the line BC and the centre of the circumcircle are denoted by E and F, respectively. Finally, let K stand for the mid-point of $[EA]$. Prove that:

(a) the circle passing through the mid-points of the edges of the triangle ABC, also passes through K;

(b) the line passing through K and the mid-point of $[BC]$ is perpendicular to AF.

Solution

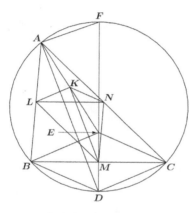

(a) Letting L, M, and N be the mid-points of AB, BC, and CA, respectively, we have $LM \parallel AC$ and $MN \parallel AB$. Thus,

$$\angle LMN = \angle LAN = \angle BAC.$$

Since K is the mid-point of AE, we see that $LK \parallel BE$ and $KN \parallel EC$. Thus, $\angle LKN = \angle BEC$. Since E is the reflection of D with respect to BC, we have $\angle BEC = \angle BDC$, and then $\angle LKN = \angle BDC$. Hence,

$$\angle LKN + \angle LMN = \angle BDC + \angle BAC = 180°.$$

Therefore, L, M, N, and K are concyclic.

(b) Since D is the mid-point of the arc BC, we have $BD = DC$. Thus, $BDCE$ is a rhombus, and M is the mid-point of DE. Since K and M are mid-points of AE and DE, respectively, we get $KM \parallel AD$.

Since F is symmetric to D with respect to the centre of the circumcircle of $\triangle ABC$, we see that DF is a diameter of this circle. Thus, $\angle DAF = 90°$; that is, $AD \perp AF$. Since $KM \parallel AD$, we obtain $KM \perp AF$.

Let ABC be an acute-angled triangle; M, N and P are the feet of the perpendiculars from the centroid G of the triangle upon its sides AB, BC and CA respectively. Prove that

$$\frac{4}{27} < \frac{\text{area}(MNP)}{\text{area}(ABC)} \le \frac{1}{4}.$$

Solution

As usual, let $a = BC$, $b = CA$, and $c = AB$, and let $[XYZ]$ denote the area of $\triangle XYZ$. Let $\rho = \frac{[MNP]}{[ABC]}$. We will prove that $\frac{2}{9} < \rho \le \frac{1}{4}$, which is slightly stronger than requested.

First recall that $[GBC] = [GAC] = [GAB] = \frac{1}{3}[ABC]$. This follows at once be remarking that, for instance, GN is a third of the altitude from A in $\triangle ABC$. Now, since $\angle MGN = 180° - \angle B$,

$$
\begin{aligned}
2[GMN] &= GM \cdot GN \cdot \sin B \\
&= \frac{2[GAB]}{c} \cdot \frac{2[GBC]}{a} \sin B = \frac{4}{9} \frac{[ABC]^2}{ac} \sin B \, .
\end{aligned}
$$

Similar results hold for $[GNP]$ and $[GMP]$. Thus,

$$[MNP] = \frac{2[ABC]^2}{9} \left(\frac{\sin A}{bc} + \frac{\sin B}{ca} + \frac{\sin C}{ab} \right) .$$

Since $[ABC] = \frac{1}{2}ab\sin C = \frac{1}{2}bc\sin A = \frac{1}{2}ca\sin B$, it follows that

$$\rho = \tfrac{1}{9}(\sin^2 A + \sin^2 B + \sin^2 C) \, .$$

By the usual trigonometric formulas, we get

$$
\begin{aligned}
\sin^2 A + \sin^2 B + \sin^2 C &= \tfrac{3}{2} - \tfrac{1}{2}(\cos 2A + \cos 2B + \cos 2C) \\
&= 2(1 + \cos A \cos B \cos C) \, .
\end{aligned}
$$

Since $\triangle ABC$ is acute-angled, $\cos A \cos B \cos C > 0$, and hence $\rho > \frac{2}{9}$. Furthermore, by the Law of Cosines,

$$\cos A \cos B \cos C = \frac{(b^2 + c^2 - a^2)(c^2 + a^2 - b^2)(a^2 + b^2 - c^2)}{8a^2b^2c^2} \, .$$

By the AM–GM Inequality,

$$
\begin{aligned}
\sqrt{(b^2 + c^2 - a^2)(c^2 + a^2 - b^2)} &\le \tfrac{1}{2}(2c^2) = c^2 \, , \\
\sqrt{(c^2 + a^2 - b^2)(a^2 + b^2 - c^2)} &\le a^2 \, , \\
\sqrt{(a^2 + b^2 - c^2)(b^2 + c^2 - a^2)} &\le b^2 \, .
\end{aligned}
$$

Multiplying these inequalities gives

$$(b^2 + c^2 - a^2)(c^2 + a^2 - b^2)(a^2 + b^2 - c^2) \le a^2b^2c^2 \, ,$$

which implies that $\cos A \cos B \cos C \le \frac{1}{8}$. The inequality $\rho \le \frac{1}{4}$ follows immediately.

On the base of the isosceles triangle ABC ($|AB| = |AC|$) we choose a point D such that $|BD| : |DC| = 2 : 1$, and on $[AD]$ we choose a point P such that $m(\widehat{BAC}) = m(\widehat{BPD})$.

Prove that $m(\widehat{DPC}) = m(\widehat{BAC})/2$.

Solution

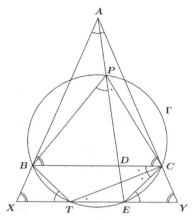

We denote the circumcircle of $\triangle PBC$ by Γ. Let E be the second intersection of PD with Γ. The line through E parallel to BC meets Γ at T, and it meets AB and AC at X and Y, respectively.

Then $XE : EY = BD : DC = 2 : 1$. Hence, we get

$$XE = 2EY . \qquad (1)$$

Note that $\angle CEY = \angle BCE = \angle BPE = \angle BPD = \angle BAC$ and $\angle CYE = \angle ACB$. It follows that $\triangle ECY \sim \triangle ABC$. Thus,

$$\angle ECY = \angle ABC = \angle ACB = \angle CYE .$$

Hence, we have $EC = EY$. Since $\angle BTX = \angle BPE = \angle BPD = \angle BAC$ and $\angle BXT = \angle ABC$, it follows that

$$\angle XBT = \angle ACB = \angle ABC = \angle BXT ;$$

whence, $TB = TX$.

Since $TE \parallel BC$ and $\angle BTX = \angle CEY$, we get $TB = EC$. Thus, we have $TX = TB = EC = EY$. Using (1), we get $XE = 2TX$. Then $TE = XE - TX = TX = EY = EC$. Therefore,

$$\angle CPE = \angle CTE = \angle ECT = \tfrac{1}{2}\angle CEY = \tfrac{1}{2}\angle BAC .$$

This implies that $\angle DPC = \tfrac{1}{2}\angle BAC$.

Given the angle XOY, variable points M and N are considered on the arms $[OX]$ and $[OY]$, respectively, so that $|OM| + |ON|$ is constant. Determine the geometric locus of the mid-point of $[MN]$.

Solution

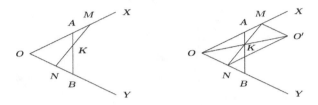

Let $OM + ON = 2a$, and let $A \in OX$ and $B \in OY$ such that $OA = OB = a$. Then $AM = NB$. (See the diagram on the left above.) We will prove that the geometric locus of the mid-point of MN is $[AB]$.

Let $K = AB \cap MN$. Applying the Theorem of Menelaus to $\triangle OMN$ with AKB as transversal, we get

$$\frac{AM}{AO} \cdot \frac{KN}{KM} \cdot \frac{BO}{BN} = 1,$$

which implies that $KN = KM$. Thus, the mid-point of MN belongs to AB.

Conversely, if $K \in [AB]$, let O' be such that K is the mid-point of OO'. (See the diagram on the right above.) Let $M \in OX$ and $N \in OY$ such that $O'M \parallel OY$ and $O'N \parallel OX$. Then $ONO'M$ is a parallelogram. Applying the Theorem of Menelaus to $\triangle OMN$, we deduce that $AM = BN$. Then $OM + ON = a + AM + a - BN = 2a$. Thus, K belongs to the geometric locus.

Let L and N be the mid-points of the diagonals $[AC]$ and $[BD]$ of the cyclic quadrilateral $ABCD$, respectively. If BD is the bisector of the angle ANC, then prove that AC is the bisector of the angle BLD.

Solution

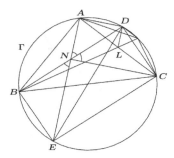

We denote the circumscribed circle of $ABCD$ by Γ. Let E be a point on Γ such that $CE \parallel BD$. Since $CE \parallel BD$, we have $BE = DC$ and $\angle NBE = \angle NDC$. Also, we are given that $BN = DN$. Therefore, $\triangle BNE \cong \triangle DNC$, which implies that $\angle BNE = \angle DNC = \angle DNA$. Hence, A, N, and E are collinear.

Since AE bisects BD, triangles BAE and DAE have the same area. Thus,

$$\tfrac{1}{2}AB \cdot BE \sin \angle ABE = \tfrac{1}{2}AD \cdot DE \sin \angle ADE.$$

Since $\angle ABE + \angle ADE = 180°$, we have $\sin \angle ABE = \sin \angle ADE$, and consequently,

$$AB \cdot BE = AD \cdot DE.$$

Since $CE \parallel BD$, we have $BE = CD$ and $DE = BC$. Thus, the above equation becomes

$$AB \cdot CD = AD \cdot BC. \tag{1}$$

Let S be the point on Γ such that $DS \parallel AC$. Then $AD = CS$ and $CD = AS$. It follows from (1) that $AB \cdot AS = CS \cdot BC$. This, together with the relation $\angle BAS + \angle BCS = 180°$, implies that triangles ABS and CBS have the same area. Therefore, BS bisects AC. Consequently, BS passes through L.

Since $DS \parallel AC$, we have $AD = CS$ and $\angle DAL = \angle SCL$. Hence, $\triangle ALD \cong \triangle CLS$, and therefore,

$$\angle ALD = \angle CLS = \angle ALB.$$

Thus, AC bisects $\angle BLD$.

Prove that the plane is not a union of the inner regions of finitely many parabolas. (The outer region of a parabola is the union of the lines not intersecting the parabola. The inner region of a parabola is the set of points of the plane that do not belong to the outer region of the parabola.)

Solution

Suppose, to the contrary, that the plane is the union of the inner regions of finitely many parabolas, say P_1, P_2, ..., P_k. For each $i = 1, 2, ..., k$, let ℓ_i be the axis of symmetry of the parabola P_i. Choose a line ℓ which is *not* parallel to any of the lines ℓ_1, ℓ_2, ..., ℓ_k. This choice ensures us that if ℓ meets a parabola P_i at all, then either it is tangent to P_i or it meets P_i at two distinct points A_i and B_i. By renumbering, if necessary, assume that P_1, P_2, ..., P_m ($m \leq k$) are the parabolas that meet line ℓ at two distinct points. Since every point on ℓ must be in the inner region of at least one of the parabolas P_1, P_2, ..., P_k, we find that

$$\text{length of } \ell \ \leq \ \sum_{1}^{m} \|A_i B_i\| \ < \ +\infty,$$

an obvious contradiction.

Two circles intersect each other in points M and N. An arbitrary point A of the first circle, which is not M or N, is connected with M and N, and the straight lines AM and AN intersect the second circle again in the points B and C. Prove that the tangent to the first circle at A is parallel to the straight line BC.

Solution

Let AT be the tangent to the first circle at A. Since

$$\angle TAM = \angle ANM = \angle MBC,$$

we have $\angle TAB = \angle ABC$. Thus, $AT \parallel BC$.

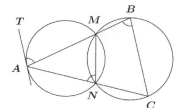

Let $ABCD$ be a rectangle, P a point on the line CD. Let M and N be the mid-points of AD and BC, respectively. PM intersects AC in Q. Show that MN is the bisector of the angle QNP.

Solution

Let O be the centre of the rectangle, and let R be the intersection of the lines CD and QN. From Thales' Theorem, we have

$$\frac{PC}{MO} = \frac{CQ}{OQ} = \frac{CR}{ON}.$$

Since $OM = ON$, we deduce that $PC = CR$. Thus, C is the mid-point of PR. Since $CN \perp PR$, we deduce that N belongs to the perpendicular bisector of PR. It follows that the triangle PNR is isosceles, and

$$\angle CPN = \angle NRP. \qquad (1)$$

Case 1: Points P and D are on opposite sides of C (see figure to the right).

Then CN is the internal bisector of $\angle QNP$. Since $MN \perp CN$, it follows that MN is the external bisector of $\angle QNP$.

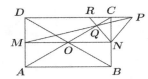

Case 2: Points P and D are on the same side of C (see figure below).

Then $\angle CPN = \angle PNM$ (since MN and CP are parallel) and $\angle NRP = \angle QNM$ (since MN and PR are parallel). From (1), it follows that $\angle PNM = \angle QNM$; that is, MN is the internal bisector of $\angle QNP$.

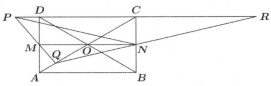

A square is partitioned into rectangles whose sides are parallel to the sides of the square. For each rectangle, the ratio of its shorter side to its longer side is determined. Prove that the sum S of these ratios is always at least 1.

Solution

Assume that the side of the square has length 1 and that the sides of rectangle i have lengths a_i, b_i where $a_i \geq b_i$. Then $1 \geq a_i \geq b_i$ and $\sum a_i b_i = 1$. Therefore, $S = \sum b_i / a_i \geq \sum b_i \geq \sum a_i b_i = 1$.

Let D be a point on side BC of triangle ABC such that $AD > BC$. Point E on side AC is defined by the equation $\dfrac{AE}{EC} = \dfrac{BC}{AD - BC}$. Show that $AD > BE$.

Solution

The condition $\dfrac{AE}{EC} = \dfrac{BC}{AD - BC}$ is incorrect. The correct condition is $\dfrac{AE}{EC} = \dfrac{BD}{AD - BC}$, which is what we shall use in our proof.

Let F be the point such that $AF \parallel BD$ and $BF \parallel AD$. Since $AFBD$ is a parallelogram, we have $FB = AD$ and $FA = BD$.

Let G be the intersection of EF with BC. Since $FA \parallel CG$, it follows that

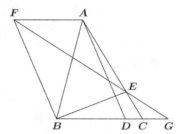

$$\frac{FA}{CG} = \frac{AE}{EC} = \frac{BD}{AD - BC}.$$

Since $FA = BD$, we have

$$\frac{BD}{CG} = \frac{BD}{AD - BC}.$$

Thus, $CG = AD - BC$, which implies that

$$AD = BC + CG = BG.$$

Since $BF = AD$, we have $BF = BG$. Consequently,

$$\angle BEF > \angle BGF = \angle BFG = \angle BFE.$$

Therefore, $BF > BE$. That is, $AD > BE$.

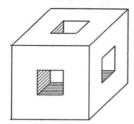

Consider a cube of edge 18 cm. In the centre of three different (and not opposite) faces we bore a square perforation of side 6 cm that goes across the cube as far as the opposite face. We thus obtain the following figure:

Determine the surface area of the resulting solid.

Solution

Each outside face of the solid has area $18^2 - 6^2 = 288$ cm^2, for a total area of $6 \cdot 288 = 1728$ cm^2. The tunnels are made up of 7 removed identical cubes, but they only contribute 6 groups of four squares of side 6 cm to the area of the solid. Thus, the inside area of the solid is $6 \cdot 4 \cdot 6^2 = 864$ cm^2. Hence, the solid has total area 2592 cm^2.

Two circles intersect at A and B. P is a point on arc $\overset{\frown}{AB}$ on one of the circles. PA and PB intersect the other circle at R and S (see figure). If P' is any point on the same arc as P and if R' and S' are the points in which $P'A$ and $P'B$ intersect the second circle, prove that $\overset{\frown}{RS} = \overset{\frown}{R'S'}$.

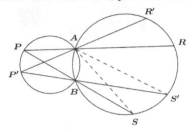

Solution

Since A, B, P, P' are concyclic we have

$$\angle APS \;=\; \angle APB \;=\; \angle AP'B \;=\; \angle AP'S'. \qquad (1)$$

Since A, B, S, S' are concyclic we have

$$\angle ASP \;=\; \angle ASB \;=\; \angle AS'B \;=\; \angle AS'P'. \qquad (2)$$

From (1) and (2), we get

$$\angle RAS \;=\; \angle APS + \angle ASP \;=\; \angle AP'S' + \angle AS'P' \;=\; \angle R'AS'.$$

Hence, we have $\overset{\frown}{RS} = \overset{\frown}{R'S'}$.

The point C is on the segment AB. A straight line through C intersects the circle with diameter AB at E and F, the circle with diameter AC again at M, and the circle with diameter BC again at N. Prove that $MF = EN$.

Solution

In the figure, the line AM is extended to meet the circle with diameter AB at M'. Since AC and AB are diameters, $\angle AMC$ and $\angle AM'B$ are right angles. The two chords EF and BM', both perpendicular to AM', are parallel to each other. Hence, $EFM'B$ is an isosceles trapezoid.

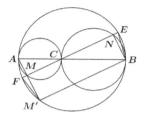

   Since BC is a diameter, $\angle BNC = 90°$. The right triangles MFM' and NEB are congruent, and hence, $MF = EN$.

The sides of a heptagon $A_1A_2A_3A_4A_5A_6A_7$ have equal length. From a point O inside, perpendiculars are dropped to the sides A_1A_2, A_2A_3, ..., A_7A_1, meeting them, and not their extensions, at H_1, H_2, ..., H_7, respectively. Prove that

$$A_1H_1 + A_2H_2 + \cdots + A_7H_7 = H_1A_2 + H_2A_3 + \cdots + H_7A_1.$$

Solution

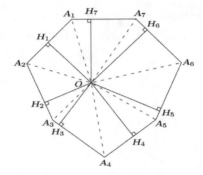

We let a denote the length of the sides of the heptagon, and we put $A_8 = A_1$. For $i = 1, 2, \ldots, 7$, since $OH_i \perp A_iA_{i+1}$, we have

$$
\begin{aligned}
OA_i^2 - OA_{i+1}^2 &= A_iH_i^2 - H_iA_{i+1}^2 \\
&= (A_iH_i + H_iA_{i+1})(A_iH_i - H_iA_{i+1}) \\
&= a(A_iH_i - H_iA_{i+1}).
\end{aligned}
$$

Thus,

$$\sum_{i=1}^{7}(OA_i^2 - OA_{i+1}^2) = a\sum_{i=1}^{7}(A_iH_i - H_iA_{i+1}).$$

Since the sum on the left side is equal to zero, the sum on the right side is also zero. Consequently,

$$\sum_{i=1}^{7} A_iH_i = \sum_{i=1}^{7} H_iA_{i+1},$$

which is the desired result.

In triangle ABC, the sides satisfy $AB + AC = 2BC$. Prove that the bisector of $\angle A$ is perpendicular to the line segment joining the incentre and circumcentre of ABC.

Solution

We assume that $AB \neq AC$. Let I and O be the incentre and circumcentre of $\triangle ABC$, respectively, and let D be the intersection of AI with BC. Since BI and CI bisect $\angle ABD$ and $\angle ACD$, respectively, we have

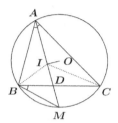

$$\begin{aligned} \frac{AI}{ID} &= \frac{AB}{BD} = \frac{AC}{CD} \\ &= \frac{AB + AC}{BD + CD} = \frac{AB + AC}{BC} = 2. \end{aligned}$$

Hence, $AB = 2BD$ and $AI = 2ID$. Consequently,

$$AD = 3ID. \tag{1}$$

Let M be the second intersection of AD with the circumcircle of $\triangle ABC$. Then

$$\angle MBD = \angle MBC = \angle MAC = \angle MAB.$$

Since $\angle BMD = \angle BMA$, we get $\triangle MBD \sim \triangle MAB$. It follows that

$$\frac{DM}{BM} = \frac{BM}{AM} = \frac{BD}{AB} = \frac{1}{2}.$$

Thus,

$$\frac{DM}{AM} = \frac{DM}{BM} \cdot \frac{BM}{AM} = \left(\frac{1}{2}\right)^2 = \frac{1}{4}.$$

Hence, $AM = 4DM$, from which we obtain

$$AD = 3DM. \tag{2}$$

From (1) and (2) we get $ID = DM$. Thus, $AI = 2ID = ID + DM = IM$. Therefore, $OI \perp AM$. This implies that $AI \perp OI$.

Segments AC and BD intersect at point E. Points K and M, on segments AB and CD, respectively, are such that the segment KM passes through E. Prove that $KM \leq \max\{AC, BD\}$.

Solution

The following lemma is well known, and its proof will not be given.

Lemma. If P is a point on the side BC of triangle ABC, then $AP \leq \max\{AB, AC\}$.

Case 1. $AB \parallel CD$. (See the diagram on the left below.)
Let X, Y be points on CD such that $KX \parallel AC$ and $KY \parallel BD$. Since $AKXC$ and $BKYD$ are both parallelograms, we have

$$KX = AC \quad \text{and} \quad KY = BD.$$

Since M is a point on the segment XY, we have, by the lemma,

$$KM \leq \max\{KX, KY\}.$$

Therefore,

$$KM \leq \max\{AC, BD\}.$$

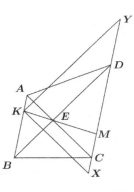 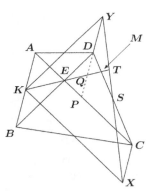

Case 2. $AB \nparallel CD$. (See the diagram on the right above.)
In this case, when we consider quadrilateral $ABCD$, we have either $\angle A + \angle D > 180°$ or $\angle B + \angle C > 180°$. We may assume without loss of generality that $\angle A + \angle D > 180°$. The line through D parallel to AB meets EC and EM at P and Q, respectively. Then P and Q are points on the segments EC and EM, respectively. By Menelaus' Theorem for $\triangle DPC$, we have

$$\frac{PQ}{QD} \cdot \frac{DM}{MC} \cdot \frac{CE}{EP} = 1.$$

Therefore,

$$\frac{PQ}{QD} \cdot \frac{DM}{MC} = \frac{EP}{CE} < 1;$$

that is, $\frac{CM}{MD} > \frac{PQ}{QD}$. Since $DP \parallel AB$, we get $\frac{PQ}{QD} = \frac{AK}{KB}$. Thus,

$$\frac{CM}{MD} > \frac{AK}{KB}. \tag{1}$$

Let X be a point such that $CX \parallel AK$ and $KX \parallel AC$. Let Y be a point such that $DY \parallel BK$ and $KY \parallel BD$. Let S be the intersection of XY with CD.

Then $CX = AK$, $KX = AC$, $YD = KB$, and $KY = BD$. Since $CX \parallel AB \parallel YD$, we have

$$\frac{CS}{SD} = \frac{CX}{YD} = \frac{AK}{KB}.$$

Consequently, using (1), we have $\frac{CS}{SD} < \frac{CM}{MD}$. Hence, M is a point on the segment DS.

Let T be the intersection of KM with SY. Then M is a point on the segment KT. Thus, $KM \leq KT$. Since T is a point on the segment XY, we have, by the lemma,

$$KT \leq \max\{KX, KY\} = \max\{AC, BD\}.$$

Therefore, $KM \leq \max\{AC, BD\}$.

The plane is divided into regions by n lines in general positions. Prove that at least $n - 2$ of the regions are triangles.

Solution

First note that, if the line ℓ meets the interior of the non-degenerate triangle ABC, then ℓ must cross two sides of the triangle, say $[AB]$ at M and $[AC]$ at N. It follows that AMN is a non-degenerate triangle. Thus, if a line meets the interior of a triangle, it divides the triangle into two regions, at least one of which is a triangle.

Let $n \geq 3$ be an integer. Let the plane be divided into regions by n lines $\ell_1, \ell_2, \ldots, \ell_n$ in general position. Without loss of generality, we may suppose that, for $i = 1, 2, \ldots, n - 1$, the line ℓ_i meets ℓ_n at M_i, such that the points $M_1, M_2, \ldots, M_{n-1}$ are pairwise distinct (since the lines are in general position) and in this order on ℓ_n.

For $i \leq n - 2$, the lines ℓ_i, ℓ_{i+1}, and ℓ_n form a triangle T_i, where M_i and M_{i+1} are two vertices of T_i. Moreover, from the order of the M_i's on the line ℓ_n, any two of the triangles $T_1, T_2, \ldots, T_{n-2}$ have no interior point in common. Thus, we have exactly $n - 2$ triangles.

Let $k \leq n - 2$ be fixed. If none of the lines ℓ_i meets the interior of T_k, then T_k is one of the regions. Otherwise, a line ℓ_i meets the interior of T_k. Let i_1 be the least integer such that ℓ_{i_1} meets the interior of T_k. Then, from the initial remark above, the line ℓ_{i_1} divides T_k into two regions, at least one of which is a triangle, say T_{k_1}. Note that none of the lines ℓ_i meets the interior of T_{k_1} for $i \leq i_1$.

If, for $i > i_1$, none of the lines ℓ_i meets the interior of T_{k_1}, then T_{k_1} is one of the regions. In the other case, substituting T_{k_1} for T_k, we follow the same reasoning as above. Since, at each step, the number of lines remaining to be considered is decreasing, this process will eventually stop, giving us a region which is a triangle.

With this process, each of the T_i's leads to a triangular region. Since any two of the regions T_i have no interior point in common, the triangular regions are distinct, and we are done.

From each of k points on a plane, a few rays are drawn. No two rays intersect. Prove that one can choose $k - 1$ of the segments connecting these points such that they are disjoint from one another and from any of the rays, except possibly at those k points.

Solution

We interpret the hypothesis that no two rays intersect as implying that no ray goes through any of the k points, other than the one from which it emanates.

For $k \geq 2$, let $\mathcal{P}_k$ be the claim. "For any configuration of k points in the plane satisfying the assumptions of the problem, it is possible to draw some segments connecting these points so as to form a connected planar simple graph, whose vertices are the k given points, and whose edges are not intersected by any ray (except possibly at the vertices)". In the sequel, such a graph will be called a *good* graph.

The desired conclusion will follow immediately from the proof that $\mathcal{P}_k$ holds and from the well-known result that a connected graph with k vertices has at least $k - 1$ edges.

Now, we prove $\mathcal{P}_k$ by induction on k. For $k = 1$, there is nothing to prove. For $k = 2$, let M_1 and M_2 be the given points. Since the segment $M_1 M_2$ is not cut by a ray, the claim $\mathcal{P}_2$ clearly holds.

Let $k \geq 3$ be fixed. Suppose that $\mathcal{P}_q$ holds for all $q \in \{2, \ldots, k - 1\}$. Let us give a configuration with k points satisfying the assumptions of the problem.

Since there is a finite number of points, they determine by pairs only a finite number of directions. Thus, we may choose an orthonormal system of coordinates such that the "vertical" coordinate of the points are pairwise distinct. With no loss of generality, we may suppose that the points are $M_1, M_2, \ldots, M_k$ with $y_{M_1} = \min_{i \geq 1} y_{M_i}$ and $y_{M_2} = \min_{i \geq 2} y_{M_i}$. Note that M_1 is the unique point belonging to the half plane $y \leq y_{M_1}$.

In the following, we will say that the ray r (or the segment s) *separates* the points A and B if r (or s) intersects the interior of the line segment AB.

First case. A ray r from M_1 separates two of the points, say A and B.

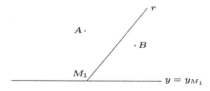

By the induction hypothesis, we may construct a good graph $\mathcal{G}_1$ whose vertices are the points on the left side of r including M_1, and a good graph $\mathcal{G}_2$ whose vertices are the points on the right side of r including M_1. Since two rays never intersect, none of the edges of $\mathcal{G}_1$ (respectively, $\mathcal{G}_2$) can be separated by a ray issued from a vertex of $\mathcal{G}_2$ (respectively, $\mathcal{G}_1$), nor by an edge of $\mathcal{G}_2$ (respectively, $\mathcal{G}_1$).

Thus, the graph $\mathcal{G} = \mathcal{G}_1 \cup \mathcal{G}_2$ is a good graph (it is connected via M_1) for the whole set of points.

Second case. No ray from M_1 separates two of the points.

We may use the induction hypothesis to construct a good graph $\mathcal{G}$ whose vertices are $M_2, \ldots, M_k$.

In the following, we will say that the point M *separates* the points A and B if M is an interior point of the line segment AB or if a ray from M separates A and B, or if an edge with end-point M separates A and B.

By adding the vertex M_1, we separate no pair of points. Now, it suffices to prove that M_1 may be joined by an edge to at least one of the other points, so as to form a good graph.

From the minimality of M_1 and M_2, no M_i belongs to the interior of the line segment $M_1 M_2$, and no edge of $\mathcal{G}$ separates M_1 and M_2.

(1) If M_1 and M_2 can be joined, we are done.

(2) If M_1 and M_2 cannot be joined, then there is a ray which separates M_1 and M_2. Since the number of rays is finite, there is a finite number of intersection points between the interior of the line segment $M_1 M_2$ and the set of rays. With no loss of generality, we may suppose that the ray r_3 issued from M_3 separates M_1 and M_2, with $M_1 H_3$ minimal, where H_3 is the point in common between r_3 and the interior of line segment $M_1 M_2$. Note that M_2 is exterior to $\triangle M_1 M_3 H_3$. Let n_3 be the number of the M_i's which are not exterior to $\triangle M_1 M_3 H_3$.

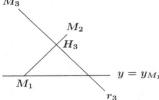

(3) If M_1 and M_3 can be joined, we are done.

(4) If not, note that, from the minimality of H_3 and M_2, the interior of the line segment $M_1 H_3$ cannot be cut by any edge or ray. Moreover, since the segment $M_3 H_3$ belongs r_3, we see that $M_3 H_3$ cannot be cut by any edge or any other ray. It follows that any ray or edge which separates M_1 and M_3 has one of its end-points in the interior of $\triangle M_1 M_3 H_3$ or in the interior of the segment $M_1 M_3$.

(5) If no ray or edge separates M_1 and M_3, then they are separated only by points belonging from the interior of $M_1 M_3$. Let P be the point which separates M_1 and M_3 with $M_1 P$ minimal (along $M_1 M_3$). From above, M_1 and P are not separated. We may join M_1 and P by an edge, and we are done.

(6) If M_1 and M_3 are separated by a ray or an edge, then with no loss of generality, we may suppose that they are separated by an edge or a ray issued from M_4, which intersects the interior of $M_1 M_3$ at H_4, with $M_1 H_4$ minimal.

Note that $\triangle M_1 M_4 H_4$ is included in $\triangle M_1 M_3 H_3$, and (from the minimality of H_3) the interior of the segment $M_1 H_3$ cannot be cut by any edge or ray. Let n_4 be the number of the M_i's which are not exterior to $\triangle M_1 M_4 H_4$.

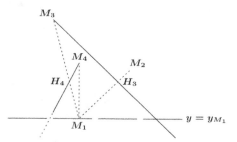

Thus, we are in the same situation as in (5) except that, since M_3 is exterior to $\triangle M_1 M_4 H_4$, we have $n_4 < n_3$. (*)

Repeating the reasoning above, the process will eventually stop (because of (*)) at some step similar to (3) or (5). Thus, M_1 can be joined by an edge with some M_p, to form a good graph from $\mathcal{G}$.

This ends the induction step, and proves that $\mathcal{P}_k$ holds.

Remark. The value $k - 1$ is minimal in the sense that it can be achieved, as in the configuration at right.

A straight line passes through the centre of a regular $2n$–gon. Prove that the sum of distances to this line from the vertices on one side of this line equals the sum of the distances from the remaining vertices.

Solution

Let A_0, A_1, ..., A_{2n-1} be the points with respective complex affixes 1, z, ..., z^{2n-1}, where $z = \exp\left(\dfrac{2\pi i}{2n}\right) = \exp\left(\dfrac{\pi i}{n}\right)$. Since any regular $2n$–gon is similar to the $2n$–gon $A_0 A_1 \ldots A_{2n-1}$, it is sufficient to prove the result for $A_0 A_1 \ldots A_{2n-1}$.

We partition the set of vertices into n pairs: $\{A_0,\ A_n\}$, $\{A_1,\ A_{n+1}\}$, ..., $\{A_{n-1},\ A_{2n-1}\}$. Since $-z^k = z^n z^k = z^{n+k}$, the two points in each pair are symmetrical about the centre O of $A_0 A_1 \ldots A_{2n-1}$. Consider one of these pairs $\{A_k,\ A_{n+k}\}$, and let L be the given line through O. Because the symmetry through O exchanges the two half-planes determined by L, if A_k is on one side of L, then A_{n+k} is on the other side (and if A_k is on L, then A_{n+k} is also on L). Now, since the symmetry through O preserves distances, and since L passes through O, we have $d(A_k, L) = d(A_{n+k}, L)$. The result follows immediately.

Each of n lines on a plane is cut by the others into 2 rays and $n - 2$ equal segments. Prove that $n = 3$.

Solution

First, we note that the problem makes sense only for $n \geq 2$. The case $n = 2$ is possible but trivial, since any two intersecting lines cut one another into 2 rays and 0 line segments. This case is apparently disallowed. For $n = 3$, it is easy to to come up with 3 lines that satisfy the given conditions.

Now suppose, by way of contradiction, that $n \geq 4$. Note that no three of the given lines have a common point and no two are parallel. In the following, each of the lines which are considered is one of the n given lines.

Let ℓ be one of the lines, and let B, C, D be three consecutive intersection points, in that order, on ℓ. Then $BC = CD$, and none of the lines passes through the interior of the segments BC or CD. Let ℓ_B be a line which intersects ℓ at B, and let ℓ_C and ℓ_D be defined in the same way. Let A be the common point of ℓ_B and ℓ_C, and let E be the common point of ℓ_D and ℓ_C. We claim that one of the lines meets the interior of $\triangle ABC$ or $\triangle ECD$.

Case 1. C between A and E. (Figure 1).

Suppose that our claim is false. Then A, C, E are three consecutive intersection points, in that order, on ℓ_C. Thus, $AC = CE$.

Using Thales' Theorem, since $BC = CD$, we deduce that $\ell_B = AB$ is parallel to $ED = \ell_D$, a contradiction. Thus, our claim is true in this case.

Figure 1

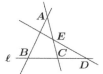

Figure 2

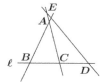

Figure 3

Case 2. E between A and C. (Figure 2)

Then ℓ_D meets the interior of $\triangle ABC$.

Case 3. A between C and E. (Figure 3)

Then ℓ_B meets the interior of $\triangle ECD$.

Thus, in every case, one of the lines meets the interior of $\triangle ABC$ or $\triangle ECD$. With no loss of generality, we may suppose that one of the lines meets the interior of $\triangle ABC$.

Any line which meets the interior of $\triangle ABC$ is neither ℓ_B nor ℓ_C nor ℓ, and must intersect the interior of each of the segments AB and AC, from above. Then the number of intersection points in the interior of segment AB is equal to the number of intersection points in the interior of segment AC. Let $k \geq 1$ be this common value.

Let B_1 be the intersection point in the interior of AB such that AB_1 is minimal. Let ℓ_1 be the line which meets AB at B_1, and let C_1 be the intersection of ℓ_1 and the interior of AC. Note that $\ell_1 \neq \ell$.

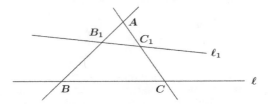

Case (a). None of the lines meets the interior of $\triangle AB_1C_1$.

Then C_1 is the intersection point in the interior of AC such that AC_1 is minimal. Thus, $\overrightarrow{AB_1} = \frac{1}{k}\overrightarrow{AB}$ and $\overrightarrow{AC_1} = \frac{1}{k}\overrightarrow{AC}$. It follows that the line $\ell_1 = B_1C_1$ is parallel to $BC = \ell$, a contradiction.

Case (b). One of the lines meets the interior of $\triangle AB_1C_1$.

We note that none of the lines intersects the interior of AB_1, and that the area of $\triangle AB_1C_1$ is strictly less than the area of $\triangle ABC$, We may use the same reasoning as above, with $\triangle AB_1C_1$ in place of $\triangle ABC$. Since the number of triangles XYZ (where X, Y, Z are three intersection points) is finite, this process eventually stops, at which time we obtain the same contradiction as in (a).

In every case, we obtain a contradiction. It follows that $n \leq 3$, and we are done.

H is a given point inside a circle. Prove that a fixed circle passes through the mid-points of the sides of any triangle inscribed in the circle and having H as its orthocentre.

Solution

Let Γ be the given circle and O be its centre. Let $\triangle ABC$ be inscribed in Γ and have H as its orthocentre. Since the circumcentre O and the orthocentre H of $\triangle ABC$ are fixed points, the same is true of its centroid G (because of Euler's relation $\overrightarrow{OG} = \frac{1}{3}\overrightarrow{OH}$, valid in all triangles). The triangle whose vertices are the mid-points of the sides AB, BC, CA is the homothetic of $\triangle ABC$ under the homothety h with centre G and scale factor $-\frac{1}{2}$. Thus, the circumcircle of this triangle is the image of Γ under h and, as such, is the fixed circle with centre O' defined by $\overrightarrow{GO'} = -\frac{1}{2}\overrightarrow{GO}$ and radius $\frac{1}{2}R$, where R is the radius of Γ.

A triangle T_1 is constructed with the medians of a right triangle T. If R_1 and R are the circumradii of T_1 and T, respectively, prove that $R_1 > 5R/6$.

Solution

The inequality should be $R_1 \geq 5R/6$ since equality occurs for an isosceles right triangle. If a, b, c are the sides of T with $c^2 = a^2 + b^2$, then

$$4m_a{}^2 = 4b^2 + a^2, \quad 4m_b{}^2 = 4a^2 + b^2, \quad 4m_c{}^2 = a^2 + b^2,$$

where m_a, m_b, m_c are the medians corresponding to a, b, c respectively. Also,

$$R_1 = \frac{m_a m_b m_c}{4F_1} = \frac{m_a m_b m_c}{3F}$$

where $F = ab/2$ is the area of T, F_1 the area of T_1. Also $R = c/2$. The given inequality now becomes $8m_a m_b m_c \geq 5abc$ or, squaring,

$$(a^2 + b^2)(a^2 + 4b^2)(4a^2 + b^2) = 64(m_a m_b m_c)^2 \geq 25a^2b^2c^2 = 25a^2b^2(a^2 + b^2).$$

Expanding out and factoring, we obtain the obvious inequality

$$(a^2 + b^2)(a^2 - b^2)^2 \geq 0.$$

There is equality if and only if $a = b$.

A plane is partitioned into an infinite set of unit squares by parallel lines. A triangle ABC is constructed with vertices at line intersections. Show that if $|AB| > |AC|$, then $|AB| - |AC| > 1/p$, where p is the perimeter of the triangle. (Grades 8, 9, 10)

Solution

Without loss of generality we can take the rectangular coordinates of A,B,C to be $(0,0)$, (x,y), (u,v), respectively, where x,y,u,v are integers. Then letting $c^2 = |AB|^2 = x^2 + y^2$, $b^2 = |AC|^2 = u^2 + v^2$, $a^2 = |BC|^2 = (x-u)^2 + (y-v)^2$, we have to show that

$$(c-b)(c+b+a) = c^2 - b^2 + (c-b)a > 1.$$

Finally, since $c^2 - b^2$ is a positive integer it is ≥ 1; also $(c-b)a > 0$.

In a convex quadrilateral the sum of the distances from any point within the quadrilateral to the four straight lines along which the sides lie is constant. Show that the quadrilateral is a parallelogram. (Grade 9)

Solution

Assume for the quadrilateral $ABCD$ that lines AD and BC are not parallel; so they must meet in a point E as in the figure. Now draw a chord $c = GH$ of $ABCD$ perpendicular to the angle bisector of angle E. It follows by considering the area of the isosceles triangle EGH that the sum of the distances from any point on c to lines AD and BC is constant. Consequently, by hypothesis, the sum of the distances from any

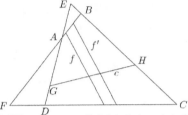

point of c to lines AB and CD is constant. If AB and CD are not parallel, let their point of intersection be F and draw 2 chords f and f' of $ABCD$ perpendicular to the angle bisector of angle F, with f nearer to F. It follows easily that the sum of the perpendiculars to lines AB and CD from a point on f is less than from a point on f'. Consequently, AB must be parallel to CD. Proceeding in a similar way using another chord c' parallel to c, it follows also that AD must be parallel to BC, whence the figure must be a parallelogram.

It is to be noted that a non-convex quadrilateral cannot have the given property. Also as a rider, show that if the sum of the six distances from any point within a hexahedron is constant, the hexahedron must be a parallelepiped.

If **a** and **b** are given nonparallel vectors, solve for x in the equation

$$\frac{a^2 + x\mathbf{a} \cdot \mathbf{b}}{|\mathbf{a}||\mathbf{a} + x\mathbf{b}|} = \frac{b^2 + \mathbf{a} \cdot \mathbf{b}}{|\mathbf{b}||\mathbf{a} + \mathbf{b}|}.$$

Solution

One can solve by squaring out and solving the rather messy quadratic in x. However, it is easier to proceed geometrically. Referring to the figure, the given equation requires that $\angle SPQ = \angle PRQ \, (= \phi$, say). Thus $\triangle PQS \sim \triangle RQP$.

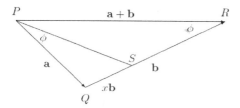

Thus, putting $a = |\mathbf{a}|$ and $b = |\mathbf{b}|$, $xb/a = a/b$ or $x = a^2/b^2$.
Also, $x = -x'$ can be negative as in the following figure.

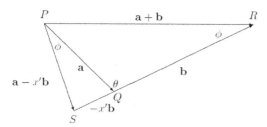

By the law of sines, $a/\sin(\theta - \phi) = x'b/\sin\phi$, and $a/\sin\phi = b/\sin(\theta + \phi)$. Hence,

$$\sin(\theta + \phi) - \sin(\theta - \phi) = \frac{b\sin\phi}{a} - \frac{a\sin\phi}{x'b}$$

or $2\cos\theta = b/a - a/x'b$. Finally,

$$x = -x' = \frac{-a^2}{b(b - 2a\cos\theta)} = \frac{-a^2}{b^2 + 2\mathbf{a} \cdot \mathbf{b}}.$$

Cut the regular (equilateral) triangle AXY from rectangle $ABCD$ in such a way that the vertex X is on side BC and the vertex Y is on side CD. Prove that among the three remaining right triangles there are two the sum of whose areas equals the area of the third.

Solution

First such a triangle is not possible in every rectangle. In fact a necessary condition is that the sides $a \leq b$ of the rectangle must satisfy $a \geq b\sqrt{3}/2$.

Let us assume such a triangle is possible. Let s be the length of the side of the equilateral triangle. We claim that $[XYC] = [ABX] + [ADY]$ where T denotes the area of triangle T. Indeed

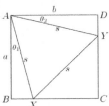

$$[ABX] = \frac{1}{2}s^2 \cos\theta_1 \sin\theta_1 = \frac{1}{4}s^2 \sin 2\theta_1$$

and

$$[ADY] = \frac{1}{2}s^2 \cos\theta_2 \sin\theta_2 = \frac{1}{4}s^2 \sin 2\theta_2 = \frac{1}{4}s^2 \sin\left(\frac{\pi}{3} - 2\theta_1\right)$$

$$= \frac{1}{4}s^2 \frac{\sqrt{3}}{2} \cos 2\theta_1 - \frac{1}{8}s^2 \sin 2\theta_1,$$

thus

$$[ABX] + [ADY] = \frac{1}{8}s^2 \sin 2\theta_1 + \frac{\sqrt{3}}{8}s^2 \cos 2\theta_1. \tag{1}$$

Now for $\triangle XYC$ $\angle YXC = \pi/6 + \theta_1$. Therefore

$$[XYC] = \frac{s^2}{4} \sin\left(\frac{\pi}{3} + 2\theta_1\right)$$

$$= \frac{s^2}{4}\frac{\sqrt{3}}{2} \cos 2\theta_1 + \frac{s^2}{4}\frac{1}{2} \sin 2\theta_1.$$

This is exactly (1) the sum of the areas.

Consider points A and B on given rays (semilines) starting from C, such that the sum $CA + CB$ is a given constant. Show that there is a point $D \neq C$ such that for each position of A and B the circumcircle of triangle ABC passes through D.

Solution

Let A and B be given and let Γ be the circumcircle of $\triangle ABC$. The interior bisector of $\angle ACB$ intersects Γ for the second time in the required point D. To see this, consult the figure. If $CA' + CB' = CA + CB$ then $AA' = BB'$ (1). Also $DA = DB$ (2) since $\angle ABD = \angle ACD = \angle DCB = \angle DAB$. Assume without loss that $CB \geq CA$. Quadrilateral $DBCA$ is inscribed in a circle, hence $\angle DAA' = \angle DBB'$ (3). From (1), (2) and (3) $\triangle DAA' \cong \triangle DBB'$. Thus $\angle ADA' = \angle BDB'$ and $\angle A'DB' = \angle ADB$. Thus D is a point on the circumcircle of $\triangle A'B'C$.

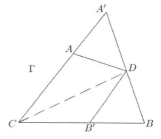

In the triangle ABC with circumcentre O, $AB = AC$, D is the midpoint of AB, and E is the centroid of triangle ACD. Prove that OE is perpendicular to CD.

Solution

Join the lines DE, DO, and AO, and let F be the intersection of DE and AC, G the intersection of AO and CD, and H the intersection of AO and BC. Find the point I on BC such that $HI = \frac{1}{3}HC$. Since $\triangle ABC$ is isosceles and O is the circumcentre, AO is the central line of BC. Since D is the midpoint of AB, G is the centroid of the triangle, and $GH = \frac{1}{3}AH$. Thus $GI \parallel AC$. Therefore $\angle HGI = \angle HAC = \angle DAO$. Since O is the circumcentre and D is the midpoint of AB, OD is perpendicular to AB. Also, we have $\angle GHI = 90°$. Then $\triangle GHI \sim \triangle ADO$. From this we have $GH/AD = HI/DO$. Now, since $DE = \frac{2}{3}DF = \frac{2}{3}CH = 2HI$ and $AG = 2GH$, we have

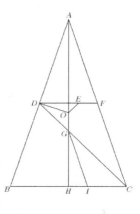

$$\frac{AG}{AD} = \frac{DE}{DO}.$$

Obviously, DE is perpendicular to AH, so that $\angle ODE = 90° - \angle ADE = \angle DAG$. From this, $\triangle ADG \sim \triangle DOE$. Since the angle between AD and DO is $90°$, the angle between DG and EO must be $90°$, too. Thus OE is perpendicular to CD.

West Point Proposals 1984

Given six segments $S_1, S_2, \ldots, S_6$ congruent to the edges AB, AC, AD, CD, DB, BC, respectively, of a tetrahedron $ABCD$, show how to construct with straightedge and compass a segment whose length equals that of the *bialtitude* of the tetrahedron relative to opposite edges AB and CD (i.e., the distance between the lines AB and CD).

Solution

We use the known construction for an altitude of a tetrahedron [1] and the known theorem [2] that the volume of a tetrahedron equals one-sixth the product of two opposite edges times the sine of the angle between those edges and times the shortest distance between those edges. The volume also equals one-third the product of an altitude and the area of the corresponding face.

Let $s_1 = |S_1|$, etc. Let θ be the angle between edges AB and CD and let d be the distance between AB and CD. Also let h_D be the altitude of the tetrahedron from D and h' be the altitude of triangle ABC from C. Then six times the volume of the tetrahedron equals

$$s_4 s_1 d \sin\theta = 2h_D[ABC] = h_D s_1 s_2 \sin \angle CAB = h_D s_1 h'. \tag{1}$$

Here $[ABC]$ denotes the area of triangle ABC. To express $\sin\theta$ as a ratio of two constructible segments, we have

$$s_4 s_1 \cos\theta = |(\mathbf{A} - \mathbf{B}) \cdot \mathbf{C}| = |\mathbf{A} \cdot \mathbf{C} - \mathbf{B} \cdot \mathbf{C}| = |s_3 s_4 \cos \angle ADC - s_5 s_4 \cos \angle BDC|, \tag{2}$$

where $\mathbf{A}, \mathbf{B}, \mathbf{C}$ are respective vectors from D to A, B, C. Now if AA' and BB' are the respective altitudes in triangles ACD and BCD, then $s_3 \cos \angle ADC = A'D$ and $s_5 \cos \angle BDC = B'D$. Hence from (2),

$$\cos\theta = \frac{|A'D - B'D|}{s_1} = \frac{A'B'}{s_1}.$$

where the length $A'B'$ is constructible. From this, we easily can obtain $\sin\theta = \alpha/s_1$ where $\alpha = \sqrt{s_1^2 - (A'B')^2}$ is also constructible. Finally from (1),

$$d = \frac{h_D h' s_1}{s_4 \alpha}$$

which is constructible in the usual way.

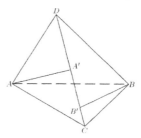

We are given a unit circle C with center M and a closed convex region R in the interior of C. From every point P of circle C, there are two tangents to the boundary of R that are inclined to each other at $60°$. Prove that R is a closed circular disk with center M and radius $1/2$.

Solution

Let P be on C and let the two tangents from P to R meet C again at Q and Q'. Let the other tangent from $Q(Q')$ meet the circle again at $S(S')$ respectively. Since angles P, Q, Q' are all $60°$, QS must coincide with $Q'S'$ so that PQS is an equilateral triangle. Hence R is the envelope of all inscribed equilateral triangles in a circle. This envelope is known to be a circle concentric with C and with radius half that of C.

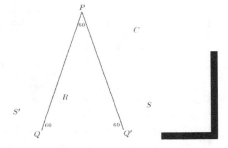

Let A_1, A_2, A_3 be three points in the plane, and for convenience, let $A_4 = A_1$, $A_5 = A_2$. For $n = 1, 2$ and 3 suppose that B_n is the midpoint of $A_n A_{n+1}$, and suppose that C_n is the midpoint of $A_n B_n$. Suppose that $A_n C_{n+1}$ and $B_n A_{n+2}$ meet at D_n, and that $A_n B_{n+1}$ and $C_n A_{n+2}$ meet at E_n. Calculate the ratio of the area of triangle $D_1 D_2 D_3$ to the area of triangle $E_1 E_2 E_3$.

Solution

Let X denote the centroid of $\triangle A_1 A_2 A_3$. Then

$$B_1 X = \frac{1}{3} A_3 B_1 \,, \quad B_2 X = \frac{1}{3} A_1 B_2 \,, \quad B_3 X = \frac{1}{3} A_2 B_3.$$

Using perspectives from A_1 the cross-ratios $(A_2, A_3; B_2, C_2)$ and $(B_1, A_3; X, D_1)$ are equal. Therefore

$$\frac{A_2 B_2}{B_2 A_3} \cdot \frac{C_2 A_3}{A_2 C_2} = \frac{B_1 X}{X A_3} \cdot \frac{D_1 A_3}{B_1 D_1}$$

from which

$$1 \cdot 3 = \frac{1}{2} \cdot \frac{D_1 A_3}{B_1 D_1}.$$

This gives $D_1 A_3 = 6 B_1 D_1$ and so $B_1 D_1 = \frac{1}{7} B_1 A_3$. Hence

$$\frac{D_1 X}{B_1 X} = \frac{B_1 X - B_1 D_1}{B_1 X} = \frac{\frac{1}{3} - \frac{1}{7}}{\frac{1}{3}} = \frac{4}{7}.$$

Similarly $D_2 X / B_2 X = \frac{4}{7}$ and $\triangle D_1 D_2 X$ is similar to $\triangle B_1 B_2 X$. Thus

$$\frac{[D_1 D_2 X]}{[B_1 B_2 X]} = \left(\frac{4}{7}\right)^2 = \frac{16}{49}.$$

where $[T]$ denotes the area of triangle T. In similar fashion

$$\frac{[D_2 D_3 X]}{[B_2 B_3 X]} = \frac{[D_1 D_3 X]}{[B_1 B_3 X]} = \frac{16}{49}.$$

It follows that

$$[D_1 D_2 D_3] = \frac{16}{49} [B_1 B_2 B_3] = \frac{4}{49} [A_1 A_2 A_3],$$

using the fact that triangles $B_1 B_2 B_3$, $B_3 A_1 B_1$, $B_2 B_1 A_2$ and $A_3 B_3 B_2$ are congruent. Now, with A_2 as the centre

$$(A_1, A_3; B_3, C_3) = (B_1, A_3; X, E_3)$$

and so

$$1 \cdot \frac{1}{3} = \frac{A_1 B_3}{B_3 A_3} \cdot \frac{C_3 A_3}{A_1 C_3} = \frac{B_1 X}{X A_3} \cdot \frac{E_3 A_3}{B_1 E_3} = \frac{1}{2} \cdot \frac{E_3 A_3}{B_1 E_3}.$$

Since $X A_3 = \frac{2}{3} B_1 A_3$, this means

$$X E_3 = \left[\frac{2}{3} - \frac{2}{5}\right] B_1 A_3 = \frac{4}{15} B_1 A_3.$$

Hence $X E_3 = \frac{2}{5} X A_3$ and $[X E_3 E_1] = \frac{4}{25} [X A_3 A_1]$. Finally $[E_1 E_2 E_3] = \frac{4}{25} [A_1 A_2 A_3]$ so that

$$[D_1 D_2 D_3] = \frac{25}{49} [E_1 E_2 E_3].$$

The consecutive vertices of a given convex n-gon are $A_0, A_1, \ldots, A_{n-1}$. The n-gon is partitioned into $n-2$ triangles by diagonals which are non-intersecting (except possibly at the vertices). Show that there exists an enumeration $\Delta_1, \Delta_2, \ldots, \Delta_{n-2}$ of these triangles such that A_i is a vertex of Δ_i for $1 \leq i \leq n-2$. How many enumerations of this kind exist?

Solution

There is always just one such enumeration.

We argue by induction on n. The cases $n = 3$ and $n = 4$ are trivial. Suppose $n > 4$.

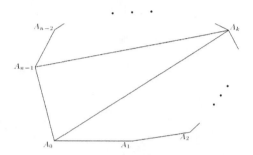

The side $A_0 A_{n-1}$ and another vertex, say A_k, $1 \leq k \leq n-2$, form a triangle. It is immediate that the triangle is Δ_k (since 0 and $n-2$ are not available labels). If $k = 1$ or $k = n-2$, by considering the remaining $(n-1)$-gon formed using the diagonal $A_{n-1} A_1$ or $A_0 A_{n-2}$ as appropriate and relabelling A_i as A'_{i-1} in the former case, the result follows.

So suppose $1 < k < n-2$. Now the triangle formed divides the polygon into two convex polygons $[A_0, \ldots, A_k]$ and $[A_k, \ldots, A_{n-1}]$. Also the original triangulation induces a triangulation of each of these, since the diagonals do not intersect except at endpoints. Existence of a numbering is now immediate. Uniqueness follows since the triangles $\Delta_1, \ldots, \Delta_{k-1}$ must be in $[A_0, \ldots, A_k]$ and $\Delta_{k+1}, \ldots, \Delta_{n-2}$ must be in $[A_k, \ldots, A_{n-1}]$.

If in triangle ABC, $C = 2A$ and $AC = 2BC$, show that it is a right triangle. (Grade 8, 9)

Solution

Choose D on the line BC (extended) so that $CD = AC$. Then $BD = 3BC$. The triangles ADB and CAB are similar because $\angle CAD = \angle ADB = A$ (= α, say). Thus $AB/BD = BC/AB$ and $AB^2 = BD \cdot BC = 3 \cdot BC^2$. Therefore in triangle ABC, $AB^2 + BC^2 = AC^2$, and $B = 90°$, as desired.

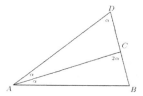

In a given tetrahedron $ABCD$, $\angle BAC + \angle BAD = 180°$. If AK is the bisector of $\angle CAD$, determine $\angle BAK$. (Grade 10)

Solution

If the triangle ABD is rotated with axis AB, the point D describes a circle in a plane orthogonal to AB. The bisector of $\angle CAD$ meets CD at K. Then K divides CD in the constant ratio AC/AD. Thus K describes a circle in a plane parallel to the plane described by D. Now A is a point of this circle [the condition $\angle BAC + \angle BAD = 180°$ means that at some stage in the rotation of $\triangle ABD$ the point A will lie on the line CD]; therefore $\angle BAK = 90°$.

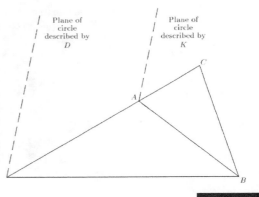

Plane of circle described by D

Plane of circle described by K

Show that it is possible to place non-zero numbers at the vertices of a given regular n-gon P so that for any set of vertices of P which are vertices of a regular k-gon ($k \leq n$), the sum of the corresponding numbers equals zero. (Grade 10)

Solution

Consider a coordinate system with $O(0,0)$ the centre of the n-gon (and therefore the centre of all regular k-gons ($k \leq n$) which have vertices some of those of the n-gon). At the vertices of the n-gon, place the x-coordinates. [The n-gon can be rotated so that none of these x-coordinates are zero.] But we have $\sum_{i=1}^{k} \overrightarrow{OA_i} = \mathbf{0}$, where the A_i are the vertices of a regular k-gon. From this, looking at the x-coordinates we have $\sum_{i=1}^{k} x_i = 0$, where $x_1, x_2, \ldots, x_k$ are the x-coordinates of $A_1, \ldots, A_k$. This solves the problem.

The angles of a triangle are in arithmetical progression. The altitudes of the triangle are also in arithmetical progression. Show that the triangle is equilateral.

Solution

Let A, B, C be the angles of the given triangle and let h_a, h_b, h_c be the corresponding altitudes. Without loss of generality, we may assume $A \leq B \leq C$. Since the angles are in arithmetic progression $A + C = 2B$, and since $A + B + C = 180°$, $B = 60°$. Now also $h_c \leq h_b \leq h_a$ and $a \leq b \leq c$ where a, b, c are the side lengths opposite A, B, C, respectively.

From the law of cosines $b^2 = a^2 + c^2 - 2ac \cos 60° = a^2 + c^2 - ac$. Now $2h_b = h_a + h_c$ implies that $4F/b = 2F/a + 2F/c$, where F is the area of triangle ABC, so

$$\frac{2}{b} = \frac{1}{a} + \frac{1}{c} = \frac{a+c}{ac}, \quad \text{or} \quad b = \frac{2ac}{a+c}.$$

Since $b^2 = a^2 + c^2 - ac$, $4a^2c^2 = (a+c)^2(a^2 + c^2 - ac)$. From this we get

$$\begin{aligned}
0 &= (a+c)^2(a^2 + c^2 - ac) - 4a^2c^2 \\
&= [(a-c)^2 + 4ac][(a-c)^2 + ac] - 4a^2c^2 \\
&= (a-c)^4 + 5ac(a-c)^2 \\
&= (a-c)^2[(a-c)^2 + 5ac],
\end{aligned}$$

and so $a = c$. This gives $a = b = c$ since $a \leq b \leq c$, and the given triangle is equilateral.

Let ABC be a triangle with sides a, b, c. Each side is divided in n equal parts. Let S be the sum of the squares of distances from each vertex to each one of the points of subdivision of the opposite side (excepting the vertices). Show that

$$\frac{S}{a^2 + b^2 + c^2}$$

is rational.

Solution

Consider the triangle shown with sides represented by vectors. Let $\mathbf{B}_j$ be the vector joining the vertex B to the corresponding point of subdivision on side $\mathbf{b}$, and define $\mathbf{C}_j$ and $\mathbf{A}_j$ analogously. Then

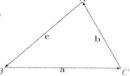

$$\mathbf{B}_j = \mathbf{a} + \frac{j}{n}\mathbf{b},$$

so

$$|\mathbf{B}_j|^2 = |\mathbf{a}|^2 + \frac{j^2}{n^2}|\mathbf{b}|^2 + \frac{2j}{n}(\mathbf{a} \cdot \mathbf{b}).$$

Therefore

$$\sum_{j=1}^{n-1} |\mathbf{B}_j|^2 = (n-1)a^2 + b^2 \sum_{j=1}^{n-1} \frac{j^2}{n^2} + \frac{2}{n} \sum_{j=1}^{n-1} j(\mathbf{a} \cdot \mathbf{b})$$

$$= (n-1)a^2 + b^2\frac{(n-1)(2n-1)}{6n} + (n-1)(\mathbf{a} \cdot \mathbf{b}).$$

Similarly

$$\sum_{j=1}^{n-1} |\mathbf{C}_j|^2 = (n-1)b^2 + c^2\frac{(n-1)(2n-1)}{6n} + (n-1)(\mathbf{b} \cdot \mathbf{c}),$$

$$\sum_{j=1}^{n-1} |\mathbf{A}_j|^2 = (n-1)c^2 + a^2\frac{(n-1)(2n-1)}{6n} + (n-1)(\mathbf{a} \cdot \mathbf{c}).$$

Therefore

$$S = \sum_{j=1}^{n-1}(|\mathbf{A}_j|^2 + |\mathbf{B}_j|^2 + |\mathbf{C}_j|^2) = (n-1)(a^2 + b^2 + c^2) +$$

$$\frac{(a^2 + b^2 + c^2)(n-1)(2n-1)}{6n} + (n-1)(\mathbf{a} \cdot \mathbf{b} + \mathbf{b} \cdot \mathbf{c} + \mathbf{a} \cdot \mathbf{c}) \quad (1)$$

Since $\mathbf{a} + \mathbf{b} + \mathbf{c} = \mathbf{0}$,

$$0 = |\mathbf{a} + \mathbf{b} + \mathbf{c}|^2 = a^2 + b^2 + c^2 + 2(\mathbf{a} \cdot \mathbf{b} + \mathbf{a} \cdot \mathbf{c} + \mathbf{b} \cdot \mathbf{c}).$$

Substituting this into (1) gives

$$S = (a^2 + b^2 + c^2)\left(n - 1 + \frac{(n-1)(2n-1)}{6n} - \frac{n-1}{2}\right).$$

Hence

$$\frac{S}{a^2 + b^2 + c^2} = \frac{(n-1)(5n-1)}{6n}.$$

L and M are points on the sides AB and AC, respectively, of triangle ABC such that $\overline{AL} = 2\overline{AB}/5$ and $\overline{AM} = 3\overline{AC}/4$. If BM and CL intersect at P, and AP and BC intersect at N, determine $\overline{BN}/\overline{BC}$.

Solution

From Ceva's theorem one has

$$\frac{AL}{LB} \cdot \frac{BN}{NC} \cdot \frac{CM}{MA} = 1$$

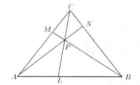

This gives $BN/NC = 9/2$ and so $BN/BC = 9/11$.

Let O be the centre of the circle through the points A, B, C, and let D be the midpoint of AB. Let E be the centroid of the triangle ACD. Prove that the line CD is perpendicular to the line OE if and only if $AB = AC$.

Solution

Set $\overrightarrow{OA} = \mathbf{a}$, $\overrightarrow{OB} = \mathbf{b}$, $\overrightarrow{OC} = \mathbf{c}$. Then

$$\overrightarrow{OE} = \overrightarrow{OA} + \overrightarrow{OC} + \overrightarrow{OD} = \frac{3}{2}\,\overrightarrow{OA} + \frac{1}{2}\,\overrightarrow{OB} + \overrightarrow{OC} = \frac{1}{6}(3\mathbf{a} + \mathbf{b} + 2\mathbf{c})$$

and

$$\overrightarrow{CD} = \frac{1}{2}\,(\overrightarrow{CA} + \overrightarrow{CB}) = \frac{1}{2}\,(\overrightarrow{OA} - \overrightarrow{OC} + \overrightarrow{OB} - \overrightarrow{OC}) = \frac{1}{2}\,(\mathbf{a} + \mathbf{b} - 2\mathbf{c}).$$

Hence CD is perpendicular to OE if and only if $(3\mathbf{a} + \mathbf{b} + 2\mathbf{c}, \mathbf{a} + \mathbf{b} - 2\mathbf{c}) = 0$. Using the fact that $(\mathbf{a}, \mathbf{a}) = (\mathbf{b}, \mathbf{b}) = (\mathbf{c}, \mathbf{c})$, this is equivalent to $(\mathbf{a}, \mathbf{b} - \mathbf{c}) = (\mathbf{a}, \mathbf{b}) - (\mathbf{a}, \mathbf{c}) = 0$. This just the condition that $OA \perp CB$, or that $AB = AC$.

In a Cartesian coordinate system, the circle C_1 has center $O_1 = (-2, 0)$ and radius 3. Denote the point $(1, 0)$ by A and the origin by O. Prove that there is a positive constant c such that for any point X which is exterior to C_1,

$$\overline{OX} - 1 \geq c \, \min\{\overline{AX}, \overline{AX}^2\}.$$

Find the smallest possible c.

Solution

Denote by D_1 and D_2 the disks bounded by C_1 and the circle C_2 with center A and radius 1. Clearly, $\min\{\overline{AX}, \overline{AX}^2\} = \overline{AX}$ if $X \notin D_2$ and $\min\{\overline{AX}, \overline{AX}^2\} = \overline{AX}^2$ if $X \in D_2$.

If $X \notin D_1 \cup D_2$, set $t = \overline{OX}/\overline{AX}$. Then X lies on the Apollonius circle S_t. On S_t, $(\overline{OX} - 1)/\overline{AX} = t - 1/\overline{AX}$ is minimized when $\overline{AX}$ is minimal; this is clearly the case when X is on the boundary of $D_1 \cup D_2$. If X is on C_2, $\overline{AX} = 1$ and $t - 1/\overline{AX} = t - 1$ is minimized when X is as close to O as possible; this means that X is the intersection X_0 of C_1 and C_2. By some elementary trigonometry, $t = \overline{OX_0} = \sqrt{5/3}$. If $X \in C_1$, one calculates that

$$t - 1/\overline{AX} = \frac{\sqrt{1 + 24\sin^2(\omega/2)} - 1}{6\sin(\omega/2)},$$

where ω is the angle XO_1A. This is an increasing function of ω. So even here $t - 1/\overline{AX}$ is minimized at X_0.

If $X \in D_2 \setminus D_1$, we again consider S_t such that $X \in S_t$. On S_t, $(\overline{OX} - 1)/\overline{AX}^2 = t/\overline{AX} - 1/\overline{AX}^2$. This function of $\overline{AX}$ assumes its minimum either when AX takes its largest value or when it takes its smallest value, i.e., either on the boundary C_2 or the x-axis, where it reduces in either case to $t - 1$ and is minimized at X_0, or on the boundary C_1, where its expression is

$$\frac{\sqrt{1 + 24\sin^2(\omega/2)} - 1}{[6\sin(\omega/2)]^2}.$$

This decreases with ω and is minimized at X_0. So one can choose $c = \sqrt{5/3} - 1$. It is also the smallest possible value of c.

IMO Proposal by Poland (1987)

Let F be a one-to-one mapping of the plane into itself which maps closed rectangles into closed rectangles. Show that F maps squares into squares. Continuity of F is not assumed.

Solution

We consider an arbitrary rectangle $ABCD$. Let O be the center of the rectangle, and X, Y, Z, T the midpoints of the sides AB, BC, CD, DA respectively. Let P, P_{AB}, P_{BC}, P_{CD}, P_{DA} denote the rectangles $ABCD$, $ABYT$, $BCZX$, $CDTY$, $DAXZ$, and a, b the segments YT, XZ, respectively. Thus we have

$$P = P_{AB} \cup P_{CD} = P_{BC} \cup P_{DA}, \quad a = P_{AB} \cap P_{CD}, \quad b = P_{BC} \cap P_{DA}.$$

We denote by Q, Q_{AB}, Q_{BC}, Q_{CD}, Q_{DA}, a', b' the respective images, i.e. $Q = F(P)$, $Q_{AB} = F(P_{AB})$, etc. We have

(1) $Q = Q_{AB} \cup Q_{CD}, \quad a' = Q_{AB} \cap Q_{CD}$.

This implies that

(2) Q_{AB} and Q_{CD} are rectangles such that for some two parallel sides of Q one of them is a side of Q_{AB} and another is a side of Q_{CD}.

This in turn implies that

(3a) a' is a line segment whose endpoints lie on sides of the rectangle Q and which is parallel to its two sides, or

(3b) a' is a rectangle whose vertices lie on sides of Q and whose sides are parallel to the sides of Q.

From (3a) and (3b), and from similar conditions for the set b', it follows that

(4) the set $a' \cap b'$ consists of a single point iff the sets a' and b' are perpendicular line segments which are parallel to sides of the rectangle Q and whose endpoints lie on sides of Q.

Since $F(O) = a' \cap b'$, the set $a' \cap b'$ is a single point. From this, from the definition of a, b, a', b', and from (4) we obtain the following

Lemma: *F maps line segments into line segments, sides of rectangles into sides of rectangles, vertices of rectangles into vertices of rectangles, and perpendicular line segments into perpendicular line segments.*

From the lemma it follows that if $ABCD$ is a square, then $F(A)F(B)F(C)F(D)$ is its image and it is a rectangle. F maps diagonals of $ABCD$ onto diagonals of its image. Since AC and BD are perpendicular, their images $F(A)F(C)$ and $F(B)F(D)$ are perpendicular, too. But this is possible if and only if $F(A)F(B)F(C)F(D)$ is a square.

Suppose $\triangle ABC$ and $\triangle DEF$ in the figure are congruent. Prove that the perpendicular bisectors of AD, BE, and CF intersect at the same point.

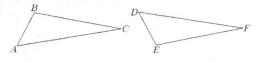

Solution

The problem is obviously false as stated, as the accompanying diagram illustrates.

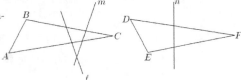

ℓ is the $\perp$ bisector of AD.
m is the $\perp$ bisector of BE.
n is the $\perp$ bisector of CF.

However, there is a result about perpendicular bisectors of congruent triangles:

Let $\triangle ABC$ be a triangle in the plane and R any other point. If $\triangle DEF$ is the image of $\triangle ABC$ under any isometry which fixes R, then the perpendicular bisectors of AD, BE and CF intersect at R.

(This result follows since the perpendicular bisector of a line segment is the locus of all points which are equidistant from the two endpoints.)

In triangle ABC, angle C is $30°$. D is a point on AC and E is a point on BC such that $AD = BE = AB$. Prove that $OI = DE$ and OI is perpendicular to DE, where O and I are respectively the circumcentre and incentre of triangle ABC.

Solution

We generalize the problem by considering an arbitrary triangle ABC with $c < a$, $c < b$. The projection of O on CB is F, that on CA is G. The projection of I on CB is H, that on CA is K. Now

$$HF = BF - BH = \frac{1}{2}a - (s - b) = \frac{1}{2}(b - c) = \frac{1}{2}CD$$

and $KG = \frac{1}{2}(a - c) = \frac{1}{2}CE$. The production of GO intersects IH (or its production) in L. Consider triangle OIL. Angle $\angle ILO = \gamma\ (= \angle C)$, since $OL \perp CA$, $IL \perp CB$. It is easy to verify that

$$IL = \frac{KG}{\sin \gamma} = \frac{CE}{2 \sin \gamma}$$

and

$$OL = \frac{HF}{\sin \gamma} = \frac{CD}{2 \sin \gamma}.$$

We see that triangles LIO and CED are similar, for $LI : LO = CE : CD$. Moreover $LI \perp CE$ and $LO \perp CD$ imply $IO \perp ED$. Also

$$IO = \frac{DE}{2 \sin \gamma},$$

and for $\gamma = 30°$ this gives $IO = DE$, as desired.

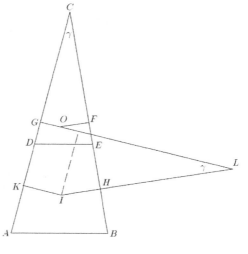

Side AB of a square $ABCD$ is divided into n segments in such a way that the sum of lengths of the even numbered segments equals the sum of lengths of the odd numbered segments. Lines parallel to AD are drawn through each point of division, and each of the n "strips" thus formed is divided by diagonal BD into a left region and a right region. Show that the sum of the areas of the left regions with odd numbers is equal to the sum of the areas of the right regions with even numbers.

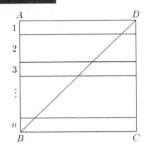

Solution

We show that the conclusion holds when $ABCD$ is any rectangle. Let $AD = a$ and $AB = b$. Denote by h_i the height of the ith strip, so that $\sum_{i \ \text{odd}} h_i = \sum_{i \ \text{even}} h_i$ and $\sum_{i=1}^{n} h_i = b$. Also let L_i and R_i denote the area of the ith left region and right region, respectively, $i = 1, 2, \ldots, n$. Then

$$\sum_{i \ \text{odd}} L_i + \sum_{i \ \text{even}} L_i = \frac{1}{2} ab$$

and

$$\sum_{i \ \text{even}} L_i + \sum_{i \ \text{even}} R_i = a \sum_{i \ \text{even}} h_i = \frac{1}{2} ab.$$

From these we immediately get

$$\sum_{i \ \text{odd}} L_i = \sum_{i \ \text{even}} R_i.$$

Points M and P are the midpoints of sides BC and CD of convex quadrilateral $ABCD$. If $AM + AP = a$, show that the area of the region $ABCD$ is less than $a^2/2$.

Solution

Denote by $[P]$ the area of polygon P. Since $BM = CM$, $[ABM] = [ACM]$. Similarly $[ADP] = [ACP]$ so that $[ABCD] = 2[AMCP]$. Now MP is parallel to BD, and C is at the same distance from MP as BD is from MP. Since $ABCD$ is convex, A is on the opposite side to C of BD. Now AMP and CMP have the same base. Since AMP has the greater altitude, $[AMP] > [CMP]$. Finally, note that

$$[AMP] = \frac{1}{2}AM \cdot AP \sin MAP \leq \frac{1}{2}AM \cdot AP \leq \frac{1}{8}a^2$$

by the Arithmetic-Mean Geometric-Mean Inequality. Hence

$$[ABCD] = 2[AMCP] = 2[AMP] + 2[CMP] < 4[AMP] \leq \frac{1}{2}a^2$$

as desired.

Segments AC and BD intersect in point P so that $PA = PD$, $PB = PC$. Let O be the circumcentre of triangle PAB. Prove that lines OP and CD are perpendicular.

Solution

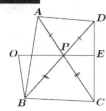

Because $PA = PD$, $PB = PC$,

and $\angle APB = \angle DPC$,

we get $\triangle PAB \equiv \triangle PDC$, so that

$$\angle BAP = \angle CDP. \qquad (1)$$

At least one of $\angle PAB$ and $\angle PBA$ is acute, so we may assume without loss of generality that $\angle PAB$ is acute. Since O is the circumcentre of $\triangle PAB$ we get $OB = OP$ and $\angle BOP = 2\angle BAP$, so that

$$\angle OPB = 90° - \frac{1}{2}\angle BOP = 90° - \angle BAP. \qquad (2)$$

Let E be the intersection of OP with CD. Then

$$\angle EPD = \angle OPB. \qquad (3)$$

From (1), (2) and (3) we have

$$\angle EPD = 90° - \angle CDP.$$

Thus $\angle EPD + \angle EDP = \angle EPD + \angle CDP = 90°$. Therefore $OP \perp CD$.

Comment: Generally if A, B, C, D are concyclic, we have $OP \perp CD$ and this theorem is an extension of Brahmagupta's theorem.

Let triangle ABC be such that its circumradius $R = 1$. Let r be the inradius of ABC and let p be the inradius of the orthic triangle $A'B'C'$ of triangle ABC. Prove that $p \leq 1 - 1/3(1 + r)^2$.

Solution

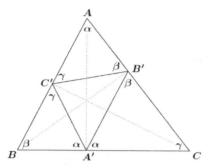

Now $r_{\triangle ABC} = R(\cos \alpha + \cos \beta + \cos \gamma - 1)$. From $R = 1$, we obtain $r = \cos \alpha + \cos \beta + \cos \gamma - 1$. Similarly,

$$p = \frac{1}{2}[\cos(\pi - 2\alpha) + \cos(\pi - 2\beta) + \cos(\pi - 2\gamma) - 1]$$
$$= 2 \cos \alpha \cos \beta \cos \gamma.$$

We are to show that $p + \frac{1}{3}(1 + r)^2 \leq 1$. $\hspace{2cm}$ (1)

Equivalently,

$$2 \cos \alpha \cos \beta \cos \gamma + \frac{1}{3}(\cos \alpha + \cos \beta + \cos \gamma)^2 \leq 1. \hspace{1cm} (2)$$

Now

$$\left.\begin{array}{c} -1 < \cos \alpha \cos \beta \cos \gamma \leq \frac{1}{8}, \\ 1 < \cos \alpha + \cos \beta + \cos \gamma \leq \frac{3}{2}. \end{array}\right\} \hspace{1cm} (3)$$

Consider the triangle ABC, its circumcircle k of centre O and radius R, and its incircle of centre I and radius r. Another circle K_c is tangent to the sides CA, CB at D, E, respectively, and it is internally tangent to k. Show that I is the midpoint of DE.

Solution

Assume (see figure) that $\beta > \gamma$. Let F be the centre of K_c and ρ its radius. Then F lies on the production of AI. Now $FD = \rho$, so

$$AF = \frac{\rho}{\sin\frac{\alpha}{2}}.$$

Also $AO = R$, $OF = R - \rho$, and $\angle FAO = \varphi = \frac{1}{2}(\beta - \gamma)$.

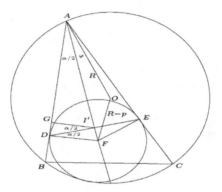

Apply the Law of Cosines to $\triangle AFO$:

$$OF^2 = AF^2 + AO^2 - 2AF \cdot AO \cos\varphi,$$

or

$$(R - \rho)^2 = \frac{\rho^2}{\sin^2\frac{\alpha}{2}} + R^2 - \frac{2R\rho \cos\left(\frac{\beta-\gamma}{2}\right)}{2\sin\frac{\alpha}{2}}; \quad \rho \neq 0.$$

From this we obtain

$$-2R + \rho = \frac{\rho}{\sin^2\frac{\alpha}{2}} - \frac{2R\cos\left(\frac{\beta-\gamma}{2}\right)}{\cos\left(\frac{\beta+\gamma}{2}\right)},$$

or

$$\frac{\rho\cos^2\frac{\alpha}{2}}{\sin^2\alpha/2} = \frac{4R\sin\frac{\beta}{2}\sin\frac{\gamma}{2}}{\sin\alpha/2}.$$

Thus

$$\rho = \frac{4R\sin\frac{\alpha}{2}\sin\frac{\beta}{2}\sin\frac{\gamma}{2}}{\cos^2\frac{\alpha}{2}} = \frac{r}{\cos^2\frac{\alpha}{2}} = FD.$$

Now let DE intersect AF at I'. Then $DI' = DF\cos\frac{\alpha}{2} = \frac{r}{\cos\frac{\alpha}{2}}$.
Let G be the foot of the perpendicular from I' to AB.
Then $I'G = I'D\cos\frac{\alpha}{2} = \frac{r}{\cos\frac{\alpha}{2}}\cos\frac{\alpha}{2} = r$. So I' coincides with I.

34th IMO Proposal by Spain (1993)

Given the triangle ABC, let D, E be points on the side BC such that $\angle BAD = \angle CAE$. If M and N are respectively, the points of tangency with BC of the incircles of the triangles ABD and ACE, show that

$$\frac{1}{BM} + \frac{1}{MD} = \frac{1}{NC} + \frac{1}{NE}.$$

Solution

We are to show $\frac{1}{MB} + \frac{1}{MD} = \frac{1}{NC} + \frac{1}{NE}$, or equivalently

$$BD \cdot NC \cdot NE = CE \cdot MB \cdot MD. \tag{1}$$

We denote $\angle BAD = \angle CAE = \varphi$.

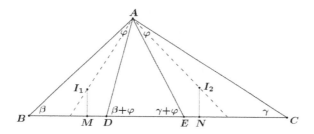

Applying the law of sines to $\triangle ABD$ we obtain

$$BD = \frac{c \sin \varphi}{\sin(\beta + \varphi)}, \qquad AD = \frac{c \sin \beta}{\sin(\beta + \varphi)}. \tag{2}$$

The sine law for $\triangle ACE$ gives

$$CE = \frac{b \sin \varphi}{\sin(\gamma + \varphi)}, \qquad AE = \frac{b \sin \gamma}{\sin(\gamma + \varphi)}. \tag{2'}$$

From $\triangle ABD$:

$$2MB = AB + BD - AD$$
$$2MD = -AB + BD + AD,$$

and from $\triangle ACE$:

$$2NC = AC + CE - AE$$
$$2NE = -AC + CE + AE.$$

From this we see that to show (1) we must show

$$BD(AC + CE - AE)(-AC + CE + AE)$$
$$= CE(AB + BD - AD)(-AB + BD + AD),$$

or equivalently

$$BD(CE^2 - AC^2 - AE^2 + 2AC \cdot AE)$$
$$= CE(BD^2 - AB^2 - AD^2 + 2AB \cdot AD). \qquad (3)$$

Now use the law of cosines in $\triangle ACE$, and in $\triangle ABD$ to obtain

$$\left. \begin{array}{l} CE^2 - AC^2 - AE^2 = -2AC\,AE \cos \varphi \\ BD^2 - AB^2 - AD^2 = -2AB\,AD \cos \varphi. \end{array} \right\} \qquad (4)$$

Combining (3) and (4) we see that we must show

$$BD \cdot AC \cdot AE(1 - \cos \varphi) = CE \cdot AB \cdot AD(1 - \cos \varphi).$$

As $1 - \cos \varphi \neq 0$, we find with (2) and (2') that we must verify that

$$\frac{c \sin \varphi}{\sin(\beta + \gamma)} \cdot b \cdot \frac{b \sin \gamma}{\sin(\gamma + \varphi)} = \frac{b \sin \varphi}{\sin(\gamma + \varphi)} \cdot c \cdot \frac{c \sin \beta}{\sin(\beta + \varphi)},$$

and as $b \sin \gamma = c \sin \beta$, this holds.

ABC is an isosceles triangle with $AB = AC$. Suppose that

(i) M is the midoint of BC and D is the point on the line AM such that OB is perpendicular to AB;

(ii) Q is an arbitrary point on the segment BC different from B and C;

(iii) E lies on the line AB and F on the line AC such that E, Q and F are distinct and collinear.

Prove that OQ is perpendicular to EF if and only if $QE = QF$.

Solution

($\Longrightarrow$). See Figure 1. Assume $OQ \perp EF$. We want to show $QE = QF$.

Note that quadrilateral $OBEQ$ is inscribed on the circle with diameter OE. Thus $\angle OEQ = \angle OBQ = \angle OQB = \frac{\alpha}{2}$. Also $OFCQ$ is cyclic and thus $\angle OFQ = \angle OCQ = \angle OAC = \frac{\alpha}{2}$. Together these give $\angle OEQ = \angle OFQ$ and $OQ \perp EF$, so $QE = QF$.

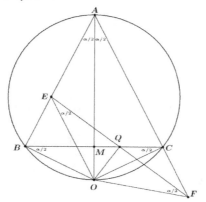

Figure 1.

($\Longleftarrow$). See Figure 2. Assume that $QE = QF$. We want to show that $OQ \perp EF$.

Let D lie on AC with QD parallel to AB. As $QE = QF$ we see that D is the midpoint of AF. As $AB = AC$ we have $DQ = DC$. $\qquad$ (1)
Also,

$$QE = 2DQ = 2CD \qquad\qquad (2)$$

$$BE = AB - AE. \qquad\qquad (3)$$

From (2) and (3)

$$BE = AC - 2CD = (AC - CD) - CD$$
$$= AD - CD = DF - CD.$$

Thus $BE = CF$. $\qquad\qquad\qquad\qquad\qquad\qquad\qquad\qquad$ (4)

Draw OB, OE, OC, and OF.

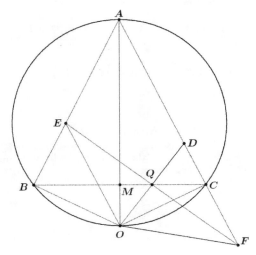

Figure 2.

Then

$$\triangle OBE \cong \triangle COF[BE = CF, \ OB = OC, \ \angle OBE = \angle OCF = n/2].$$
$$\qquad\qquad\qquad\qquad\qquad\qquad\qquad\qquad\qquad\qquad (5)$$

Now this implies that $OE = OF$, $QE = QF$ giving $OQ \perp EF$.

Remark. This direction could be shortened by using the law of sines in triangles BQF and CQF, but the given solution is, I think, more elementary, and therefore more elegant.

The rectangular $2n$-gon is the base of a regular pyramid with vertex S. A sphere passing through S cuts the lateral edges SA_i in the respective points B_i $(i = 1, 2, \ldots, 2n)$. Show that

$$\sum_{i=1}^{n} SB_{2i-1} = \sum_{i=1}^{n} SB_{2i}.$$

Solution

Let S be the origin $(0, 0, 0)$ of a rectangular coordinate system and let the coordinates origin $(0, 0, 0)$ of a rectangular coordinate system and let the coordinates of the vertices A_k of the regular $2n$-gon be given by $(r \cos \theta_k, r \sin \theta_k, a)$, $k = 1, 2, \ldots, 2n$ where $\theta_k = \pi k / n$. A general sphere through S is given by

$$(x - h)^2 + (y - k)^2 + (z - l)^2 = h^2 + k^2 + l^2.$$

Since the parametric equation of the line SA_k is given by

$$x = tr \cos \theta_k, \quad y = tr \sin \theta_k, \quad z = ta,$$

its intersection with the sphere is given by

$$(tr \cos \theta_k - h)^2 + (tr \sin \theta_k - k)^2 + (ta - l)^2 = h^2 + k^2 + l^2.$$

Solving for t, $t = 0$ corresponding to point S and

$$t = \frac{(hr \cos \theta_k + kr \sin \theta_k + al)}{(r^2 + a^2)}.$$

Since $SB_k = t\sqrt{r^2 + a^2}$, the desired result will follow if

$$\sum \cos \theta_{2k-1} = \sum \cos \theta_{2k} \quad \text{and} \quad \sum \sin \theta_{2k-1} = \sum \sin \theta_{2k}$$

(where the sums are over $k = 1, 2, \ldots, n$). Since in the plane

$$(\cos \theta_{2k-1}, \sin \theta_{2k-1}), \quad k = 1, 2, \ldots, n,$$

are the vertices of a regular n-gon, both $\sum \cos \theta_{2k-1}$ and $\sum \sin \theta_{2k-1}$ vanish and the same for $\sum \cos \theta_{2k}$ and $\sum \sin \theta_{2k}$.

Nordic Mathematical Contest, 1992

3

Prove that among all triangles with given incircle, the equilateral one has the least perimeter.

Solution

Let the three sides be a, b, c. Then the inradius r times the semiperimeter is the area $A = rs$, $r = 1$ so, using Heron's formula

$$\sqrt{s(s-a)(s-b)(s-c)} = s$$

or

$$\sqrt{(s-a)(s-b)(s-c)} = \sqrt{s}$$

so

$$s = (s-a)(s-b)(s-c). \quad (1)$$

Also

$$s = (s-a) + (s-b) + (s-c). \quad (2)$$

We minimize the perimeter and therefore s by the AM–GM inequality and (1) and (2)

$$\sqrt{(s-a)(s-b)(s-c)} \le \frac{(s-a)+(s-b)+(s-c)}{3}$$

The RHS is minimized when we have equality, that is $s-a = s-b = s-c$, and $a = b = c$.

Let O be the intersection of diagonals of the convex quadrilateral $ABCD$. If P and Q are the centres of the circumcircles of AOB and COD show that

$$PQ \geq \frac{AB + CD}{4}.$$

Solution

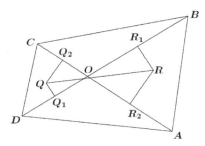

Let P_1, Q_1, P_2, Q_2 be the midpoints of OB, OD, OA and OC respectively.

Then

$$PQ \geq P_1Q_1 \Rightarrow PQ \geq \tfrac{1}{2}BD,$$

$$PQ \geq P_2Q_2 \Rightarrow PQ \geq \tfrac{1}{2}AC.$$

From this, we get

$$PQ \geq \frac{1}{4}(BD + AC)$$
$$\geq \frac{1}{4}(OB + OD + OA + OC)$$
$$\geq \frac{1}{4}[(OB + OA) + (OC + OD)].$$

Now $OB + OA > AB$ and $OC + OD > CD$. Thus $PQ \geq \tfrac{1}{4}(AB + CD)$.

Let $\triangle ABC$ be an isosceles triangle with $AB = AC$. Suppose that the angle bisector of $\angle B$ meets AC at D and that $BC = BD + AD$. Determine $\angle A$.

Solution

Let $BE = BD$ with E on BC, so that $AD = EC$:

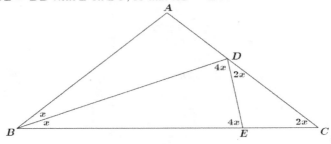

By a standard theorem, $\dfrac{AB}{CB} = \dfrac{AD}{DC}$; so in $\triangle CED$ and $\triangle CAB$ we have a common angle and

$$\frac{CE}{CD} = \frac{AD}{CD} = \frac{AB}{CB} = \frac{CA}{CB} .$$

Thus, $\triangle CED \sim \triangle CAB$, so that $\angle CDE = \angle DCE = \angle ABC = 2x$.

Hence $\angle BDE = \angle BED = 4x$, whence $9x = 180°$ so $x = 20°$.

Thus $\angle A = 180° - 4x = 100°$.

In the right triangle ABC ($A = 90°$), let the internal bisectors of B and C intersect each other at I and the opposite sides D and E respectively. Prove that the area of quadrilateral $BCDE$ is twice the area of the triangle BIC.

Solution

If b and c are the legs, a the hypotenuse, s the semiperimeter and r the inradius of the given right triangle then it is known that $r = s - a$.

The area of such a triangle is $bc/2$. On the other hand, the area of any triangle is sr. Setting the two expressions equal we have

$$bc = 2sr = 2s(s - a) \tag{1}$$

We see that (see figure 1.1)

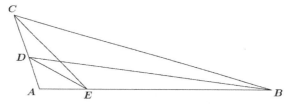

Figure 1.1

area of quadrilateral $BCDE$ = area ($\triangle ABC$) − area ($\triangle AED$). (2)

Since $AE = bc/(a + b)$ and $AD = bd/(a + c)$ we have Area ($\triangle AED$) = $\frac{1}{2}\frac{bc}{a+b} \cdot \frac{bc}{a+c}$. Substituting, using (2), we have

$$\begin{aligned}
\text{area of quadrilateral } & BCDE \\
&= \frac{1}{2}bc - \frac{1}{2}\frac{bc}{a + c} \cdot \frac{bc}{a+c} \\
&= \frac{1}{2}bc \left(1 - \frac{bc}{(a + b)(a + c)}\right) \\
&= \frac{1}{2}bc\frac{a(a + b + c)}{(a + b)(a + c)} = \frac{abcs}{(a + b)(a + c)}.
\end{aligned} \tag{3}$$

Since $(a + b)(a + c) = a(a + b + c) + bc = 2as + 2s(s - a) = 2s^2$ we can write (3) in the form

$$\text{Area of quadrilateral } BCDE = \frac{abc}{2s}.$$

Finally, we substitute $2rs$ for bc from (1), simplify, and obtain Area of quadrilateral $BCDE = ar = 2$(area of $\triangle BIC$), which was to be proved.

In the triangle ABC we have $A \leq 90°$ and $B = 2C$. Let the internal bisector of C intersect the median AM (M is the mid-point of BC) at D. Prove that $\angle MDC \leq 45°$. What is the condition for $\angle MDC = 45°$?

Solution

It suffices to show that $\tan(\angle MDC) \leq 1$.

If $\triangle ABC$ has sides a, b, c, in the usual order, then the condition $B = 2C$ is equivalent to the condition $b^2 = c(c + a)$ (see this journal [1976: 74] and [1984: 287]). \hfill (1)

We introduce a Cartesian frame with origin at B and x-axis along BC:

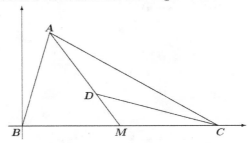

Figure 5

The coordinates of A are $(c \cdot \cos B, c \cdot \sin B)$, the coordinates of C are $(a, 0)$, and those of M are $(a/2, 0)$.

The internal angle bisector of C has slope

$$m_1 = \tan(180° - C/2) = -\tan(C/2)$$

and the slope of the median AM is

$$m_2 = \frac{c \cdot \sin B}{c \cdot \cos B - a/2}. \tag{2}$$

The law of cosines gives

$$b^2 = c^2 + a^2 - 2ca \cdot \cos B.$$

Substituting for b^2 from (1), we obtain

$$c(c + a) = c^2 + a^2 - 2ca \cdot \cos B,$$

and hence

$$c \cdot \cos B = (a - c)/2.$$

Substituting this into (2), we obtain

$$m_2 = -2 \cdot \sin B.$$

Since $B = 2C$ and $\sin 2C = 2 \sin C \cos C$, this equation may be rewritten as

$$m_2 = -4 \sin C \cos C.$$

Using the formula for the tangent of the angle between two lines, we get

$$\tan(\angle MDC) = \frac{m_1 - m_2}{1 + m_1 m_2} = \frac{-\tan(C/2) + 4\sin C \cos C}{1 + 4(\tan(C/2)) \cdot \sin C \cos C}. \qquad (3)$$

We express $\sin C$ and $\cos C$ in terms of $\tan(C/2)$. Putting $t = \tan(C/2)$, we get

$$\sin C = \frac{2t}{(1 + t^2)}, \quad \cos C = \frac{(1 - t^2)}{(1 + t^2)}.$$

When these are substituted into (3), it becomes

$$\tan(\angle MDC) = \frac{-t + \frac{8t(1-t)^2}{(1+t^2)^2}}{1 + \frac{8t^2(1-t^2)}{(1+t^2)^2}} = \frac{-t(1 + t^2)^2 + 8t(1 - t^2)}{(1 + t^2)^2 + 8t^2(1 - t^2)}.$$

We now prove that $\tan(\angle MDC) \leq 1$. This holds if and only if

$$8t(1 - t^2) - t(1 + t^2)^2 \leq 8t^2(1 - t^2) + (1 + t^2)^2,$$

or, equivalently,

$$8t(1 - t^2) - 8t^2(1 - t^2) \leq (1 + t^2)^2 + t(1 + t^2)^2,$$

or

$$8t(1 - t^2)(1 - t) \leq (1 + t^2)^2(1 + t).$$

Dividing both sides by the positive number $1 + t$, we get

$$8t(1 - t)^2 \leq (1 + t^2)^2,$$

equivalent to

$$8t - 16t^2 + 8t^3 \leq 1 + 2t^2 + t^4,$$

which is indeed true since

$$t^4 - 8t^3 + 18t^2 - 8t + 1 = (t^2 - 4t + 1)^2 \geq 0.$$

Equality $\angle MDC = 45°$ occurs if and only if $t^2 - 4t + 1 = 0$, where $t = \tan(C/2)$. This is satisfied when $t = 2 - \sqrt{3}$, i.e. $C = 30° + 360°k$; or $t = 2 + \sqrt{3}$, i.e. $C = 150° + 360°k$ $(k = \ldots, -2, -1, 0, 1, 2, \ldots)$.

The only acceptable value for C is $30°$.

We conclude that $\angle MDC = 45°$ iff $A = 90°$, $B = 60°$, $C = 30°$.

Let ABC be a triangle with $\overline{BC} = a$, $\overline{CA} = b$, $\overline{AB} = c$. Find the point P for which

$$a \cdot \overline{AP}^2 + b \cdot \overline{BP}^2 + c \cdot \overline{CP}^2$$

is minimal, and find the minimum.

Solution

Let P be a point in the plane of a triangle ABC and M be an arbitrary point in space. Then $\overrightarrow{MP} = (\sum x_i \, \overrightarrow{MA})/(\sum x_i)$, where x_1, x_2, x_3 are real numbers, and summations are taken cyclically. The following generalization of the well-known Leibnitz identity is valid:

$$\left(\sum x_i\right)^2 \overline{MP}^2 = \left(\sum x_i\right) \sum x_i \overline{MA}^2 - \sum a^2 x_2 x_3.$$

For $P = I$, (where I is the incentre of $\triangle ABC$), we get (because we can take $\sum x_i = 2s$, $\sum a^2 x_i x_j = abc \cdot 2s$)

$$\sum a\overline{MA}^2 = 2s\overline{MI}^2 + abc,$$

and as a consequence we have the following inequality,

$$\sum a\overline{MA}^2 \geq abc,$$

and equality holds only for $M = I$.

From this take $M = P$,

$$a\overline{AP}^2 + b\overline{BP}^2 + c\overline{CP}^2 \geq abc$$

and

$$\min(a\overline{AP}^2 + b\overline{BP}^2 + c\overline{CP}^2) = abc$$

with $P = I$.

Let ABC be a triangle with $\overline{BC} = a$, $\overline{CA} = b$ and $\overline{AB} = c$. Let D be the mid-point of the side BC, and let E be the point on BC for which the line segment AE is the bisector of angle A. Let the circle passing through A, D, E intersect with the sides CA, AB at F, G respectively. Finally let H be the point on AB for which $\overline{BG} = \overline{GH}$, i.e. $\overline{BH} = 2\overline{BG}$. Prove that the triangles EBH and ABC are similar and then find the ratio $\frac{\triangle EBH}{\triangle ABC}$ of these areas.

Solution

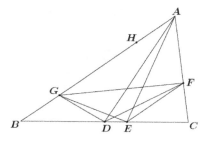

Now $\angle EAF = \angle EGF = \angle FDE$ and $\angle GAD = \angle GFD = \angle GED$. Thus $\triangle GED \sim \triangle ABD$ since two angles are the same. Thus

$$\frac{BE}{AB} = \frac{BG}{BD} = \frac{GE}{AD} \quad \text{and} \quad \frac{BE}{AB} = \frac{BH}{BC} = \frac{HE}{AC}.$$

Thus $\triangle BHE \sim \triangle ABC$.

The ratio $\frac{\triangle BHE}{\triangle ABC} = \left(\frac{BE}{c}\right)^2$. By the sine rule

$$\frac{BE}{\sin \frac{A}{2}} = \frac{AE}{\sin B}$$

$$\frac{a - BE}{\sin \frac{A}{2}} = \frac{AE}{\sin C}.$$

Therefore $BE \sin B = (a - BE) \sin C$, and so

$$BE = \frac{a \sin C}{\sin B + \sin C} = \frac{a \frac{c}{2R}}{\frac{b}{2R} + \frac{c}{2R}}$$

$$= \frac{ac}{b + c},$$

and

$$\left(\frac{BE}{c}\right)^2 : 1 = \left(\frac{ac}{c(b + c)}\right)^2 : 1 = \frac{a^2}{(b + c)^2}.$$

Let M be the circumcentre of an acute-angled triangle ABC, and assume the circle (BMA) intersects the segment $[BC]$ at P, and the segment $[AC]$ at Q. Show that the line CM is perpendicular to the line PQ.

Solution

Let triangle ABC have angles A, B, and C. $\angle AMC = 2\angle B$ in circle (ABC). Thus

$$\angle MCA = \frac{180° - 2B}{2} \quad \text{(in isosceles triangle } AMC)$$
$$= 90° - B;$$
$$\angle PQC = \angle ABP \quad \text{(in circle } (AMB))$$
$$= B.$$

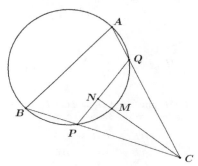

Thus, extending CM to meet PQ in N we have $\angle QCN = \angle MCA = 90° - B$ and $\angle NQC = \angle PQC = B$.

It follows that

$$\angle QNC = 180° - (\angle QCN + \angle NQC)$$
$$= 180° - (90° - B + B)$$
$$= 90°.$$

That is, $CM \perp PQ$.

On a semicircle with diameter AB and centre O points E and C are marked in such a way that OE is perpendicular to AB, and the chord AC intersects the segment OE at a point D which is interior to the semicircle. Find all values of the angle $\angle CAB$ such that a circle can be inscribed into the quadrilateral $OBCD$.

Solution

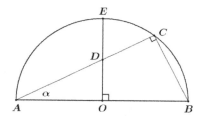

We set $OA = OB = 1$ and denote $\angle BAC = \alpha$. Then $OD = \tan\alpha$, $OB = 1$ and $BC = 2\sin\alpha$, $CD = 2\cos\alpha - \frac{1}{\cos\alpha}$.

For a circle to be inscribed in quadrilateral $OBCD$, we have

$$
\begin{aligned}
OB + CD &= OD + BC \\
1 + 2\cos\alpha - \frac{1}{\cos\alpha} &= \tan\alpha + 2\sin\alpha \\
\cos\alpha + 2\cos^2\alpha - 1 &= \sin\alpha + 2\sin\alpha\cos\alpha \\
\cos\alpha + \cos 2\alpha &= \sin\alpha + \sin 2\alpha \\
2\cos\frac{3}{2}\alpha\cos\frac{\alpha}{2} &= 2\sin\frac{3}{2}\alpha\cos\frac{\alpha}{2}.
\end{aligned}
$$

Since $\cos\frac{\alpha}{2} \neq 0$, we have

$$
\begin{aligned}
\tan\frac{3\alpha}{2} &= 1 \\
\frac{3\alpha}{2} &= \frac{\pi}{4} \\
\alpha &= \frac{\pi}{6}.
\end{aligned}
$$

The line l is tangent to the circle S at the point A; B and C are points on l on opposite sides of A and the other tangents from B, C to S intersect at a point P. If B, C vary along l in such a way that the product $|AB| \cdot |AC|$ is constant, find the locus of P.

Solution

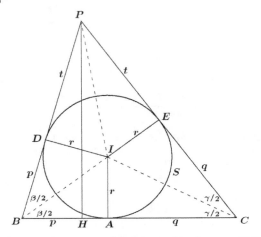

Let S be the incircle $s(I, 2)$ of $\triangle BCP$. We denote $\angle PBA = \beta$, $\angle PCA = \gamma$

$$\overline{AB} = p \quad \overline{AC} = q$$

with $pq = k^2$, a constant.

Let S touch BP and CP at D and E respectively. For $\triangle PEI$ we have $\angle EIP = \frac{1}{2}(\beta + \gamma)$. Thus

$$t = r \tan \frac{1}{2}(\beta + \gamma) = \frac{(p + q)r^2}{pq - r^2}.$$

The semiperimeter of $\triangle BCP$ is

$$p + q + t = p + q + \frac{(p + q)r^2}{pq - r^2} = \frac{pq(p + q)}{pq - r^2}.$$

The area, F, of $\triangle BCP$ is

$$r\frac{pq(p + q)}{pq - r^2} = \frac{1}{2}(p + q)PH,$$

where PH is the altitude to BC. It follows immediately that

$$PH = \frac{2pqr}{pq - r^2} = \frac{2k^2 r}{k^2 - r}.$$

So the locus of P is a line parallel to BC.

The vertices of six squares coincide in such a way that they enclose triangles; see the picture. Prove that the sum of the areas of the three outer squares (I, II and III) equals three times the sum of the areas of the three inner squares (IV, V and VI).

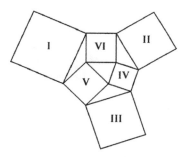

Solution

Let the figure on the next page be labelled as shown:

Let $MN = x_1$, $LU = x_3$, $UY = x_2$, $AC = x_4$, $AB = x_5$, $BC = x_6$, $\angle MBN = \alpha$, $\angle LAU = \beta$, $\angle VCY = \gamma$, $\angle BAC = A$, $\angle ACB = C$ and $\angle ABC = B$.

Then we have $\alpha + \beta = \pi$, $\beta + A = \pi$, $\gamma + C = \pi$

$$\left. \begin{aligned} x_1^2 &= x_6^2 + x_5^2 - 2x_5x_6 \cos \alpha \\ x_2^2 &= x_4^2 + x_6^2 - 2x_4x_6 \cos \gamma \\ x_3^2 &= x_4^2 + x_5^2 - 2x_4x_5 \cos \beta \end{aligned} \right\} \dots \tag{1}$$

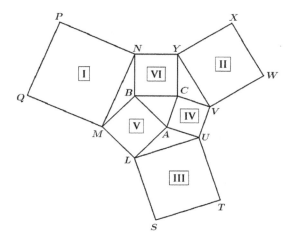

$$x_4^2 = x_5^2 + x_6^2 - 2x_5x_6 \cos B$$
$$x_4^2 = x_4^2 + x_6^2 - 2x_4x_6 \cos C \qquad \left.\right\} \ldots \qquad (2)$$
$$x_6^2 = x_4^2 + x_5^2 - 2x_4x_6 \cos A$$

From (2), we have

$$
\begin{aligned}
x_4^2 + x_5^2 + x_6^2 &= 2x_4x_5 \cos A + 2x_5x_6 \cos B + 2x_4x_6 \cos C \\
&= -2x_4x_5 \cos \beta - 2x_5x_6 \cos \alpha - 2x_4x_6 \cos \gamma \quad \ldots (3)
\end{aligned}
$$

From (1), we have

$$
\begin{aligned}
x_1^2 + x_2^2 + x_3^2 &= 2(x_4^2 + x_5^2 + x_6^2) - 2x_5x_6 \cos \alpha \\
&\qquad - 2x_4x_5 \cos \beta - 2x_4x_6 \cos \gamma
\end{aligned}
$$

$$\text{using (3)}$$

$$
\begin{aligned}
&= 2(x_4^2 + x_5^2 + x_6^2) + x_4^2 + x_5^2 + x_6^2 \\
&= 3(x_4^2 + x_5^2 + x_6^2).
\end{aligned}
$$

That is, Area of $(I + II + III) = 3$ Area of $(IV + V + VI)$.

We consider regular n-gons with a fixed circumference 4. We call the distance from the centre of such a n-gon to a vertex r_n and the distance from the centre to an edge a_n.

    a) Determine a_4, r_4, a_8, r_8.

    b) Give an appropriate interpretation for a_2 and r_2.

    c) Prove: $a_{2n} = \frac{1}{2}(a_n + r_n)$ and $r_{2n} = \sqrt{a_{2n}r_n}$.

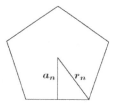

Let $u_0, u_1, u_2, u_3, \dots$ be defined as follows:

$$u_0 = 0, \ u_1 = 1; \ u_n = \frac{1}{2}(u_{n-2} + u_{n-1}) \text{ for } n \text{ even and}$$

$$u_n = \sqrt{u_{n-2} \cdot u_{n-1}} \text{ for } n \text{ odd}.$$

    d) Determine: $\lim_{n \to \infty} u_n$.

Solution

Let O be the centre of the regular n-gon. Let $A_1 A_2$ denote one side of the regular n-gon

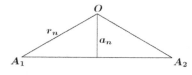

Then we have $\angle A_1 O A_2 = \frac{2\pi}{n}$, $\angle O A_1 A_2 = \angle O A_2 A_1 = \frac{\pi}{2} - \frac{\pi}{n}$. Thus

$$
\begin{aligned}
|\overrightarrow{A_1 A_2}| &= \sqrt{r_n^2 + r_n^2 - 2r_n^2 \cos \frac{2\pi}{n}} \\
&= \sqrt{2r_n^2 \left(1 - \cos \frac{2\pi}{n}\right)} \\
&= \sqrt{4r_n^2 \sin^2 \frac{\pi}{n}} = 2r_n \sin \frac{\pi}{n}.
\end{aligned}
$$

The circumference of the regular n-gon is $2nr_n \sin \frac{\pi}{n} = 4$ whence

$$r_n = \frac{2}{n \sin \frac{\pi}{n}},$$

$$a_n = r_n \sin \left(\frac{\pi}{2} - \frac{\pi}{n}\right) = r_n \cos \frac{\pi}{n} = \frac{2}{n} \cot \frac{\pi}{n}.$$

In particular

$$r_4 = \frac{1}{2}\frac{1}{\sin\frac{\pi}{4}} = \frac{\sqrt{2}}{2}, \qquad a_4 = \frac{2}{4}\cot\frac{\pi}{4} = \frac{1}{2},$$

$$r_8 = \frac{2}{8\sin\frac{\pi}{8}} = \frac{1}{4\sin\frac{\pi}{8}}.$$

Now, $\cos\frac{\pi}{4} = \frac{1}{\sqrt{2}} = 1 - 2\sin^2\frac{\pi}{8}$ gives

$$\sin\frac{\pi}{8} = \frac{1}{2}\sqrt{2 - \sqrt{2}},$$

so

$$r_8 = \frac{1}{4}\frac{2}{\sqrt{2-\sqrt{2}}} = \frac{1}{2}\cdot\frac{1}{\sqrt{2-\sqrt{2}}},$$

and

$$a_8 = r_8\cos\frac{\pi}{8} = \frac{1}{4}\sqrt{\frac{2+\sqrt{2}}{2-\sqrt{2}}} = \frac{1}{4}\frac{1}{2-\sqrt{2}}\sqrt{2},$$

since $\cos\frac{\pi}{4} = 2\cos^2\frac{\pi}{8} - 1$.

For (b), $r_2 = 1$, $a_2 = 0$ as the 2-gon is a straight line with O lying at the middle of A_1 and A_2.

For (c), we have

$$
\begin{aligned}
a_n + r_n &= r_n\left(1 + \cos\frac{\pi}{n}\right) = 2r_n\cos^2\frac{\pi}{2n} \\
&= \frac{4}{n\sin\frac{\pi}{n}}\cos^2\frac{\pi}{2n} \\
&= \frac{4}{2n\sin\frac{\pi}{2n}\cos\frac{\pi}{2n}}\cos^2\frac{\pi}{2n} = \frac{2}{n}\cot\frac{\pi}{2n}.
\end{aligned}
$$

Thus $\frac{1}{2}(a_n + r_n) = \frac{1}{n}\cot(\frac{\pi}{2n}) = a_{2n}$, and

$$a_{2n}r_n = \frac{1}{n}\frac{\cos\frac{\pi}{2n}}{\sin\frac{\pi}{2n}}\cdot\frac{2}{n\sin\frac{\pi}{n}} = \frac{1}{n^2}\frac{\cos\frac{\pi}{2n}}{\sin^2\frac{\pi}{2n}\cos\frac{\pi}{2n}} = \frac{1}{n^2\sin^2\frac{\pi}{2n}},$$

so $\sqrt{a_{2n}r_n} = \frac{1}{n\sin\frac{\pi}{2n}} = r_{2n}$.

For (d), note $u_0 = 0$, $u_1 = 1$, and $u_2 = \frac{1}{2}$. For $n \geq 2$ we have that u_n is either the arithmetic or geometric mean of u_{n-1} and u_{n-2} and in either case lies between them. It is also easy to show by induction that $u_0, u_2, u_4, \ldots$ form an increasing sequence, and $u_1, u_3, u_5, \ldots$ form a decreasing sequence with $u_{2l} \leq u_{2s+1}$ for all $l, s \geq 0$. Let $\lim_{k\to\infty}u_{2k} = P$ and $\lim_{k\to\infty}u_{2k+1} = I$. Then $P \leq I$. We also have from $u_{2n} = \frac{1}{2}(u_{2n-1} + u_{2n-2})$ that $P = \frac{1}{2}(I + P)$ so that $I = P$ and $\lim_{n\to\infty}u_n$ exists. Let $\lim_{n\to\infty}u_n = L$.

With $a_2 = 0$ and $r_2 = 1$, let $\overline{u}_{2k} = a_{2^{k+1}}$ and $\overline{u}_{2k+1} = r_{2^{k+1}}$, for $k = 0, 1, 2, \ldots$. From (c), $\overline{u}_0 = a_{2^1} = a_2 = 0$ and $\overline{u}_1 = r_{2^1} = r_2 = 1$. Also for $n = 2k + 2$, $\overline{u}_{2k+2} = a_{2^{k+1+1}} = a_{2\cdot 2^{k+1}} = \frac{1}{2}(a_{2^{k+1}} + b_{2^{k+1}}) = \frac{1}{2}(\overline{u}_{2k} + \overline{u}_{2k+1})$; that is $\overline{u}_n = \frac{1}{2}(\overline{u}_{n-2} + \overline{u}_{n-1})$ and for $n = 2k + 3$

$$
\begin{aligned}
\overline{u}_{2k+3} &= \overline{u}_{2(k+1)+1} = r_{2^{k+1+1}} = r_{2(2^{k+1})} \\
&= \sqrt{a_{2(2^{k+1})}\cdot r_{2^{k+1}}} = \sqrt{a_{2^{k+1+1}}\cdot r_{2^{k+1}}} \\
&= \sqrt{\overline{u}_{2(k+1)}\cdot\overline{u}_{2k+1}}
\end{aligned}
$$

so $\overline{u}_n = \sqrt{\overline{u}_{n-1}\cdot\overline{u}_{n-2}}$. Thus u_n and $\overline{u}_n$ satisfy the same recurrence and it follows that $L = \lim_{k\to\infty}a_{2^{k+1}} = \lim_{k\to\infty}r_{2^{k+1}}$. Now, from the solution to (c),

$$r_n = \frac{2}{n\sin\frac{\pi}{n}} = \frac{2}{\pi}\frac{\frac{\pi}{n}}{\sin\frac{\pi}{n}},$$

so $\lim_{n\to\infty}r_n = \frac{2}{\pi}$ since $\frac{\pi}{n} \to 0$. Therefore $\lim_{n\to\infty}u_n = \frac{2}{\pi}$.

Let $\triangle ABC$ be equilateral. On side AB produced, we choose a point P such that A lies between P and B. We now denote a as the length of sides of $\triangle ABC$; r_1 as the radius of incircle of $\triangle PAC$; and r_2 as the exradius of $\triangle PBC$ with respect to side BC. Determine the sum $r_1 + r_2$ as a function of a alone.

Solution

Looking at the figure, we see that $\angle T_1 O_1 R = 60°$ since it is the supplement of $\angle T_1 A R = 120°$ (as an exterior angle for $\triangle ABC$). Hence, $\angle AO_1 R = 30°$. Similarly, we obtain $\angle BO_2 S = 30°$.

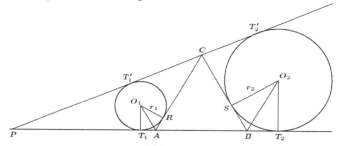

Since tangents drawn to a circle from an external point are equal, we have

$$T_1 T_2 = T_1 A + AB + BT_2 = RA + AB + SB$$
$$= r_1 \tan 30° + a + r_2 \tan 30° = \frac{r_1 + r_2}{\sqrt{3}} + a,$$

and

$$T_1' T_2' = T_1' C + C T_2' = CR + CS = (a - RA) + (a - SB) = 2a - \frac{r_1 + r_2}{\sqrt{3}}.$$

Since common external tangents to two circles are equal, $T_1 T_2 = T_1' T_2'$. Hence,

$$\frac{r_1 + r_2}{\sqrt{3}} + a = 2a - \frac{r_1 + r_2}{\sqrt{3}},$$

whence we find that

$$r_1 + r_2 = \frac{a\sqrt{3}}{2}.$$

A semicircle Γ is drawn on one side of a straight line ℓ. C and D are points on Γ. The tangents to Γ at C and D meet ℓ at B and A respectively, with the center of the semicircle between them. Let E be the point of intersection of AC and BD, and F be the point on ℓ such that EF is perpendicular to ℓ. Prove that EF bisects $\angle CFD$.

Solution

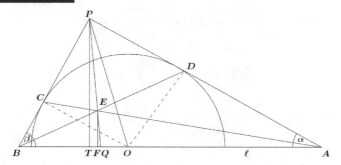

Let P be the intersection of AD and BC. Then $\angle PCO = \angle PDO = 90°$, $\angle CPO = \angle DPO$ and $PC = PD$. Let Q be the intersection of PE with AB. Then by Ceva's Theorem, we get

$$\frac{BQ}{QA} \cdot \frac{AD}{DP} \cdot \frac{PC}{CB} = \frac{BQ}{QA} \cdot \frac{AD}{CB} = 1.$$

Thus we get

$$\frac{BQ}{QA} = \frac{BC}{AD}. \tag{1}$$

Since $\angle BPO = \angle APO$ we get

$$\frac{PB}{PA} = \frac{BO}{AO}. \tag{2}$$

We put $\angle PAB = \alpha$, $\angle PBA = \beta$.

Let T be the foot of the perpendicular from P to AB. Then from (1) and (2) we have

$$\frac{BC}{AD} = \frac{BO \cos \beta}{AO \cos \alpha} = \frac{PB \cos \beta}{PA \cos \alpha} = \frac{PT}{TA}. \tag{3}$$

From (1) and (3) we have

$$\frac{BQ}{QA} = \frac{PT}{TA}.$$

Hence Q coincides with T so that P, E, F are collinear.

Because $\angle PCO = \angle PDO = \angle PFO = 90°$, P, C, F, O, D are concyclic. Hence $\angle CFE = \angle CFP = \angle CDP = \angle DCP = \angle DFP = \angle DFE$. Thus EF bisects $\angle CFD$.

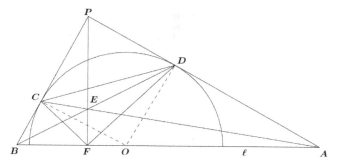

A circle ω is tangent to two parallel lines ℓ_1 and ℓ_2. A second circle ω_1 is tangent to ℓ_1 at A and to ω externally at C. A third circle ω_2 is tangent to ℓ_2 at B, to ω externally at D and to ω_1 externally at E. AD intersects BC at Q. Prove that Q is the circumcentre of triangle CDE.

Solution

We denote the three circles as $\omega(O, R)$, $\omega_1(O_1, R_1)$, $\omega_2(O_2, R_2)$. Now let ω touch ℓ_1 at F and ℓ_2 at F'. Let the line through O_2 parallel to ℓ_1 intersect FF' at G and the production of AO_1 at H.

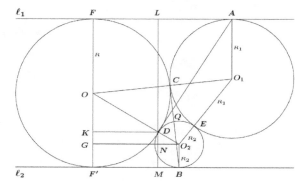

Let the line through D parallel to ℓ_1 intersect FF' at K.

Let the line through D parallel to FF' intersect ℓ_1 at L, ℓ_2 at M and GO_2 at N. Now AF is a common tangent of ω and ω_1, so

$$AF = 2\sqrt{RR_1} \tag{1}$$

and

$$BF' = 2\sqrt{RR_2} = GO_2. \tag{2}$$

It follows that

$$HO_2 = |2\sqrt{RR_2} - 2\sqrt{RR_1}|;$$

$$HO_1 = 2R - R_1 - R_2.$$

In right triangle O_1HO_2,

$$(2\sqrt{RR_2} - 2\sqrt{RR_1})^2 + (2R - R_1 - R_2)^2 = (R_1 + R_2)^2.$$

After some reduction $R = 2\sqrt{R_1R_2}$.

Next consider triangle GOO_2.

$$GO = R - R_2, \quad GO_2 = 2\sqrt{RR_2}, \quad DO_2 = R_2, \quad DO = R, \quad KD\|GO_2.$$

We find that $GN = FL = \dfrac{R}{R + R_2} \cdot GO_2 = \dfrac{2R\sqrt{RR_2}}{R + R_2}$.

With (1) we have

$$AL = 2\sqrt{RR_1} - \frac{2R\sqrt{RR_2}}{R + R_2}. \tag{3}$$

Furthermore $DN = \dfrac{R_2}{R + R_2} \cdot GO = \dfrac{R_2(R - R_2)}{R + R_2}$ and

$$DL = 2R - R_2 - \frac{R_2(R - R_2)}{R + R_2} = \frac{2R^2}{R + R_2}. \qquad (4)$$

Now $AD^2 = AL^2 + DL^2$. With (3) and (4),

$$\left(2\sqrt{RR_1} - \frac{2R\sqrt{RR_2}}{R_1 + R_2}\right)^2 + \left(\frac{2R^2}{R_1 + R_2}\right)^2 = 4RR_1 = AE^2.$$

So $AD = AF$.

That means that AD touches ω at D and AD is a common tangent and the radical axis of ω and ω_2.

In the same way BC is the radical axis of ω and ω_1 and Q is the radical point of ω, ω_1 and ω_2.

So $QC = QD = QE$, as required.

A line ℓ does not meet a circle ω with center O. E is the point on ℓ such that OE is perpendicular to ℓ. M is any point on ℓ other than E. The tangents from M to ω touch it at A and B. C is the point on MA such that EC is perpendicular to MA. D is the point on MB such that ED is perpendicular to MB. The line CD cuts OE at F. Prove that the location of F is independent of that of M.

Solution

As MA, MB are tangent to ω at A, B respectively, we get $\angle OAM = \angle OBM = 90°$ and $OM \perp AB$. Let N, P be the intersections of AB with OM and OE respectively.

Since M, E, P, N lie on the circle with diameter MP we get $ON \cdot OM = OB^2 = r^2$ where r is the radius of ω. Hence P is a fixed point. (P is the pole of ℓ.)

Let G be the foot of the perpendicular from E to AB. As $\angle OBM = \angle OAM = \angle OEM = 90°$, O, B, M, E, A are concyclic, so that by Simson's Theorem C, D, G are collinear.

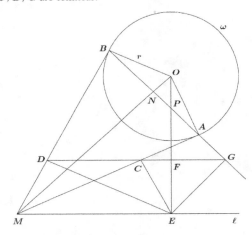

Since A, C, E, G lie on the circle with diameter AE we get

$$\angle EGF = \angle EGC = \angle EAC = \angle EAM. \tag{1}$$

As O, M, E, A are concyclic and OM is parallel to EG we have

$$\angle EAM = \angle EDM = \angle DEG = \angle FEG. \tag{2}$$

From (1) and (2) we get

$$\angle EGF = \angle FEG. \tag{3}$$

Since $\angle EGP = 90°$ we get

$$\angle FGP = \angle FPG. \tag{4}$$

From (3) and (4) we have $EF = FG = FP$. Thus F is the midpoint of EP. Hence F is a fixed point.

$ABCD$ is a quadrilateral with BC parallel to AD. M is the midpoint of CD, P that of MA and Q that of MB. The lines DP and CQ meet at N. Prove that N is not outside triangle ABM.

Solution

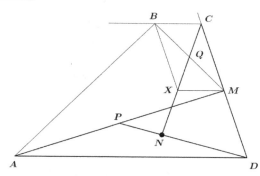

We draw a triangle ADM and denote the midpoint of MA by P. Let C be a point on the half-line DM such that M is the midpoint of CD.

Let N be any point of the segment PD, *inside* triangle ADM.

We construct a parallelogram $MCBX$ such that MX and BC are parallel to AD and X lies on the segment CN.

Let us denote the point where the diagonal MB of this quadrilateral meets CN by Q. Q is then the midpoint of MB.

Connect points A and B. We have thus constructed a quadrilateral $ABCD$ with BC parallel to AD, M is the midpoint of CD, P that of MA and Q that of MB. Lines DP and CQ meet at N.

N is inside triangle ADM; hence it is outside triangle ABM.

Given five points P_1, P_2, P_3, P_4, P_5 in the plane having integer coordinates, prove that there is at least one pair (P_i, P_j) with $i \neq j$ such that the line $P_i P_j$ contains a point Q having integer coordinates and lying strictly between P_i and P_j.

Solution

The points can be characterized according to the parity of their x and y coordinates. There are only four such classes: (even, even), (even, odd), (odd, even), (odd, odd).

Since we are given five such points, at least two must have the same parity of coordinates by the Pigeonhole Principle. Suppose they are P_i and P_j, $P_i = (x_i, y_i)$, $P_j = (x_j, y_j)$. Then $x_i + x_j$ is even and $y_i + y_j$ is even, since the x_i, x_j have the same parity and y_i, y_j have the same parity. Hence the midpoint

$$Q = \left(\frac{x_i + x_j}{2}, \frac{y_i + y_j}{2} \right)$$

has integral coordinates.

N is an arbitrary point on the bisector of $\angle BAC$. P and O are points on the lines AB and AN, respectively, such that $\angle ANP = 90° = \angle APO$. Q is an arbitrary point on NP, and an arbitrary line through Q meets the lines AB and AC at E and F respectively. Prove that $\angle OQE = 90°$ if and only if $QE = QF$.

Solution

First assume that $\angle OQE = 90°$. Extend PN to meet AC at R. Now $OEPQ$ and $ORFQ$ are cyclic quadrilaterals. Hence $\angle OEQ = \angle OPQ = \angle ORQ = \angle OFQ$. It now follows that we have $\triangle OEQ \equiv \triangle OFQ$ and $QE = QF$.

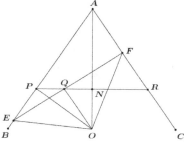

Now suppose that $\angle OQE \neq 90°$. Let the perpendicular through O to EF meet NP at $Q' \neq Q$. Draw the line through Q' parallel to EF, meeting the lines AB and AC at E' and F', respectively. Then $Q'E' = Q'F'$ as before. Let AQ' meet EF at $M \neq Q$. Then $ME = MF$ so that $QE \neq QF$. It follows that if $QE = QF$, then $\angle OQE = 90°$. (See next page for the diagram.)

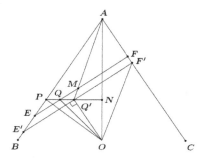

Show that in any triangle, the diameter of the incircle is not bigger than the circumradius.

Solution

Let a, b, c, r, R and Δ denote the side lengths, the inradius, the circumradius and the area of the given triangle, respectively. Then it is well known that $r = \dfrac{\Delta}{s}$ and $R = \dfrac{abc}{4\Delta}$ where $s = \dfrac{1}{2}(a + b + c)$ denotes the semiperimeter of the triangle. Hence $2r \leq R$ is equivalent to $8\Delta^2 \leq sabc$, which by virtue of Heron's formula

$$\Delta = \sqrt{s(s - a)(s - b)(s - c)}$$

becomes $\qquad 8(s - a)(s - b)(s - c) \leq abc,$

or $\qquad (b + c - a)(c + a - b)(a + b - c) \leq abc. \qquad (1)$

To show (1), note that $a^2 - (b - c)^2 \leq a^2$, $b^2 - (c - a)^2 \leq b^2$, and $c^2 - (a - b)^2 \leq c^2$. Multiplying, we obtain

$$(b + c - a)^2(c + a - b)^2(a + b - c)^2 \leq a^2b^2c^2. \qquad (2)$$

Since $b + c - a$, $c + a - b$ and $a + b - c$ are all positive, (1) follows from (2) by taking the square roots of both sides.

Clearly, equality holds if and only if $a = b = c$, that is, when the triangle is equilateral.

The point O is situated inside the parallelogram $ABCD$ so that

$$\angle AOB + \angle COD = 180° .$$

Prove that $\angle OBC = \angle ODC$.

Solution

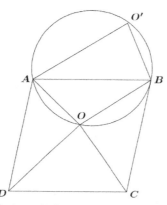

Consider a translation which maps D to A. It will map $O \rightarrow O'$ with $\overrightarrow{OO'} = \overrightarrow{DA}$, and C will be mapped to B because $\overrightarrow{CB} = \overrightarrow{DA}$.

This translation keeps angles invariant, so $\angle AO'B = \angle DOC = 180° - \angle AOB$.

Therefore $AOBO'$ is a cyclic quadrilateral. And further, $\angle ODC = \angle O'AB = \angle O'OB$. But, since $O'O$ is parallel to BC,

$$\angle O'OB = \angle OBC.$$

Therefore

$$\angle ODC = \angle OBC.$$

Solution by Adrian Chan, Upper Canada College, Toronto, ON.

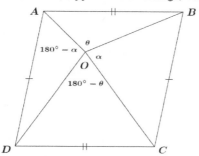

Let $\angle AOB = \theta$ and $\angle BOC = \alpha$. Then $\angle COD = 180° - \theta$ and $\angle AOD = 180° - \alpha$.

Since $AB = CD$ (parallelogram) and $\sin \theta = \sin(180° - \theta)$, the sine law on $\triangle OCD$ and $\triangle OAB$ gives

$$\frac{\sin \angle CDO}{OC} = \frac{\sin(180° - \theta)}{CD} = \frac{\sin \theta}{AB} = \frac{\sin \angle ABO}{OA}$$

so

$$\frac{OA}{OC} = \frac{\sin \angle ABO}{\sin \angle CDO}. \tag{1}$$

Similarly, the Sine Law on $\triangle OBC$ and $\triangle OAD$ gives

$$\frac{\sin \angle CBO}{OC} = \frac{\sin \alpha}{BC} = \frac{\sin(180° - \alpha)}{AD} = \frac{\sin \angle ADO}{OA}$$

so

$$\frac{OA}{OC} = \frac{\sin \angle ADO}{\sin \angle CBO}. \tag{2}$$

Equations (1) and (2) show that

$$\sin \angle ABO \cdot \sin \angle CBO = \sin \angle ADO \cdot \sin \angle CDO.$$

Hence

$$\frac{1}{2}[\cos(\angle ABO + \angle CBO) - \cos(\angle ABO - \angle CBO)]$$
$$= \frac{1}{2}[\cos(\angle ADO + \angle CDO) - \cos(\angle ADO - \angle CDO)].$$

Since $\angle ADC = \angle ABC$(parallelogram) and $\angle ADO + \angle CDO = \angle ADC$ and $\angle ABO + \angle CBO = \angle ABC$ it follows that

$$\cos(\angle ABO - \angle CBO) = \cos(\angle ADO - \angle CDO).$$

There are two cases to consider.

Case (i): $\angle ABO - \angle CBO = \angle ADO - \angle CDO$.

Since $\angle ABO + \angle CBO = \angle ADO + \angle CDO$, subtracting gives $2 \angle CBO = 2 \angle CDO$ so $\angle CBO = \angle CDO$, and we are done.

Case (ii): $\angle ABO - \angle CBO = \angle CDO - \angle ADO$.

Since we know that $\angle ABO + \angle CBO = \angle CDO + \angle ADO$, adding gives $2 \angle ABO = 2 \angle CDO$ so $\angle ABO = \angle CDO$ and $\angle CBO = \angle ADO$.

Substituting this into (1), it follows that $OA = OC$.

Also, $\angle ADO + \angle ABO = \angle CBO + \angle ABO = \angle ABC$.

Now, $\angle ABC = 180° - \angle BAD$ since $ABCD$ is a parallelogram.

Hence $\angle BAD + \angle ADO + \angle ABO = 180°$ so $\angle DOB = 180°$ and D, O, B are collinear.

We now have the diagram

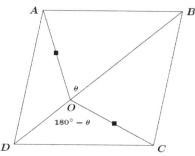

Then $\angle COD + \angle BOC = 180°$, so $\angle BOC = \theta = \angle AOB$.

$\triangle AOB$ is congruent to $\triangle COB$ (SAS, OB is common, $\angle AOB = \angle COB$ and $AO = CO$), so $\angle ABO = \angle CBO$. Since also $\angle ABO = \angle CDO$ we conclude that $\angle CBO = \angle CDO$.

Since it is true in both cases, then $\angle CBO = \angle CDO$.

In the acute-angled triangle ABC, let D, E, F be the feet of altitudes through A, B, C, respectively, and H the orthocentre. Prove that

$$\frac{AH}{AD} + \frac{BH}{BE} + \frac{CH}{CF} = 2.$$

Solution

$$
\begin{aligned}
\frac{AH}{AD} + \frac{BH}{BE} + \frac{CH}{CF} &= 3 - \left(\frac{HD}{AD} + \frac{HE}{BE} + \frac{HF}{CF} \right) \\
&= 3 - \left(\frac{[BHC]}{[ABC]} + \frac{[CHA]}{[ABC]} + \frac{[AHB]}{[ABC]} \right) \\
&= 3 - \frac{[ABC]}{[ABC]} = 2.
\end{aligned}
$$

Australian Mathematical Olympiad, 1993

The vertices of triangle ABC in the xy-plane have integer coordinates, and its sides do not contain any other points having integer coordinates. The interior of ABC contains only one point, G, that has integer coordinates. Prove that G is the centroid of ABC.

Solution

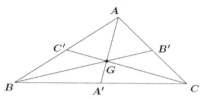

By Pick's Theorem

$$[ABC] = 1 + 3\left(\frac{1}{2}\right) - 1 = \frac{3}{2},$$

$$[ABG] = 0 + 3\left(\frac{1}{2}\right) - 1 = \frac{1}{2},$$

$$[BCG] = \frac{1}{2} \quad \text{and}$$

$$[CAG] = \frac{1}{2}.$$

Therefore

$$\frac{[ABG]}{[ABC]} = \frac{[BCG]}{[ABC]} = \frac{[CAG]}{[ABC]} = \frac{1}{3}.$$

Hence

$$\frac{GA'}{AA'} = \frac{GB'}{BB'} = \frac{GC'}{CC'} = \frac{1}{3}.$$

The unique point satisfying this above is well-known to be the centroid.

Quadrangle $ABCD$ is inscribed in a circle with radius 1 in such a way that one diagonal, AC, is a diameter of the circle, while the other diagonal, BD, is as long as AB. The diagonals intersect in P. It is known that the length of PC is $\frac{2}{5}$. How long is the side CD?

Solution

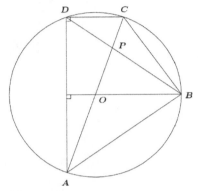

The triangle ABD is isosceles because $AB = BD$. Let O be the centre of the circumcircle. Then $BO \perp AD$. Because $CD \perp AD$ (AC is a diameter), we get $CD \| BO$; that is, $\triangle PCD \sim \triangle POB$, and it follows that

$$\frac{CD}{OB} = \frac{PC}{PO}; \qquad \text{that is}$$

$$CD = \frac{OB \cdot PC}{PO} = \frac{1 \cdot \frac{2}{5}}{\frac{3}{5}} = \frac{2}{3}.$$

Show that in a non-obtuse triangle the perimeter of the triangle is always greater than two times the diameter of the circumcircle.

Solution

In this solution R, r, s will denote the circumradius, inradius and semi-perimeter of a triangle. We shall show that in a non-obtuse triangle the perimeter is always greater than or equal to $2(2R) + 2r$.

Lemma. If A is an angle of triangle ABC, then $\cos A$ is a root of the equation

$$4R^2t^3 - 4R(R + r)t^2 + (s^2 + r^2 - 4R^2)t + (2R + r)^2 - s^2 = 0 \qquad (*)$$

Proof. Since $a = 2R \sin A$, and $s - a = r \cot(\frac{A}{2})$,

$$s = a + (s - a) = 2R \sin A + r \cot\left(\frac{A}{2}\right)$$

$$= 2R\sqrt{(1 - \cos A)(1 + \cos A)} + r\sqrt{\frac{1 + \cos A}{1 - \cos A}}.$$

Thus

$$s^2 = 4R^2(1 - \cos A)(1 + \cos A) + 4Rr(1 + \cos A) + r^2\frac{1 + \cos A}{1 - \cos A}$$

so

$$4R^2(1 - \cos A)^2(1 + \cos A) + 4Rr(1 + \cos A)(1 - \cos A)$$
$$+ r^2(1 + \cos A) - s^2(1 - \cos A) = 0.$$

Hence

$$rR^2\cos^3 A - 4R(R + r)\cos^2 A + (s^2 + r^2 - 4R^2)\cos A$$
$$+ (2R + r)^2 - s^2 = 0$$

making $\cos A$ a root of the equation $(*)$.

Corollary 1. If A, B, and C are the angles of triangle ABC, then $\cos A$, $\cos B$, and $\cos C$ are the roots of the equation $(*)$.

Corollary 2. If A, B, and C are the angles of triangle ABC, then

$$\cos A \cos B \cos C = \frac{s^2 - (2R + r)^2}{4R^2}.$$

Corollary 3. If A is the largest angle of triangle ABC, then

$$s > 2R + r \quad \text{if} \quad A < 90°$$
$$s = 2R + r \quad \text{if} \quad A = 90°$$
$$\text{and} \quad s < 2R + r \quad \text{if} \quad A > 90°.$$

Corollary 4. In a non-obtuse triangle the perimeter of the triangle is always greater than or equal to $2(2R) + 2r$.

Proof. If the triangle is an acute triangle, then $s > 2R + r$, and $2s > 2(2R) + 2r$. If the triangle is a right triangle, then $s = 2R + r$. Thus $2s = 2(2R) + 2r$.

Corollary 5. In a non-obtuse triangle the perimeter of the triangle is always greater than twice the diameter of the circumcircle.

Let C be a circle in the plane. Let C_1 and C_2 be nonintersecting circles touching C internally at points A and B respectively. Let t be a common tangent of C_1 and C_2, touching them at points D and E respectively, such that both C_1 and C_2 are on the same side of t. Let F be the point of intersection of AD and BE. Show that F lies on C.

Solution

Let SA be the tangent to C_1 and C at A and TB be the tangent to C_2 and C at B, as shown.

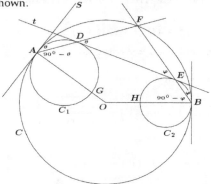

Let $\angle SAD = \theta$ and $\angle TBE = \varphi$. Let O be the centre of C. AO meets C_1 again at G and since it is a common radius, AG is a diameter of C_1. BO meets C_2 again at H and BH is likewise a diameter of C_2.

We have $\angle DAG = 90° - \theta$ and $\angle DGA = \theta$. By the alternate segment theorem $\angle GDE = 90° - \theta$ and since $\angle ADG = 90°$ (angle in a semicircle) it follows that $\angle FDE = \theta$. Similarly $\angle FED = \varphi$ and so $\angle DFE = 180° - \theta - \varphi$. Also $\angle EBH = 90° - \varphi$.

Considering the angles of the (re-entrant) quadrilateral $FAOB$ we have reflex $\angle AOB = 360° - (90° - \theta) - (90° - \varphi) - (180° - \theta - \varphi) = 2\theta + 2\varphi$. So $\angle AOB = 360° - 2\theta - 2\varphi = 2\angle DFE$. But O is the centre of circle C, and AB is an arc of C, so F lies on C. (Converse of the angle at the centre = twice angle at circumference).

Mathematical Contest Baltic Way, 1992

20

Let $a \leq b \leq c$ be the sides of a right triangle, and let $2p$ be its perimeter. Show that $p(p-c) = (p-a)(p-b) = S$ (the area of the triangle).

Solution

Since the triangle is a right triangle we have $c^2 = a^2 + b^2$, $p = \frac{a+b+c}{2}$, and $S = \frac{ab}{2}$.

Then

$$\begin{aligned} p(p-c) &= \frac{a+b+c}{2}\left(\frac{a+b+c}{2} - c\right) = \frac{(a+b)^2 - c^2}{4} \\ &= \frac{a^2 + b^2 + 2ab - c^2}{4} = \frac{ab}{2} = S, \end{aligned}$$

and

$$\begin{aligned} (p-a)(p-b) &= \left(\frac{a+b+c}{2} - a\right)\left(\frac{a+b+c}{2} - b\right) \\ &= \frac{c+b-a}{2}\frac{c-b+a}{2} \\ &= \frac{c^2 - (b-a)^2}{4} = \frac{c^2 - (b^2+a^2) + 2ab}{4} = \frac{ab}{2} = S, \end{aligned}$$

as required.

Show that for any convex polygon of unit area, there exists a parallelogram of area 2 which contains the polygon.

Solution

We shall show more generally that there exists a rectangle of area 2 containing the polygon. The result is obviously true for a triangle. To prove this, construct a rectangle on the longest side of the triangle and circumscribing the triangle. If the area of the triangle is 1, then the rectangle will have area 2.

If the polygon has more than three vertices, then choose the two vertices of the polygon which are furthest apart. Call them B and C. Draw perpendiculars to the line BC at B and at C to give lines l_1 and l_2, respectively.

All the vertices of the polygon must lie between these two lines. (Otherwise there would be two vertices further apart than $|BC|$.)

Now consider the smallest rectangle which circumscribes the polygon and with one pair of opposite sides lying on l_1 and l_2. Suppose this polygon touches the polygon again at D and E.

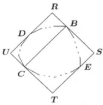

Let the vertices of the rectangle be R, S, T and U with D on UR and E on ST. Then it is easy to see that

$$[RUCB] = 2[BCD]$$

and

$$[BSTC] = 2[BEC]$$

since $BC \| RU$ and $BC \| ST$. $[RSUT] = 2[CDBE] \leq 2(\text{area of polygon}) = 2$ since the polygon is convex. We can find an even larger rectangle of area 2 containing the polygon.

Let ABC be an equilateral triangle, and Γ its incircle. If D and E are points of the sides AB and AC, respectively, such that DE is tangent to Γ, show that

$$\frac{AD}{DB} + \frac{AE}{EC} = 1.$$

Solution

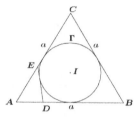

Let $AB = AC = BC = a$ and $BD = p$; that is, $AD = a - p$, and $CE = q$; that is, $AE = a - q$. The circle Γ is inscribed in the quadrilateral and we get

$$ED + BC = BD + CE$$

or

$$ED + a = p + q$$

or

$$ED = p + q - a. \qquad (*)$$

By the law of cosines for the triangle ADE, it follows that

$$ED^2 = AE^2 + AD^2 - 2AE \cdot AD \cos 60°,$$

so, from $(*)$

$$(p + q - a)^2 = (a - q)^2 + (a - p)^2 - (a - q)(a - p)$$

and from this we obtain

$$a = \frac{3pq}{p + q}.$$

Now, we have

$$AD = a - p = \frac{p(2q - p)}{p + q}$$

and

$$AE = a - q = \frac{q(2p - q)}{p + q};$$

that is,

$$\frac{AD}{DB} + \frac{AE}{EC} = \frac{p}{p}\frac{(2q - p)}{p + q} + \frac{q}{q}\frac{(2p - q)}{p + q} = \frac{p + q}{p + q} = 1,$$

as required.

Let r be a line in the plane and let ABC be a triangle contained in one of the half-planes determined by r. Let A', B', C' be the points symmetric to A, B, C with respect to r; draw the line through A' parallel to BC, the line through B' parallel to AC and the line through C' parallel to AB. Show that these three lines have a common point.

Solution

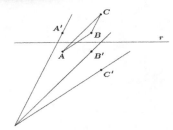

There is no need that $\triangle ABC$ be contained in one of the half planes determined by r.

If the coordinates of A are (x_1, y_1), the coordinates of B are (x_2, y_2) and those of C are (x_3, y_3) in a Cartesian coordinate system with r as x-axis, then A' has coordinates $(x_1, -y_1)$, B' has coordinates $(x_2, -y_2)$ and C' has coordinates $(x_3, -y_3)$.

We have:

The equation of the line through A' parallel to BC is

$$(y_2 - y_3)x - (x_2 - x_3)y - x_1(y_2 - y_3) - y_1(x_2 - x_3) = 0.$$

The equation of the line through B' parallel to CA is

$$(y_3 - y_1)x - (x_3 - x_1)y - x_2(y_3 - y_1) - y_2(x_2 - x_1) = 0.$$

The equation of the line through C' parallel to AB is

$$(y_1 - y_2)x - (x_1 - x_2)y - x_3(y_1 - y_2) - y_3(x_1 - x_2) = 0.$$

Since the three equations when added together vanish identically, the lines represented by them meet in a point.

Its coordinates are found, by solving between any two, to be

$$\left(\frac{(x_1^2 + x_2 x_3)(y_2 - y_3) + (x_2^2 + x_3 x_1)(y_3 - y_1) + (x_3^2 + x_1 x_2)(y_1 - y_2)}{x_1(y_2 - y_3) + x_2(y_3 - y_1) + x_3(y_1 - y_2)}, \right.$$

$$\left. \frac{(y_1^2 + y_2 y_3)(x_2 - x_3) + (y_2^2 + y_3 y_1)(x_3 - x_1) + (y_3^2 + y_1 y_2)(x_1 - x_2)}{x_1(y_2 - y_3) + x_2(y_3 - y_1) + x_3(y_1 - y_2)} \right).$$

The inscribed circumference in the triangle ABC is tangent to BC, CA and AB at D, E and F, respectively. Suppose that this circumference meets AD again at its mid-point X; that is, $AX = XD$. The lines XB and XC meet the inscribed circumference again at Y and Z, respectively. Show that $EY = FZ$.

Solution

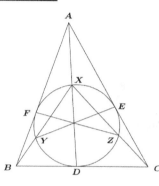

Since $\angle BFY = \angle BXF$ and $\angle FBY = \angle XBF$ we have $\triangle BFY$ and $\triangle BXF$ are similar, so that

$$FY : FX = BF : BX. \qquad (1)$$

Similarly we get

$$DY : DX = BD : BX. \qquad (2)$$

As $BF = BD$, we have from (1) and (2) that

$$FY : FX = DY : DX.$$

Since $AX = DX$ we get

$$FY : FX = DY : AX. \qquad (3)$$

Since X, F, Y, D are concyclic we have

$$\angle FYD = \angle AXF. \qquad (4)$$

Thus we get from (3) and (4) that $\triangle FYD$ is similar to $\triangle FXA$.

Hence $\angle YFD = \angle XFA = \angle XDF$ so that $FY \| XD$. Similarly we have $EZ \| XD$. Thus $FY \| EZ$.

Therefore $FYZE$ is an isosceles trapezoid and then $EY = FZ$.

Let A, B and C be non-collinear points. Prove that there is a unique point X in the plane of ABC such that $XA^2 + XB^2 + AB^2 = XB^2 + XC^2 + BC^2 = XC^2 + XA^2 + CA^2$.

Solution

From the hypothesis we have

$$AX^2 + AB^2 = CX^2 + CB^2. \tag{1}$$

If B_1 is the midpoint of BX, applying the first theorem of the median in the triangles $\triangle ABX$, $\triangle CBX$ we get

$$2AB_1^2 + 2BB_1^2 = 2CB_1^2 + 2BB_1^2 \quad \text{or}$$
$$AB_1 = CB_1. \tag{2}$$

This indicates that the perpendicular bisector of the side AC passes through the point B_1. Let A_1, C_1 be the midpoints of AX and CX, respectively.

Similarly, we obtain that the perpendicular bisectors of BC and AB pass through the midpoints A_1 and C_1, respectively. $\hspace{1cm}$ (3)

Furthermore we obtain $AB \| A_1B_1$, $AC \| A_1C_1$ and $BC \| B_1C_1$. $\hspace{0.5cm}$ (4)

From (3) and (4) we get that the circumcentre O of ABC is the ortho-centre H_1 of $A_1B_1C_1$. $\hspace{1cm}$ (5)

Also from (4) the triangles ABC and $A_1B_1C_1$ are similar with X the centre of similarity and ratio $\frac{1}{2}$. $\hspace{1cm}$ (6)

So, their orthocentres H and H_1 lie in the same straight line with the point X and $HH_1 = H_1X$. $\hspace{1cm}$ (7)

Combining (5) and (7) we get $HO = OX$; that is the point X is known (constant), because X is symmetric to H with respect to the orthocentre O of ABC.

The incircle of ABC touches BC, CA and AB at D, E and F respectively. X is a point inside ABC such that the incircle of XBC touches BC at D also, and touches CX and XB at Y and Z, respectively. Prove that $EFZY$ is a cyclic quadrilateral.

Solution

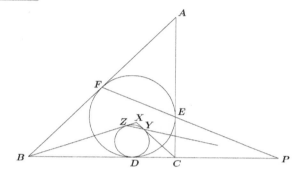

Let P be the intersection of EF with BC. Then by Menelaus' Theorem we have

$$\frac{BP}{PC} \cdot \frac{CE}{EA} \cdot \frac{AF}{FB} = 1. \qquad (1)$$

Since $CE = CD$, $EA = AF$, and $FB = BD$, we get

$$\frac{BP}{PC} \cdot \frac{CD}{BD} = 1$$

so that

$$\frac{BP}{PC} = \frac{BD}{CD}. \qquad (2)$$

Since $XZ = XY$, $BZ = BD$ and $CY = CD$, we have from (2)

$$\frac{BP}{PC} \cdot \frac{CY}{YX} \cdot \frac{XZ}{ZB} = \frac{BD}{CD} \cdot \frac{CD}{YX} \cdot \frac{XY}{BD} = 1.$$

Hence by Menelaus' Theorem P, Z and Y are collinear. Since $PF \cdot PE = PD^2$ and $PZ \cdot PY = PD^2$ we have $PF \cdot PE = PZ \cdot PY$.

Hence $EFZY$ is a cyclic quadrialteral.

An acute triangle ABC is given. Points A_1 and A_2 are taken on the side BC (with A_2 between A_1 and C), B_1 and B_2 on the side AC (with B_2 between B_1 and A) and C_1 and C_2 on the side AB (with C_2 between C_1 and B) so that

$$\angle AA_1A_2 = \angle AA_2A_1 = \angle BB_1B_2 = \angle BB_2B_1 = \angle CC_1C_2 = \angle CC_2C_1.$$

The lines AA_1, BB_1, and CC_1 bound a triangle, and the lines AA_2, BB_2 and CC_2 bound a second triangle. Prove that all six vertices of these two triangles lie on a single circle.

Solution

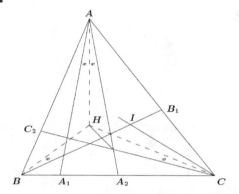

Let AA_1, BB_1 meet at the point E; AA_1, CC_2 meet at the point F; and BB_1, CC_1 meet at the point I. Also

$$\angle A_1AA_2 = \angle B_1BB_2 = \angle C_1CC_2 = 2x. \tag{1}$$

The bisectors of the angles at A_1, B_1 and C in triangles $\triangle A_1AA_2$, $\triangle B_1BB_2$ and $\triangle C_1CC_2$ respectively are perpendicular to their respective bases. Hence they are the altitudes of $\triangle ABC$. Let H be the orthocentre of $\triangle ABC$.

Since $\angle A_1AH = \angle B_1BH = x$ and $\angle A_1AH = \angle C_1CH = x$ each one of the quadrilaterals $AHEB$, $AHDC$ is inscribable in a circle.

These two circles have a common chord, the segment AH and since $\angle ABH = \angle ACH = 90° - \angle BAC$, then the circles have equal radii.

Thus, since the inscribed angles $\angle EAH$, $\angle DAH$ are equal, the corresponding chords HE and HD are equal.

Therefore $HE = HD$. Similarly, we prove that $HD = HI$, and so on for all six vertices of these two triangles of the problem.

Thus, all six vertices lie at the same distance from the point H, and the points are concyclic.

Let P be a point inside triangle ABC such that

$$\angle APB - \angle ACB = \angle APC - \angle ABC.$$

Let D, E be the incentres of triangles APB, APC respectively. Show that AP, BD and CE meet at a point.

Solution

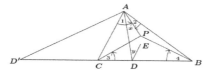

Figure 1.

We will first prove the converse of the proposition and then apply it to prove the stated problem.

Stage I. The equality $\angle APB - \angle APC = \angle ACB - \angle ABC$ is equivalent to

$$\angle A_1 - \angle A_2 = \angle C_3 - \angle B_4 \tag{1}$$

(see figure 1).

Stage II. Assume the conclusion of the problem; that is. assume that the bisectors of the angles $\angle PCA$ and $\angle PBA$ concur at a point I on AP. Then we have

$$\frac{AC}{PC} = \frac{AI}{PI} = \frac{AB}{PB}$$

or

$$\frac{AC}{AB} = \frac{PC}{PB}. \tag{2}$$

This ratio indicates that if AD is the bisector of the angle $\angle BAC$, then PD is the bisector of the angle $\angle BPC$, or equivalently

"the points A, P belong to the "circle of Apollonius" whose diameter DD' lies on the line CB, with D, D' harmonic conjugates to the points C, B" $\tag{3}$

Stage III. If (3) holds then (1) holds. Since AD bisects $\angle CAB$, then

$$\angle PAD = x = \frac{\angle A_1 - \angle A_2}{2}. \tag{4}$$

Since PD bisects $\angle CPB$ then

$$\angle PDB - \angle PDC = \angle C_3 - \angle B_4$$

and if we draw the bisector DE of the straight angle $\angle BDC$ we get

$$\angle PDE = y = \frac{\angle C_3 - \angle B_4}{2}. \tag{5}$$

Because of (3), and since $DE \perp CD$ we obtain that DE is tangent at D to the circumcircle of the triangle $\triangle APD$.

Hence $x = y$. (6)

Combining (4), (5) and (6) we get that

$$\angle A_1 - A_2 = \angle C_3 - \angle B_4$$

so the converse of the proposition is true.

Stage IV. If (1) holds then (3) holds.

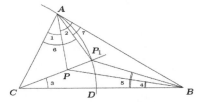

Figure 2.

Consider the circle of Apollonius with respect to the angle A of the triangle ABC with DD' as diameter. Let P_1 be the point at which the circle intersects line CP. We want to show that $P \equiv P_1$ to complete the proof.

Suppose $P \not\equiv P_1$. We distinguish two cases:

Case a. P_1 is external to the segment CP (see figure 2). Denote

$$\angle A_1 = \angle CAP, \quad \angle A_2 = \angle BAP,$$

$$\angle A_6 = \angle CAP_1, \quad \angle A_7 = \angle BAP_1,$$

$$\angle B_4 = \angle CBP \quad \text{and} \quad \angle B_5 = \angle CBP_1.$$

Then we have

$$\angle A_1 \; < \; \angle A_6$$
$$\angle A_2 \; > \; \angle A_7 \tag{7}$$
$$\angle B_4 \; < \; \angle B_5. \tag{8}$$

So from the hypothesis and the conclusion of Stage III

$$\begin{aligned}
\angle C_3 - \angle B_4 \; &= \; \angle A_1 - \angle A_2 \\
&< \; \angle A_6 - \angle A_7 \\
&= \; \angle C_3 - \angle B_5 \\
&< \; \angle C_3 - \angle B_4.
\end{aligned}$$

or

$$\angle C_3 - \angle B_4 < \angle C_3 - \angle B_4,$$

a contradiction.

Case b. P_1 is internal to the segment CD. The proof is similar. This completes the proof.

Let ABC be a triangle. A circle passing through B and C intersects the sides AB and AC again at C' and B', respectively. Prove that BB', CC' and HH' are concurrent, where H and H' are the orthocentres of triangles ABC and $AB'C'$ respectively.

Solution

Let BH, CH meet AC, AB at D, E respectively. Since $\angle BDC = \angle BEC = 90°$, B, C, D, E are concyclic and thus $\angle ADE = \angle ABC$.

Now, since B, C, B', C' are concyclic we have

$$\angle AB'C' = \angle ABC.$$

Thus $\angle ADE = \angle AB'C'$, so that $DE \| B'C'$. Let Q be the intersection of DC' with EB'. As $HE \perp AB$, $B'H' \perp AB$, we get $HE \| H'B'$. Similarly we have $HD \| H'C'$.

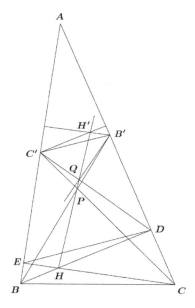

Since $DE \| C'B'$, $HD \| H'C'$ and $HE \| H'B'$, DC', EB' and HH' are concurrent, so that H, Q, H' are collinear.

By Pappus' Theorem H, P, Q are collinear.

Hence H, P, Q, H' are collinear. So BB', CC', and HH' are concurrent.

A triangle ABC is given. From the vertex B, n rays are constructed intersecting the side AC. For each of the $n+1$ triangles obtained, an incircle with radius r_i and excircle (which touches the side AC) with radius R_i is constructed. Prove that the expression

$$\frac{r_1 r_2 \ldots r_{n+1}}{R_1 R_2 \ldots R_{n+1}}$$

depends on neither n nor on which rays are constructed.

Solution

If A, B, C are the angles of a triangle, then

$$r = s \tan \frac{A}{2} \tan \frac{B}{2} \tan \frac{C}{2} \qquad \text{and} \qquad r_a = s \tan \frac{A}{2},$$

where r, r_a are the inradius and the radius of the excircle opposite A, and s is the semiperimeter.

It follows that

$$\frac{r}{r_a} = \tan \frac{B}{2} \tan \frac{C}{2}.$$

Next we apply this result to each of $n+1$ triangles obtained (see figure at the top of the next page). This yields

$$
\begin{aligned}
\frac{r_1}{R_1} &= \tan \frac{A}{2} \tan \frac{\alpha_1}{2} \\
\frac{r_2}{R_2} &= \tan \frac{180° - \alpha_1}{2} \tan \frac{\alpha_2}{2} \\
&\cdots\cdots\cdots \\
&\cdots\cdots\cdots \\
\frac{r_n}{R_n} &= \tan \frac{180° - \alpha_{n-1}}{2} \tan \frac{\alpha_n}{2} \\
\frac{r_{n+1}}{R_{n+1}} &= \tan \frac{180° - \alpha_n}{2} \tan \frac{C}{2}.
\end{aligned}
$$

Multiplying these equalities, we observe that the product of all the right hand members is

$$\tan \frac{A}{2} \cdot \left(\tan \frac{\alpha_1}{2} \cot \frac{\alpha_1}{2} \right) \cdot \left(\tan \frac{\alpha_2}{2} \cot \frac{\alpha_2}{2} \right) \cdots \left(\tan \frac{\alpha_n}{2} \cot \frac{\alpha_n}{2} \right) \cdot \tan \frac{C}{2}$$

$$= \tan \frac{A}{2} \cdot \tan \frac{C}{2},$$

and we get

$$\frac{r_1 r_2 \cdots r_{n-1}}{R_1 R_2 \cdots R_{n+1}} = \tan \frac{A}{2} \cdot \tan \frac{C}{2}$$

which depends on neither n nor on which rays are constructed.

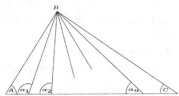

Let $ABCD$ be an inscribed quadrilateral. Its diagonals intersect at O. Let the midpoints of AB and CD be U and V. Prove that the lines through O, U and V, perpendicular to AD, BD and AC respectively, are concurrent.

Solution

Case 1. Neither is AC orthogonal to BD, nor is AD a diameter.

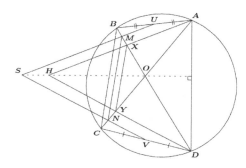

Let M, N be the feet of the perpendiculars from U, V to BD, AC respectively, and let S be the intersection of UM and VN. Let X, Y be the feet of the perpendiculars from A, D to BD, AC respectively, and let H be the intersection of AX and DY. Since U is the midpoint of AB, and $UM\|AX$, M is the midpoint of BX. Similarly N is the midpoint of CY.

Since $\angle AXD = \angle AYD = 90°$, A, X, Y, D are concyclic. Therefore $\angle YXD = \angle YAD = \angle CAD = \angle CBD$. Thus we have $XY\|BC$.

Since M, N are the midpoints of BX, CY respectively, we have $MN\|XY$.

Since $SM\|HX$, $XN\|HY$, and $MN\|XY$, MX, NY and SH are concurrent at O. Therefore S, H, O are collinear.

Since $AH \perp OD$ and $DH \perp OA$, H is the orthocentre of $\triangle OAD$, so that $HO \perp AD$. Thus we have $SO \perp AD$.

Thus the lines through O, U and V, perpendicular to AD, BD and AC respectively, are concurrent at S.

Case 2. AC is orthogonal to BD.

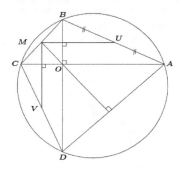

Let M be the midpoint of BC. Since U is the midpoint of AB, we get $UM \perp AC$, so that $UM \perp BD$. Similarly we have $VM \perp AC$.

Since $AC \perp BD$ and M is the midpoint of BC, by Brahmagupta's Theorem we have $MO \perp AD$. (See: H.S.M. Coxeter and S.L. Greitzer, *Geometry Revisited*, p. 59).

Thus the lines through O, U and V, perpendicular to AD, BD and AC respectively, are concurrent at M.

Case 3. AD is a diameter.

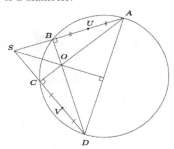

Let S be the intersection of AB and CD. Since $AB \perp BD$ and $CD \perp AC$, S is the orthocentre of $\triangle OAD$. Thus $SO \perp AD$.

Hence the lines through O, U and V, perpendicular to AD, BD and AC respectively, are concurrent at S.

Let $ABCD$ be a quadrilateral with $\overline{AD} = \overline{BC}$ and let $\angle A + \angle B = 120°$. Three equilateral triangles $\triangle ACP$, $\triangle DCQ$ and $\triangle DBR$ are drawn on $\overline{AC}$, $\overline{DC}$ and $\overline{DB}$ away from $\overline{AB}$. Prove that the three new vertices P, Q and R are collinear.

Solution

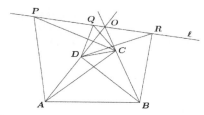

Let O be the intersection of AD and BC. Since $\angle A + \angle B = 120°$, we get $\angle AOB = 60°$. Let l be the exterior bisector of angle AOB. Since $\angle APC = 60° = \angle AOC$, we have that O, P, A, C are concyclic. Hence $\angle POA = \angle PCA = 60°$. The exterior angle of $\angle AOB$ is $120°$, showing that PO bisects the exterior angle of $\angle AOB$. Thus P lies on l. Similarly Q and R lie on l. Hence, P, Q and R are collinear.

Let ABC be a triangle with $\angle BAC = 40°$ and $\angle ABC = 60°$. Let D and E be the points lying on the sides AC and AB, respectively, such that $\angle CBD = 40°$ and $\angle BCE = 70°$. Let F be the point of intersection of the lines BD and CE. Show that the line AF is perpendicular to the line BC.

Solution

Suppose H is the foot of the perpendicular line from A to BC; construct equilateral $\triangle ABG$, with C on BG. I will prove that if F is the point where AH meets BD, then $\angle FCB = 70°$. (Because that means AH, and the given lines BD and CE meet at one point, this answers the question.) Suppose BD extended meets AG at I.

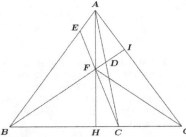

Now $BF = GF$ and $\angle FBG = \angle FGB = 40°$, so that $\angle IGF = 20°$. Also $\angle IFG = \angle FBG + \angle FGB = 80°$, so that

$$
\begin{aligned}
\angle FIG &= 180° - \angle IFG - \angle IGF \\
&= 180° - 80° - 20° \\
&= 80°.
\end{aligned}
$$

Therefore $\triangle GIF$ is an isosceles triangle, so

$$GI = GF = BF. \tag{1}$$

But $\triangle BGI$ and $\triangle ABC$ are congruent, since $BG = AB$, $\angle GBI = \angle BAC$, $\angle BGI = \angle ABC$.

Therefore

$$GI = BC. \tag{2}$$

From (1) and (2) we get

$$BC = BF.$$

So in $\triangle BCF$,

$$\angle BCF = \frac{180° - \angle FBC}{2} = \frac{180° - 40°}{2} = 70°.$$

Thus $\angle FCB = 70°$ and that proves that the given lines CE and BD and the perpendicular line AH meet at one point.

A triangle with perimeter $2p$ has sides a, b and c. If possible, a new triangle with the sides $p - a$, $p - b$ and $p - c$ is formed. The process is then repeated with the new triangle. For which original triangles can the process be repeated indefinitely?

Solution

Let $a \leq b \leq c$ and Δ be the difference between the longest and the shortest side.

Original Triangle	New Triangle
Perimeter $= 2p$	Perimeter$^{(1)} = 3p - (a + b + c) = p$
$\Delta = c - a$	$\Delta^{(1)} = (p - a) - (p - c) = c - a$

We can see that the perimeter of the new triangle is half the previous perimeter, but Δ is the same. Then, if $\Delta > 0$, repeating this process we can obtain

$$\text{Perimeter}^{(k)} = \frac{2p}{2^k} < \Delta^{(k)} = c - a.$$

If $c^{(k)}$ is the longest side we obtain the absurd relation $c^{(k)} < \text{Perimeter}^{(k)} < \Delta^{(k)} < c^{(k)}$. Finally, only with an equilateral triangle as the original triangle ($\Delta = 0$) can we repeat the process indefinitely.

Given is a triangle ABC, $\angle A = 90°$. D is the midpoint of BC, F is the midpoint of AB, E the midpoint of AF and G the midpoint of FB. AD intersects CE, CF and CG respectively in P, Q and R. Determine the ratio $\frac{PQ}{QR}$.

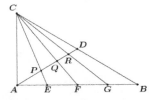

Solution

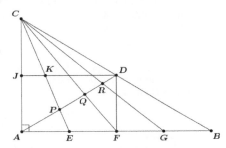

We know that two medians in a triangle divide each other in 2 : 1 ratio, or in other words the point of intersection is $\frac{2}{3}$ the way from the vertex.

Since CF and AD are both medians in $\triangle ABC$, then $\frac{AQ}{QD} = \frac{2}{1}$, where Q is the point of intersection.

Also, since D is the midpoint of the hypotenuse in the right triangle ABC, then it is the centre of the circumscribed circle with radius $DA = DC = DB$.

Drop a perpendicular from D onto sides AB and CA. The feet of the perpendiculars will be F and J, respectively, where J is the midpoint of AC, since DF and DJ are altitudes in isosceles triangles $\triangle ADB$ and $\triangle ADC$, respectively. Now consider $\triangle CFB$. The segments CG and FD are medians and therefore intersect at H say in the ratio 2 : 1 so, $\frac{HD}{FD} = \frac{1}{3}$. From here it can be seen that $\triangle ARC$ and $\triangle DRH$ are similar, since their angles are the same. Also, since we know that $\overline{FD} = \overline{JA}$, and $2\overline{JA} = \overline{AC}$ then $\overline{HD} = \frac{1}{6}\overline{CA}$ and $\triangle ARC$ is 6 times bigger than $\triangle DRH$. Now we can see that $\frac{\overline{AR}}{\overline{RD}} = \frac{6}{1}$ and since $\overline{AR} + \overline{RD} = \overline{AD}$, then $\frac{\overline{RD}}{\overline{AD}} = \frac{1}{7}$.

Similarly $\triangle APE \sim \triangle KPD$, where medians DJ and CE meet at K. We know that $\overline{AE} = \frac{1}{4}\overline{AB}$, so then $\overline{JK} = \frac{1}{4}\overline{JD}$, since JD is parallel to AB. It now follows that $\frac{\overline{AE}}{\overline{KD}} = \frac{2}{3}$, and from the similarity of the triangles $\frac{\overline{AP}}{\overline{PD}} = \frac{2}{3}$. Also, since $\overline{AP} + \overline{PD} = \overline{AD}$, then $\frac{\overline{AP}}{\overline{AD}} = \frac{2}{5}$. Combining these results we have $\overline{AP} = \frac{2}{5}\overline{AD}$, $\overline{AQ} = \frac{2}{3}\overline{AD}$, $\overline{QD} = \frac{1}{3}\overline{AD}$ and $\overline{RD} = \frac{1}{7}\overline{AD}$.

Thus

$$\overline{PQ} = \overline{AQ} - \overline{AP} = \frac{2}{3}\overline{AD} - \frac{2}{5}\overline{AD} = \frac{4}{15}\overline{AD}$$

and

$$\overline{QR} = \overline{QD} - \overline{RD} = \frac{1}{3}\overline{AD} - \frac{1}{7}\overline{AD} = \frac{4}{21}\overline{AD}.$$

From these $\frac{\overline{PQ}}{\overline{QR}} = \frac{7}{5}$.

A convex polygon and point O inside it are given. Prove that for any $n > 1$ there exist points $A_1, A_2, \ldots, A_n$ on the sides of the polygon such that $\overrightarrow{OA_1} + \overrightarrow{OA_2} + \ldots + \overrightarrow{OA_n} = \overrightarrow{0}$.

Solution

It follows by continuity that there always exists a chord $A_1 O A_1'$ such that $A_1 O = A_1' O$ and hence $\overrightarrow{OA_1} + \overrightarrow{OA_1'} = \overrightarrow{0}$. Similarly, there exists a chord $A_2 A_3'$ which is bisected by the midpoint O_1 of OA_1'. It follows by the parallelogram law that $\overrightarrow{OA_2} + \overrightarrow{OA_3'} = \overrightarrow{OA_1'}$ and hence $\overrightarrow{OA_1} + \overrightarrow{OA_2} + \overrightarrow{OA_3'} = \overrightarrow{0}$. Again similarly there exists a chord $A_3 A_4'$ which is bisected by the midpoint of OA_3' so that $\overrightarrow{OA_1} + \overrightarrow{OA_2} + \overrightarrow{OA_3} + \overrightarrow{OA_4'} = \overrightarrow{0}$, and so on for any number of vectors $n > 1$.

In a triangle $\triangle ABC$, $\angle C = 2\angle B$. P is a point in the interior of $\triangle ABC$ satisfying that $AP = AC$ and $PB = PC$. Show that AP trisects the angle $\angle A$.

Solution

Let $\angle PAC$ and $\angle BAP$ be 2α and β respectively. Then, since $\angle C = 2\angle B$, we deduce from $A + B + C = 180°$ that

$$2\alpha + \beta + 3B = 180°. \tag{1}$$

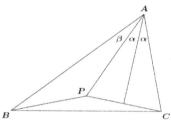

The angles at the base of the isosceles triangle PAC are each $90° - \alpha$. Also $\triangle BPC$ is isosceles, having base angles

$$C - (90° - \alpha) = 2B + \alpha - 90°,$$

and so

$$
\begin{aligned}
\angle BPA &= 180° - (\angle PBA + \angle BAP) \\
&= 180° - [B - (2B + \alpha - 90°) + 180° - 2\alpha - 3B] \\
&= 4B + 3\alpha - 90°.
\end{aligned}
$$

As usual, let a, b and c denote the lengths of the sides BC, AC and AB. By the Law of Cosines, applied to $\triangle BPA$, where $\overline{PA} = b$ and $\overline{PB} = \overline{PC} = 2b \sin \alpha$,

$$c^2 = b^2 + (2b \sin \alpha)^2 - 2 \cdot b \cdot 2b \sin \alpha \cdot \cos(4B + 3\alpha - 90°),$$

so that

$$c^2 = b^2[1 + 4 \sin^2 \alpha - 4 \sin \alpha \sin(4B + 3\alpha)]. \tag{2}$$

We now use the fact that $\angle C = 2\angle B$ is equivalent to the condition $c^2 = b(b + a)$, which has appeared before in **CRUX** [1976: 74], [1984: 278] and [1996: 265–267]. Since $a = 2 \cdot \overline{PC} \cdot \cos(2B + \alpha - 90°) = 4b \sin \alpha \sin(2B + \alpha)$, we have

$$c^2 = b^2[1 + 4 \sin \alpha \sin(2B + \alpha)]. \tag{3}$$

Therefore, from (2) and (3), we get

$$b^2[1 + 4 \sin^2 \alpha - 4 \sin \alpha \sin(4B + 3\alpha)] = b^2[1 + 4 \sin \alpha \sin(2B + \alpha)],$$

which simplifies to

$$\sin\alpha - \sin(4B + 3\alpha) \;=\; \sin(2B + \alpha).$$

Since $\sin\alpha - \sin(4B + 3\alpha) = -2\cos(2B + 2\alpha)\sin(2B + \alpha)$, this equation may be rewritten as

$$\sin(2B + \alpha)\cdot[1 + 2\cos(2B + 2\alpha)] \;=\; 0.$$

Since, from (1), $2B + \alpha < 180°$, we must have $1 + 2\cos(2B + 2\alpha) = 0$, giving $\cos(2B + 2\alpha) = -1/2$; that is,

$$2B + 2\alpha = 120° \tag{4}$$

since, again from (1), $2B + 2\alpha < 180°$.

Finally, we may eliminate B between (1) and (4) to obtain $\alpha = \beta$. The result follows.

In a plane V a circle C is given with centre M. P is a point not on the circle C.

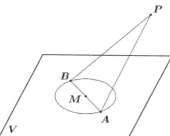

(a) Prove that for a fixed point P, $\overline{AP}^2 + \overline{BP}^2$ is a constant for every diameter AB of the circle C.

(b) Let AB be any diameter of C and P a point on a fixed sphere S not intersecting V. Determine the point(s) P on S such that $\overline{AP}^2 + \overline{BP}^2$ is minimal.

Solution

(a) With $\triangle PAB$, we can join P and M to create two new triangles, $\triangle PMA$ and $\triangle PMB$. Let $\angle PMA = \theta$. Then $\angle PMB = 180° - \theta$. Because M is the centre of circle C and A and B both lie on circle C, we have $\overline{MA} = \overline{MB} = r$, the radius of the circle.

By the Law of Cosines,

$$\begin{aligned} \overline{BP}^2 &= \overline{MP}^2 + r^2 - 2\overline{MP}r\cos(180° - \theta) \\ &= \overline{MP}^2 + r^2 + 2\overline{MP}r\cos\theta \end{aligned}$$

and

$$\overline{AP}^2 = \overline{MP}^2 + r^2 - 2\overline{MP}r\cos\theta$$

so $\overline{AP}^2 + \overline{BP}^2 = 2\overline{MP}^2 + 2r^2$.

The right hand side is a constant depending only on the radius of the circle and the distance of P from the centre.

(b) From (a), we know that $\overline{AP}^2 + \overline{BP}^2 = 2\overline{MP}^2 + 2r^2$. For any point P on sphere S, the radius of the circle will remain constant. Therefore the only variable affecting the sum $\overline{AP}^2 + \overline{BP}^2$ is $\overline{MP}$, the distance from the point P to the centre of the circle. $\overline{AP}^2 + \overline{BP}^2$ will be a minimum when $\overline{MP}$ is minimum. Therefore we are looking for the point on the sphere closest to M.

Let T be the centre of the sphere S, D be the point on the segment MT that lies on the sphere, and D' be any other point on S.

We know that $\overline{MD} + \overline{DT} < \overline{MD'} + \overline{D'T}$ because the shortest distance between M and T is a straight line. We know that $\overline{DT} = \overline{D'T}$. Thus $\overline{MD} < \overline{MD'}$. Thus D is the point on the sphere which minimizes the sum.

Let $A_1, A_2, \ldots, A_8$ be the vertices of a parallelepiped and let O be its centre. Show that

$$4(OA_1^2 + OA_2^2 + \cdots + OA_8^2) \leq (OA_1 + OA_2 + \cdots + OA_8)^2.$$

Solution

Let one of the vertices be the origin and let the vectors $B + C$, $C + A$, $A + B$ denote the three coterminal edges emanating from this origin. Then the vectors to the remaining four vertices are $S + A$, $S + B$, $S + C$, and $2S$ where $S = A + B + C$ and which is also the vector to the centre. The inequality now becomes

$$2(S^2 + A^2 + B^2 + C^2) \leq (|S| + |A| + |B| + |C|)^2,$$

or

$$S^2 + A^2 + B^2 + C^2 \leq 2|S|\{|A| + |B| + |C|\} + 2\{|B|\,|C| + |C|\,|A| + |A|\,|B|\}.$$

Since

$$S^2 = A^2 + B^2 + C^2 + 2B \cdot C + 2C \cdot A + 2A \cdot B,$$

the inequality now becomes

$$S^2 - B \cdot C - C \cdot A - A \cdot B \leq |S|\{|A| + |B| + |C|\} + \{|B|\,|C| + |C|\,|A| + |A|\,|B|\}.$$

Clearly,

$$S^2 \leq |S|\{|A| + |B| + |C|\}$$

and

$$-B \cdot C - C \cdot A - A \cdot B \leq |B|\,|C|\,|A| + |A|\,|B|.$$

There is equality if and only if the parellelepiped is degenerate, for example, $B = C = O$.

Let A, B, C be three collinear points with B between A and C. Equilateral triangles ABD, BCE, CAF are constructed with D, E on one side of the line AC and F on the opposite side. Prove that the centroids of the triangles are the vertices of an equilateral triangle. Prove that the centroid of this triangle lies on the line AC.

Solution

We introduce a rectangular Cartesian system with origin at B and x–axis along AC. Let $\overline{AB} = a$ and $\overline{BC} = b$. The centroids O_1, O_2, O_3 of equilateral triangles ABD, BCE and CAF are

$$G_1 = \left(\frac{-a}{2}, \frac{a}{2\sqrt{3}}\right), \qquad G_2 = \left(\frac{b}{2}, \frac{b}{2\sqrt{3}}\right) \qquad \text{and}$$

$$G_3 = \left(\frac{-a+b}{2}, -\frac{a+b}{2\sqrt{3}}\right).$$

Hence the centroid G of triangle $\triangle G_1 G_2 G_3$ is

$$G = \left(\frac{-a+b}{3}, 0\right).$$

It is straightforward to verify that

$$\overline{G_1 G_2} = \overline{G_2 G_3} = \overline{G_3 G_1} = \sqrt{\frac{a^2 + ab + b^2}{3}}.$$

Therefore $\triangle G_1 G_2 G_3$ is equilateral.

Finally, since the y–coordinate of G is 0, clearly G is on the x–axis; that is to say, G lies on the line AC.

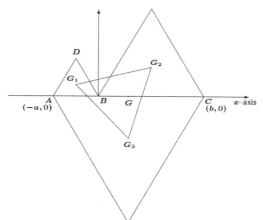

Let triangle ABC have orthocentre H, and let P be a point on its circumcircle, distinct from A, B, C. Let E be the foot of the altitude BH, let $PAQB$ and $PARC$ be parallelograms, and let AQ meet HR in X. Prove that EX is parallel to AP.

Solution

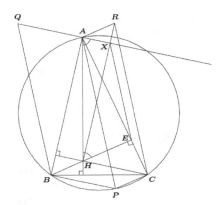

Since $AX \| BP$ and A, B, P, C are concyclic we have

$$\angle XAP = \angle APB = \angle ACB.$$

As $AH \perp BC$ and $BH \perp AC$, we get $\angle ACB = \angle AHE$, so that

$$\angle XAP = \angle AHE. \qquad (1)$$

Since $APCR$ is a parallelogram and A, B, P, C are concyclic we have $\angle ARC = \angle APC = \angle ABC$. As $AH \perp BC$ and $CH \perp AB$, we get

$$\angle AHC + \angle ABC = 180°,$$

so that

$$\angle AHC + \angle ARC = 180°.$$

Hence A, H, C, R are concyclic.

It follows that

$$\angle AHR = \angle ACR = \angle CAP. \qquad (2)$$

From (1) and (2) we have

$$\angle XAE = \angle XAP - \angle CAP = \angle AHE - \angle AHR = \angle XHE.$$

Hence X, A, H, E are concyclic, and

$$\angle AEX = \angle AHX = \angle AHR.$$

Hence we have, from (2), that $\angle AEX = \angle CAP$. Thus $EX \| AP$.

Let ABC be an acute-angled triangle with $|BC| > |CA|$, and let O be the circumcentre, H its orthocentre, and F the foot of its altitude CH. Let the perpendicular to OF at F meet the side CA at P. Prove that $\angle FHP = \angle BAC$.

Solution

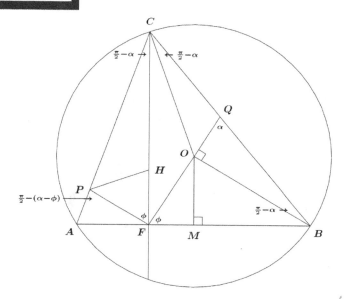

We denote $\angle CFP = \angle OFB = \phi$. M is the mid-point of AB. Now

$$OM \;=\; R\cos\gamma, \qquad FM \;=\; R\sin(\alpha - \beta),$$

so that

$$\tan\varphi \;=\; \frac{\cos\gamma}{\sin(\alpha - \beta)}. \tag{1}$$

From the Law of Sines in $\triangle CPF$,

$$
\begin{aligned}
CF &= 2R\sin\alpha\sin\beta \\
\angle FCP &= \frac{\pi}{2} - \alpha \\
\angle FPC &= \frac{\pi}{2} + \alpha - \varphi
\end{aligned}
\tag{2}
$$

so $CP : CF = \sin\varphi : \cos(\alpha - \varphi)$.

With (2)

$$CP = \frac{2R \sin\alpha \sin\beta \sin\varphi}{\cos(\alpha - \varphi)} = \frac{2R \sin\alpha \sin\beta}{\cos\alpha \cot\varphi + \sin(\alpha)}. \tag{3}$$

From (1) and (3),

$$CP = \frac{2R \sin\alpha \cos\gamma}{\sin\beta(\sin^2\alpha - \cos^2\alpha)} = \frac{-2R \sin\alpha \cos\gamma}{\sin\beta \cos 2\alpha} \tag{4}$$

$$OQ \perp OB, \qquad \angle OBQ = \frac{\pi}{2} - \alpha \Longrightarrow \angle OQB = \alpha.$$

Now

$$CQ = a - QB = R\left(2\sin\alpha - \frac{1}{\sin\alpha}\right) = -R\frac{\cos 2\alpha}{\sin\alpha}.$$

Furthermore, $CH = 2R\cos\gamma, \quad CO = R$.

It is easy to verify that $CP : CH = CO : CQ$, and

$$-2R\frac{\sin\alpha \cos\gamma}{\sin\beta \cos 2\alpha} : 2R\cos\gamma = R : \frac{-R\cos 2\alpha}{\sin\alpha}. \tag{5}$$

We also have

$$\angle PCH = \angle OCQ = \frac{\pi}{2} - \alpha. \tag{6}$$

From (5) and (6), we have that $\triangle PCH$ and $\triangle OCQ$ are similar. Thus $\angle PHC = \angle OQC = \pi - \alpha$. Thus $\angle FHP = \alpha$.

Let ABC be equilateral, and let P be a point in its interior. Let the lines AP, BP, CP meet the sides BC, CA, AB in the points A_1, B_1, C_1 respectively. Prove that

$$A_1B_1 \cdot B_1C_1 \cdot C_1A_1 \geq A_1B \cdot B_1C \cdot C_1A.$$

Solution

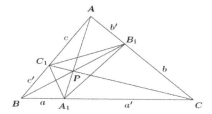

We put $A_1B = a$, $A_1C = a'$, $B_1C = b$, $B_1A = b'$, $C_1A = c$ and $C_1B = c'$. Then we have by Ceva's Theorem

$$abc = a'b'c'. \tag{1}$$

Since $\angle B_1AC_1 = 60°$ we have

$$\begin{aligned} B_1C_1^2 &= (b')^2 + c^2 - 2b'c\cos 60° \\ &= (b')^2 + c^2 - b'c \geq b'c. \end{aligned}$$

Similarly we have

$$C_1A_1^2 \geq c'a \quad \text{and} \quad A_1B_1^2 \geq a'b.$$

Multiplying these three inequalities, we get

$$B_1C_1^2 \cdot C_1A_1^2 \cdot A_1B_1^2 \geq b'c \cdot c'a \cdot a'b. \tag{2}$$

From (1) and (2) we have

$$B_1C_1^2 \cdot C_1A_1^2 \cdot A_1B_1^2 \geq a^2b^2c^2.$$

Thus we have

$$B_1C_1 \cdot C_1A_1 \cdot A_1B_1 \geq abc.$$

That is

$$B_1C_1 \cdot C_1A_1 \cdot A_1B_1 \geq A_1B \cdot B_1C \cdot C_1A.$$

Let ABC be an acute-angled triangle with circumcentre O and circumradius R. Let AO meet the circle BOC again in A', let BO meet the circle COA again in B' and let CO meet the circle AOB again in C'. Prove that

$$OA' \cdot OB' \cdot OC' \geq 8R^3 .$$

When does equality hold?

Solution

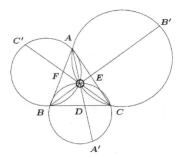

Let D, E, F be the intersections of AO, BO, CO with BC, CA, AB, respectively. We denote the area of $\triangle PQR$ by $[PQR]$. Since $\dfrac{AD}{OD} = \dfrac{[ABC]}{[OBC]}$, we get

$$\frac{OA}{OD} = \frac{AD}{OD} - 1 = \frac{[ABC] - [OBC]}{[OBC]} = \frac{[OCA] + [OAB]}{[OBC]} .$$

We put $[OBC] = x$, $[OCA] = y$ and $[OAB] = z$. Then we have $\dfrac{OA}{OD} = \dfrac{y+z}{x}$; that is $\dfrac{R}{OD} = \dfrac{y+z}{x}$.

Similarly we have $\dfrac{R}{OE} = \dfrac{z+x}{y}$ and $\dfrac{R}{OF} = \dfrac{x+y}{z}$. Multiplying these three equations, we have

$$\frac{R^3}{OD \cdot DE \cdot OF} = \frac{(y+z)(z+x)(x+y)}{xyz} . \qquad (1)$$

Since $y + z \geq 2\sqrt{yz}$, $z + x \geq 2\sqrt{zx}$ and $x + y \geq 2\sqrt{xy}$, we have $(y+z)(z+x)(x+y) \geq 8xyz$, with equality holding when $x = y = z$.

Hence from (1),

$$\frac{R^3}{OD \cdot OE \cdot OF} \geq 8 . \qquad (2)$$

Since O, B, A', C are concyclic we get

$$\angle OA'C = \angle OBC = \angle OCB = \angle OCD,$$

so that we get $OD \cdot OA' = OC^2 = R^2$. Thus we have $OA' = \frac{R^2}{OD}$.

Similarly, we have $OB' = \frac{R^2}{OE}$, and $OC' = \frac{R^2}{OF}$. Multiplying these three equations we get

$$OA' \cdot OB' \cdot OC' = \frac{R^6}{OD \cdot DE \cdot OF}. \tag{3}$$

Therefore, we obtain from (2) and (3)

$$OA' \cdot OB' \cdot OC' \geq 8R^3.$$

Equality holds when $[OBC] = [OCA] = [OAB]$; that is when $\triangle ABC$ is equilateral.

In the plane five points P_1, P_2, P_3, P_4, P_5 are chosen having integer coordinates. Show that there is at least one pair (P_i, P_j), for $i \neq j$ such that the line $P_i P_j$ contains a point Q, with integer coordinates, and is strictly between P_i and P_j.

Solution

With respect to parity, there are only 4 kinds of points (x, y). They are (E, E), (E, O), (O, E) and (O, O), where E denotes an even integer, and O denotes an odd integer. Since there are 5 points, there must be at least two (x_1, y_1) and (x_2, y_2) such that x_1 and x_2 have the same parity and also y_1 and y_2. Hence Q can be taken as the mid-point of these two points.

Construct a triangle ABC if the lengths $|AO|$, $|AU|$ and radius r of incircle are given, where O is orthocentre and U the centre of the incircle.

Solution

Denote the orthocentre, the incentre and the circumcentre of triangle ABC by H, I, and O, respectively.

Figure 1

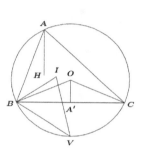

Figure 2

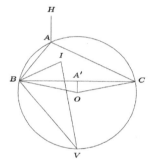

Figure 3

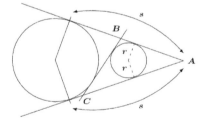

Figure 4

Analysis. Imagine the construction completed (Figures 2 and 3), with A' the mid-point of side BC and V the midpoint of arc BC. It is a standard exercise (for example #1.8 and #3.4 in Trajan Lalesco, La Géométrie du Triangle) to show that

$$OA' = \frac{1}{2}AH \qquad \text{and} \qquad BV = VI.$$

Geometrical Construction. Since AI and r are given, $\angle A$ and $s - a$ are known (Figure 1).

If $\angle A = 90°$ (or equivalently, $AI = r\sqrt{2}$), then A and H coincide and there are an infinite number of triangles circumscribing the r circle.

Suppose $\angle A \neq 90°$. In *isosceles* triangle BOC we then know

$$\angle BOC = \begin{cases} 2 \cdot \angle A & \text{if } \angle A < 90° \\ & \text{(or, equivalently } AI > r\sqrt{2}) \\ 2 \cdot (180° - \angle A), & \text{if } \angle A > 90° \\ & \text{(or, equivalently } AI < r\sqrt{2}), \end{cases}$$

and altitude OA' $(= \frac{1}{2}AH)$, whence $\triangle BOC$ and the circumcircle of $\triangle ABC$ can be constructed. Then,

Solution 1. Triangle BOC and the circumcircle of $\triangle ABC$ being constructed, draw XY parallel to BC and a distance r from it (on the same side as O if $\angle A < 90°$ and on the opposite side if $\angle A > 90°$). Bisect the arc BC at V and let the circle, centre V, radius VB, cut XY at I and I'. These points will be the incentres for the two (symmetrical) solutions. Let VI meet the circumcircle again at A. Then ABC is the required triangle.

Solution 2. Triangle BOC being constructed, we then know $\angle A$, r and s $(= a + (s - a))$ where s is the semiperimeter of $\triangle ABC$ and $a = \overline{BC}$.

These elements suffice to determine the incircle and the excircle lying in $\angle A$, which are readily constructed.

The common internal tangents of these circles intersect the sides of the angle A at B and C to form the required triangle (Figure 4).

The details of the construction may be omitted since they are obvious.

Given a triangle ABC, $\angle A = 90°$. D is the mid-point of BC, F is the mid-point of AB, E the midpoint of AF and G the mid-point of FB. AD intersects CE, CF and CG respectively in P, Q and R. Determine the ratio $\frac{PQ}{QR}$.

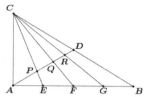

Solution

We first establish the following:

Lemma.
$$\frac{PQ}{QR} = \frac{CP}{CE} \cdot \frac{EF}{FG} \cdot \frac{CG}{CR}.$$

Proof.
$$\frac{PQ}{QR} = \frac{[CPQ]}{[CQR]} = \frac{[CPQ]}{[CEF]} \cdot \frac{[CEF]}{[CFG]} \cdot \frac{[CFG]}{[CQR]}$$
$$= \frac{CP \cdot CQ}{CE \cdot CF} \cdot \frac{EF}{FG} \cdot \frac{CF \cdot CG}{CQ \cdot CR} = \frac{CP}{CE} \cdot \frac{EF}{FG} \cdot \frac{CG}{CR}.$$

We now solve the problem, without using the hypothesis that $\angle A = 90°$.

By the lemma
$$\frac{PQ}{QR} = \frac{CP}{CE} \cdot \frac{EF}{FG} \cdot \frac{CG}{RC} = \frac{CP}{CE} \cdot \frac{CG}{RC}.$$

By Menelaus' Theorem we have

$$\frac{CD}{DB} \cdot \frac{BA}{AE} \cdot \frac{EP}{PC} = 1, \quad \text{hence} \quad \frac{EP}{PC} = \frac{1}{4}, \quad \frac{CP}{CE} = \frac{4}{5}; \quad (1)$$

$$\frac{CD}{DB} \cdot \frac{BA}{AG} \cdot \frac{GR}{CR} = 1, \quad \text{hence} \quad \frac{GR}{CR} = \frac{3}{4}, \quad \frac{CG}{CR} = \frac{7}{4}. \quad (2)$$

Consequently $\frac{PQ}{QR} = \frac{4}{5} \cdot \frac{7}{4} = \frac{7}{5}$.

This method can be used with different ratios $CD : DB$ and $AE : EF : FG : GB$.

A convex hexagon $ABCDEF$ satisfies the following conditions:

(a) The opposite sides are parallel (that is, $AB \parallel DE$, $BC \parallel EF$, $CD \parallel FA$).

(b) The distances between the opposite sides are equal (that is, $d(AB, DE) = d(BC, EF) = d(CD, FA)$, where $d(g, h)$ denotes the distance between lines g and h).

(c) $\angle FAB$ and $\angle CDE$ are right angles.

Show that diagonals BE and CF intersect at an angle of $45°$.

Let X, Y be the feet of the perpendiculars from C to AF, EF, respectively. (See figure.)

Since $AF \parallel CD$, it follows that $CX = d(AF, CD)$.

Since $BC \parallel EF$, it follows that $CY = d(BC, EF)$.

Since $d(AF, CD) = d(BC, EF)$, we have $CX = CY$. Thus, CF bisects $\angle AFE$. Similarly, BE bisects $\angle DEF$. Let T be the intersection of AF and DE. Since $AB \parallel DE$ and $\angle A = 90°$, we get

$$\angle FTE = 90°.$$

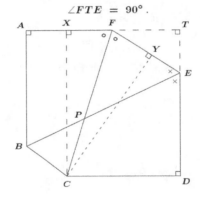

Then,

$$\begin{aligned}
\angle AFE &+ \angle DEF \\
&= (\angle T + \angle TEF) + (\angle T + \angle TFE) \\
&= 2\angle T + (\angle TEF + \angle TFE) \\
&= 90° \times 2 + 90° = 270°.
\end{aligned}$$

Thus, we have

$$\angle PFE + \angle PEF = \tfrac{1}{2}(\angle AFE + \angle DEF) = 135°.$$

Hence, we get

$$\begin{aligned}
\angle FPE &= 180° - (\angle PFE + \angle PEF) \\
&= 180° - 135° = 45°.
\end{aligned}$$

For an acute triangle ABC, k_1, k_2, k_3 are the circles with diameters $[BC]$, $[CA]$, $[AB]$, respectively. If K is the radical centre of these circles, $[AK] \cap k_1 = \{D\}$, $[BK] \cap k_2 = \{E\}$, $[CK] \cap k_3 = \{F\}$ and area$(ABC) = u$, area$(DBC) = x$, area$(ECA) = y$, and area$(FAB) = z$, show that $u^2 = x^2 + y^2 + z^2$.

Solution

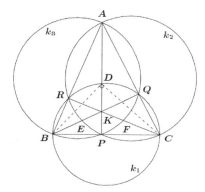

Let P, Q, and R be the feet of the perpendiculars from A, B, and C, to BC, CA, and AB, respectively.

AP, BQ, and CR are common chords of k_2, k_3; k_3, k_1; and k_1, k_2, respectively. Thus, K is the orthocentre of $\triangle ABC$. Since $\angle BDC = 90°$ and $DP \perp BC$, we get

$$DP^2 = BP \cdot CP. \qquad (1)$$

Since $BK \perp AC$ and $AP \perp BC$, we have $\angle BKP = \angle ACP$. Further, we have $\triangle BKP \sim \triangle ACP$. It follows that $BP : AP = KP : CP$; that is

$$AP \cdot KP = BP \cdot CP. \qquad (2)$$

From (1) and (2) we have

$$DP^2 = AP \cdot KP.$$

Hence, we have

$$DP^2 \cdot BC^2 = (AP \cdot BC) \times (KP \cdot BC).$$

From this we get

$$x^2 = u \times \text{area}\,(KBC). \qquad (3)$$

Similarly, we have

$$y^2 = u \times \text{area}\,(KCA), \qquad (4)$$

and

$$z^2 = u \times \text{area } (KAB).\tag{5}$$

Therefore, we obtain from (3), (4), and (5),

$$\begin{aligned}
x^2 + y^2 + z^2 &= u \times \{\text{area } (KBC) + \text{area } (KCA) + \text{area } (KAB)\} \\
&= u \times \text{area } (ABC) \\
&= u^2.
\end{aligned}$$

In a triangle ABC with $|AB| \neq |AC|$, the internal and external bisectors of the angle A intersect the line BC at D and E, respectively. If the feet of the perpendiculars from a point F on the circle with diameter $[DE]$ to the lines BC, CA, AB are K, L, M, respectively, show that $|KL| = |KM|$.

Solution

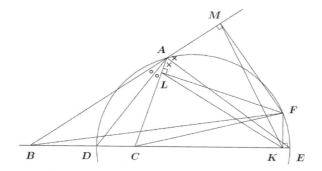

Since the circle with diameter DE is the Apollonius circle, we have

$$\frac{FB}{FC} = \frac{AB}{AC}. \qquad (1)$$

By the Law of Sines, we have

$$\frac{AB}{AC} = \frac{\sin C}{\sin B}. \qquad (2)$$

From (1) and (2), we get

$$\frac{FB}{FC} = \frac{\sin C}{\sin B};$$

that is,

$$FB \sin B = FC \sin C. \qquad (3)$$

Since the circle with diameter BF passes through K and M, we have

$$KM = FB \sin B.$$

Similarly, we have

$$KL = FC \sin C.$$

Therefore, we obtain from (3)

$$KL = KM.$$

In a parallelogram $ABCD$ with $m(\hat{A}) < 90°$, the circle with diameter $[AC]$ intersects the lines CB and CD at E and F besides C, and the tangent to this circle at A intersects the line BD at P. Show that the points P, F, E are collinear.

Solution

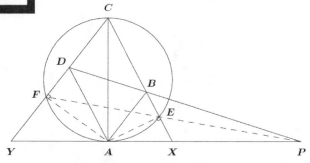

Since AC is a diameter we get $\angle AEC = \angle AFC = 90°$. Since AP is tangent to the circle with diameter AC we have $AP \perp AC$.

Let X and Y be the intersections of AP with BC and CD, respectively.

Since $\angle XAC = 90°$ and $AE \perp XC$, we have $AX^2 = XE \cdot XC$ and $AC^2 = EC \cdot XC$, so

$$AX^2 : AC^2 = XE : EC. \tag{1}$$

Similarly, we have

$$AY^2 : AC^2 = YF : FC. \tag{2}$$

It follows that, from (1) and (2),

$$\frac{XE}{EC} \cdot \frac{CF}{FY} = \frac{AX^2}{AC^2} \cdot \frac{AC^2}{AY^2} = \frac{AX^2}{AY^2}. \tag{3}$$

Since $AB \parallel CY$ and $AD \parallel XC$, we get

$$\frac{AX}{AY} = \frac{XB}{BC} \quad \text{and} \quad \frac{AX}{AY} = \frac{CD}{DY}.$$

Hence, we have

$$\frac{AX^2}{AY^2} = \frac{XB}{BC} \cdot \frac{CD}{DY}. \tag{4}$$

By Menelaus' Theorem for triangle CXY, we have

$$\frac{YP}{PX} \cdot \frac{XB}{BC} \cdot \frac{CD}{DY} = 1. \tag{5}$$

Thus, we obtain from (3), (4) and (5),

$$\frac{YP}{PX} \cdot \frac{XE}{EC} \cdot \frac{CF}{FY} = 1.$$

Therefore, P, F, E are collinear, by the converse of Menelaus' Theorem.

In a convex quadrilateral $ABCD$, $\text{Area}(ABC) = \text{Area}(ADC)$ and $[AC] \cap [BD] = \{E\}$. The parallels from E to the line segments $[AD]$, $[DC]$, $[CB]$, $[BA]$ intersect $[AB]$, $[BC]$, $[CD]$, $[DA]$ at the points K, L, M, N, respectively. Compute the ratio

$$\frac{\text{Area}(KLMN)}{\text{Area}(ABCD)} .$$

Solution

We denote the area of polygon $A_1 A_2 \cdots A_n$ by $[A_1 A_2 \cdots A_n]$. Let B', D' be the feet of perpendiculars from B, D to AC, respectively. (See figure below.)

Since $[ABC] = [ADC]$, we get $BB' = DD'$, so that

$$BE : ED \ = \ BB' : DD' \ = \ 1 : 1 .$$

Thus, we have $BE = ED$. Since $EK \parallel DA$, we have

$$BK : KA = BE : ED = 1 : 1 .$$

Hence, $BK = KA$. Similarly, we have

$$BL \ = \ LC , \quad CM \ = \ MD \quad \text{and} \quad DN \ = \ NA .$$

In triangle ABD, note that K, E and N are the mid-points of AB, BD and DA, respectively. Thus,

$$[ENK] \ = \ \tfrac{1}{4}[ABD] .$$

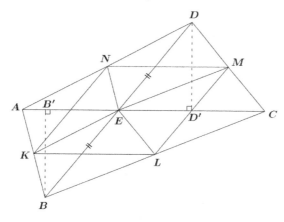

Similarly, we have

$$[EKL] = \tfrac{1}{4}[ABC], \quad [ELM] = \tfrac{1}{4}[BCD] \quad \text{and} \quad [EMN] = \tfrac{1}{4}[CDA].$$

Hence,

$$
\begin{aligned}
[KLMN] &= [ENK] + [EKL] + [ELM] + [EMN] \\
&= \tfrac{1}{4}[ABD] + \tfrac{1}{4}[ABC] + \tfrac{1}{4}[BCD] + \tfrac{1}{4}[CDA] \\
&= \tfrac{1}{4}([ABD] + [BCD]) + \tfrac{1}{4}([ABC] + [CDA]) \\
&= \tfrac{1}{4}[ABCD] + \tfrac{1}{4}[ABCD] \\
&= \tfrac{1}{2}[ABCD].
\end{aligned}
$$

Therefore, we obtain

$$\frac{[KLMN]}{[ABCD]} = \frac{1}{2}.$$

Let $ABCDE$ be a convex pentagon such that $BC = CD = DE$ and each diagonal of the pentagon is parallel to one of its sides. Prove that all the angles in the pentagon are equal, and that all sides are equal.

Solution

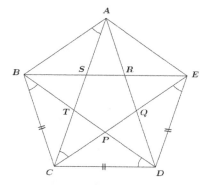

As shown in the figure, we label the intersections of diagonals.

Since $BE \parallel CD$ and $AC \parallel ED$, $SCDE$ is a parallelogram, so that $CS = DE = CB$.

Hence, $\angle CBE = \angle CBS = \angle CSB = \angle DEB$.

Since $\angle CBE = \angle DEB$ and $BC = ED$, it follows that $BCDE$ is an isosceles quadrilateral, so that B, C, D, E are concyclic. Since $AB \parallel CE$, $AC \parallel DE$, we have

$$\angle BAC = \angle ACE = \angle CED = \angle CBD = \angle BDC.$$

Thus, A, B, C, D are concyclic, giving that A, B, C, D, E are concyclic. Since $BC \parallel AD$, we get $AB = CD$, and since $AC \parallel ED$, we have $AE = CD$. Therefore, $AB = BC = CD = DE = EA$.

Consequently, corresponding minor arcs AB, BC, CD, DE and EA are equal, and also corresponding inscribed angles are equal. We put $\angle BAC = \alpha$. Then we have

$$\angle EAB = \angle ABC = \angle BCD = \angle CDE = \angle DEA = 3\alpha.$$

Let $ABCD$ be a cyclic quadrilateral and let P and Q be points on the sides AB and AD, respectively, such that $AP = CD$ and $AQ = BC$. Let M be the point of intersection of AC and PQ. Show that M is the mid-point of PQ.

Solution

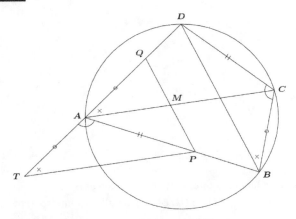

Let T be a point on AD produced beyond A such that

$$AT = BC.$$

Since $AT = BC$, $AP = CD$ and $\angle TAP = \angle TAB = \angle BCD$, we get $\triangle ATP \equiv \triangle CBD$, so that

$$\angle ATP = \angle CBD.$$

Since $\angle CBD = \angle CAD$, we have

$$\angle ATP = \angle CAD.$$

Thus, $TP \parallel AC$; that is, $TP \parallel AM$.

Hence, we get $PM : MQ = TA : AQ = BC : AQ = 1 : 1$. Therefore, $PM = MQ$.

Given is a triangle ABC and a point P inside it satisfying the conditions: $\angle PBC = \angle PCA < \angle PAB$. Line BP cuts the circumcircle of ABC at B and E. The circumcircle of triangle APE meets line CE at E and F. Show that the points A, P, E, F are consecutive vertices of a quadrilateral. Also show that the ratio of the area of quadrilateral $APEF$ to the area of triangle ABP does not depend on the choice of P.

Solution

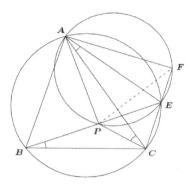

Since

$$
\begin{aligned}
\angle PFC &= \angle PAE = \angle PAC + \angle EAC = \angle PAC + \angle EBC \\
&= \angle PAC + \angle PBC \\
&< \angle PAC + \angle PAB = \angle BAC = \angle BEC = \angle PEC.
\end{aligned}
$$

Thus, F is a point on CE beyond E.

Therefore, A, P, E, F are consecutive vertices of a quadrilateral. Since $\angle EAC = \angle EBC = \angle PBC = \angle PCA$, we have $PC \| AE$. Thus, we have $[APE] = [ACE]$, where $[A_1 A_2 \ldots A_n]$ denotes the area of n-gon $A_1, A_2, \ldots, A_n$.

Hence,

$$
[APEF] = [APE] + [AEF] = [ACE] + [AEF] = [ACF].
$$

Since

$$
\angle ACF = \angle ACE = \angle ABE = \angle ABP,
$$

and

$$
\angle AFC = \angle AFE = \angle APB,
$$

we have $\triangle ACF \sim \triangle ABP$.

Thus, we get $[ACF] : [ABP] = AC^2 : AB^2$; that is

$$
[APEF] : [ABP] = AC^2 : AB^2 \quad (= \text{constant}).
$$

Therefore, $[APEF] : [ABP]$ does not depend on the choice of P.

Let $ABCD$ be a tetrahedron with

$$\angle BAC = \angle ACD \quad \text{and} \quad \angle ABD = \angle BDC.$$

Show that edges AB and CD have equal lengths.

Solution

It is to be noted that there is a tacit assumption the figure is 3-dimensional. The result is not valid if $ABCD$ is a trapezoid with AB parallel to CD.

Letting $b = AB$, $c = AC$, $d = AD$, $b_1 = CD$, $c_1 = BD$, and $d_1 = BC$, and applying the Law of Cosines, we get

$$2c \cos \angle BAC = \frac{b^2 + c^2 - d_1^2}{b} = \frac{b_1^2 + c^2 - d^2}{b_1}, \tag{1}$$

$$2c_1 \cos \angle ABD = \frac{b_1^2 + c_1^2 - d_1^2}{b_1} = \frac{b^2 + c_1^2 - d^2}{b}. \tag{2}$$

Equations (1) and (2) reduce to

$$(bb_1 - c^2)(b - b_1) = b_1 d_1^2 - bd^2, \tag{1'}$$

$$(bb_1 - c_1^2)(b - b_1) = b_1 d^2 - bd_1^2. \tag{2'}$$

Adding the latter two equations, we get

$$(b - b_1)(2bb_1 + d^2 + d_1^2 - c^2 - c_1^2) = 0. \tag{3}$$

We now show that the second factor of (3) is > 0, so that $b = b_1$. Letting $\mathbf{B}$, $\mathbf{C}$, $\mathbf{D}$ denote the vectors AB, AC, and AD, respectively, the second factor is also given by

$$2|\mathbf{B}||\mathbf{C} - \mathbf{D}| + \mathbf{D}^2 + (\mathbf{B} - \mathbf{C})^2 - \mathbf{C}^2 - (\mathbf{B} - \mathbf{D})^2 = 2(|\mathbf{B}||\mathbf{C} - \mathbf{D}| - \mathbf{B}(\mathbf{C} - \mathbf{D})).$$

Hence, this factor is > 0 provided AB is not parallel to CD. It now also follows from (1) or (2) that $d = d_1$.

A circle has the altitude from A in a triangle ABC as a diameter, and intersects AB and AC in the points D and E, respectively, different from A. Prove that the circumcentre of triangle ABC lies on the altitude from A in triangle ADE, or it produced.

Solution

Let H be the foot of the altitude from A to BC. Then

$$AH \perp BC.$$

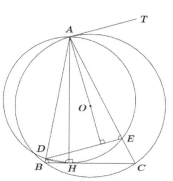

Since AH is the diameter of the circle $ADHE$, we have

$$\angle ADH = 90°.$$

Since $\angle AHB = 90°$ and $HD \perp AB$, we get

$$\angle AHD = \angle ABH = \angle ABC.$$

Since $\angle AHD = \angle AED$ (because A, D, H, E are concyclic), we have

$$\angle ABC = \angle AED. \qquad (1)$$

Let O be the circumcentre of $\triangle ABC$, and let AT be the tangent at A to the circumcircle of $\triangle ABC$. Then

$$\angle TAC = \angle ABC. \qquad (2)$$

From (1) and (2) we get $\angle AED = \angle TAC$. Thus, $DE \perp AT$. Since $AT \perp AO$, we have $AO \perp DE$.

Therefore, the perpendicular from A to DE passes through O.

On a segment AB a point P is chosen. On AP and PB, isosceles right-angled triangles AQP and PRB are constructed with Q and R on the same side of AB. M is the mid-point of QR. Determine the set of all points M for all points P on the segment AB.

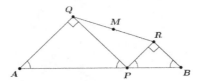

Solution

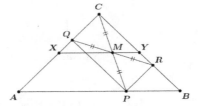

We consider the problem on one side of AB. Let C be the intersection of AQ and BR. Since $\angle CAB = \angle QAP = 45°$ and $\angle CBA = \angle RBP = 45°$, we have that $\triangle CAB$ is isosceles and a right-angled triangle.

Since $\angle QPA = \angle RBP$ $(= 45°)$, we have $PQ\|BR$. Similarly we have $PR\|AQ$, so that $CQPR$ is a parallelogram.

Since M is the mid-point of QR, M is also the mid-point of CP.

Let X and Y be the mid-points of CA and CB respectively.

Since X, M are mid-points of CA, CP respectively, we have $XM\|AP$.

Similarly we have $MY\|PB$. Hence, X, M, Y are collinear.

If P varies on the segment AB from A to B, then M varies on the segment XY from X to Y.

Thus, the set of all points M is the segment XY.

A number of spheres, all with radius 1, are being placed in the form of a square pyramid. First, there is a layer in the form of a square with $n \times n$ spheres. On top of that layer comes the next layer with $(n-1) \times (n-1)$ spheres, and so on. The top layer consists of only one sphere. Determine the height of the pyramid.

Solution

We observe that there is a plane parallel to the base containing all the centres of the spheres of a layer, and we first determine the distance d between the planes so associated to two successive layers. Any sphere (S) of the $(k+1)^{\text{th}}$ layer rests on four spheres (S_1), (S_2), (S_3), (S_4) of the kth layer so that (S) is tangent to these four spheres and (S_1), (S_2) [and (S_2), (S_3), and (S_3), (S_4) and (S_4), (S_1)] are tangent to each other

Let Ω, A, B, C, D be the centres of (S), (S_1), (S_2), (S_3), (S_4) respectively. Then d is the height of the regular pyramid $\Omega ABCD$ and we have

$$\Omega A = \Omega B = \Omega C = \Omega D = AB = BC = CD = DA = 2.$$

Let H be the projection of Ω on the plane $(ABCD)$ and K be the projection of H on, say, AB. Then K is also the projection of Ω on AB and Pythagoras' theorem gives:

$$d^2 = \Omega H^2 = \Omega K^2 - HK^2 = \left(2\frac{\sqrt{3}}{2}\right)^2 - \left(\frac{2}{2}\right)^2 = 2.$$

Hence, $d = \sqrt{2}$.

Now, there are n planes associated to the different layers, so that the distance between the lowest (P_1) and the highest (P_n) of these planes is $(n-1)\sqrt{2}$.

Taking into account that the base is lower than (P_1) by a radius of the spheres and that the apex is higher than (P_n) by a radius as well, we finally obtain the height of the pyramid: $2 + (n-1)\sqrt{2}$.

Let h_a, h_b and h_c be the altitudes of the triangle with edges a, b and c, and r be the radius of the inscribed circle in the triangle. Prove that the triangle is equilateral if and only if $h_a + h_b + h_c = 9r$.

Solution

Clearly $h_a + h_b + h_c = 9r$ when the triangle is equilateral since in that case, we have

$$h_a \;=\; h_b \;=\; h_c \;=\; a\frac{\sqrt{3}}{2} \quad \text{and} \quad r \;=\; \frac{1}{3} \cdot a\frac{\sqrt{3}}{2}\,.$$

Conversely, let S denote the area of a $\triangle ABC$ in which $h_a + h_b + h_c = 9r$. Then, on the one hand,

$$2S = ah_a = bh_b = ch_c \quad \text{so that } h_a + h_b + h_c = 2S\left(\frac{1}{a} + \frac{1}{b} + \frac{1}{c}\right)$$

and on the other hand

$$2S = ar + br + cr\,, \quad \text{so that} \quad r = \frac{2S}{a+b+c}\,.$$

From the hypothesis, we get

$$\frac{1}{3}\left(\frac{1}{a} + \frac{1}{b} + \frac{1}{c}\right) \;=\; \frac{3}{a+b+c}\,.$$

In other words, the harmonic mean of a, b, c equals their arithmetic mean. This implies $a = b = c$ and the triangle is equilateral.

Let AH, BK and CL be the altitudes of arbitrary triangle ABC. Prove that

$$\overline{AK} \cdot \overline{BL} \cdot \overline{CH} = \overline{AL} \cdot \overline{BH} \cdot \overline{CK} = \overline{HK} \cdot \overline{KL} \cdot \overline{LH}.$$

Solution

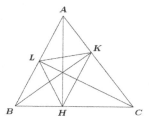

Since $\angle BKC = \angle BLC = 90°$, B, C, K, L are concyclic. Hence, $\angle AKL = \angle ABC$, so that we have

$$\triangle AKL \sim \triangle ABC.$$

Thus,

$$\frac{\overline{AK}}{\overline{KL}} = \frac{\overline{AB}}{\overline{BC}}. \qquad (1)$$

Similarly we have

$$\frac{\overline{BL}}{\overline{LH}} = \frac{\overline{BC}}{\overline{CA}}, \qquad (2)$$

and

$$\frac{\overline{CH}}{\overline{HK}} = \frac{\overline{CA}}{\overline{AB}}. \qquad (3)$$

From (1), (2), (3) we get

$$\frac{\overline{AK}}{\overline{KL}} \cdot \frac{\overline{BL}}{\overline{LH}} \cdot \frac{\overline{CH}}{\overline{HK}} = \frac{\overline{AB}}{\overline{BC}} \cdot \frac{\overline{BC}}{\overline{CA}} \cdot \frac{\overline{CA}}{\overline{AB}} = 1.$$

It follows that

$$\overline{AK} \cdot \overline{BL} \cdot \overline{CH} = \overline{HK} \cdot \overline{KL} \cdot \overline{LH}.$$

Similarly we have

$$\overline{AL} \cdot \overline{BH} \cdot \overline{CK} = \overline{HK} \cdot \overline{KL} \cdot \overline{LH}.$$

A finite number of points in the plane are given such that not all of them are collinear. A real number is assigned to each point. The sum of the numbers for each line containing at least two of the given points is zero. Prove that all numbers are zeros.

Solution

Let M_1, M_2, ..., M_n be the points. Then $n \geq 3$. Denote by a_i, the real number assigned to M_i, and let $S = a_1 + a_2 + \cdots + a_n$.

For a fixed $i_0 \in \{1, \ldots, n\}$, denote by n_{i_0} the number of lines containing M_{i_0} and at least one of the M_j for $j \neq i_0$.

Since not all the M_i are collinear, we have $n_i \geq 2$ for each i. Let Δ be one of the lines containing M_{i_0} and another of the M_j.

We then have

$$S(\Delta) = \sum_{M_j \in \Delta} a_j = 0.$$

Adding all these equalities, for all such Δ, we obtain

$$\sum_{M_{i_0} \in \Delta} S(\Delta) = 0 = S + (n_{i_0} - 1)a_{i_0}.$$

Since M_{i_0} is arbitrary, we then have

$$S + (n_i - 1)a_i \quad \text{for each } i. \tag{1}$$

Suppose that $S \neq 0$. Then there exists $i_0 \in \{1, \ldots, n\}$ such that a_{i_0} has the same sign as S.

For this choice of i_0, we cannot have $S + (n_{i_0} - 1)a_{i_0} = 0$. This is a contradiction.

Then $S = 0$, and, from (1), we have $a_i = 0$ for each i.

Two circles with radii R and r touch from inside. Find the side of an equilateral triangle having one vertex at the common point of the circles and the other two vertices lying on the two circles.

Solution

Let Γ, γ denote the two given circles (with centres Ω, ω and radii R, r respectively) and let A be their point of tangency.

An equilateral triangle ABC having B on γ and C on Γ is easily obtained by drawing the circle Γ' image of Γ under a rotation ρ with centre A and angle $60°$. B is the point other than A common to γ and Γ', and C is the image of B under ρ^{-1}. [There are two such triangles — because we can use either a direct or an indirect rotation; they are symmetrical about the line $A\Omega$ and, consequently, have the same length of sides].

Let Ω' be the centre of Γ' (so that $A\Omega = A\Omega' = R$). Then $AB = 2h$ where h is the length of the altitude from A in $\triangle A\omega\Omega'$. Since $A\omega = r$, $A\Omega' = R$ and $\angle\omega A\Omega' = 60°$, the Cosine Law gives: $\omega\Omega'^2 = r^2 + R^2 - rR$.

Now, the area of $\triangle A\omega\Omega'$ is $\frac{1}{2}h \times \omega\Omega'$ as well as $\frac{1}{2} \times rR\sin(\angle\omega A\Omega') = \frac{\sqrt{3}}{4}rR$. This provides immediately:

$$h = \frac{\sqrt{3}}{2}\frac{rR}{\sqrt{r^2 + R^2 - rR}} \quad \text{and} \quad AB = \sqrt{3}\frac{rR}{\sqrt{r^2 + R^2 - rR}}.$$

Let $ABCD$ be a parallelogram which is not a rectangle and E be a point in its plane, such that $AE \perp AB$ and $BC \perp EC$. Prove that $\angle DAE = \angle CEB$. [Ed. We know this is incorrect — can any reader supply the correct version?]

Solution

Try to prove that $\angle DAE = \angle DCE$.

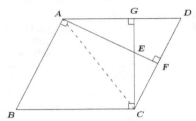

Proof. Extend AE to meet CD at F; CE to meet AD at G. Therefore, $ABCD$ is a parallelogram. Therefore, $AB \parallel DC$, $AD \parallel BC$, and

$$\left. \begin{array}{l} EC \perp BC \implies EC \perp AD \\ AE \perp AB \implies AE \perp CD \end{array} \right\} \implies \left\{ \begin{array}{l} CG \perp AD, \\ AF \perp CD. \end{array} \right.$$

With base AC, and since $\angle AGC = \angle AFC = 90°$, we have that $ACFG$ is a cyclic quadrilateral. Therefore, $\angle DAE = \angle DCE$.

Let $\mathcal{P}$ be the set of all polygons in the plane and let $M : \mathcal{P} \to \mathbb{R}$ be a mapping which satisfies:

(i) $M(P) \geq 0$ for each polygon P;

(ii) $M(P) = x^2$ if P is an equilateral triangle of side x;

(iii) If P is a polygon separated into two polygons S and T, then

$$M(P) = M(S) + M(T); \quad \text{and}$$

(iv) If P and T are congruent polygons, then $M(P) = M(T)$.

Find $M(P)$ if P is a rectangle with edges x and y.

Solution

We will prove that, if P is a rectangle with edges x and y, then

$$M(P) = \frac{4xy}{\sqrt{3}}.$$

Lemma. Let a be a positive real number. Denote by R_a the rectangle with edges a and $a\sqrt{3}$. Then $M(R_a) = 4a^2$.

Proof of the Lemma. Let T be an equilateral triangle with edges $2a$. From (ii), we have $M(T) = 4a^2$. Using a median, we separate T into two congruent right-angled triangles T_1 and T_2.

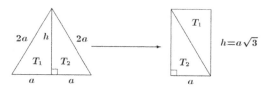

From (iii) we have

$$M(T) = M(T_1) + M(T_2).$$

With these two right-angled triangles, we can form a rectangle R_a with edges a and $h = \sqrt{3}a$.

From (iii) and (iv) we have $M(R_a) = M(T_1) + M(T_2) = 4a^2$. ∎

Now, let x, y be two positive real numbers. Denote by P a rectangle with edges x and y.

Let $n \in \mathbb{N}^*$ such that

$$0 < \frac{1}{n} < x \quad \text{and} \quad 0 < \frac{1}{n} < \frac{y}{\sqrt{3}}. \tag{1}$$

Let p, q be the largest positive integers such that

$$\frac{p}{n} \leq x \quad \text{and} \quad \frac{q}{n} \leq \frac{y}{\sqrt{3}}. \tag{1'}$$

It follows that

$$\frac{pq}{n^2} \leq \frac{xy}{\sqrt{3}} \tag{2}$$

and

$$x < \frac{p+1}{n}, \quad \frac{y}{\sqrt{3}} < \frac{q+1}{n}. \tag{3}$$

Thus,

$$\left(x - \frac{1}{n}\right)\left(\frac{y}{\sqrt{3}} - \frac{1}{n}\right) < \frac{pq}{n^2}. \tag{4}$$

From (1'), note that pq rectangles $R_{1/n}$ can be placed, without overlapping, into P. Note that the part of P which is not covered by these rectangles is a polygon P_1.

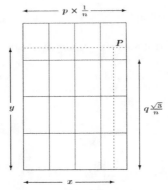

From (iii) and (i), we have

$$
\begin{aligned}
M(P) &= pqM(R_{1/n}) + M(P_1) \\
&\geq pqM(R_{1/n}) \quad \text{from (i),} \\
&= \frac{4pq}{n^2} \quad \text{from the lemma,} \\
&\geq 4\left(x - \frac{1}{n}\right)\left(\frac{y}{\sqrt{3}} - \frac{1}{n}\right) \quad \text{from (4)}.
\end{aligned}
$$

From (3), P is covered by $(p+1)(q+1)$ rectangles $R_{1/n}$.

As above, we have

$$\begin{aligned}
M(P) & \leq (p+1)(q+1)M(R_{1/n}) = \frac{4(p+1)(q+1)}{n^2} \\
& = \frac{4pq}{n^2} + \frac{4p}{n^2} + \frac{4q}{n^2} + \frac{4}{n^2} \\
& \leq \frac{4xy}{\sqrt{3}} + \frac{4x}{n} + \frac{4y}{n\sqrt{3}} + \frac{4}{n^2}
\end{aligned}$$

(from (1$'$) and (2)).

Finally, we have

$$4\left(x - \frac{1}{n}\right)\left(\frac{y}{\sqrt{3}} - \frac{1}{n}\right) \leq M(P) \leq \frac{4xy}{\sqrt{3}} + \frac{4x}{n} + \frac{4y}{n\sqrt{3}} + \frac{4}{n^2}.$$

As n tends to infinity, we get

$$M(P) = \frac{4xy}{\sqrt{3}},$$

as claimed.

Let F be the mid-point of the side BC of the triangle ABC. Isosceles right-angled triangles ABD and ACE are constructed externally on the sides AB and AC with the right angles at D and E, respectively.

Prove that DEF is a right-angled isosceles triangle.

Solution

Let R_1 be the rotation with centre D which transforms B into A and R_2 be the rotation with centre E which transforms A into C. Then $S = R_2 \circ R_1$ is a rotation by angle $180°$; that is, a symmetry about a point, and, since $S(B) = C$, this point is F.

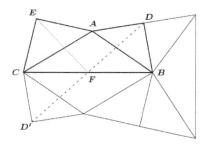

Now, $S(D) = R_2 \circ R_1(D) = R_2(D) = D'$ (say).

From $S(D) = D'$, we see that F is the mid-point of DD', and from $R_2(D) = D'$, we deduce that $\triangle DED'$ is isosceles and right-angled at E.

Therefore, $FD = FD' = FE$ and $EF \perp DD'$ and the result follows.

Let ABC be an acute-angled triangle and let D, E, F be the feet of the perpendiculars from A, B, C onto the sides BC, CA, AB, respectively. Let P, Q, R be the feet of the perpendiculars from A, B, C onto the lines EF, FD, DE respectively. Prove that the lines AP, BQ, CR (extended) are concurrent.

Solution

Let H_B and H_C be the points symmetrical to the orthocentre H about the lines AC and AB, respectively. Then E, F are the mid-points of HH_B, HH_C, respectively, so that $H_B H_C \parallel EF$. Hence, $AP \perp H_B H_C$, and, since $AH_B = AH_C \ (= AH)$, AP is the perpendicular bisector of the segment $H_B H_C$. Since, as is well known, H_B and H_C lie on the circumcircle of $\triangle ABC$, we can conclude: AP passes through the circumcentre O of $\triangle ABC$.

Similarly, BQ and CR pass through O. Thus, the lines AP, BQ, CR are concurrent (at O).

$\angle C$ in $\triangle ABC$ is a right angle and the legs BC and AC are both of length 1. For an arbitrary point P on the leg BC construct points Q, respectively, R, on the hypotenuse, respectively, on the other leg, such that PQ is parallel to AC and QR is parallel to BC. This divides the triangle into three parts.

Determine positions of the point P on BC such that the rectangular part has greater area than each of the other two parts.

Solution

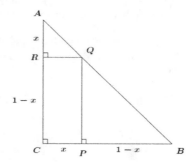

Denote $x = CP$, $x \in (0,1)$. Then $PB = 1 - x$, and, from Thales' Theorem,

$$QB = (1-x)\sqrt{2}, \quad QA = x\sqrt{2}, \quad RC = 1-x, \quad AR = x.$$

Thus,

$$[RQPC] = x(1-x), \quad [PBQ] = \tfrac{1}{2}(1-x)^2, \quad [AQR] = \tfrac{1}{2}x^2.$$

It remains to solve

$$\begin{cases} x(1-x) > \tfrac{1}{2}(1-x)^2, \\ x(1-x) > \tfrac{1}{2}x^2, \end{cases}$$

which is equivalent to

$$\begin{cases} x > \tfrac{1}{3}, \\ x < \tfrac{2}{3}. \end{cases}$$

Thus, we will have the desired result if and only if $PC = x$ with $x \in \left(\tfrac{1}{3}, \tfrac{2}{3}\right)$.

This year's idea for a gift is from "BabyMath", namely a series of 9 coloured plastic figures of decreasing sizes, alternating cube, sphere, cube, sphere, etc. Each figure may be opened and the succeeding one may be placed inside, fitting exactly. The largest and the smallest figures are both cubes. Determine the ratio between their side-lengths.

Solution

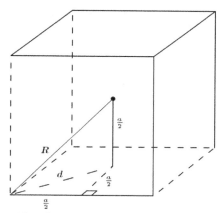

If a sphere with radius R is circumscribed to a cube with edge a then the sphere and the cube have the same centre, and the vertices of the cube are points of the sphere.

From Pythagoras' Theorem:

$$R^2 = d^2 + \frac{a^2}{4} = \frac{3a^2}{4}.$$

Thus,

$$R = \frac{\sqrt{3}}{2}a. \qquad (1)$$

If a sphere with radius R is inscribed in a cube with edge b, then the sphere and the cube have the same centre, and the centres of the sides of the cube are points of the sphere. Then

$$R = \frac{b}{2}. \qquad (2)$$

From (1) and (2), it follows that the ratio between the side-lengths of the "outside cube" and the "inside cube" is

$$\frac{b}{a} = \sqrt{3}.$$

Since there are 5 cubes, the ratios between the side-lengths of the largest and the smallest figures is $\left(\sqrt{3}\right)^4 = 9$.

No three diagonals of a convex 1996–gon meet in one point. Prove
that the number of the triangles lying in the interior of the 1996–gon and
having sides on its diagonals is divisible by 11.

Solution

If $ABCDEF$ is a 6–gon such that no three diagonals meet in one point,
then the triangle formed by AD, BE and CF is the **only one** having sides on
its diagonals. Hence, the number of such triangles for a 1996–gon is $\binom{1996}{6}$,
but since $1991 = 11 \times 181$, we deduce the desired result.

Points A' and C' are taken on the diagonal BD of a parallelogram $ABCD$ so that $AA'\|CC'$. Point K lies on the segment $A'C$, the line AK meets the line $C'C$ at the point L. A line parallel to BC is drawn through K, and a line parallel to BD is drawn through C. These two lines meet at point M. Prove that the points D, M, L are collinear.

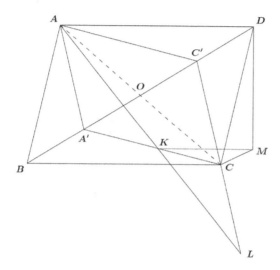

Let O be the intersection of AC and BD. Since $ABCD$ is a parallelogram we have $AO = OC$.

Since $AA'\|CC'$, we obtain $A'O : OC' = AO : OC = 1 : 1$, so that $A'O = OC'$. Thus, $AA'CC'$ is a parallelogram, and further, $AC'\|A'C$. Since $AD\|KM$, $C'D\|CM$, $AC'\|KC$, and $AC' \neq KC$, we have AK, $C'C$, and DM are concurrent at L.

Therefore, D, M, L are collinear.

In a convex pentagon $ABCDE$, $AB = BC$, $\angle ABE + \angle DBC = \angle EBD$, and $\angle AEB + \angle BDE = 180°$. Prove that the orthocentre of triangle BDE lies on diagonal AC.

Solution

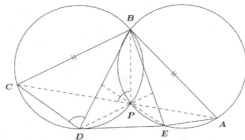

(The condition $\angle AEB + \angle BDE = 180°$ is incorrect. The correct condition is $\angle AEB + \angle BDC = 180°$. After correcting, we shall solve the problem.)

Let P be the second intersection of the circumcircles of $\triangle BCD$ and $\triangle BAE$. Then

$$\angle APB = \angle AEB \quad \text{and} \quad \angle BPC = \angle BDC.$$

Therefore,

$$\angle APB + \angle BPC = \angle AEB + \angle BDC = 180°.$$

Thus, A, P, C are collinear. That is, P is a point on the diagonal AC.

We put $\angle BAC = \angle BCA = \theta$ (because $AB = BC$). Then

$$\angle BEP = \angle BAP = \theta, \quad \text{and} \quad \angle BDP = \angle BCP = \theta.$$

Since $\angle ABE + \angle DBC = \angle EBD$, so that

$$\angle ABC = 2\angle EBD.$$

Since $\angle ABC + \angle BAC + \angle BCA = 180°$, we have

$$2\angle EBD + 2\theta = 180°.$$

Hence,

$$\angle EBD + \theta = 90°.$$

Since $\angle EBD + \angle BDP = \angle EBD + \theta = 90°$, and

$$\angle EBD + \angle BEP = \angle EBD + \theta = 90°,$$

we have $DP \perp BE$ and $EP \perp BD$.

Hence, P is the orthocentre of $\triangle BDE$.

Thus, the orthocentre of $\triangle BDE$ lies on diagonal AC.

Segments AE and CF of equal length are taken on the sides AB and BC of a triangle ABC. The circle going through the points B, C, E and the circle going through the points A, B, F intersect at points B and D. Prove that the line BD is the bisector of angle ABC.

Solution

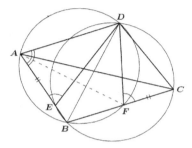

Since A, B, F, D are concyclic, we have

$$\angle EAD = \angle BAD = \angle CFD. \qquad (1)$$

Similarly, we have

$$\angle AED = \angle FCD. \qquad (2)$$

Since $AE = CF$, we get from (1) and (2) that $\triangle DAE \equiv \triangle DFC$. Therefore, $DA = DF$. Hence, we have

$$\angle ABD = \angle AFD = \angle FAD = \angle FBD = \angle CBD.$$

Thus, BD is the bisector of $\angle ABC$.

In a triangle ABC the angle A is $60°$. A point O is taken inside the triangle such that $\angle AOB = \angle BOC = 120°$. A point D is chosen on the half-line CO such that the triangle AOD is equilateral. The mid-perpendicular to the segment AO meets the line BC at point Q. Prove that the line OQ divides the segment BD into two equal parts.

Solution

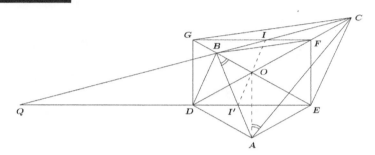

We have $\angle BAC = 60°$, and

$$\angle BOC = \angle AOB = \angle AOC = 120°.$$

Then

$$\angle OBA = 60° - \angle BAO = \angle BAC - \angle BAO = \angle OAC.$$

Thus, $\triangle OAB$ and $\triangle OCA$ are similar. It follows that

$$\frac{OB}{OA} = \frac{OA}{OC}. \tag{1}$$

Let E be the point such that $OEAD$ is a diamond. Let G, F be the points such that $EDGF$ is a rectangle, whose diagonals intersect with an angle of $120°$.

Then $G \in (OE)$, $F \in (OD)$, and $B \in (GE)$.

It follows that:

$$\frac{OB}{OE} = \frac{OB}{OA} = \frac{OA}{OC} = \frac{OD}{OC} \quad \text{(from (1).)}$$

Then (BD) is parallel to (EC).

Moreover,

$$\frac{OB}{OG} = \frac{OB}{OA} = \frac{OA}{OC} = \frac{OF}{OC}.$$

Then (BF) is parallel to (GC).

Let I, I' be respectively the intersection of (BC) and (GF), of (OI) and (ED). Since O is the centre of $DEFG$, O is the mid-point of (II').

From Thales' Theorem,

- In IGC and IFB: $\quad \dfrac{BF}{GC} = \dfrac{BI}{IC}$.

- In OBF and OGC: $\quad \dfrac{BF}{GC} = \dfrac{OB}{OG} = \dfrac{OB}{OE}$.

It follows that (OI) is parallel to (EC), and then to (BD).

Since Q, C, I, B are collinear, and Q, D, I' are collinear, since (OQ) divides (II') into two equal parts, then (OQ) divides (BD) into two equal parts.

Through the vertices of a triangle tangents to the circumcircle are constructed. The distances of an arbitrary point of the circle to the straight lines containing the sides of the triangle are equal to a, b and c and to the tangents are equal to x, y and z. Prove that $a^2 + b^2 + c^2 = xy + xz + yz$.

Solution

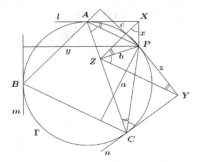

Let the triangle be ABC, and let Γ be the circumcircle of $\triangle ABC$, and let l, m, n be the tangents to Γ at A, B, C, respectively. Suppose that P is a point on Γ and that a, b, c, are the distances from P to BC, CA, AB, respectively, and that x, y, z, be the distances from P to l, m, n, respectively.

Let X, Y and Z, be the feet of the perpendiculars from P to l, n and AC, respectively. Then $PX = x$, $PY = z$, and $PZ = b$.

Since $\angle PXA = \angle PZA = 90°$, we have that P, X, A, Z, are concyclic, and similarly P, Y, C, Z, are concyclic. Since AX is tangent to Γ, we have

$$\angle PZX = \angle PAX = \angle PCA = \angle PCZ = \angle PYZ. \qquad (1)$$

Similarly we have

$$\angle PXZ = \angle PAZ = \angle PAC = \angle PCY = \angle PZY. \qquad (2)$$

From (1) and (2), we get $\triangle PXZ \sim \triangle PZY$, so that $PX : PZ = PZ : PY$; that is

$$PZ^2 = PX \cdot PY.$$

This implies that $b^2 = xz$. Similarly, we have $a^2 = yz$ and $c^2 = xy$. [Ed.: this is stronger than what was asked for.] Thus, we obtain

$$a^2 + b^2 + c^2 = xy + xz + yz.$$

Two disjoint circles C_1 and C_2 with centres O_1 and O_2 are given. A common exterior tangent touches C_1 and C_2 at points A and B, respectively. The segment O_1O_2 cuts C_1 and C_2 at points C and D, respectively. Prove that:

(a) the points A, B, C and D are concyclic;

(b) the straight lines (AC) and (BD) are perpendicular.

Solution

(a) Letting the base angles in isosceles triangles AO_1C and BO_2D be x and y, respectively, the sum of the angles in quadrilateral $ABDC$ is

$$(90° - x) + (90° - y) + (180° - y) + (180° - x) = 360°,$$

and we have

$$x + y = 90°. \qquad (1)$$

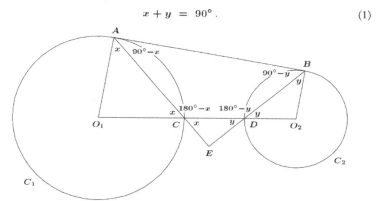

Hence, in $ABDC$, the angles at A and D add up to

$$(90° - x) + (180° - y) = 270° - (x + y) = 270° - 90° = 180°,$$

and thus, $ABDC$ is cyclic. This proves (a).

(b) Let $E = AC \cap CD$. It follows from equation (1) that in triangle CED the angles at C and D add up to $90°$. Thus, CED is a right-angled triangle with the right angle at E and AC and BD are in fact perpendicular.

The perpendicular bisector to the side $[BC]$ of a triangle ABC intersects the straight line (AC) at a point M and the perpendicular bisector to the side $[AC]$ intersects the straight line (BC) at a point N. Let O be the centre of the circumcircle to the triangle ABC. Prove that:

(a) points A, B, M, N and O lie on a circle S;

(b) the radius of S equals the radius of the circumcircle of the triangle MNC.

Solution

(a) If $\angle C = 90°$ then O is the mid-point of AB, and if we consider the line AB as a degenerate circle, it also contains the (infinite) points M and N.

Suppose that in $\triangle ABC$, we have $\angle C < 90°$.

Since M lies on the perpendicular bisector to the side BC, $\triangle BMC$ is isosceles and its exterior angle at M is $\angle AMB = 2\angle C$.

Similarly, $\angle ANB = 2\angle C$.

Now, AB subtends at the centre O twice the angle it subtends at C on the circumcircle, implying that

$$\angle AOB = 2\angle C.$$

Consequently, we deduce that the three points O, M, N all lie on the arc of a circle S on the chord AB which contains the angle $2\angle C$.

This proves (a).

(b) Since quadrilateral $AMNB$ is cyclic, we immediately have that $\angle CAB = 180° - \angle MNB = \angle MNC$, so that triangles MNC and BAC are similar.

Hence,

$$\frac{MN}{AB} = \frac{CM}{BC} = \frac{CM}{2 \cdot CA'},$$

where A' is the mid-point of the side BC.

Now, in right triangle $CA'M$,

$$CA' = CM \cdot \cos C,$$

and therefore,

$$\frac{MN}{AB} = \frac{1}{2 \cos C}.$$

Hence, the ratio between the corresponding circumradii of $\triangle MNC$ and $\triangle ABC$ will be $1 : 2\cos C$, yielding

$$
\begin{aligned}
\text{Circumradius of } \triangle MNC \quad &= \quad \frac{\text{circumradius of } \triangle ABC}{2\cos C} \\
&= \quad \frac{\frac{c}{2\sin C}}{2\cos C} \\
&= \quad \frac{c}{2\sin 2C} \\
&= \quad \text{circumradius of } \triangle AMB \\
&= \quad \text{radius of } S .
\end{aligned}
$$

The present solution can be applied with minor modifications to the case $\angle C > 90°$ as well.

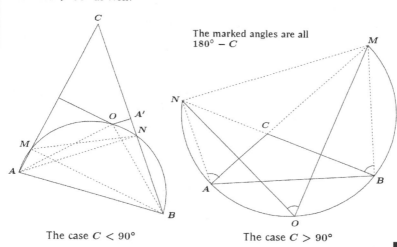

The marked angles are all $180° - C$

The case $C < 90°$ The case $C > 90°$

On a sphere distinct points A, B, C and D are chosen so that segments $[AB]$ and $[CD]$ cut each other at point F, and points A, C and F are equidistant to a point E. Prove that the straight lines (BD) and (EF) are perpendicular

Solution

Points A, C, F are on a sphere S with centre E, and the plane P determined by these points cuts S along a circle Γ. The centre I of Γ is the projection of E onto P so that $(EI) \perp P$. Hence, $(EI) \perp (BD)$, since points B, D are in P.

Now, P cuts the given sphere along a circle γ containing the points A, B, C, D and, in the plane P, the circles γ and Γ intersect at A and C.

In P, consider the inversion with centre F and power $\overline{FA} \cdot \overline{FB} = \overline{FC} \cdot \overline{FD} =$ power of F with respect to γ. Under this inversion, the line (BD) is transformed into Γ, so that the centre I of Γ is on the perpendicular to (BD) through F. Hence, $(IF) \perp (BD)$.

Since (BD) is perpendicular to (EI) and to (IF), it is perpendicular to the plane (EIF) and consequently to the line (EF).

Let ABC be an equilateral triangle of altitude 1. A circle with radius 1 and centre on the same side of AB as C rolls along the segment AB. Prove that the arc of the circle that is inside the triangle always has the same length.

Solution

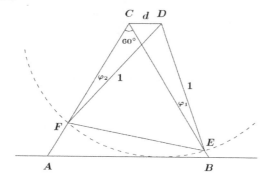

The rolling circle intersects CB at E and CA at F. D is the centre of the rolling circle.

$$\angle CED = \varphi_1, \quad \angle CFD = \varphi_2, \quad \angle DCE = 60°, \quad \angle DCF = 120°,$$

$$\overline{CD} = d, \quad DE = DF = 1.$$

From the Sine Law in $\triangle CDE$, we have

$$d : \sin\varphi_1 = 1 : \sin 60° \implies \sin\varphi_1 = d\sin 60°.$$

From the Sine Law in $\triangle CDF$, we have

$$d : \sin\varphi_2 = 1 : \sin 120° \implies \sin\varphi_2 = d\sin 120°$$
$$\implies \sin\varphi_1 = \sin\varphi_2 \implies \varphi_1 = \varphi_2 = \varphi.$$
$$\implies \text{Quad}CDEF \text{ can be inscribed in a circle}$$
$$\implies \angle EDF = \angle ECF = \angle BCA = 60° = \text{constant.}$$

A regular polygon with 1996 vertices is given. What minimal number of vertices can we delete so that we do not have four remaining vertices which form: (a) a square? (b) a rectangle?

Solution

(a) Let A_1, A_2, ..., A_{1996} be the vertices, in that order, of the regular polygon. There are exactly 499 squares whose vertices are vertices of the polygon, which are $A_i A_{i+499} A_{i+998} A_{i+1497}$ (subscripts are modulo 1996), for $i = 1, 2, \ldots, 499$.

Then, we have to delete at least one of the vertices of each of these squares in order not to have a remaining square. Conversely, if we delete one of the vertices of the 499 squares, there is no remaining square.

Thus, the minimal number to delete is 499.

(b) A rectangle is formed by the vertices of two diameters of the circumcircle. There are 998 diameters whose vertices are vertices of the polygon, which are $A_i A_{i+998}$ for $i = 1, \ldots, 998$.

Then, there will be no remaining rectangles if and only if we delete at least one vertex of all these 998 diameters, except one eventually.

Thus, the minimal number is 997.

Let O be the centre of the parallelogram $ABCD$, $\angle AOB > \pi/2$. We take the points A_1, B_1 on the half lines OA, OB respectively so that $A_1B_1 \parallel AB$ and $\angle A_1B_1C = \angle ABC/2$.

Prove that $A_1D \perp B_1C$.

Solution

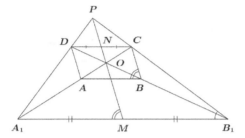

Let P be the intersection of A_1D and B_1C. Since $DC \parallel AB \parallel A_1B_1$, we get $DC \parallel A_1B_1$, so that

$$\frac{PD}{DA_1} = \frac{PC}{CB_1}. \tag{1}$$

Let M and N be the intersections of PO with A_1B_1 and DC respectively. By Ceva's Theorem we have

$$\frac{A_1M}{MB_1} \cdot \frac{B_1C}{CP} \cdot \frac{PD}{DA_1} = 1.$$

Thus, we have from (1)

$$\frac{A_1M}{MB_1} = 1; \quad \text{that is,} \quad A_1M = MB_1.$$

Since $DC \parallel A_1B_1$, we have

$$\frac{DN}{A_1M} = \frac{PN}{PM} = \frac{NC}{MB_1}, \quad \text{giving} \quad DN = NC.$$

Because $DN = NC$ and $DO = OB$, we have $NO \parallel CB$; that is $PM \parallel CB$.

Since $A_1B_1 \parallel AB$ and $PM \parallel CB$, we get

$$\angle A_1MP = \angle ABC = 2\angle A_1B_1C = 2\angle A_1B_1P.$$

Thus, $\angle MPB_1 = \angle A_1MP - \angle A_1B_1P = \angle A_1B_1P$. Further, we obtain that $A_1M = B_1M = PM$. Thus, $\angle A_1PB_1 = 90°$. This implies that $A_1D \perp B_1C$.

Among the triangles with an assigned side l and with given area S, determine all those for which the product of the three altitudes is maximum.

Solution

Let the altitudes be d, e, f so that

$$d = \frac{2S}{a}, \quad e = \frac{2S}{b}, \quad f = \frac{2S}{c}.$$

Let $a = l$, so that with S fixed, so is d. One maximizes def when ef is maximum. Now $ef = \frac{4S^2}{bc}$, so that maximum ef occurs for minimum bc.

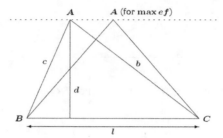

Now S is fixed, so that A lies on the dotted line parallel to BC through a point A perpendicular distance d from BC. Also, $S = \frac{1}{2}bc \sin A$ is constant, so that bc is minimized when $\angle A$ is maximized. This is true when $AB = AC$, and the triangle is isosceles.

Let a circle C and a point A exterior to C be given. For each point P on C construct the square $APQR$, with anticlockwise ordering of the letters A, P, Q, R. Find the locus of the point Q when P runs over C.

Solution

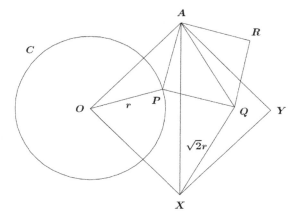

Let O and r be the centre and radius of the circle C. Construct square $AOXY$ with anticlockwise ordering of the letters A, O, X, Y.

$\triangle APQ$ and $\triangle AOX$ are both right-angled isosceles triangles, and they are directly similar, so

$$\triangle AOP \sim \triangle AXQ.$$

Thus, we have

$$OP : XQ = AP : AQ = 1 : \sqrt{2}.$$

Therefore, $XQ = \sqrt{2}\, OP = \sqrt{2}\, r$.

Hence, when P runs over C, point Q describes the circle with centre X and radius $\sqrt{2}\, r$.

Therefore, the locus of Q is the circle with centre X and radius $\sqrt{2}\, r$.

ABC is a triangle with $\angle A > \angle C$, and D is the point on BC such that $\angle BAD = \angle ACB$. The perpendicular bisectors of AD and DC intersect in the point E. Prove that $\angle BAE = 90°$.

Solution

E is the circumcentre of $\triangle ADC$. Denote its circumcircle by Γ.

Since $\angle DAB = \angle ACD$ we have that AB is tangent to Γ at A, so that $\angle BAE = 90°$.

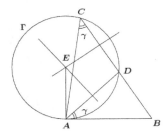

Three circles, with radii p, q, r, and centres A, B, C respectively, touch one another externally at points D, E, F. Prove that the ratio of the areas of $\triangle DEF$ and $\triangle ABC$ equals

$$\frac{2pqr}{(p+q)(q+r)(r+p)}.$$

Solution

We denote circles with radii p, q, r and centres A, B, C by Γ_1, Γ_2, Γ_3 respectively. Let D, E, F be the points of tangency of Γ_2, Γ_3; Γ_3, Γ_1; and Γ_1, Γ_2 respectively.

By the assumption D, E, F are points on segments BC, CA, AB respectively.

Since $\angle FAE = \angle BAC$ we get

$$\frac{[AFE]}{[ABC]} = \frac{\frac{1}{2}AF \cdot AE \sin\angle FAE}{\frac{1}{2}AB \cdot AC \sin\angle BAC} = \frac{AF \cdot AE}{AB \cdot AC} = \frac{p^2}{(p+q)(p+r)},$$

where $[PQR]$ denotes the area of triangle PQR.

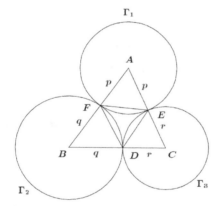

Similarly we have

$$\frac{[BDF]}{[ABC]} = \frac{q^2}{(p+q)(q+r)}, \quad \text{and} \quad \frac{[CED]}{[ABC]} = \frac{r^2}{(q+r)(p+r)}.$$

Hence, we have

$$\frac{[DEF]}{[ABC]} = 1 - \frac{[AFE]}{[ABC]} - \frac{[BDF]}{[ABC]} - \frac{[CED]}{[ABC]}$$

$$= 1 - \frac{p^2}{(p+q)(p+r)} - \frac{q^2}{(p+q)(q+r)} - \frac{r^2}{(q+r)(p+r)}$$

$$= \frac{(p+q)(q+r)(p+r) - p^2(q+r) - q^2(p+r) - r^2(p+q)}{(p+q)(q+r)(p+r)}$$

$$= \frac{2pqr}{(p+q)(q+r)(r+p)}.$$

The convex quadrilateral $ABCD$ has area 1, and AB is produced to E, BC to F, CD to G and DA to H, such that $AB = BE$, $BC = CF$, $CD = DG$ and $DA = AH$. Find the area of the quadrilateral $EFGH$.

Solution

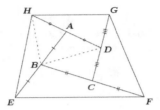

We denote the area of n-gon $P_1 P_2 \ldots P_n$ by $[P_1 P_2 \ldots P_n]$. Since B and A are the mid-points of AE and DH respectively, we get $[HEB] = [HAB] = [ABD]$, so that

$$[AEH] = 2[ABD].$$

Similarly we have $[CFG] = 2[CBD]$. Thus,

$$
\begin{aligned}
[AEH] + [CFG] &= 2[ABD] + 2[CBD] \\
&= 2[ABCD] \\
&= 2.
\end{aligned}
$$

Similarly, we get

$$[BEF] + [DGH] = 2.$$

Thus, we have

$$
\begin{aligned}
[EFGH] &= [ABCD] + \{[AEH] + [CFG]\} + \{[BEF] + [DGH]\} \\
&= 1 + 2 + 2 \\
&= 5.
\end{aligned}
$$

The circumcircle of $\triangle ABC$ has radius 1 and centre O, and P is a point inside the triangle such that $OP = x$. Prove that

$$AP \cdot BP \cdot CP \leq (1 + x)^2(1 - x),$$

with equality only if $P = O$.

Solution

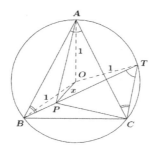

If we assume that

$$\angle PBA + \angle PCA < \angle BAC, \tag{1}$$

that

$$\angle PAB + \angle PCB < \angle ABC, \tag{2}$$

and that

$$\angle PAC + \angle PBC < \angle ACB, \tag{3}$$

then, adding (1) and (2) to (3), we have

$$\angle BAC + \angle ABC + \angle ACB < \angle BAC + \angle ABC + \angle ACB.$$

This is a contradiction. Therefore, (1), (2) and (3) do not hold simultaneously, so that at least one of them is not true.

Without loss of generality we may assume that (1) is not true, so that we have

$$\angle PBA + \angle PCA \geq \angle BAC.$$

Let T be the second intersection of BP with the circumcircle of $\triangle ABC$. Then, we have $\angle BTC = \angle BAC$ and $\angle ACT = \angle ABT$.

Thus, $\angle PCT = \angle ACP + \angle ACT = \angle ACP + \angle ABT = \angle ACP + \angle ABP \geq \angle BAC = \angle BTC = \angle PTC$; that is, $\angle PCT \geq \angle PTC$. Thus, we have $PT \geq CP$. Since

$$BP \cdot PT = OT^2 - OP^2 = 1 - x^2,$$

we have

$$BP \cdot CP \leq BP \cdot PT = 1 - x^2. \tag{4}$$

Since

$$AP \leq AO + OP = 1 + x,\tag{5}$$

we obtain, from (4) and (5), that

$$AP \cdot BP \cdot CP \leq (1+x)(1-x^2) = (1+x)^2(1-x).\tag{6}$$

Next, we consider when equality in (6) holds. This is when equalities in (4) and (5) hold simultaneously.

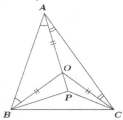

In (5), equality holds if and only if P is a point on AO produced beyond O or $P = O$.

If $\triangle ABC$ is not an acute triangle, O is not an interior point of $\triangle ABC$, so that equality in (5) does not hold.

When $\triangle ABC$ is an acute triangle, let P be a point on AO produced beyond O. Then $\angle ABP + \angle ACP > \angle ABO + \angle ACO = \angle BAO + \angle CAO = \angle BAC$. Thus, $BP \cdot CP < 1 - x^2$. Thus, equality in (4) does not hold.

If $P = O$, in (4), (5) and (6), then all equalities hold.

Therefore, in (6) equality holds if and only if $P = O$.

Let A and B be two fixed points on a fixed circle. Let a point P move on this circle and let M be a corresponding point such that either M is on the segment PA with $AM = MP + PB$ or M is on the segment PB with $AP + MP = PB$. Determine the locus of such points P.

Solution

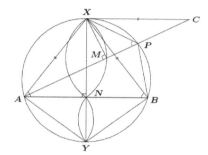

The perpendicular bisector of AB meets the circle at X and Y. Then $XA = XB$ and $YA = YB$.

Let P be a point on the minor arc XB. Then $PA \geq PB$.

Let C be a point on AP produced beyond P such that $PC = PB$. Since $AM = MP + PB = MP + PC = MC$, M is the mid-point of AC.

Since $\angle XPA = \angle XBA = \angle XAB$, we have

$$\angle XPC = 180° - \angle XPA = 180° - \angle XAB = \angle XPB.$$

Since $PC = PB$ and $XP = XP$ we get $\triangle XPC \equiv \triangle XPB$. Hence, $XC = XB = XA$.

Since M is the mid-point of AC we have $XM \perp AC$; that is, $\angle XMA = 90°$.

Let N be the mid-point of AB. Then $\angle XNA = 90°$.

If P moves on the minor arc BX from B to X, then M moves on the minor arc NX of the circle with diameter XA. Similarly, if P moves on the minor arc XA from X to A, then M moves on the minor arc XN of the circle with diameter XB.

And if P moves on the minor arc AY, then m moves on the minor arc NY of the circle with diameter BY.

And if P moves on the minor arc YB, then M moves on the minor arc NY of the circle with diameter AY.

Thus, the locus of M is the union of the four minor arcs as shown in the figure as a shape of a "figure-eight" loop.

(a) $n = 2k + 1$ points are given in the plane. Construct an n–gon such that these points are mid-points of its sides.

(b) Arbitrary $n = 2k$, $k > 1$, points are given in the plane. Prove that it is impossible to construct an n–gon, in each case, such that these points are mid-points of its sides.

Solution

We will denote by H_A the half-turn around point A and by T_U the translation with vector U. Note the following formula: $H_B \circ H_A = T_U$ where $U = 2\overrightarrow{AB}$.

Suppose now that A_1, A_2, ..., A_n are the mid-points of the sides of the n-gon $M_1 M_2 \ldots M_n$ (with A_1 the mid-point of $M_1 M_2$, etc. ...). Then

$$M_1 = H_{A_n}(M_n) = H_{A_n} \circ H_{A_{n-1}}(M_{n-1})$$
$$= \cdots = H_{A_n} \circ H_{A_{n-1}} \circ \cdots \circ H_{A_1}(M_1)$$

so that M_1 is invariant under the transformation $H = H_{A_n} \circ H_{A_{n-1}} \circ \cdots \circ H_{A_1}$.

If $n = 2k$, then $H = T_{U_k} \circ T_{U_{k-1}} \circ \cdots \circ T_{U_1}$ where $U_i = 2\overrightarrow{A_{2t-1}A_{2t}}$ ($i = 1, \ldots, k$). Hence, H is the translation with vector $U = U_1 + \cdots + U_k$. Unless $U = \overrightarrow{0}$, H has no invariant point so that no n–gon $M_1 M_2 \ldots M_n$ can be obtained. (If $U = \overrightarrow{0}$, M_1 can be any point in the plane and we obtain an infinity of solutions; see figure 2.)

If $n = 2k + 1$, then

$$
\begin{aligned}
H &= H_{A_n} \circ T_U \quad \text{(with the notation above)} \\
&= H_{A_n} \circ H_{A_n} \circ H_B \quad \text{where } B \text{ is such that } 2\overrightarrow{BA_n} = U \\
&= H_B .
\end{aligned}
$$

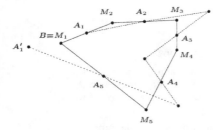

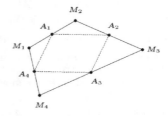

figure 1 (for $n = 5$) figure 2 (for $n = 4$ and $U = \overrightarrow{0}$)

Hence, H is the half-turn around B and, necessarily, $M_1 = B$. Note that B is easily constructed: just construct $A_1' = H(A_1)$ and B is the mid-point of $A_1 A_1'$.

Conversely, taking $M_1 = B$ and constructing successively the points $M_2 = H_{A_1}(M_1)$, ..., $M_n = H_{A_{n-1}}(M_{n-1})$, we obtain a suitable n–gon $M_1 M_2 \ldots M_n$ (since $H_{A_n}(M_n) = H(M_1) = M_1$). Thus, when n is odd, there is a unique solution (see figure 1).

The side-length of the square $ABCD$ equals a. Two points E and F are given on sides $\overline{BC}$ and $\overline{AB}$ such that the perimeter of the triangle BEF equals $2a$. Determine the angle $\angle EDF$.

Solution

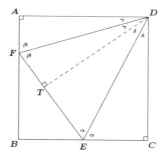

Since $BA = BC = a = \frac{1}{2}(BE + EF + FB)$, the excircle of $\triangle BEF$ opposite to B touches BA and BC at A and C respectively. Since $DA \perp AB$ and $DC \perp BC$, D is the excentre, so that DF and DE are the bisectors of $\angle AFE$ and $\angle FEC$, respectively.

Let T be the foot of the perpendicular from D to EF. Since $\angle AFD = \angle TFD$, and $\angle DAF = \angle DTF\ (= 90°)$, we get

$$\angle ADF = \angle TDF.$$

Similarly we have $\angle CDE = \angle TDE$.

Therefore, $\angle ADF + \angle CDE = \angle TDF + \angle TDE = \angle EDF$. Thus, $\angle ADC = 2\angle EDF$.

Therefore, $\angle EDF = \frac{1}{2}\angle ADC = 45°$.

Let A_1, A_2, ..., A_n be a regular n-gon inscribed in the circle of radius 1 with the centre at O. A point M is given on the ray OA_1 outside the n-gon. Prove that

$$\sum_{k=1}^{n} \frac{1}{|MA_k|} \geq \frac{n}{|OM|}.$$

Solution

We may suppose that a system of coordinates has been chosen so that the complex numbers associated to O, A_1, A_2, ..., A_n, M are respectively 0, 1, u, ..., u^{n-1}, r, where $u = \exp(\frac{2\pi i}{n})$ and r is a real number > 1.

Note that 1, u, ..., u^{n-1} are the nth roots of unity. Hence we have the identity

$$z^n - 1 = (z - 1)(z - u) \ldots (z - u^{n-1}). \tag{1}$$

Now,

$$
\begin{aligned}
\frac{1}{n} \sum_{k=1}^{n} \frac{1}{|MA_k|} &= \frac{1}{n} \sum_{k=0}^{n-1} \frac{1}{|r - u^k|} \\
&\geq \sqrt[n]{\frac{1}{|r-1|} \cdot \frac{1}{|r-u|} \cdot \ldots \cdot \frac{1}{|r-u^{n-1}|}} \quad \text{(by AM-GM)} \\
&= \sqrt[n]{\frac{1}{|r^n - 1|}} \quad \text{(using (1))} \\
&= \sqrt[n]{\frac{1}{r^n - 1}} > \sqrt[n]{\frac{1}{r^n}} = \frac{1}{r} = \frac{1}{|OM|}.
\end{aligned}
$$

The result follows.

Let L be a line in the plane of an acute triangle ABC. Let the lines symmetric to L with respect to the sides of ABC intersect each other in the points A', B' and C'. Prove that the incentre of triangle $A'B'C'$ lies on the circumcircle of triangle ABC.

Solution

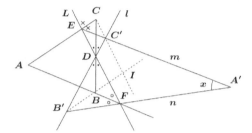

Let D, E, F be the intersections of L with BC, CA, AB respectively.

Let l, m, n be the lines symmetric to L with respect to BC, CA, AB, respectively, and let A', B', C' be the intersections of m, n; n, l; l, m, respectively.

Since BF and BD are bisectors of $\angle B'FD$ and $\angle B'DF$, respectively, we have B is the incentre of $\triangle B'FD$. Hence $B'B$ bisects $\angle FB'D$.

Since DC bisects $\angle EDC'$ and CE bisects the exterior angle of $\angle DEC'$, we have C is the excentre of $\triangle DEC'$ opposite to D. Hence CC' bisects the exterior angle of $\angle DC'E$, so that CC' is the bisector of $\angle B'C'A'$.

Let I be the intersection of BB' and CC'.

Since BB' and CC' are bisectors of $\angle A'B'C'$ and $\angle A'C'B'$ respectively, we have I is the incentre of $\triangle A'B'C'$.

We put $\angle B'A'C' = \angle FA'E = x$.

Since I is the incentre of $\triangle A'B'C'$ we get

$$\angle B'IC = 90° + \frac{x}{2}; \quad \text{that is}$$
$$\angle BIC = \angle B'IC' = 90° + \frac{x}{2}. \tag{1}$$

In triangle $A'EF$, FA and EA are the exterior bisectors of $\angle A'FE$ and $\angle A'EF$, respectively, so that A is the excentre of $\triangle A'EF$ opposite to A'. Thus, we have $\angle FAE = 90° - \frac{x}{2}$; that is

$$\angle BAC = 90° - \frac{x}{2}. \tag{2}$$

From (1) and (2), it follows that

$$\angle BIC + \angle BAC = \left(90° + \frac{x}{2}\right) + \left(90° - \frac{x}{2}\right) = 180°.$$

Therefore A, B, I, C are concyclic.

Thus the incentre of $\triangle A'B'C'$ lies on the circumcircle of $\triangle ABC$.

In triangle ABC we have $\angle A = 60°$. Let O, H, I, and I' be the circumcentre, orthocentre, incentre, and the excentre with respect to A of the triangle ABC. Consider points B' and C' on AC and AB such that $AB = AB'$ and $AC = AC'$. Prove that

(a) Eight points B, C, H, O, I, I', B', and C' are concyclic.

(b) If OH intersects AB and AC in E and F respectively, then triangle AEF has a perimeter equal to $AC + AB$.

(c) $OH = |AB - AC|$.

Solution

In the figure we assume that $\triangle ABC$ is acute and $AB < AC$. But the following proof works in other cases with minor changes.

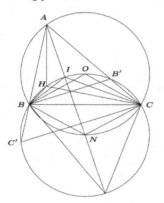 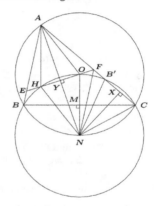

(a) Let N be the second intersection of AI with the circumcircle of $\triangle ABC$. It is well known that $BN = CN = IN$, so that N is the circumcentre of $\triangle IBC$. Since $BH \perp AC$, $CH \perp AB$, we have $\angle BHC = 180° - 60° = 120°$.

Since I is the incentre of $\triangle ABC$, we have $\angle BIC = 90° + \frac{1}{2}\angle A = 90° + 30° = 120°$. Since O is the circumcentre of $\triangle ABC$, we have $\angle BOC = 2\angle BAC = 120°$.

Similarly, $\triangle ACC'$ is equilateral, so that $\angle BC'C = \angle AC'C = 60°$. Also, H, I, O, B' lie on the same side of A with respect to BC, and C', I' lie on the opposite side of A.

Now,

$$\angle BHC = \angle BIC = \angle BOC = \angle BB'C(=120°), \text{ and}$$
$$\angle BC'C + \angle BIC = \angle BI'C + \angle BIC = 60° + 120° = 180°.$$

Hence B, C, H, I, O, B', I' lie on the circle with centre N.

(b) Let M be the intersection of ON with BC. Since $BN = CN$, we have that M is the mid-point of BC and that $OM \perp BC$.

Since $\angle BOM = \frac{1}{2}\angle BOC = \angle BAC = 60°$ and $OB = ON$, we have that $\triangle OBN$ is equilateral. Hence $OM = MN$. As is well known, $AH = 2OM$, so that $AH = ON = OA$. Since H, O lie on the circle with centre N, we have $HN = ON$. Thus, $AH = AO = ON = HN$, so that $AHNO$ is a rhombus. Therefore, HO is the perpendicular bisector of AN.

Since $\angle EAN = \angle FAN$ and $AN \perp EF$, we have $\angle AFE = 90° - \angle NAF = 90° - 30° = 60°$. Since EF is the perpendicular bisector of AN, we get $\angle NFE = \angle AFE = 60°$, so that $\angle NFC = 60°$. Hence, $\angle EFN = \angle NFC$, and $\angle EAN = \angle NAF$, so that N is the excentre of $\triangle AEF$. Let X be the foot of the perpendicular from N to AC. Then X is the point of tangency of the excircle to AC.

Thus, we have $2AX = AE + AF + EF$.

Since $NB' = NC$, X is the mid-point of $B'C$, so $2AX = AB' + AC = AB + AC$. Hence, we have $AE + AF + EF = AB + AC$. Thus, the perimeter of $\triangle AEF$ is equal to $AB + AC$.

(c) Let Y be the intersection of AN with OH. Then $NY \perp OH$. Since $\angle NFY = \angle NFX$, we have $NY = NX$. Since H, O, B', C lie on the circle with centre N, we get from $NY = NX$ that $OH = B'C = AC - AB' = AC - AB$. That is, $OH = |AB - AC|$.

13th Iranian Mathematical Olympiad, 1995 (Final Round)

5

Let ABC be a non-isosceles triangle. Medians of the triangle ABC intersect the circumcircle in points L, M, N. If L lies on the median of BC and $LM = LN$, prove that $2a^2 = b^2 + c^2$.

Solution

Let G be the centroid of $\triangle ABC$. Since $\triangle ACG$ and $\triangle NGL$ are similar, and since $\triangle MLG$ and $\triangle ABG$ are similar, we have

$$\frac{LN}{AC} = \frac{LG}{CG}, \quad \frac{LM}{AB} = \frac{GL}{BG}.$$

Thanks to $LM = LN$, we obtain

$$\frac{AB}{AC} = \frac{BG}{CG}.$$

We have

$$\frac{c^2}{b^2} = \frac{2c^2 + 2a^2 - b^2}{2b^2 + 2a^2 - c^2},$$

which yields

$$(b^2 - c^2)(2a^2 - c^2 - b^2) = 0.$$

Finally, we have $2a^2 = b^2 + c^2$.

Points D and E are situated on the sides AB and AC of triangle ABC in such a way that $DE\|BC$. Let P be an arbitrary point inside the triangle ABC. Lines PB and PC intersect DE at F and G, respectively. Let O_1 be the circumcentre of triangle PDG and let O_2 be that of PFE. Show that $AP \perp O_1O_2$.

Solution

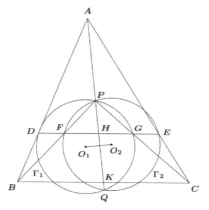

Let Γ_1 and Γ_2 be the circumcircles of $\triangle PDG$ and $\triangle PFE$, respectively, so that O_1 and O_2 are centres of Γ_1 and Γ_2, respectively. Let Q be the intersection of Γ_1 and Γ_2 other than P. Then $O_1O_2 \perp PQ$.

Let H and K be the intersections of AP with DE and BC, respectively.

Since $DE\|BC$, we get

$$DH : BK \;=\; AH : AK \;=\; HE : KC, \text{ so that}$$

$$DH : HE \;=\; BK : KC. \tag{1}$$

Since $FG\|BC$, we similarly get

$$FH : HG \;=\; BK : KC. \tag{2}$$

From (1) and (2), we have

$$DH : HE \;=\; FH : HG.$$

Thus,

$$DH \cdot HG \;=\; FH \cdot HE.$$

Note that $DH \cdot HG$ and $FH \cdot HE$ are the powers of H with respect to Γ_1 and Γ_2, respectively. Hence, H is a point on the radical axis of Γ_1 and Γ_2.

Since P and Q are intersections of Γ_1 and Γ_2, we have that PQ is the radical axis of Γ_1 and Γ_2. Therefore, H is a point on the line PQ, so that A, P, Q are collinear.

Since, $PQ \perp O_1O_2$, we have $AP \perp O_1O_2$.

Let H be the orthocentre of an obtuse triangle ABC and A_1, B_1, C_1 arbitrary points taken on the sides BC, AC, AB, respectively. Prove that the tangents drawn from the point H to the circles with diameters AA_1, BB_1, CC_1 are equal.

Solution

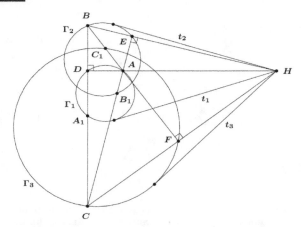

The lines HA, HB, HC meet BC, CA, AB at D, E, F, respectively. Then, $AD \perp BC$, $BE \perp AC$ and $CF \perp AB$.

Let Γ_1, Γ_2, Γ_3 be circles with diameters AA_1, BB_1, CC_1, respectively.

Since $\angle ADA_1 = \angle BEB_1 = CFC_1 = 90°$, we have that Γ_1, Γ_2, Γ_3 pass through D, E, F, respectively.

Let t_1, t_2, t_3 be the tangent segments from H to Γ_1, Γ_2, Γ_3, respectively.

Since $\angle ADB = \angle AEB = 90°$, A, D, B, E are concyclic, so that

$$HA \cdot HD = HB \cdot HE.$$

Hence, we have

$$t_1^2 = HA \cdot HD = HB \cdot HE = t_2^2.$$

Thus, $t_1 = t_2$.

Similarly, we have $t_1 = t_3$. Therefore, $t_1 = t_2 = t_3$.

Let $ABCD$ be a quadrilateral and let P and Q be the trisecting points of the diagonal BD (that is, P and Q are the points on the line segment BD for which the lengths BP, PQ and QD are all the same). Let E be the intersection of the straight line through A and P with BC, and let F be the intersection of the straight line through A and Q with DC. Prove the following:

(i) If $ABCD$ is a parallelogram, then E and F are the mid-points of BC and CD, respectively.

(ii) If E and F are the mid-points of BC and CD, respectively, then $ABCD$ is a parallelogram.

Solution

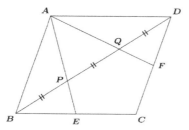

(i) Since $ABCD$ is a parallelogram $AD \| BC$ and $AD = BC$. Thus, we have $BE : AD = BP : PD = 1 : 2$.

Therefore, $BE = \frac{1}{2}AD = \frac{1}{2}BC$, so that $BE = EC$. Similarly, we get $DF : DC = DF : AB = DQ : QB = 1 : 2$. Thus, $DF = \frac{1}{2}DC$; that is $DF = FC$.

Therefore, E and F are mid-points of BC and CD, respectively.

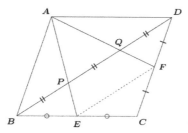

(ii) Since E, F are mid-points of BC, CD, respectively, we get $EF \| BD$ and $EF = \frac{1}{2}BD$.

Since $PQ \| EF$ we have

$$AP : AE = PQ : EF = \frac{1}{3}BD : \frac{1}{2}BD = 2 : 3 = DP : DB.$$

Therefore, $AD \| BE$; that is, $AD \| BC$. Similarly we have $AB \| DC$.

Hence, $ABCD$ is a parallelogram.

The picture below shows a triangle $\triangle ABC$ in which the length AB is smaller than that of BC, and the length of BC is smaller than that of AC. The points A', B' and C' are such that AA' is perpendicular to BC and the length of AA' equals that of BC; BB' is perpendicular to AC and the length of BB' equals that of AC; CC' is perpendicular to AB and the length of CC' equals that of AB. Moreover $\angle AC'B$ is a $90°$ angle. Prove that A', B' and C' are collinear.

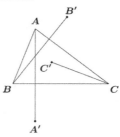

Solution

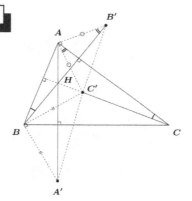

AA', BB' and CC' are concurrent at the orthocentre H of $\triangle ABC$. Since $BH \perp AC$ and $CH \perp AB$ we get

$$\angle ABB' = \angle ABH = \angle ACH = \angle ACC'.$$

Since $BA = CC'$ and $BB' = CA$, we have

$$\triangle BAB' \equiv \triangle CC'A.$$

Thus, $AB' = C'A$ and $\angle AB'B = \angle C'AC$. Since $BB' \perp AC$ we have

$$\angle B'AC' = \angle B'AC + \angle C'AC = \angle B'AC + \angle AB'B = 90°.$$

Since $AB' = AC'$ and $\angle B'AC' = 90°$ we get $\angle AC'B' = 45°$.

Similarly we have $BA' = BC'$ and $\angle A'BC' = 90°$. Thus, we get $\angle BC'A' = 45°$.

Since $\angle AC'B = 90°$, we have

$$\angle B'C'A' = \angle AC'B' + \angle AC'B + \angle BC'A' = 45° + 90° + 45° = 180°.$$

Therefore, A', B' and C' are collinear.

A given convex polyhedron has no vertex which is incident with exactly 3 edges. Prove that the number of faces of the polyhedron which are triangles, is at least 8.

Solution

Let E, F, V denote the respective number of edges, faces, and vertices of the polyhedron. As is known, $E + 2 = F + V$. Also, let V_r denote the number of vertices with valence r and F_s the number of faces with s sides. It follows that

$$2E \;=\; 3F_3 + 4F_4 + \cdots + sF_s \;=\; 4V_4 + 5V_5 + \cdots + rV_r \,.$$

Since

$$V \;=\; V_4 + V_5 + \cdots + V_r \quad \text{and} \quad F \;=\; F_3 + F_4 + \cdots + F_s \,,$$

we get from

$$2E + 4 \;=\; 2\left(V_4 + V_5 + \cdots + V_r\right) + 2\left(F_3 + F_4 + \cdots + F_s\right) \,,$$

that

$$F_3 + 2F_4 + \cdots + (s-2)F_s + 4 \;=\; 2\left(V_4 + V_5 + \cdots + V_r\right)$$

and

$$2V_4 + 3V_5 + \cdots + (r-2)V_r + 4 \;=\; 2\left(F_3 + F_4 + \cdots + F_s\right) \,.$$

Adding the last two equations, we get

$$8 + V_5 + 2V_6 + \cdots + (r-4)V_r + F_5 + 2F_6 + \cdots + (s-4)F_s \;=\; F_3 \,.$$

Hence, F_3 is at least 8.

Two circles, of radii R and r, $R > r$, are externally tangent. Consider the common tangent of the circles, not passing through their common point. Determine the maximal radius of a circle drawn in the domain bounded by this tangent line and the circles.

Solution 1

We will denote by D the domain bounded by the given circles C, Γ (with respective centres O, Ω) and their common tangent T.

We take for granted that the circle γ_m with maximal radius ρ_m contained in D is the one that is tangent to C, Γ and T (which may seem obvious).

We shall make use of the following result (R) [see proof below]: If C_i, with centre O_i and radius R_i, $(i = 1, 2)$ are two circles tangent externally at I, and T is their common tangent (not through I) touching C_1 at K_1 and C_2 at K_2, then $K_1 K_2 = 2\sqrt{R_1 R_2}$.

Applying (R) to the three pairs of circles (C, Γ), (γ_m, C), (γ_m, Γ), we readily obtain

$$2\sqrt{rR} = 2\sqrt{r\rho_m} + 2\sqrt{R\rho_m}\,,$$

so that $\rho_m = \dfrac{rR}{(\sqrt{r} + \sqrt{R})^2}$.

Proof of (R) (see figure)

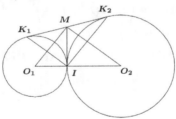

We introduce the point M where the tangent at I to the circles intersects T. Then $MI = MK_1 = MK_2$ so that $\triangle K_1 I K_2$ is right-angled at I. It follows that $\triangle O_1 M O_2$ is right-angled at M. Since MI is the altitude from M in this triangle, we get:

$$IM^2 = IO_1 \cdot IO_2 = R_1 R_2 \quad \text{and} \quad K_1 K_2 = 2MI = 2\sqrt{R_1 R_2}\,.$$

Consider an arbitrary circle γ with radius ρ contained in D. We may suppose that γ is tangent to C and Γ [otherwise we take instead the circle with the same radius ρ and centre at the point of intersection in D of the circles with centres O, Ω and radii $r + \rho$, $R + \rho$].

Now invert the figure in a circle with centre the common point I of C and Γ and radius k, cutting C at A, B and Γ at E, F.

Thus, C, Γ invert into the parallel lines AB, EF respectively, T inverts into a circle τ passing through I and γ into a circle γ'. Note that τ and γ' are both tangent to AB and EF with γ' exterior to τ.

Since $d(I, AB) = \dfrac{k^2}{2r}$ and $d(I, EF) = \dfrac{k^2}{2R}$, the common radius of τ and γ' is given by

$$u = \frac{1}{2} d(AB, EF) = \frac{k^2}{2}\left(\frac{1}{2r} + \frac{1}{2R}\right).$$

From a known formula, ρ is related to u by the relation

$$\rho = k^2 \frac{u}{d^2 - u^2}, \tag{1}$$

where d is the distance from I to the centre of γ'. Clearly, the maximal value ρ_m of ρ is obtained when d is minimal; that is, when γ' is tangent (externally) to the circle τ. In this case, some simple calculations give (see figure below)

$$l^2 = \frac{k^4}{4}\left(\frac{1}{2r} - \frac{1}{2R}\right)^2 \quad \text{and} \quad d^2 - u^2 = l^2 + (2u + l')^2 - u^2$$

where $l'^2 = u^2 - l^2 = \dfrac{k^4}{4rR}$. Hence,

$$d^2 - u^2 = \frac{k^4}{4}\left(\frac{1}{r} + \frac{1}{R}\right)\left(\frac{1}{\sqrt{r}} + \frac{1}{\sqrt{R}}\right)^2.$$

With the help of (1), we get

$$\rho_m = \frac{1}{\left(\dfrac{1}{\sqrt{r}} + \dfrac{1}{\sqrt{R}}\right)^2} = \frac{rR}{(\sqrt{r} + \sqrt{R})^2}.$$

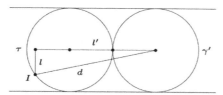

Let $n \geq 3$. Find a configuration of n points in the plane such that the mutual distance of no pair of points exceeds 1 and exactly n pairs of points have a mutual distance equal to 1.

Solution

Let $\mathcal{C}$ be the circle with centre P_1 and radius 1. Let P_2, P_n be two distinct points on $\mathcal{C}$ such that $P_1 P_2 P_n$ is equilateral.

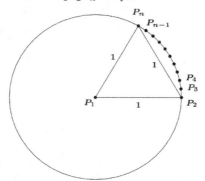

We choose any $n - 3$ points on the arc $\overset{\frown}{P_2 P_n}$ (see figure above). Then:

$$P_1 P_i = 1 \quad \text{for} \quad i = 2, \ldots, n$$
$$P_2 P_n = 1$$

and

$$P_i P_j < 1 \quad \text{in all other cases.}$$

The area of a given trapezoid is 2 cm^2 and the sum of its diagonals equals 4 cm. Find the altitude of the trapezoid.

Solution

Now, it is not difficult to see that trapezoid $ABCD$ is isosceles. Draw perpendiculars AA' and DD' from A and D to the line BC. Right triangles $AA'C$ and $DD'B$ have two sides respectively equal, making them congruent, and giving $A'C = BD'$.

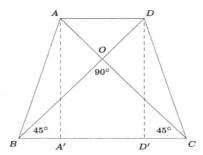

Subtracting $A'D'$ from each side gives $D'C = BA'$.

Hence, $AB = DC$, because they are hypotenuses in congruent right triangles $AA'B$ and $DD'C$.

Let O be the intersection of the diagonals. Since angle BOC is a right angle, we have immediately that BOC is an isosceles right-angled triangle. The right triangle $DD'B$ has a $45°$ angle and therefore, is also an isosceles right-angled triangle. Hence,

$$BD' = DD'. \qquad (1)$$

Moreover, since $ABCD$ is an isosceles trapezoid, we have the special relation that

$$\text{area of } ABCD = \overline{BD'} \cdot \overline{DD'}. \qquad (2)$$

This is clear from the following figure.

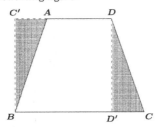

From (1) and (2) it follows that

$$\overline{DD'} = \sqrt{\text{area of } ABCD}$$

so that the required altitude is equal to $\sqrt{2}$.

Prove that in any triangle the following inequality holds: $pR \geq 2S$, where p, R, S are respectively the semiperimeter, the radius of circumcircle and the area of the triangle.

Solution

Let a, b, c be the sides of the triangle. Since $R = \dfrac{abc}{4S}$, the inequality to be proved is equivalent to

$$p \cdot abc \geq 8S^2$$

or

$$abc \geq (a + b - c)(a + c - b)(b + c - a) \tag{1}$$

[via Heron's formula $S = \sqrt{p(p - a)(p - b)(p - c)}$].

Now denote by x, y, z the positive real numbers $\dfrac{-a + b + c}{2}$, $\dfrac{a - b + c}{2}$, $\dfrac{a + b - c}{2}$ (respectively). Then we have $a = y + z$, $b = z + x$, $c = x + y$ and (1) becomes

$$(y + z)(z + x)(x + y) \geq 8xyz .$$

But this inequality is certainly true since $y + z \geq 2\sqrt{yz}$, $z + x \geq 2\sqrt{zx}$ and $x + y \geq 2\sqrt{xy}$, so that we are done.

Let AB be a given line segment. Find all possible points C in the plane such that in $\triangle ABC$, the height from the vertex A and the length of the median from the vertex B are equal.

Solution

Let A_1 be symmetric to A about B. If C is any point not on the line AB, denote by I the mid-point of AC and by H, K, L the projections of A onto BC, A onto BI, B onto CA_1 respectively (see figure). Note that $AK = BL$.

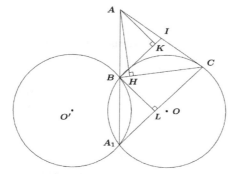

The relation $[ABC] = 2[ABI]$ yields $AH \cdot BC = 2AK \cdot BI$ or $AH \cdot BC = 2BL \cdot BI$. It follows that $AH = BI$ if and only if $\dfrac{BL}{BC} = \dfrac{1}{2}$; that is, if and only if $\angle BCA_1 = 30°$ or $150°$. Therefore, the locus of points C such that $AH = BI$ is the union of the two circles passing through B and A_1 and centred at O and O' defined by

$$\angle BOA_1 = \angle BO'A_1 = 60°$$

[points B and A_1 must be deleted for $\triangle ABC$ to be non-degenerate].

Let $\triangle ABC$ be an acute triangle with circumcentre O and circumradius R. Show that if AO meets the circle OBC again at D, BO meets the circle OCA again at E, and CO meets the circle OAB again at F, then $OD \cdot OE \cdot OF \geq 8R^3$.

Solution

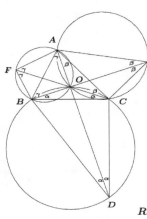

First note the following similar triangles:
$\triangle BCE \sim \triangle DCA$, $\triangle CAF \sim \triangle EAB$, $\triangle ABD \sim \triangle FBC$.

Hence,

$EC : CB : BE = AC : CD : DA$, etc.
Use Ptolemy's Theorem in the three cyclic quadrilaterals that share O as a vertex. In these cyclic quadrilaterals, we have

$$OD \cdot BC = OC \cdot BD + OB \cdot DC$$
$$OD = R\left(\frac{BD}{BC} + \frac{DC}{BC}\right), \text{ etc.}$$
$$= R\left(\frac{AD}{CF} + \frac{AD}{BE}\right), \text{ etc.}$$

Therefore, $OD \cdot OE \cdot OF =$

$$R^3\left[\left(\frac{AD}{CF} + \frac{CF}{AD}\right) + \left(\frac{AD}{BE} + \frac{BE}{AD}\right) + \left(\frac{BE}{CF} + \frac{CF}{BE}\right) + 2\right]$$

$$\geq R^3(2 + 2 + 2 + 2) = 8R^3.$$

Let M be the mid-point of the median AD of the triangle ABC (D belongs to the side BC). The line BM meets the side AC at the point N. Show that AB is tangent to the circumcircle of the triangle NBC if and only if the equality

$$\frac{BM}{MN} = \frac{BC^2}{BN^2}$$

holds.

Solution

By Menelaus' Theorem for $\triangle BCN$ we get

$$\frac{BM}{MN} \cdot \frac{NA}{AC} \cdot \frac{CD}{DB} = 1 \,.$$

Since $BD = DC$ we have

$$\frac{BM}{MN} = \frac{AC}{AN} \,. \tag{1}$$

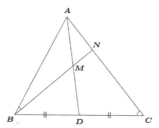

(a) If AB is tangent to the circumcircle of $\triangle NBC$, then we have

$$\frac{BM}{MN} = \frac{BC^2}{BN^2} \,.$$

Since $\angle ABN = \angle ACB$, we get $\triangle ABN \sim \triangle ACB$, so that

$$\frac{AN}{AB} = \frac{AB}{AC} = \frac{BN}{CB} \,.$$

Thus, $\dfrac{AN}{AB} \times \dfrac{AB}{AC} = \left(\dfrac{BN}{CB}\right)^2$; that is

$$\frac{AC}{AN} = \frac{BC^2}{BN^2} \,.$$

Therefore, we obtain from (1)

$$\frac{BM}{MN} = \frac{BC^2}{BN^2} \,.$$

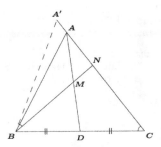

(b) If $\dfrac{BM}{MN} = \dfrac{BC^2}{BN^2}$, then BA is tangent to the circumcircle of $\triangle NBC$.

From (1) we get

$$\frac{AC}{AN} = \frac{BM}{MN} = \frac{BC^2}{BN^2}. \tag{2}$$

Let the tangent to the circumcircle of $\triangle NBC$ at B meet AC at A'. Then we have

$$\frac{A'C}{A'N} = \frac{BC^2}{BN^2}. \tag{3}$$

Thus, we obtain from (2) and (3)

$$\frac{AC}{AN} = \frac{A'C}{A'N}.$$

Hence, A coincides with A', so AB is tangent to the circumcircle of $\triangle NBC$.

Therefore, AB is tangent to the circumcircle of $\triangle NBC$ if and only if the equality $\dfrac{BM}{MN} = \dfrac{BC^2}{BN^2}$ holds.

We have n distinct points $A_1, \ldots, A_n$ in the plane. To each point A_i a real number $\lambda_i \neq 0$ is assigned, in such a way that

$$\overline{A_i A_j}^2 = \lambda_i + \lambda_j, \quad \text{for all } i, j \text{ with } i \neq j.$$

Show that

(a) $n \leq 4$.

(b) If $n = 4$, then

$$\frac{1}{\lambda_1} + \frac{1}{\lambda_2} + \frac{1}{\lambda_3} + \frac{1}{\lambda_4} = 0.$$

Solution

The following lemma is a well-known theorem.

Lemma. A, B, C and D are four distinct points.
If $AB^2 + CD^2 = BC^2 + AD^2$, then $AC \perp BD$.

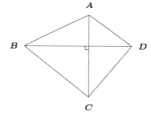 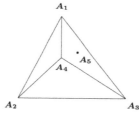

(a) We assume that $n \geq 5$.

Since $\overline{A_1 A_2}^2 + \overline{A_3 A_4}^2 = (\lambda_1 + \lambda_2) + (\lambda_3 + \lambda_4) = (\lambda_1 + \lambda_3) + (\lambda_2 + \lambda_4) = \overline{A_1 A_3}^2 + \overline{A_2 A_4}^2$, we have by, the lemma, $A_2 A_3 \perp A_1 A_4$.

Similarly, we get

$$\begin{aligned}
\overline{A_1 A_2}^2 + \overline{A_3 A_4}^2 &= (\lambda_1 + \lambda_2) + (\lambda_3 + \lambda_4) \\
&= (\lambda_1 + \lambda_4) + (\lambda_2 + \lambda_3) = \overline{A_1 A_4}^2 + \overline{A_2 A_3}^2.
\end{aligned}$$

Hence, we have $A_1 A_3 \perp A_2 A_4$. Therefore, A_4 is the orthocentre of $\triangle A_1 A_2 A_3$.

Similarly, A_5 is the orthocentre of $\triangle A_1 A_2 A_3$. Thus, A_5 coincides with A_4. This contradicts $A_4 \neq A_5$. Therefore, $n < 5$; that is, $n \leq 4$.

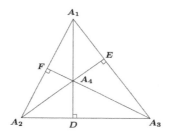

(b) By the above argument A_4 is the orthocentre of $\triangle A_1A_2A_3$. We may assume, without loss of generality, that A_4 is the orthocentre of acute triangle $A_1A_2A_3$, A_1A_4, A_2A_4 and A_3A_4 meet A_2A_3, A_3A_1 and A_1A_2 at D, E and F respectively, and we have $A_1D \perp A_2A_3$, $A_2E \perp A_3A_1$ and $A_3F \perp A_1A_2$. Since

$$2\lambda_1 = (\lambda_1 + \lambda_2) + (\lambda_1 + \lambda_4) - (\lambda_2 + \lambda_4) = \overline{A_1A_2}^2 + \overline{A_1A_4}^2 - \overline{A_2A_4}^2$$

$$= 2\overline{A_1A_2} \cdot \overline{A_1A_4} \cos \angle A_2A_1A_4 = 2\overline{A_1A_2} \cdot \overline{A_1F},$$

so that
$$\lambda_1 = \overline{A_1A_2} \cdot \overline{A_1F}. \tag{1}$$

Similarly, we have

$$\lambda_2 = \overline{A_2A_1} \cdot \overline{A_2F}, \tag{2}$$

$$\lambda_3 = \overline{A_3A_2} \cdot \overline{A_3A_4} \cos \angle A_2A_3A_4 = \overline{A_3A_4} \cdot \overline{A_3F} \tag{3}$$

$$\lambda_4 = \overline{A_4A_2} \cdot \overline{A_4A_3} \cos \angle A_2A_4A_3 = -\overline{A_3A_4} \cdot \overline{A_4F}. \tag{4}$$

It follows from (1) and (2)

$$\frac{1}{\lambda_1} + \frac{1}{\lambda_2} = \frac{1}{\overline{A_1A_2} \cdot \overline{A_1F}} + \frac{1}{\overline{A_1A_2} \cdot \overline{A_2F}} = \frac{\overline{A_2F} + \overline{A_1F}}{\overline{A_1A_2} \cdot \overline{A_1F} \cdot \overline{A_2F}}$$

$$= \frac{\overline{A_1A_2}}{\overline{A_1A_2} \cdot \overline{A_1F} \cdot \overline{A_2F}} = \frac{1}{\overline{A_1F} \cdot \overline{A_2F}}. \tag{5}$$

Since $\angle FA_1A_4 = \angle FA_3A_2$ we get $\triangle A_1FA_4 \sim \triangle A_3FA_2$, we have

$$\overline{A_1F} : \overline{A_3F} = \overline{A_4F} : \overline{A_2F} \text{; that is } \overline{A_1F} \cdot \overline{A_2F} = \overline{A_3F} \cdot \overline{A_4F}. \tag{6}$$

Thus, we have from (3), (5) and (6),

$$\frac{1}{\lambda_1} + \frac{1}{\lambda_2} + \frac{1}{\lambda_3} = \frac{1}{\overline{A_3F} \cdot \overline{A_4F}} + \frac{1}{\overline{A_3A_4} \cdot \overline{A_3F}}$$

$$= \frac{\overline{A_3A_4} + \overline{A_4F}}{\overline{A_3F} \cdot \overline{A_4F} \cdot \overline{A_3A_4}} = \frac{\overline{A_3F}}{\overline{A_3F} \cdot \overline{A_4F} \cdot \overline{A_3A_4}} = \frac{1}{\overline{A_3A_4} \cdot \overline{A_4F}}. \tag{7}$$

Hence, we obtain from (4) and (7)

$$\frac{1}{\lambda_1} + \frac{1}{\lambda_2} + \frac{1}{\lambda_3} + \frac{1}{\lambda_4} = \frac{1}{\overline{A_3A_4} \cdot \overline{A_4F}} - \frac{1}{\overline{A_3A_4} \cdot \overline{A_4F}} = 0.$$

In tetrahedron $ABCD$ let A', B', C', and D' be the circumcentres of faces BCD, ACD, ABD and ABC. We mean by $S(X, YZ)$, the plane perpendicular from point X to the line YZ. Prove that the planes $S(A, C'D')$, $S(B, D'A')$, $S(C, A'B')$, and $S(D, B'C')$ are concurrent.

Solution

Let R_3 and R_4 be the circumradii of $\triangle ABD$ and $\triangle ABC$, respectively. Then $AC' = R_3$ and $AD' = R_4$ so that $A \in \{M : MC'^2 - MD'^2 = R_3^2 - R_4^2\}$. This set of points, which is known to be a plane orthogonal to $C'D'$, is thus, $S(A, C'D')$.

Now let Σ be the circumsphere of the tetrahedron $ABCD$ (centre O, radius R) and Σ' be the circumsphere of the tetrahedron $A'B'C'D'$ (centre O', radius R'). The circumcircle of $\triangle ABC$ is the intersection of Σ with the plane (ABC). Hence, D' is the orthogonal projection of O onto (ABC) and $OD'^2 = AO^2 - AD'^2 = R^2 - R_4^2$. Similarly, $OC'^2 = R^2 - R_3^2$ and therefore, $OC'^2 - OD'^2 = R_4^2 - R_3^2$. Now, let Ω be the reflection of O in O'. Then, using $O'C' = O'D' = R'$,

$$\Omega C'^2 - \Omega D'^2$$
$$= \Omega O'^2 + O'C'^2 + 2\overrightarrow{\Omega O'} \cdot \overrightarrow{O'C'} - \Omega O'^2 - O'D'^2 - 2\overrightarrow{\Omega O'} \cdot \overrightarrow{O'D'}$$
$$= 2\overrightarrow{OO'} \cdot \overrightarrow{O'D'} - 2\overrightarrow{OO'} \cdot \overrightarrow{O'C'}$$
$$= OD'^2 - OO'^2 - O'D'^2 - (OC'^2 - OO'^2 - O'C'^2)$$
$$= R_3^2 - R_4^2.$$

It follows that $\Omega \in S(A, C'D')$. Similarly, Ω belongs to the planes $S(B, D'A')$, $S(C, A'B')$, and $S(D, B'C')$, and we are done.

Consider a circle of centre O, radius r, and let P be an external point. We draw a chord AB parallel to OP.

(a) Show that $PA^2 + PB^2$ is constant.

(b) Find the length of the chord AB which maximizes the area of the $\triangle ABP$.

Solution

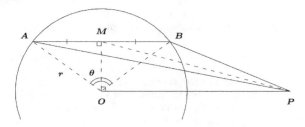

(a) Let M be the mid-point of AB, then $OM \perp AB$. Since $AB \parallel OP$, we have $OM \perp OP$.

Since M is the mid-point of AB, we get

$$
\begin{aligned}
PA^2 + PB^2 &= 2(PM^2 + AM^2) \\
&= 2\{(OM^2 + OP^2) + (OA^2 - OM^2)\} \\
&= 2(OP^2 + OA^2) \\
&= 2(OP^2 + r^2) = \text{ constant.}
\end{aligned}
$$

(b) Since $AB \parallel OP$ we have $[ABP] = [ABO]$, where $[XYZ]$ denotes the area of triangle XYZ.

We put $\angle AOB = \theta$, so

$$
[ABO] = \tfrac{1}{2}OA \cdot OB \sin\theta = \tfrac{1}{2}r^2 \sin\theta \leq \tfrac{1}{2}r^2 :
$$

equality holds when $\theta = 90°$, and $AB = \sqrt{2}\,r$. Therefore, $[ABP]$ is a maximum when $AB = \sqrt{2}\,r$.

The triangle ABC has $\widehat{A} = 90°$, and AD is the altitude from A. The bisectors of the angles $\widehat{ABD}$ and $\widehat{ADB}$ intersect at I_1; the bisectors of the angles $\widehat{ACD}$ and $\widehat{ADC}$ intersect at I_2.

Find the acute angles of $\triangle ABC$, given that the sum of distances from I_1 and I_2 to AD is $BC/4$.

Solution

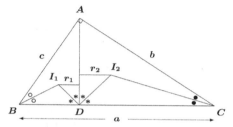

We denote the distances from I_1 and I_2 to AD by r_1 and r_2, respectively.

Since I_1 and I_2 are incentres of $\triangle ABD$ and $\triangle ACD$, respectively, then r_1 and r_2 are inradii of $\triangle ABD$ and $\triangle ACD$, respectively.

Since $\angle ADB = \angle ADC = 90°$, we have

$$2r_1 = AD + BD - AB \quad \text{and} \quad 2r_2 = AD + DC - AC$$

so that

$$2(r_1 + r_2) = 2AD + BC - AB - AC. \tag{1}$$

We put $BC = a$, $CA = b$ and $AB = c$. Since $\angle BAC = 90°$ and $AD \perp BC$ we get

$$AD \cdot BC = AB \cdot AC.$$

Thus, we have $AD = \dfrac{bc}{a}$. Since $r_1 + r_2 = \dfrac{BC}{4}$, we obtain from (1)

$$\frac{a}{2} = \frac{2bc}{a} + a - b - c.$$

Multiplying both sides by $2a$, we get

$$a^2 = 4bc + 2a^2 - 2a(b + c).$$

Thus, $a^2 - 2a(b + c) + 4bc = 0$, so that

$$(a - 2b)(a - 2c) = 0.$$

Therefore, either $a - 2b = 0$ or $a - 2c = 0$. If $a - 2b = 0$, then $a = 2b$, since $\angle A = 90°$ so that we get $\angle B = 30°$ and $\angle C = 60°$. If $a - 2c = 0$, similarly, we get $\angle C = 30°$ and $\angle B = 60°$. Therefore, the acute angles of $\triangle ABC$ are $60°$ and $30°$.

P is the common point of straight lines l_1 and l_2. Two circles S_1 and S_2 are externally tangent at P and l_1 is their common tangent line. Similarly, two circles T_1 and T_2 are externally tangent at P and l_2 is their common tangent line. The circles S_1 and T_1 have common points P and A, the circles S_1 and T_2 have common points P and B, the circles S_2 and T_2 have common points P and C, and the circles S_2 and T_1 have common points P and D. Prove that the points A, B, C, D lie on a circle if and only if the lines l_1 and l_2 are perpendicular.

Solution

Let O_1, O_2, O_3 and O_4 be centres of S_1, T_1, S_2 and T_2, respectively. Since S_1 and S_2 touch l_1 at P, then $O_1P \perp l_1$ and $O_3P \perp l_1$. Thus, O_1, P, and O_3 are collinear and $O_1O_3 \perp l_1$.

Similarly, O_2, P, and O_4 are collinear and $O_2O_4 \perp l_2$. Let PA meet O_1O_2 at M_1. Since S_1, T_1 intersect at P and A, M_1 is the mid-point of PA, and $PM_1 \perp O_1O_2$.

Let M_2, M_3 and M_4 be the intersections of PD, O_2O_3, PC, O_3O_4 and PB, O_4O_1, respectively. Then M_2, M_3 and M_4 are mid-points of O_2O_3,

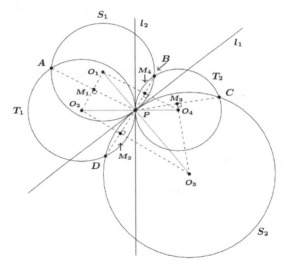

O_3O_4 and O_4O_1, respectively, and $PM_2 \perp O_2O_3$, $PM_3 \perp O_3O_4$, and $PM_4 \perp O_4O_1$.

Since M_1, M_2, M_3, and M_4 are mid-points of PA, PD, PC and PB, respectively, we have

A, B, C, D are concyclic $\iff$ M_1, M_2, M_3, M_4 are concyclic.

$\qquad\qquad\qquad\qquad\iff$ $\angle M_2M_1M_4 + \angle M_2M_3M_4 = 180°$.

Since $\angle PM_1O_1 = \angle PM_4O_1 = 90°$, it follows that O_1, M_1, P, M_4 are concyclic, so that $\angle PM_1M_4 = \angle PO_1M_4 = \angle PO_1O_4$. Similarly, we have $\angle PM_1M_2 = \angle PO_2O_3$, $\angle PM_3M_2 = \angle PO_3O_2$ and $\angle PM_3M_4 = \angle PO_4O_1$.

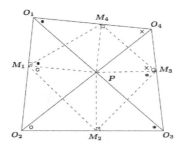

Thus,

$$\angle M_2M_1M_4 + \angle M_2M_3M_4$$
$$= \angle PM_1M_4 + \angle PM_1M_2 + \angle PM_3M_2 + \angle PM_3M_1$$
$$= \angle PO_1O_4 + \angle PO_2O_3 + \angle PO_3O_2 + \angle PO_4O_1$$
$$= (\angle PO_1O_4 + \angle PO_4O_1) + (\angle PO_2O_3 + \angle PO_3O_2)$$
$$= \angle O_1PO_2 + \angle O_1PO_2 = 2\angle O_1PO_2 .$$

It follows that

$$\angle M_2M_1M_4 + \angle M_2M_3M_4 = 180° \iff 2\angle O_1PO_2 = 180°$$
$$\iff \angle O_1PO_2 = 90° .$$

Since $O_1P \perp l_1$ and $O_2P \perp l_2$, we have that l_1 and l_2 coincide with O_2P and O_1P, respectively.

Thus, $\angle O_1PO_2 = 90°$ if and only if $l_1 \perp l_2$. Therefore, we have that A, B, C, D are concyclic if and only if $l_1 \perp l_2$.

In a convex quadrilateral $ABCD$ the sides AB and CD are parallel, the diagonals AC and BD intersect at point E and points F and G are the orthocentres of the triangles EBC and EAD, respectively. Prove that the midpoint of the segment GF lies on the line k perpendicular to AB such that $E \in k$.

Solution

We denote
$$\angle DAB = \alpha, \quad \angle ABC = \beta, \quad BC = b, \quad AD = d.$$

$$AB \parallel CD \implies d\sin\alpha = b\sin\beta \tag{1}$$

Write $\angle AED = \angle BEC = \varepsilon$ and let G', E', F' be the projections onto AB of G, E, and F, respectively. Then $\angle EGG' = \alpha$, $\angle EFF' = \beta$.

Denote by R_1 the circumradius of $\triangle AED$, and by R_2 that of $\triangle BEC$.

$$d = 2R_1\sin\varepsilon \implies R_1 = \frac{d}{2\sin\varepsilon}; EG = 2R_1\cos\varepsilon = d\cot\varepsilon$$
$$\implies E'G' = EG\sin\alpha = d\cot\varepsilon\sin\alpha. \tag{2}$$

In the same way:

$$E'F' = b\cot\varepsilon\sin\beta \tag{3}$$

$$(1), (2) \text{ and } (3) \implies E'G' = E'F'. \tag{4}$$

$(4) \implies M$, the mid-point of GF, lies on EE' ($= k$).

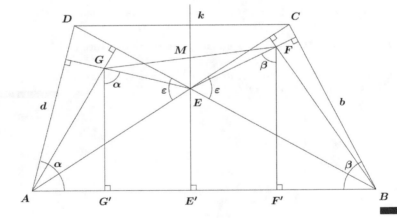

Quadrilateral $ABCD$ is inscribed in a circle. Line AB meets DC at point P. Line AD meets BC at point Q. Tangent lines QE and QF touch the circle at points E and F, respectively. Prove that points P, E and F are collinear.

Solution

Let O and r be the centre and radius of the circle. Let S be the second intersection of PQ with the circumcircle of $\triangle PAD$. Then we have

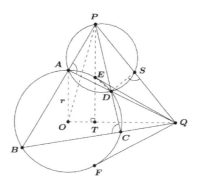

$$\angle DSQ \,=\, \angle PAD \,=\, \angle DCB \,.$$

Thus, C, D, S, Q are concyclic. Hence, $PS \cdot PQ = PD \cdot PC = PO^2 - r^2$. Similarly, we have

$$QS \cdot QP \,=\, QD \cdot QA \,=\, QO^2 - r^2 \,.$$

Therefore,

$$
\begin{aligned}
PQ^2 &= (PS + SQ) \cdot PQ \,=\, PS \cdot PQ + QS \cdot QP \\
&= (PO^2 - r^2) + (QO^2 - r^2) \\
&= PO^2 + QO^2 - 2r^2 \,.
\end{aligned}
$$

Thus,

$$
\begin{aligned}
2r^2 &= PO^2 + QO^2 - PQ^2 \\
&= 2PO \cdot QO \cos \angle POQ \,.
\end{aligned}
$$

so that we get

$$r^2 \,=\, PO \cdot QO \cos \angle POQ \,. \tag{1}$$

Let T be the foot of perpendicular from P to OQ, then

$$PO \cos \angle POQ \,=\, OT \,.$$

Thus, we obtain from (1)

$$r^2 = OT \cdot OQ. \tag{2}$$

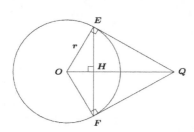

Let H be the intersection of EF with OQ. Since QE and QF are tangent to the circle at E and F, we have

$$\angle OEQ = \angle OFQ = 90°$$

and

$$EF \perp OQ.$$

Since $\angle OEQ = 90°$ and $EH \perp OQ$, we get

$$OE^2 = OH \cdot OQ;$$

that is,

$$r^2 = OH \cdot OQ. \tag{3}$$

It follows that from (2) and (3)

$$OT \cdot OQ = OH \cdot OQ.$$

Hence, $OT = OH$. Therefore, T coincides with H. Since $PT \perp OQ$ and $EH \perp OQ$, the line PT coincides with the line EF. This implies that P, E and F are collinear.

Through an arbitrary interior point of a triangle lines parallel to the sides of the triangle are drawn dividing the triangle into six regions, three of which are triangles. Let the areas of these three triangles be T_1, T_2, and T_3 and let the area of the original triangle be T. Prove that

$$T = (\sqrt{T_1} + \sqrt{T_2} + \sqrt{T_3})^2 \,.$$

Solution

Let P be the given interior point of $\mathcal{T} = \triangle ABC$ (with area T) and $\mathcal{T}_1$, $\mathcal{T}_2$, $\mathcal{T}_3$ be the triangles with respective areas T_1, T_2, T_3. We denote by I, J, K the points of intersection of AP with BC, BP with AC, CP with AB, respectively.

We are required to prove that $\sqrt{\frac{T_1}{T}} + \sqrt{\frac{T_2}{T}} + \sqrt{\frac{T_3}{T}} = 1$.
[Ed. T_1 is the area of the small triangle with base on side BC, and so on.]

Solution I. Clearly, triangles $\mathcal{T}_1$ and $\mathcal{T}$ are similar (even homothetic). It follows that $\frac{T_1}{T} = \left(\frac{IP}{IA}\right)^2$. Similar results hold for $\frac{T_2}{T}$ and $\frac{T_3}{T}$, so that

$$
\begin{aligned}
\sqrt{\frac{T_1}{T}} + \sqrt{\frac{T_2}{T}} + \sqrt{\frac{T_3}{T}} &= \frac{IP}{IA} + \frac{JP}{JB} + \frac{KP}{KC} \\
&= \frac{[PBC]}{[ABC]} + \frac{[PCA]}{[ABC]} + \frac{[PAB]}{[ABC]} = \frac{[ABC]}{[ABC]} = 1
\end{aligned}
$$

(using, for instance, that $\triangle PBC$ and $\triangle ABC$, which share the base BC, have their areas $[PBC]$ and $[ABC]$ in the ratio of their altitudes from P and A, respectively, and this ratio is also $\frac{IP}{IA}$).

Solution II. We use barycentric coordinates with respect to (A, B, C). There exist positive real numbers r, s, t such that $P = rA + sB + tC$ and $r + s + t = 1$. From the hypotheses, it is easy to obtain that the other two vertices of $\mathcal{T}_1$ are given by $(r + s)B + tC$ and $sB + (r + t)C$. It follows that

$$
\frac{T_1}{T} = \left| \det \begin{pmatrix} r & 0 & 0 \\ s & r+s & s \\ t & t & r+t \end{pmatrix} \right| = |r(r^2 + rs + rt)| = r^2 \,.
$$

Similarly, $\frac{T_2}{T} = s^2$, $\frac{T_3}{T} = t^2$, so that $\sqrt{\frac{T_1}{T}} + \sqrt{\frac{T_2}{T}} + \sqrt{\frac{T_3}{T}} = r + s + t = 1$.

A pentagon $ABCDE$ is inscribed in a circle. The angles at A, B, C, D, E form an increasing sequence. Show that the angle at C is $> \pi/2$. Also, prove that this lower bound is best possible.

Solution

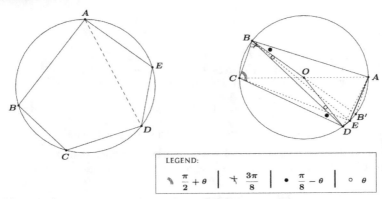

LEGEND:

$\frac{\pi}{2} + \theta$ | $\frac{3\pi}{8}$ | $\frac{\pi}{8} - \theta$ | θ

Since $\angle A < \angle B < \angle C$, we have $\angle BAD < \angle BAE < \angle BCD$. Thus, $\angle BAD + \angle BCD < 2\angle BCD$; that is $\pi < 2\angle BCD$. Hence, $\angle BCD > \frac{\pi}{2}$.

We now need to show that $\frac{\pi}{2}$ is the best possible lower bound. Let Γ be a circle with centre O. Let BD be a chord of Γ such that $\angle OBD = \angle ODB = \theta < \frac{\pi}{16}$.

Also, let C be a point on the minor arc BD such that $\angle CBD = \frac{3}{8}\pi$. Since the major angle $BOD = \pi + 2\theta$, we get $\angle BCD = \frac{\pi}{2} + \theta$, and $\angle BDC = \frac{\pi}{8} - \theta$.

Let CA and BB' be diameters of Γ, and let E be a point on the minor arc $B'D$. Since BB' is a diameter, we have $\angle EAB < \angle B'AB = \frac{\pi}{2}$. Since CA is a diameter, $\angle ABC = \frac{\pi}{2}$, so that $\angle EAB < \angle ABC$. Since $\angle BCD = \frac{\pi}{2} + \theta > \frac{\pi}{2}$, we have $\angle BCD > \angle ABC$. Since CA and BB' are diameters, we get
$$\angle ABB' = \angle ABO = \angle BAO = \angle BAC = \angle BDC = \frac{\pi}{8} - \theta.$$
Thus, $\angle CDE = \angle CDA + \angle ADE = \frac{\pi}{2} + \angle ABE > \frac{\pi}{2} + \angle ABB' = \frac{\pi}{2} + \left(\frac{\pi}{8} - \theta\right) > \frac{\pi}{2} + \theta$ (since $\theta < \frac{\pi}{16}$).

Thus, $\angle CDE > \angle BCD$.

Since $\angle CDE = \angle CDA + \angle ADE = \frac{\pi}{2} + \angle ABE < \frac{\pi}{2} + \angle ABD = \frac{\pi}{2} + \angle ABB' + \angle B'BD = \frac{\pi}{2} + \left(\frac{\pi}{8} - \theta\right) + \theta = \frac{\pi}{2} + \frac{\pi}{8}$, and
$$\angle DEA = \angle DEC + \angle CEA = \angle DBC + \frac{\pi}{2} = \frac{3}{8}\pi + \frac{\pi}{2} > \frac{\pi}{2} + \frac{\pi}{8},$$
we get $\angle CDE < \angle DEA$.

Thus, the inscribed pentagon $ABCDE$ has the property $\angle A < \angle B < \angle C < \angle D < \angle E$. We can choose positive angle θ as small as we like. Therefore, $\frac{\pi}{2}$ is the best possible lower bound of $\angle C$.

In a triangular pyramid $ABCD$, the medians of the lateral faces ABD, ACD, BCD drawn from vertex D form equal angles with the corresponding edges AB, AC, BC. Prove that the area of each lateral face is less than the sum of the areas of the two other lateral faces.

Solution

Let A', B', C' be the respective mid-points of BC, CA, AB, and θ be the common angle formed by DA' and BC, DB' and CA, DC' and AB. We denote by $[KLM]$ the area of $\triangle KLM$.

Since $[DA'B] = [DA'C]$, we have

$$[DBC] \;=\; 2[DA'B] \;=\; 2 \times \frac{1}{2} \times \frac{BC}{2} \times DA' \times \sin\theta \;=\; B'C' \cdot DA' \cdot \sin\theta \,.$$

Similar relations hold for $[DCA]$ and $[DAB]$, and so we are required to prove that, for instance,

$$B'C' \cdot DA' \;<\; A'C' \cdot DB' + A'B' \cdot DC' \,. \tag{1}$$

Denoting by X, Y, Z, the vectors $\overrightarrow{DA'}$, $\overrightarrow{DB'}$, $\overrightarrow{DC'}$, respectively, it amounts to proving that

$$\|X\| \cdot \|Z - Y\| \;<\; \|Y\| \cdot \|Z - X\| + \|Z\| \cdot \|X - Y\|$$

or, since X, Y, Z are non-zero vectors, that

$$\frac{\|Z - Y\|}{\|Z\| \, \|Y\|} \;<\; \frac{\|Z - X\|}{\|Z\| \, \|X\|} + \frac{\|X - Y\|}{\|X\| \, \|Y\|} \,. \tag{2}$$

From $\left\| \frac{1}{\|X\|^2} X \right\| = \frac{1}{\|X\|}$ and $\|X - Y\|^2 = \|X\|^2 + \|Y\|^2 - 2X \cdot Y$ (where $X \cdot Y$ is the scalar product of X and Y), we deduce that

$$\frac{\|X - Y\|^2}{\|X\|^2 \|Y\|^2} \;=\; \frac{1}{\|Y\|^2} + \frac{1}{\|X\|^2} - 2\frac{X \cdot Y}{\|X\|^2 \|Y\|^2} \;=\; \left\| \frac{1}{\|X\|^2} X - \frac{1}{\|Y\|^2} Y \right\|^2 \,.$$

Thus, (2) may be rewritten as

$$\|Z' - Y'\| \;<\; \|Z' - X'\| + \|X' - Y'\| \,, \tag{3}$$

where $X' = \frac{1}{\|X\|^2} X$, $Y' = \frac{1}{\|Y\|^2} Y$, $Z' = \frac{1}{\|Z\|^2} Z$.

Since (3) results from the triangular inequality (a strict inequality since X', Y', Z' are not coplanar), (2) and (1) follow and the proof is complete.

Given is a convex pentagon $ABCDE$ with

$$DC = DE \quad \text{and} \quad \angle DCB = \angle DEA = 90°.$$

Let F be the point on AB such that $AF : BF = AE : BC$. Show that

$$\angle FCE = \angle ADE \quad \text{and} \quad \angle FEC = \angle BDC.$$

Solution

Let $X \mapsto X'$ be the linear transformation that rotates each non-zero vector counterclockwise by 90° while preserving its length. This transformation preserves dot products: $X' \cdot Y' = X \cdot Y$.

Let $V = \overrightarrow{DE}$, $W = \overrightarrow{DC}$ ($|V| = |W|$). There exist $x, t > 0$ such that $\overrightarrow{EA} = sV'$, $\overrightarrow{CB} = -tW'$.

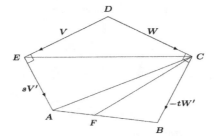

Note that $\tan \angle ADE = \dfrac{EA}{DE} = \dfrac{s|V'|}{|V|} = s$, giving us that $\cos \angle ADE = \dfrac{1}{\sqrt{s^2 + 1}}$.

We have $\overrightarrow{CA} = \overrightarrow{CE} + \overrightarrow{EA} = V - W + sV'$. Since

$$\frac{AF}{BF} = \frac{AE}{BC} = \frac{s|V'|}{t|W'|} = \frac{s}{t},$$

it follows that

$$\overrightarrow{CF} = \frac{1}{s+t}(s\overrightarrow{CB} + t\overrightarrow{CA}) = \frac{t}{s+t}((V - W) + s(V - W)').$$

Therefore, $\overrightarrow{CF} \cdot \overrightarrow{CE} = \dfrac{t}{s+t}|V - W|^2$. Also,

$$|\overrightarrow{CF}|^2 = \overrightarrow{CF} \cdot \overrightarrow{CF} = \frac{t^2}{(s+t)^2}(s^2 + 1)|V - W|^2.$$

Thus,

$$\cos \angle FCE = \frac{\overrightarrow{CF} \cdot \overrightarrow{CE}}{|\overrightarrow{CF}| \cdot |\overrightarrow{CE}|} = \frac{1}{\sqrt{s^2 + 1}} = \cos \angle ADE.$$

Hence, $\angle FCE = \angle ADE$.

The second part of the conclusion is analogous to the first.

Consider n points ($n \geq 2$) on the circumference of a circle of radius 1. Let q be the number of segments having those points as endpoints and having length greater than $\sqrt{2}$. Prove that $3q \leq n^2$.

Solution

Mark the n points on the circle Γ with center O and radius 1. For every $M, P \in \Gamma : MP > \sqrt{2}$ if and only if $\widehat{MOP} > \frac{\pi}{2}$. Since the number of marked points is finite, we may divide Γ into four arcs by two perpendicular diameters $[AC]$ and $[BD]$ such that none of the points A, B, C, D is marked.

Denote by a, b, c, d the number of marked points in the arcs AB, BC, CD, DA, respectively. Thus,

$$a + b + c + d = n. \tag{1}$$

With no loss of generality, we may suppose that $ab = \max(ab, bc, cd, da)$. There are $\binom{n}{2} - q$ segments having the marked points as endpoints and having length not greater than $\sqrt{2}$.

First note that if M, P are two marked points in the same arc then $\widehat{MOP} < \frac{\pi}{2}$ and then $MP < \sqrt{2}$. Thus, we may count $\binom{a}{2} + \binom{b}{2} + \binom{c}{2} + \binom{d}{2}$ such segments.

Secondly, there are $abcd$ choices for four marked points M, N, P, Q such that $M \in \widehat{AB}$, $N \in \widehat{BC}$, $P \in \widehat{CD}$, $Q \in \widehat{DA}$. Note that for such a choice, O is interior to the convex quadrilateral $MNPQ$. Thus, $\widehat{MON} + \widehat{NOP} + \widehat{POQ} + \widehat{QOM} = 2\pi$. It follows that at least one of these four angles is not greater than $\frac{\pi}{2}$. Thus, for every choice of four such points we may find a segment whose length is not greater than $\sqrt{2}$. Such a segment must have its endpoints belonging to two consecutive arcs. For example, $NP \leq \sqrt{2}$. This segment may be counted at most ad times in the $abcd$ segments above. And $ad \leq ab$. Thus, each of the segments is counted at most ab times. It follows that, in this case, we may find at least $\frac{abcd}{ab} = cd$ segments having length not greater than $\sqrt{2}$. It follows that

$$\binom{n}{2} - q \geq cd + \binom{a}{2} + \binom{b}{2} + \binom{c}{2} + \binom{d}{2}.$$

Using (1), we deduce that

$$-q \geq cd - \frac{1}{2}n^2 + \frac{1}{2}(a^2 + b^2 + c^2 + d^2).$$

Thus,

$$
\begin{aligned}
n^2 - 3q &\geq -\frac{n^2}{2} + 3cd + \frac{3}{2}(a^2 + b^2 + c^2 + d^2) \\
&= \left(\frac{1}{2}(a+b) - (c+d)\right)^2 + \frac{3}{4}(a-b)^2 \quad \text{(from (1))} \\
&\geq 0,
\end{aligned}
$$

and we are done.

Is there a set A of n points ($n \geq 3$) in the plane such that:

(i) A does not contain three collinear points; and

(ii) given any three points in A, the centre of the circle which contain these points also belongs to A?

Solution

No.

Suppose, by way of contradiction, that such a set A does exist.

Since A is finite, we may consider two points P and Q in A which are adjacent points in the convex hull of A. It follows, using (i), that no other point of A is on the line (PQ) and that all these points in A are on the same side of (PQ). Denote by E the region delimited by the lines perpendicular to (PQ) at P and at Q respectively (including the borders).

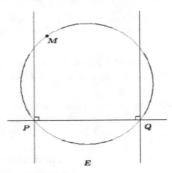

Since $n \geq 3$, there exists a point $M \in A - \{P, Q\}$. From (ii) the circle through M, P, Q has centre Ω with $\Omega \in A$. Moreover, Ω belongs to the line perpendicular to (PQ) through the middle of (PQ). Then $\Omega \in E$. It follows that the set $A' = A \cap E$ is non-empty, and finite.

Let $M \in A'$ such that the distance from M to the line (PQ) is minimal. Let Ω be the centre of the circle through M, P, Q.

From (ii) we have $\Omega \in A'$. Since $M \in E$, we have $\widehat{MPQ} \leq \frac{\pi}{2}$ and $\widehat{MQP} \leq \frac{\pi}{2}$.

If $\widehat{MPQ} = \frac{\pi}{2}$, then Ω is the mid-point of $[MQ]$, which contradicts (i). Thus, $\widehat{MPQ} < \frac{\pi}{2}$. In a similar way, we have $\widehat{MQP} < \frac{\pi}{2}$.

If $\widehat{PMQ} \leq \frac{\pi}{2}$, then PMQ is non-obtuse and Ω is an interior point of MPQ or the mid-point of (PQ). In the first case, it contradicts the minimality of M; in the second case, it contradicts (i).

If $\widehat{PMQ} > \frac{\pi}{2}$, then M and Ω are on distinct sides of the line (PQ), which contradicts the choice of P and Q.

Thus, in every case we have a contradiction, and the conclusion follows.

Let D be a point of the side $\overline{BC}$ of the acute-angled triangle ABC ($D \neq B$ and $D \neq C$), O_1 be the circumcentre of $\triangle ABD$, O_2 be the circumcentre of $\triangle ACD$ and O be the circumcentre of $\triangle AO_1O_2$. Determine the locus described by the point O when D runs through the side $\overline{BC}$ ($D \neq B$ and $D \neq C$).

Solution

Since O_1 and O_2 are the circumcentres of $\triangle ABD$ and $\triangle ACD$, respectively, we have that O_1O_2 is the perpendicular bisector of AD. Thus, $\triangle AO_1O_2 \equiv \triangle DO_1O_2$. Hence, we have

$$\angle AO_1O_2 = \tfrac{1}{2}\angle AO_1D$$
$$= \angle ABD = \angle ABC.$$

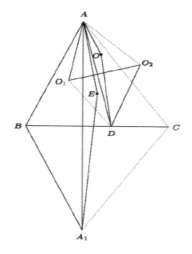

Similarly, we have $\angle AO_2O_1 = \angle ACB$, so that $\triangle AO_1O_2$ is directly similar to $\triangle ABC$.

Let A_1 be the reflection of A in BC. Since D is the reflection of A in O_1O_2, the quadrilateral AO_1DO_2 is directly similar to the quadrilateral ABA_1C.

Let E be the circumcentre of $\triangle ABC$. Since O, E, and D, A_1 are the pairs of corresponding points, $\triangle ADO$ is directly similar to $\triangle AA_1E$.

Let $\triangle ABP$ and $\triangle ACQ$ be directly similar to $\triangle AA_1E$. Then $\triangle ABP$, $\triangle ADO$ and $\triangle ACQ$ are directly similar. It follows that $\triangle APO \sim \triangle ABD$, and $\triangle AOQ \sim \triangle ADC$. Hence, we have

$$\angle AOP = \angle ADB \quad \text{and}$$
$$\angle AOQ = \angle ADC.$$

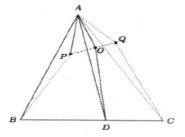

Thus,

$$\angle AOP + \angle AOQ = \angle ADB + \angle ADC = 180°,$$

so that P, O, Q are collinear. When D runs through the side BC ($D \neq B$ and $D \neq C$), O runs through the line segment PQ ($O \neq P$ and $O \neq Q$). Therefore, the locus of O is the line segment PQ, excluding P and Q.

Let $ABCD$ be a tetrahedron with $BC = a$, $CA = b$, $AB = c$, $DA = a_1$, $DB = b_1$, $CD = c_1$.

Prove that there exists one and only one point P satisfying the conditions:

$$PA^2 + a_1^2 + b^2 + c^2 = PB^2 + b_1^2 + c^2 + a^2$$
$$= PC^2 + c_1^2 + a^2 + b^2 = PD^2 + a_1^2 + b_1^2 + c_1^2,$$

and that for this point P, we have $PA^2 + PB^2 + PC^2 + PD^2 \geq 4R^2$, where R is the radius of the circumscribed sphere of the tetrahedron $ABCD$. Find a necessary and sufficient condition on the lengths of the edges so that the preceding inequality becomes an equality.

Solution

Let

$$\mathcal{P}_1 = \{M : MA^2 - MB^2 = b_1^2 + a^2 - b^2 - a_1^2\},$$

$$\mathcal{P}_2 = \{M : MB^2 - MC^2 = c_1^2 + b^2 - c^2 - b_1^2\}$$

and

$$\mathcal{P}_3 = \{M : MC^2 - MD^2 = a_1^2 + b_1^2 - b^2 - a^2\}.$$

If P exists, it must belong to $\mathcal{P}_1$, $\mathcal{P}_2$ and $\mathcal{P}_3$ which are planes orthogonal respectively to AB, BC, and CD. The planes $\mathcal{P}_1$ and $\mathcal{P}_2$ are not parallel (since A, B, C are not collinear) and their intersection is a line L orthogonal to the plane (ABC). It follows that L intersects $\mathcal{P}_3$ (otherwise CD would be orthogonal to L, hence parallel to (ABC)) and P must be their point of intersection. This shows the uniqueness of P.

Conversely, this common point to L and $\mathcal{P}_3$ belongs to $\mathcal{P}_1$, $\mathcal{P}_2$ and $\mathcal{P}_3$, hence satisfies all the given conditions.

Let O be the centre of the circumscribed sphere of $ABCD$. For convenience, we denote by $\vec{M}$ the vector $\overrightarrow{OM}$. Note that

$$\left(\vec{A}\right)^2 = \left(\vec{B}\right)^2 = \left(\vec{C}\right)^2 = \left(\vec{D}\right)^2 = R^2.$$

We have

$$PA^2 + PB^2 + PC^2 + PD^2$$
$$= \left(\vec{A} - \vec{P}\right)^2 + \left(\vec{B} - \vec{P}\right)^2 + \left(\vec{C} - \vec{P}\right)^2 + \left(\vec{D} - \vec{P}\right)^2$$
$$= 4\left(\vec{P}\right)^2 + 4R^2 - 2\vec{P} \cdot \left(\vec{A} + \vec{B} + \vec{C} + \vec{D}\right) \qquad (1)$$

Transforming in the same manner the conditions expressing that $P \in \mathcal{P}_1$ and $P \in \mathcal{P}_3$, we get

$$\vec{P} \cdot \vec{B} - \vec{P} \cdot \vec{A} = \vec{A} \cdot \vec{D} - \vec{B} \cdot \vec{D} + \vec{A} \cdot \vec{C} - \vec{B} \cdot \vec{C}$$

and

$$\vec{P} \cdot \vec{D} - \vec{P} \cdot \vec{C} = \vec{A} \cdot \vec{C} - \vec{A} \cdot \vec{D} + \vec{B} \cdot \vec{C} - \vec{B} \cdot \vec{D} .$$

Then a simple calculation yields

$$\left(\vec{B} - \vec{A} + \vec{D} - \vec{C} \right) \cdot \left(\vec{P} + \vec{A} + \vec{B} + \vec{C} + \vec{D} \right) = 0,$$

which means that $\vec{P} + \vec{A} + \vec{B} + \vec{C} + \vec{D}$ is orthogonal to $\overrightarrow{AB} + \overrightarrow{CD}$. Permuting the roles of A, B, C, D, we obtain that $\vec{P} + \vec{A} + \vec{B} + \vec{C} + \vec{D}$ is also orthogonal to $\overrightarrow{CA} + \overrightarrow{BD}$ and $\overrightarrow{BC} + \overrightarrow{AD}$.

Note: it is easy to check that $\overrightarrow{AB} + \overrightarrow{CD}$, $\overrightarrow{CA} + \overrightarrow{BD}$, $\overrightarrow{BC} + \overrightarrow{AD}$ are three independent vectors in space. It follows that $\vec{P} + \vec{A} + \vec{B} + \vec{C} + \vec{D} = \vec{0}$ or $\vec{A} + \vec{B} + \vec{C} + \vec{D} = - \vec{P}$.

Substituting in (1) gives $PA^2 + PB^2 + PC^2 + PD^2 = 4R^2 + 6 \left(\vec{P} \right)^2$. Thus, we have $PA^2 + PB^2 + PC^2 + PD^2 \geq 4R^2$ with equality only when $\vec{0} = \vec{P}$. Returning to the defining conditions for P, we see at once that equality occurs if and only if $a = a_1$, $b = b_1$, and $c = c_1$. (Such a tetrahedron $ABCD$ is called an equifacial tetrahedron.)

The line t has no common points with a circle w centered at O.
Point E lies on t; $OE \perp t$. Point M is another point on t; MA and MB
are tangents to w, A and B being the points of tangency; AB intersects OE
at X.

Prove that X does not depend on M.

Solution

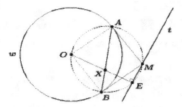

On a $OA \perp MA$, $OB \perp MB$ et $OE \perp ME$, donc les points A, B et
E appartiennent au cercle de diamètre OM.

On en déduit (puissance de X par rapport au cercle) :

$$XO \times XE = XA \times XB.$$

D'autre part, la puissance de X par rapport à w donne :

$$XA \times XB = OA^2 - OX^2.$$

Les deux relations précédentes permettent alors d'écrire :

$$OX \times XE = OA^2 - OX^2,$$

soit

$$OX \times XE + OX^2 = OA^2 \implies OX(XE + OX) = OA^2$$
$$\implies OX \times OE = OA^2.$$

Finalement

$$OX = \frac{OA^2}{OE}$$

qui est un réel indépendant de la position de M sur t. Donc X ne dépend
pas de M.

An equilateral triangle of side 1 is dissected into n triangles. Prove that the sum of squares of all sides of all triangles is at least 3.

Solution

For any triangle of sides a, b, c and area F it is a known elementary inequality that $a^2 + b^2 + c^2 \geq 4F\sqrt{3}$ and with equality if and only if the triangle is equilateral. (For a proof, just square both sides and use the identity $16F^2 = 2(b^2c^2 + c^2a^2 + a^2b^2) - a^4 - b^4 - c^4$. This reduces the inequality to $(b^2 - c^2)^2 + (c^2 - a^2)^2 + (a^2 - b^2)^2 \geq 0$).

Summing over the squares of all the sides of all the triangles, we get

$$\sum \left(a_j^2 + b_j^2 + c_j^2\right) \geq \sum \frac{4F_j}{\sqrt{3}} = 3.$$

There is equality if and only if the triangle can be dissected into n equilateral triangles.

It is to be noted the given result holds for any polygon of area $\frac{\sqrt{3}}{4}$.

Let $ABCD$ be a parallelogram. The bisector of A cuts BC at M and cuts the extension of CD at N. The circumcentre of MCN is O. Prove that B, O, C, D are concyclic.

Solution

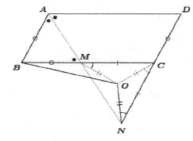

Since $AD \parallel BC$ and $AB \parallel DC$, we get
$$\angle CMN = \angle DAM = \angle BAN = \angle CNM.$$
Thus, we have $CM = CN$. Since $OM = ON = OC$, we get
$$\triangle OCM \equiv \triangle OCN,$$
so that $\angle OMC = \angle ONC = \angle OCN$. Consequently we have
$$\angle OMB = \angle OCD. \qquad (1)$$
Since $\angle BMA = \angle DAM = \angle BAM$, we get
$$BM = BA = CD. \qquad (2)$$
Since $OM = OC$, it follows that from (1) and (2)
$$\triangle OMB \equiv \triangle OCD.$$
Thus, $\angle OBM = \angle ODC$; that is
$$\angle OBC = \angle ODC.$$
Therefore, B, O, C, D are concyclic.

In an isosceles triangle ABC with the base $\overline{AB}$, point M lies on the side $\overline{BC}$. Let O be the centre of its circumscribed circle, and S be the centre of the inscribed circle in the triangle ABC. Prove that:

$$SM \parallel AC \iff OM \perp BS.$$

Solution

First, let the line BS meet the lines MO and CA at K and N, respectively. Also, let the points of tangency of the incircle with the sides BA and CA be L and L', respectively. Notice that BS bisects $\angle B$ and that the line COS bisects $\angle C$ and is perpendicular to AB at L. Moreover, it is easy to see that

$$\angle OBS = \frac{\angle B - \angle C}{2} = \angle NSL'. \tag{1}$$

Now if SM is parallel to AC, then $\angle SMB = \angle C = \angle SOB$; that is, $SOMB$ is cyclic. Hence,

$$\begin{aligned}
\angle OMB &= \angle OMS + \angle SMB = \angle OBS + \angle SMB \\
&= \frac{\angle B - \angle C}{2} + \angle C = \frac{\angle B + \angle C}{2},
\end{aligned}$$

and thus,

$$\angle KOS + \angle SKO = \angle SBM + \angle OMB = \frac{\angle B}{2} + \frac{\angle B + \angle C}{2} = 90°,$$

which means that OM is perpendicular to BS at K.

Conversely, if OM is perpendicular to BS at K, then the right triangles OKB and OKS are similar to the right triangles $NL'S$ by (1) and BLS, respectively. Thus,

$$\frac{NS}{SL} = \frac{NS}{SL'} = \frac{OB}{KB} = \frac{CO}{KB} \quad \text{and} \quad \frac{SL}{SB} = \frac{SK}{OS}.$$

By multiplying, we get

$$\frac{NS}{SB} = \frac{CO}{KB} \cdot \frac{SK}{OS} = \frac{CM}{MB},$$

where the last equality follows from the Theorem of Menelaus in the triangle CSB for the line MOK. Therefore, SM is parallel to AC and the proof is complete.

(a) Let A_1, B_1, C_1 be the points of contact of the circle inscribed in the triangle ABC and the sides BC, CA, AB, respectively. Let B_1C_1, A_1C_1, B_1A_1 be the arcs which do not contain points A_1, B_1, C_1 respectively. Let I_1, I_2, I_3 be their respective arc lengths. Prove the following inequality:

$$\frac{a}{I_1} + \frac{b}{I_2} + \frac{c}{I_3} \geq 9\frac{\sqrt{3}}{\pi}$$

(where a, b, c denote the lengths of sides of the given triangle).

(b) Let $ABCD$ be a tetrahedron with:

$$AB = CD = a,$$
$$BC = AD = b,$$
$$AC = BD = c.$$

Express the height of the tetrahedron in terms of the lengths a, b and c.

Solution

(a) Denote the incentre and inradius of triangle ABC by I and r, respectively.

The perpendiculars IA_1, IB_1, IC_1 partition the triangle into three quadrilaterals, each of which is clearly cyclic. If A, B, C denote the angles in radians of $\triangle ABC$, then

$$I_1 = r(\pi - A), \quad I_2 = r(\pi - B), \quad I_3 = r(\pi - C).$$

We employ the AM–GM inequality and obtain

$$\frac{a}{I_1} + \frac{b}{I_2} + \frac{c}{I_3} = \frac{1}{r}\left(\frac{a}{\pi - A} + \frac{b}{\pi - B} + \frac{c}{\pi - C}\right)$$

$$\geq \frac{1}{r} \cdot 3\sqrt[3]{\frac{abc}{(\pi - A)(\pi - B)(\pi - C)}}. \qquad (1)$$

Now,

$$\sqrt[3]{(\pi - A)(\pi - B)(\pi - C)} \leq \frac{(\pi - A) + (\pi - B) + (\pi - C)}{3} = \frac{2\pi}{3},$$

whence by (1)

$$\frac{a}{I_1} + \frac{b}{I_2} + \frac{c}{I_3} \geq \frac{1}{r} \cdot \frac{9}{2\pi}\sqrt[3]{abc} = \frac{9}{2\pi r}\sqrt[3]{4Rrs}$$

$$\geq \frac{9}{\pi r}\sqrt[3]{r^2 s} = \frac{9}{\pi}\sqrt[3]{\frac{s}{r}} \qquad (2)$$

where R and s are the circumradius and semiperimeter of $\triangle ABC$ and we have used Euler's Inequality $R \geq 2r$.

Finally, using the inequality $\frac{s}{r} \geq 3\sqrt{3}$ (item 5.3 of Bottema et al. *Geometric inequalities*) we obtain from (2)

$$\frac{a}{I_1} + \frac{b}{I_2} + \frac{c}{I_3} \geq \frac{9}{\pi}\sqrt[3]{3\sqrt{3}} = \frac{9\sqrt{3}}{\pi}.$$

Equality occurs only if $\triangle ABC$ is equilateral.

Let AA_1, BB_1, CC_1 be the altitudes of acute triangle ABC, let O be an arbitrary point inside the triangle $A_1B_1C_1$. Let us denote by M and N the bases of perpendiculars drawn from O to lines AA_1 and BC, respectively, by P and Q — ones from O to lines BB_1 and CA, respectively, by R and S — ones from O to lines CC_1 and AB, respectively. Prove that the lines MN, PQ, RS are concurrent.

Solution

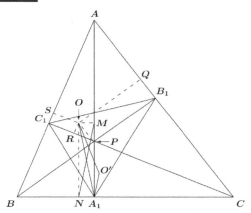

Since $\angle BB_1C = \angle BC_1C = 90°$, the points B, C, B_1, C_1 are concyclic. Similarly, C, A, C_1, A_1 are concyclic, and A, B, A_1, B_1 are concyclic. Hence, $\angle B_1A_1A = \angle B_1BA = \angle ACC_1 = \angle AA_1C_1$.

Let O' be the isogonal conjugate of O with respect to $\triangle A_1B_1C_1$. Then

$$\begin{aligned}\angle AA_1O &= \angle AA_1B_1 - \angle OA_1B_1 \\ &= \angle C_1A_1A - \angle C_1A_1O' = \angle O'A_1A.\end{aligned} \qquad (1)$$

Since OMA_1N is a rectangle, we get from (1)

$$\angle A_1MN = \angle OA_1M = \angle OA_1A = \angle O'A_1A.$$

Therefore, $MN \parallel A_1O'$.

Let L be the intersection of OA_1 and MN. Then L is the mid-point of OA_1. Let T be the intersection of OO' with MN. Since $MN \parallel A_1O'$, we have

$$OT : TO' = OL : LA_1 = 1 : 1.$$

Thus, $OT = TO'$, and MN passes through the mid-point of OO'.

Similarly, PQ and RS pass through the mid-point of OO'. Hence, MN, PQ, and RS are concurrent at the mid-point of OO'.

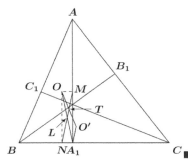

On the sides BC and AB of the equilateral triangle ABC the points D and E, respectively, are taken such that $CD : DB = BE : EA = (\sqrt{5} + 1)/2$. The straight lines AD and CE intersect in the point O. The points M and N are interior points of the segments OD and OC, respectively, such that $MN \parallel BC$ and $AN = 2OM$. The parallel to the straight line AC, drawn through the point O, intersects the segment MC in the point P. Prove that the half-line AP is the bisectrix of the angle MAN.

Solution

The conditions of the problem statement cannot all be true. We will show that the condition $AN = 2OM$ cannot be true if the other conditions are true.

Since $CD : DB = (\sqrt{5} + 1) : 2$, we get $CD : CB = (\sqrt{5} + 1) : (\sqrt{5} + 3)$. By Menelaus' Theorem for $\triangle ABD$, we have

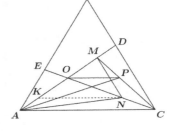

$$\frac{BE}{EA} \cdot \frac{AO}{OD} \cdot \frac{DC}{CB} = 1;$$

that is, $\dfrac{\sqrt{5} + 1}{2} \cdot \dfrac{AO}{OD} \cdot \dfrac{\sqrt{5} + 1}{\sqrt{5} + 3} = 1$. Thus,

$$\frac{AO}{OD} = \frac{2(\sqrt{5} + 3)}{(\sqrt{5} + 1)^2} = 1;$$

whence, $AO = OD$.

We are given that M and N are points on the segments OD and OC, respectively, such that $MN \parallel DC$. Let K be the point on OA such that $KN \parallel AC$. Then $OK : OA = ON : OC = OM : OD$. Since $OA = OD$, we see that $OK = OM$. Since $\angle KMN = \angle ADC > \angle ABC = 60°$ and $\angle KNM = \angle ACD = 60°$, we have $\angle KMN > \angle KNM$. Therefore, $KN > KM = 2OM$. Since

$$\angle AKN = 180° - \angle DAC > 180° - \angle BAC = 120°,$$

it follows that $AN > KN$. Therefore, $AN > 2OM$.

Thus, it is not true that $AN = 2OM$.

On the sides BC, AC and AB of the equilateral triangle ABC the points M, N and P, respectively, are considered such that $AP : PB = BM : MC = CN : NA = \lambda$. Find all the values λ for which the circle with the diameter AC covers the triangle bounded by the straight lines AM, BN and CP. (In the case of concurrent straight lines, the mentioned triangle degenerates into a point.)

Solution

Let the intersections of AM and BN, BN and CP, and CP and AM be X, Y, and Z, respectively, and let O be the circumcentre of $\triangle ABC$.

Since $AP = BM = CN$, we see that $\triangle PAC \equiv \triangle MBA \equiv \triangle NCB$, from which we have

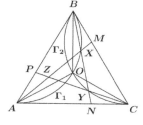

$$\angle PCA = \angle MAB = \angle NBC.$$

It follows that $\angle AXB = \angle BYC = \angle CZA = 120°$.

We denote the circumcircles of $\triangle OAB$ and $\triangle OBC$ by Γ_1 and Γ_2, respectively. Since $\angle AOB = \angle BOC = 120°$, we have $\angle AXB = \angle AOB$ and $\angle BYC = \angle BOC$. Therefore, X lies on the minor arc AOB of Γ_1, and Y lies on the minor arc BOC of Γ_2.

If M varies on the side BC from B to C, then X moves on the arc BOA from B to A, and if N varies on the side CA from C to A, then Y moves on the arc BOC from C to B.

If $\lambda = 1$, then X, Y, and Z coincide with O. If $\lambda < 1$, then X lies on the minor arc BO of Γ_1 and Y lies on the minor arc CO of Γ_2. If $\lambda > 1$, then X lies on the minor arc AO of Γ_1 and Y lies on the minor arc BO of Γ_2.

Now we consider the case $\lambda = \frac{1}{2}$. In this case we denote M, N, and X by M_0, N_0, and X_0, respectively.

Let T be the second intersection of BN_0 with the circumcircle of $\triangle ABC$. Then

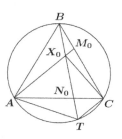

$$\angle ATN_0 = \angle ATB = \angle ACB = 60°$$
and $\quad \angle CTN_0 = \angle CTB = \angle CAB = 60°.$

Thus, $\angle ATN_0 = \angle CTN_0$; whence,

$$AT : TC = AN_0 : N_0C = 1 : \lambda = 2 : 1,$$

which implies that $AT = 2CT$.

Since $\angle AX_0T = 60°$ and $\angle ATX_0 = 60°$, we see that $\triangle ATX_0$ is equilateral. Hence, $X_0T = AT = 2CT$. Since $\angle X_0TC = 60°$, it follows that $\angle X_0CT = 90°$. Hence, $\angle TX_0C = 30°$. Therefore,

$$\angle AX_0C = \angle AX_0T + \angle TX_0C = 60° + 30° = 90°.$$

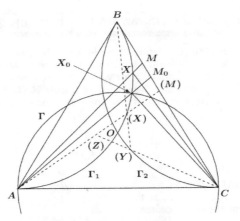

We denote the circle with diameter AC by Γ.

If $\lambda < \frac{1}{2}$, then X lies on the minor arc BX_0 of Γ_1, which means that $\angle AXC < \angle AX_0C = 90°$. Thus, X is an exterior point of Γ, from which we see that $\triangle XYZ$ is not contained in Γ.

If $\frac{1}{2} \leq \lambda \leq 1$, then X lies on the minor arc X_0O of Γ_1. Thus,

$$\angle AXC \;\geq\; \angle AX_0C \;=\; 90°,$$
$$\angle AYC \;\geq\; \angle AXC \;\geq\; 90°,$$
$$\text{and} \quad \angle AZC \;\geq\; \angle AXC \;\geq\; 90°.$$

Hence, X, Y, and Z are contained in Γ. Thus, $\triangle XYZ$ is contained in Γ.

Finally, suppose that $\lambda > 1$. Let $\mu = 1/\lambda$. Then $0 < \mu < 1$, and $AN : NC = CM : MB = BP : PA = \mu$. The above argument shows that for $\frac{1}{2} \leq \mu \leq 1$ the triangle XYZ is contained in Γ, and for $\mu < \frac{1}{2}$, this is not the case. Therefore, $\triangle XYZ$ is contained in Γ if and only if $\frac{1}{2} \leq \lambda \leq 2$.

Points D and E are given on the sides AB and AC of $\triangle ABC$ in such a way that DE is parallel to BC and tangent to the incircle of $\triangle ABC$. Prove that

$$DE \leq \tfrac{1}{8}(AB + BC + CA).$$

Solution

We set $BC = a$, $CA = b$, $AB = c$, and $2s = a + b + c$. Let the incircle touch BC, CA, AB at P, Q, R, respectively.

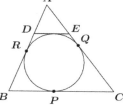

Since DE is parallel to BC, we have $\triangle ADE \sim \triangle ABC$. Thus,

$$\frac{AD + DE + AE}{AB + BC + AC} = \frac{DE}{BC} = \frac{DE}{a}.$$

Since $AD + DE + AE = AR + AQ = b + c - a$, we have

$$\frac{b + c - a}{a + b + c} = \frac{DE}{a};$$

whence, $DE = \dfrac{a(b + c - a)}{a + b + c}$. Then

$$\tfrac{1}{8}(AB + BC + CA) - DE$$

$$= \frac{a + b + c}{8} - \frac{a(b + c - a)}{a + b + c} = \frac{(a + b + c)^2 - 8a(b + c - a)}{8(a + b + c)}$$

$$= \frac{(b + c)^2 - 6a(b + c) + 9a^2}{8(a + b + c)} = \frac{(b + c - 3a)^2}{8(a + b + c)} \geq 0.$$

Thus, $\tfrac{1}{8}(AB + BC + CA) \geq DE$.

Given an angle $\angle ABC$ and rays $\ell_1, \ldots, \ell_{n-1}$ dividing the angle into n congruent angles, for a line ℓ denote $\ell \cap (AB) = A_1$, $\ell \cap (BC) = A_{n+1}$ and $\ell \cap \ell_i = A_{i+1}$ for $1 \leq i < n$, show that the quotient

$$\frac{\left(\dfrac{1}{|BA_1|} + \dfrac{1}{|BA_{n+1}|} \right)}{\left(\dfrac{1}{|BA_1|} + \dfrac{1}{|BA_2|} + \cdots + \dfrac{1}{|BA_n|} + \dfrac{1}{|BA_{n+1}|} \right)}$$

is a constant which does not depend on ℓ, and find the value of this constant knowing $\angle ABC = \varphi$.

Solution

Let $\theta = \angle BA_1 A_{n+1}$. For $k = 1, 2, \ldots, n$, the Law of Sines provides

$$\frac{|BA_1|}{|BA_{k+1}|} = \frac{\sin(\angle A_1 A_{k+1} B)}{\sin \theta} = \frac{\sin \left(\theta + \dfrac{k\varphi}{n} \right)}{\sin \theta}.$$

It follows that

$$1 + \frac{|BA_1|}{|BA_{n+1}|} = 1 + \frac{\sin(\theta + \varphi)}{\sin \theta} = \frac{2 \cos \left(\dfrac{\varphi}{2} \right) \sin \left(\theta + \dfrac{\varphi}{2} \right)}{\sin \theta} \tag{1}$$

and

$$1 + \sum_{k=1}^{n} \frac{|BA_1|}{|BA_{k+1}|} = 1 + \frac{1}{\sin \theta} \sum_{k=1}^{n} \sin \left(\theta + \frac{k\varphi}{n} \right) = \frac{1}{\sin \theta} \sum_{k=0}^{n} \sin \left(\theta + \frac{k\varphi}{n} \right)$$

$$= \frac{1}{\sin \theta} \left(\sin \left(\theta + \frac{\varphi}{2} \right) \frac{\sin \left(\dfrac{(n+1)\varphi}{2n} \right)}{\sin \left(\dfrac{\varphi}{2n} \right)} \right), \tag{2}$$

where the last line follows by a well-known classical calculation.

Dividing equation (1) by equation (2), we find that the quotient to which the problem refers is equal to

$$\frac{2 \cos \left(\dfrac{\varphi}{2} \right) \sin \left(\dfrac{\varphi}{2n} \right)}{\sin \left(\dfrac{(n+1)\varphi}{2n} \right)} = 1 - \frac{\sin \left(\dfrac{(n-1)\varphi}{2n} \right)}{\sin \left(\dfrac{(n+1)\varphi}{2n} \right)},$$

which is independent of θ and, therefore, independent of the line ℓ.

A point M lies on the side AC of a triangle ABC. The circle γ with the diameter BM intersects the lines AB, BC, at points P, Q, respectively. Find the locus of intersection points of the tangents of the circle γ at the points P, Q, when the point M varies.

Solution

In the following proof, we assume that $\triangle ABC$ is acute. In other cases, the proof works with minor changes.

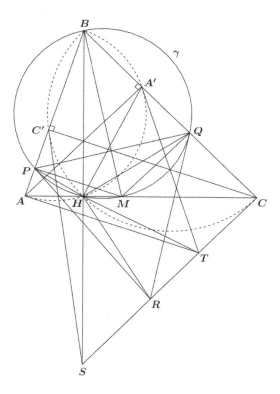

Let H be the second intersection of γ with AC. Then $\angle BHM = 90°$; hence, $BH \perp AC$. Let R be the intersection of the tangents to γ at P and Q. Let A' and C' be the feet of the perpendiculars from A and C to BC and AB, respectively. Let T be the point such that TA and TA' are tangent to the circumcircle of $\triangle BAA'$, and let S be the point such that SC and SC' are tangent to the circumcircle of $\triangle BCC'$.

Since A, B, A', and H are concyclic, we have

$$\angle HA'A = \angle HBA = \angle HBP = \angle HQP,$$

and

$$\angle HAA' = \angle HBA' = \angle HBQ = \angle HPQ.$$

Hence, $\triangle HAA' \sim \triangle HPQ$. Also, $\triangle TAA' \sim \triangle RPQ$, because

$$\angle TAA' = \angle TA'A = \angle ABA' = \angle PBQ = \angle RPQ = \angle RQP.$$

Consequently, $\triangle HA'T \sim \triangle HQR$. It follows that $\triangle HA'Q \sim \triangle HTR$. Thus, $\angle HQA' = \angle HRT$.

In the same way, since $\angle HCC' = \angle HQP$ and $\angle HC'C = \angle HPQ$, we have $\triangle HC'C \sim \triangle HPQ$. Also, $\triangle SCC' \sim \triangle RPQ$, and hence, $\triangle HCS \sim \triangle HQR$. Then $\triangle HQC \sim \triangle HRS$. Thus, $\angle HQC = \angle HRS$.

Therefore, $\angle HRT + \angle HRS = \angle HQA' + \angle HQC = 180°$, which shows that the point R is on the segment TS.

Since $\triangle HTR \sim \triangle HA'Q$ and $\triangle HRS \sim \triangle HQC$, we get

$$TR : A'Q = HR : HQ = RS : QC.$$

Then $TR : RS = A'Q : QC$. Since $AA' \perp BC$ and $MQ \perp BC$, we have $AA' \parallel MQ$, and therefore, $A'Q : QC = AM : MC$. We conclude that $TR : RS = AM : MC$.

When the point M varies on the side AC from A to C, the point R varies on the segment TS from T to S, satisfying $TR : RS = AM : MC$. Therefore, the locus of R is the segment TS.

Let ABC be a triangle such that $\angle A = 90°$ and $\angle B < \angle C$. The tangent at A to its circumcircle k meets the line BC at D. Let E be the reflection of A across BC, X the foot of the perpendicular from A to BE, and Y the mid-point of AX. Let the line BY meet k again in Z. Prove that the line BD is tangent to the circumcircle of triangle ADZ.

Solution

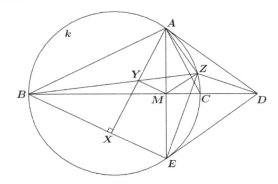

Since BC is a diameter of k, we see that E is a point on k. Let M be the intersection of AE with BC. Then M is the mid-point of AE, and $\angle AMD = 90°$. Since Y and M are mid-points of AX and AE, respectively, we have $YM \parallel XE$; that is, $YM \parallel BE$.

Thus, $\angle ZYM = \angle ZBE = \angle ZAE = \angle ZAM$, which implies that A, Y, M, and Z are concyclic. Hence, $\angle YAM = \angle YZM$. Therefore,

$$\angle BAX = \angle BAE - \angle YAM = \angle BZE - \angle YZM = \angle MZE.$$

Also, since $\angle ABX = \angle ABE = \angle EAD = \angle MAD$, we have

$$\angle BAX = 90° - \angle ABX = 90° - \angle MAD = \angle ADM = \angle EDM.$$

Consequently, $\angle MZE = \angle EDM$. Then M, E, D, and Z are concyclic. Thus,

$$\angle ZDM = \angle ZEM = \angle ZEA = \angle ZAD.$$

Therefore, BD is tangent to the circumcircle of $\triangle ADZ$.

Given a rectangular sheet with sides a and b, with $a > b$, fold it along a diagonal. Determine the area of the overlapped triangle (the shaded triangle in the picture).

Solution

Note that $\triangle ABE \cong \triangle CDE$ (AAS). Thus, $BE = DE$ and $AE = CE$. Letting $x = BE = DE$, we get $a - x = AE = CE$. By the Theorem of Pythagoras, we have $(a - x)^2 + b^2 = x^2$, or $a^2 + b^2 = 2ax$. Then $x = \dfrac{a^2 + b^2}{2a}$.

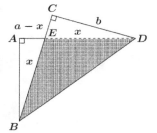

Using $BE = x$ as a base in $\triangle BDE$, the corresponding height is $CD = b$. Therefore, the area of $\triangle BDE$ is

$$\frac{1}{2}xb \;=\; \frac{1}{2}\left(\frac{a^2 + b^2}{2a}\right)b \;=\; \frac{b(a^2 + b^2)}{4a}\,.$$

The incircle of triangle ABC with centre O touches the side AC at K. Another circle with the same centre intersects each side at two points. The points of intersection on AC are B_1 and B_2, with B_1 closer to A. E is the point of intersection on AB closer to B, and F is the point of intersection on BC closer to B. Let P be the point of intersection of B_2E and B_1F. Prove that B, K, and P are collinear.

Solution

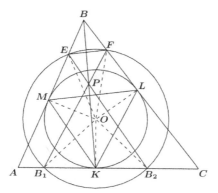

Let the incircle meet BC and BA at L and M, respectively. Let r be the radius of the incircle, and let r' be the radius of the other circle centred at O. Since $OK = OL = OM = r$ and $OB_1 = OB_2 = OE = OF = r'$, and since $\angle OKB_1 = \angle OKB_2 = \angle OLF = \angle OME = 90°$, we have

$$\triangle OKB_1 \cong \triangle OKB_2 \cong \triangle OLF \cong \triangle OME .$$

Hence, $KB_1 = KB_2 = LF = ME$. Since $AK = AM$ and $KB_2 = ME$, we have $AK : KB_2 = AM : ME$. Thus, $MK \parallel EB_2$; that is, $MK \parallel EP$. Then, by symmetry, $LK \parallel FP$.

Similarly, since $BM = BL$ and $EM = FL$, we obtain $ML \parallel EF$. In triangles KLM and PFE, we have $KM \parallel PE$, $KL \parallel PF$, and $ML \parallel EF$. It follows that KP, LF, and ME are concurrent. Therefore, B, K, and P are collinear.

Let ABC be an acute triangle.

(a) Prove that there exist unique points A', B', and C', on BC, CA, and AB, respectively, such that A' is the mid-point of the orthogonal projection of $B'C'$ onto BC, B' is the mid-point of the orthogonal projection of $C'A'$ onto CA, and C' is the mid-point of the orthogonal projection of $A'B'$ onto AB.

(b) Prove that $A'B'C'$ is similar to the triangle formed by the medians of ABC.

Solution

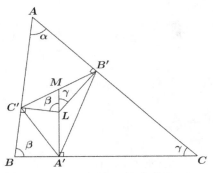

The points A', B', C' are the projections onto BC, CA, AB of the Lemoine Point (or symmedian point) L of $\triangle ABC$. We denote

$$\lambda = \frac{LA'}{a} = \frac{LB'}{b} = \frac{LC'}{c}.$$

(a) Let M be the point of intersection of $A'L$ and $B'C'$. Rectangle $BA'LC'$ is cyclic, which implies that $\angle C'LM = \beta$. Rectangle $CA'LB'$ is cyclic, implying that $\angle B'LM = \gamma$.

By the Sine Law, first in $\triangle B'C'L$ and then in $\triangle ABC$, we have

$$\frac{\sin \angle LC'B'}{\sin \angle LB'C'} = \frac{LB'}{LC'} = \frac{\lambda b}{\lambda c} = \frac{\sin \beta}{\sin \gamma} = \frac{\sin \angle C'LM}{\sin \angle B'LM}. \qquad (1)$$

Equation (1) is a necessary and sufficient condition for LM to be a median in $\triangle B'C'L$. It follows that A' is the mid-point of the orthogonal projection of $B'C'$ onto BC. By symmetry, analogous statements are true for B' and C'.

Now we will prove the uniqueness. Let L' be a point not on AL, and denote its projections onto BC, CA, and AB by D, E, and F respectively. Let DL' intersect EF at N.

Since $L'E : L'F \neq b : c$, equation (1) does not hold for $\triangle L'EF$, and N is not the mid-point of EF. Thus, A', B', C' are unique indeed.

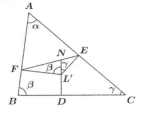

(b) Let us denote the length of the median from A to BC by m_a. Applying the Law of Cosines, first in $\triangle B'C'L$ and then in $\triangle ABC$, we obtain

$$
\begin{aligned}
(B'C')^2 &= (LB')^2 + (LC')^2 - 2(LB')(LC')\cos(\beta + \gamma) \\
&= \lambda^2(b^2 + c^2 + 2bc\cos\alpha) \\
&= 4\lambda^2\left(\tfrac{1}{2}(b^2 + c^2) - \tfrac{1}{4}a^2\right) \\
&= 4\lambda^2 m_a^2 \,;
\end{aligned}
$$

whence, $B'C' = \lambda m_a$. Similarly, $C'A' = \lambda m_b$ and $A'B' = \lambda m_c$, where m_b and m_c are the lengths of the medians (in $\triangle ABC$) to sides b and c, respectively. Therefore, $\triangle A'B'C'$ is similar to the triangle formed by the medians of $\triangle ABC$.

In triangle ABC, we have $CA = CB$. Let D be the mid-point of AB and E an arbitrary point on AB. Let O be the circumcentre of $\triangle ACE$. Prove that the line through D perpendicular to DO, the line through E perpendicular to BC, and the line through B parallel to AC are concurrent.

Solution

Take rectangular Cartesian coordinates with $D(0,0)$, $A(-k,0)$, $B(k,0)$, $C(0,h)$, $E(t,0)$. The mid-point of AE is $(\frac{1}{2}(t-k), 0)$; hence, the x–coordinate of O is $\frac{1}{2}(t-k)$.

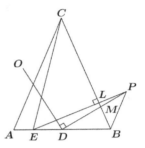

The equation of AC is $ky - hx = hk$, and the mid-point of AC is $(-\frac{1}{2}k, \frac{1}{2}h)$. The perpendicular bisector of AC is then $hy + kx = \frac{1}{2}(h^2 - k^2)$. It follows that the coordinates of O are $\left(\frac{1}{2}(t-k), \dfrac{h^2 - tk}{2h}\right)$.

Therefore, the slope of OD is $\dfrac{h^2 - tk}{h(t-k)}$.

The equation of the line through D perpendicular to OD is $(h^2 - tk)y = h(k - t)x$. The line through B parallel to AC has equation $ky = h(x - k)$, and the line through E perpendicular to BC has equation $hy = k(x - t)$. It is easy to check that all three lines pass through the point P with coordinates

$$\left(\frac{k(h^2 - kt)}{h^2 - k^2}, \frac{hk(k - t)}{h^2 - k^2}\right).$$

It appears that we must exclude the case when $h = \pm k$; that is, when $\angle ACB = 90°$. However, in this case, the three lines of the problem are all perpendicular to BC and thus "meet at infinity".

Let $ABCD$ be a quadrilateral with AB parallel to DC. A line ℓ intersects AD, AC, BD, and BC, forming three segments of equal lengths between consecutive points of intersection. Does it follow that ℓ is parallel to AB?

Solution

We cannot conclude that l is parallel to AB. Here is a counterexample.

Let $ABCD$ be a trapezoid with $AB \parallel CD$ and $AB = 2CD$. Let P and S be interior points of the sides AD and BC, respectively, such that $\frac{AP}{PD} = \frac{CS}{SB} \neq 1$, which implies that PS is not parallel to AB. Let Q and R be the intersections of PS with AC and BD, respectively. We shall prove that $PQ = QR = RS$.

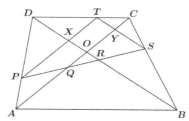

Let T be the point on the side CD such that

$$\frac{CT}{TD} = \frac{AP}{PD} = \frac{CS}{SB}.$$

Since $\frac{CT}{TD} = \frac{AP}{PD}$, we have $PT \parallel AC$. Since $\frac{CT}{TD} = \frac{CS}{SB}$, we have $TS \parallel DB$.

Let X and O be the intersections of BD with PT and AC, respectively, and let Y be the intersection of TS with AC.

Since $XR \parallel TS$, $PT \parallel AC$, and $AB \parallel CD$, we obtain

$$\frac{PR}{RS} = \frac{PX}{XT} = \frac{AO}{OC} = \frac{AB}{CD} = \frac{2}{1}; \quad \text{hence} \quad PR = 2RS. \quad (1)$$

Since $QY \parallel PT$, $TS \parallel DB$, and $AB \parallel CD$, we have

$$\frac{PQ}{QS} = \frac{TY}{YS} = \frac{DO}{OB} = \frac{CD}{AB} = \frac{1}{2}; \quad \text{hence} \quad QS = 2PQ. \quad (2)$$

It follows from (1) and (2) that $PQ = QR = RS$.

In an acute triangle ABC, $AC > BC$ and M is the mid-point of AB. Let AP be the altitude from A. Let BQ be the altitude from B meeting AP at H. Let the lines AB and PQ meet at R. Prove that the lines RH and CM are perpendicular to each other.

Solution 1

Since $\angle BQA = \angle BPA = 90°$, the circle Γ with diameter AB passes through P and Q. Thus, the point H, as the intersection of the diagonals of $QPBA$, is on the polar of R with respect to Γ (since the sides QP and AB meet at R). Similarly, H is on the polar of C; whence, CR is the polar of H. Since M is the centre of Γ, it follows that CR is perpendicular to HM. Note that since H is the orthocentre of $\triangle ABC$, we also have $CH \perp RM$. As a result, H is the intersection of two altitudes in triangle CRM and, as such, H is the orthocentre of $\triangle CRM$. The result, $RH \perp CM$, follows.

Solution 2

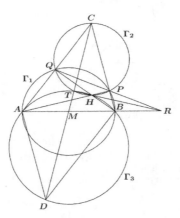

Since $\angle APB = \angle AQB = 90°$, the points A, B, P, and Q lie on a circle Γ_1. Let T be the foot of the perpendicular from H to CM. Since

$$\angle CPH = \angle CQH = \angle CTH = 90°,$$

we see that C, P, Q, T, and H all lie on a circle Γ_2.

On CM produced beyond M, let D be the point such that $CM = MD$. Then quadrilateral $CADB$ is a parallelogram. Since $BD \parallel CA$ and $BQ \perp AC$, we have $BQ \perp BD$. Similarly, $AD \perp AP$. Thus,

$$\angle HBD = \angle HAD = \angle HTD = 90°.$$

Therefore A, D, B, H, and T all lie on a circle Γ_3.

Note that PQ is a common chord of Γ_1 and Γ_2, HT is a common chord of Γ_2 and Γ_3, and AB is a common chord of Γ_3 and Γ_1. It follows that PQ, HT, and AB are concurrent at R. Thus, T, H, and R are collinear. Therefore, $RH \perp CM$.

Construct the point P inside a given triangle such that the feet of the perpendiculars from P to the sides of the triangle determine a triangle whose centroid is P.

Solution

Let the given triangle be ABC, and let D, E, and F denote the feet of the perpendiculars from P to the sides BC, CA, and AB, respectively.

First, suppose that P is the centroid of $\triangle DEF$. Then the areas $[PEF]$, $[PFD]$, and $[PDE]$ are equal. Hence,

$$PE \cdot PF \cdot \sin A \ = \ PF \cdot PD \cdot \sin B \ = \ PD \cdot PE \cdot \sin C \,.$$

(Note that $\angle EPF = 180° - A$, since A, P, E, F all lie on the circle with diameter AP, and similarly, $\angle DPF = 180° - B$ and $\angle EPD = 180° - C$.) It follows that

$$\frac{PE}{PD} = \frac{\sin B}{\sin A} = \frac{b}{a} \quad \text{and} \quad \frac{PF}{PE} = \frac{\sin C}{\sin B} = \frac{c}{b} \,,$$

where, as usual, $a = BC$, $b = CA$, $c = AB$.

Thus, $\dfrac{PD}{a} = \dfrac{PE}{b} = \dfrac{PF}{c}$, and P is the point inside $\triangle ABC$ such that the distances $d(P, BC)$, $d(P, CA)$, $d(P, AB)$ are proportional to a, b, c, respectively. This point is the well-known Lemoine point of $\triangle ABC$.

Conversely, if P is the Lemoine point of $\triangle ABC$, then we have $\dfrac{PD}{a} = \dfrac{PE}{b} = \dfrac{PF}{c} = \lambda$, which implies that

$$[PEF] \ = \ PE \cdot PF \cdot \sin A \ = \ \lambda^2 bc \, \frac{a}{2R} \ = \ \frac{\lambda^2}{2R} \, abc$$

(where R is the circumradius of $\triangle ABC$). Thus, $[PEF] = [PFD] = [PDE]$, and P is the centroid of $\triangle DEF$.

To construct P, note that any point M on the median AA', where A' is the mid-point of BC, satisfies

$$\frac{d(M, AB)}{d(M, AC)} \ = \ \frac{d(A', AB)}{d(A', AC)} \ = \ \frac{b}{c} \,.$$

(The latter follows because $[A'AB] = [A'AC]$.)

Thus, if S_A is the reflection of AA' in the internal bisector of $\angle BAC$, then, for any point M' of S_A, we have $\dfrac{d(M', AB)}{c} = \dfrac{d(M', AC)}{b}$. The line S_A is the symmedian through A. Constructing similarly the symmedian S_B through B, we obtain P at the intersection of S_A and S_B.

Triangles $A_3 A_1 O_2$ and $A_1 A_2 O_3$ are constructed outside triangle $A_1 A_2 A_3$, with $O_2 A_3 = O_2 A_1$ and $O_3 A_1 = O_3 A_2$. A point O_1 is outside $A_1 A_2 A_3$ such that $\angle O_1 A_3 A_2 = \frac{1}{2} \angle A_1 O_3 A_2$ and $\angle O_1 A_2 A_3 = \frac{1}{2} \angle A_1 O_2 A_3$, and T is the foot of the perpendicular from O_1 to $A_2 A_3$. Prove that:

(a) $A_1 O_1$ is perpendicular to $O_2 O_3$;

(b) $\dfrac{A_1 O_1}{O_2 O_3} = 2 \dfrac{O_1 T}{A_2 A_3}$.

Solution

Let $X \longmapsto X'$ be the linear transformation that rotates a vector X counterclockwise by $90°$. Let M and N be the mid-points of $A_1 A_3$ and $A_1 A_2$, respectively. Let $\theta = \angle O_1 A_2 A_3$ and $\varphi = \angle O_1 A_3 A_2$. Then $\angle A_3 O_2 M = \angle A_1 O_2 M = \theta$ and $\angle A_2 O_3 N = \angle A_1 O_3 N = \varphi$. Let $a = \cot\theta$, $b = \cot\varphi$, and $c = a + b$. Let $P = \overrightarrow{A_1 N} = \overrightarrow{N A_2}$, $Q = \overrightarrow{A_1 M} = \overrightarrow{M A_3}$, $R = \overrightarrow{T O_1}$, $H = \overrightarrow{A_1 T}$, and $V = \overrightarrow{N M}$.

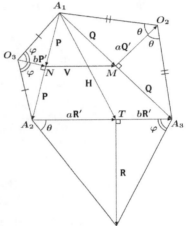

Now $\overrightarrow{M O_2} = a Q'$, $\overrightarrow{O_3 N} = b P'$, $\overrightarrow{A_2 T} = a R'$, and $\overrightarrow{T A_3} = b R'$. Note that $(a+b)R' = 2V$; that is, $V = \frac{c}{2} R'$. Also, since $A_2 T : T A_3 = a : b$, we have

$$H = \frac{a}{a+b}(2Q) + \frac{b}{a+b}(2P) = \frac{2}{c}(aQ + bP).$$

Thus, $aQ + bP = \frac{c}{2}H$.

Now, $\overrightarrow{A_1 O_1} = H + R$ and

$$\overrightarrow{O_3 O_2} = bP' + V + aQ' = (aQ + bP)' + V = \frac{c}{2}H' + \frac{c}{2}R' = \frac{c}{2}(\overrightarrow{A_1 O_1})'.$$

This proves assertion (a).

Also, $A_1 O_1 : O_2 O_3 = 2 : c$ and $2 O_1 T : A_2 A_3 = 2|R| : c|R'| = 2 : c$, which proves (b).

Let O be the circumcentre and H the orthocentre of an acute triangle ABC. Prove that there exist points D, E, and F on sides BC, CA, and AB, respectively, such that $OD + DH = OE + EH = OF + FH$ and the lines AD, BE, and CF are concurrent.

Solution

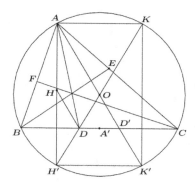

Let Γ be the circumcircle of $\triangle ABC$. It is well known that the reflection H' of H in BC lies on Γ. Note that O and H' are on opposite sides of BC (because $\triangle ABC$ is acute). Let D be the point of intersection of BC and OH', and let E and F be similarly constructed on CA and AB, respectively. We show that the points D, E, F satisfy the conditions in the problem.

First, $OD + DH = OE + EH = OF + FH = R$, the radius of Γ. This follows from $OD + DH = OD + DH' = OH' = R$, for example. Now consider the points K and K' which are diametrically opposite to H' and A, respectively, on Γ. Then $AKK'H'$ is a rectangle with centre O whose sides are parallel to AH and BC. As a result, AO meets BC at D', the point which is symmetrical to D about the mid-point A' of BC (see the diagram). A similar property holds for the points E' and F' at which BO and CO meet CA and AB, respectively. Since AO, BO, CO are concurrent, Ceva's Theorem yields

$$\frac{BD'}{D'C} \cdot \frac{CE'}{E'A} \cdot \frac{AF'}{F'B} = 1.$$

Hence,

$$\frac{-CD}{-DB} \cdot \frac{-BE}{-EC} \cdot \frac{-BF}{-FA} = 1.$$

By the converse of Ceva's Theorem, it follows that AD, BE, and CF are concurrent (they cannot be parallel, since D, E, F are on the segments BC, CA, AB, respectively).

Ten gangsters are standing on a flat surface. The distances between them are all distinct. Simultaneously each of them shoots at the one
among the other nine who is the nearest. At least how many gangsters will
be shot at?

Solution

The problem can be stated mathematically as follows: A set S of ten
points in the plane is given. The distances between them are all distinct. For
each point $P \in S$, we colour red the point $Q \in S$ nearest to P ($Q \neq P$).
Find the least possible number of red points.

Note that if a red point Q is assigned (as the closest neighbour) to two
distinct points P_1 and P_2 in S, then the angle $P_1 Q P_2$ must be greater than
$60°$, because $P_1 P_2$ must be the longest side in the (non-isosceles) triangle
$P_1 Q P_2$. It follows that no red point can be assigned to more than five distinct
points in S.

Let AB be the shortest segment with end-points A, $B \in S$. Clearly, A
and B are both red. We are going to show that there exists at least one more
red point. Assume instead that, for each one of the remaining eight points,
its closest neighbour is either A or B. In view of the previous observation, A
must be assigned to four points M_1, M_2, M_3, M_4 and B must be assigned to
the remaining four points, N_1, N_2, N_3, N_4. Choose labelling such that the
angles $M_i A M_{i+1}$, $i = 1$, 2, 3, are successively adjacent, as are the angles
$N_i B N_{i+1}$, with the points M_1 and N_1 on one side of the line AB, and M_4
and N_4 on the opposite side.

The angles $M_i A M_{i+1}$ and $N_i B N_{i+1}$ are each greater than $60°$.
Therefore, $\angle M_1 A M_4$ and $\angle N_1 B N_4$ are each less than $180°$. Hence,

$$(\angle M_1 A B + \angle N_1 B A) + (\angle M_4 A B + \angle N_4 B A) < 360° \, .$$

At least one of the two sums on the left side
is less than $180°$, say, $\angle M_1 A B + \angle N_1 B A < 180°$.
From here on, we write M and N in place of M_1
and N_1, for the sake of brevity.

Since $MA < MB$ and $NB < NA$, the
points A and M lie on one side of the perpendicular bisector of AB, and the points B and N lie
on the other side. Hence, because M and N lie
on the same side of AB, the points A, B, N, M
are consecutive vertices of a quadrilateral. Since
AB is the shortest side of the triangle BNA, the
angle BNA is acute. Since MA is not the longest
side in the triangle ANM, the angle ANM is
acute. Therefore, the internal angle BNM of the
quadrilateral $ABNM$ is less than $180°$. Similarly,
the internal angle NMA is less than $180°$. Thus,
$ABNM$ is a convex quadrilateral.

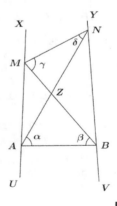

Choose points U, V, X, Y arbitrarily on the rays MA, NB, AM, BN produced beyond the quadrilateral. Recall that $\angle MAB + \angle NBA < 180°$. This implies that

$$\angle UAB + \angle ABV \; > \; 180° \quad \text{and} \quad \angle XMN + \angle MNY \; < \; 180°\,.$$

Let $\alpha = \angle NAB$, $\beta = \angle ABM$, $\gamma = \angle BMN$, and $\delta = \angle MNA$. In $\triangle NAB$, we have $AB < NB$, which implies that $\angle ANB < \angle NAB = \alpha$, and, thus, $\angle ABV = \angle NAB + \angle ANB < 2\alpha$. In $\triangle BMN$, we have $MN > BN$, which implies that $\angle MBN > \angle BMN = \gamma$, and, consequently, $\angle MNY = \angle BMN + \angle MBN > 2\gamma$. Analogously, $\angle UAB < 2\beta$ and $\angle XMN > 2\delta$. Hence,

$$2\alpha+2\beta \; > \; \angle ABV+\angle UAB \; > \; 180° \; > \; \angle MNY+\angle XMN \; > \; 2\gamma+2\delta\,.$$

But $\alpha + \beta = \gamma + \delta = \angle AZM$, where Z is the point of intersection of AN and BM. We have a contradiction. Thus, indeed, there exists a third red point.

The following example shows that a fourth red point need not exist, so that *three* is the minimum sought. The two tangent circles in the figure differ slightly in size. The acute central angles are greater than $60°$. Six points of S are just a bit outside the circles, two points are the centres of the circles, one point is the point of tangency of the circles, and one point is on the common tangent to the circles at a distance which is slightly greater than the radius of the larger circle. The only three points which will be marked red are the two centres and the point of tangency. (If some of the distances happen to be equal, one can slightly perturb the positions of any points without changing the nearest neighbours.)

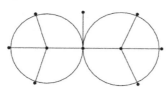

In the plane we are given two circles intersecting at X and Y. Prove that there exist four points such that for every circle touching the two given circles at A and B, and meeting the line XY at C and D, each of the lines AC, AD, BC, and BD passes through one of those four points.

Solution

The four points of contact of the two given circles with their common tangents have the required property, as we will now prove.

Let Γ be a circle that touches the two given circles at points A and B and meets the line XY at points C and D. Then Γ touches the two given circles either both externally or both internally. In the latter case, the two given circles may be situated inside Γ or outside Γ. The latter subcase is illustrated in the diagram; however, the reasoning that follows is valid for any other situation, without any modifications.

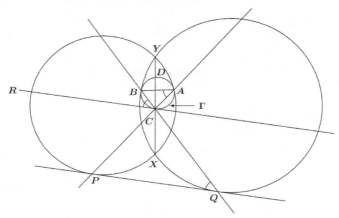

It is enough to consider the lines CA and CB. Let CA meet the circle (AXY) again at P, and let CB meet the circle (BXY) again at Q. Since C lies on XY, we have $CA \cdot CP = CX \cdot CY = CB \cdot CQ$, by the Power of the Point Theorem. Thus, the triangles CAB and CQP are similar, implying that $\angle CAB = \angle CQP$.

Draw the line CR tangent to Γ, with R lying on the same side of line XY as B. Then $\angle BCR = \angle CAB = \angle CQP$, implying that $CR \parallel PQ$. Consider the two homotheties, centred at A and B, respectively, that map Γ onto the two given circles. One of the homotheties transforms the line CR to the line tangent at P to one of these circles, and the other homothety takes CR to the line tangent at Q to the other circle. Both these image lines are parallel to CR; hence, they coincide with the line PQ, which is, therefore, a common tangent to those circles.

The tangents at B and A to the circumcircle of an acute triangle ABC meet the tangent at C at T and U, respectively. The lines AT and BC meet at P, and Q is the mid-point of AP; the lines BU and CA meet at R, and S is the mid-point of BR.

(a) Prove that $\angle ABQ = \angle BAS$.

(b) Determine, in terms of ratios of side lengths, the triangles for which this angle is a maximum.

Solution

In $\triangle ABC$, let $\alpha = \angle A$, $\beta = \angle B$, $\gamma = \angle C$. By the tangent-chord theorem, we get $\angle TBC = \angle TCB = \angle BAC = \alpha$. Let R denote the circumradius of $\triangle ABC$. The isosceles triangle BCT gives

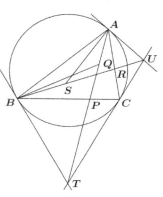

$$BT = \frac{BC}{2\cos\alpha} = R\tan\alpha.$$

By the Law of Sines in $\triangle ABT$, we have $\dfrac{AB}{BT} = \dfrac{\sin\angle ATB}{\sin\angle BAT}$. Let $\varphi = \angle BAT$. Noting that $\angle ABT = \alpha + \beta$, we get

$$\frac{AB}{BT} = \frac{\sin(\alpha+\beta+\varphi)}{\sin\varphi}.$$

Using the relations $AB = 2R\sin\gamma$, $BT = R\tan\alpha$, and $\alpha + \beta + \gamma = 180°$, we obtain

$$\cot\varphi = \cot\gamma + 2\cot\alpha. \tag{1}$$

Next, we set $\angle ABQ = \psi$ and apply the Law of Sines to $\triangle BAQ$ and $\triangle BPQ$. This gives

$$\frac{BQ}{QA} = \frac{\sin\varphi}{\sin\psi} \quad\text{and}\quad \frac{BQ}{PQ} = \frac{\sin\angle APB}{\sin(\beta-\psi)} = \frac{\sin(\beta+\varphi)}{\sin(\beta-\psi)}.$$

Since Q is the mid-point of AP, we have $PQ = QA$. Thus, the ratios in the two equations above are equal. This gives $\dfrac{\sin\varphi}{\sin\psi} = \dfrac{\sin(\beta+\varphi)}{\sin(\beta-\psi)}$, or $\dfrac{\sin(\beta+\varphi)}{\sin\varphi} = \dfrac{\sin(\beta-\psi)}{\sin\psi}$. Hence, $\sin\beta\cot\varphi + \cos\beta = \sin\beta\cot\psi - \cos\beta$, leading to $\cot\psi = 2\cot\beta + \cot\varphi$. In this last equation, we use (1) to get

$$\cot\angle ABQ = \cot\psi = 2(\cot\alpha + \cot\beta) + \cot\gamma. \tag{2}$$

It follows, by symmetry, that $\cot\angle BAS = \cot\angle ABQ$. Then $\angle ABQ = \angle BAS$ (since the cotangent function is strictly decreasing in the open interval $(0°, 180°)$). We have proved (a).

Maximizing ψ is equivalent to minimizing $\cot \psi$, which can be done using formula (2). Since

$$
\begin{aligned}
\cot \alpha + \cot \beta &= \frac{\sin \beta \cos \alpha + \sin \alpha \cos \beta}{\sin \alpha \sin \beta} = \frac{\sin \gamma}{\sin \alpha \sin \beta} \\
&= \frac{2 \sin \gamma}{\cos(\alpha - \beta) - \cos(\alpha + \beta)} = \frac{2 \sin \gamma}{\cos(\alpha - \beta) + \cos \gamma} \\
&\geq \frac{2 \sin \gamma}{1 + \cos \gamma},
\end{aligned}
$$

we have

$$
\begin{aligned}
\cot \psi &\geq \frac{4 \sin \gamma}{1 + \cos \gamma} + \cot \gamma \\
&= 4 \tan \tfrac{\gamma}{2} + \frac{1 - \tan^2 \tfrac{\gamma}{2}}{2 \tan \tfrac{\gamma}{2}} = \tfrac{7}{2} \tan \tfrac{\gamma}{2} + \frac{1}{2 \tan \tfrac{\gamma}{2}}.
\end{aligned}
$$

Applying the AM–GM Inequality, we obtain

$$
\cot \psi \geq \sqrt{7 \tan \tfrac{\gamma}{2} \cdot \frac{1}{\tan \tfrac{\gamma}{2}}} = \sqrt{7}.
$$

For equality, it is necessary that $\alpha = \beta = 90° - \gamma/2$ and $7 \tan \tfrac{\gamma}{2} = 1/\tan \tfrac{\gamma}{2}$. These conditions give $\sin \gamma = \sqrt{7}/4$ and $\sin \alpha = \sin \beta = \sqrt{14}/4$. Hence, by the Law of Sines, the angle ψ is a maximum when the ratios of side lengths of $\triangle ABC$ are

$$
a : b : c = \sqrt{2} : \sqrt{2} : 1.
$$

We are given a triangle ABC having $k(U, r)$ as its circumcircle. Next we construct the 'doubled' circle $k(U, 2r)$ and its two tangents parallel to $c = AB$. Among them we select the one (and designate it c') for which C lies between c and c'. In a similar way we get the tangents a' and b'.

Let $A'B'C'$ be the triangle having its sides on a', b', and c', respectively. Prove: The lines joining the mid-points of corresponding sides of the two triangles intersect in a single point.

Solution

Triangles ABC and $A'B'C'$ have equal corresponding angles and are therefore similar. Corresponding sides of these triangles are parallel, which means that the triangles are homothetic. It follows that AA', BB', CC' are concurrent at a point P. Likewise, if L, M, N are the mid-points of ABC and L', M', N' are the mid-points of $A'B'C'$, then (L, L'), (M, M'), and (N, N') are pairs of corresponding points; that is, LL', MM', NN' pass through P.

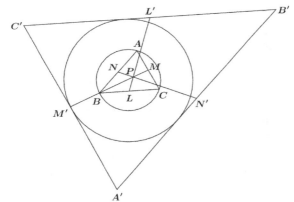

We are given a semicircle s with diameter AB. On s we choose any two points C and D such that $AC = CD$. The tangent at C intersects line BD in a point E. Line AE intersects s at point F.

Prove that $CD < FD$.

Solution

Presumably, the question should read: Prove that $CF < FD$ (and not $CD < FD$).

Take rectangular Cartesian coordinates with origin $O(0,0)$ at the centre of S and with $A(-1,0)$ and $B(1,0)$. Let θ be the angle subtended at O by AC. Then $0 < \theta < \frac{\pi}{2}$, and $C(-\cos\theta, \sin\theta)$ and $D(-\cos 2\theta, \sin 2\theta)$.

Letting M be the mid-point of the arc CD, we have $M\left(-\cos(\frac{3}{2}\theta), \sin(\frac{3}{2}\theta)\right)$.

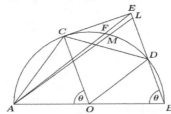

Since $AC = CD$, the angle subtended at B by AD is equal to θ. Hence, BD is parallel to OC and has equation $x\sin\theta + y\cos\theta = \sin\theta$. The equation of the tangent at C is $-x\cos\theta + y\sin\theta = 1$. Letting E be the point at which these two lines meet, we find that the coordinates of E are

$$x = 1 - (1 + \cos\theta)\cos\theta \quad \text{and} \quad y = (1 + \cos\theta)\sin\theta.$$

It follows that $\overrightarrow{BE} = [-(1 + \cos\theta)\cos\theta, (1 + \cos\theta)\sin\theta]$.

Now, $\overrightarrow{AM} = [1 - \cos(\frac{3}{2}\theta), \sin(\frac{3}{2}\theta)]$. The slope of AM is therefore

$$\frac{\sin(\frac{3}{2}\theta)}{1 - \cos(\frac{3}{2}\theta)} = \frac{2\sin(\frac{3}{4}\theta)\cos(\frac{3}{4}\theta)}{2\sin^2(\frac{3}{4}\theta)} = \cot(\frac{3}{4}\theta),$$

and the equation of AM is $y\sin(\frac{3}{4}\theta) = (x + 1)\cos(\frac{3}{4}\theta)$.

Let L be the point at which AM meets BD. The coordinates of L are

$$x = -\frac{\cos(\frac{7}{4}\theta)}{\cos(\frac{1}{4}\theta)} \quad \text{and}$$

$$y = \frac{2\cos(\frac{3}{4}\theta)\sin\theta}{\cos(\frac{1}{4}\theta)} = \frac{2\left(4\cos^3(\frac{1}{4}\theta) - 3\cos(\frac{1}{4}\theta)\right)\sin\theta}{\cos(\frac{1}{4}\theta)}$$

$$= 2\left(4\cos^2(\frac{1}{4}\theta) - 3\right)\sin\theta.$$

We aim to show that $BL < BE$, which implies that $CF < FD$ (see the diagram). It is thus sufficient to prove that

$$2\left(4\cos^2(\frac{1}{4}\theta) - 3\right)\sin\theta < (1 + \cos\theta)\sin\theta.$$

Since $\theta \neq 0$, this is true if and only if

$$8\cos^2\left(\tfrac{1}{4}\theta\right) \;<\; 7 + \cos\theta\,. \tag{1}$$

Now consider $f(\theta) = 7 + \cos\theta - 8\cos^2\left(\tfrac{1}{4}\theta\right)$. We have $f(0) = 0$, and

$$\begin{aligned}
\frac{df}{d\theta} &= -\sin\theta + 4\cos\left(\tfrac{1}{4}\theta\right)\sin\left(\tfrac{1}{4}\theta\right) \;=\; -\sin\theta + 2\sin\left(\tfrac{1}{2}\theta\right) \\
&= -2\sin\left(\tfrac{1}{2}\theta\right)\cos\left(\tfrac{1}{2}\theta\right) + 2\sin\left(\tfrac{1}{2}\theta\right) \;=\; 2\sin\left(\tfrac{1}{2}\theta\right)\left(1 - \cos\left(\tfrac{1}{2}\theta\right)\right)\,,
\end{aligned}$$

which is positive for $0 < \theta \leq \tfrac{\pi}{2}$. Therefore, (1) holds, and the inequality is proved.

In the triangle ABC, the bisector of angle B meets AC at D, and the bisector of angle C meets AB at E. The bisectors intersect at O, and $OD = OE$. Prove that either $\triangle ABC$ is isosceles or $\angle BAC = 60°$.

Solution

The bisector of $\angle BAC$ is AO. Let α, β, γ, θ, and φ be angles as shown in the diagram. Since

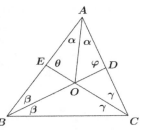

$$\frac{\sin \theta}{\sin \alpha} = \frac{AO}{OE} = \frac{AO}{OD} = \frac{\sin \varphi}{\sin \alpha},$$

we have $\sin \theta = \sin \varphi$. Thus, either $\theta = \varphi$, or θ and φ are supplementary.

(a) If $\theta = \varphi$, then $2\beta + \gamma = \beta + 2\gamma$. Consequently, $\beta = \gamma$ and $\triangle ABC$ is isosceles.

(b) If θ and φ are supplementary, then $(2\beta + \gamma) + (\beta + 2\gamma) = 180°$. It follows that $\beta + \gamma = 60°$. Hence, $\angle BAC = 60°$.

Two circles touch each other externally at A. A common tangent touches one circle at B and the other at C ($B \neq C$). The segments BD and CE are diameters of the circles. Prove that D, A, and C are collinear.

Solution

Let the tangent at A meet BC at P. Then $PA = PB = PC$ (since these three segments are tangents from the external point P). Hence, P is the centre of the circle BAC. Thus, BC is a diameter of this circle, and $\angle BAC = 90°$. Similarly, $\angle BAD = 90°$, since BD is a diameter of the circle BAD. Therefore,

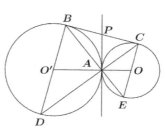

$$\angle DAC = \angle BAD + \angle BAC$$
$$= 90° + 90° = 180°.$$

Hence, D, A, C are collinear.

Next we give the presentation by Bataille.

Consider the homothety h with centre A which transforms the circle ACE into the circle ABD. Since the lines CE and BD are both perpendicular to the line BC, we have $CE \parallel BD$. In addition, CE and BD pass through the centres O and O' of ACE and ABD (respectively) and $h(O) = O'$; whence, the image of the line CE under h is the line BD. Therefore $h(C)$ is a point on the line BD and on the circle ABD. But $h(C)$ cannot be B (since C, A, B are not collinear); thus, we must have $h(C) = D$, and D, A, C are collinear.

An acute triangle ABC, with $AC \neq BC$, is inscribed in a circle ω. The points A, B, C divide the circle into disjoint arcs $\overset{\frown}{AB}$, $\overset{\frown}{BC}$, and $\overset{\frown}{CA}$. Let M and N be the mid-points of $\overset{\frown}{BC}$ and $\overset{\frown}{AC}$, respectively, and let K be an arbitrary point of $\overset{\frown}{AB}$. Let D be the point of $\overset{\frown}{MN}$ such that $CD \parallel NM$. Let O, O_1, O_2 be the incentres of triangles ABC, CAK, CBK, respectively. Let L be the intersection point of the line DO and the circle ω, where $L \neq D$. Prove that the points K, O_1, O_2, L are concyclic.

Solution

Since M and N are the mid-points of $\overset{\frown}{BC}$ and $\overset{\frown}{AC}$, respectively, we see that AM and BN are the bisectors of $\angle CAB$ and $\angle CBA$, respectively. Thus, the intersection of AM and BN is the incentre O of $\triangle ABC$. Since O is the incentre of $\triangle ABC$, we have $\angle ACO = \angle BCO$. Hence,

$$\begin{aligned} \angle MOC &= \angle ACO + \angle CAM &= \angle BCO + \angle BAM \\ &= \angle BCO + \angle BCM &= \angle MCO. \end{aligned}$$

Thus, $MO = MC = MB$. Similarly, we get $NO = NC = NA$.

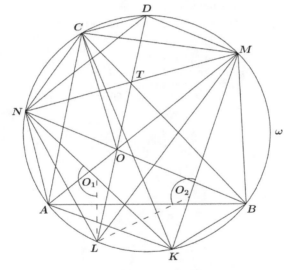

Since O_1 and O_2 are the incentres of $\triangle CAK$ and $\triangle CBK$, respectively, we similarly obtain

$$NO_1 = NC = NA, \quad \text{and} \quad MO_2 = MC = MB.$$

Since $CD \parallel MN$, we have $MD = NC = NO$, and $DN = CM = MO$. Hence, quadrilateral $MDNO$ is a parallelogram. Let T be the intersection of DO and MN. Then $NT = TM$.

Since $\triangle NLT \sim \triangle DMT$, and $\triangle MLT \sim \triangle DNT$, we obtain

$$NL : DM = LT : MT = LT : NT = ML : DN.$$

Hence, $NL : ML = DM : DN$. Since $DM = CN = NO_1$, and $DN = CM = MO_2$, we have

$$NL : ML = NO_1 : MO_2. \tag{1}$$

Since $\angle LNO_1 = \angle LNK = \angle LMK = \angle LMO_2$, we get from (1)

$$\triangle NLO_1 \sim \triangle MLO_2.$$

Thus, $\angle NO_1L = \angle MO_2L$. Hence,

$$\angle LO_1K = 180° - \angle NO_1L = 180° - \angle MO_2L = \angle LO_2K.$$

Therefore, K, O_1, O_2, L are concyclic.

The incircle γ of triangle ABC touches the side AB at T. Let D be the point on γ diametrically opposite to T, and let S be the intersection of the line through C and D with the side AB. Show that $AT = SB$.

Solution

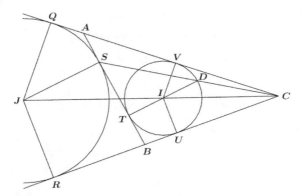

Let γ touch BC at U and CA at V. Let I be the incentre and J be the point of intersection of the line CI and the perpendicular to AB at S. Let Q, R be the projections of J onto the lines CA, CB, respectively (see figure). Note that $ID \parallel JS$, $UI \parallel JR$, $IV \parallel JQ$. It follows that $\dfrac{CI}{CJ} = \dfrac{IU}{JR} = \dfrac{ID}{JS}$. Since $IU = ID$ (the inradius), we obtain $JR = JS$. Similarly, $JQ = JS$. Hence, $JQ = JR = JS$ (and clearly $J \neq I$). Thus, J is the excentre in $\angle ACB$, and the excircle with centre J touches CA, AB, CB at Q, S, R, respectively.

Now, it is well known that $AT = BS = s - a$ (with the standard notations) [briefly, $b - a = BR - QA = BS - SA = 2BS - c$ and $b - a = AV - BU = AT - BT = 2AT - c$, from which we obtain $BS = AT = \frac{1}{2}(b + c - a) = s - a$].

Let $ABCD$ be a parallelogram, and let K and L be points lying on the sides BC and CD, respectively, such that $BK \cdot AD = DL \cdot AB$. The segments DK and BL intersect at P. Show that $\angle DAP = \angle BAC$.

Solution

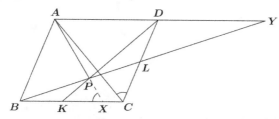

Let X and Y be the intersections of AP and BL with BC and AD, respectively. Since $BX \parallel AY$, we have

$$BK : BX = YD : YA.$$

Since $DL \parallel AB$, we see that $YD : YA = DL : AB$, and then $BK : BX = DL : AB$; that is,

$$BK : DL = BX : AB. \tag{1}$$

Since $BK \cdot AD = DL \cdot AB$, we have

$$BK : DL = AB : AD. \tag{2}$$

It follows from (1) and (2) that

$$BX : AB = AB : AD = DC : AD. \tag{3}$$

Since $\angle ABX = \angle ADC$, we have from (3)

$$\triangle ABX \sim \triangle ADC.$$

Thus,

$$\angle AXB = \angle ACD. \tag{4}$$

Since $AD \parallel BX$, and $AB \parallel DC$, we have $\angle AXB = \angle DAX = \angle DAP$ and $\angle ACD = \angle BAC$. Therefore, using (4), we get $\angle DAP = \angle BAC$.

Points A, B, C, D lie on the line ℓ, in that order. Find the locus of points P in the plane for which $\angle APB = \angle CPD$.

Solution

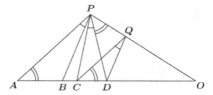

Let P be a point such that $\angle APB = \angle CPD$. Let Q be the point such that $QC \parallel PA$ and $QD \parallel PB$. Then $\triangle PAB \sim \triangle QCD$, implying that $\angle CQD = \angle APB = \angle CPD$. Thus, P, C, D, and Q are concyclic.

Case 1. $AB = CD$.

Then $\triangle PAB \equiv \triangle QCD$. Thus, $PB = QD$. Therefore, $PBDQ$ is a parallelogram. Hence, $PQ \parallel BD$; that is $PQ \parallel CD$. Since P, C, D, Q are concyclic, we have $PC = QD$. Hence, $PB = PC$. Thus, the locus of P is the perpendicular bisector of BC (excluding the mid-point of BC).

Case 2. $AB \neq CD$.

Let O be the point of intersection of PQ with AD. Since $PA \parallel QC$, we have $OA : OC = PA : QC$. Also, since $\triangle PAB \sim \triangle QCD$, we have $PA : QC = AB : CD$. Therefore, $OA : OC = AB : CD$, which is a constant ratio. Thus, O is a fixed point.

Since P, C, Q, D are concyclic, we have $\angle QPD = \angle QCD = \angle PAB$; that is, $\angle OPD = \angle PAO$, from which we get $OP^2 = OA \cdot OD$. Thus, $OP = \sqrt{OA \cdot OD}$, a constant. Therefore, the locus of P is the circle with centre O and radius $\sqrt{OA \cdot OD}$ (excluding the points of intersection with the line ℓ).

A triangle ABC is given. The mid-points of sides AC and AB are B_1 and C_1, respectively. The centre of the incircle of $\triangle ABC$ is I. The lines $B_1 I$, $C_1 I$ meet the sides AB, AC at C_2, B_2, respectively. Given that the areas of $\triangle ABC$ and $\triangle AB_2C_2$ are equal, what is $\angle BAC$?

Solution

We set $BC = a$, $CA = b$, $AB = c$, $AC_2 = x$ and $AB_2 = y$. Since $[AB_2C_2] = [ABC]$ (where $[PQR]$ denotes the area of triangle PQR), we have $xy = bc$.

Let D and E be the intersections of BI and CI with AC and AB, respectively. Since AI and CI are the bisectors of $\angle BAD$ and $\angle BCD$, we have

$$\frac{BI}{ID} = \frac{AB}{AD} = \frac{BC}{CD} = \frac{AB + BC}{AD + CD} = \frac{AB + BC}{AC} = \frac{a + c}{b}.$$

Similarly, $\dfrac{CI}{IE} = \dfrac{a+b}{c}$.

Since BD is the bisector of $\angle ABC$, we have

$$AD : DC = AB : BC = c : a.$$

From this, we get $AD = \dfrac{bc}{a+c}$. Similarly, $AE = \dfrac{bc}{a+b}$.

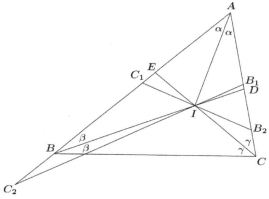

Case 1. $c = a$.

Then B_1 coincides with D, and therefore C_2 coincides with B. Thus, $x = c$ and $y = b$. Hence, B_2 coincides with C, and C_1 coincides with E. Thus, $AC = BC$; that is $b = a$. Thus, $a = b = c$. Hence, $\triangle ABC$ is equilateral, and we get $\angle BAC = 60°$.

Case 2. $a < c$.

Then $x > c$, and $y < b$, from which we get $a > b$. By Menelaus' Theorem for $\triangle ABD$, we have

$$\frac{AC_2}{C_2B} \cdot \frac{BI}{ID} \cdot \frac{DB_1}{B_1A} = 1 . \tag{1}$$

Since $DB_1 = AD - AB_1 = \dfrac{bc}{a+c} - \dfrac{b}{2} = \dfrac{b(c-a)}{2(a+c)}$, we have $\dfrac{DB_1}{B_1A} = \dfrac{c-a}{a+c}$.

Now (1) becomes

$$\frac{x}{x-c} \cdot \frac{a+c}{b} \cdot \frac{c-a}{a+c} = 1 ;$$

whence, $\dfrac{x}{x-c} = \dfrac{b}{c-a}$. Thus, $x = \dfrac{bc}{b-c+a}$. Similarly, $y = \dfrac{bc}{c-b+a}$.
Since $xy = bc$, we get

$$bc = \frac{b^2c^2}{(b-c+a)(c-b+a)} .$$

Then $a^2 - (b-c)^2 = bc$, or equivalently, $a^2 = b^2 - bc + c^2$. Since $a^2 = b^2 + c^2 - 2bc \cos \angle BAC$, we get $\cos \angle BAC = \frac{1}{2}$. Thus, $\angle BAC = 60°$.

Case 3. $a > c$.

As in case 2, we can prove that $\angle BAC = 60°$.

Let I and O be the incentre and circumcentre, respectively, of $\triangle ABC$. Assume $\triangle ABC$ is not equilateral (so that $I \neq O$). Prove that $\angle AIO \leq 90°$ if and only if $2BC \leq AB + CA$.

Solution

We will prove that $\angle AIO \leq 90°$ if and only if $2BC \leq AB + CA$ (as required), and we will also prove that equality holds on one side of this equivalence if and only if it holds on the other side. We will use standard notation for the elements of the triangle ABC.

By the Cosine Law in $\triangle AIO$, we have

$$AO^2 = AI^2 + IO^2 - 2(AI)(IO)\cos\angle AIO \,.$$

Since $\angle AIO \leq 90°$ if and only if $\cos\angle AIO \geq 0$, we deduce that

$$\angle AIO \leq 90° \quad \Longleftrightarrow \quad AO^2 \leq AI^2 + IO^2 \,. \tag{1}$$

Furthermore, equality occurs on one side of this equivalence if and only if it occurs on the other side.

We have

$$AI^2 = \frac{(s-a)^2}{\cos^2(A/2)} = \frac{(b+c-a)^2}{2(1+\cos A)} = \frac{bc(b+c-a)}{2s} \,,$$

where the last step makes use of the Cosine Law in $\triangle ABC$. Now $rs = \frac{abc}{4R}$ (since both expressions are equal to the area of $\triangle ABC$), and therefore,

$$AI^2 = \frac{2Rr}{a}(b+c-a) \,.$$

We also have $AO^2 = R^2$ and $IO^2 = R^2 - 2Rr$. Hence,

$$\begin{aligned} AI^2 + IO^2 &= \frac{2Rr}{a}(b+c-a) + (R^2 - 2Rr) \\ &= AO^2 + \frac{2Rr}{a}(b+c-2a) \,. \end{aligned}$$

Thus, $AI^2 + IO^2 \geq AO^2$ if and only if $b + c \geq 2a$, and equality in either of these inequalities implies equality in the other. Recalling (1), we obtain the desired conclusion.

Let ABC be a non-isosceles acute triangle, and let E be an interior point of the median AD, with D on BC. Let F be the orthogonal projection of E onto the line BC. Let M be an interior point of the segment EF, and let N and P be the orthogonal projections of M onto the lines AC and AB, respectively. Prove that the bisectors of angles PMN and PEN are parallel.

Solution

Since $\triangle ABC$ is not isosceles, we may assume that $AB < AC$.

As usual, we set $\alpha = \angle CAB$, $\beta = \angle ABC$, and $\gamma = \angle BCA$. We further set $\alpha_1 = \angle BAD$ and $\alpha_2 = \angle CAD$. Then

$$\sin \alpha_1 : \sin \alpha_2 \; = \; \sin \beta : \sin \gamma \; = \; b : c . \tag{1}$$

Let K and L be the points on AC and AB, respectively, such that $EK \perp AC$ and $EL \perp AB$. Then $EK = AE \sin \alpha_2$ and $EL = AE \sin \alpha_1$. Hence, using (1), we get

$$EK : EL \; = \; \sin \gamma : \sin \beta . \tag{2}$$

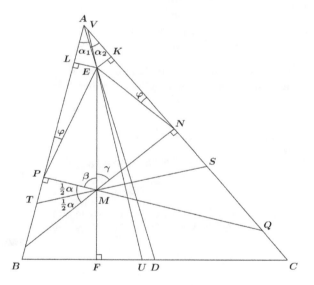

Since quadrilateral $BFMP$ is cyclic, we have $\angle PME = \beta$. Similarly, $\angle NME = \gamma$ and $\angle NMQ = \alpha$, where Q is the point where the production of PM meets the line AC. Then $KN = EM \sin \gamma$ and $LP = EM \sin \beta$. This, together with (2), implies that $EK : EL = KN : LP$. Since we also have $\angle NKE = \angle PLE = 90°$, it follows that

$$\triangle EKN \sim \triangle ELP . \tag{3}$$

Setting $\varphi = \angle ENK = \angle EPL$, we see that

$$\angle PEN = 360° - (180° - \alpha) - 2(90° - \varphi) = 2\varphi + \alpha.$$

Let the bisector of $\angle PEN$ meet BC at U. Then $\angle UEN = \varphi + \frac{1}{2}\alpha$. Let the production of UE intersect AC at V. In $\triangle NEV$, we see that $\angle EVN + \angle VNE = \varphi + \frac{1}{2}\alpha$. Since $\angle VNE = \varphi$, we have $\angle EVN = \frac{1}{2}\alpha$. This implies that EU is parallel to the bisector of $\angle BAC$.

Let the bisector of $\angle NMQ$ intersect AC at S, and the production of SM intersect AB at T. It is easy to see that $\triangle ATS$ is isosceles, since both $\angle ATS$ and $\angle AST$ have the value $90° - \frac{1}{2}\alpha$. Thus, the bisector of $\angle BAC$ is perpendicular to ST. The bisector of $\angle PMN$ is also perpendicular to ST, since it is perpendicular to the bisector of $\angle NMQ$.

Thus, the bisectors of angles PMN and PEN are both parallel to that of $\angle BAC$.

The lengths of the sides of triangle ABC are 4, 5, 6. For any point D on one of the sides, drop the perpendiculars DP, DQ onto the other two sides (P, Q are on the sides). What is the minimal value of PQ?

Solution

First we consider an arbitrary acute triangle ABC. We set $a = BC$, $b = CA$, $c = AB$, $\alpha = \angle A$, $\beta = \angle B$, and $\gamma = \angle C$, and we denote by R the circumradius of $\triangle ABC$.

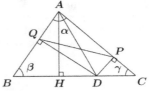

Suppose that D is on the side BC. Let H be the foot of the perpendicular from A to BC, and let P and Q be the feet of the perpendiculars from D to AC and AB, respectively. Since $AQDP$ is a cyclic quadrilateral, Ptolemy's Theorem implies that

$$PQ = AD \sin \angle PAQ = AD \sin \alpha \geq AH \sin \alpha.$$

Since

$$AH = AB \sin \beta = c \sin \beta = 2R \sin \gamma \cdot \sin \beta,$$

we see that $AH \sin \alpha = 2R \sin \alpha \sin \beta \sin \gamma$. Thus, the minimal value of PQ is $2R \sin \alpha \sin \beta \sin \gamma$.

If D is a point on either AB or AC, the minimal value of PQ is also $2R \sin \alpha \sin \beta \sin \gamma$. Thus, the minimal value of PQ for any point D on the perimeter of $\triangle ABC$ is $2R \sin \alpha \sin \beta \sin \gamma$; that is, $AH \sin \alpha$.

Now let $a = 6$, $b = 5$, and $c = 4$. Since $a > b > c$, we have $\alpha > \beta > \gamma$. By the Law of Cosines, $a^2 = b^2 + c^2 - 2bc \cos \alpha$, which means that $a^2 = 5^2 + 4^2 - 2 \cdot 5 \cdot 4 \cos \alpha$. Hence, $40 \cos \alpha = 5^2 + 4^2 - 6^2 = 5$, or $\cos \alpha = \frac{1}{8}$. Therefore, α is acute.

Since $\alpha > \beta > \gamma$, we see that $\triangle ABC$ is an acute triangle. Thus, the minimal value of PQ is $AH \sin \alpha$.

Since $\cos \alpha = \frac{1}{8}$, we have $\sin^2 \alpha = 1 - \cos^2 \alpha = 1 - \frac{1}{64} = \frac{63}{64}$. Since $AH \cdot BC = AB \cdot AC \sin \alpha$, we also have $AH \cdot a = bc \sin \alpha$; that is, $AH = \frac{bc \sin \alpha}{a}$. Hence,

$$AH \sin \alpha = \frac{bc \sin^2 \alpha}{a} = \frac{5 \cdot 4}{6} \cdot \frac{63}{64} = \frac{105}{32}.$$

Therefore, the minimal value of PQ is $\frac{105}{32}$.

Let $ABCDE$ be a regular pentagon such that the star $ACEBD$ has area 1. Let P be the point of intersection of AC and BE, and let Q be the point of intersection of BD and CE. Find the area of $APQD$.

Solution

Let R be the point of intersection of AD and BE, and S that of AD and CE. Each corner angle of a regular pentagon is trisected by the two diagonals passing through its vertex into three $36°$ angles. It follows that $PQ \parallel AR$ and $AP \parallel RQ$.

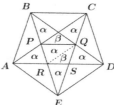

Let $\alpha = [PQR]$ and $\beta = [QRS]$. Then

$$[APQD] = 3\alpha + \beta = \tfrac{1}{2}(6\alpha + 2\beta) = \tfrac{1}{2}[ACEBD] = \tfrac{1}{2}.$$

In the triangle ABC, the point D is the mid-point of the side AB. Point E divides BC in the ratio $BE : EC = 2 : 1$. Given that $\angle ADC = \angle BAE$, determine $\angle BAC$.

Solution

Let the lines CD and AE intersect at O. Let F be the intersection of BO and CA and let P be the intersection of EF and CD.

Then, by Ceva's Theorem, $\dfrac{CF}{FA} \cdot \dfrac{AD}{DB} \cdot \dfrac{BE}{EC} = 1$. But we are assuming that $AD = DB$. Hence, $\dfrac{CF}{FA} = \dfrac{CE}{EB}$, which implies that EF is parallel to AB and

$$\angle EFC = \angle BAC. \tag{1}$$

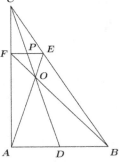

Triangles OAD and OEP have equal corresponding angles and therefore are similar; and since $\triangle OAD$ is isosceles, so is $\triangle OEP$ with $OE = OP$.

Similarly, $\triangle CFE$ is similar to $\triangle CAB$. It follows that

$$\frac{EF}{AD} = \frac{EF}{\frac{1}{2}AB} = 2 \cdot \frac{EF}{AB} = 2 \cdot \frac{CE}{BC}$$

and

$$\frac{AE}{CD} = \frac{PD}{CD} = \frac{BE}{BC}$$

because $AE = AO + OE = DO + OP = PD$.

Since $BE : EC = 2 : 1$, we have $2 \cdot \dfrac{CE}{BC} = \dfrac{BE}{BC} \left(= \dfrac{2}{3} \right)$. Thus, $\dfrac{EF}{AD} = \dfrac{AE}{CD}$ (from above). Therefore, triangles EFA and DAC are similar (SAS) with

$$\angle EFA = \angle DAC = \angle BAC. \tag{2}$$

Now $\angle EFA$ and $\angle EFC$ are supplementary angles and thus sum to $180°$. It follows from (1) and (2) that $\angle BAC = 90°$.

A line divides both the area and the perimeter of a triangle into two equal parts. Prove that this line passes through the incentre of the triangle. Does the converse statement always hold?

Solution

Let ABC be a given triangle with incentre I. We may assume without loss of generality that the line in the problem intersects the sides AB and AC at P and Q, respectively.

We set $a = BC$, $b = CA$, and $c = AB$. Let D be the intersection of AI with BC. Since BI and CI are the bisectors of $\angle ABD$ and $\angle ACD$, respectively, we have

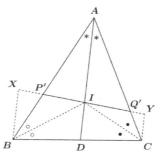

$$\frac{AI}{ID} = \frac{AB}{BD} = \frac{AC}{CD}$$
$$= \frac{AB + AC}{BD + CD}$$
$$= \frac{AB + AC}{BC} = \frac{b + c}{a}.$$

Let ℓ be a line through I which intersects sides AB and AC at P' and Q', respectively. Let X and Y be points on the line $P'Q'$ such that $BX \parallel AD$ and $CY \parallel AD$. Then

$$\frac{P'B}{AP'} = \frac{BX}{AI}, \quad \text{and} \quad \frac{Q'C}{AQ'} = \frac{CY}{AI}.$$

Since $BD : DC = AB : AC = c : b$, and $BX \parallel DI \parallel CY$, we get

$$b \cdot BX + c \cdot CY = (b + c) \cdot DI.$$

Hence,

$$b\frac{BX}{AI} + c\frac{CY}{AI} = (b + c)\frac{DI}{AI};$$

that is,

$$b\frac{P'B}{AP'} + c\frac{Q'C}{AQ'} = (b + c)\frac{DI}{AI}.$$

Conversely, if P' and Q' are points on the sides AB and AC, respectively, and if

$$b\frac{P'B}{AP'} + c\frac{Q'C}{AQ'} = (b + c)\frac{ID}{AI}, \tag{1}$$

then P', Q', and I are collinear. (*Proof:* Let I' be the intersection of $P'Q'$ with AD. Then

$$b\frac{P'B}{AP'} + c\frac{Q'C}{AQ'} = (b + c)\frac{I'D}{AI'},$$

from which we have $\frac{I'D}{AI'} = \frac{ID}{AI}$. Then I' coincides with I.)

Therefore, P, Q, and I are collinear if and only if (1) holds.
We set $x = AP$ and $y = AQ$. Then (1) becomes

$$b\frac{c-x}{x} + c\frac{b-y}{y} = (b+c)\frac{a}{b+c} = a \, ;$$

that is,

$$bc\left(\frac{1}{x} + \frac{1}{y}\right) = a+b+c. \tag{2}$$

If PQ divides both the area and the perimeter of $\triangle ABC$ into two equal parts, then $xy = \frac{1}{2}bc$ and $x+y = \frac{1}{2}(a+b+c)$. Thus,

$$bc\left(\frac{1}{x} + \frac{1}{y}\right) = bc\frac{x+y}{x} = a+b+c,$$

and (2) holds. Therefore, PQ passes through I.

Next we consider converses.

I. If PQ passes through I and divides the area of $\triangle ABC$ into two equal parts, then PQ divides the perimeter of $\triangle ABC$ into two equal parts.

Since $bc\left(\frac{1}{x} + \frac{1}{y}\right) = a+b+c$ and $xy = \frac{1}{2}bc$, we obtain $x+y = \frac{a+b+c}{2}$. Thus, PQ divides the perimeter of $\triangle ABC$ into two equal parts.

II. If PQ passes through I and divides the perimeter of $\triangle ABC$ into two equal parts, then PQ divides the area of $\triangle ABC$ into two equal parts.

Since $bc\left(\frac{1}{x} + \frac{1}{y}\right) = a+b+c$ and $x+y = \frac{a+b+c}{2}$, we have $xy = \frac{1}{2}bc$. Thus, PQ divides the area of $\triangle ABC$ into two equal parts.

III. If PQ passes through I, then PQ divides both the area and the perimeter of $\triangle ABC$ into two equal parts.

This converse is not correct.

Circles C_1 and C_2 intersect at points A and B. A line r through B inter-sects C_1 and C_2 again at points P_r and Q_r, respectively. Prove that there is a point M, which depends only on C_1 and C_2, such that the perpendicular bisector of P_rQ_r passes through M.

Solution

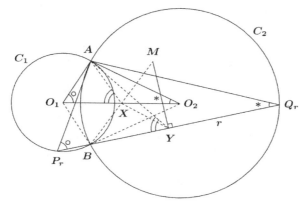

Let O_1 and O_2 be the centres of C_1 and C_2, respectively. Then O_1O_2 is the perpendicular bisector of AB. We have $\triangle AO_1O_2 \sim \triangle AP_rQ_r$, since

$$\angle AO_1O_2 = \tfrac{1}{2}\angle AO_1B = \angle AP_rB = \angle AP_rQ_r$$
$$\text{and} \quad \angle AO_2O_1 = \tfrac{1}{2}\angle AO_2B = \angle AQ_rB = \angle AQ_rP_r \, .$$

Let X and Y be the mid-points of O_1O_2 and P_rQ_r, respectively. Since O_1O_2 and P_rQ_r are corresponding sides in the similar triangles AP_rQ_r and AP_rQ_r, we get $\triangle AXO_1 \sim \triangle AYP_r$, and hence, $\angle AXO_1 = \angle AYP_r$.

Thus, $\angle AYB = \angle AYP_r = \angle AXO_1 = \tfrac{1}{2}\angle AXB$. Since $AX = BX$ and $\angle AXB = 2\angle AYB$, we see that X is the circumcentre of $\triangle AYB$. Then $AX = BX = YX$.

Let M be the reflection of B with respect to X. Then X is the mid-point of BM. Since $MX = BX = YX$, we have $\angle BYM = 90°$. Thus, the perpendicular bisector of P_rQ_r passes through the fixed point M.

Four points are placed in a square of side 1. Show that the distance between some two of them is less than or equal to 1.

Solution

First note that the maximum distance between two points in a square (in its interior or on its boundary) is $\sqrt{2}$.

Let A, B, C, and D be four points placed in a square of side 1. Let $\mathcal{C}$ be the convex hull of $\{A, B, C, D\}$. Clearly, $\mathcal{C}$ is contained in the square.

Case 1. $\mathcal{C}$ is a line segment.

Without loss of generality, we may assume that A, B, C, and D are collinear in that order. Thus, $AB + BC + CD = AD \leq \sqrt{2}$, so that $\min\{AB, BC, CD\} \leq \frac{\sqrt{2}}{3} < 1$, and we are done with this case.

Case 2. $\mathcal{C}$ is a triangle.

Without loss of generality, we may assume that D is inside or on the boundary of ABC, and that $\theta = \angle CDA = \max\{\angle ADB, \angle BDC, \angle CDA\}$.

Since $\angle ADB + \angle BDC + \angle CDA = 2\pi$, we see that $\theta \geq \frac{2\pi}{3}$ and $\cos \theta \leq -\frac{1}{2}$. If AD and DC are greater than 1, then, from the Law of Cosines,

$$AC^2 = AD^2 + DC^2 - 2AD \cdot DC \cos \theta \geq 1 + 1 + AD \cdot DC > 3,$$

which leads to $AC > \sqrt{3} > \sqrt{2}$, a contradiction.

Then $AD \leq 1$ or $DC \leq 1$, and we are done again. In fact, the above argument can easily be strengthened to show that $AD < 1$ or $CD < 1$.

Case 3. $\mathcal{C}$ is a (convex) quadrilateral, say $ABCD$.

Since the convex quadrilateral $ABCD$ is contained in the square, it follows that its perimeter is not greater than the perimeter of the square; that is, $AB + BC + CD + DA \leq 4$. Therefore, $\min\{AB, BC, CD, DA\} \leq 1$, and we are done.

We note that equality occurs if and only if $ABCD$ is the square itself.

In an acute triangle ABC with $|AC| > |BC|$, let M be the mid-point of AB. Let AP be the altitude from A and BQ be the altitude from B. These altitudes meet at H, and the lines AB and PQ meet at R. Prove that the two lines RH and CM are perpendicular.

Solution

We will use vectors with the circumcentre O as origin and $x = \overrightarrow{OA}$, $y = \overrightarrow{OB}$, $z = \overrightarrow{OC}$. It is known that QP meets AB at R, where

$$\overrightarrow{OR} = \frac{-(a\cos B)x + (b\cos A)y}{b\cos A - a\cos B}$$

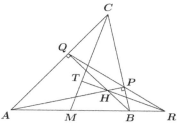

and $\overrightarrow{OH} = x + y + z$. We also have $\overrightarrow{CM} = \frac{1}{2}(x + y) - z$. Hence,

$$\overrightarrow{RH}(b\cos A - a\cos B)$$
$$= (b\cos A)x - (a\cos B)x$$
$$+ (b\cos A - a\cos B)z .$$

Thus, if ρ is the radius of the circumcircle of $\triangle ABC$, we get

$$2(b\cos A - a\cos B)\overrightarrow{RH} \cdot \overrightarrow{CM}$$
$$= (-b\cos A + a\cos B)\rho^2 + (b\cos A - a\cos B)x \cdot y$$
$$+ (b\cos A + a\cos B)(y - x) \cdot z$$
$$= \rho^2(a\cos B - b\cos A)(1 - \cos 2C) + c(\cos 2A - \cos 2B)$$
$$= 2\rho^2 c(a\cos B - b\cos A)\sin C((\sin A\cos B - \sin B\cos A)$$
$$+ \sin(B - A))$$
$$= 0 .$$

Hence, $RH \perp CM$.

Let T be a point in the plane of the non-equilateral triangle ABC which is different from the vertices of the triangle. Let the lines AT, BT, and CT meet the circumcircle of the triangle at A_T, B_T, and C_T, respectively. Prove that there are exactly two points P and Q in the plane for which the triangles $A_PB_PC_P$ and $A_QB_QC_Q$ are equilateral. Prove, furthermore, that the line PQ passes through the circumcentre of the triangle ABC.

Solution

We embed the figure in the complex plane and, for simplicity, denote a point or its complex representation by the same small letter. Without loss of generality, we suppose that a, b, and c lie on the unit circle Γ, so that $a\bar{a} = b\bar{b} = c\bar{c} = 1$. Note that the points p and q we seek cannot lie on Γ.

Let $a' \in \Gamma$ and $m \notin \Gamma$. The line aa' passes through m if and only if $m + aa'\bar{m} = a + a'$; that is, $a' = \overline{T_m(a)}$, where T_m denotes the Möbius transformation defined by $T_m(z) = \dfrac{1 - \bar{m}z}{m - z}$. As a result, for a', b', c' on Γ, the lines aa', bb' and cc' concur at m if and only if $a' = \overline{T_m(a)}$, $b' = \overline{T_m(b)}$ and $c' = \overline{T_m(c)}$.

The statement that $a'b'c'$ is equilateral is successively equivalent to

- $\dfrac{a' - c'}{a' - b'} \in \{-\omega, -\omega^2\}$, where $\omega = \exp(2\pi i/3)$,

- $\overline{[T_m(m), T_m(a), T_m(b), T_m(c)]} \in \{-\omega, -\omega^2\}$, where $[\cdot, \cdot, \cdot, \cdot]$ denotes the cross ratio,

- $[T_m(m), T_m(a), T_m(b), T_m(c)] \in \{-\omega, -\omega^2\}$ (since $-\omega$ and $-\omega^2$ are conjugates),

- $[m, a, b, c] \in \{-\omega, -\omega^2\}$ (since T_m preserves the cross ratio).

The conclusion follows, since p and q are the two points given by $[p, a, b, c] = -\omega$, $[q, a, b, c] = -\omega^2$. Note that p, $q \neq \infty$ since ABC is not equilateral. Also, from $[q, a, b, c] = \overline{[p, a, b, c]}$, an easy calculation yields $q = 1/\bar{p}$. Thus, 0, p, and q are collinear (p and q are even inverses in Γ).

Let A, B, C, and D be circles such that (i) A and B are externally tangent at P, (ii) B and C are externally tangent at Q, (iii) C and D are externally tangent at R, and (iv) D and A are externally tangent at S. Assume that A and C do not intersect and that B and D do not intersect.

(a) Prove that P, Q, R, and S lie on a circle.

(b) Assume further that A and C have radius 2, B and D have radius 3, and the distance between the centres of A and C is 6. Determine the area of $PQRS$.

Solution

(a)

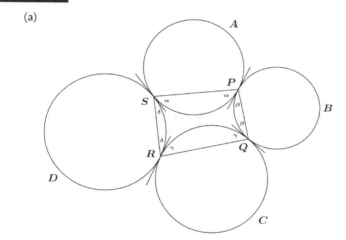

Draw the common internal tangents at P, Q, R, and S, and label angles α, β, γ, and δ as shown in the diagram above. Since the sum of the internal angles in quadrilateral $PQRS$ is $360°$, it follows that $\alpha + \beta + \gamma + \delta = 180°$. Hence, opposite angles of $PQRS$ are supplementary. Thus, $PQRS$ is cyclic.

(b) Let A', B', C', D' be the centres of the circles A, B, C, D, and let $A'C'$ and $B'D'$ meet at E. Since $A'B'C'D'$ is a rhombus, the diagonals $A'C'$ and $B'D'$ are the perpendicular bisectors of one another. Then, since the distance between A' and C' is 6, we have $A'E = 3$. Hence, $D'E = 4$ and $D'B' = 8$. Since $SP \parallel D'B' \parallel RQ$ and $SR \parallel A'C' \parallel PQ$, it follows that $PQRS$ is a rectangle.

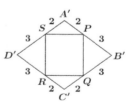

We have

$$\frac{SP}{D'B'} = \frac{2}{5} \quad \text{and} \quad \frac{SR}{A'C'} = \frac{3}{5}.$$

Therefore, $SP = \frac{2}{5} \cdot 8 = \frac{16}{5}$ and $SR = \frac{3}{5} \cdot 6 = \frac{18}{5}$. Finally,

$$[PQRS] = SP \cdot SR = \frac{288}{25}.$$

Let ABC be a triangle with $\angle B > 90°$ such that, for some point H on AC, we have $AH = BH$, and BH is perpendicular to BC. Let D and E be the mid-points of AB and BC, respectively. Through H a parallel to AB is drawn, intersecting DE at F. Prove that $\angle BCF = \angle ACD$.

Solution

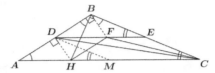

Since D and E are the mid-points of AB and BC, respectively, we have $DE \parallel AC$. Let M be the mid-point of AC; then $DM \parallel BC$. These imply that

$$\angle BED = \angle BCA = \angle DMA. \tag{1}$$

Since $DF \parallel AH$ and $HF \parallel AD$, quadrilateral $DAHF$ is a parallelogram. Thus, $HF = AD = DB$; hence, quadrilateral $BDHF$ is a parallelogram, and we have $BF \parallel DH$. Since $AH = BH$ and $AD = BD$, we get $HD \perp AB$. Thus, $\angle DBF = \angle ADH = 90°$.

Since $\angle HBE = 90°$, we have $\angle DBF = \angle HBE$; that is,

$$\angle DBH + \angle HBF = \angle HBF + \angle FBE.$$

Thus, $\angle DBH = \angle FBE$. Since $AH = BH$, we have $\angle DAH = \angle DBH$, and hence,

$$\angle FBE = \angle DAH. \tag{2}$$

It follows from (1) and (2) that $\triangle FBE \sim \triangle DAM$. Thus,

$$EF : DM = BE : AM = EC : MC. \tag{3}$$

Since $\angle FEC = 180° - \angle BEF = 180° - \angle DMA = \angle DMC$, it follows (in view of (3)) that $\triangle FEC \sim \triangle DMC$. Hence, $\angle ECF = \angle MCD$; that is, $\angle BCF = \angle ACD$.

Given a triangle ABC with side AB greater than BC, let M be the mid-point of AC, and let L be the point at which the bisector of $\angle B$ cuts side AC. A straight line is drawn through M parallel to AB, cutting the bisector BL at D, and another straight line is drawn through L parallel to BC, cutting the median BM at E. Show that ED is perpendicular to BL.

Solution

Let N be the mid-point of BC. The line through M parallel to AB intersects BC at N and bisects EL at a point P. Triangle PDL is isosceles, since

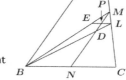

$$\angle PLD = \angle LBC = \tfrac{1}{2}\angle B$$
$$\text{and} \quad \angle PDL = \angle ABL = \tfrac{1}{2}\angle B.$$

We then have $DP = PL = PE$, which implies that $\triangle DEL$ is right-angled at D; that is, $DE \perp BL$.

Next we give Bataille's solution.

Let $a = BC$, $b = CA$, and $c = AB$, as usual.

First, we note that L is between A and C, and $\dfrac{LC}{LA} = \dfrac{BC}{BA} = \dfrac{a}{c}$. Thus,

$$c\overrightarrow{LC} + a\overrightarrow{LA} = \vec{0}. \tag{1}$$

Hence, $c(\overrightarrow{BC} - \overrightarrow{BL}) + a(\overrightarrow{BA} - \overrightarrow{BL}) = \vec{0}$, which gives

$$(a+c)\overrightarrow{BL} = c\overrightarrow{BC} + a\overrightarrow{BA}. \tag{2}$$

Also, using (1),

$$(a+c)(\overrightarrow{LM} + \overrightarrow{MC}) = (a+c)\overrightarrow{LC} = a(\overrightarrow{LC} - \overrightarrow{LA}) = a\overrightarrow{AC} = 2a\overrightarrow{MC};$$

whence $\overrightarrow{ML} = \dfrac{c-a}{c+a}\overrightarrow{MC}$. Since $LE \parallel BC$, we see that $\overrightarrow{ME} = \dfrac{c-a}{c+a}\overrightarrow{MB}$. Similarly, using (1) again, we get $\overrightarrow{LM} = \dfrac{c-a}{2c}\overrightarrow{LA}$, and since $MD \parallel AB$, we have $\overrightarrow{MD} = \dfrac{c-a}{2c}\overrightarrow{AB}$. Now,

$$\frac{a-c}{2(a+c)}(\overrightarrow{BC} + \overrightarrow{BA}) = \frac{a-c}{a+c}\overrightarrow{BM} = \overrightarrow{ME} = \overrightarrow{MD} + \overrightarrow{DE}$$
$$= \frac{c-a}{2c}\overrightarrow{AB} + \overrightarrow{DE},$$

which easily yields

$$\frac{2c(a+c)}{a-c}\overrightarrow{DE} = c\overrightarrow{BC} - a\overrightarrow{BA}. \tag{3}$$

Now we note that the right sides of (2) and (3) are orthogonal vectors:

$$(c\overrightarrow{BC} + a\overrightarrow{BA}) \cdot (c\overrightarrow{BC} - a\overrightarrow{BA}) = c^2a^2 - a^2c^2 = 0.$$

It follows that $\overrightarrow{BL}$ and $\overrightarrow{DE}$ are orthogonal. Thus, $ED \perp BL$.

Let a, b, c be the sides of a triangle, and let α, β, γ be the angles opposite the sides a, b, c, respectively.

(a) Prove that $\gamma = 2\alpha$ if and only if $c^2 = a(a+b)$.

(b) Find all triangles such that a, b, c are natural numbers, b is a prime, and $\gamma = 2\alpha$.

Solution

(a) First, suppose that $c^2 = a(a+b)$. Then, using the Law of Cosines,

$$c^2(a-b) \;=\; a(a^2 - b^2) \;=\; a(c^2 - 2bc\cos\alpha)\,.$$

This simplifies to $c = 2a\cos\alpha$. Since $c\sin\alpha = a\sin\gamma$ (from the Law of Sines), we obtain $\sin\gamma = \sin 2\alpha$. It follows that $\gamma = 2\alpha$ or $\gamma = \pi - 2\alpha$. In the latter case, since we also have $\gamma = \pi - \alpha - \beta$, we find that $\alpha = \beta$, which implies that $a = b$. Then $c^2 = 2a^2$ and $\triangle ABC$ is isosceles and right-angled with hypotenuse c; thus $\alpha = \pi/4$ and $\gamma = \pi/2$. In both cases, $\gamma = 2\alpha$.

Conversely, if $\gamma = 2\alpha$, then $\sin\gamma = 2\sin\alpha\cos\alpha$, or (using the Law of Sines and the Law of Cosines)

$$\frac{c}{a} \;=\; \frac{\sin\gamma}{\sin\alpha} \;=\; 2\cos\alpha \;=\; 2\left(\frac{b^2 + c^2 - a^2}{2bc}\right),$$

which yields $c^2(b-a) = a^2(b^2 - a^2)$. If $a \neq b$, we obtain $c^2 = a(a+b)$. If $a = b$, then $\alpha = \beta$. Since $\gamma = 2\alpha$, it follows that $\triangle ABC$ is isosceles and right-angled with $c^2 = 2a^2$, and $c^2 = a(a+b)$ is still true.

(b) Suppose that $\gamma = 2\alpha$. From the hypotheses and part (a), we see that $c^2 - a^2 = ab$; thus $c > a$. Let $d = \gcd(a, c)$, and let a' and c' be the coprime integers defined by $a = da'$ and $c = dc'$. Then $d(c' - a')(c' + a') = ba'$. Since b is prime, $b \mid d$ or $b \mid (c' - a')$ or $b \mid (c' + a')$. If $b \mid d$ or $b \mid (c' - a')$, then $b \mid (c - a)$, which implies that $b \leq c - a$, contradicting the triangle inequality. Thus, $c' + a' = kb$ for some positive integer k.

Now $kd(c' - a') = a'$, implying that k divides a'. Since k also divides $c' + a'$, we see that k divides both c' and a'. It follows that $k = 1$, $b = a' + c'$, and $d(c' - a') = a'$. As a result, $d \mid a'$ and $dc' = a'(d+1)$. Since a' and c' are coprime, the latter shows that $a' \mid d$. Hence, $a' = d$ and $c' = d+1$. We finally have $b = 2d + 1$, $a = d^2$, and $c = d(d+1)$. Note that $d > 1$, since $b < a + c$, and hence, $b \geq 5$.

Conversely, let $b = 2d + 1$ be a prime with $b \geq 5$, and let $a = d^2$ and $c = d(d+1)$. Then $c - a < b < c + a$ is easily checked (since $d > 1$), and thus, there exists a triangle with sides a, b, and c. Moreover, the relation $c^2 = a(a+b)$ is obtained at once, and (a) shows that $\gamma = 2\alpha$ in this triangle.

In conclusion, the suitable triangles are those with sides $b = 2d + 1$, $a = d^2$, and $c = d(d+1)$ for some prime $b \geq 5$.

Let ABC be a right triangle with hypotenuse AB and altitude CF, where F lies on AB. The circle through F centred at B and another circle of the same radius centred at A intersect on the side CB. Determine $FB : BC$.

Solution

Let the circle through F centred at B intersect BC at P. Let M be the foot of the perpendicular from P to AB.

Since the circle with radius BF centred at A passes through P, we have $AP = BF = BP$. Thus, triangle APB is isosceles, which implies that M is the mid-point of AB. From similar triangles PBM and CBF, we get $\frac{BP}{MB} = \frac{BC}{FB}$; from similar triangles ABC and CBF, we get $\frac{AB}{BC} = \frac{BC}{FB}$. Hence,

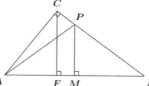

$$\frac{FB}{BC} = \frac{FB}{MB} \cdot \frac{MB}{BC} = \frac{BP}{MB} \cdot \frac{\frac{1}{2}AB}{BC} = \frac{BC}{FB} \cdot \frac{\frac{1}{2}BC}{FB}.$$

It follows that $\left(\frac{FB}{BC}\right)^3 = \frac{1}{2}$; that is, $\frac{FB}{BC} = \frac{1}{\sqrt[3]{2}}$.

Prove that, if ABC is an acute-angled triangle, then

$$\frac{a^2 + b^2}{a + b} \cdot \frac{b^2 + c^2}{b + c} \cdot \frac{c^2 + a^2}{c + a} \geq 16 \cdot R^2 \cdot r \cdot \frac{m_a}{a} \cdot \frac{m_b}{b} \cdot \frac{m_c}{c}.$$

Solution

Using the formulas $4m_a^2 = 2(b^2 + c^2) - a^2$ and

$$w_a^2 = \frac{bc(b + c + a)(b + c - a)}{(b + c)^2} = \frac{4bcs(s - a)}{(b + c)^2},$$

it can be shown that

$$m_a \leq w_a \cdot \frac{b^2 + c^2}{2bc}. \tag{1}$$

Substituting $w_a = \dfrac{2\sqrt{bcs(s - a)}}{b + c}$ in (1), we get

$$m_a \leq \frac{b^2 + c^2}{b + c} \sqrt{\frac{s(s - a)}{bc}}.$$

Letting K denote the area of $\triangle ABC$, we have $K = \sqrt{s(s - a)(s - b)(s - c)}$ (Heron's formula). We will also use the formulas $abc = 4RK = 4Rrs$. We have

$$\begin{aligned} 16R^2 r \prod_{\text{cyclic}} \frac{m_a}{a} &\leq 16R^2 r \prod_{\text{cyclic}} \frac{b^2 + c^2}{a(b + c)} \sqrt{\frac{s(s - a)}{bc}} \\ &= \frac{16R^2 rs}{(abc)^2} \sqrt{s(s - a)(s - b)(s - c)} \prod_{\text{cyclic}} \frac{b^2 + c^2}{b + c} \\ &= \frac{16R^2 rs}{(4RK)(4Rrs)}(K) \prod_{\text{cyclic}} \frac{b^2 + c^2}{b + c} = \prod_{\text{cyclic}} \frac{b^2 + c^2}{b + c}, \end{aligned}$$

as required.

Let $ABCDE$ be a regular pentagon with its sides of length one. Let F be the mid-point of AB, and let G and H be points on the sides CD and DE, respectively, such that $\angle GFD = \angle HFD = 30°$. Prove that the triangle GFH is equilateral. A square is inscribed in the triangle GFH with one side of the square along GH. Prove that FG has length

$$t = \frac{2\cos 18°(\cos 36°)^2}{\cos 6°},$$

and that the square has side length $\dfrac{t\sqrt{3}}{2+\sqrt{3}}$.

Solution

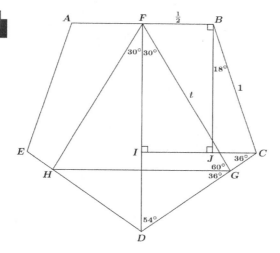

By symmetry, we have $FG = FH$; thus, $\triangle FGH$ is equilateral. Also, $\angle FDC = \frac{1}{2}\angle EDC = 54°$. Drop a perpendicular CI from C to DF, and a perpendicular BJ from B to CI. We have

$$\begin{aligned} DF &= DI + JB = \sin 36° + \cos 18° = 2\cos 18°\left(\sin 18° + \tfrac{1}{2}\right) \\ &= 2\cos 18° \cdot CI = 2\cos 18° \cos 36°. \end{aligned}$$

By the Law of Sines,

$$\frac{t}{\sin 54°} = \frac{DF}{\sin 96°};$$

whence,

$$t = \frac{\cos 36°}{\cos 6°} \cdot DF = \frac{2\cos 18°(\cos 36°)^2}{\cos 6°}.$$

Let x be the length of a side of the square under consideration. It is clear from the diagram that $\dfrac{x}{\sqrt{3}} = \dfrac{t-x}{2}$, from which it follows easily that

$$x = \frac{t\sqrt{3}}{2+\sqrt{3}}.$$

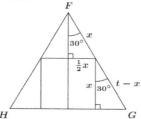

Let $ABCD$ be a cyclic quadrilateral and R the radius of the circumcircle. Let a, b, c, d be the lengths of the sides of $ABCD$, and let Q be its area. Prove that

$$R^2 = \frac{(ab + cd)(ac + bd)(ad + bc)}{16Q^2}.$$

Deduce that $R \geq \dfrac{(abcd)^{\frac{3}{4}}}{Q\sqrt{2}}$, with equality if and only if $ABCD$ is a square.

Solution

Let $t = AC$ and $u = BD$. Let $[XYZ]$ denote the area of $\triangle XYZ$. By a well-known formula, we have $4R[ABC] = abt$ and $4R[ADC] = cdt$; hence, $4RQ = (ab + cd)t$. Analogously, $4RQ = (ad + bc)u$. Consequently,

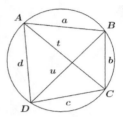

$$16R^2Q^2 = (ab + cd)tu(ad + bc).$$

By Ptolemy's Theorem, $tu = ac + bd$; thus, we easily obtain the desired expression for R^2.

By the AM–GM Inequality, each of $ab + cd$, $ac + bd$, $ad + bc$ is greater than or equal to $2(abcd)^{1/2}$. Therefore,

$$R^2 \geq \frac{(abcd)^{3/2}}{2Q^2}; \quad \text{that is,} \quad R \geq \frac{(abcd)^{3/4}}{Q\sqrt{2}}.$$

If equality holds, then $ab = cd$, $ac = bd$, and $ad = bc$, which implies that $a = b = c = d$. Thus, $ABCD$ is a rhombus and, being cyclic, a square. The converse is obvious.

Two circles intersect at points P and Q. A line ℓ that intersects the line segment PQ intersects the two circles at the points A, B, C, and D (in that order along the line ℓ). Prove that $\angle APB = \angle CQD$.

Solution

We have $\angle PBD = \angle PQD$ (since these angles are subtended by the same arc) and $\angle PQD = \angle CQD + \angle CQP$. Hence, $\angle PBD = \angle CQD + \angle CQP$. Also, since $\angle PBD$ is an exterior angle to $\triangle APB$, we have $\angle PBD = \angle APB + \angle PAB$. Thus,

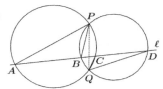

$$\angle APB + \angle PAB = \angle CQD + \angle CQP.$$

But $\angle PAB = \angle PAC = \angle CQP$ (since these angles are subtended by the same arc). Therefore, $\angle APB = \angle CQD$.

Triangle ABC is isosceles with a right angle at B and $AB = BC = x$. Point D on the side AB and point E on the side BC are chosen such that $BD = BE = y$. The line segments AE and CD intersect at the point P. What is the area of the triangle APC, expressed in terms of x and y?

Solution

We consider the more general problem of determining the area of $\triangle APC$ if $BD = y$ and $BE = z$. The given problem is the special case where $y = z$.

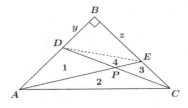

We connect DE and let $\triangle_1$, $\triangle_2$, $\triangle_3$, $\triangle_4$ denote the areas of the triangles labelled by 1, 2, 3, 4, respectively. We are to determine $\triangle_2$ in terms of x, y, and z.

From the diagram, it is easily seen that

$$\triangle_1 + \triangle_2 = \tfrac{1}{2}x(x - y), \qquad (1)$$

$$\triangle_1 + \triangle_4 = \tfrac{1}{2}z(x - y), \qquad (2)$$

$$\text{and} \quad \triangle_2 + \triangle_3 = \tfrac{1}{2}x(x - z). \qquad (3)$$

Since $\dfrac{\triangle_1}{\triangle_2} = \dfrac{DP}{CP} = \dfrac{\triangle_4}{\triangle_3}$, we have, using (2) and (3),

$$\frac{\triangle_1}{\triangle_2} = \frac{\triangle_1 + \triangle_4}{\triangle_2 + \triangle_3} = \frac{\tfrac{1}{2}z(x - y)}{\tfrac{1}{2}x(x - z)};$$

that is, $\triangle_1 = \dfrac{z(x - y)}{x(x - z)}\triangle_2$. Substituting into (1), we get

$$\frac{z(x - y)}{x(x - z)}\triangle_2 + \triangle_2 = \tfrac{1}{2}x(x - y),$$

$$\text{or} \quad (z(x - y) + x(x - z))\triangle_2 = \tfrac{1}{2}x^2(x - y)(x - z).$$

Hence, $\triangle_2 = \dfrac{x^2(x - y)(x - z)}{2(x^2 - yz)}$.

For the original problem, where $y = z$, we have $\triangle_2 = \dfrac{x^2}{2}\left(\dfrac{x - y}{x + y}\right)$.

Let ABC be an isosceles triangle with $AB = AC$. Let M be the mid-point of side BC. The circle with diameter AB cuts side AC at point P. The parallelogram $MPDC$ is constructed so that $PD = MC$ and $PD \parallel MC$. Prove that triangles APD and APM are congruent.

Solution

It is not necessary to assume that $\triangle ABC$ is isosceles.

Let Q be the point of intersection of AC and MD. Since $MPDC$ is a parallelogram, we have $MQ = QD$. Also, $BPDM$ is a parallelogram; in particular, $BP \parallel MD$. Since $\angle APB$ is a right angle, so is $\angle AQM$. Thus, AC is the perpendicular bisector of MD. Therefore, $AM = AD$ and $PM = PD$, and it follows that $\triangle APD \cong \triangle APM$ by SSS.

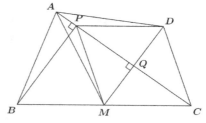

On sides AC and BC of an acute-angled triangle ABC, rectangles $ACPQ$ and $BKCL$ are erected outwardly. Assuming that these rectangles have equal areas, show that the vertex C, the circumcentre of triangle ABC, and the mid-point of segment PL are collinear.

Solution

Let O be the circumcentre of $\triangle ABC$. Let OC (produced) intersect PL at M. We will prove that M is the mid-point of PL. The desired conclusion follows from this.

Let S and T be the feet of the perpendiculars to OC from L and P, respectively, and let U and V be the feet of the perpendiculars from O to BC and CA, respectively. Since $\angle OCU$ is a complementary angle for both $\angle LCS$ and $\angle COU$, we have $\angle LCS = \angle COU$. It follows that the right triangles OUC and CSL are similar. Hence, $LS/UC = CL/OC$. Similarly, $PT/VC = CP/OC$. Therefore,

$$LS = \frac{UC \cdot CL}{OC} = \frac{\frac{1}{2}[BKLC]}{OC} = \frac{\frac{1}{2}[ACPQ]}{OC} = \frac{VC \cdot CP}{OC} = PT.$$

This implies that $LM = MP$; that is M is the mid-point of PL.

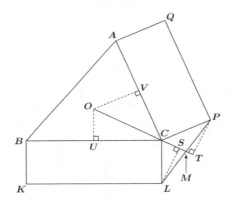

In an acute-angled triangle ABC with circumcentre O, points P and Q lying respectively on sides AC and BC are such that

$$\frac{AP}{PQ} = \frac{BC}{AB} \quad \text{and} \quad \frac{BQ}{PQ} = \frac{AC}{AB}.$$

Show that the points O, P, Q, and C are concyclic.

Solution

We will use standard notation for the sides, angles, and circumradius of $\triangle ABC$. Define $k = AP/a$. Using the given equations, we get

$$k = \frac{AP}{a} = \frac{BQ}{b} = \frac{PQ}{c}.$$

Then $CP = b - AP = b - ka$ and $CQ = a - BQ = a - kb$.

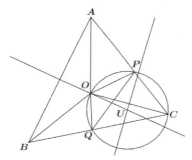

The Law of Cosines gives

$$\begin{aligned}
k^2 c^2 &= PQ^2 = (a - kb)^2 + (b - ka)^2 - 2(a - kb)(b - ka)\cos C \\
&= (1 + k^2)(a^2 + b^2 - 2ab\cos C) - 4kab + 2k(a^2 + b^2)\cos C \\
&= (1 + k^2)c^2 - 2k(2ab - (a^2 + b^2)\cos C),
\end{aligned}$$

and hence,

$$c^2 = 2k(2ab - (a^2 + b^2)\cos C).$$

But, using the Law of Sines, we have

$$\begin{aligned}
2ab &- (a^2 + b^2)\cos C \\
&= 8R^2 \sin A \sin B - 4R^2 \cos C(\sin^2 A + \sin^2 B) \\
&= 4R^2 [\cos(A - B) - \cos(A + B) - \cos C(\sin^2 A + \sin^2 B)] \\
&= 4R^2 \sin^2 C \cos(A - B) = c^2 \cos(A - B),
\end{aligned}$$

where we have used the identity

$$\begin{aligned}
\cos(A - B)\cos(A + B) &= \cos^2 A(1 - \sin^2 B) - \sin^2 B(1 - \cos^2 A) \\
&= \cos^2 A - \sin^2 B.
\end{aligned}$$

It follows that $k = \dfrac{1}{2\cos(A-B)}$.

Since $\angle AOC = 2B$ and $OA = OC$, we have $\angle OAP = 90° - B$. Thus,

$$
\begin{aligned}
OP^2 &= OA^2 + AP^2 - 2OA \cdot AP \cos(90° - B) \\
&= R^2 + k^2 a^2 - 2kRa \sin B \\
&= 4R^2 k^2 \left(\frac{1}{4k^2} + \sin^2 A - \frac{1}{k} \sin A \sin B \right) \\
&= 4R^2 k^2 \left[\cos^2(A-B) + \sin^2 A - 2\cos(A-B)\sin A \sin B \right] \\
&= 4R^2 k^2 \left[\cos^2(A-B) + \sin^2 A \right. \\
&\qquad\qquad \left. - \cos(A-B)(\cos(A-B) - \cos(A+B)) \right] \\
&= 4R^2 k^2 (\sin^2 A + \cos^2 A - \sin^2 B) \; = \; 4R^2 k^2 \cos^2 B \,.
\end{aligned}
$$

Therefore, $OP = 2kR\cos B$. Similarly, $OQ = 2kR\cos A$. Now,

$$
\begin{aligned}
OP &\cdot CQ + OQ \cdot CP \\
&= 4kR^2 (\cos B \sin A - k\sin B \cos B + \cos A \sin B - k\sin A \cos A) \\
&= 4kR^2 \left[\sin(A+B) - k\sin(A+B)\cos(A-B) \right] \\
&= 4kR^2 \left(\sin C - \tfrac{1}{2}\sin C \right) \; = \; 2kR^2 \sin C \; = \; R \cdot kc \; = \; OC \cdot PQ \,,
\end{aligned}
$$

where we have used the identity

$$
\sin(A+B)\cos(A-B) \; = \; \sin A \cos A + \sin B \cos B \,.
$$

It follows from Ptolemy's Theorem that O, P, Q, C are concyclic.

A circle passes through the vertex C of a rectangle $ABCD$ and touches its sides AB and AD at points M and N, respectively. Suppose the distance from C to MN is 2 cm. Find the area of $ABCD$ in cm^2.

Solution

The answer is $[ABCD] = 4$ cm^2.

More generally, let d be the distance from C to MN. We introduce additional notation as shown in the diagram. Since AB is tangent to the circle at M, we have

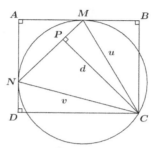

$$\angle BMC \ = \ \angle MNC \ = \ \angle PNC \,.$$

Hence, $\triangle BMC$ is similar to $\triangle PNC$. Similarly, $\triangle DNC$ is similar to $\triangle PMC$. Consequently,

$$\frac{BC}{d} \ = \ \frac{u}{v} \quad \text{and} \quad \frac{DC}{d} \ = \ \frac{v}{u} \,.$$

From these two equations, we get $BC \cdot DC = d^2$; that is, $[ABCD] = d^2$.

Let A and B be two points of the plane, and let M be the mid-point of AB. Let r be a line, and let R and S be the projections of A and B onto r. Assuming that A, M, and R are not collinear, prove that the circumcircle of triangle AMR has the same radius as the circumcircle of BSM.

Solution

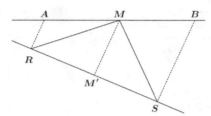

Let M' be the projection of M onto r. Then M' is the mid-point of RS (since M is the mid-point of AB) and $MM' \perp RS$. It follows that $\triangle RMS$ is isosceles with

$$RM = MS. \tag{1}$$

Now, let ρ_a and ρ_b be the circumradii of $\triangle AMR$ and $\triangle BMS$, respectively. We have

$$2\rho_a = \frac{RM}{\sin(\angle RAM)}, \quad 2\rho_b = \frac{SM}{\sin(\angle SBM)}. \tag{2}$$

But $\angle RAM + \angle SBM = 180°$ (since $AR \parallel BS$); hence,

$$\sin(\angle RAM) = \sin(\angle SBM). \tag{3}$$

From (1), (2), and (3), we obtain $\rho_a = \rho_b$.

The quadrilateral $ABCD$ is inscribed in a circle. The diagonals AC and BD meet at Q. The sides DA, extended beyond A, and CB, extended beyond B, meet at P.

Given that $CD = CP = DQ$, prove that $\angle CAD = 60°$.

Solution

We set $\alpha = \angle QCD$ and $\beta = \angle BDA$. Then

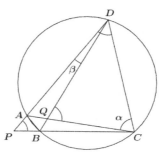

$$\angle DQC = \angle QCD = \alpha,$$
$$\angle PCA = \angle BCA$$
$$= \angle BDA = \beta,$$
$$\angle CAD = \angle DAQ$$
$$= \angle DQC - \angle QDA$$
$$= \alpha - \beta,$$
$$\angle CDQ = 180° - 2\alpha,$$

and

$$\angle APC = \angle DPC = \angle CDP = \angle CDQ + \angle BDA = (180° - 2\alpha) + \beta.$$

By the External Angle Theorem applied to $\triangle APC$ at A,

$$\angle CAD = \angle APC + \angle PCA = (180° - 2\alpha + \beta) + \beta$$
$$= 180° - 2(\alpha - \beta) = 180° - 2 \cdot \angle CAD.$$

Hence, $\angle CAD = 60°$.

The altitude from one of the vertices of an acute-angled triangle ABC meets the opposite side at D. From D, perpendiculars DE and DF are drawn to the other two sides. Prove that the length of EF is the same whichever vertex is chosen.

Solution

Suppose that D is the foot of the altitude from A. Since $\angle AED$ and $\angle DFA$ are right angles, the quadrilateral $AEDF$ may be inscribed in a circle. Therefore,

$$\angle AEF \ = \ \angle ADF \ = \ 90° - \angle FAD \ = \ 90° - \angle CAD \ = \ \angle BCA,$$

making $\triangle AFE$ similar to $\triangle ABC$. Then $\dfrac{EF}{BC} = \dfrac{AF}{AB}$; that is,

$$EF \ = \ \frac{AF \cdot BC}{AB}. \tag{1}$$

We have $AF = AD \cdot \sin \angle ADF = AD \cdot \sin \angle BCA = AD \cdot AB/(2R)$ and $AD \cdot BC = 2S$, where R and S denote the circumradius and the area of $\triangle ABC$, respectively. On substituting into (1), we find that $EF = S/R$. Since this quantity depends only on R and S, the same expression would be obtained if we had chosen the altitude from B or C.

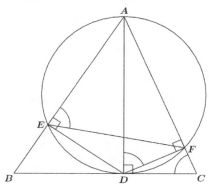

Let ABC be an acute triangle, and let O be its circumcircle. Let the perpendicular line from A to BC meet O at D. Let P be a point on O, and let Q be the foot of the perpendicular line from P to the line AB. Prove that if Q is on the outside of O and $2\angle QPB = \angle PBC$, then D, P, Q are collinear.

Solution

Let $w = \angle QPB$. Then $\angle PBC = 2w$ and $\angle QBP = 90° - w = \angle ABC$.

Case 1. The line PQ intersects the circle O at a point D' between P and Q.

Let F be the intersection of AD' and BC. We have $\angle BAD' = \angle BPD'$ (since these angles subtend the same arc), and hence $\angle BAD' = \angle BPQ = w$. Then

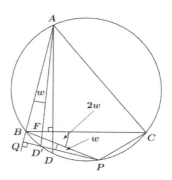

$$
\begin{aligned}
\angle AFB &= 180° - \angle BAD' - \angle ABC \\
&= 180° - w - (90° - w) \\
&= 90°.
\end{aligned}
$$

Then $D' = D$. Thus, D, P, Q are collinear.

Case 2. The line PQ intersects the circle O at a point D' such that P is between D' and Q.

Let F be the intersection of AD' and BC. Since quadrilateral $BPD'C$ is inscribed in the circle O, we see that $\angle BCD' = 180° - \angle BPD' = w$. Hence, $\angle BAD' = w$. In the triangle ABF, we have $\angle BAF = \angle BAD' = w$ and $\angle ABF = \angle ABC = 90° - w$. Therefore, $\angle AFB = 90°$. Then $D' = D$. Thus, D, P, Q are collinear.

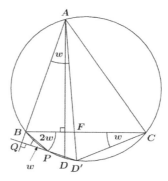

Case 3. The line PQ is tangent to the circle O at P.

The proof is similar to Case 2. Quadrilateral $BPD'C$ now degenerates into triangle BPC. Then $\angle BCP = w$ by the Tangent-Chord Theorem, and the rest of Case 2 follows.

Let p be the semiperimeter of the triangle ABC. Let the points E and F lie on the line AB such that $CE = CF = p$. Prove that the circumcircle of the triangle EFC and the circle that touches the side AB and the extension of the sides AC and BC of the triangle ABC meet in one point.

Solution

Tangency invites inversion; thus, we invert in the circle with centre C and radius $p = CE = CF$.

The circumcircle of $\triangle EFC$ becomes the straight line through E and F.

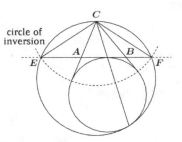

Since the tangents from C (or any other vertex) to the excircle beyond the opposite side are of length p, the excircle that touches the side AB is invariant under this inversion.

Tangency is preserved under inversion; therefore, the circumcircle of $\triangle EFC$ and the excircle beyond AB meet in one point.

Triangle ABC is given in a plane. Draw the bisectors of all three of its angles. Then draw the line that connects the points where the bisectors of angles ABC and ACB meet the sides AC and AB, respectively. Through the point of intersection of the bisector of angle BAC and the previously drawn line, draw another line, parallel to the side BC. Let this line intersect the sides AB and AC in points M and N. Prove that $2MN = BM + CN$.

Solution

Lemma. In triangle ABC, the bisector of $\angle ACB$ meets the side AB at D, and the bisector of $\angle ABC$ meets the side AC at E. Let P be any point on the segment DE. Let X, Y, and Z be the orthogonal projections of P onto the sides BC, AC, and AB, respectively. Then $PX = PY + PZ$.

Proof: Let R and S be the orthogonal projections of D onto the sides BC and AC, respectively. Let T and U be the orthogonal projections of E onto the sides BC and AB, respectively. Note that $DR = DS$ and $ET = EU$.

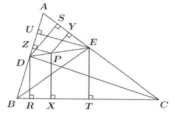

Let $r = DP/DE$. Then $0 < r < 1$ and $PE/DE = 1 - r$. Since $PY \parallel DS$, we have $PY = (1-r)DS = (1-r)DR$; similarly, since $PZ \parallel EU$, we also have $PZ = rEU = rET$. Then

$$PY + PZ = (1-r)DR + rET = PX,$$

since $DR \parallel PX \parallel ET$ and $DP/PE = r/(1-r)$.

Now we turn to the given problem. As in the lemma, we let D and E be the points where the bisectors of $\angle ACB$ and $\angle ABC$ meet the sides AB and AC, respectively. Let P be any point on the segment DE. (Later, we will require P to be on the bisector of $\angle BAC$, as required in the problem.)

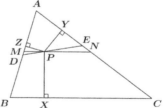

Let $[UVW]$ denote the area of a triangle UVW. Since $MN \parallel BC$, we see that $[MBP] = [MXP]$ and $[PCN] = [PXN]$. Hence,

$$[MBP] + [PCN] = [MXP] + [PXN] = [MXN].$$

Since the area of $\triangle MBP$ may be expressed by $\frac{1}{2}BM \cdot PZ$, the area of $\triangle PCN$ by $\frac{1}{2}CN \cdot PY$, and that of $\triangle MXN$ by $\frac{1}{2}MN \cdot PX$, we may write the above equation as

$$BM \cdot PZ + CN \cdot PY = MN \cdot PX. \qquad (1)$$

Now assume that P lies on the bisector of $\angle BAC$. Then $PZ = PY$ and, by the lemma, $PX = 2PY$. Substituting into (1) and dividing by PY, we obtain the desired result.

Let the vertices of the convex quadrilateral $ABCD$ and the intersecting point S of its diagonals be integer points in the plane. Let P be the area of the quadrilateral $ABCD$ and P_1 the area of triangle ABS. Prove the following inequality:

$$\sqrt{P} \geq \sqrt{P_1} + \frac{\sqrt{2}}{2}.$$

Solution

Lemma. If X_1, X_2, and X_3 are non-collinear points with integer coordinates, then $[X_1 X_2 X_3] \geq \frac{1}{2}$.

Proof: Let X_i have coordinates (a_i, b_i), with $a_i, b_i \in \mathbb{Z}$, for $i = 1, 2, 3$. Then

$$2[X_1 X_2 X_3] = \begin{vmatrix} a_1 & b_1 & 1 \\ a_2 & b_2 & 1 \\ a_3 & b_3 & 1 \end{vmatrix} \in \mathbb{Z}_+^*.$$

Hence, $2[X_1 X_2 X_3] \geq 1$; that is, $[X_1 X_2 X_3] \geq \frac{1}{2}$. ∎

Let P_2, P_3, and P_4 be the areas of triangles BCS, CDS, ADS, respectively. We have $P_1/P_2 = AS/CS$, because $\triangle BAS$ has the same height from the base AS as does $\triangle BCS$ from the base CS. Similarly, $P_4/P_3 = AS/CS$. Thus, $P_1/P_2 = P_4/P_3$. Then $P_1 = P_2 P_4/P_3 \leq 2P_2 P_4$, since $P_3 \geq \frac{1}{2}$ by the lemma. Hence,

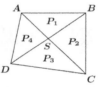

$$\sqrt{2P_1} \leq 2\sqrt{P_2 P_4} \leq P_2 + P_4,$$

using the AM–GM Inequality. Then

$$\begin{aligned} P = P_1 + P_2 + P_3 + P_4 &\geq P_1 + P_3 + \sqrt{2P_1} \\ &\geq P_1 + \tfrac{1}{2} + \sqrt{2P_1} = \left(\sqrt{P_1} + \tfrac{\sqrt{2}}{2}\right)^2. \end{aligned}$$

Taking square roots gives the desired result.

There are 212 points inside or on a circle with radius 1. Prove that there are at least 2001 pairs of these points having distances at most 1.

Solution

We may partition the disk into 6 congruent sectors, each with a central angle of 60°, by rays from the centre O of the disk. Since the number of given points is finite, we may choose the rays so that none of the points lie on a ray, except that the centre O may be one of the points. In each of the 6 sectors, the distance between any two points is at most 1. Let $n_1, \ldots, n_6$ be the respective number of the given points in each of the 6 sectors (if O is one of the points, it is counted only once, say in n_1). Thus, $\sum\limits_{i=1}^{6} n_i = 212$.

In sector i, the number of pairs of points is $\frac{1}{2} n_i(n_i - 1)$, and each of these pairs has distance at most 1. Hence, the total number N of pairs of points having distances at most 1 satisfies

$$N \geq \sum_{i=1}^{6} \frac{1}{2} n_i(n_i - 1) = \frac{1}{2}\left(\sum_{i=1}^{6} n_i^2 - 212 \right).$$

Then, using Jensen's Inequality for the function $f(x) = x^2$, we deduce that

$$N \geq \frac{1}{2}\left(\frac{1}{6}\left(\sum_{i=1}^{6} n_i \right)^2 - 212 \right) = \frac{1}{2}\left(\frac{1}{6}(212)^2 - 212 \right) > 3639.$$

Thus, $N \geq 3640$, which is better than required.

In a triangle ABC, $AB = 20$, $AC = 21$, and $BC = 29$. The points D and E lie on the line segment BC, with $BD = 8$ and $EC = 9$. Calculate the angle $\angle DAE$.

Solution

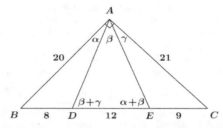

Let $\alpha = \angle BAD$, $\beta = \angle DAE$, and $\gamma = \angle EAC$. Since $BA = BE$, we have $\angle AEB = \alpha + \beta$; similarly, since $CA = CD$, we have $\angle ADC = \beta + \gamma$. Therefore,

$$180° = (\alpha + \beta) + (\beta + \gamma) + \beta = (\alpha + \beta + \gamma) + 2\beta.$$

But $\alpha + \beta + \gamma = 90°$, since $20^2 + 21^2 = 29^2$. Consequently, $\beta = 45°$.

Let ABC be a triangle whose side lengths are all integers, and let D and E be the points at which the incircle of ABC touches BC and AC, respectively. If $|AD^2 - BE^2| \leq 2$, show that $AC = BC$.

Solution

We have $CE = CD = (a + b - c)/2$. By the Cosine Law,

$$AD^2 = b^2 + \frac{(a + b - c)^2}{4} - b(a + b - c)\cos C$$

$$\text{and} \quad BE^2 = a^2 + \frac{(a + b - c)^2}{4} - a(a + b - c)\cos C.$$

Thus,

$$BE^2 - AD^2 = a^2 - b^2 - (a + b - c)(a - b)\cos C.$$

By the Cosine Law, we have $\cos C = \dfrac{a^2 + b^2 - c^2}{2ab}$, and hence,

$$BE^2 - AD^2 = a^2 - b^2 - (a + b - c)(a - b)\frac{a^2 + b^2 - c^2}{2ab}$$

$$= \frac{a - b}{2ab}\left(a^2(-a + b + c) + b^2(a - b + c) + c^2(a + b - c)\right).$$

For the purpose of contradiction, we assume that $a \neq b$. Without loss of generality, we may assume $a > b$. If $c = 1$, then, since $a < b + c$, we have $b < a < b + 1$, which is impossible for integers a and b. Therefore, $c \geq 2$.

Let $a - b = k$. If $k = 1$, then

$$BE^2 - AD^2 = \frac{(b + 1)^2(c - 1) + b^2(c + 1) + c^2(2b + 1 - c)}{2(b + 1)b}.$$

We must have $2 \leq c \leq a + b - 1 = 2b$. It is not hard to show that the minimum value of $f(c) = c^2(2b + 1 - c)$ for $2 \leq c \leq 2b$ is $f(2) = 4(2b - 1)$. Therefore,

$$BE^2 - AD^2 \geq \frac{(b + 1)^2(1) + b^2(3) + 4(2b - 1)}{2(b + 1)b} = \frac{4b^2 + 10b - 3}{2b^2 + 2b}$$

$$= 2 + \frac{3(2b - 1)}{2b^2 + 2b} > 2.$$

If $k \geq 2$, then

$$BE^2 - AD^2 = \frac{k}{2(b + k)b}\left[(b + k)^2(c - k) + b^2(c + k) + c^2(2b + k - c)\right]$$

$$\geq \frac{2}{2(b + k)b}\left[(b + k)^2 + b^2\right] = \frac{2b^2 + 2kb + k^2}{b^2 + kb} > 2.$$

Thus, in both cases, $BE^2 - AD^2 > 2$, a contradiction. Hence, $a = b$; that is, $AC = BC$.

Let A_1, A_2, ..., A_n ($n \geq 4$) be points in the plane such that no three of them are collinear. Some pairs of distinct points among A_1, A_2, ..., A_n are connected by line segments in such a way that each point is connected to at least three others. Prove that there exists $k > 1$ and distinct points X_1, X_2, ..., $X_{2k} \in \{A_1, A_2, ..., A_n\}$ such that for each $1 \leq i \leq 2k - 1$, X_i is connected to X_{i+1} and X_{2k} is connected to X_1.

Solution

An equivalent formulation is the following: A finite simple graph for which each vertex has degree at least 3 contains an even cycle.

Consider the longest path (using pairwise distinct vertices) in the graph, say X_1, X_2, ..., X_p. According to the maximality of the path, each vertex adjacent to X_1 must belong in the path. Since X_1 has degree at least 3, X_1 is adjacent to X_r and X_s, where $2 < r < s$.

Now, among the three integers 2, r, and s, at least two have the same parity. Then, X_1 is adjacent to X_a and to X_b, where $2 \leq a < b \leq p$ and $a \equiv b \pmod 2$. Thus, X_1–X_a–X_{a+1}–...–X_b–X_1 is the desired even cycle.

Prove that the mid-points of the altitudes of a triangle are collinear if and only if the triangle is right.

Solution

Consider $\triangle ABC$, with $\angle C = 90°$. Then AC and BC are two of its altitudes. The line connecting their mid-points bisects every line segment connecting C and AB. Now let C be the largest angle in ABC, $C < 90°$. The feet D and E of the altitudes from A and B are on the segments BC and AC. Thus, the distances of the mid-points P and Q of AD and BE from AB is less than the distance of the mid-point S of the altitude CF. Hence, P and Q are in the half-plane determined by the parallel to AB through S. Therefore, P, Q and S are not collinear. Finally, let $C > 90°$. In this case, the feet D and E of the altitudes dropped from A and B lie on the extensions to BC and AC. Their mid-points P and Q now lie farther away from AB than the mid-point S of the altitude CF. Again, P and Q are both in one of the half-planes determined by the parallel to AB through S. Thus, P, Q, and S are not collinear.

Let $OABC$ be a tetrahedron such that $OA \perp OB \perp OC \perp OA$, let r be the radius of its inscribed sphere, and let H be the orthocentre of triangle ABC. Prove that $OH \leq r(\sqrt{3}+1)$.

Solution

Let Δ_A, Δ_B, Δ_C, and Δ_O be the area of triangles OBC, OAC, OAB, and ABC, respectively. Taking into account that triangles OBC, OAC, and OAB are projections of ABC in mutually orthogonal directions, we have

$$\Delta_O^2 = \Delta_A^2 + \Delta_B^2 + \Delta_C^2.$$

Applying the AM–QM Inequality, we get

$$\Delta_O^2 = \Delta_A^2 + \Delta_B^2 + \Delta_C^2 \geq \tfrac{1}{3}(\Delta_A + \Delta_B + \Delta_C)^2,$$

and hence,

$$\frac{\Delta_A + \Delta_B + \Delta_C}{\Delta_O} \leq \sqrt{3}. \tag{1}$$

Since OH is perpendicular to triangle ABC, the volume of the tetrahedron $OABC$ is

$$\tfrac{1}{3}OH \cdot \Delta_O = \tfrac{1}{3}r(\Delta_A + \Delta_B + \Delta_C + \Delta_O),$$

from which we get

$$OH = r\frac{\Delta_A + \Delta_B + \Delta_C + \Delta_O}{\Delta_O} = r\left(1 + \frac{\Delta_A + \Delta_B + \Delta_C}{\Delta_O}\right).$$

Finally, using (1), we obtain $OH \leq r(1 + \sqrt{3})$.

Let $ABCD$ be a rhombus with $\angle A < 90°$. Let its two diagonals AC and BD meet at a point M. A point O on the line segment MC is selected such that $O \neq M$ and $OB < OC$. The circle centred at O passing through points B and D meets the line AB at point B and a point X (where $X = B$ when the line AB is tangent to the circle) and meets the line BC at point B and a point Y. Let the lines DX and DY meet the line segment AC at P and Q, respectively. Express the value of $\dfrac{OQ}{OP}$ in terms of t when $\dfrac{MA}{MO} = t$.

Solution

Since the quadrilateral $DXBY$ is cyclic, we have

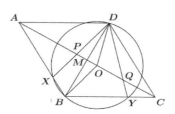

$$\angle AXD = \angle BYD$$
$$= \angle BOA = \angle BOP;$$

hence, quadrilateral $BOPX$ is cyclic. Consider the inversion I of pole O and power OB^2. Then the circle circumscribing $BOPX$ maps to the line AB. Thus, $I(P) = A$, which implies that $OP \cdot OA = OB^2$.

Similarly, we obtain $OQ \cdot OC = OB^2$. Therefore,

$$\frac{OQ}{OP} = \frac{OA}{OC} = \frac{MA + MO}{MA - MO} = \frac{\dfrac{MA}{MO} + 1}{\dfrac{MA}{MO} - 1} = \frac{t + 1}{t - 1}.$$

Suppose that the incircle of $\triangle ABC$ is tangent to the sides AB, BC, CA at points P, Q, R, respectively. Prove the following inequality:

$$\frac{BC}{PQ} + \frac{CA}{QR} + \frac{AB}{RP} \geq 6.$$

Solution

We use the standard notation a, b, c for the sides of triangle ABC, and s for the semiperimeter.

We have

$$PQ = 2(s-b)\sin\frac{B}{2} = 2(s-b)\sqrt{\frac{(s-c)(s-a)}{ca}},$$

$$QR = 2(s-c)\sin\frac{C}{2} = 2(s-c)\sqrt{\frac{(s-a)(s-b)}{ab}},$$

$$RP = 2(s-a)\sin\frac{A}{2} = 2(s-a)\sqrt{\frac{(s-b)(s-c)}{bc}}.$$

We apply the AM–GM Inequality and use the above expressions for PQ, QR, and RP to get

$$\frac{BC}{PQ} + \frac{CA}{QR} + \frac{AB}{RP} \geq 3 \cdot \sqrt[3]{\frac{BC \cdot CA \cdot AB}{PQ \cdot QR \cdot RP}} = 3 \cdot \sqrt[3]{\frac{(abc)^2}{8[(s-a)(s-b)(s-c)]^2}}.$$

Finally, we use the well-known inequality $abc \geq 8(s-a)(s-b)(s-c)$, which is equivalent to Euler's Inequality, to obtain

$$\frac{BC}{PQ} + \frac{CA}{QR} + \frac{AB}{RP} \geq 3\sqrt[3]{8} = 6.$$

Equality occurs only if $\triangle ABC$ is equilateral.

Two circles are externally tangent to each other at a point A and internally tangent to a third circle Γ at points B and C. Let D be the mid-point of the secant of Γ which is tangent to the smaller circles at A. Show that A is the incentre of the triangle BCD if the centres of the circles are not collinear.

Solution

Let E and F be the end-points of the diameter of Γ which is perpendicular to AD. Since the perpendicular bisector of a chord of a circle is a diameter of this circle, EF passes through D. The diameters of the smaller circles through A are perpendicular to AD and hence are parallel to EF. Therefore points B, A, and F are collinear, and C, A, and E are collinear. (*Proof:* (1) Proposition 1 of the book of Lemmas of Archimedes states: "two circles touch at P and if TU, VW be parallel diameters in them, PUW is a right line". (2) Points A and B are corresponding points in the inversion centred at F with the power of the inversion equal to $FD \cdot FE$, and points A and C are corresponding points in the inversion centred at F with the power of the inversion equal to $ED \cdot EF$.)

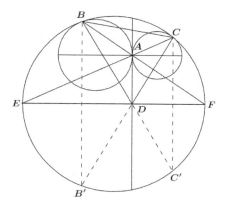

Let B' and C' be the reflections of B and C, respectively, across EF. Then B' and C' lie on Γ. Since $BB'C'C$ is an isosceles trapezoid, BC' and $B'C$ intersect at D. Thus,

$$\angle CBA = \angle CBF = \angle CEF = \angle FBC' = \angle ABD$$
$$\text{and} \quad \angle ACB = \angle ECB = \angle EFB = \angle B'CE = \angle DCA,$$

making A the incentre of triangle ABC.

In an acute triangle ABC with $|BC| < |AC| < |AB|$, the points D on side AB and E on side AC satisfy the condition $|BD| = |BC| = |CE|$. Show that the circumradius of the triangle ADE is equal to the distance between the incentre and the circumcentre of the triangle ABC.

Solution

Let O be the circumcentre of $\triangle ABC$ and I its incentre. Let the projections of O and I onto AC be O_2 and I_2, respectively, and let the projections of O and I onto AB be O_3 and I_3, respectively. Let the projections of O onto II_2 and II_3 be D_1 and E_1, respectively.

We have

$$OD_1 = O_2I_2 = \tfrac{1}{2}(c - a) = \tfrac{1}{2}AD$$

and

$$OE_1 = O_3I_3 = \tfrac{1}{2}(b - a) = \tfrac{1}{2}AE.$$

Also, $\angle D_1OE_1 = \angle DAE$. Hence, $\triangle OD_1E_1$ is similar to $\triangle ADE$, and the scale factor of the similarity is $\tfrac{1}{2}$. Since

$$\angle OD_1I = \angle OE_1I = 90°,$$

we see that OI is the diameter of the circumcircle of $\triangle OD_1E_1$. Then OI is the circumradius of $\triangle ADE$.

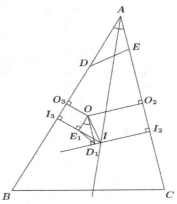

Remark. The points O, E_1, D_1, and I are concyclic if and only if $\angle OIE_1 = \angle OD_1E_1 = \angle ADE$. Since $IE_1 \perp AB$, it follows that $OI \perp DE$.

A point P lies in a triangle ABC. The edge AC meets the line BP at Q, and AB meets CP at R. Suppose that $AR = RB = CP$ and $CQ = PQ$. Find $\angle BRC$.

Solution

Let S be the second point of intersection of the circumcircles of triangles BPR and RCA.

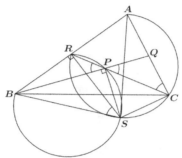

Since B, S, P, and R are concyclic, we have $\angle BSR = \angle BPR$; since A, R, S, and C are concyclic, $\angle RCA = \angle RSA$. Then

$$\angle BSR = \angle BPR = \angle QPC = \angle PCQ = \angle RCA = RSA.$$

Thus, SR bisects $\angle BSA$. Since $BR = RA$, the angle bisector theorem gives us $BS = SA$. Consequently, $\angle BRS = 90°$. Then $\angle BPS = 90°$ (because B, S, P, and R are concyclic).

We have

$$\angle CPS = 90° - \angle QPC = 90° - \angle BSR = \angle RBS = \angle ABS$$

and $\quad \angle SCP = \angle SCR = \angle SAR = \angle SAB$.

Therefore, triangles ABS and CPS are similar. Since $\triangle ABS$ is isosceles with $BS = SA$, it follows that $\triangle CPS$ is isosceles with $PS = SC$. Also,

$$\frac{PS}{BS} = \frac{CP}{AB} = \frac{\frac{1}{2}AB}{AB} = \frac{1}{2},$$

making $\angle SBP = 30°$ in right triangle PBS. Therefore,

$$\angle BRC = \angle BRS + \angle SRC = \angle BRS + \angle SRP$$
$$= \angle BRS + \angle SBP = 90° + 30° = 120°.$$

Let ABC be a triangle. We drop a perpendicular from A to the internal bisectors starting from B and C, their feet being A_1 and A_2. In the same way we define B_1, B_2 and C_1, C_2. Prove that

$$2(A_1A_2 + B_1B_2 + C_1C_2) = AB + BC + CA.$$

Solution

Let I be the incentre of $\triangle ABC$. Then,

$$\angle BAA_1 = \frac{\pi}{2} - \frac{B}{2} = \frac{A+C}{2} > \frac{A}{2} = \angle BAI,$$

$$\angle CAA_2 = \frac{\pi}{2} - \frac{C}{2} = \frac{A+B}{2} > \frac{A}{2} = \angle CAI.$$

Thus, A_1 and A_2 are on opposite sides of the bisector AI. Moreover,

$$\angle IAA_1 = \frac{\pi}{2} - \angle AIA_1 = \frac{\pi}{2} - \left(\frac{A}{2} + \frac{B}{2}\right) = \frac{C}{2}$$

(since $\angle AIA_1 = \pi - \angle AIB$) and similarly, $\angle IAA_2 = \frac{B}{2}$. It follows that

$$IA_1 = AI\sin\left(\frac{C}{2}\right) \quad \text{and} \quad IA_2 = AI\sin\left(\frac{B}{2}\right). \qquad (1)$$

With the familiar notations $a = BC$, $b = CA$, and $c = AB$, we also have

$$AA_1 = c\sin\left(\frac{B}{2}\right) \quad \text{and} \quad AA_2 = b\sin\left(\frac{C}{2}\right). \qquad (2)$$

Now, observe that A, A_2, I, and A_1 are (in this order) on the circle with diameter AI. Ptolemy's Theorem gives $A_1A_2 \cdot AI = IA_2 \cdot AA_1 + IA_1 \cdot AA_2$, from which, using (1) and (2), we get

$$A_1A_2 = c\sin^2\left(\frac{B}{2}\right) + b\sin^2\left(\frac{C}{2}\right).$$

There are analogous results for B_1B_2 and C_1C_2. Now we have

$$
\begin{aligned}
2(A_1A_2 &+ B_1B_2 + C_1C_2) \\
&= 2(a+b)\sin^2\left(\frac{C}{2}\right) + 2(b+c)\sin^2\left(\frac{A}{2}\right) + 2(c+a)\sin^2\left(\frac{B}{2}\right) \\
&= (a+b)(1-\cos C) + (b+c)(1-\cos A) + (c+a)(1\cos B) \\
&= 2(a+b+c) - \big[(c\cos B + b\cos C) \\
&\qquad\qquad + (a\cos C + c\cos A) + (a\cos B + b\cos A)\big] \\
&= 2(a+b+c) - (a+b+c) = a+b+c = AB + BC + CA.
\end{aligned}
$$

The triangle ABC, where $AB < AC$, has circumcircle S. The perpendicular from A to BC meets S again at P. The point X lies on the line segment AC, and BX meets S again at Q.

Show that $BX = CX$ if and only if PQ is a diameter of S.

Solution

Suppose that $BX = CX$. Then

$$\angle XCB = \angle XBC$$
$$= \angle QBC = \angle QAC;$$

whence, $AQ \parallel BC$. It follows that $\angle PAQ = 90°$, which means that PQ is a diameter of S.

The argument is reversible.

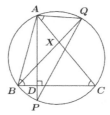

Let ABC be a triangle, and let D be a point on AB such that $4AD = AB$. The half-line ℓ is drawn on the same side of AB as C, starting from D and making an angle of θ with DA, where $\theta = \angle ACB$. If the circumcircle of ABC meets the half-line ℓ at P, show that $PB = 2PD$.

Solution

Let Q be the second point of intersection of the line DP with the circumcircle (see figure). Then

$$\angle ADQ = \angle BDP = \pi - \angle ADP = \pi - \angle ACB = \angle AQB$$

and $\angle QAD = \angle BAQ$. Therefore, $\triangle ADQ$ and $\triangle AQB$ are similar. Then $\dfrac{AD}{AQ} = \dfrac{AQ}{AB}$. Since $AB = 4AD$, it follows that $AB = 2AQ$. But $\triangle PDB$ and $\triangle AQB$ are also similar, since $\angle BDP = \angle AQB$ (from above) and $\angle DPB = \angle QPB = \angle QAB$. From this similarity and the relation $AB = 2AQ$, we conclude that $PB = 2PD$.

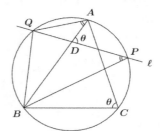

Angles B and C of triangle ABC are acute. Side KN of rectangle $KLMN$ belongs to segment BC, points L and M belong to segments AB and AC, respectively. Let O be the intersection point of the diagonals of $KLMN$. Let C_1 be the intersection point of lines BO and MN, and let B_1 be the intersection point of lines CO and LK. Prove that lines AO, BB_1, and CC_1 are concurrent.

Solution

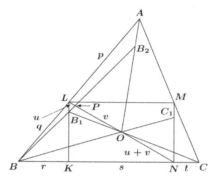

Let line BB_1 meet LN and OA at P and B_2, respectively. Let C_2 (not shown in the diagram) be the point of intersection of line CC_1 and OA. We use the following notation: $AL = p$, $LB = q$; $BK = r$, $KN = LM = s$, $NC = t$; $LP = u$, $PO = v$.

Since $\triangle ALM \sim \triangle ABC$, we have $\dfrac{p}{s} = \dfrac{p+q}{r+s+t} = \dfrac{q}{r+t}$; that is, $\dfrac{p}{q} = \dfrac{s}{r+t}$.

Now we apply Menelaus' Theorem to the triangle-transversal pairs $(\triangle LKN; B_1C)$ and $(\triangle LKN; PB)$ to get

$$\frac{LO}{ON} \cdot \frac{t}{s+t} = \frac{LB_1}{B_1K} = \frac{u}{u+2v} \cdot \frac{r+s}{r}.$$

Consequently, $\dfrac{u+2v}{u} = \dfrac{r+s}{r} \cdot \dfrac{s+t}{t}$; that is,

$$\frac{v}{u} = \frac{1}{2}\left(\frac{(r+s)(s+t)}{rt} - 1\right) = \frac{s(r+s+t)}{2rt}.$$

Applying Menelaus' Theorem to the pair $(\triangle OAL; B_2B)$, we obtain

$$\frac{OB_2}{B_2A} = \frac{v}{u} \cdot \frac{q}{p+q} = \frac{s(r+s+t)}{2rt} \cdot \frac{r+t}{r+s+t} = \frac{s(r+t)}{2rt}.$$

By symmetry, C_2 divides OA in the same ratio; that is, the points B_2 and C_2 coincide. Thus, AO, BB_1, and CC_1 concur at $B_2 (= C_2)$.

Prove that for any triangle, if S denotes its area and r denotes the radius of its inscribed circle, then

$$\frac{S}{r^2} \geq 3\sqrt{3}.$$

Solution

Denote the side lengths of the triangle by a, b, and c and the semi-perimeter by s. Applying the AM–GM Inequality to the positive numbers $s - a$, $s - b$, and $s - c$, we obtain $\sqrt[3]{(s-a)(s-b)(s-c)} \leq \frac{1}{3}s$; that is,

$$(s-a)(s-b)(s-c) \leq \frac{s^3}{27}. \tag{1}$$

Using Heron's Formula along with (1) and the known formula $S = rs$, we obtain

$$S^2 = s(s-a)(s-b)(s-c) \leq \frac{s^4}{27} \leq \frac{S^4}{27r^4}.$$

Then, $\frac{S^2}{r^4} \geq 27$, and hence, $\frac{S}{r^2} \geq 3\sqrt{3}$.

Let A', B', C' be the mid-points of the sides BC, CA, AB, respectively, of an acute non-isoceles triangle ABC, and let D, E, F be the feet of the altitudes through the vertices A, B, C on these sides, respectively. Consider the arc DA' of the nine-point circle of triangle ABC lying outside the triangle. Let the point of trisection of this arc closer to A' be A''. Define analogously the points B'' (on arc EB') and C'' (on arc FC'). Show that triangle $A''B''C''$ is equilateral.

Solution

Let N be the centre of the nine-point circle $\mathcal{N}$ of triangle ABC. The perpendicular bisectors of $B'C'$ and $A'D$ coincide (both pass through N and are perpendicular to BC); hence, A' and D are symmetrical in the diameter of $\mathcal{N}$ perpendicular to BC. It follows that the mid-point of the (smaller) arc $B'C'$ and the mid-point of the arc DA' lying outside the triangle are diametrically opposite.

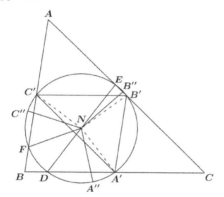

Without loss of generality, we may suppose that $\mathcal{N}$ is the unit circle in the complex plane, with $\triangle A'B'C'$ positively oriented (see figure). We may even suppose that the angles $\alpha = \angle B'A'C'$, $\beta = \angle C'B'A'$, and $\gamma = \angle A'C'B'$ satisfy $\frac{\pi}{2} > \beta > \alpha > \gamma$ and that the complex affix of B' is 1. It is readily seen that the affixes of C' and A' are $e^{2i\alpha}$ and $e^{-2i\gamma} = e^{2i(\pi-\gamma)}$, respectively. The affix of the mid-point of the arc $B'C'$ is $e^{i\alpha}$; hence, the affix of the mid-point of the arc DA' is $e^{i(\pi+\alpha)}$. Since $\pi + \alpha < 2\pi - 2\gamma$ (note that $\alpha + 2\gamma < \alpha + \beta + \gamma - \pi$), we find D, A'', and A' in that order on the circle positively oriented. It follows that the affix of A'' is

$$e^{i(\pi+\alpha+(2\pi-2\gamma-\pi-\alpha)/3)} = e^{4\pi i/3} \cdot e^{2i(\alpha-\gamma)/3}.$$

In a similar way, we find that the affix of B'' is $e^{2i(\alpha-\gamma)/3}$ and the affix of C'' is $e^{2\pi i/3} \cdot e^{2i(\alpha-\gamma)/3}$. Thus, the affixes of B'', C'', and A'' are of the form $e^{i\theta}$, $e^{i\theta} \cdot e^{2\pi i/3}$, and $e^{i\theta} \cdot e^{4\pi i/3}$; whence, $\triangle A''B''C''$ is equilateral.

Let ABC be a triangle, and let r, r_1, r_2, r_3 denote its inradius and the exradii opposite the vertices A, B, C, respectively. Suppose $a > r_1$, $b > r_2$, $c > r_3$. Prove that

(a) triangle ABC is acute, (b) $a + b + c > r + r_1 + r_2 + r_3$.

Solution

(a) Let s denote the semipermieter of $\triangle ABC$. From the known formula $\tan(A/2) = r_1/s$ and the given inequality $a > r_1$, we obtain $\tan(A/2) < a/s < 1$. Similarly, $\tan(B/2) < 1$ and $\tan(C/2) < 1$. Then $A < \frac{\pi}{2}$, $B < \frac{\pi}{2}$, and $C < \frac{\pi}{2}$. Hence, $\triangle ABC$ is acute.

(b) Since the triangle ABC is acute, we have the known inequality $s > r + 2R$, where R is the circumradius of $\triangle ABC$. We also have $r_1 + r_2 + r_3 = r + 4R$. Hence,

$$r + r_1 + r_2 + r_3 = 2r + 4R < 2s = a + b + c.$$

In the interior of a triangle ABC, circles K_1, K_2, K_3, and K_4 of the same radii are defined such that K_1, K_2, and K_3 touch two sides of the triangle and K_4 touches K_1, K_2, and K_3, as shown in the figure.

Prove that the centre of K_4 is located on the line through the incentre and the circumcentre.

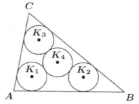

Solution

Let O_i be the centre of the circle K_i (for $i = 1, 2, 3, 4$), and let ρ be the common radius of the circles. Let γ (centre I, radius r) and Γ (centre O, radius R) denote the incircle and the circumcircle of $\triangle ABC$, respectively.

Circle K_1 is the image of γ under the homothety with centre A and scale factor $k = \rho/r$; hence, $\overrightarrow{AO_1} = k\overrightarrow{AI}$, so that $\overrightarrow{IO_1} = (1-k)\overrightarrow{IA}$. Similarly, $\overrightarrow{IO_2} = (1-k)\overrightarrow{IB}$ and $\overrightarrow{IO_3} = (1-k)\overrightarrow{IC}$. Therefore, $\triangle O_1O_2O_3$ is the image of $\triangle ABC$ under the homothety with centre I and factor $1 - k$. It follows that the circumcentre of $\triangle O_1O_2O_3$, namely O_4, is the image of O through this homothety. As a result, O_4, I, and O are collinear, as required.

Note. The circumradius 2ρ of $\triangle O_1O_2O_3$ satisfies $2\rho = \left(1 - \frac{\rho}{r}\right)R$. Thus, $\rho = \dfrac{rR}{2r + R}$, a useful result when drawing the figure.

Let A_1, B_1, and C_1 be the mid-points of the sides of the acute-angled triangle ABC. The 6 lines through these points perpendicular to the other sides meet in the points A_2, B_2, and C_2, as shown in the figure. Prove that the area of the hexagon $A_1C_2B_1A_2C_1B_2$ equals half of the area of $\triangle ABC$.

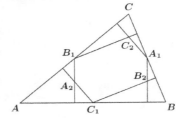

Solution

Denote the area of $\triangle XYZ$ by $[XYZ]$. Since $\triangle A_1B_1C_1$ is the image of $\triangle ABC$ under the homothety with centre at the centroid and factor $-\frac{1}{2}$, we have $[A_1B_1C_1] = \frac{1}{4}[ABC]$. Similarly, using the homothety h with centre A and factor $\frac{1}{2}$, we have $[AB_1C_1] = \frac{1}{4}[ABC]$.

Now, let O and H be the circumcentre and orthocentre of $\triangle ABC$, respectively. Note that these points are interior to the acute-angled $\triangle ABC$. Letting h_a be the length of the altitude from A to BC in $\triangle ABC$, we have

$$[BHC] = \tfrac{1}{2} \cdot BC \cdot (h_a - AH) = [ABC] - \tfrac{1}{2}BC \cdot AH .$$

Using the well-known relation $AH = 2OA_1$, we deduce that

$$[BHC] = [ABC] - BC \cdot OA_1 = [ABC] - 2[OBC] .$$

Observing that $h(H) = A_2$ (where h is the homothety defined above), we obtain

$$[B_1A_2C_1] = \tfrac{1}{4}[BHC] = \tfrac{1}{4}[ABC] - \tfrac{1}{2}[OBC] .$$

In the same way, we can show that $[C_1B_2A_1] = \frac{1}{4}[ABC] - \frac{1}{2}[OCA]$ and $[A_1C_2B_1] = \frac{1}{4}[ABC] - \frac{1}{2}[OAB]$. It follows that

$$\begin{aligned}
[A_1C_2B_1A_2C_1B_2] &= [A_1B_1C_1] + [B_1A_2C_1] + [C_1B_2A_1] + [A_1C_2B_1] \\
&= \tfrac{1}{4}[ABC] + \tfrac{3}{4}[ABC] \\
&\quad - \tfrac{1}{2}([OBC] + [OCA] + [OAB]) \\
&= [ABC] - \tfrac{1}{2}[ABC] = \tfrac{1}{2}[ABC] ,
\end{aligned}$$

as required.

The incircle of triangle ABC with $AB \neq BC$ touches sides BC and AC at points A_1 and B_1, respectively. The segments AA_1 and BB_1 meet the incircle at A_2 and B_2, respectively. Prove that the lines AB, A_1B_1, and A_2B_2 are concurrent.

Solution

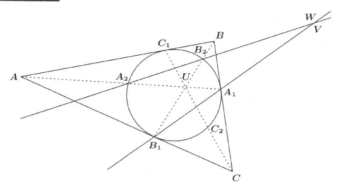

Let the incircle Γ touch the side AB at C_1 and let $a = BC$, $b = CA$, $c = AB$, and $s = \frac{1}{2}(a + b + c)$. Since

$$\frac{AB_1}{B_1C} \cdot \frac{CA_1}{A_1B} \cdot \frac{BC_1}{C_1A} = \frac{s-a}{s-c} \cdot \frac{s-c}{s-b} \cdot \frac{s-b}{s-a} = 1,$$

Ceva's Theorem shows that the lines AA_1, BB_1, and CC_1 are concurrent, say at U (U is the Gergonne Point of the triangle).

Let V be the pole of the line CC_1 with respect to the circle Γ. Since CA_1 and CB_1 are tangent to Γ at A_1 and B_1, respectively, the polar of C with respect to Γ is the line A_1B_1. By polar reciprocity, V is on A_1B_1. Similarly, the polar of C_1 is the line AB; hence, V is on AB. Now, let A_1B_1 and A_2B_2 meet at W. Since A_1A_2 and B_1B_2 meet at U, the polar of W with respect to Γ passes through U. But this polar also passes through C (since W is on A_1B_1). Thus, the polar of W is $CU = CC_1$ and $W = V$. Finally, V is on AB, A_1B_1, and A_2B_2 and the result follows.

Let A_1, B_1, and C_1 be the respective mid-points of the sides BC, AC, and AB of triangle ABC. Take a point K on the segment C_1A_1 and a point L on the segment A_1B_1 such that

$$\frac{C_1K}{KA_1} = \frac{BC + AC}{AC + AB} \quad \text{and} \quad \frac{A_1L}{LB_1} = \frac{AC + AB}{AB + BC}.$$

Let $S = BK \cap CL$. Show that $\angle C_1 A_1 S = \angle B_1 A_1 S$.

Solution

As usual, let $a = BC$, $b = CA$, and $c = AB$. Denote by $d(X, YZ)$ the distance from point X to the line YZ and by $[XYZ]$ the area of triangle XYZ. Since S is interior to $\triangle A_1 B_1 C_1$, the desired conclusion is successively equivalent to

$$S \text{ is on the internal bisector of } \angle B_1 A_1 C_1\,,$$
$$d(S, A_1 C_1) = d(S, A_1 B_1)\,,$$
$$A_1 B_1 \cdot A_1 C_1 \cdot d(S, A_1 C_1) = A_1 C_1 \cdot A_1 B_1 \cdot d(S, A_1 B_1)\,,$$
$$c \cdot [SA_1 C_1] = b \cdot [SA_1 B_1]\,. \tag{1}$$

Denote by $\overrightarrow{X}$ the vector to X from a fixed origin. From the hypotheses, we have

$$(a + 2b + c)\overrightarrow{K} = (a + b)\overrightarrow{A}_1 + (b + c)\overrightarrow{C}_1$$
$$(a + b + 2c)\overrightarrow{L} = (a + c)\overrightarrow{A_1} + (b + c)\overrightarrow{B}_1$$
$$\overrightarrow{B} = \overrightarrow{A}_1 - \overrightarrow{B}_1 + \overrightarrow{C}_1 \quad \text{and} \quad \overrightarrow{C} = \overrightarrow{A}_1 + \overrightarrow{B}_1 - \overrightarrow{C}_1\,.$$

Thus,

$$(a + 2b + c)\overrightarrow{K} - b\overrightarrow{B} = (a + b + 2c)\overrightarrow{L} - c\overrightarrow{C} = a\overrightarrow{A}_1 + b\overrightarrow{B}_1 + c\overrightarrow{C}_1\,;$$

whence (since $S = BK \cap CL$),

$$(a + b + c)\overrightarrow{S} = a\overrightarrow{A}_1 + b\overrightarrow{B}_1 + c\overrightarrow{C}_1\,.$$

As a result, $a : b : c = [SB_1 C_1] : [SC_1 A_1] : [SA_1 B_1]$, and (1) follows.

Note: Since $B_1 C_1 = \frac{1}{2}a$, $C_1 A_1 = \frac{1}{2}b$, and $A_1 B_1 = \frac{1}{2}c$, the result just obtained even shows that S is the incentre of $\triangle A_1 B_1 C_1$.

Let A and B be two fixed points in the plane. Let $ABCD$ be a convex quadrilateral such that $AB = BC$, $AD = DC$, and $\angle ADC = 90°$. Prove that there is a fixed point P such that, for every such quadrilateral $ABCD$ on the same side of the line AB, the line DC passes through P.

Solution

On the same side of AB as the quadrilateral $ABCD$, draw the semi-circle (S) with centre B and radius BA, and the ray (R) originating at B and perpendicular to BA. We will show that all the lines CD pass through the point of intersection of (S) and (R).

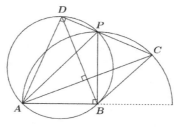

Let $ABCD$ be an arbitrary quadrilateral satisfying the given conditions, and let P be the point of intersection of CD and (R).

We complete the proof by showing that this point P is on (S); that is, $BP = BC$. Let $\angle(\ell, \ell')$ denote the directed angle of the lines ℓ and ℓ'. Our goal will be reached if we prove the equality $\angle(PB, PC) = \angle(CP, CB)$.

We will use the fact that $\triangle ADC$ is right-angled and isosceles and that A, D, P, and B are concyclic (on the circle with diameter AP). Note also that BD is perpendicular to AC (since $BA = BC$ and $DA = DC$).

First, $\angle(PB, PC) = \angle(PB, PD) - \pi = \angle(AB, AD)$. Then,

$$\begin{aligned}
\angle(CP, CB) &= \angle(CP, CA) + \angle(CA, CB) \\
&= \angle(AC, AD) + \angle(AB, AC) \\
&\qquad \text{(since } AD = DC \text{ and } AB = BC\text{)} \\
&= \angle(AB, AD),
\end{aligned}$$

and the result follows.

In a triangle ABC, define C_a to be the circle tangent to AB, to AC, and to the incircle of the triangle ABC, and let r_a be the radius of C_a. Define r_b and r_c in the same way. Prove that $r_a + r_b + r_c \geq 4r$, where r is the inradius of the triangle ABC.

Solution

The given inequality is false (for example $r_a = r_b = r_c = \frac{r}{3}$ in an equilateral triangle). We will prove instead that

$$r_a + r_b + r_c \geq r. \tag{1}$$

The circle C_a is the image of the incircle in the homothety with centre A and scale factor r_a/r. Hence, if I is the incentre and I_a is the centre of C_a, we have $\overrightarrow{AI_a} = \frac{r_a}{r} \overrightarrow{AI}$, which can be rewritten as

$$\overrightarrow{II_a} = \left(\frac{r_a}{r} - 1\right) \overrightarrow{AI}.$$

Since $r_a < r$ and $II_a = r + r_a$, it follows that

$$\frac{r_a}{r} = \frac{AI - r}{AI + r} = \frac{2AI}{AI + r} - 1 = \frac{2}{1 + (r/AI)} - 1 = \frac{2}{1 + \sin(A/2)} - 1.$$

Similar results hold for r_b and r_c. Thus, we see that (1) is equivalent to

$$\frac{1}{1 + \sin(A/2)} + \frac{1}{1 + \sin(B/2)} + \frac{1}{1 + \sin(C/2)} \geq 2. \tag{2}$$

The function $f(x) = 1/(1+\sin x)$ is strictly convex on $\left(0, \frac{\pi}{2}\right)$ (its second derivative is $f''(x) = (1 + \sin x)^{-3}(1 + \sin x + \cos^2 x)$, which is positive); hence,

$$f\left(\frac{A}{2}\right) + f\left(\frac{B}{2}\right) + f\left(\frac{C}{2}\right) \geq 3f\left(\frac{A+B+C}{3}\right) = 3f\left(\frac{\pi}{6}\right) = 2.$$

Therefore, (2) holds. Equality is attained in (2) if and only if $A = B = C$; that is, if and only if $\triangle ABC$ is equilateral.

Let ABC be a triangle. We drop a perpendicular from A to the internal bisectors starting from B and C, their feet being A_1 and A_2. In the same way we define B_1, B_2 and C_1, C_2. Prove that

$$2(A_1A_2 + B_1B_2 + C_1C_2) = AB + BC + CA.$$

Solution

We shall see that

$$A_1A_2 = s - a, \quad B_1B_2 = s - b, \quad C_1C_2 = s - c,$$

where s is the semiperimeter of $\triangle ABC$ and a, b, c are the sides. Then it will follow at once that

$$2(A_1A_2 + B_1B_2 + C_1C_2) = 2(s - a + s - b + s - c) = 2s,$$

which is the desired result.

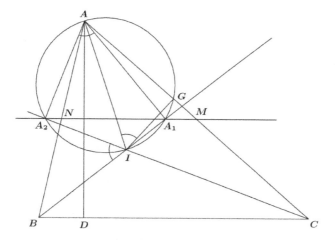

To this end, we denote the incentre (where BA_1 intersects CA_2) by I and look at the circle on diameter AI. Because of the right angles at A_1 and A_2, the quadrangle AA_2IA_1 is cyclic; whence, $\angle A_2AA_1 = \angle A_2IB$. This last angle is an exterior angle of $\triangle BIC$, so that

$$\angle A_2AA_1 = \angle A_2IB = \frac{B}{2} + \frac{C}{2} = \frac{\pi}{2} - \frac{A}{2}.$$

Let G be the foot of the perpendicular from I to AC. Then $\angle GIA$ is the complement of $\angle IAG$ in the right triangle IAG, which implies that

$$\angle A_2AA_1 = \angle GIA.$$

Because G is the point where the incircle of $\triangle ABC$ touches the side AC, we have $AG = s - a$. Furthermore, AI subtends the right angle at G, so that G is another point on the circle AA_2IA_1G whose diameter is AI. Because the inscribed angles $\angle A_2AA_1$ and $\angle GIA$ are equal, the chords that subtend them, namely A_1A_2 and AG must have the same length; that is, $A_1A_2 = s - a$ as claimed. Similarly $B_1B_2 = s - b$ and $C_1C_2 = s - c$, which completes the proof.

Find the area of the convex pentagon $ABCDE$, given that $AB = BC$, $CD = DE$, $\angle ABC = 150°$, $\angle CDE = 30°$, and $BD = 2$.

Solution

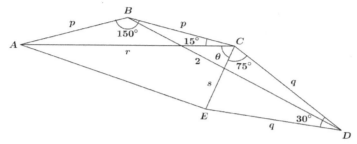

Let $p = AB = BC$ and $q = CD = DE$. Let $r = AC$, $s = CE$, and $\theta = \angle ACE$. From the given information, we see that $\angle ACB = 15°$ and $\angle DCE = 75°$. Then $r = 2p\cos 15°$ and $s = 2q\cos 75° = 2q\sin 15°$. Thus, $rs = 2pq \cdot 2\sin 15° \cos 15° = 2pq\sin 30° = pq$. By applying the Cosine Law to $\triangle BCD$, we get

$$4 = p^2 + q^2 - 2pq\cos(\theta + 90°) = p^2 + q^2 + 2pq\sin\theta.$$

Consequently,

$$
\begin{aligned}
[ABCDE] &= [ABC] + [CDE] + [ACE] \\
&= \tfrac{1}{2}p^2\sin 150° + \tfrac{1}{2}q^2\sin 30° + \tfrac{1}{2}rs\sin\theta \\
&= \tfrac{1}{4}(p^2 + q^2 + 2pq\sin\theta) = \tfrac{1}{4}(4) = 1.
\end{aligned}
$$

The quadrilateral $ABCD$ is cyclic and has the property that $AB = BC = AD + CD$. Given that $\angle BAD = \alpha$ and that the diagonal $AC = d$, find the area of the triangle ABC.

We will show that $[ABC] = \frac{1}{2}d^2 \sin \alpha$ (here and in what follows, $[\cdot]$ denotes area).
Let $a = AB = BC = AD + CD$ and $\theta = \angle ABC$. Then

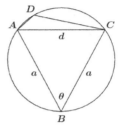

$$
\begin{aligned}
[ABCD] \\
&= [DAB] + [DCB] \\
&= \tfrac{1}{2}AB \cdot AD \sin \alpha + \tfrac{1}{2}BC \cdot CD \sin \alpha \\
&= \tfrac{1}{2}a(AD + CD) \sin \alpha = \tfrac{1}{2}a^2 \sin \alpha
\end{aligned}
$$

and

$$
\begin{aligned}
[ABCD] &= [ABC] + [ADC] = \tfrac{1}{2}AB \cdot BC \sin \theta + \tfrac{1}{2}AD \cdot CD \sin \theta \\
&= \tfrac{1}{2}(a^2 + AD \cdot CD) \sin \theta
\end{aligned}
$$

Thus,

$$
a^2 \sin \alpha = (a^2 + AD \cdot CD) \sin \theta . \tag{1}
$$

By the Law of Cosines,

$$
d^2 = AB^2 + BC^2 - 2AB \cdot BC \cos \theta = 2a^2(1 - \cos \theta) ;
$$

that is, $2(1 - \cos \theta) = d^2/a^2$. Also,

$$
\begin{aligned}
d^2 &= AD^2 + CD^2 + 2AD \cdot CD \cos \theta \\
&= (AD + CD)^2 - 2AD \cdot CD(1 - \cos \theta) = a^2 - AD \cdot CD(d^2/a^2) ,
\end{aligned}
$$

which implies that $a^2 + AD \cdot CD = a^4/d^2$. Using this result in (1), we get $a^2 \sin \alpha = (a^4/d^2) \sin \theta$; that is, $d^2 \sin \alpha = a^2 \sin \theta$.
Finally, $[ABC] = \frac{1}{2}AB \cdot BC \sin \theta = \frac{1}{2}a^2 \sin \theta = \frac{1}{2}d^2 \sin \alpha$.

Prove that a right-angled triangle can be inscribed in the parabola $y = x^2$ so that its hypotenuse is parallel to the x–axis if and only if the altitude from the right angle is equal to 1. (A triangle is inscribed in a parabola if all three vertices of the triangle are on the parabola.)

Solution

Let ABC be a triangle with $\angle A = 90°$, placed so that the hypotenuse BC is parallel to the x-axis and the vertices B and C lie on the parabola $y = x^2$. Suppose that the coordinates of B are (b, b^2), where $b > 0$. Then the coordinates of C are $(-b, b^2)$. Let (x_0, y_0) be the coordinates of A.

Note that $\overrightarrow{AB} = [b - x_0, b^2 - y_0]$ and $\overrightarrow{AC} = [-b - x_0, b^2 - y_0]$. Since $\angle A = 90°$, we have $\overrightarrow{AB} \cdot \overrightarrow{AC} = 0$; that is,

$$x_0^2 - b^2 + (b^2 - y_0)^2 = 0. \qquad (1)$$

If $\triangle ABC$ is inscribed in the parabola $y = x^2$, then A lies on the parabola, which implies that $y_0 = x_0^2$. This, together with (1), gives $y_0 - b^2 + (b^2 - y_0)^2 = 0$, or $(b^2 - y_0)(b^2 - y_0 - 1) = 0$. Since $b^2 \neq y_0$, we obtain $b^2 - y_0 = 1$, which means that the altitude from A is equal to 1.

Conversely, if the altitude from A is equal to 1, then $b^2 - y_0 = 1$. Setting $b^2 = y_0 + 1$ in (1), we obtain $x_0^2 - (y_0 + 1) + 1 = 0$, or $y_0 = x_0^2$. Thus, A lies on the parabola and $\triangle ABC$ is inscribed in the parabola.

The diagonals A_1A_4, A_2A_5, and A_3A_6 of the convex hexagon $A_1A_2A_3A_4A_5A_6$ meet at a point K. Given that $A_2A_1 = A_2A_3 = A_2K$, $A_4A_3 = A_4A_5 = A_4K$, and $A_6A_5 = A_6A_1 = A_6K$, prove that the hexagon is cyclic.

Solution

We first observe that A_2A_4 is the perpendicular bisector of KA_3, A_4A_6 is the perpendicular bisector of KA_5, and A_6A_2 is the perpendicular bisector of KA_1. Let the points at which these perpendicular bisections occur be denoted by P, Q, and R, respectively. Then

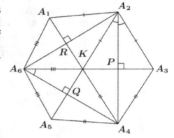

$$\triangle A_2PA_3 \cong \triangle A_2PK \sim \triangle A_6QK .$$

Thus,

$$\angle A_3A_6A_4 = \angle A_5A_2A_4 = \angle A_3A_2A_4 .$$

Hence, the quadrilateral $A_2A_3A_4A_6$ is cyclic; that is, A_3 lies on the circumcircle of $\triangle A_2A_4A_6$. Similarly, A_5 and A_1 lie on the same circumcircle. Therefore, the hexagon is cyclic.

Distinct points A_0, A_1, ..., A_{1000} on one side of an angle and distinct points B_0, B_1, ..., B_{1000} on the other side are spaced so that $A_0A_1 = A_1A_2 = \cdots = A_{999}A_{1000}$ and $B_0B_1 = B_1B_2 = \cdots = B_{999}B_{1000}$. Find the area of the quadrilateral $A_{999}A_{1000}B_{1000}B_{999}$ if the areas of the quadrilaterals $A_0A_1B_1B_0$ and $A_1A_2B_2B_1$ are equal to 5 and 7, respectively.

Solution

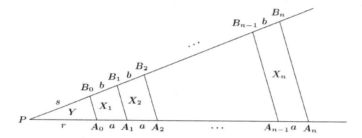

Let P denote the vertex of the angle, and let $r = PA_0$, $a = A_0A_1$, $s = PB_0$, $b = B_0B_1$, $Y = [PA_0B_0]$, and $X_n = [A_{n-1}A_nB_nB_{n-1}]$, where $[\cdot]$ denotes area, as usual. Furthermore, set $\alpha = a/r$ and $\beta = b/s$. We have

$$
\begin{aligned}
\frac{X_n}{Y} &= \frac{[PA_nB_n]}{Y} - \frac{[PA_{n-1}B_{n-1}]}{Y} \\
&= \frac{(r+na)(s+nb)}{rs} - \frac{(r+(n-1)a)(s+(n-1)b)}{rs} \\
&= (1+n\alpha)(1+n\beta) - (1+(n-1)\alpha)(1+(n-1)\beta) \\
&= \alpha + \beta + (2n-1)\alpha\beta\,;
\end{aligned}
$$

that is, $X_n = (\alpha+\beta+(2n-1)\alpha\beta)Y$. Consequently, $X_{n+1} - X_n = 2\alpha\beta Y$. Thus, X_1, X_2, X_3, ... is an arithmetic progression.

In the case where $X_1 = 5$ and $X_2 = 7$, the common difference is 2; therefore, $X_{1000} = 5 + 999 \cdot 2 = 2003$.

A quadrilateral $ABCD$ is cyclic with $AB = 2AD$ and $BC = 2CD$. Given that $\angle BAD = \alpha$, and diagonal $AC = d$, find the area of the triangle ABC.

Solution

Note that A and C lie on the circle consisting of all points P such that $PB = 2PD$, which is centred on the line BD. It follows that A and C are on opposite sides of BD (otherwise, we would have $A = C$); that is, $ABCD$ is convex.

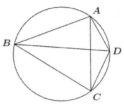

Denote area by $[\cdot]$. We will show that $[ABC] = \frac{1}{2}d^2 \sin \alpha$.

First,

$$[ABC] = \tfrac{1}{2}BA \cdot BC \sin \angle ABC = 2AD \cdot CD \sin \angle ADC = 4[ACD];$$

thus,

$$[ABC] = \tfrac{4}{5}[ABCD]. \qquad (1)$$

Now,

$$[ABCD] = [ABD] + [DCB] = \tfrac{1}{2}AB \cdot AD \sin \alpha + \tfrac{1}{2}CB \cdot CD \sin \alpha$$
$$= (AD^2 + CD^2) \sin \alpha. \qquad (2)$$

From the Law of Cosines, we have

$$d^2 = AD^2 + CD^2 - 2AD \cdot CD \cos \angle ADC$$

and also

$$d^2 = AB^2 + BC^2 - 2AB \cdot BC \cos \angle ABC$$
$$= 4AD^2 + 4CD^2 + 8DA \cdot DC \cos \angle ADC,$$

from which it readily follows that $8(AD^2 + CD^2) = 5d^2$. With (1) and (2), this immediately yields

$$[ABC] = \tfrac{4}{5} \cdot \tfrac{5}{8}d^2 \cdot \sin \alpha = \tfrac{1}{2}d^2 \sin \alpha.$$

Let $ABCD$ be a cyclic quadrilateral. Let P, Q, R be the feet of the perpendiculars from D to the lines BC, CA, AB, respectively. Show that $PQ = QR$ if and only if the bisectors of $\angle ABC$ and $\angle ADC$ are concurrent with AC.

Solution

Let A, B, C denote the angles of $\triangle ABC$. Let M be the point of intersection of the internal bisector of $\angle ABC$ with AC. Recall that M is the point of the line segment AC characterized by $\dfrac{MA}{MC} = \dfrac{BA}{BC}$.

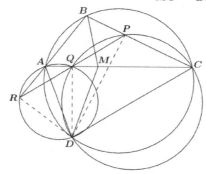

Points Q and R lie on the circle with diameter AD; hence, by the Law of Sines, $QR = DA \sin \angle RAQ = DA \sin A$. Similarly, $QP = DC \sin C$. Then

$$\frac{QR}{QP} = \frac{DA \sin A}{DC \sin C} = \frac{DA}{DC} \cdot \frac{BC}{BA} = \frac{DA}{DC} \cdot \frac{MC}{MA}.$$

Now $PQ = QR$ if and only if $\dfrac{MA}{MC} = \dfrac{DA}{DC}$, which is equivalent to DM being the internal bisector of $\angle ADC$.

Let ABC be a triangle, and let P be a point in its interior. Denote by D, E, F the feet of the perpendiculars from P to the lines BC, CA, AB, respectively. Suppose that $AP^2 + PD^2 = BP^2 + PE^2 = CP^2 + PF^2$. Denote by I_A, I_B, I_C the excentres of the triangle ABC. Prove that P is the circumcentre of the triangle $I_A I_B I_C$.

Solution

Let $a = BC$, $b = CA$, $c = AB$, and $s = \frac{1}{2}(a + b + c)$. From the hypothesis, $BD^2 = BP^2 - PD^2 = AP^2 - PE^2 = AE^2$; hence, $BD = AE$. Similarly, $CE = BF$ and $AF = CD$. Since $BD + DC = a$, $CE + EA = b$, and $AF + FB = c$, we find that $BD = AE = s - c$, $CE = BF = s - a$, and $AF = CD = s - b$, which implies that D, E, and F are the points of tangency of the excircles with the sides BC, CA, and AB, respectively. In particular, D is on the line PI_A, and similar results hold for E and F.

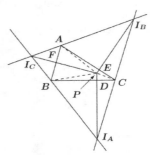

Now, $\angle BCI_A = \frac{1}{2}(\pi - C)$, since $I_A I_B$ is the external bisector of $\angle ACB$. Using this and similar equalities, we obtain the angles of $\triangle I_A I_B I_C$:

$$\angle I_A = \tfrac{1}{2}(\pi - A), \quad \angle I_B = \tfrac{1}{2}(\pi - B), \quad \angle I_C = \tfrac{1}{2}(\pi - C).$$

The internal bisector $I_A A$ is perpendicular to the external bisector $I_B I_C$; whence, $I_A A$ is the altitude from I_A in $\triangle I_A I_B I_C$. Moreover,

$$I_C I_A A = \tfrac{\pi}{2} - \angle A I_C I_A = \tfrac{1}{2} C$$

and

$$\angle D I_A C = \tfrac{\pi}{2} - \angle B C I_A = \tfrac{1}{2} C.$$

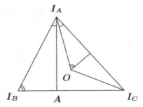

Therefore, $I_A D$ is the image of the altitude $I_A A$ in the internal bisector of $\angle I_B I_A I_C$. It follows that $I_A D$ passes through the circumcentre of $\triangle I_A I_B I_C$ (see the figure for a proof without words). Similarly, $I_B E$ and $I_C F$ pass through this circumcentre. The required result follows.

Let ABC be an isosceles triangle with $AC = BC$, whose incentre is I.
Let P be a point on the circumcircle of the triangle AIB lying inside the
triangle ABC. The lines through P parallel to CA and CB meet AB at D
and E, respectively. The line through P parallel to AB meets CA and CB
at F and G, respectively. Prove that the lines DF and EG intersect on the
circumcircle of the triangle ABC.

Solution

Set $\alpha = \angle CAB = \angle CBA$. Then $\angle ACB = 180° - 2\alpha$. Since P lies
on the circumcircle of triangle AIB, we have $\angle APB = \angle AIB = 180° - \alpha$.
Set $\theta = \angle FAP$ and $\phi = \angle PAB$. Then $\phi = \alpha - \theta$,

$$\angle PBA = 180° - \angle PAB - \angle APB = 180° - (\alpha - \theta) - (180° - \alpha) = \theta,$$

and $\angle PBG = \angle CBA - \angle PBA = \alpha - \theta = \phi$. Also, since $FG \parallel AB$, we
have $\angle APF = \angle PAB = \phi$ and $\angle BPG = \angle PBA = \theta$.
    Since $\angle FPE = \angle FGB = 180° - \alpha$ and $\angle FAE = \angle CAB = \alpha$, we
see that $\angle FPE + \angle FAE = 180°$; hence, quadrilateral $FPEA$ is cyclic. Let
GE produced intersect the circle $FPEA$ at T. Then $\angle FTP = \angle FAP = \theta$,
$\angle ATF = \angle APF = \phi$, and $\angle PTG = \angle PTE = \angle PAE = \phi$.

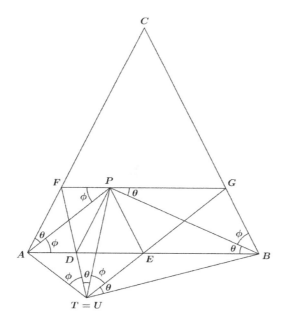

Likewise, quadrilateral $DPGB$ is cyclic. Let FD produced intersect the circle $DPGB$ at U. Then $\angle PUG = \angle PBG = \phi$, $\angle BUG = \angle BPG = \theta$, and $\angle FUP = \angle DUP = \angle DBP = \angle PBA = \theta$.

Now we have $\angle FTP = \angle FUP = \theta$ and $\angle PTG = \angle PUG = \phi$, meaning that segments FP and PG are seen from both U and T with angles θ and ϕ, respectively; hence, $U = T$. Therefore,

$$\begin{aligned} \angle ATB &= \angle ATF + \angle FTP + \angle PTG + \angle GTB \\ &= (\alpha - \theta) + \theta + (\alpha - \theta) + \theta = 2\alpha . \end{aligned}$$

Finally, $\angle ACB + \angle ATB = (180° - 2\alpha) + 2\alpha = 180°$, which implies that T is on the circumcircle of triangle ABC.

Let a, b, and c denote the sides of a triangle opposite the angles A, B, and C, respectively. Let r be the inradius and R the circumradius of the triangle. If $\angle A \geq 90°$, prove that

$$\frac{r}{R} \leq \frac{a \sin A}{a + b + c}.$$

Solution

If we let F be the area of $\triangle ABC$ and let h_a be the altitude from A, the proposed inequality is successively equivalent to

$$
\begin{aligned}
r(a + b + c) &\leq aR \sin A, \\
2F &\leq \tfrac{1}{2}a \cdot 2R \sin A, \\
ah_a &\leq \tfrac{1}{2}a^2, \\
h_a &\leq \tfrac{1}{2}a.
\end{aligned}
\tag{2}
$$

Now, the median m_a from A satisfies

$$
\begin{aligned}
m_a^2 &= \tfrac{1}{2}(b^2 + c^2) - \tfrac{1}{4}a^2 \\
&= \tfrac{1}{2}(a^2 + 2bc \cos A) - \tfrac{1}{4}a^2 \\
&= \tfrac{1}{4}a^2 + bc \cos A \leq \tfrac{1}{4}a^2,
\end{aligned}
$$

where the final inequality follows from $\cos A \leq 0$ (since $\angle A \geq 90°$).

Thus, $m_a \leq \tfrac{1}{2}a$, and (2) follows from the obvious inequality $h_a \leq m_a$.

Let ABC be an acute triangle, and let P be a point on side AB. Draw lines through P parallel to AC and BC, and let them cut BC and AC at X and Y, respectively. Construct (with straightedge and compass) the point P which gives the shortest length XY. Prove that the shortest XY is perpendicular to the median of ABC through C.

Solution

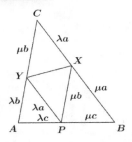
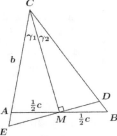

Let λ and μ be the positive real numbers such that $AP = \lambda AB = \lambda c$ and $BP = \mu AB = \mu c$. Then $\lambda + \mu = 1$, and we also have

$$PY = \lambda a, \quad AY = \lambda b, \quad BX = \mu a, \quad XC = \lambda a, \quad YC = \mu b.$$

Let $f(\lambda, \mu)$ be the square of the distance from X to Y. If $\gamma = \angle C = \angle XPY$, then, by the Law of Cosines in $\triangle PXY$ and $\triangle ABC$, we have

$$
\begin{aligned}
f(\lambda, \mu) \;=\; XY^2 &= \lambda^2 a^2 + \mu^2 b^2 - 2\lambda\mu ab \cos\gamma \\
&= \lambda^2 a^2 + \mu^2 b^2 - \lambda\mu(a^2 + b^2 - c^2) \\
&= \lambda^2 a^2 + (\lambda^2 - 2\lambda + 1)b^2 + \lambda(\lambda - 1)(a^2 + b^2 - c^2) \\
&= \lambda^2(2a^2 + 2b^2 - c^2) - \lambda(a^2 + 3b^2 - c^2) + b^2 \\
&= \lambda^2 \cdot 4m_c^2 - \lambda(a^2 + 3b^2 - c^2) + b^2.
\end{aligned}
$$

Setting $\frac{df}{d\lambda} = 0$, we get

$$\lambda \;=\; \frac{a^2 + 3b^2 - c^2}{8m_c^2} \qquad \left(\text{and} \quad \mu \;=\; 1 - \lambda \;=\; \frac{3a^2 + b^2 - c^2}{8m_c^2}\right).$$

Therefore,

$$CX \;=\; \lambda a \;=\; a\frac{a^2 + 3b^2 - c^2}{8m_c^2} \quad \text{and} \quad CY \;=\; \mu b \;=\; b\frac{3a^2 + b^2 - c^2}{8m_c^2}. \tag{1}$$

Let M be the mid-point of AB and set $\gamma_1 = \angle ACM$ and $\gamma_2 = \angle BCM$. By the Law of Cosines in $\triangle ACM$,

$$AM^2 = CA^2 + CM^2 - 2CA \cdot CM \cdot \cos \gamma_1 ,$$
$$\text{or} \quad c^2 = 4b^2 + 4m_c^2 - 8bm_c \cos \gamma_1 .$$

Similarly, we get $c^2 = 4a^2 + 4m_c^2 - 8am_c \cos \gamma_2$. Since $4m_c^2 = 2a^2 + 2b^2 - c^2$, we have

$$\cos \gamma_1 = \frac{a^2 + 3b^2 - c^2}{4bm_c} \quad \text{and} \quad \cos \gamma_2 = \frac{3a^2 + b^2 - c^2}{4am_c} ,$$

from which we have

$$\frac{\cos \gamma_1}{\cos \gamma_2} = \frac{a(a^2 + 3b^2 - c^2)}{b(3a^2 + b^2 - c^2)} .$$

Let the line through M perpendicular to CM intersect BC at D and AC at E. Applying the Law of Sines to $\triangle CDE$, we obtain

$$\frac{CD}{CE} = \frac{\sin \angle CED}{\sin \angle CDE} = \frac{\cos \gamma_1}{\cos \gamma_2} = \frac{a(a^2 + 3b^2 - c^2)}{b(3a^2 + b^2 - c^2)} . \qquad (2)$$

By (1) and (2), we have

$$\frac{CX}{CY} = \frac{a(a^2 + 3b^2 - c^2)}{b(3a^2 + b^2 - c^2)} = \frac{CD}{CE} .$$

Since $\triangle CXY$ and $\triangle CDE$ also have the angle at C in common, we see that they must be similar. Since $CM \perp ED$, it follows that $CM \perp XY$.

Consider the three disjoint arcs of a circle determined by three points on the circle. For each of these arcs, draw a circle centred at the mid-point of the arc and passing through the end-points of the arc. Prove that the three circles have a common point.

Solution

The following theorem is well-known:
Let I be the incentre of $\triangle ABC$. Then the lines AI, BI, and CI intersect the circumcircle for the second time in the mid-points A_1, B_1, and C_1 of the arcs BC, CA, and AB, respectively. Furthermore,

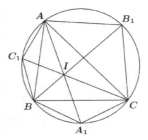

$$A_1B = A_1I = A_1C,$$
$$B_1C = B_1I = B_1A,$$
$$\text{and} \quad C_1A = C_1I = C_1B.$$

The common point of the three circles is thus the incentre of $\triangle ABC$.

Two circles with radii r and R are externally tangent at a point P. Determine the length of the segment cut from the common tangent through P by the other common tangents.

Solution

Without loss of generality, we may assume that $r \leq R$. Let the circle with radius r have centre O_1 and the circle with radius R have centre O_2. Let P be their point of tangency. Let the common external tangents meet the circles at A, B, C, and D, as in the diagram. Let the internal common tangent meet the external common tangents at K and L.

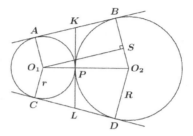

Let S be the point on O_2B such that $O_1S \perp O_2B$. Then $O_1S = AB$ and $O_2S = R - r$. Also

$$O_1S = \sqrt{(O_1O_2)^2 - (O_2S)^2} = \sqrt{(R+r)^2 - (R-r)^2} = 2\sqrt{Rr}.$$

Thus, $KP = \frac{1}{2}AB = \sqrt{Rr}$. Similarly, since $CD = AB = 2\sqrt{Rr}$, we have $PL = \sqrt{Rr}$, which implies that $KL = 2\sqrt{Rr}$.

Let r and s be two parallel lines in the plane, and P and Q two points such that $P \in r$ and $Q \in s$. Consider circles C_P and C_Q such that C_P is tangent to r at P, C_Q is tangent to s at Q, and C_P and C_Q are tangent externally to each other at some point, say T. Find the locus of T when (C_P, C_Q) varies over all pairs of circles with the given properties.

Solution

Let KH be the common tangent of the circles C_P and C_Q. It is obvious that quadrilaterals PO_1TH and QO_2TK are cyclic, and the fact that $\angle K = \angle H$ means that $\angle PO_1T = \angle TO_2Q$.

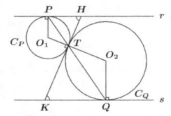

Thus, $\triangle PO_1T \sim \triangle TO_2Q$ (similar triangles), and the fact that O_1TO_2 is a straight line tells us that PTQ is also a straight line.

Consequently, T belongs to the constant line PQ. Also, we get from the above similarity of triangles that $PT = PQ \cdot \dfrac{R}{R+r}$.

Let P be a point inside the triangle ABC. Say that the lines AP, BP, and CP meet the sides of ABC at A', B', and C', respectively. Let

$$x = \frac{AP}{PA'}, \quad y = \frac{BP}{PB'}, \quad z = \frac{CP}{PC'}.$$

Prove that $xyz = x + y + z + 2$.

Solution

Define positive real numbers α, β, and γ by $\alpha + \beta + \gamma = 1$ and $P = \alpha A + \beta B + \gamma C$. Then $P - \alpha A = \beta B + \gamma C = (1 - \alpha)A'$; hence, $\alpha \overrightarrow{PA} + (1 - \alpha)\overrightarrow{PA'} = \overrightarrow{0}$. It follows that

$$\frac{AP}{PA'} = x = \frac{1 - \alpha}{\alpha}.$$

Similarly, $y = \frac{1 - \beta}{\beta}$ and $z = \frac{1 - \gamma}{\gamma}$; hence,

$$xyz = \frac{(1 - \alpha)(1 - \beta)(1 - \gamma)}{\alpha\beta\gamma}$$

and

$$x + y + z + 2 = \frac{1 - \alpha}{\alpha} + \frac{1 - \beta}{\beta} + \frac{1 - \gamma}{\gamma} + 2.$$

Thus, it is sufficient to show that

$$(1 - \alpha)(1 - \beta)(1 - \gamma) = \beta\gamma(1 - \alpha) + \gamma\alpha(1 - \beta) + \alpha\beta(1 - \gamma) + 2\alpha\beta\gamma.$$

Recalling that $\alpha + \beta + \gamma = 1$, this identity is easily checked.

Let AB be a chord of length 6 of a circle of radius 5 centred at O. Let $PQRS$ denote the square inscribed in the sector OAB such that P is on the radius OA, S is on the radius OB, and Q and R are points on the arc of the circle between A and B. Find the area of $PQRS$.

Solution

Construct points F, G, and H, as in the diagram. Since $OA = 5$ and $AG = 3$, we see that $OG = 4$, from the Theorem of Pythagoras. Since $\triangle OPF \sim \triangle OAG$, it follows that $PF = 3t$ and $OF = 4t$ for some t. Then

$$OH = OF + FH = 4t + 6t = 10t$$

and $QH = 3t$. It now follows from the Theorem of Pythagoras (in $\triangle OQH$) that $(10t)^2 + (3t)^2 = 25$. Hence, $t^2 = \frac{25}{109}$ and

$$[PQRS] = (6t)^2 = \frac{900}{109}.$$

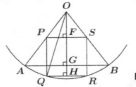

Let A and B be distinct points on a circle T. Let C be a point distinct from B such that $|AB| = |AC|$ and such that BC is tangent to T at B. Suppose that the bisector of $\angle ABC$ meets AC at a point D inside T. Show that $\angle ABC > 72°$.

Solution

Let O be the centre of T, let $AB = AC = b$ and $BC = a$, and let $\angle ABC = \alpha$. We then have $\cos \alpha = \frac{a}{2b}$, $\angle ABO = 90° - \alpha$, and $\angle OBD = 90° - \frac{\alpha}{2}$. In the isosceles triangle AOB, we have

$$OB = \frac{AB}{2 \cos \angle ABO} = \frac{b}{2 \sin \alpha}.$$

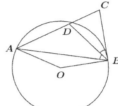

It is known that $BD = \frac{2ab \cos \frac{\alpha}{2}}{a + b}$ and that $\sin 18° = \frac{-1 + \sqrt{5}}{4}$. The Law of Cosines gives

$$OD^2 = OB^2 + BD^2 - 2\,OB \cdot BD \cdot \cos\left(90° - \frac{\alpha}{2}\right).$$

Thus, $OD^2 < OB^2$ if and only if $BD^2 < 2 \cdot OB \cdot BD \cdot \sin \frac{\alpha}{2}$; that is, D is inside T if and only if

$$\frac{2ab \cos \frac{\alpha}{2}}{a + b} < 2 \cdot \frac{b}{2 \sin \alpha} \cdot \sin \frac{\alpha}{2}.$$

If we cancel $2b$, write $\sin \alpha = 2 \sin \frac{\alpha}{2} \cos \frac{\alpha}{2}$, and $a = 2b \cos \alpha$, we get

$$\frac{2 \cos \alpha \cos \frac{\alpha}{2}}{2 \cos \alpha + 1} < \frac{1}{4 \cos \frac{\alpha}{2}}.$$

This gives $4 \cos \alpha \cdot 2 \cos^2 \frac{\alpha}{2} - (2 \cos \alpha + 1) < 0$, which, by employing the identity $2 \cos^2 \frac{\alpha}{2} = 1 + \cos \alpha$, is equivalent to $4 \cos^2 \alpha + 2 \cos \alpha - 1 < 0$. Therefore, $\cos \alpha \in \left(\frac{-1 - \sqrt{5}}{4}, \frac{-1 + \sqrt{5}}{4} \right)$; thus,

$$\cos \alpha < \frac{-1 + \sqrt{5}}{4} = \sin 18°.$$

However, $\sin 18° = \cos 72°$; hence, $\alpha > 72°$ since $\alpha < 90°$.

Let I be the incentre of triangle ABC, and let A', B', and C' be the reflections of I in BC, CA, and AB, respectively. The circle through A', B', and C' passes also through B. Find the angle $\angle ABC$.

Solution

Let X, Y, and Z be the feet of the perpendiculars from I to the sides BC, CA, and AB, respectively.

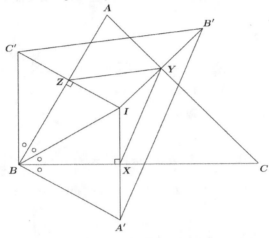

Then X, Y, Z are the mid-points of segments IA', IB', IC' respectively. Therefore XY is parallel to $A'B'$ and YZ is parallel to $B'C'$, so we have

$$\angle A'B'C' = \angle XYZ = \tfrac{1}{2}\angle XIZ = \tfrac{1}{2}(180° - \angle ZBX)$$
$$= \tfrac{1}{2}(180° - \angle ABC) = 90° - \tfrac{1}{2}\angle ABC$$

On the other hand, since BI bisects $\angle ABC$, we have

$$\angle C'BZ = \angle ZBI = \tfrac{1}{2}\angle ABC = \angle IBX = \angle XBA';$$

whence,

$$\angle C'BA' = \angle C'BZ + \angle ZBI + \angle IBX + \angle XBA'$$
$$= 4 \cdot \tfrac{1}{2}\angle ABC = 2\angle ABC.$$

Since A', B', C', and B are concyclic, we have $\angle C'BA' + \angle A'B'C' = 180°$, which, on substitution, gives $2 \cdot \angle ABC + (90° - \tfrac{1}{2}\angle ABC) = 180°$. Therefore, $\angle ABC = 60°$.

Let I be the incentre of triangle ABC. Let points $A_1 \neq A_2$ lie on the line BC, points $B_1 \neq B_2$ lie on the line AC, and points $C_1 \neq C_2$ lie on the line AB so that $AI = A_1I = A_2I$, $BI = B_1I = B_2I$, $CI = C_1I = C_2I$. Prove that $A_1A_2 + B_1B_2 + C_1C_2 = P$, where P is the perimeter of $\triangle ABC$.

Solution

Let X, Y, Z be the feet of the perpendiculars from I to the sides BC, CA, AB respectively. Then $IX = IY = IZ$. Right triangles IAZ, IA_1X, IA_2X, IYA are congruent, and since X is the mid-point of segment A_1A_2, we have

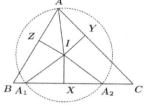

$$A_1A_2 = A_1X + XA_2 = AZ + YA.$$

Similarly, we obtain

$$B_1B_2 = B_1Y + YB_2 = BX + ZB$$
$$\text{and} \quad C_1C_2 = C_1Z + ZC_2 = CY + XC.$$

Therefore,

$$
\begin{aligned}
A_1A_2 + B_1B_2 + C_1C_2 &= (AZ + YA) + (BX + ZB) + (CY + XC) \\
&= (AZ + ZB) + (BX + XC) + (CY + YA) \\
&= AB + BC + CA = P.
\end{aligned}
$$

Let O be the circumcentre of the acute triangle ABC. The circles centred at the mid-points of the triangle's sides and passing through O intersect one another at the points K, L, and M. Prove that O is the incentre of triangle KLM.

Solution

Let X, Y, and Z be the mid-points of BC, CA, and AB, respectively. Since OK is perpendicular to the line through the centres Y and Z, and $YZ \parallel BC$, we see that KO is perpendicular to BC and it follows that O lies on the line KX. Similarly, O is on LY and MZ. Note that O is the orthocentre of $\triangle XYZ$ and that K, L, and M are

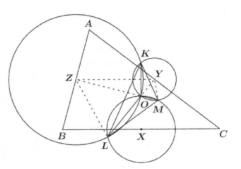

the reflections of O in the sides YZ, ZX, and XY, respectively. It follows that K, L, and M are on the circumcircle Γ of $\triangle XYZ$. Since O is interior to $\triangle XYZ$ (an acute-angled triangle, as it is similar to $\triangle ABC$), K is on the arc YZ of Γ which does not contain X. Analogous observations can be made for L and M, so that X, M, Y, K, Z, L, and X occur in this order on Γ. In addition, ZX is clearly the internal bisector of $\angle LZO$, so that X is the mid-point of the arc LM of Γ (recall that Z, O, and M are collinear). Thus, KX is the internal bisector of $\angle MKL$. The result follows.

Triangle ABC has $\angle A = 70°$ and $CA + AI = BC$, where I is the incentre of triangle ABC. Find $\angle B$.

Solution

First note that IA bisects $\angle BAC$, and IB bisects $\angle ABC$. Extend BA to a point D such that $AD = AI = a - b$. Let F be the foot of the perpendicular from I onto AB; F is the point of contact of the incircle with AB. It is well-known that $BF = s - b$ and $AF = s - a$. Then

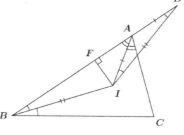

$$DF = (a-b)+(s-a) = s-b = BF,$$

so $IB = ID$. Consequently,

$\angle IBF = \angle IDA = \angle AID = \frac{1}{2}\angle BAI$; hence, $\angle ABC = \angle BAI = \frac{1}{2}\angle BAC$. We were given that $\angle BAC = 70°$, so $\angle ABC = 35°$.

Thai Mathematical Olympiad, 2003

6

Let $ABCD$ be a convex quadrilateral. Prove that

$$[ABCD] \leq \tfrac{1}{4}\left(AB^2 + BC^2 + CD^2 + DA^2\right).$$

Solution

We have

$$\begin{aligned}
[ABCD] &= [ABC] + [CDA] \\
&= \tfrac{1}{2}\cdot AB\cdot BC\cdot \sin\angle ABC + \tfrac{1}{2}CD\cdot DA\cdot \sin\angle CDA \\
&\leq \tfrac{1}{2}AB\cdot BC + \tfrac{1}{2}CD\cdot DA \\
&\leq \tfrac{1}{2}\left(\tfrac{1}{2}(AB^2 + BC^2) + \tfrac{1}{2}(CD^2 + DA^2)\right) \\
&= \tfrac{1}{4}(AB^2 + BC^2 + CD^2 + DA^2).
\end{aligned}$$

Equality holds if and only if $ABCD$ is a square.

Given a right triangle ABC with $\angle B = 90°$, let P be a point on the angle bisector of $\angle A$ inside ABC and let M be a point on the side AB (with $A \neq M \neq B$). Lines AP, CP, and MP intersect BC, AB, and AC at D, E, and N, respectively. Suppose that $\angle MPB = \angle PCN$ and $\angle NPC = \angle MBP$. Find $[APC]/[ACDE]$.

Solution

Let $a = BC$, $b = CA$, and $c = AB$, and let $c_a = AD$, the bisector of $\angle A$. We have

$$c_a = \frac{2bc \cos \frac{A}{2}}{b + c}.$$

By the Bisector Theorem, we deduce that

$$DC = \frac{ab}{b + c}, \qquad BD = \frac{ac}{b + c}.$$

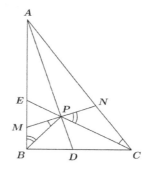

We have $\angle BMP = \angle CNP$; thus, $\triangle AMN$ is isosceles. Hence, $AM = AN$ and P is the mid-point of MN. Let x be the common length of AM and AN. It follows that

$$MP = NP = x \sin \frac{A}{2}, \qquad AP = x \cos \frac{A}{2}.$$

Since $\triangle MBP$ and $\triangle CPN$ are similar, we have $\dfrac{BM}{PN} = \dfrac{PM}{NC}$, which yields successively

$$(b - x)(c - x) = x^2 \sin^2 \frac{A}{2};$$

$$x^2 \left(1 - \sin^2 \frac{A}{2}\right) - (b + c)x + bc = 0;$$

$$x^2 \cdot \frac{1 + \cos A}{2} - (b + c)x + bc = 0;$$

$$(b + c)x^2 - 2b(b + c)x + 2b^2c = 0.$$

Solving this equation we obtain

$$x = \frac{b(b + c) \pm \sqrt{b^2(b + c)^2 - 2b^2c(b + c)}}{b + c}$$

$$= \frac{b(b + c) \pm b\sqrt{(b + c)(b - c)}}{b + c}$$

$$= \frac{b(b + c \pm a)}{b + c},$$

and since $x < b$, we take $x = \dfrac{b(b + c - a)}{b + c}$.

We now have

$$\frac{AP}{PD} = \frac{x \cos \frac{A}{2}}{c_a - x \cos \frac{A}{2}} = \frac{(b+c)x \cos \frac{A}{2}}{(b+c)c_a - (b+c)x \cos \frac{A}{2}}$$

$$= \frac{b(b+c-a) \cos \frac{A}{2}}{2bc \cos \frac{A}{2} - b(b+c-a) \cos \frac{A}{2}}$$

$$= \frac{b(b+c-a)}{2bc - b(b+c-a)} = \frac{b+c-a}{a+c-b}.$$

Menelaus' Theorem applied to $\triangle ABD$ gives $\frac{CD}{CB} \cdot \frac{EB}{EA} \cdot \frac{PA}{PD} = 1$; hence, $\frac{EB}{EA} = \frac{CB}{CD} \cdot \frac{PD}{PA}$. Substituting the previously obtained expressions gives

$$\frac{EB}{EA} = \frac{(b+c)(a-b+c)}{b(b+c-a)}.$$

If r is the ratio $EB : EA$, then the ratio $EB : c$ is equal to $r : 1 + r$. Hence,

$$EB = \frac{(b+c)(a-b+c)}{a+b+c}.$$

Finally, we have

$$[ACDE] = [ABC] - [BDE]$$

$$= \frac{ac}{2} - \frac{ac}{2(b+c)} \cdot \frac{(b+c)(a-b+c)}{a+b+c}$$

$$= \frac{ac}{2}\left(1 - \frac{a-b+c}{a+b+c}\right) = \frac{abc}{a+b+c},$$

and also

$$[APC] = \frac{AP \cdot AC \cdot \sin \frac{A}{2}}{2} = \frac{x \cos \frac{A}{2} \cdot b \sin \frac{A}{2}}{2}$$

$$= \frac{bx \sin A}{4} = b \cdot \frac{b(b+c-a)}{4(b+c)} \cdot \frac{a}{b} = \frac{ab(b+c-a)}{4(b+c)};$$

hence,

$$\frac{[APC]}{[ACDE]} = \frac{(b+c-a)(a+b+c)}{4c(b+c)}.$$

Let M, N, and P be the respective mid-points of sides BC, CA, and AB of triangle ABC, and let G be the intersection point of its medians. Prove that if $BN = \frac{\sqrt{3}}{2}AB$ and $BMGP$ is a cyclic polygon, then triangle ABC is equilateral.

Solution

Since $BMGP$ is a cyclic polygon we obtain

$$
\begin{aligned}
AG \cdot AM &= AP \cdot AB, \\
\frac{2}{3}AM \cdot AM &= \frac{1}{2}AB \cdot AB, \\
AM^2 = \frac{3}{4}AB^2 &= BN^2, \\
AM &= BN,
\end{aligned}
$$

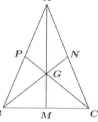

hence $AC = BC$. The segment CP is also an altitude, that is $\angle GPB = 90°$, and since opposite angles of a cylic quadrilateral add to 180°, we also have $\angle GMB = 90°$. Therefore AM is also an altitude, hence $AB = AC$, which together with $AC = BC$ shows that triangle ABC is equilateral.

In an acute-angled triangle ABC, Let H be the orthocenter, and let d_a, d_b, and d_c be the distances from H to the sides BC, CA, and AB, respectively. Prove that $d_a + d_b + d_c \leq 3r$, where r is the radius of the incircle of triangle ABC.

Solution

Let a, b, and c be the lengths of the sides opposite A, B, and C, respectively, and let $s = \frac{1}{2}(a + b + c)$ be the semiperimeter. Let R be the circumradius of triangle ABC, and let O and A' be the circumcentre and the mid-point of the side BC, respectively.

Letting h_a be the length of the altitude from A to BC in $\triangle ABC$, and using the well-known relation $AH = 2 \cdot OA'$, we deduce that

$$d_a = h_a - AH = h_a - 2 \cdot OA' = h_a - 2R \cos A.$$

By symmetry, we have $d_b = h_b - 2R \cos B$ and $d_c = h_c - 2R \cos C$. It follows that

$$d_a + d_b + d_c = h_a + h_b + h_c - 2R(\cos A + \cos B + \cos C).$$

We have the relation $h_a = \frac{2rs}{a}$ and its symmetric analogues, and also we have the well-known relations

$$abc = 4Rrs,$$
$$ab + bc + ca = s^2 + r^2 + 4Rr,$$
$$\cos A + \cos B + \cos C = \frac{R + r}{R}.$$

Using these we deduce that

$$d_a + d_b + d_c = \frac{s^2 + r^2 - 4Rr}{2R},$$

and hence the given inequality is equivalent to

$$s^2 + r^2 - 4R^2 \leq 6Rr. \qquad (1)$$

To establish the validity of (1), we make use of the linear transformation $a = y + z$, $b = z + x$, and $c = x + y$, where x, y, and z are uniquely determined positive numbers. Ater applying the transformation, (1) becomes

$$(x + y + z)^2 + \frac{xyz}{x + y + z} - \frac{(x + y)^2(y + z)^2(z + x)^2}{4xyz(x + y + z)}$$
$$\leq 6 \cdot \frac{(x + y)(y + z)(z + x)}{4(x + y + z)},$$

or equivalently

$$4xyz(x + y + z)^3 + 4x^2y^2z^2 - (x + y)^2(y + z)^2(z + x)^2$$
$$\leq 6xyz(x + y)(y + z)(z + x).$$

We substitute $x^3 + y^3 + z^3 + 3(x+y)(y+z)(z+x)$ for $(x+y+z)^3$, simplify, and obtain

$$4xyz(x^3 + y^3 + z^3) \quad + \quad 6xyz(x+y)(y+z)(z+x) \quad + \quad 4x^2y^2z^2$$
$$\leq \quad [(x+y)(y+z)(z+x)]^2.$$

We substitute $2xyz + \sum_{\text{sym}} x^2 y$ for $(x+y)(y+z)(z+x)$ (the symmetric sum is over the six permutations of x, y, and z) to obtain

$$4xyz(x^3 + y^3 + z^3) \ + \ 6xyz \left(2xyz + \sum_{\text{sym}} x^2 y \right) \ + \ 4x^2y^2z^2$$
$$\leq \ \left(2xyz + \sum_{\text{sym}} \right)^2 x^2 y \ = \ \left(\sum_{\text{sym}} x^2 y \right)^2 + \ 4xyz \left(\sum_{\text{sym}} x^2 y \right) \ + \ 4x^2y^2z^2.$$

We have the expansion

$$\left(\sum_{\text{sym}} x^2 y \right)^2 \ = \ \left(\sum_{\text{sym}} x^4 y^2 \right) \ + \ 2xyz(x^3 + y^3 + z^3) \ + \ 2xyz \left(\sum_{\text{sym}} x^2 y \right)$$
$$+ \ 2(x^3 y^3 + y^3 z^3 + z^3 x^3) \ + \ 6x^2 y^2 z^2,$$

which we substitute into the above and then simplify to obtain

$$2xyz(x^3 + y^3 + z^3) \ + \ 6x^2 y^2 z^2 \ \leq \ \left(\sum_{\text{sym}} x^4 y^2 \right) + 2(x^3 y^3 + y^3 z^3 + z^3 x^3).$$

However, this is equivalent to

$$2 \left[(xy)^3 + (yz)^3 + (zx)^3 - 3x^2 y^2 z^2 \right]$$
$$+ \ x^4 (y-z)^2 + \ y^4 (z-x)^2 + \ z^4 (x-y)^2 \ \geq \ 0,$$

which is true, since $(xy)^3 + (yz)^3 + (zx)^3 \geq 3x^2 y^2 z^2$ holds by the AM-GM Inequality.

Equality occurs only if $x = y = z$, that is, if and only if the triangle ABC is equilateral.

The acute-angled triangle ABC is given. Let O be the centre of its circumcircle. The perpendicular bisector of the side AC intersects the side AB and the line BC at the points P and Q, respectively. Prove that $\angle PQB = \angle PBO$.

Solution

In triangle BOA we have $OA = OB$. Thus

$$
\begin{aligned}
\angle PBO &= \frac{180° - \angle BOA}{2} = \frac{180° - \widehat{BKA}}{2} \\
&= \frac{180° - \widehat{BK} - \widehat{AK}}{2} \\
&= \frac{180° - \widehat{BK} - \widehat{CK}}{2} \\
&= \frac{\widehat{KM} - \widehat{BK} - \widehat{CK}}{2} \\
&= \frac{\widehat{CM} - \widehat{BK}}{2} = \angle PQB .
\end{aligned}
$$

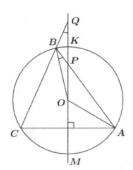

Let ω be the inscribed circle of the triangle ABC. Let L, N, and E be the points of tangency of ω with the sides AB, BC, and CA, respectively. Lines LE and BC intersect at the point H, and lines LN and AC intersect at the point J (all the points H, J, N, E lie on the same side of the line AB). Let O and P be the mid-points of the segments EJ and NH, respectively. Find $S(HJNE)$ if $S(ABOP) = u^2$ and $S(COP) = v^2$. (Here $S(\mathcal{F})$ is the area of figure $\mathcal{F}$.)

As usual we write $a = BC$, $b = CA$, $c = AB$, and $s = \frac{1}{2}(a + b + c)$.

It is well known that $AL = AE = s - a$, $BL = BN = s - b$, and $CN = CE = s - c$.

Assume that $c > b$. In order that the points H, J, N, and E all lie on the same side of the line AB, we must have $c > a$.

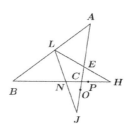

By Menelaus' Theorem applied to $\triangle ABC$ and transversal HEL, we have

$$\frac{HC}{HB} \cdot \frac{LB}{LA} \cdot \frac{EA}{EC} = 1 \Rightarrow \frac{HC}{HC + a} = \frac{s - c}{s - b} \Rightarrow HC = \frac{a(s - c)}{c - b},$$

and by symmetry we have $JC = \frac{b(s - c)}{c - a}$. Therefore we deduce

$$
\begin{aligned}
NH &= NC + CH = (s - c) + \frac{a(s - c)}{c - b} \\
&= \frac{(s - c)(c - b + a)}{c - b} = \frac{2(s - b)(s - c)}{c - b},
\end{aligned}
$$

and by symmetry we have $EJ = \frac{2(s - a)(s - c)}{c - a}$. Using the expressions we have obtained so far, we have

$$
\begin{aligned}
S(HJNE) &= \frac{NH \cdot JE \cdot \sin C}{2} \\
&= \frac{2(s - a)(s - b)(s - c)^2}{(c - b)(c - a)} \cdot \sin C, \qquad (1)
\end{aligned}
$$

$$
\begin{aligned}
CP &= NP - NC = \frac{1}{2}NH - NC \\
&= \frac{(s - b)(s - c)}{c - b} - (s - c) \\
&= \frac{(s - c)(s - b - c + b)}{c - b} = \frac{(s - c)^2}{c - b},
\end{aligned}
$$

and by symmetry, $CO = \dfrac{(s-c)^2}{c-a}$. It follows that

$$S(COP) \;=\; v^2 \;=\; \frac{(s-c)^4 \sin C}{2(c-b)(c-a)}\,. \tag{2}$$

Continuing with our calculations,

$$
\begin{aligned}
AO \;&=\; AC + CO \;=\; b + \frac{(s-c)^2}{c-a} \\
&=\; \frac{-c(2s-c-b)+s^2-ab}{c-a} \;=\; \frac{s^2-ab-ac}{c-a} \\
&=\; \frac{s^2-(a(b+c))}{c-a} \;=\; \frac{s^2-2as+a^2}{c-a} \;=\; \frac{(s-a)^2}{c-a}\,,
\end{aligned}
$$

and by symmetry $BP = \dfrac{(s-b)^2}{c-b}$, hence

$$S(ABOP) \;=\; u^2 \;=\; \frac{(s-a)^2(s-b)^2}{(c-a)(c-b)} \cdot \frac{\sin C}{2}\,. \tag{3}$$

Combining (1), (2), and (3) we obtain the desired result

$$
\begin{aligned}
S(HJNE) \;&=\; \frac{2(s-a)(s-b)(s-c)^2}{(c-b)(c-a)} \cdot \sin C \\
&=\; 4\sqrt{\frac{(s-a)^2(s-b)^2 \cdot \sin C}{2(c-b)(c-a)}} \cdot \sqrt{\frac{(s-c)^4 \sin C}{2(c-b)(c-a)}} \;=\; 4uv\,.
\end{aligned}
$$

Let EF be a diameter of the circle Γ, and let e be the tangent line to Γ at E. Let A and B be any two points of e such that E is an interior point of the segment AB, and $AE \cdot EB$ is a fixed constant. Let AF and BF meet Γ at A' and B', respectively. Prove that all such segments $A'B'$ pass through a common point.

Solution

Let G be the point of intersection of $A'B'$ and EF. Let $FA' = p$, $FB' = q$, $EA' = r$, $EB' = s$, $AE = t$, and $EB = u$. It is given that $tu = k$, where k is a fixed constant.

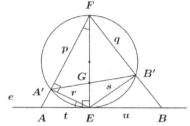

We have that $\angle EAF$ and $\angle AEF$ are right angles. The pair of angles $\angle FEA'$ and $\angle A'FE$ are supplementary, as are the pair of angles $\angle FEA'$ and $\angle A'EA$. Therefore, $\angle A'FE = \angle A'EA$, and hence, $\triangle EFA' \sim \triangle AEA'$. Consequently, $pt = r \cdot EF$, and by analogy, $qu = s \cdot EF$. Therefore, $pqk = rs \cdot EF^2$.

Now $\angle A'FB'$ and $\angle A'EB'$ are supplementary angles, hence,

$$\frac{FG}{GE} = \frac{[A'FB']}{[A'EB']} = \frac{pq}{rs} = \frac{EF^2}{k},$$

which is a fixed ratio. Thus, all such segments $A'B'$ pass through G.

A circle (O, r) and a point A outside the circle are given. From A we draw a straight line ε, different from the line AO, which intersects the circle at B and Γ, with B between A and Γ. Next we draw the symmetric line of ε with respect to the axis AO, which intersects the circle at E and Δ, with E between A and Δ.

Prove that the diagonals of the quadrilateral $B\Gamma\Delta E$ pass through a fixed point; that is, they always intersect at the same point, independent of the position of the line ε.

Solution

Let $AO \cap B\Delta = \{P\}$. By symmetry, $\angle A\Gamma P = \angle B\Delta A$. Since $\angle B\Delta A = \frac{1}{2}\angle BOE = \angle BOA$, we have $\angle A\Gamma P = \angle BOA$. Thus, triangles $A\Gamma P$ and AOB are similar, so

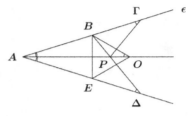

$$\frac{AP}{AB} = \frac{A\Gamma}{AO}, \text{ or } AP = \frac{AB \cdot A\Gamma}{AO}.$$

Since $AB \cdot A\Gamma = AO^2 - r^2$, we have

$AP = \dfrac{AO^2 - r^2}{AO}$, which is independent of the line ϵ. By symmetry, $E\Gamma$ and AO also intersect at the point P, and the proof is complete.

Let ABC be a triangle in a plane. The internal angle bisector of $\angle ACB$ cuts the side AB at D.

Consider an arbitrary circle Γ_1 passing through C and D so that the lines BC and CA are not its tangents. This circle cuts the lines BC and CA again at M and N, respectively.

(a) Prove that there exists a circle Γ_2 touching the line DM at M and touching the line DN at N.

(b) The circle Γ_2 from part (a) cuts the lines BC and CA again at P and Q, respectively. Prove that the measures of the segments MP and NQ are constant as Γ_1 varies.

Solution

(a) Let $\gamma = \frac{1}{2}\angle ACB$. Consider the perpendiculars to DM at M and to DN at N. Clearly they intersect in a point R on Γ_1, where DR is a diameter of the circle. Since $\angle NRD = \gamma = \angle MRD$, then $NR = MR$. Thus, Γ_2 exists, namely Γ_2 is the circle with centre at R and passing through the points M and N.

(b) Using the facts established in part (a), the Law of Sines, and the fact that $DMRC$ is cyclic with a right angle at M, we have

$$\frac{PC}{\sin \angle PRC} = \frac{CR}{\sin \angle CPR} = \frac{MR}{\sin \angle RCM}$$
$$= \frac{MR}{\sin \angle RDM} = \frac{MR}{\cos \gamma}.$$

Since $\angle RMC = \angle RNC$, then triangles MRP and NRQ are congruent and it is easy to show that $\angle PRC = \angle CDN$. Then

$$PC = \frac{MR}{\cos \gamma} \cdot \sin \angle CDN .$$

On the other hand,

$$\frac{CM}{\sin \angle CDM} = \frac{MD}{\sin \gamma},$$

from which we obtain

$$CM = \frac{MD}{\sin \gamma} \cdot \sin \angle CDM$$
$$= \frac{MR \tan \gamma}{\sin \gamma} \cdot \sin \angle CDM = \frac{MR}{\cos \gamma} \cdot \sin \angle CDM .$$

Hence,

$$
\begin{aligned}
PC + CM &= \frac{MR}{\cos\gamma} \cdot (\sin\angle CDN + \sin\angle CDM) \\
&= \frac{2MR}{\cos\gamma} \cdot \sin\left(\frac{\angle NDM}{2}\right) \cdot \cos\left(\frac{\angle CDN - \angle CDM}{2}\right) \\
&= 2MR \cdot \cos\left(\frac{\angle CDN - \angle CDM}{2}\right).
\end{aligned}
$$

However,

$$
\begin{aligned}
&\angle CDN - \angle CDM \\
&= (\angle RDN - (90^\circ - \angle CMD)) - (\angle RDM + 90^\circ - \angle CMD) \\
&= 2\angle CMD - 180^\circ.
\end{aligned}
$$

Then

$$
\begin{aligned}
PC + CM &= 2MR \cdot \sin\angle CMD \\
&= 2CD \cdot \sin\gamma \cdot \frac{MR}{MD} \\
&= 2CD \cdot \cos\gamma,
\end{aligned}
$$

which is a constant. The same holds for NQ, since $MP = NQ$.

Given an acute triangle ABC inscribed in a circle Γ in a plane, let H be its orthocentre. On the arc BC of Γ not containing A, take a point P distinct from B and C. Let D be the point such that $\overrightarrow{AD} = \overrightarrow{PC}$. Let K be the orthocentre of triangle ACD, and let E and F be the orthogonal projections of K onto the lines BC and AB, respectively. Prove that the line EF passes through the mid-point of HK.

Solution

Since $\overrightarrow{AD} = \overrightarrow{PC}$, the quadrilateral $ADCP$ is a parallelogram and so $AP\|CD$ and $CP\|AD$. Since we have $AK \perp CD$, we also have $AK \perp AP$. It follows that the circle with diameter KP passes through A. Similarly, this circle passes through C. Finally, this circle is Γ and in particular, K is on Γ. As a result, the line EF is just the Simson line of K relative to $\triangle ABC$ and it is a well-known result that this line bisects the segment joining K to the orthocentre H.

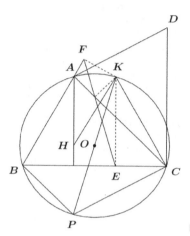

Suppose that the points D and E lie on the circumcircle of $\triangle ABC$, ray $\overrightarrow{AD}$ is the interior angle bisector of $\angle BAC$, and ray $\overrightarrow{AE}$ is the exterior angle bisector of $\angle BAC$. Let F be the symmetrical point of A with respect to D, and let G be the symmetrical point of A with respect to E. Prove that, if the circumcircle of $\triangle ADG$ and the circumcircle of $\triangle AEF$ intersect at P, then AP is parallel to BC.

Solution

Suppose that the parallel to AD and passing through E intersects the parallel to AE and passing through D at the point T. Let O_1 be the circumcentre of triangle ADG and let O_2 be the circumcentre of triangle AEF.

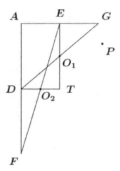

Since O_1 is on the perpendicular bisector of AP, and O_2 is on the perpendicular bisector of AP, it follows that $O_1O_2 \perp AP$.

Since $AE \perp AD$, the point O_1 is the mid-point of DG and the mid-point of ET; the point O_2 is the mid-point of EF and the mid-point of DT. It follows that $O_1O_2 \| DE$.

Since AD is the internal bisector of $\angle BAC$, the point D is the mid-point of arc BC; we deduce that DE is a diameter of the circumcircle of $\triangle ABC$, hence $DE \perp BC$.

We have now shown that $O_1O_2 \perp AP$, $O_1O_2 \| DE$, and $DE \perp BC$, hence, AP is parallel to BC.

Let O and H be the circumcentre and orthocentre of an acute triangle ABC. Suppose that the bisectrix of $\angle BAC$ intersects the circumcircle of $\triangle ABC$ at D, and that the points E and F are symmetrical points of D with respect to BC and O, respectively. If AE and FH intersect at G and if M is the mid-point of BC, prove that GM is perpendicular to AF.

Solution

The point D is the mid-point of the arc BC, and FD is the perpendicular bisector of BC. If $AB = AC$, then points D, M, O, E, G, A, and F are collinear, so we assume $AB \neq AC$.

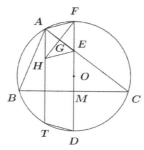

We will prove that $AHEF$ is a parallelogram. In that case it follows that G is the mid-point of AE, and since M is the mid-point of DE, we see (in $\triangle ADE$) that $GM \| AD$. Since DF is a diameter, $AD \perp AF$, hence $GM \perp AF$. We offer two demonstrations.

Proof 1: As usual, $a = BC$ and R is the circumradius of $\triangle ABC$. Since $\angle MBD = \frac{1}{2}\angle BAC$, we have that $MD = \frac{a}{2}\tan\frac{A}{2}$. We obtain

$$
\begin{aligned}
EF &= 2R - 2MD = 2R - a\tan\frac{A}{2} \\
&= 2R - 2R\cdot\sin A\tan\frac{A}{2} \\
&= 2R\left(1 - 2\sin\frac{A}{2}\cos\frac{A}{2}\tan\frac{A}{2}\right) \\
&= 2R\left(1 - 2\sin^2\frac{A}{2}\right) = 2R\cos A\,.
\end{aligned}
$$

It is known that $AH = 2R\cos A$; because $AH \perp BC$, $EF \perp BC$, and $AH = EF$, it follows that $AHEF$ is a parallelogram.

Proof 2: Let AH intersect the circumcircle at T.

It is known that T is the symmetric point of H with respect of BC. It follows that the trapezoid $HTDE$ is isosceles. Since the trapezoid $ATDF$ is isosceles, we have

$$\angle HED = \angle EDT = \angle AFE\,,$$

hence $AF \| HE$. However, $AH \| EF$, therefore the quadrilateral $AHEF$ is a parallelogram.

In an acute-angled triangle ABC, let H be the orthocentre, and let d_a, d_b, and d_c be the distances from H to the sides BC, CA, and AB, respectively. Prove that $d_a + d_b + d_c \leq 3r$, where r is the radius of the incircle of triangle ABC.

Solution

Let $a = BC$, $b = CA$, and $c = AB$, and $s = \frac{1}{2}(a + b + c)$. Without loss of generality, assume that $a \leq b \leq c$. Then

$$\begin{aligned} d_a &= CH \cos B \leq CH \cos A = d_b \\ &= AH \cos C \leq AH \cos B = d_c. \end{aligned}$$

Denote by $[ABC]$ the area of triangle ABC. By Chebyshev's Inequality,

$$sr = [ABC] = \frac{1}{2}(ad_a + bd_b + cd_c) \geq \frac{1}{3}s(d_a + d_b + d_c),$$

completing the proof.

Let $ABCD$ be a rhombus. Let E, F, G, and H be points on the sides AB, BC, CD, and DA, respectively, so that EF and GH are tangent to the incircle of $ABCD$. Show that EH and FG are parallel.

Solution

The hexagon $AEFCGH$ circumscribes the incircle of the rhombus, so Brianchon's theorem implies that the lines AC, EG, and FH are concurrent. Let U be their common point and let h denote the homothety with centre U which transforms A into C. Since AE and CG are parallel and E, U, and G are collinear, we see that $h(E) = G$. Similarly, $h(H) = F$ and $EH \| FG$ follows.

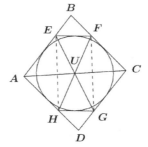

Let ABC be an acute-angled triangle with orthocentre H and circumcentre O. The inscribed and circumscribed circles have radii r and R, respectively. If P is an arbitrary point of the segment $[OH]$, prove that $6r \le PA + PB + PC \le 3R$.

Solution

Let $\overrightarrow{PO} = t\overrightarrow{HO}$, $t \in [0, 1]$ and let $X \in \{A, B, C\}$. Then

$$
\begin{aligned}
\overrightarrow{PX} &= \overrightarrow{PO} + \overrightarrow{OX} = t\overrightarrow{HO} + \overrightarrow{OX} \\
&= t\left(\overrightarrow{HX} + \overrightarrow{XO}\right) + \overrightarrow{OX} = (1-t)\overrightarrow{OX} + t\overrightarrow{HX}.
\end{aligned}
$$

Since $|\overrightarrow{PX}| = |(1-t)\overrightarrow{OX} + t\overrightarrow{HX}| \le (1-t)|\overrightarrow{OX}| + t|\overrightarrow{HX}|$, we have

$$
\begin{aligned}
PA + PB + PC &= \sum_{\text{cyclic}} |\overrightarrow{PA}| \le \sum_{\text{cyclic}} \left((1-t)|\overrightarrow{OA}| + t|\overrightarrow{HA}|\right) \\
&= 3(1-t)R + t\sum_{\text{cyclic}} HA.
\end{aligned}
$$

For any vertex X, $HX = 2R\cos X$. Also, $\cos A + \cos B + \cos C = 1 + \dfrac{r}{R}$ and Euler's Inequality, $R \ge 2r$, holds. Thus,

$$
\begin{aligned}
PA + PB + PC &\le 3(1-t)R + 2Rt(\cos A + \cos B + \cos C) \\
&= 3(1-t)R + t(2R + 2r) \\
&\le 3(1-t)R + t(2R + R) = 3R.
\end{aligned}
$$

Next we prove the inequality $6r \le PA + PB + PC$ for *any* interior point P in the acute-angled triangle ABC.

For each vertex X let R_X be the distance from P to X. Let h_a, h_b, and h_c be the heights of the triangle to the corresponding side, and let d_a, d_b, and d_c be the distances from P to the corresponding side.

Since $R_A + d_a \ge h_a$ we have $\sum_{\text{cyclic}} (R_a + d_a) \ge \sum_{\text{cyclic}} h_a$. By the Erdös–Mordell Inequality in the form $\sum_{\text{cyclic}} d_a \le \frac{1}{2} \sum_{\text{cyclic}} R_A$ and the preceding inequality we have $\frac{3}{2} \sum_{\text{cyclic}} R_A \ge \sum_{\text{cyclic}} h_a$, or equivalently $\frac{2}{3} \sum_{\text{cyclic}} h_a \le \sum_{\text{cyclic}} R_A$.

Since

$$
h_a + h_b + h_c = 2F\left(\frac{1}{a} + \frac{1}{b} + \frac{1}{c}\right) \ge 2F\left(\frac{9}{a+b+c}\right) = \frac{9F}{2s} = 9r,
$$

where F is the area of triangle ABC, we finally obtain

$$
6r \le \frac{2}{3}(h_a + h_b + h_c) \le R_a + R_b + R_c.
$$

Equality occurs if and only if P is the circumcenter and $a = b = c$.

Let ABC be an isosceles triangle with $AC = BC$, and let I be its incentre. Let P be a point on the circumcircle of the triangle AIB lying inside the triangle ABC. The straight lines through P parallel to CA and CB meet AB at D and E, respectively. The line through P parallel to AB meets CA and CB at F and G, respectively. Prove that the straight lines DF and GE intersect on the circumcircle of the triangle ABC.

Solution

For convenience let

$$\angle CAB = \alpha, \ \angle ACB = \gamma,$$
$$\angle DFP = \xi, \ \angle GPB = \omega.$$

We then have

$$\angle APB = \angle AIB = \alpha + \gamma,$$
$$\angle APF = 180° - (\gamma + \alpha) - \omega$$
$$= \alpha - \omega,$$
$$\angle GBP = \alpha - \omega,$$
$$\angle PAF = \omega.$$

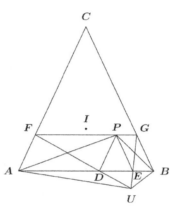

Thus, $GBEP \sim FPDA$, so that $\angle EGP = \angle DFA = 180° - \alpha - \xi = \alpha + \gamma - \xi$.

Let U be the intersection of the lines EG and FD. We then have

$$\angle GUF = 180 - \angle DFP - \angle EGP$$
$$= (2\alpha + \gamma) - \xi - (\alpha + \gamma - \xi) = \alpha.$$

Now, $UBGD$ is inscribable, since $\angle DUG = \angle DBG = \alpha$. Also, $PGBD$ is inscribable, since $\angle DPG + \angle GBD = 180°$. Thus, $PGBUD$ is inscribable and $\angle GUB = \angle GPB = \omega$. Similarly, $\angle FUA = \angle FPA = \alpha - \omega$ and $\angle AUB = 2\alpha$; hence, U is on the circumcircle of triangle ABC.

Let AD be the common chord of two circles Γ_1 and Γ_2. A line through D intersects Γ_1 at B and Γ_2 at C. Let E be a point on the segment AD different from A and D. The line CE intersects Γ_1 at P and Q. The line BE intersects Γ_2 at M and N.

(i) Prove that P, Q, M, and N lie on the circumference of a circle Γ_3.

(ii) If the centre of Γ_3 is O, prove that OD is perpendicular to BC.

Solution

(i) We have $EP \cdot EQ = EA \cdot ED$, since the chords PQ and AD of Γ_1 intersect at E. Similarly, we obtain $EM \cdot EN = EA \cdot ED$. It follows that $EP \cdot EQ = EM \cdot EN$ and so P, Q, M, and N are concyclic.

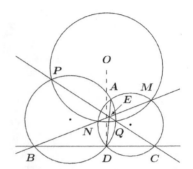

(ii) Since MN and CD intersect at B, we have $BD \cdot BC = BM \cdot BN$. But $BM \cdot BN$ is the power of B with respect to Γ_3, so $BM \cdot BN = BO^2 - \rho^2$ where ρ is the radius of Γ_3. Similarly,

$$CD \cdot CB = CP \cdot CQ = CO^2 - \rho^2,$$

and therefore

$$
\begin{aligned}
BO^2 - CO^2 &= BD \cdot BC - CD \cdot CB = BC(BD - DC) \\
&= (BD + DC)(BD - DC) = BD^2 - DC^2.
\end{aligned}
$$

From $BO^2 - CO^2 = BD^2 - DC^2$, it follows that OD is perpendicular to BC.

Let a, b, c, and R be the side lengths and the circumradius of a triangle. Show that

$$\frac{1}{ab} + \frac{1}{bc} + \frac{1}{ca} \geq \frac{1}{R^2}.$$

Solution

Let s, r, and P be the semiperimeter, the inradius, and the area of the triangle. It is well known that

$$\begin{aligned}
\frac{1}{R^2} &= \left(\frac{4P}{abc}\right)^2 = \frac{16P^2}{(abc)^2} \\
&= \frac{16(s(s-a)(s-b)(s-c))}{(abc)^2} \\
&= \frac{(a+b+c)(b+c-a)(c+a-b)(a+b-c)}{(abc)^2},
\end{aligned}$$

so it is enough to prove

$$\begin{aligned}
\frac{1}{ab} + \frac{1}{bc} + \frac{1}{ca} &= \frac{a+b+c}{abc} \\
&\geq \frac{(a+b+c)(b+c-a)(c+a-b)(a+b-c)}{(abc)^2},
\end{aligned}$$

which is equivalent to

$$(a+b-c)(c+a-b)(b+c-a) \leq abc.$$

There are several ways to prove this last inequality.

One may, for instance, expand the left-hand side and reduce the inequality to Schur's Inequality. We give another proof, where we use the fact that $a+b-c > 0$, $b+c-a > 0$, $c+a-b > 0$, and $\sqrt{ab} \leq \frac{a+b}{2}$:

$$\begin{aligned}
(a+b-c)(b+c-a)(a+c-b) \\
= \prod_{\text{cyclic}} \sqrt{(a+b-c)(b+c-a)} \\
= \prod_{\text{cyclic}} \frac{(a+b-c)+(b+c-a)}{2} = \prod_{\text{cyclic}} b = abc.
\end{aligned}$$

Equality holds if and only if $a = b = c$, in which case the triangle is equilateral.

Let A and B be distinct points on a circle T. Let C be a point distinct from B such that $|AB| = |AC|$ and such that BC is tangent to T at B. Suppose that the bisector of $\angle ABC$ meets AC at a point D inside T. Show that $\angle ABC > 72°$.

Solution

Let $D' \neq B$ be the second point of intersection of BD with the circle T. Let $\angle ABD = \angle DBC = \beta$. Since $AB = AC$, we have $\angle ACB = 2\beta$. Also, BC is tangent to the circle and AB is a chord, hence $\angle D'AB = \beta$. Let $\angle ABO = \gamma$.

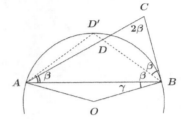

Since BC is tangent to T, we have $2\beta + \gamma = 90°$. Adding the angles in the isosceles triangle ABC yields $4\beta + \angle CAB = 180°$. From these two equations it follows that $\angle CAB = 2\gamma$. Since D is inside T we have

$$\beta = \angle D'AB > \angle CAB = 2\gamma,$$

and therefore $\frac{\beta}{2} > \gamma$. This last inequality together with $2\beta + \gamma = 90°$ yields $2\beta + \frac{\beta}{2} > 90°$, or $\frac{5\beta}{2} > 90°$. Hence, $\beta > 36°$ and $\angle ABC = 2\beta > 72°$.

A $\triangle ABC$ is given with side lengths a, b, and c. A point P lies inside $\triangle ABC$, and the distances from P to the three sides are p, q, and r, respectively. Prove that

$$R \leq \frac{a^2 + b^2 + c^2}{18 \sqrt[3]{pqr}},$$

where R is the circumradius of $\triangle ABC$. When does equality hold?

Solution

Let F denote the area of $\triangle ABC$. We have the well-known relation $2F = \frac{abc}{2R}$, but also from the definition of p, q, and r we have the equation $2F = ap + bq + cr$. Thus, the proposed inequality is equivalent to

$$\frac{abc}{2(ap + bq + cr)} \leq \frac{a^2 + b^2 + c^2}{18 \sqrt[3]{pqr}}$$

or

$$(a^2 + b^2 + c^2)(ap + bq + cr) \geq 9abc \sqrt[3]{pqr}. \tag{1}$$

By the AM–GM Inequality,

$$a^2 + b^2 + c^2 \geq 3\sqrt[3]{a^2b^2c^2} \quad \text{and} \quad ap + bq + cr \geq 3\sqrt[3]{abcpqr},$$

and the inequality (1) now follows from

$$(a^2 + b^2 + c^2)(ap + bq + cr) \geq 9\sqrt[3]{a^2b^2c^2} \cdot \sqrt[3]{abc} \cdot \sqrt[3]{pqr}.$$

Let A, B, and C be three distinct points on the circle k. Let the lines h and g each be perpendicular to BC with h passing through B and g passing through C. The perpendicular bisector of AB meets h in F and the perpendicular bisector of AC meets g in G. Prove that the product $|BF| \cdot |CG|$ is independent of the choice of A, whenever B and C are fixed.

Solution

Let A' be the point diametrically opposite to A. Let M and N be the midpoints of the segments AB and AC, respectively. Let B' and C' be the second points of intersection of the lines g and h with the circle k, respectively.

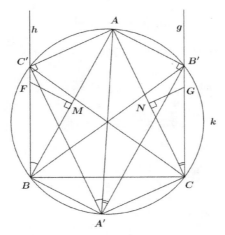

Since $C'BC$ and BCB' are right angles, the segments BB' and CC' are diameters of the circle k. Thus, the two quadrilaterals $AC'A'C$ and $ABA'B'$ are rectangles, and hence parallelograms, so we have

$$|C'A'| \ = \ |CA| \quad \text{and} \quad |A'B'| \ = \ |AB| \, .$$

Since the right triangles BMF and $A'C'A$ are similar, as are the right triangles CNG and $A'B'A$, we have

$$\frac{BF}{AA'} \ = \ \frac{BM}{C'A'} \ = \ \frac{\frac{1}{2}AB}{CA}$$

and

$$\frac{CG}{AA'} \ = \ \frac{CN}{A'B'} \ = \ \frac{\frac{1}{2}CA}{AB} \, ,$$

from which we obtain

$$BF \cdot CG \ = \ \frac{1}{4}|AA'|^2$$

as the square of the radius of k, which is independent of the choice of A.

A lamp is placed at each lattice point (x, y) in the plane (that is, x and y are both integers). At time $t = 0$ exactly one lamp is switched on. At any integer time $t \geq 1$, exactly those lamps are switched on which are at a distance of 2005 from some lamp which is already switched on. Prove that every lamp will be switched on at some time.

Solution

Assume that at time $t = 0$ the lamp at $O(0, 0)$ is switched on. Since $2005 = \sqrt{1357^2 + 1476^2}$ then at some time the lamps at the following lattice points will be switched on:

$$A_1(1357, 1476), \qquad O_1(2 \cdot 1357, 0),$$
$$A_2(3 \cdot 1357, 1476), \qquad O_2(4 \cdot 1357, 0),$$

$$\vdots \qquad\qquad\qquad \vdots$$

$$A_k((2k - 1) \cdot 1357, 1476), \qquad O_k(2k \cdot 1357, 0);$$

and then the lamps at these lattice points will be switched on:

$$B_1(2k \cdot 1357 - 2005, 0),$$
$$B_2(2k \cdot 1357 - 2 \cdot 2005, 0),$$
$$B_3(2k \cdot 1357 - 3 \cdot 2005, 0),$$

$$\vdots$$

$$B_t(2k \cdot 1357 - t \cdot 2005, 0).$$

The equation $2k \cdot 1357 - 2005t = 1$ is the same as $2714k - 2005t = 1$, which has a solution in positive integers k, t because $\gcd(2714, 2005) = 1$, for example, $2714 \cdot 1134 - 2005 \cdot 1535 = 1$. Thus the lamp at $(1, 0)$ will be switched on at some time. It follows (by symmetry) that every lamp will be switched on at some time.

The quadrilateral $ABCD$ is cyclic. Prove that

$$\frac{AC}{BD} = \frac{DA \cdot AB + BC \cdot CD}{AB \cdot BC + CD \cdot DA}.$$

Solution

This is Ptolemy's theorem about cyclic quadrilaterals. Here is a proof:

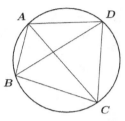

We denote by $[XY \cdots Z]$ the area of the polygon $XY \cdots Z$. Using the known fact that $[ABC] = (AB \cdot BC \cdot CA)/4R$, where R is the circumradius, we have the two equations

$$[ABCD] = [ABC] + [ADC]$$
$$= \frac{AB \cdot BC \cdot CA}{4R} + \frac{AD \cdot DC \cdot AC}{4R};$$

$$[ABCD] = [ABD] + [BCD] = \frac{AB \cdot BD \cdot AD}{4R} + \frac{BC \cdot CD \cdot BD}{4R}.$$

It follows that

$$AC(AB \cdot BC + CD \cdot DA) = BD(DA \cdot AB + BC \cdot CD).$$

Let $ABCD$ be a trapezoid with parallel sides AB and CD. Let E be a point on the side AB such that EC and AD are parallel. Further, let the area of the triangle determined by the lines AC, BD, and DE be t, and the area of ABC be T. Determine the ratio $AB : CD$, if $t : T$ is maximal.

Solution

Let M be the intersection of diagonals AC and BD, and N be the intersection of AC and DE.

Since $EC\|AD$ and $AE\|DC$, the quadrilateral $AECD$ is a parallelogram, hence N is the midpoint of AC.

Let $a = AB$, $b = CD$. Since $\triangle MCD$ is similar to $\triangle MAB$ we obtain

$$\frac{MC}{MA} = \frac{b}{a} \Leftrightarrow \frac{NC - MN}{NA + MN} = \frac{b}{a} \Leftrightarrow \frac{AC - 2MN}{AC + 2MN} = \frac{b}{a}.$$

By the last equality and some algebra we obtain $\dfrac{MN}{AC} = \dfrac{a - b}{2(a + b)}$. If h_t is the altitude of $\triangle DMN$ from D, and h_T is the altitude of $\triangle ABC$ from B, we have

$$\frac{h_t}{h_T} = \frac{DM}{MB} = \frac{b}{a}.$$

It follows that

$$\frac{t}{T} = \frac{MN \cdot h_t}{AC \cdot h_T} = \frac{b}{a} \cdot \frac{a - b}{2(a + b)} = \frac{\frac{a}{b} - 1}{2\frac{a}{b}(\frac{a}{b} + 1)},$$

and we have to find $\dfrac{a}{b} = x$ when $\dfrac{x - 1}{x(x + 1)}$ takes its maximum value.

Setting $f(x) = \dfrac{x - 1}{x(x + 1)}$, we have $f'(x) = \dfrac{-x^2 + 2x + 1}{x^2(x + 1)^2}$, hence f takes its maximum value for $x = 1 + \sqrt{2}$. Hence, $t : T$ is maximized when $AB : CD = 1 + \sqrt{2}$.

In triangle ABC, the points B_1 and C_1 are on BC, point B_2 is on AB, and point C_2 is on AC such that the segment B_1B_2 is parallel to AC and the segment C_1C_2 is parallel to AB. Let the lines B_1B_2 and C_1C_2 meet at D. Denote the areas of triangles BB_1B_2 and CC_1C_2 by b and c, respectively.

(a) Prove that if $b = c$, then the centroid of ABC is on the line AD.

(b) Find the ratio $b : c$ if D is the incentre of ABC and $AB = 4$, $BC = 5$, and $CA = 6$.

Solution

(a) Let F denote the area of $\triangle ABC$ and let $M = \overline{AD} \cap \overline{BC}$. For convenience, replace b and c by F_b and F_c, respectively. Since $B_1B_2 \| AC$ and $C_1C_2 \| AB$, we have

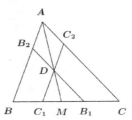

$$\frac{F_B}{F} = \left(\frac{BB_1}{BC}\right)^2 ; \qquad \frac{F_C}{F} = \left(\frac{CC_1}{BC}\right)^2 ,$$

hence $BB_1 = CC_1$ (and $BC_1 = CB_1$) since $F_B = F_C$. By Menelaus' theorem applied to $\triangle ABM$ and the traverse B_1DB_2 we obtain

$$\frac{B_1M}{B_1B} \cdot \frac{B_2B}{B_2A} \cdot \frac{DA}{DM} = 1 .$$

Similarly, by applying Menelaus' theorem to $\triangle ACM$ and the traverse C_1DC_2 we obtain

$$\frac{C_1M}{C_1C} \cdot \frac{C_2C}{C_2A} \cdot \frac{DA}{DM} = 1 .$$

The last two equations imply that

$$B_1M \cdot \frac{B_2B}{B_2A} = C_1M \cdot \frac{C_2C}{C_2A} .$$

Since $\dfrac{B_2B}{B_2A} = \dfrac{B_1B}{B_1C} = \dfrac{C_1C}{C_1B} = \dfrac{C_2C}{C_2A}$, it follows that $B_1M = C_1M$, hence M is the midpoint of BC (recall that $BC_1 = CB_1$). It follows that the centroid of ABC is on the line AD.

(b) Let $a = BC$, $b = CA$, $c = AB$, r be the inradius of $\triangle ABC$, and h_b and h_c be the altitudes of $\triangle ABC$ from B and C, respectively. Since $\triangle BB_1B$ and $\triangle CC_1C_2$ are similar, we have

$$\frac{F_B}{F_C} = \left(\frac{BB_1}{CC_1}\right)^2 = \left(\frac{BB_1}{BC}\right)^2\left(\frac{BC}{CC_1}\right)^2 = \left(\frac{h_b - r}{h_b} \cdot \frac{h_c}{h_c - r}\right)^2 .$$

By substituting $h_b = \dfrac{2F}{b}$, $h_c = \dfrac{2F}{c}$, and $r = \dfrac{2F}{a+b+c}$ in the above we deduce that

$$
\begin{aligned}
\frac{F_B}{F_C} &= \left(\frac{\frac{2F}{b} - \frac{2F}{a+b+c}}{\frac{2F}{b}} \cdot \frac{\frac{2F}{c}}{\frac{2F}{c} - \frac{2F}{a+b+c}} \right)^2 \\
&= \left(\frac{a+c}{a+b+c} \cdot \frac{a+b+c}{a+b} \right)^2 = \left(\frac{a+c}{a+b} \right)^2 .
\end{aligned}
$$

Since $a = 5$, $b = 6$, and $c = 4$ were given, we obtain $\dfrac{F_B}{F_C} = \dfrac{81}{121}$.

Triangle ABC is acute angled, $\angle BAC = 60°$, $AB = c$, and $AC = b$ with $b > c$. The orthocentre and the circumcentre of ABC are M and O, respectively. The line OM intersects AB and CA at X and Y, respectively.

(a) Prove that the perimeter of triangle AXY is $b + c$.

(b) Prove that $OM = b - c$.

Solution

(a) Let α and β be the angles at A and B, respectively. Since

$$AM = 2R \cos \alpha = R = AO,$$

we have that $\angle AMO = \angle AOM$. Also, since

$$\angle XAM = \angle YAO = 90° - \beta,$$

it follows that $\triangle XAM \sim \triangle YAO$. Therefore, $\angle AXY = \angle AYX = 60°$ and $\triangle AXY$ is equilateral.

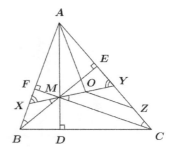

    Now $\angle ABM = 30°$, hence $\angle XMB = 30°$ and $XB = XM$. In the same way we can prove that $YC = YM$. It now follows that the perimeter of $\triangle AXY$ is $b + c$.

(b) Let Z be the point on AC such that $AZ = AB = c$. Then we have $ZC = b - c$, and from part (a)

$$YZ = BX = MX = OY.$$

Therefore, $\triangle YOZ$ is isosceles, and $\angle YOZ = \angle YZO = 30°$. Since we have $\angle MCZ = \angle CMO = 30°$, we conclude that $MCZO$ is an isosceles trapezoid. This establishes that $OM = ZC = b - c$, as desired.

Let A, B, and C be three points on a line with B between A and C. Let Γ_1, Γ_2, and Γ_3 be semicircles, all on the same side of AC, and with AC, AB, and BC as diameters, respectively. Let l be the line perpendicular to AC through B. Let Γ be the circle which is tangent to the line l, tangent to Γ_1 internally, and tangent to Γ_3 externally. Let D be the point of contact of Γ and Γ_3. The diameter of Γ through D meets l in E. Show that $AB = DE$.

Solution

Let O, P, and Q, be the centres of Γ_1, Γ_3, and Γ, respectively. Let r, s, and t be the radii of Γ_2, Γ_3, and Γ, respectively. Let Γ meet l at the point F. The tangent to Γ at D meets l at the point G. Let u denote the common length of the tangent segments GB, GD, and GF. Let $\alpha = \angle BPD$.

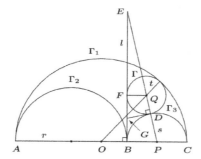

By the Law of Cosines in $\triangle OPQ$ we have

$$
\begin{aligned}
(r + s - t)^2 &= OQ^2 = OP^2 + PQ^2 - 2OP \cdot PQ \cos \angle OPQ, \\
&= r^2 + (s + t)^2 - 2r(s + t) \cos \alpha \, ;
\end{aligned}
$$

hence

$$
\cos \alpha = \frac{2st + rt - rs}{rs + rt}. \tag{1}
$$

Applying the Law of Cosines to the triangles BPD, BGD, DGF, and DQF we have

$$
\begin{aligned}
2s^2(1 - \cos \alpha) &= BD^2 = 2u^2(1 + \cos \alpha), \\
2u^2(1 - \cos \alpha) &= FD^2 = 2t^2(1 + \cos \alpha) \, ;
\end{aligned}
$$

thus, $(1 + \cos \alpha)t = (1 - \cos \alpha)s$. We substitute for $\cos \alpha$ the expression in equation (1) and simplify successively to obtain

$$\left(\frac{rt + st}{rs + rt}\right)t = \left(\frac{rs - st}{rs + st}\right)s\,,$$

$$(r + s)t^2 + s^2 t - rs^2 = 0\,,$$

$$((r + s)t - rs)(t + s) = 0\,.$$

Since $t > 0$, we have $t = \dfrac{rs}{r + s}$.

Let $d = ED$. We observe that the triangles EFQ and EBP are homothetic. Hence,

$$d - t = EQ = \frac{FQ \cdot EP}{BP} = \frac{t(d + s)}{s}\,,$$

so that $s(d - t) = t(d + s)$.

Therefore,

$$DE = d = \frac{2st}{s - t} = \frac{2s \cdot \dfrac{rs}{r + s}}{s - \dfrac{rs}{r + s}} = \frac{2rs^2}{s^2} = 2r = AB\,,$$

and the proof is complete.

Let ABC be a triangle and let P be an exterior point in the plane of the triangle. Let AP, BP, and CP meet the (possibly extended) sides BC, CA, and AB in D, E, and F, respectively. If the areas of the triangles PBD, PCE, and PAF are all equal, prove that their common area is equal to the area of the triangle ABC.

Solution

Let $[XYZ]$ denote the area of $\triangle XYZ$. We assume without loss of generality that $[ABC] = 1$. Let (a, b, c) be the barycentric coordinates of P with respect to $\triangle ABC$. The oriented (signed) area of $\triangle PBD$ is then

$$[PBD] = \begin{pmatrix} a & b & c \\ 0 & 1 & 0 \\ 0 & \frac{b}{b+c} & \frac{c}{b+c} \end{pmatrix} = \frac{ac}{b+c}.$$

Similarly, we have $[PCE] = \dfrac{ab}{a+c}$ and $[PAF] = \dfrac{ab}{a+c}$. The assumption $|[PBD]| = |[PCE]| = |[PAF]|$ implies $|a(a+b)| = |b(b+c)| = |c(c+a)|$, where at least two of the real numbers $a(a+b)$, $b(b+c)$, $c(c+a)$ are equal. Without loss of generality assume that $a(a+b) = c(c+a)$. We can scale the barycentric coordinates so that $a = 1$. Therefore, $1(1+b) = c(c+1)$, that is

$$b = c^2 + c - 1. \tag{1}$$

The equation $|b(b+c)| = |a(a+b)| = |1+b|$ leads to two cases.

Case 1. $b(b+c) = 1+b$. We subsitute for b as in (1) and obtain

$$(c^2 + c - 1)(c^2 + 2c - 1) = c^2 + c;$$
$$c^4 + 2c^3 - c^2 - 4c + 1 = (c-1)(c^3 + 4c^2 + 3c - 1) = 0.$$

If $c = 1$ then also $b = a = 1$, which contradicts the hypothesis that P is an exterior point of $\triangle ABC$. Consequently, $c^3 + 4c^2 + 3c - 1 = 0$. It follows from (1) that

$$[PBD] = \frac{c}{(c^2 + 2c)(c^2 + 2c - 1)}$$
$$= \frac{1}{c^3 + 4c^2 + 3c - 2} = -1 = -[ABC],$$

which is the desired conclusion.

Case 2. $b(b + c) = -1 - b$. We substitute according to (1) to obtain

$$\begin{aligned}(c^2 + c - 1)(c^2 + 2c - 1) &= -c^2 - c \, ; \qquad\qquad (2)\\ c^4 + c^3 + c^2 - 2c + 1 &= 0 \, .\end{aligned}$$

We will prove that $f(x) = x^4 + 3x^3 + x^2 - 2x + 1$ is positive for $x \in \mathbb{R}$, thus proving that (3) is impossible. Since $f(x) = x^4 + 3x^3 + (x - 1)^2$, we see that $f(x) > 0$ for $x \in (-\infty, -3] \cup [0, \infty)$.

It suffices to show that $f(x) > 0$ for $x \in [-3, 0]$. Let $t = -x$. The AM–GM Inequality yields

$$\begin{aligned}f(x) &= -4t\left(\frac{t}{2}\right)\left(\frac{t}{2}\right)(3 - t) + (t + 1)^2\\ &\geq -4t\left(\frac{1}{3}\left(\frac{t}{2} + \frac{t}{2} + 3 - t\right)\right)^3 + (t + 1)^2 = (t - 1)^2 \geq 0 \, ,\end{aligned}$$

where at least one of the last two inequalities is strict. This completes the proof.

Let PQR be an acute triangle. Let SRP, TPQ, and UQR be isosceles triangles exterior to PQR, with $SP = SR$, $TP = TQ$, and $UQ = UR$, such that $\angle PSR = 2\angle QPR$, $\angle QTP = 2\angle RQP$, and $\angle RUQ = 2\angle PRQ$. Let S', T', and U' be the points of intersection of SQ and TU, TR and US, and UP and ST, respectively. Determine the value of

$$\frac{SQ}{SS'} + \frac{TR}{TT'} + \frac{UP}{UU'}.$$

Solution

Let $\angle RPQ = \alpha$, $\angle PQR = \beta$, and $\angle QRP = \gamma$. Let $\bar{P}$, $\bar{Q}$, and $\bar{R}$ be the reflections of P, Q, and R, with respect to the axes ST, TU, and US, respectively. Since $PT = \bar{P}T$, $\bar{P}$ is on the circle Γ_T with centre T and radius TP. Since $PS = \bar{P}S$, $\bar{P}$ is on the circle Γ_S with centre S and radius SP. Therefore, $\angle P\bar{P}Q = 180° = \beta$ and $\angle R\bar{P}P = 180° - \alpha$. We now have that $\angle Q\bar{P}R = 360° - (180° - \alpha) - (180° - \beta) = 180° - \gamma$. Hence, $\bar{P}$ is also on the circle Γ_U with centre U and radius UR.

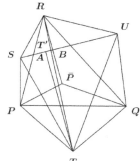

We conclude that the three circles Γ_S, Γ_T, and Γ_U intersect at $\bar{P}$. By symmetry, $\bar{P}$ coincides with $\bar{Q}$ and with $\bar{R}$, so we have $\triangle PST \cong \triangle \bar{P}ST$, $\triangle QTU \cong \triangle \bar{P}TU$, and $\triangle RUS \cong \triangle \bar{P}US$.

Let A and B be the feet of the perpendiculars from T and R to SU, respectively. Then we have

$$\frac{RT'}{TT'} = \frac{RB}{TA} = \frac{[RUS]}{[STU]} = \frac{[\bar{P}US]}{[STU]},$$

thus

$$\frac{TR}{TT'} = 1 + \frac{[\bar{P}US]}{[STU]}.$$

We finally obtain

$$\frac{SQ}{SS'} + \frac{TR}{TT'} + \frac{UP}{UU'}$$
$$= \left(1 + \frac{[\bar{P}TU]}{[STU]}\right) + \left(1 + \frac{[\bar{P}US]}{[STU]}\right) + \left(1 + \frac{[\bar{P}ST]}{[STU]}\right) = 4.$$

Through a point P exterior to a given circle pass a secant and a tangent to the circle. The secant intersects the circle at A and B, and the tangent touches the circle at C on the same side of the diameter through P as A and B. The projection of C onto the diameter is Q. Prove that QC bisects $\angle AQB$.

Solution

Let O be the centre of the given circle.

By the theorem of the power of a point with respect to a circle applied to P,

$$PA \cdot PB = PC^2.$$

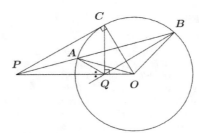

Now, in right triangle CPO, CQ is the altitude to the hypotenuse. By a standard mean proportion we then have

$$PC^2 = PO \cdot PQ.$$

Hence,

$$PA \cdot PB = PO \cdot PQ,$$

or equivalently, $\frac{PQ}{PA} = \frac{PB}{PO}$ and $\frac{PQ}{PB} = \frac{PA}{PO}$, so that triangles APQ, APO are similar to triangles BPQ, APO; respectively. Observing proportional sides, we have $\frac{AQ}{PA} = \frac{OB}{PO}$ and $\frac{QB}{PB} = \frac{OA}{PO}$. Since $OA = OB$, it follows that $\frac{AQ}{PA} = \frac{QB}{PB}$, hence PO is the external bisector of the angle at Q in triangle AQB. However $CQ \perp PQ$, so CQ is the internal bisector of the angle at Q in triangle AQB, yielding $\angle AQC = \angle CQB$, as required.

Consider a rectangle with sides of lengths 3 and 4, and on each side pick an arbitrary point that is not a corner. Let x, y, z, and u be the lengths of the sides of the quadrilateral spanned by these points. Prove that

$$25 \leq x^2 + y^2 + z^2 + u^2 \leq 50.$$

Solution

We assume that the four points divide the respective sides in the ratios $\dfrac{a}{4-a}$, $\dfrac{b}{3-b}$, $\dfrac{c}{4-c}$, and $\dfrac{d}{3-d}$.

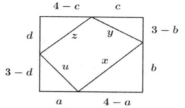

We have

$$
\begin{aligned}
&x^2 + y^2 + z^2 + u^2 \\
&= (4-a)^2 + b^2 + (3-b)^2 + c^2 + (4-c)^2 + d^2 + (3-d)^2 + a^2 \\
&= 25 + 2(a-2)^2 + 2\left(b - \frac{3}{2}\right)^2 + 2(c-2)^2 + 2\left(d - \frac{3}{2}\right)^2 .
\end{aligned}
$$

The desired bounds now follow readily from the inequalities

$$0 \leq (a-2)^2 \leq 4; \qquad 0 \leq \left(b - \frac{3}{2}\right)^2 \leq \frac{9}{4};$$

$$0 \leq (c-2)^2 \leq 4; \qquad 0 \leq \left(d - \frac{3}{2}\right)^2 \leq \frac{9}{4}.$$

A ray emanating from the vertex A of the triangle ABC intersects the side BC at X and the circumcircle of ABC at Y. Prove that

$$\frac{1}{AX} + \frac{1}{XY} \geq \frac{4}{BC}.$$

Solution

The proposed inequality can be rewritten as

$$BC \cdot AY \geq 4AX \cdot XY. \tag{1}$$

First, we suppose $AY < BC$. Since $XY = AY - AX$, the inequality (1) is equivalent to each of the following, the latter being obvious:

$$4AX^2 - 4AX \cdot AY + BC \cdot AY \geq 0,$$
$$(2AX - AY)^2 + AY(BC - AY) \geq 0.$$

Now, suppose that $AY \geq BC$. Observing that $BC = XB + XC$ and $AX \cdot XY = XB \cdot XC$ (by the Intersecting Chord Theorem), inequality (1) may be written as

$$AY(XB + XC) \geq 4XB \cdot XC.$$

This inequality certainly holds, since

$$AY(XB + XC) \geq BC(XB + XC) = (XB + XC)^2 \geq 4XB \cdot XC.$$

In triangle ABC let D be the midpoint of BC and let M be a point on the side BC such that $\angle BAM = \angle DAC$. Let L be the second intersection point of the circumcircle of triangle CAM with AB, and let K be the second intersection point of the circumcircle of triangle BAM with the side AC. Prove that $KL \parallel BC$.

Solution

Let $\alpha_1 = \angle BAM = \angle CAD$ and $\alpha_2 = \angle BAD = \angle CAM$, so $\alpha_1 + \alpha_2 = \alpha = \angle BAC$. Let $\beta = \angle ABC$, $\gamma = \angle ACB$. From the Sine Law in $\triangle ABM$ and $\triangle CAM$, we see that

$$AM = \frac{BM \sin \beta}{\sin \alpha_1} = \frac{CM \sin \gamma}{\sin \alpha_2}.$$

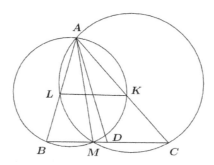

Therefore,

$$BM \sin \beta \sin \alpha_2$$
$$= CM \sin \gamma \sin \alpha_1 . \quad (1)$$

Similarly, by the Sine Law in $\triangle BAD$ and $\triangle CAD$ we deduce that

$$BC \sin \beta \sin \alpha_1 = CD \sin \gamma \sin \alpha_2 . \qquad (2)$$

Now $BD = CD$, so (1), (2) imply $BM : CM = c^2 : b^2$, hence $CM = \dfrac{ab^2}{b^2 + c^2}$.

As $CK \cdot CA = CM \cdot CB$, we find that $CK : b = a^2 : (b^2 + c^2)$ and $BL : c = a^2 : (b^2 + c^2)$, hence $KL \parallel BC$.

Three circular arcs w_1, w_2, and w_3 with common end-points A and B are on the same side of the line AB, and w_2 lies between w_1 and w_3. Two rays emanating from B intersect these arcs at M_1, M_2, M_3 and K_1, K_2, K_3, respectively. Prove that

$$\frac{M_1 M_2}{M_2 M_3} = \frac{K_1 K_2}{K_2 K_3}.$$

Solution

One less an index is so many dashes.

We have $\angle AKB = \angle AMB$ and $\angle AK'B = \angle AM'B$, because these are inscribed angles. It follows that $\triangle AKK'$ is similar to $\triangle AMM'$, and hence $\frac{KK'}{MM'} = \frac{AK'}{AM'}$.

Similarly, $\triangle AK'K''$ is similar to $\triangle AM'M''$, hence $\frac{K'K''}{M'M''} = \frac{AK'}{AM'}$.

Thus, $\frac{KK'}{MM'} = \frac{K'K''}{M'M''}$, and it follows that $\frac{MM'}{M'M''} = \frac{KK'}{K'K''}$, as desired.

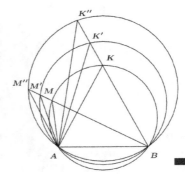

Let A be a fixed exterior point with respect to a given circle with centre O and radius r. Let M be a point on the circle and let N be diametrically opposite to M with respect to O. Find the locus of the centres of the circles passing through A, M, and N, as the point M is varied on the circle.

Solution

Let U be the circum-centre of $\triangle AMN$. Since O is the midpoint of MN, UO is orthogonal to MN and $UM^2 = UO^2 + r^2$. But $UM = UA$, so we have $UA^2 - UO^2 = r^2$. It follows that U is on a line ℓ perpendicular to AO. More precisely, if $M_0 N_0$ is the diameter perpendicular to AO and U_0 is the circumcentre of $\triangle AM_0 N_0$, then ℓ is the perpendicular to AO through U_0. Note that $U_0 \neq O$.

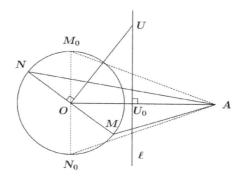

Conversely, Let U be any point on ℓ (so that $UA^2 - UO^2 = r^2$) and let MN be the diameter perpendicular to UO. Then $UO^2 + r^2 = UM^2 = UN^2$ so that $UM = UN = UA$ and U is the circumcentre of $\triangle AMN$ (note that A, M, and N are not collinear because $U_0 \neq O$).

In a scalene triangle ABC, the interior bisectors of the angles A, B, and C meet the opposite sides at points A', B', and C' respectively. Let A'' be the intersection of BC with the perpendicular bisector of AA', let B'' be the intersection of AC with the perpendicular bisector of BB', and let C'' be the intersection of AB with the perpendicular bisector of CC'. Prove that A'', B'', and C'' are collinear.

Solution

Let $a = BC$, $b = CA$, and $c = AB$. Let M be the midpoint of AA'. By the Bisector Theorem we have $A'C = \dfrac{ab}{b+c}$, $BA' = \dfrac{ac}{b+c}$, and (with $\alpha = \dfrac{A}{2}$) it is known that $AA' = \dfrac{2bc\cos\alpha}{b+c}$. Since $\angle MA'A'' = \alpha + C$, in the

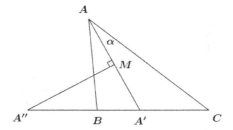

triangle $A''A'M$ we obtain

$$A'A'' = \frac{MA'}{\cos(\alpha + B)} = \frac{AA'}{2\cos(\alpha + C)} = \frac{bc\cos\alpha}{(b+c)\cos(\alpha + C)}.$$

Using the Law of Sines we obtain:

$$\frac{A''B}{A''C} = \frac{A'A'' - A'B}{A'A'' + A'C} = \frac{bc\cos\alpha - ac\cos(\alpha + C)}{bc\cos\alpha + ab\cos(\alpha + C)}$$

$$= \frac{c}{b} \cdot \frac{\sin B \cos\alpha - \sin A \cos(\alpha + C)}{\sin C \cos\alpha + \sin A \cos(\alpha + C)}$$

$$= \frac{c}{b} \cdot \frac{\sin B \cos\alpha - 2\sin\alpha\cos\alpha\cos(\alpha + C)}{\sin C \cos\alpha + 2\sin\alpha\cos\alpha\cos(\alpha + C)}.$$

Since $\cos\alpha \neq 0$, we obtain

$$\frac{A''B}{A''C} = \frac{c}{b} \cdot \frac{\sin B - 2\sin\alpha\cos(\alpha + C)}{\sin C + 2\sin\alpha\cos(\alpha + C)}$$

$$= \frac{c}{b} \cdot \frac{\sin B - \sin(\alpha + \alpha + C) - \sin(\alpha - \alpha - C)}{\sin C + \sin(\alpha + \alpha + C) + \sin(\alpha - \alpha - C)}$$

$$= \frac{c}{b} \cdot \frac{\sin B - \sin(A + C) + \sin C}{\sin C + \sin(A + C) - \sin C}$$

$$= \frac{c}{b} \cdot \frac{\sin B - \sin B + \sin C}{\sin C + \sin B - \sin C} = \frac{c}{b} \cdot \frac{\sin C}{\sin B},$$

hence $\dfrac{A''B}{A''C} = \dfrac{c^2}{b^2}$.

By the converse of Menelaus' theorem, it follows that A'', B'', and C'' are collinear.

The cities A, B, C, D, and E are connected by straight roads (more than two cities may lie on the same road). The distance from A to B, and from C to D, is 3 km. The distance from B to D is 1 km, from A to C it is 5 km, from D to E it is 4 km, and finally, from A to E it is 8 km. Determine the distance from C to E.

Solution

Since $AB + BD + DE = 3 + 1 + 4 = 8 = AE$, it follows that the cities A, B, D, and E are collinear (on the same road).

We have

$$AC^2 = 5^2 = 3^2 + 4^2$$
$$= CD^2 + AD^2,$$

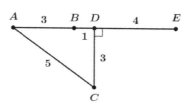

hence, by the converse of the Pythagorean Theorem, CD is perpendicular to AD. By the Pythagorean Theorem, we now obtain $CE = 5$.

Let $2n$ (where $n \geq 1$) points lie in the plane so that no straight line contains more than two of them. Paint n of the points blue and paint the other n points yellow. Show that there are n segments, each with one blue endpoint and one yellow endpoint, such that each of the $2n$ points is an endpoint of one of the n segments and none of the segments have a point in common.

Solution

There are finitely many (namely $n!$) bijective correspondences between the blue and the yellow points. Hence, there is at least one correspondence, Γ, where the sum, $s(\Gamma)$, of the Euclidean lengths of its n segments has minimum value. We will prove that each such Γ has the desired property.

Assume the contrary. Then, there are two blue points, say A and B, and two yellow points, say X and Y, such that the segments AX and BY are drawn and intersect in a point, say S. We construct another correspondence Γ' from Γ by removing the segments AX and BY and adding the segments AY and BX [*Ed.: note that by the hypotheses AY and BX contain no coloured points except their endpoints*]. The correspondence Γ' is also bijective. By the triangle inequality,

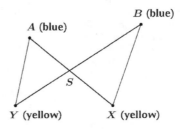

$$\begin{aligned} s(\Gamma') &= s(\Gamma) + AY + BX - AX - BY \\ &= s(\Gamma) + (AY - AS - YS) + (BX - SX - SB) < s(\Gamma), \end{aligned}$$

contradicting the fact that $s(\Gamma)$ has minimum value. The proof is complete.

Two circles in the plane of the same radius R intersect at a right angle. How large is the area of the region which lies inside both circles?

Solution

Since $\angle O_1 A O_2 = 90°$, half the area of the lens-shaped region of intersection equals the area of a quarter circle minus the area of $\triangle A O_2 B$. Hence, the required area is

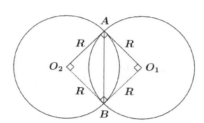

$$2 \left(\frac{1}{4} \pi R^2 - \frac{1}{2} R^2 \right) = \frac{\pi - 2}{2} \cdot R^2.$$

(a) Let $\triangle ABC$ be isosceles with $AB = AC$, and let D be the midpoint of BC. The points P and Q lie respectively on the segments AD and AB such that $PQ = PC$ and $Q \neq B$. Show that $\angle PQC = \frac{1}{2}\angle BAC$.

(b) Let $ABCD$ be a rhombus with $\angle BAD = 60°$. Let F, G, and H be points on the segments AD, CA, and DC respectively such that $DFGH$ is a parallelogram. Show that $\triangle BHF$ is equilateral.

Solution

(a) Since $PB = PC$, we have $PB = PC = PQ$. If the base angles in isosceles triangles PQB, PBC, and PCQ are x, y, and z, respectively, then in $\triangle BCQ$ we have $(x+y)+(y+z)+(z+x) = 180°$, hence $z = 90° - (x+y)$. Thus, $\angle PQC = z = 90° - (x + y) = 90° - \angle ABD = \angle BAD = \frac{1}{2}\angle BAC$.

(b) Since $GH \| AD$, we have $\angle CGH = \angle CAD$. However, $ABCD$ is a rhombus, so $\angle CAD = \angle ACD$. Therefore, $\angle CGH = \angle ACD = \angle GCH$, and hence $CH = GH = FD$. Since $\triangle ABD$ and $\triangle BCD$ are equilateral, we also have $BC = BD$ and $\angle BCH = \angle BDF$. Thus, $\triangle BCH$ and $\triangle BDF$ are congruent with (i) $BH = BF$, and (ii) $\angle CHB = \angle DFB$. By (i), $\triangle BFH$ is isosceles; by (ii) $DFBH$ is a cyclic quadrilateral, so that $\angle FBH = 180° - \angle HDF = 180° - (60° + 60°) = 60°$. We conclude that $\triangle BHF$ is equilateral, as desired.

Figure A

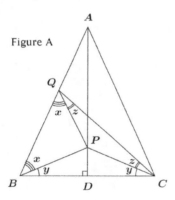

Figure B

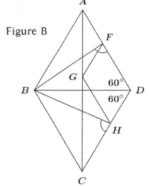

Let a, b, and c be the sides of a triangle and let x, y, and z be real numbers such that $x + y + z = 0$. Prove that

$$a^2 yz + b^2 zx + c^2 xy \leq 0.$$

Solution

More generally, let α, β, γ, x, y, and z be real numbers and suppose that $x + y + z = 0$.

For real numbers u and v we have $(u + v)^2 \leq 2(u^2 + v^2)$, hence

$$(\beta + \gamma)^2 yz + (\gamma + \alpha)^2 zx + (\alpha + \beta)^2 xy$$

$$\leq 2[(\beta^2 + \gamma^2) yz + (\gamma^2 + \alpha^2) zx + (\alpha^2 + \beta^2) xy]$$

$$= 2[\alpha^2 x(y + z) + \beta^2 y(z + x) + \gamma^2 z(x + y)]$$

$$= -2(\alpha^2 x^2 + \beta^2 y^2 + \gamma^2 z^2) \leq 0.$$

Equality occurs only if $\alpha = \beta = \gamma$ and $\alpha x = \beta y = \gamma z = 0$.

To establish the proposed inequality, we make use of the linear transformation $a = \beta + \gamma$, $b = \gamma + \alpha$, and $c = \alpha + \beta$, where α, β, and γ are uniquely determined positive numbers and apply the above inequality.

Equality holds only if the triangle is equilateral and $x = y = z = 0$.

Points M and N are on the sides AB and BC of the triangle ABC, respectively. It is given that $\frac{AM}{MB} = \frac{BN}{NC} = 2$ and $\angle ACB = 2\angle MNB$. Prove that ABC is an isosceles triangle.

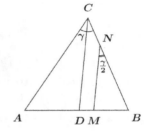

Solution

Let $\gamma = \angle ACB$, so that $\angle MNB = \frac{1}{2}\gamma$. The line through C parallel to NM meets AB at D. Then $2:3 = BN : BC = BM : BD$, hence $BD = \frac{3}{2}BM = \frac{1}{2}AB$. Since the bisector of $\angle ACB$ is also a median, $CA = CB$.

The two diagonals of a trapezoid divide it into four triangles. The areas of three of them are 1, 2, and 4 square units. What values can the area of the fourth triangle have?

Solution

Let $[XYZ]$ be the area of triangle XYZ. Then $[ABD] = [ABC]$, as the two triangles have equal altitudes from their common base AB. Therefore,

$$[OAD] + [OAB] = [OBC] + [OAB],$$

hence $[OAD] = [OBC]$.

Triangles OAB and OCD are similar, so we have $\dfrac{OA}{OC} = \dfrac{OB}{OD}$, that is $\dfrac{OA}{OC} \cdot \dfrac{OD}{OB} = 1$, and hence $\dfrac{[OAB]}{[OBC]} \cdot \dfrac{[ODC]}{[OBC]} = 1$, so $[OBC]^2 = [OAB][OBC]$. It follows that $[OBC] = 2 = [OAD]$, $[OAB] = 1$, and $[ODC] = 4$, that is, the fourth triangle has area 2 square units.

The ratio of the lengths of the diagonals of a rhombus is $a : b$. Find the ratio of the area of the rhombus to the area of an inscribed circle.

Solution

Let r be the radius of the circle inscribed in the rhombus. The required ratio is then

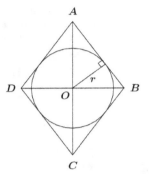

$$\frac{4 \cdot \frac{1}{2} OA \cdot OB}{\pi r^2} = \frac{2}{\pi} \cdot OA \cdot OB \cdot \frac{1}{r^2}$$

$$= \frac{2}{\pi} \cdot OA \cdot OB \left(\frac{1}{OA^2} + \frac{1}{OB^2} \right)$$

$$= \frac{2}{\pi} \left(\frac{OB}{OA} + \frac{OA}{OB} \right) = \frac{2}{\pi} \left(\frac{b}{a} + \frac{a}{b} \right)$$

$$= \frac{2(a^2 + b^2)}{\pi ab},$$

where $\dfrac{1}{r^2} = \dfrac{1}{OA^2} + \dfrac{1}{OB^2}$ holds since r is the altitude of the right triangle OAB.

Let H be the orthocentre of an acute-angled triangle ABC. Prove that the midpoints of AB and CH and the intersection point of the interior bisectors of $\angle CAH$ and $\angle CBH$ are collinear.

Solution

Let us denote $\alpha = \angle CAB$, $\beta = \angle ABC$, $\gamma = \angle BCA$, and let $A' = AH \cap BC$, $B' = BH \cap AC$. Let M, N, O be the midpoints of segments AB, $A'B'$, CH, respectively, let $P = CH \cap A'B'$, and let Q be the intersection point of the bisectors of $\angle CAA'$ and $\angle CBB'$, respectively. We are to show that the points M, O, Q are collinear.

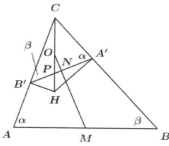

It is a well-known fact that the midpoints of the diagonals of a complete quadrilateral are collinear. Applying this to the complete quadrilateral generated by the quadrilateral $A'CB'H$, we see that the points M, N, and O are collinear. Due to the fact that $\angle HA'C = \angle CB'H = 90°$, the quadrilateral $A'CB'H$ is cyclic with circumcentre O.

Hence, $ON \perp A'B'$, which implies that

$$\begin{aligned}
\angle HOM &= \angle PON = 90° - \angle NPO = 90° - \angle A'PC \\
&= 90° - (180° - \angle PA'C - \angle A'CP) \\
&= \angle PA'C + \angle BCH - 90° \\
&= \alpha + (90° - \beta) - 90° = \alpha - \beta;
\end{aligned}$$

thus,

$$\angle AMO = 90° - \angle HOM = 90° - \alpha + \beta. \tag{1}$$

Since $\angle BAA' = 90° - \beta$ and $\angle A'AC = 90° - \gamma$, we have

$$\begin{aligned}
\angle BAQ &= \angle BAA' + \frac{1}{2}\angle A'AC \\
&= 90° - \beta + \frac{1}{2}(90° - \gamma) = 135° - \beta - \frac{1}{2}\gamma.
\end{aligned}$$

Similarly, $\angle ABQ = 135° - \alpha - \frac{1}{2}\gamma$. Hence,

$$\begin{aligned}
\angle AQB &= 180° - \angle BAQ - \angle ABQ \\
&= 180° - \left(135° - \beta - \frac{1}{2}\gamma\right) - \left(135° - \alpha - \frac{1}{2}\gamma\right) \\
&= \alpha + \beta + \gamma - 90° = 90°.
\end{aligned}$$

We deduce that $\triangle AMQ$ is isosceles with $AM = MQ$. Thus,

$$\angle AMQ = 180° - 2\angle MAQ = 180° - 2\left(135° - \beta - \frac{1}{2}\gamma\right)$$
$$= 90° - \alpha + \beta. \tag{2}$$

From (1) and (2) it is readily seen that $\angle AMO = \angle AMQ$, that is, the points M, O, and Q are collinear. This completes the proof.

Given are a circle and its diameter PQ. Let t be a tangent to the circle, touching it at T, and let A be the intersection of the lines t and PQ. Let p and q be the tangents to the circle at P and Q respectively, and let

$$PT \cap q = \{N\} \quad \text{and} \quad QT \cap p = \{M\}.$$

Prove that the points A, M, and N are collinear.

Solution

Equivalently, we will prove that: Let T be a point of a circle with a given diameter PQ. Let p and q be the tangents to the circle at P and Q, respectively, and let

$$PT \cap q = \{N\}, \quad QT \cap p = \{M\}, \quad \text{and} \quad MN \cap PQ = \{A\}.$$

Then AT touches the given circle at T.

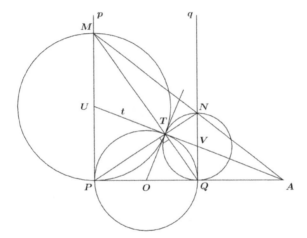

Let $AT \cap p = \{U\}$. Then, by Ceva's Theorem,

$$\frac{MU}{UP} \cdot \frac{PQ}{QA} \cdot \frac{AN}{NM} = 1.$$

But $p \perp PQ$ and $q \perp PQ$, so that $p \| q$, implying that $\frac{PQ}{QA} = \frac{NM}{AN}$. Hence, $\frac{MU}{UP} = 1$ and $MU = UP$.

Let $AT \cap q = \{V\}$. Since

$$\frac{NV}{MU} = \frac{AV}{AU} = \frac{VQ}{UP},$$

we obtain $NV = VQ$.

Thus, U and V are the midpoints of MP and NQ, respectively.

Since $\angle PTQ$ is a right angle, so also $\angle MTP = 90° = \angle NTQ$. Hence both circles constructed with MP and NQ as diameters pass through T.

Since the distance between their centres U and V equals the sum of their radii, these circles are externally tangent to each other at T.

Let their common tangent at T intersect PQ at O. This tangent is perpendicular to the line UV through the centres, and since

$$PO \ = \ OT \ = \ OQ \, ,$$

the point O is the midpoint of PQ, making OT a radius of the given circle in our problem.

Thus, $OT \perp AT$, and the conclusion follows.

Triangle ABC is equilateral, D is a point inside the triangle such that $DA = DB$, and E is a point that satisfies the conditions $\angle DBE = \angle DBC$ and $BE = AB$. How large is the angle $\angle DEB$?

Solution

Since $DA = DB$, the point D lies on the perpendicular bisector of AB, hence $\angle DCB = 30°$. We have

$$
\begin{aligned}
BE &= BC\,; \\
\angle DBE &= \angle DBC\,; \\
BD &= BD\,.
\end{aligned}
$$

It follows that $\triangle BDE$ and $\triangle BDC$ are congruent (side-angle-side), hence

$$\angle DEB = DCB = 30°\,.$$

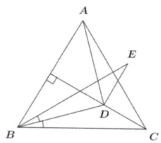

Let h be the altitude from A in an acute triangle ABC. Prove that

$$(b+c)^2 \geq a^2 + 4h^2 \,,$$

where a, b, and c are the lengths of the sides opposite A, B, and C respectively.

Solution

The triangle ABC need not be acute, as the proof will show.
Let w_a be the length of the internal bisector of angle A.
From the known relations

$$w_a = \frac{2bc}{b+c} \cos \frac{A}{2} \qquad \text{and} \qquad 4bc \leq (b+c)^2 \,,$$

we obtain

$$w_a^2 = bc \cdot \frac{4bc}{(b+c)^2} \cos^2 \frac{A}{2} \leq bc \cdot \cos^2 \frac{A}{2} \,.$$

However, $h \leq w_a$, so we have

$$h^2 \leq w_a^2 \leq bc \cdot \cos^2 \frac{A}{2} = bc \cdot \frac{1 + \cos a}{2}$$

$$= bc \cdot \frac{1 + \left(\dfrac{b^2 + c^2 - a^2}{2bc} \right)}{2} = \frac{(b+c)^2 - a^2}{4}$$

and $(b+c)^2 \geq a^2 + 4h^2$ follows, as desired.
Equality holds only if $b = c$.

CPSIA information can be obtained
at www.ICGtesting.com
Printed in the USA
BVHW01s0623011018
528559BV00012B/8/P